FOUNDATIONS OF INTERNATIONAL INCOME TAXATION

By

MICHAEL J. GRAETZ

Professor of Law
Yale Law School

FOUNDATION PRESS
New York, New York
2003

COPYRIGHT © 2003 By FOUNDATION PRESS

395 Hudson Street
New York, NY 10014
Phone Toll Free 1–877–888–1330
Fax (212) 367–6799
fdpress.com

Printed in the United States of America

ISBN 1–58778–515–3

TEXT IS PRINTED ON 10% POST CONSUMER RECYCLED PAPER

PREFACE

International transactions have grown exponentially in recent times. So has students' interest in the subject of international income taxation. In many schools, enrollment in the international income tax course now exceeds that of any other advanced course in taxation, including the venerable corporate tax course.

A course in international income taxation poses considerable difficulty for students and teachers alike. The criteria for evaluating international tax rules are contested and often at loggerheads. The statute and regulations are exemplars of stupefying complexity. Counting on cases as the principal medium to communicate the issues, the law and the underlying policy disputes of international income taxation is inadequate—considerably more inadequate in this context than in other areas of taxation. If ever there were a course that would be well served by sending students to the secondary literature, this is it. Fortunately, a number of primers and detailed treatises are available, but I, at least, have found the treatises too detailed for an introductory course, while the primers often do not explore issues in sufficient depth.

The growth of international transactions and interest in this area of law has been accompanied by an outpouring of literature in both law and economics journals. But the law journal articles, including mine—in the modern style—are overly long, and the economics articles difficult to parse for the mathematically challenged. We have attempted here to extract from the voluminous scholarly literature materials that will enhance the readers' understanding of international income tax law, the institutions that shape that law and the underlying policy debates. This text also provides context for these materials and connective tissue to tie them together.

This book is divided into eleven chapters that conform to the way in which I teach this subject. Needless to say, it is not essential that students read these materials in the order that they are presented here. The book is intended to serve as a flexible tool for teaching this difficult subject. It may be used as supplemental reading with topics assigned as they are taken up in the course or it may be assigned or recommended to students to read on their own.

We offer sufficient material here that this book might serve as a principal text, supplemented by the Internal Revenue Code, the regulations and other administrative pronouncements and some court cases. This book also could serve as a text in an international tax policy seminar. However it is used, our hope is that this book aids understanding of this difficult subject.

Due to space limitations, articles have been edited extensively. We have also freely omitted footnotes from the excerpts without designating such omissions. Readers will have to consult the original works to find the antecedent sources. Indeed, one purpose of this book is to encourage others to read the original texts of articles excerpted here. We are very grateful to all the authors and publishers who gave us permission to use their materials here.

By now, you have no doubt noticed that I am using the plural pronoun "we." This book has indeed been a collaboration among eighteen students and me over a two–year period. The students found much of the material that is excerpted here and produced chapter drafts. These students, most of whom have now graduated, are: Benjamin Alarie, Lily Batchelder, Victor Chang, Ian Crawford, Wei Cui, Alan Dale, Itai Grinberg, Larysa Gumowskyi, Sarah Holland, Bianca Micaela Locsin, Joshua Mandell, Jeffrev Manns, Melanie Markowitz, Preston Quesenberry, Scott Shuchart, Lara Slachta, Irvna Tustanovska, and Kimberly Zelnick. Simply thanking them here is inadequate to capture their crucial contributions. Ian Crawford deserves a special word of thanks for managing the entire manuscript.

I would also like to thank my friend and colleague Anne Alstott, who read and commented on a complete draft and Diane Ring, who inspired this undertaking in the first place. Gene Coakley and Scott Matheson of the Yale Law Library have once again provided invaluable assistance, as did my assistant Kris Kavanaugh who made the final changes to the book. Jeremy Robbins and Elbert Lin also deserve a word of thanks for reading the penultimate draft and saving me from countless small errors. For the remaining errors, there is no one to blame but me. Finally, I want to thank again the many authors whose fine work appears here; I hope my editing of your work has done you no disservice. This is really your book, not mine.

Let me close with an apology. Throughout this book I refer to myself in the third person. I am not trying to mimic Bob Dole; the material just seems to flow better that way.

Michael J. Graetz

New Haven, Connecticut
May 2003

ACKNOWLEDGMENTS

The editor wishes to thank all of the authors and publishers who kindly gave us permission to excerpt from their articles and books. No claim to copyright of previously copyrighted works is made here by either the editor or the publisher. The following publishers have asked that their excerpts be acknowledged in the following special way:

1.   At page 8, Nancy H. Kaufman, *Fairness and the Taxation of International Income,* 29 Law & Pol'y Int'l Bus. 145, 188–201 (1998). Reprinted with permission of the publisher, Law and Policy in International Business © 1997.

2.   At page 17, Hugh J. Ault, Comparative Income Taxation: A Structural Analysis p.p. 381-82 (1997). With kind permission from Kluwer Law International.

3.   At page 79, David Tillinghast, *"A Matter of Definition: "Foreign" and "Domestic" Taxpayers"* © 1985 by the University of California. Reprinted from Berkeley Journal of International Law. Vol. 2 No. 2, Pp: 239-272 by permission of the Regents of the University of California.

4.   At page 112, *"Tax Cheat, Inc,"* by James Surowiecki; *The New Yorker*–April 22, 2002 issue. Originally published in The New Yorker. Copyright © 2002 Condé Nast Publications Inc. Reprinted by permission. All Rights Reserved.

5.   At page 129, Arthur J. Cockfield, *Balancing National Interests in the Taxation of Electronic Commerce Business Profits,* originally published in 74 Tul. L. Rev. 133-217 (1999). Reprinted with the permission of the Tulane Law Review Association, which holds the copyright.

6.   At page 187, Martin A. Sullivan, *"Interest Allocation Reform: Time to Talk or Time to Act?"* 84 Tax Notes 1223, 1223-25 (1999). Copyright 1999 Tax Analysts. Reprinted with permission.

7.   At page 267, Ernest R. Larkins, *U.S. Income Taxation of Foreign Parties: A Primer,* 26 SYRACUSE J. INT'L L. & COM. 1 (1998). Excerpted with permission of the Syracuse Journal of International Law & Commerce.

8.   At page 287, Randolph J. Buchanan, Comment, The New-Millenium Dilemma: Does the Reliance on the Use of Computer Servers and Websites in a Global Electronic Commerce Environment Necessitate a Revision to the Current Definition of a Permanent Establishment? Originally appearing in Vol. 54, No. 4 of the

SMU Law Review. Reprinted with permission from the *SMU Law Review* and the Southern Methodist University Dedman School of Law.

9.   At page 361, Robert J. Peroni, J. Clifton Fleming, Jr., & Stephen E. Shay, Getting Serious About Curtailing Deferral of U.S. Tax on Foreign Source Income. Originally appearing in Vol. 52, No. 2 of the *SMU Law Review.* Reprinted with permission from the SMU Law Review and the Southern Methodist University Dedman School of Law.

10.   At page 411, Daniel L. Simmons, *"Worldwide Unitary Taxation: Retain and Rationalize, or Block at the Water's Edge?"* 21 Stanford Journal of International Law 157 at 162-5 (1985). Reprinted with the permission of the STANFORD JOURNAL OF INTERNATIONAL LAW. Copyright © 2002 by the Board of Trustees of the Leland Stanford Junior University.

11.   At page 415, Valerie Amerkhail, *"Pricing Methodology: Arm's Length or Formulary Apportionment? Sometimes, the Best Choice is Both,"* 8 Tax Management Transfer Pricing Report 94 (1999). Reprinted by permission of Tax Management Inc., a subsidiary of The Bureau of National Affairs Inc., All Rights Reserved.

12.   At page 505, Hugh J. Ault, Tax Competition: What (If Anything) To Do About It?, in International and Comparative Taxation p.p. 1, 2-3, 4 (Kees van Raad, ed. 2002). With kind permission from Kluwer Law International.

13.   At page 532, Hans-Werner Sinn, *Tax Harmonization and Tax Competition in Europe*, 34 European Economic Review 489, 490-91, 499, 500-01 (1990). Reprinted with permission from Elsevier.

ABOUT THE AUTHOR

Michael J. Graetz, a graduate of Emory University (B.B.A. 1966) and the University of Virginia Law School (J.D. 1969) is the Justus S. Hotchkiss Professor of Law at Yale University. Before becoming a professor at Yale in 1983, he was a professor of law at the University of Virginia and the University of Southern California law schools and Professor of Law and Social Sciences at the California Institute of Technology. His publications on the subject of Federal taxation include a leading law school text and more than 50 articles on a wide range of tax, health policy, social insurance, and tax compliance issues in books and scholarly journals. His books *True Security: Rethinking Social Insurance* (with Jerry Mashaw) and *The U.S. Income Tax: What It Is, How It Got That Way and Where We Go From Here,* were published in 1999 by Yale University Press and W. W. Norton & Co, respectively. He is also the author of *Federal Income Taxation: Principles and Policies* (Foundation Press) (with Deborah Schenk).

FOUNDATIONS OF LAW SERIES

ROBERTA ROMANO, GENERAL EDITOR

Foundations of Administrative Law
Edited by Peter H. Schuck, Yale Law School

Foundations of Contract Law
Edited by Richard Craswell, Stanford Law School and Alan Schwartz, Yale Law School

Foundations of Corporate Law
Edited by Roberta Romano, Yale Law School

Foundations of Criminal Law
Edited by Leo Katz, Michael S. Moore and Stephen J. Morse, all of the University of Pennsylvania Law School

Foundations of The Economic Approach to Law
Edited by Avery Wiener Katz, Columbia Law School

Foundations of Employment Discrimination Law
Edited by John Donohue, III, Stanford Law School

Foundations of Environmental Law and Policy
Edited by Richard L. Revesz, New York University Law School

Foundations of International Income Taxation
Edited by Michael J. Graetz, Yale Law School

Foundations of Labor Law
Edited by Samuel Estreicher, New York University Law School and Stewart J. Schwab, Cornell Law School

Foundations of Tort Law
Edited by Saul Levmore, University of Chicago Law School

CONTENTS

CONTENTS

CONTENTS

CONTENTS

CONTENTS

CONTENTS

CONTENTS

*

FOUNDATIONS OF INTERNATIONAL INCOME TAXATION

*

Chapter 1

Introduction and Overview

1.1 INTRODUCTION

The importance of international income taxation has grown dramatically over the last century. While the phrase "globalization of the economy" is now a cliché, the facts demonstrate it to have been a real phenomenon. The gross flows of capital from the United States abroad and from the rest of the world into the United States are very large and have become increasingly important to the U.S. economy, as reflected in Figure 1.1.

Figure 1.1

Net International Investment Position of the U.S., 1960 – 2001

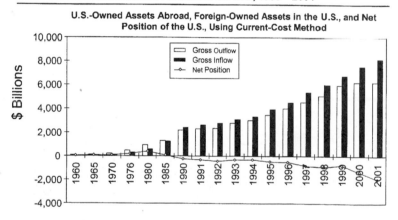

Sources: Survey of Current Business, July 2002, "The International Investment Position of the United States at Yearend 2001" by Elena L. Nguyen and Survey of Current Business, October 1972, Volume 52, Number 10, "The International Investment Position of the United States: Developments in 1971" by Russell Scholl.

This increase in international investment has occurred both for direct investments (where a U.S. person or corporation owns ten percent or more of a foreign corporation's shares) and for portfolio investments (less than ten percent ownership), as the following three figures demonstrate.

1

Figure 1.2

Direct Investment by and into the United States, 1960 - 2001

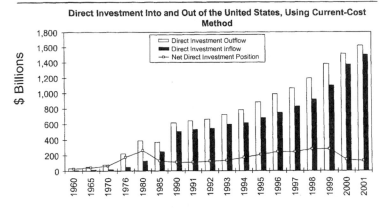

Sources: Survey of Current Business, July 2002, "The International Investment Position of the United States at Yearend 2001" by Elena L. Nguyen, and Survey of Current Business, October 1972, Volume 52, Number 10, "The International Investment Position of the United States: Developments in 1971" by Russell Scholl.

Figure 1.3

Portfolio Investment by Foreigners in the United States

Sources: U.S. Treasury Report on Foreign Holdings of U.S. Long-Term Securities as of March 31, 2000, and Summary of Report on Foreign Portfolio Investment in the United States, Office of the Asst. Sec., Int'l Affairs, Dept. of the Treasury, December 31, 1997.

Figure 1.4

Foreign Portfolio Investment by U.S. Nationals Abroad

U.S. Holdings of Foreign Long Term Securities, 1960-1999

Sources: Russell B. Scholl, *The International Investment Position of the United States in 1988,* Survey of Current Business, June 1989; Christopher L. Bach, *International Transactions, Revised Estimates for 1974-1996,* Survey of Current Business, July 1997, and U.S. Holdings of Foreign Long Term Securities, Office of the Asst. Sec., Dep of the Treasury, April 2000.

Note: 1997 and 1999 data comes from the U.S. Treasury Report on U.S. Holdings of Foreign Long Term Securities. Earlier data are only available through the standard Survey of Current Business publication and revisions, and are likely underestimated.

International tax policy exerts an important influence on business and investment activities. An examination of the incoming and outgoing flows of direct investment in the figures below makes it clear that—at least for corporations—tax considerations play a significant role. The size of direct investment to the United States from Luxembourg and the size of direct investment from the United States to Bermuda and

Figure 1.5

Direct Investment by the United States, 2001

U.S. Direct Investment Destinations, by Selected Nations, 2001

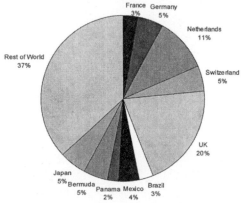

Source: Maria Borga & Daniel R. Yorgason, "Direct Investment Positions for 2001: Country and Industry Detail," *Survey of Current Business,* July 2002.

Panama surely is not justified by economic considerations alone. See Figures 1.5 and 1.6. The impact of tax considerations on the location of business activities has been confirmed by more sophisticated economic analyses.[1]

Figure 1.6
Foreign Direct Investment in the United States, 2001

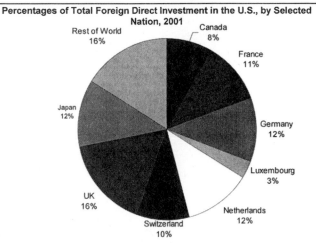

Percentages of Total Foreign Direct Investment in the U.S., by Selected Nation, 2001

Rest of World 16%
Canada 8%
France 11%
Germany 12%
Luxembourg 3%
Netherlands 12%
Switzerland 10%
UK 16%
Japan 12%

Source: Maria Borga & Daniel R. Yorgason, "Direct Investment Positions for 2001: Country and Industry Detail," *Survey of Current Business*, July 2002.

Despite the dramatic recent changes in the world economy, the fundamentals of the U.S. system of international income taxation date from the period 1918–1928. The regime of the 1920s remains largely intact probably because it has performed reasonably well; it has not proven a significant barrier to the international flow of goods, services, labor, or capital and may even have facilitated such flows. Congress, however, has revised the rules from time to time, usually to deal with one perceived abuse or another. So, while the fundamentals have remained unchanged, particular rules have become increasingly complex and cumbersome.

1. See, e.g., ROSANNE ALTSHULER ET AL., Has U.S. Investment Abroad Become More Sensitive to Tax Rates? (NBER Working Paper No. 6383, 1998) available at http://papers.nber.org/papers/W6383; Rosanne Altshuler & T. Scott Newlon, The Effect of U.S. Tax Policy on the Income Repatriation Pattern of U.S. Multinational Corporations, in STUDIES IN INTERNATIONAL TAXATION 77 (Alberto Giovannini et al. eds., 1993); Harry Grubert, Taxes and the Division of Foreign Operating Income Among Royalties, Interest, Dividends and Retained Earnings, 68 J. PUB. ECON. 269 (1998); James R. Hines, Jr., Lessons from Behavioral Responses to International Taxation, 52 NAT'L TAX J. 305 (1999).

Despite the longevity of the current U.S. system of international income taxation, disagreement rages over how best to structure an international tax system. The failure to achieve consensus is attributable in part to debate over the proper norms for evaluating an international tax system. In domestic taxation, analysts generally agree that a tax system should be evaluated on three criteria: efficiency, simplicity, and equity, although people dispute the meaning, relative weight, and priorities of these factors. Introducing multiple nations into the mix, however, makes the debate over the proper criteria much thornier. For example, should a nation be concerned with issues of equity or economic well-being for citizens of foreign countries, or should a nation instead simply attempt to maximize the well-being of its own citizens, regardless of the effects on foreigners? When a country uses its international tax regime as a way to compete to attract mobile capital, does this impose a valuable constraint on inefficient government spending or does it instead unleash a beggar-thy-neighbor spiral destined to undermine equitable taxation everywhere? There is a remarkable absence of consensus on issues such as these. In this chapter—as an introduction to the concepts that inform the policy debates throughout this book—we sample the most important contentions concerning the proper theoretical underpinnings of international income taxation.

1.2 TAXATION BASED ON RESIDENCE VERSUS SOURCE

If income is earned in one country (the "source country") by a resident or citizen of another country (the "residence country"), which country is entitled to tax this income and to what extent? Although seemingly straightforward, this question has proved quite difficult. As subsequent chapters will demonstrate, even defining residence and source—the crucial terms in the question—is not a simple task. For example, a person's country of residence may not be apparent if she resides in more than one country during the relevant period. And corporations may have considerable discretion in choosing their residences; a little paperwork may create a new corporation with a new country of residence. Likewise, a person or corporation may have a variety of sources of income from multiple "source" countries, and each may claim a share of the income.

Nations universally recognize that both the country of residence and the country of source have a valid claim to tax income. In contrast, a nation that is neither the country of source, or of residence or citizenship is generally not recognized as having a right to tax. If both the residence and the source country exercise their rights to tax simultaneously, however, the income will be taxed twice. Such "double taxation" is generally regarded as unfair and may create substantial barriers to cross-border economic activity and investments. The essential task of international tax policy is to mediate these claims of residence and source countries in an effort to ensure that income is taxed only once— and, in some cases, to ensure that it is taxed at least once. Indeed, much of this book addresses the competing claims of source and residence countries to tax income. This section sets forth the justifications for source and residence-based taxation and presents some of the approaches to reconciling these claims. The following two excerpts, from different articles by the economist Peggy Musgrave, describe the common justifications for source and residence-based taxes, respectively.

Peggy B. Musgrave, *Interjurisdictional Equity in Company Taxation: Principles and Applications to the European Union,* in TAXING CAPITAL INCOME IN THE EUROPEAN UNION 46, 52–53 (Sjibren Cnossen ed., 2000).

[W]e now examine the basis for [source] entitlement. * * *

Benefits provided

One of the most readily understood arguments on behalf of source entitlement is based on the benefit principle. Each jurisdiction should charge for the services that it has rendered. This calls for [company taxation] to be applied by the jurisdiction in which the production process occurs and the benefits are received. Such benefits may be seen in either of two ways. First, they might be looked at as being in the nature of intermediate goods which therefore lower the cost of production. In this case, a company profits tax is not as well suited to reaching those benefits as would be a more broad-based tax reaching a variety of inputs, such as value added tax. Alternatively, the benefits might be seen as arising from the government provision of part of the company's capital stock (in the form, for instance, of transportation facilities and other infrastructure) which, together with the firm's own capital, generates the profits. In this case, a company profits tax might be seen as a means of sharing in the firm's profits by the government corresponding to its provision of part of the productive capital. There is a further complication. The benefits (of whatever kind) provided to the firm may emanate from the jurisdiction of residence as well as from that of the source. * * *

National rental

From the economist's perspective, perhaps [the source jurisdiction's] entitlement to tax is best justified as a national rental charge for the use of its investment environment and natural resources by residents of another jurisdiction. This cross-border investment results in increased profits and reduced labour income in [the residence jurisdiction], with the opposite occurring in [the source jurisdiction], and with an overall net gain. [The source jurisdiction] might argue that it should be able to share, through tax participation, in [the residence jurisdiction's] increased profits, with the tax acting as a rental or royalty charge. * * *

*Territorial sovereignty and reciprocity * * **

As a matter of historical precedent * * * there is a generally accepted basis for source-based [company taxation] which simply derives from the notion of territorial sovereignty. Without further justification, this notion merely asserts the right to tax income from non-residents arising within its own borders and leaves open the questions of at what rate such income should be taxed. * * * But inasmuch as [company taxes] do not generally correspond to benefits provided by the host government, nor can they be regarded as forms of rental charges, those rates have to be set as a matter of interjurisdictional agreement based on mutually agreed notions of fairness. In this context, it seems reasonable to conclude that, in order to resolve conflict, the principle of reciprocity should apply. Reciprocity suggests that each pair of jurisdictions should tax the profits earned by residents of the other at equal rates and contrasts with the more generally applied rule of non-discrimination, which requires that each jurisdiction tax the income earned by investors from abroad at the same rate that income accruing to domestic investors is taxed.

Peggy B. Musgrave, *Sovereignty, Entitlement, and Cooperation in International Taxation*, 26 BROOK. J. INT'L L. 1335, 1336–37 (2001).

I begin with the proposition that so long as there are nation states serving populations with common purposes and interests, such states will wish to retain a degree of sovereignty over the tax treatment of the income earning activities abroad of their residents. Indeed, this national right to tax the global income of residents is recognized in international law. Residents are held to owe tax allegiance in return for the rights and privileges which they receive as residents, giving rise to what is commonly referred to as the "residence principle." Exercise of this tax sovereignty over foreign source income also is necessary to achieve equitable tax treatment of resident taxpayers by making all income, wherever earned, subject to tax, consistent with [income tax principles]. It also is needed to provide a policy instrument for affecting the outflow of capital in line with national policy objectives. It also may be justified in benefit terms, as a payment for productivity-enhancing benefits provided by the country of residence to its own factors of production prior to transfer abroad. What is important is that the country of residence is the residual taxing authority and thus has sovereignty over the total tax burden on the foreign-source income of its resident taxpayers.

If both the source country and the residence country are justified in imposing income taxes—as is now widely agreed—the question remains how to divide the tax revenues between the two countries. The following excerpt examines the idea of using considerations of "internation" equity as a basis for allocating international income taxes between residence and source countries.

Nancy H. Kaufman, *Fairness and the Taxation of International Income*, 29 LAW & POL'Y INT'L BUS. 145, 188–201 (1998).

A.   Internation Equity

Interindividual equity issues in taxation are fundamentally questions of economic justice among individuals. One can speak of the distribution of goods among individuals worldwide. However, in the present system of nation states, both revenue collection and government expenditure are matters of national, not international, prerogative. Hence, as a practical matter, interindividual equity in taxation is primarily a domestic issue. Internation equity, on the other hand, is fundamentally a question of economic justice among nations—the distribution of the competence to tax and, ultimately, tax revenue among nations. The limits of a particular country's tax base and the identification of its taxpayers in a multijurisdictional setting, although sometimes treated as matters of domestic concern, primarily affect the distribution of the competence to tax and tax revenue among nations. Hence, they are internation equity concerns. A just international tax system cannot be said to exist until each nation limits the scope of its tax base and identifies its taxpayers in a manner that effects internation equity.

The notion that internation equity should guide the formulation of international tax rules is not new. Peggy Musgrave distinguished between interindividual and internation equity over thirty years ago. Since then, only Peggy Musgrave, writing alone and with Richard Musgrave, has developed a theory of internation equity that might guide the international tax system. * * *

B.   Internation Equity Based on National Entitlements

Peggy Musgrave's view of internation equity begins with the commonly-accepted bases for the taxation of international income: source and residence. Referred to as national "entitlements," a home country has a right to tax its taxpayers' worldwide incomes, and the host country has a right to tax income arising within its geographic borders. In her early work, Musgrave viewed internation equity between the home and the host countries in terms of an equitable division of national gain and loss. A taxpayer's income is part of the "national gain" of his or her home country because a taxpayer's home country has an initial interest in all of its taxpayers' capital and incomes. Because of the home country's interest in its taxpayer's income, an income tax imposed by a host country results in a national loss to the taxpayer's home country. Whether the home country also experiences a loss of revenue or "treasury loss" depends upon the approach it takes to relieve double taxation. * * * The home country's national loss is a national gain to the host country.

In her more recent work, Musgrave has replaced the concepts of national gain and loss. Instead, she formulates the primary issue in internation equity in terms of the host country's share in the income arising within its geographic borders from the activities of foreign-owned capital. However, much of the essential structure of her earlier theory remains unchanged although * * * the interests of the home and host countries are perhaps more clearly on an equal footing in her more recent work. Still, the larger the share of international income taken in tax by the host country, the smaller the share that remains for the home country. Internation equity concerns the extent of the source entitlement and not the residence entitlement because the residence entitlement extends to worldwide income and does not result in a division of national gain and loss or of international income into shares. The extent of the source entitlement, the host country's share of international income, should flow from the theory underlying it.

Musgrave proposes several possible principles. One is host country taxation under a strict benefit rule; another consists of a system of economic rents. A strict benefit rule would allow the host country to impose a direct charge for the intermediate goods that the host country furnishes to the production process. Another possibility is that under a system of economic rents, the host country would charge an economic rent on that portion of the taxpayer's income that exceeds the amount of income the taxpayer would have earned on an investment at home. It is useful to recall that, viewed from within a home country's income tax, a strict host country benefit rule or a system of host country economic rents would not bring about shared interests in international income. Charges for intermediate goods imposed under a benefit rule at the place of production are costs of earning income. Income is a net concept. From the perspective of the home country, its taxpayers' costs of producing international income should not be included in such income. Using the same reasoning, a host country's charge of economic rent would be a cost of producing international income, not a part of international income. Thus, host country taxation under a strict benefit rule or system of economic rents arguably does not result in a division of national gain or loss or of international income into shares.

Musgrave examines two additional principles that might provide a basis for the host country's entitlement to tax and a measure of the host country's share of international income. One of these involves distributional considerations. Both Musgraves [Peggy and her husband Richard, also an economist.— ed] have suggested that "[w]ith a highly unequal distribution of resource endowments and per capita income among countries and in the absence of an adequate method for dealing with the problem, an appropriate pattern of tax-imposed national gains and losses might be used to secure some degree of adjustment." In terms of implementing a system that redistributes wealth internationally, the Musgraves have [suggested] an internationally agreed rate schedule for corporate tax and withholding tax wherein tax rates would relate inversely to per capita income in the host country and directly to per capita income in the home country. However, Musgrave ultimately settles the host country's entitlement on the legal principle of territoriality in international law under which the host country has the competence to tax income resulting from activities occurring within its borders. The legal principle of territoriality, however, does not suggest the measure of the host country's entitlement. A tempering of the territoriality principle might be found in the principle of nondiscrimination, the principle that all activity occurring within the host county's borders should be taxed alike. A related, but perhaps more appropriate, device would be the principle of reciprocity whereby two countries would agree to tax each other's taxpayers at equal rates.

* * *

Much of the modern body of international tax literature appears implicitly to accept that the home country has a superior interest in its taxpayer's worldwide income. Few modern commentators question a home country's tax on its taxpayer's foreign source income. Rather, the burden seems to be on the host country to justify its taxation of income arising within its borders. A few commentators failing to find any legitimate foundation for the host country's tax recommend a complete abandonment of source taxation in favor of an exclusive reliance on residence taxation. Their argument is framed in interindividual equity terms. In internation equity terms, their analysis suggests that the home country has an exclusive interest in its taxpayers' incomes. However, if states abolished source taxation in favor of relying exclusively on residence taxation, there would be no equitable division of national gain and loss or of interests in international income. * * *

It is very difficult to square the home country's superior interest in its taxpayers' incomes with the universality of source taxation, even in capital-exporting countries; nor is it likely that many countries view their systems of source taxation as taking that which fairly belongs to a foreign taxpayer's home country. Musgrave's more recent formulation of internation equity as concerning the host country's entitlement to a share of international income suggests that perhaps source entitlement and residence entitlement stand on equal footing. This later approach more closely conforms to today's international tax system.

NOTES

1) *Only a Little Help from Our Friends.* Although the excerpts above represent the best analyses to date of the relative claims of the source and residence countries, they do not provide much concrete guidance to the appropriate division of income tax revenues among countries. Countries of source and countries of residence both assert claims to tax international income. Working out the actual division of revenues between the countries is left to bilateral, or in a few cases, multilateral, income tax treaties. Both the OECD and the United Nations publish model treaties that are often used as a starting point for resolving nations' competing claims. The United States also publishes its own model treaty as a basis for its bilateral negotiations. There are now more than 2,000 bilateral income tax treaties in force around the world, but not all countries have treaties with each other. In the absence of a treaty, each nation's domestically enacted laws govern the taxation of international income earned by its residents or by nonresidents within its borders. The rest of this book adds detail to the kinds of issues that arise in dividing income among the nations that assert a right to tax it.

2) *International Redistribution.* Nancy Kaufman's excerpt indicates that Professor Musgrave considered—although ultimately did not settle on—a system in which taxing power is distributed based on each country's need. The idea that international tax policy should be used to redistribute income internationally is, to say the least, controversial. It certainly has not become a widely accepted norm of international tax policy. Indeed, rather than capital-exporting nations devising policies to enhance the well-being of struggling economies, it is far more common for less developed countries to shape their tax policies in an effort to attract mobile capital. As Chapter 11 details, the OECD nations[2] have sometimes responded by attempting to curb "harmful tax competition."

---

2. The OECD (Organization for Economic Co-operation and Development) is an organization consisting of thirty member countries, which attempts to "seek answers to

The following excerpt describes some concerns with using tax policy to redistribute income internationally.

Michael J. Graetz, *Taxing International Income: Inadequate Principles, Outdated Concepts, and Unsatisfactory Policies*, 54 TAX L. REV. 261, 300–01 (2001).

Achieving fairness in international income taxation is complicated further by the question whether the use of the tax law to redistribute income should stop at the nation's borders. Interrogation of this question, so far, has been largely absent from the international income tax literature, having generally been left to political philosophers. At a minimum, questions of international redistribution introduce two concerns: first, the issue of a worldwide entitlement to a minimal level of resources at least to prevent starvation, and perhaps malnutrition; second, the question of whether rich nations have any obligation to reduce misery to an "acceptable" level worldwide. The responsibility of rich nations to ensure any baseline of resources for all humanity is a controversial idea. And few observers contend that our obligations to people abroad are similar to those within our borders. As with efficiency, a national rather than worldwide perspective seems appropriate. Concerns for the economic opportunities of foreigners, indeed for their liberty, do not correspond to the commitment to equal opportunity we aspire to at home. But accepting that the international obligations required by justice, or by simple humanity, are less than those domestically does not render them nonexistent.

If fairness demands some transfer of resources across national borders, the question remains what role income taxation should play. * * * To take but one possibility, fairness between richer and poorer nations may imply that rich nations should be net exporters of capital. This could suggest that the international tax policy of rich nations should promote foreign investment, either generally (for example, by deferring to source countries) or alternatively, at least in less developed nations.

1.3 WORLDWIDE VERSUS TERRITORIAL TAXATION

The previous section discussed the theoretical arguments surrounding the claims of residence and source countries to tax income. In practice the international tax regime awards the principal right to tax income in many instances to the country where income is earned—the

common problems and work to co-ordinate domestic and international policies to help members and non-members deal with an increasingly globalised world." OECD Homepage, at http://www.oecd.org/EN/document/0,,EN-document-0-nodirectorate-no-13-26640-0,00.-html

country of source. This, for example, commonly occurs with income earned in the active conduct of a trade or business. Almost every country with an income tax imposes a source-based tax (and some countries also impose a residence-based tax). In most circumstances, therefore, the burden of preventing double taxation rests with the country of residence. This section addresses possible approaches to residence-based income taxation, given the likelihood of source-based taxation.

The residence country may want to tax foreign-source income even when the source country levies a tax. For example, the United States collects a residual tax on foreign-source income of U.S. residents when the foreign tax rate on the income is lower than the U.S. tax rate. The source country imposes its full tax rate on the income, but the United States collects any difference between that rate and the U.S. rate. This is achieved through the use of a rather complicated tax credit for foreign income taxes, the subject of Chapter 4. Other countries, such as the Netherlands, do not impose any residual residence-based tax on certain categories of income earned abroad; they exempt the foreign-source income earned by their residents from taxation.[3]

Sometimes analysts distinguish systems that tax foreign-source income from those that do not. They often call the former "worldwide systems" and the latter "territorial systems." No country, however, employs a pure "worldwide system" or a pure "territorial system." International tax regimes throughout the world are hybrid or "mixed" systems. Students should therefore be skeptical when either the label "worldwide" or "territorial" is used to ground an author's tax policy analysis or recommendations. The following excerpt attempts to define "worldwide" and "territorial" systems and compares the theoretical advantages of each, tilting the scales in favor of "worldwide" systems.

Staff of the Joint Committee on Taxation, *Background Materials on Business Tax Issues*, 53–56 (2002).

Worldwide tax system

In a pure worldwide tax system, resident individuals and entities are taxable on their worldwide income, regardless of where the income is derived. Double taxation of foreign income is mitigated through the allowance of a foreign tax credit. However, the credit is generally limited to ensure that the residence country preserves its right to tax income derived within the residence country. Since corporations are separate entities, foreign-source income earned by a resident through a foreign corporation generally is not subject to tax until repatriated. In the United States, several complex anti-deferral re-

3. See HUGH J. AULT, COMPARATIVE INCOME TAXATION: A STRUCTURAL ANALYSIS 384–85 (1997).

gimes apply as exceptions to this general rule and U.S. shareholders are taxed currently on certain mobile or passive income derived through certain foreign corporations.

Territorial tax system

In a pure territorial tax system, the country taxes only income derived within its borders, irrespective of the residence of the taxpayer. Thus, unlike in a worldwide tax system, foreign source income earned by a resident is exempt from tax. In a pure territorial system, there is no need for a foreign tax credit, because exemption generally eliminates the possibility of double taxation of foreign income. * * *

Mixed systems

No country uses a pure worldwide or territorial system. Systems may be * * * characterized as predominantly worldwide or territorial, but all systems share at least some features of both worldwide and territorial approaches. * * *

B.   Rationale for a Worldwide Tax System

Economic efficiency

A pure worldwide tax system arguably promotes economic efficiency, in that it does not distort the decision of whether to locate investment at home or abroad. * * * This efficiency norm is referred to as capital export neutrality. Common deviations from the "pure" form of the worldwide tax system, such as the foreign tax credit limitation,[4] reduce this neutrality.

Equity

A worldwide tax system arguably promotes equity in a number of ways.

Horizontal equity

First, a worldwide tax system arguably furthers the policy that taxpayers earning similar levels of income should be subject to tax at similar overall effective rates. Thus, a resident taxpayer earning income abroad should be subject to tax at the same effective rate as a taxpayer earning the same amount of income domestically. Providing a foreign tax credit mitigates the possibility that the taxpayer earning income abroad will be subject to a higher overall effective rate than the taxpayer earning income domestically; subjecting foreign-source income to residence-country tax mitigates the possibility that the taxpayer earning income abroad will be subject to a lower overall effective rate. Thus, a worldwide system provides a framework

---

4.   A detailed discussion of the foreign tax credit limitation can be found in Chapter 4.

for treating similarly situated individuals similarly—a concept known as horizontal equity.

Vertical equity

Second, a worldwide tax system arguably furthers the policy of a progressive income tax that taxes resident taxpayers earning higher levels of income at progressively higher marginal rates, on the theory that their greater ability to pay renders it fair to require them to shoulder a greater proportionate share of the tax burden. If ability to pay is regarded as important, then income earned abroad should be included in the tax base and subjected to progressive rates. Otherwise, the overall progressivity of the tax system may be eroded, as wealthier taxpayers may shift activities and income abroad. Thus, a worldwide system helps to promote the policy that higher income-earners should bear a larger proportionate share of the tax burden—a concept known as vertical equity.

Citizenship and residency as values

Taxing citizens and residents on their worldwide income arguably also reflects the notion that citizenship and residency bestow important benefits (e.g., legal and technical business infrastructure, military protection, passport and embassy services) that citizens and residents should be made to pay for, regardless of where they might earn their income. The United States is the only industrialized country in the world that taxes its citizens on their worldwide income, even if they reside outside the country.

Preservation of the U.S. tax base

A worldwide tax system arguably preserves the residence-country tax base more effectively than a pure territorial system. If foreign-source income is entirely exempt from taxation, then resident taxpayers will shift investment and income into tax havens, eroding the residence-country tax base. For this reason, even those countries that employ predominantly territorial systems (e.g., France) typically provide for current taxation of certain types of foreign source income that may easily be earned in tax havens—a significant departure from "pure" territorial taxation.

C. Rationale for a Territorial Tax System

Economic efficiency

A territorial system arguably promotes economic efficiency better than a worldwide tax system, because a territorial system treats all investment within a particular source country the same, regardless of the residence of the investor. This efficiency norm is referred to as capital import neutrality. * * *

Simplicity in compliance and administration

Some argue that territorial tax systems are less complex from an administrative and compliance standpoint than world-wide tax systems. It is certainly true that many complicated features of a worldwide system are not necessary in a *pure* territorial system. For example, the foreign tax credit and anti-deferral regimes, two of the most complex features of a world-wide tax system, are not necessary in a pure territorial system. However, a pure territorial system may not be viable because the country's tax base would be significantly eroded as residents shifted investments and activities abroad to low-tax jurisdic-tions. Thus, in order to make a territorial system work as a practical matter, various features of a worldwide system proba-bly must be incorporated, which in turn adds back much of the complexity that a pure territorial system would avoid. For example, some type of anti-deferral regime (e.g., for passive income shifted to low-tax jurisdictions) would probably be neces-sary to protect the tax base, but once adopted, such a regime would add substantial complexity to the system, both in the complexity of the anti-deferral regime itself and in the collateral consequences of having such a regime, such as the need for a foreign tax credit or other mechanism to mitigate double taxa-tion of the "tainted" income. * * *

Source vs. residence as basis for taxation

The concept of residence is the fundamental basis of taxa-tion under a worldwide tax system, whereas a pure territorial system, by relying on source, renders the concept of residence generally irrelevant. Several commentators have argued that, as applied to corporations, the concept of residence is becoming meaningless as a practical matter, since large multinational corporations are becoming "nationless" in the sense that their shareholders, employees, business activities, and income are increasingly spread throughout the world, rather than concen-trated predominantly in any one country. Thus, the de-emphasis of residence is arguably one advantage of a territorial system. Of course, in a territorial system that incorporates some attrib-utes of a worldwide system, the concept of residence would become important again, although probably less so than under a predominantly worldwide system.

As the previous excerpt indicates, in practice, no country uses a pure worldwide system or a pure territorial system. Some systems may be predominantly worldwide and others predominantly territorial, but all systems possess characteristics of both a worldwide and a territorial system. The practical overlap makes the theoretical distinction between the two systems less important than one might otherwise expect. The following two excerpts illustrate this overlap.

Michael J. Graetz & Michael M. O'Hear, *The "Original Intent" of U.S. International Taxation*, 46 Duke L.J. 1021, 1064–65 (1997).

[T]he distinction between exemption and foreign tax credit systems tends to be overdrawn. First, many countries that have an exemption system exempt foreign source income only if taxed "comparably" abroad. In addition, many countries—with France being a notable exception—have a so-called exemption with progression, and take the exempt income into account in determining the applicable tax in a progressive rate structure.

Moreover, the U.S. system has important elements of a regime designed to promote capital import neutrality. The averaging across countries inherent in an "overall" limitation on the foreign tax credit often makes it advantageous for a company that already has investments in a jurisdiction with tax rates higher than the U.S. to invest in a foreign jurisdiction with a lower tax rate. In addition, if an investment abroad is made by a foreign subsidiary of a U.S. parent, no U.S. tax is imposed until the earnings of the subsidiary are repatriated as dividends to the parent. When that happens, the U.S. allows a credit for the taxes paid to the foreign government. If the tax rate of the foreign country is low or the deferral of U.S. tax is sufficiently lengthy, the present value of the U.S. tax can be very close to zero—an exemption. In addition, by timing the payment of dividends from foreign subsidiaries, U.S. parents can minimize the impact of the FTC [foreign tax credit] limitation [and achieve results similar to those that obtain under "territorial" systems].

Hugh J. Ault, Comparative Income Taxation: A Structural Analysis 381–82 (1997).

While the exemption technique is often contrasted with the credit approach, in actual operation the two methods of relieving double taxation often yield quite similar results. In the systems here considered, exemption is usually limited to specific categories of income, most typically active business or employment income, that are likely to be subject to a level of tax comparable to that which would have been applicable in the residence country. Where rates are roughly comparable, in a credit system the residence country will not collect any additional tax on the foreign source income, a result functionally equivalent to exempting the income. Ancillary differences are reduced still further if an "exemption with progression" technique is used.

Nonetheless, there may be some important differences in the effects of the two techniques in particular situations. While rates may be roughly similar in general terms, there may be important variations across industries and with respect to different companies and the choice of exemption means that residual domestic tax may not be collected in some significant cases. In addition, great pressure is put on the source rules, as the decision that a particular item of income is foreign source may mean that it is not taxed anywhere if the source rules of the two jurisdictions are not completely congruent. Similarly, transfer pricing differences have different implications in an exemption system.

* * *

Whatever their relative advantages and disadvantages, in practice, no country uses a "pure" exemption or "pure" credit approach. All of the countries here considered combine these two methods, exempting certain classes of income and giving credit for foreign taxes imposed on others. The relative "mix" between exemption and credit varies substantially, however. The *United States*, the *United Kingdom*, and *Japan* make most use of the credit approach while the *Continental* systems have more exemption features. *Canada* and *Australia* fall somewhere in the middle.

NOTES

1) *Individuals versus Corporations.* The debate over worldwide versus territorial systems is different for corporations than for individuals. A central goal of the tax system in the United States is to impose a progressive income tax on individuals. On the other hand, the U.S. corporate tax is essentially imposed at a flat rate. It is widely believed that the only administratively feasible way to implement a progressive international tax structure for individuals is for the residence country to retain some residual taxing power over residents and perhaps citizens. Thus, the argument for residence-based taxation is considerably stronger for individuals than corporations.

2) *Cross-Reference.* An exemption alternative to the U.S. foreign tax credit system is examined in the final section of Chapter 5.

1.4   THE KEY NORMATIVE CONCEPTS OF INTERNATIONAL TAX POLICY

The previous two sections have framed the basic issue underlying international taxation policy—the need to mediate the claims of the source and residence country to tax income. This section surveys the norms most commonly used to analyze this issue. This chapter has already introduced several normative approaches. In *Fairness and the Taxation of International Income*, excerpted in Section 1.2, Nancy Kaufman offers the norm of internation equity as one possible approach. The Staff of the Joint Committee on Taxation, in the excerpt in Section 1.3 from *Background Materials on Business Tax Issues*, invokes various norms including economic efficiency, equity, and simplicity to justify international tax rules. The following excerpt from a former Assistant Secretary of the Treasury for Tax Policy summarizes the main principles underlying U.S. international tax policy.

Donald C. Lubick, Assistant Secretary of the Treasury for Tax Policy, *Remarks to the Tax Executives Institute*, March 23, 1999.

There are a number of principles that seem to have long guided policymakers in determining the appropriate taxation of international income. * * * Although there are differences over the application and relative weight to be given to them, these policy goals in the international tax area have been generally recognized.

- Meet the revenue needs determined by Congress in a fair manner
- Minimize compliance and administrative burdens
- Minimize distortion by, and maintain neutrality of, tax considerations in making of investment decisions
- Take due account of the competitive needs of U.S. multinational business, and
- Conform with international norms, to the extent possible.

The first three goals apply to income taxation in general.

Raising Revenue Fairly. The first goal is of primary importance. The credibility of our tax system depends upon the perception that revenue is being raised fairly and that the intended tax base is protected from avoidance.

Application of the concept of fairness, however, inevitably produces disagreement. For example, what is a fair tax burden on foreign business income compared to the tax burden on business income from domestic investment? And should there be a lower rate of tax imposed on income from business activities than the rate of tax imposed on income from labor? These fairness questions must be answered with significant popular satisfaction of some significant majority.

Minimizing Compliance and Administrative Burdens. The second goal, minimizing compliance and administrative burdens and avoiding complexity, receives universal acceptance, or at least lip service. The trouble is that simplification frequently comes with a cost.

* * *

Neutrality and Competitiveness. The goals of neutrality and competitiveness call for particular attention, because much of the debate * * * has revolved around these objectives. The objectives are sometimes in conflict, for example if reducing undue burdens on competitiveness requires reducing tax on foreign income. To what extent can this be accomplished without distorting investment decisions by favoring foreign investment over domestic investment? * * *

Thus we note that "competitiveness" means different things to different people. To quote a 1991 Joint Committee on Taxation Report, "although the term competitiveness is used frequently, it does not have a consistent definition."

Conforming to International Norms. Similarly, the goal of conforming with international norms is one that can mean different things to different people. As traditionally conceived, conformity requires, not rigid conformity of rates and base among countries, but that we adopt policies, such as a foreign tax credit, that have historically been adopted by developed countries to avoid double taxation. Some, however, would interpret conformity as requiring that we adopt policies that would facilitate world-wide escape from taxation. We do not accept the lowest common denominator as setting the standard in the areas of bribery, environmental regulation or fair labor laws, and we should not accept it in the tax area either.

_____

Much of the debate in both the academic literature and within the government over international tax policy has focused on norms of economic efficiency. The basic idea underlying norms of economic efficiency is that any distortions in investment decisions due to income taxation should be kept to a minimum. Unfortunately, this simple idea leads to different—and mutually inconsistent—norms. Recall that in the Joint Committee on Taxation's *Background Materials on Business Tax Issues* the first argument advanced on behalf of both a territorial and a worldwide system is economic efficiency. A pure *territorial* system is said to be efficient because a foreigner and a domestic resident investing in the same source country will both pay the same tax. This efficiency norm is known as capital import neutrality (CIN). On the other hand, a pure *worldwide* system is said to be efficient because a resident will face the same tax consequences whether she invests domestically or abroad. This efficiency norm is known as capital export neutrality (CEN). CEN is the norm of economic efficiency most widely advocated in the literature, although CIN also enjoys some support. A third norm, rarely endorsed, has been labeled national neutrality. These norms are described in more detail in the following two excerpts.

Office of Tax Policy–Department of the Treasury, *The Deferral of Income Earned Through U.S. Controlled Foreign Corporations: A Policy Study* (2000).

With respect to the broader question of how to tax foreign investment to achieve economic policy goals, a careful review of the literature reveals that capital export neutrality is probably the best policy when the goal is to provide the greatest global economic output. Capital export neutrality requires structuring taxes so that they are neutral and do not cause investors to favor either domestic or foreign investment. Put another way, if taxes were structured based on capital export neutrality, investors would make their investment decisions as if there were no taxes. Similarly, with respect to national economic welfare, a careful review of the literature provides no convincing basis for rejecting the conclusions of the basic economic analysis that a country should tax income from outward foreign investment at a rate that is at least as high as the tax rate imposed on income from domestic investment.

* * *

Policies that maximize global welfare are considered first, because maximizing global welfare is probably the best way to maximize U.S. economic welfare. All nations are likely to do best over the long term by establishing international tax policies that encourage private investors to make the best use of resources. Thus, it is probably not advisable to establish policies that promote national short-term interests at the expense of global economic welfare, because establishing such policies is likely to encourage other nations to seek to advance their own short-term national interests at the expense of global economic welfare. The need for a broad global view is particularly evident today in open economies, such as the United States, which have both substantial inbound and outbound investment. Further, the United States is often looked upon to provide global leadership in the policies it adopts.

It is also necessary, however, to determine how taxes on direct foreign investment income affect U.S. economic welfare. Although maximizing global economic welfare is probably the best policy for both capital-exporting and capital-importing countries, there may be more than one tax structure that achieves this goal, and individual countries will not necessarily be indifferent on the question of which structure should be adopted. For example, taxes on income from foreign direct investment can be structured so that for the same level of global output and total tax revenue, a capital-exporting country receives a bigger share or a smaller share of the revenue compared to a capital-importing country. The international distribution of tax revenue is thus not a matter of indifference to individual countries. Indeed, it is an important consideration when countries design their rules for taxing foreign investment.
* * *

1.   The "Standard Analysis"

Studies by Peggy Musgrave and Gary Hufbauer were among the first to carefully examine ways to structure international tax policies to maximize global economic welfare. They each used a basic model in which they assumed that there is only one form of capital investment used to produce only one type of output, that capital is freely mobile between countries, that the volume of saving is not affected by changes in the rate of return, that each country has its own tax rate that it applies to all income from investment earned within its borders, and that capital–importing countries do not change their tax policies in response to tax policy changes in the capital–exporting country. Analyzing this economic model, both Musgrave and Hufbauer found that a tax policy maximizes global economic welfare when it is consistent with the principle of capital export neutrality. According to this principle, countries should structure their taxes so that investors in a capital-exporting country are indifferent, after taxes, between foreign and domestic investments that are expected to produce the same pretax rates of return. In other words, international tax policies should be structured so that capital is allocated in the way it would be without taxes.

The logic of their analysis * * * is simple and compelling. First, consider a world without taxes. A fixed stock of privately-owned capital will be most productive if it is allocated in free, competitive markets by the owners, each independently seeking to gain the highest return from investment. All investors will be satisfied by their choices only when they cannot expect to increase their returns further by moving investments from one country to another. In other words, the allocation of capital is optimal when global output cannot be increased by reallocating capital between countries.

Now, suppose that the income from capital is taxed. Even if the countries each impose different tax rates, the optimal allocation of capital will still be achieved if each investor faces the same tax rate regardless of where the investment is placed. This will be true because the investors will be satisfied with their choices only when they can expect to receive the same after-tax return regardless of where they invest. However, because each investor would face the same tax rate regardless of where the investment is made, the expected pretax return from alternative investments would also be the same. Thus, the investors will make the same choices they would have made without taxation. The result is an optimal tax structure that provides the best international allocation of capital and maximizes global output.

By contrast, if the investors face different tax rates depending on where they invest, they will still make investments in such a way that they can expect to receive equal after-tax rates of return from alternative investments in different countries. However, because they would face different tax rates depending on where they invest, the rates of return from those alternative investments would have to differ, before taxes, in order to be equal, after taxes. The investors' choices would not result in the best allocation of capital because output could be increased if capital were instead moved from the country where the investors face the lower tax rate (and the pretax return is lower) to the country where they face the higher tax rate (and the pretax return is higher).

Michael J. Graetz, *Taxing International Income: Inadequate Principles, Outdated Concepts, and Unsatisfactory Policies*, 54 Tax L. Rev. 261, 270–75 (2001).

Frequently, the normative and policy discussions of international income taxation, including not only the academic publications of both economists and lawyers, but also—and perhaps most importantly—most of the key serious government analyses containing any normative discussion, begin and end with an assumption—not an argument—that the proper goal for U.S. international tax policy is advancing worldwide economic efficiency. Achieving such efficiency typically is said to involve two kinds of neutralities. The first is capital export neutrality (CEN), which is neutral about a resident's choice between domestic and foreign investments providing the same pretax rates of return. CEN requires that a resident of any nation pays the same marginal rate of income taxation regardless of the nation in which she invests. CEN is not only neutral about where such investments are made but also is indifferent about which country collects the tax revenue when capital originating in one country produces income in another. Typically, economists regard CEN as essential for worldwide economic efficiency, because the location of investments would be unaffected by capital income taxes.

Sometimes a second kind of neutrality, capital import neutrality (CIN), is supported. CIN requires that all investments in a given country pay the same marginal rate of income taxation regardless of the residence of the investor. CIN thus subjects all business activity within a specific country to the same overall level of taxation, whether the activity is conducted by a resident or a foreigner. If CIN holds, all savers, regardless of their residence, receive the same after-tax returns. They therefore face the same prices for future versus present consumption and the allocation of savings is efficient.

CEN usually is said to imply taxation only by the country of residence. Indeed the economic literature often suggests that if either national or worldwide economic efficiency is the goal, source countries should forgo any tax on foreign businesses operating within their borders. But countries universally impose source-based taxes whenever there is substantial business activity by both foreign and domestic companies. Thus, CEN in practice has come to mean that if the source country imposes tax, the residence country should grant a credit for the foreign tax. To fully implement CEN, the foreign tax credit should not be limited to the residence country's tax rate; income of foreign subsidiaries should be taxed currently by the residence country, and no cross crediting of foreign taxes on income taxed differently at source should be allowed. CIN, on the other hand, is said to support taxation only by the source country with the residence country exempting foreign source income from tax.

Thus, policy discussion of international income tax policy is now dominated by a simple matrix, where capital export neutrality and capital import neutrality generally constitute the normative universe. Implementing these policies requires respectively, worldwide taxation with a foreign tax credit or "territorial" taxation with foreign earnings exempt from tax. In theory, CEN gives the prime claim to tax international income to the country of residence and CIN awards that right to the country of source.

It is by now known that it is impossible to achieve CEN and CIN simultaneously in the absence of either a worldwide government or identical income tax bases and rates in all nations. This means that the analyst either must choose between these conflicting norms or—since both residence and source countries exercise their rights to tax income—urge some "compromise" between them. CEN enjoys the greatest normative support both in government analyses and in the academy. This is because distortions in the location of investments are thought to be more costly than distortions in the allocation of savings. Many economists regard the choice between CEN and CIN as essentially empirical, turning on the relative elasticities of savings and investment. Since investment is thought to be more responsive to changes in levels of taxation, a policy of CEN predominates. But the British economist Michael Keen emphasizes that "we currently know almost nothing about the quantitative welfare implications of alternative tax treatments of cross-national direct investment."

The conversation is not unanimously in favor of CEN. In the absence of perfect competition, some economists suggest that deviations from CIN may enable high marginal cost producers to co-exist with, or even drive out low-cost producers. Some legal scholars argue for the predominance of source-based taxation, government documents sometimes hedge their enthusiasm for CEN, and the U.S. business community consistently opposes CEN in the name of improving the "competitiveness" of U.S. multinationals abroad. In expressing concern for the "competitiveness" of U.S.-based multinationals, business representatives sometimes seem to be suggesting that any additional U.S. tax will be passed on to consumers in the foreign market in the form of higher prices (a somewhat unlikely scenario) but more often contend that if the U.S. tax system increases their cost of capital relative to that of foreign competitors, beneficial foreign projects will be forgone and undertaken by foreign-based companies. There is considerable debate about the welfare implications if this occurs.

Determined opposition to CEN as the goal of U.S. international income tax policy has led the U.S. business community to vigorously oppose elimination or reduction of the ability of U.S. multinationals to postpone U.S. taxation of foreign-source income until repatriated. But it has not yet resulted in the business community's embracing the CIN-linked policy of exemption of foreign source income.

The idea that CEN should be the linchpin of U.S. international tax policy was first voiced by the Kennedy administration in connection with its 1962 international tax proposals, proposals that led to the adoption of Subpart F [discussed in Chapter 5–ed.]. Treasury since that time often has expressed the view that CEN should guide policy. A few important examples include Blueprints for Tax Reform, issued in 1976, President Reagan's tax reform proposals of 1985, the 1996 Treasury White Paper on the International Taxation of Electronic Commerce, and Treasury's Study of Subpart F, issued in December 2000.

Congress has often refused to enact CEN-based proposals, however, and current law has come to be described routinely as a compromise between CEN and CIN. It is, for example, now commonplace, whenever international tax issues come before the tax-writing committees of Congress, for the pamphlets of the Staff of the Joint Committee on Taxation to describe a choice or compromise between CEN and CIN as the normative framework through which international tax policy issues should be addressed.

This is no longer just a U.S. phenomenon. The 1999 British Green Paper analyzing their foreign tax credit system and suggestions for change grounded the analysis and conclusions in a rather convoluted consideration of CEN and CIN.

Occasionally, international tax policy analysts give a brief nod to the misnamed norm of "national neutrality," which takes a national rather than worldwide point of view. This norm seeks neutrality between the pretax return on domestic investments and the return on foreign investments after the payment of foreign taxes (which is said to represent the return on foreign investments to the capital exporting country.) In essence, this norm regards domestic investment as preferable to foreign investment because the U.S. treasury gets to keep the revenue from taxing the income from domestic production. National neutrality would treat foreign taxes the same as domestic costs of doing business and allow only a deduction for foreign income taxes. The AFL–CIO urged replacing the foreign tax credit with a deduction for foreign taxes in the 1970's, and such legislation, the Burke–Hartke Bill, was introduced and debated, but Congress rejected the proposal. Today, while the national neutrality idea often is mentioned as a potential norm, national neutrality's policy of allowing only a deduction for foreign taxes generally is discussed only in passing; it is routinely dismissed as unwise and unrealistic.

NOTE

Norm Incompatibility. In the excerpt above, Michael Graetz mentions that CEN and CIN cannot be achieved simultaneously in the absence of identical income tax systems in all nations. Graetz, in an article with Michael O'Hear, elaborates:

> Our favorite way of making this point is in terms of an irreconcilable conflict among the following three simple principles:
>
> > Principle 1: People should pay equal taxes on their income regardless of the country that is the source of that income. In particular, U.S. taxpayers should be treated equally regardless of the source of their income.
> >
> > Principle 2: All investments in the United States should face the same burden regardless of whether a U.S. person or a foreign person makes the investment. In other words, U.S. and foreign-owned investments and businesses should be treated equally.
> >
> > Principle 3: Sovereign countries should be free to set their own tax rates and to vary them as their domestic economic situations demand.
>
> The essential difficulty is that the first two principles can hold simultaneously only when capital income is taxed at the same rate in all countries. This requires identical tax systems, including identical tax rates, an identical tax base, and identical choices between source and residence based taxation. That has never happened, and it never will. Even if it ever did, there would be no way to keep such a system in place without violating Principle 3. Moreover, bilateral treaties in which the United States gives benefits to certain foreign investors or foreign-owned businesses, in exchange for their countries giving reciprocal benefits to U.S. persons, will also defeat the ability to satisfy simultaneously both Principles 1 and 2. This difficulty makes compromises between these principles inevitable. Such compromises, in turn, have made the tax law governing international transactions subject to routine complaints of competitive disadvantage by U.S. companies depending on where they are competing and against whom. As a result, in practical political terms, the modern theories have proved little more useful than the ancient theories, such as "economic allegiance," which they have replaced.[5]

Failure to Achieve CEN

No nation has implemented an international tax scheme that is completely faithful to the norm of CEN, even though it is the most widely advocated norm. In particular, the U.S. system strays from the

---

5. Michael J. Graetz & Michael M. O'Hear, The "Original Intent" of U.S. International Taxation, 46 DUKE L.J. 1021, 1108–09 (1997).

ideal of CEN in several significant regards, as described in the following excerpt.

Hugh J. Ault & David F. Bradford, *Taxing International Income: An Analysis of the U.S. System and Its Economic Premises*, in TAXATION IN THE GLOBAL ECONOMY 11, 40–41 (Assaf Razin & Joel Slemrod eds., 1990).

[T]he implementation of [CEN] * * * in the real world of tax rules is enormously complex and the results often inconsistent. Some of the sources of this complexity can be identified relatively easily. In the first place, capital-export neutrality under the current system is present only when the U.S. tax rate exceeds the foreign rate. When the foreign rate of tax exceeds the U.S. rate, the theory of capital-export neutrality in principle would require the United States to credit the taxes against the U.S. taxes paid on U.S.-source income and, if necessary, refund the excess. If this step is not taken, then investment is discouraged in countries with rates of tax higher than that of the United States. In view of the revenue cost of such a policy, however, particularly when the possible reactions of foreign governments are taken into account, the credit has historically been limited to the U.S. taxes attributable to foreign-source income, though the form of the limitation has varied over the years. * * * [T]he limitations on the availability of the credit have led to much of the complexity of the legal rules.

More important, perhaps, the present form of the limitation has led to significant "second-best" issues. For example, under the current rules, averaging of foreign taxes is allowed for active business income. This means that a U.S. company that is currently paying high foreign taxes with respect to one active business investment is encouraged at the margin to undertake a new business investment in a low-tax foreign country rather than in the United States. The excess credits on the high-tax investment can in effect shelter all (or at least some) of the U.S. tax burden on the low-tax investment. In the extreme case where the foreign country does not tax the investment at all— for example, under a tax holiday—the U.S. firm is comparing the before-tax rate of return in the foreign country with the after-tax rate of return on a domestic investment. Thus, an imperfectly pursued policy of capital-export neutrality can lead to results exactly the opposite of those the policy was intended to achieve.

Similar issues arise with respect to the taxation of income earned through U.S.-controlled foreign subsidiaries. A fully implemented policy of capital-export neutrality would tax the subsidiary income to the U.S. shareholder as it accrues. On the other hand, a fully implemented policy of capital-import or competitive neutrality would lead to the complete exemption of foreign income. Historically, Congress has accepted business arguments that current U.S. taxation adversely affects the competitive position of U.S. companies in foreign markets. It has allowed the deferral of U.S. tax on subsidiary income until repatriation, but only as long as that income fell into certain categories. On repatriation, capital-export considerations reassert themselves, and the income is then taxed, with the allowance of the "deemed" foreign tax credit for the foreign taxes paid by the subsidiary. This "hybrid" mixture of capital-import and capital-export considerations again has led to the complex dividing lines required by subpart F to sort out income into deferral and accrual categories as well as the convoluted "pass through" of baskets for foreign-tax-credit purposes.

NOTE

Problems with National Neutrality. National neutrality is supposedly intended to promote the welfare of the nation's residents and citizens rather than being concerned with worldwide economic output. Peggy Musgrave has shown that a national neutrality norm implies allowing only a deduction rather than a credit for foreign income taxes. In the case of direct investments by U.S. corporations abroad, however, a deduction would offer far less relief from double taxation than does the foreign tax credit, thereby discouraging foreign investment, at least to some extent. While there can be no decisive empirical evidence, it is difficult to believe that the United States would have been better off with significantly less foreign investment than occurred in the period since 1918, when the foreign tax credit was enacted. Thus, the basic premise of the national neutrality norm is questionable.

In addition, another concern with a national neutrality approach to international tax policy is that other nations would react in kind, leading to a "beggar-thy-neighbor" contest. According to this argument, the result in practice would be a reduction in worldwide economic output and a corresponding reduction in U.S. economic output.

Norms in Addition to Economic Efficiency

Although economic efficiency is an important consideration, the emphasis on worldwide efficiency to the exclusion of other norms in the international tax policy debate is open to question. A major concern with the focus on CEN is that notions of fairness are generally ignored. The following excerpt exposes the shortcomings of the current debate and also gives some insight into normative criteria other than worldwide efficiency.

Michael J. Graetz, *Taxing International Income: Inadequate Principles, Outdated Concepts, and Unsatisfactory Policies,* **54 Tax L. Rev. 261, 276–325 (2001).**

The narrow normative focus of the international tax literature contrasts sharply with the domestic tax policy literature, of both the academy and the government, where contentions over normative issues lie at the center of the policy debates. In domestic tax policy, fairness in taxation tends to hold center stage. Achieving fair taxation with a minimal loss of economic efficiency or achieving a proper balance between economic efficiency and equity is routinely described as the appropriate quest for tax policy. Even in the economics literature concerning domestic tax policy, where economic efficiency takes precedence, discussion of other norms, particularly equity norms, is common.

The dominant normative perspective of international tax policy debates—limited to a choice or a compromise between CEN and CIN—both inhibits an adequate understanding of the normative underpinnings of international income tax policy and improperly limits serious consideration of alternative policies. There are three major problems with relying on worldwide economic efficiency (and thus CEN) as the foundation for international income tax policy. First, it seeks to improve worldwide rather than national well-being. Second, the idea of economic efficiency is too limited. Third, focusing on economic efficiency as the guiding light excludes other important values.

A. Rejecting a Worldwide Perspective

We naturally give primacy to our own citizens in setting national policy, including tax policy. This is both a matter of historical circumstance—some would say accident—and, more importantly, of political organization. In our democratic society, we the people have organized a national government to protect our safety and security, to maintain our liberty, and to promote the well-being of our citizens and residents. By assigning the task of improving the lot of the nation's citizens, including those who are least advantaged, to our government, we have made both economic growth and redistribution of income or wealth a matter of national, rather than worldwide, concern.

* * *

Why, in formulating international tax policy, should we evaluate the distribution of tax burdens (and government benefits, including transfers) within national borders, but be indifferent about where enhanced economic output occurs, whom it benefits, and what national treasury obtains the tax revenues?

Why does our higher obligation to U.S. citizens and legal residents not also apply to promoting economic output and improving economic well-being?

When we are talking, as now, about making policy, we cannot ignore history or culture. The freedom and independence, as well as the economic welfare, of people varies from nation to nation. This simply is fact. In the absence of a world government, this is how it must be.

Moreover, although I cannot develop the argument here, I believe this is how it should be. Notwithstanding the utopian philosophical ambitions for worldwide harmony implied by those who urge taking a "one-world view," I agree with those political philosophers who insist that a world government—a political entity exercising the powers now held by national governments—would likely live in a constant state of civil unrest, as various populations and regions contest for freedom, autonomy, and self-government. A "world government" would likely become a dictatorship.

* * *

Tax policy decisions, including decisions regarding a country's tax treatment of international income, should be, and inevitably are, decided based on a nation's capacity, culture, economics, politics, and history. In democracies, such decisions are determined by the votes of the nation's citizens and their representatives. Taxation without representation is still tyranny.

Unfortunately, international income tax policy does not enjoy a harmony between national and worldwide interests similar to international trade. The consensus of economists insists that a policy of free trade not only improves worldwide efficiency but also improves the economic efficiency of each nation that reduces trade barriers unilaterally. But many economists claim that the benefits of free trade are not replicated by free flows of capital, and no such confluence between national and worldwide gains has been claimed for international tax policy.

International income tax policy guided by worldwide economic efficiency is concerned with increasing economic output and reducing deadweight loss, wherever it occurs. The goal of worldwide economic efficiency tells tax policymakers—the legislators who enact the law and the representatives of the President who negotiate tax treaties—to seek improvements in the amount and/or allocation of world capital, regardless of who benefits and of the revenue consequences to the U.S. treasury.

Worldwide efficiency tells a U.S. policymaker to respond with equal vigor to avoidance of a foreign country's taxes and avoidance of U.S. taxes. This criterion is indifferent both about whose well-being is increased and which nation's treasury collects the income taxes that are assessed. If a choice must be made between benefitting the nation's own citizens and residents or benefitting people elsewhere, the principle of worldwide economic efficiency urges policymakers to embrace the larger benefit without regard to where it occurs or who benefits. Worldwide economic efficiency does not heed love of country.

But why should a U.S. President or members of Congress put aside "narrow" national interests to fashion U.S. tax policy in a manner apathetic to whether benefits flow to U.S. citizens or citizens of other nations? Why should they not care whether taxes flow into the U.S. treasury or to some foreign nation? Paying attention to the distribution of the burdens and benefits of taxation among U.S. families and to the revenue consequences of the tax law is a fundamental obligation of both legislators and the executive branch in our democracy.

Let me not be misunderstood. By urging that this nation's international tax policy be fashioned to advance the interests of the American people, I am not calling for either American imperialism or American isolationism. Nor am I suggesting any retreat from this nation's engagement in the world economy or from political cooperation with other nations and peoples. * * *

Advocates of worldwide economic efficiency as the guiding principle of U.S. international income tax policy sometimes point to the shortcomings of "national neutrality"—a policy allowing only a deduction for foreign income taxes—as a reason for eschewing a national point of view in fashioning international tax policy. But the inadequacies of that policy do not support worldwide economic efficiency as the proper goal. They serve instead simply to demonstrate that any nation must take the responses of foreign governments into account in making international tax policy, and as a reminder that cooperative multilateral policymaking may benefit both U.S. citizens and foreigners. National neutrality is an example of a policy that may advance national self-interest in the short term but prove self-defeating over the long run.

* * *

B.   Too Narrow a View of Economic Efficiency

In denying that a worldwide perspective is the proper lens for U.S. international income tax policy, I am not rejecting an important role for considerations of economic efficiency in formulating that policy. But I believe the proper function of economic efficiency in this context is to ask—from the national perspective—what international income tax rules will enhance Americans' standard of living, now and in future generations, for example, by promoting economic growth in the United States. As with domestic tax policy, the proper question is about the effects of international tax rules on the economic well-being, the welfare, of U.S. citizens and residents.

All taxes have efficiency costs; they change incentives to engage in various activities and affect the allocation of resources. If economic efficiency were the sole goal of tax policy, we would see only per capita taxes, head taxes. Margaret Thatcher tried a little experiment in the United Kingdom along these lines that proved a political disaster.

* * *

C. Economic Efficiency as the Sole Value

The focus in the international income tax literature on economic efficiency to the exclusion of all other values is antithetical to the analysis of tax policy generally, and of income tax policy especially. When assessing our domestic income tax policy or arguing for any substantial change in that policy, the debate generally is guided by a coherent, if controversial, set of multiple principles. There is great dispute over the meaning of these norms and about the priority to be accorded to each, but since Adam Smith, it has been commonplace to say that a tax system should be fair, economically efficient, and reasonably easy to administer and comply with.

* * *

If economic efficiency were the sole goal of tax policy, we would tax wages or consumption, but not income. Having decided to impose an income tax, it is mysterious why concern for fairness should disappear simply because goods or services or labor or capital, have crossed national boundaries.

To the contrary, the original motivation for the unilateral adoption by the United States of a foreign tax credit was grounded in concerns for fairness.

* * *

The enactment of the foreign tax credit was intended to ensure that the tax burden on investment and business income did not become too high (labeled "double taxation") simply because the income was earned abroad rather than in the United States. The FTC also was advanced to ensure that foreign source income of individuals and businesses not escape taxation altogether.

* * *

E.   Nondiscrimination   and   Reciprocity   as   Fairness–Based Norms

* * *

The idea of fair play between sovereign people of different nations also introduces a concern for "reciprocity" between nations as an element in securing fairness or justice in international taxation. A requirement of "reciprocity" is familiar in discussions of international relations, including international tax policy. I cannot discuss the idea in any detail here, but I believe that ideas of fair play, of reciprocity, are quite useful in explaining, for example, recent multilateral efforts to curb "harmful tax competition." In my view, the requirements of reciprocity may be more pronounced in cases of geographic proximity and more attenuated between rich and poor nations (such as those within and without the OECD).

* * *

I.   Foreign Policy and International Taxation

So far, I have argued that basing U.S. international income tax policy solely on the principle of worldwide economic efficiency is wrong both because it fails to give adequate priority to the goals and interests of the American people and omits from consideration important demands of fairness, of justice. But the process of international tax policymaking is further complicated by other considerations, including foreign policy.

For the well-being of its citizens and residents, the U.S. government necessarily takes into account—through its foreign policies—circumstances elsewhere in the world. This nation's attitudes and policies toward other nations depend on economic, political, and social relationships, as well as our history. History, for example, best explains our current relationship with the Philippines. Our alliances for defense constitute a classic example of U.S. foreign policy at work. Another example is U.S. actions to affect the flow of foreign oil. Sometimes we act simply out of altruism.

Foreign policy concerns have long played an important role in U.S. international tax policy. In 1921 Congress enacted a special exemption for businesses operating in U.S. possessions to encourage economic development there. That law became the model for the special tax advantages enacted in 1942 for Western Hemisphere Trade Corporations. In 1922 Congress passed the China Trade Act, which adopted a complicated structure providing benefits to "China Trade Corporations" to stimulate investments in China by U.S. corporations. * * *

This nation's post-war policies of using both public and private capital to rebuild the economies of Europe and Japan prompted a number of changes in U.S. international tax rules following World War II, including rules governing the calculation of the limitation on the foreign tax credit. Encouraging investments abroad by U.S. corporations and individuals was intended not only to stimulate economic development in countries devastated by the war, but also to spread capitalism and democracy through economic interdependencies and political alliances. Similar goals have been advanced more recently for U.S. investments in Eastern Europe, the former Soviet Union, and China.

* * *

The income tax also has denied foreign tax credits for companies participating in a boycott of Israel and investing in South Africa during apartheid. The former was enacted to express our distaste for the boycott and to reaffirm this nation's special relationship with Israel. In the latter case, humanitarian concerns of U.S. citizens provided a national interest in discouraging private investments in South Africa.

There are many other potential uses of international tax policy to advance U.S. foreign policy. In the late 1970's, for example, when keeping the supply of mideast oil flowing headed the U.S. foreign policy agenda, some analysts suggested that U.S. oil companies should be entering into management service contracts with oil-producing nations rather than making equity investments. To achieve such an outcome, U.S. policymakers could have readily fashioned international tax rules to favor management contracts and disfavor equity investments. Instances where government should make these kinds of distinctions may be rare, but when they are warranted, international income tax laws may facilitate the desired policies.

* * *

Indeed, tax policy may be a superior instrument of foreign policy when stimulating or inhibiting investments of private U.S. capital or transfers of technology or other knowledge to another country is important to this nation's foreign policy interests. Only the view that the tax law is always a bad way to do things other than raise revenue—the perspective of tax-expenditure religionists—would rule out the tax law as an implement of U.S. foreign policy.

In assessing the role of international tax policy as an instrument of U.S. foreign policy, we should keep in mind the relative inadequacy and costliness of other foreign policy options, including economic sanctions, military blockades, and war.

* * *

J. Compliance Costs and Administrability

Even when treated as a separate goal, rather than just a facet of economic efficiency, simplicity always seems to be the forgotten stepchild of income tax policy. Routinely lip service is offered to the idea that the tax law ought to be as simple to comply with and administer as possible; then, after a nod and a wink, vaulting complexity overleaps itself. Analyzing international tax policy solely through the competing lenses of CEN and CIN relegates simplicity to a footnote.

But wasting valuable resources through unnecessary costs of complying with a complex tax law is economically inefficient. And the Service cannot fairly administer a law its personnel cannot comprehend.

* * *

K. International Cooperation and Conformity

Conformity with international practices sometimes is advanced as an independent principle for making international income tax policy. This I think is a mistake. As I have said, I believe the United States should shape its international tax policy to serve the best interests of the nation, broadly defined. A wide range of principles must be taken into account, including what is fair, economically efficient, reasonably simple to comply with and administer, and advances the nation's foreign policy interests.

Often our national interests can be enhanced through international cooperation, cooperation that also may produce gains for other nations. And when a cooperative solution proves impossible or impractical, our national interests may best be promoted by bringing our rules into closer conformity with those of foreign countries. The flexibility that companies enjoy in determining the source of income and their country of residence may mean that the international tax policies and rules of other nations may constrain our ability to depart dramatically from international practice and still achieve our policy goals. This constraint may be especially important as a practical matter in taxing income from direct investments by corporations.

* * *

Caution, however, is warranted in assuming that conforming our nation's tax system with that of other nations—even developed nations with effective income taxes—will inevitably improve our national welfare. International harmonization of tax systems, like other changes in policy, will tend to produce winners and losers. Recent evidence, for example, suggests that European harmonization of capital income taxes might increase the welfare of citizens and residents of the United Kingdom, while producing large outflows of capital and significant diminution of tax revenues and welfare in the nations of continental Europe.

National interests and social, economic, and political conditions vary from country to country, often along important dimensions. International conformity and cooperation therefore should never be an end in itself and need not serve generally as a bedrock principle informing U.S. international tax policymaking. Rather, cooperation and sometimes conformity are properly regarded as possible means to achieve improvement of our national welfare and the development of a simpler and more just tax system.

L.   Enforceability

Collectability is an essential attribute of any tax. Enacting rules that cannot be enforced is pointless. In the international tax arena, considerations of enforceability have always shaped the law and always will. Source-based taxation of income, for example, has long been justified, at least in part, on the ground that the country of source is in the best position to collect income tax.

III.   Unsatisfactory Policy

Adherents of CEN have clear policy priorities: They would eliminate "deferral"—taxation by the United States of active business income of foreign corporations controlled by U.S. corporations or persons when repatriated to the United States rather than when earned. As I have indicated, elimination of deferral was proposed to Congress in 1962 by President Kennedy, suggested again in December 2000 by Treasury (along with reliance on CEN as a basis for U.S. international tax policy), and frequently endorsed by other CEN proponents. On the other hand, support for the other two policy changes implied by CEN—elimination of cross-crediting of foreign taxes and repeal of the foreign tax credit limitation—is scarce. The former is regarded as impractical, * * * the latter unwise. No one urges an unlimited foreign tax credit, because it would both undermine the ability of the United States to collect taxes on U.S. source income and invite other nations to impose high taxes on U.S. companies as a way to shift revenues from our treasury to theirs. Although CEN advocates insist that their policy is "worldwide" taxation of residents, a "pure" CEN policy is not in the cards.

Enthusiasts of CIN, on the other hand, endorse a territorial system of international income taxation, a system that would grant the exclusive power to tax income to countries of source, with no tax on income earned abroad by countries where the suppliers of capital reside. But, although about one-half of the OECD countries exempt from tax at least some foreign active business income, nations with substantial capital exports routinely retain residence taxation of passive and portfolio income.

Viewed through the twin lenses of CEN and CIN, U.S. international tax policies (and those of our major trading partners) can reasonably be described as a "compromise," and, as I have stressed earlier, a "compromise" between CEN and CIN can justify virtually any policy outcome. Debating CEN versus CIN as a guide to international tax policymaking is a dead end. We need to change the conversation about international tax policy, and take a fresh look at our international tax rules. And in doing so, we should avoid fruitless policy debates where one side insists that any departure from worldwide taxation of U.S. residents, including corporate residents, is an unfortunate violation of CEN, while the other side demands that only territorial taxation of income will implement CIN.

Instead, we can now ask the straightforward, but difficult to answer, question: What international tax policy is in the best interests of the people of the United States, taking into account political as well as economic considerations, and the demands of fairness as well as of efficiency, recognizing that nations believe that they have rights (or at a minimum, fair claims) to the tax revenues attributable to the economic activities that take place within their borders, and keeping in mind that the United States is now a large importer, as well as exporter, of capital? We should minimize the costs of compliance and administration and acknowledge that an unenforceable tax can be neither efficient nor fair.

NOTE

Too Many Factors? Michael Graetz discusses several considerations besides worldwide efficiency that should be relevant to policy discussions, including internation equity, nondiscrimination, reciprocity, redistribution, foreign policy, administrability, international cooperation, and enforceability. The norms of internation equity and redistribution were also discussed in Section 1.2, and nondiscrimination[6] is the subject of Chapter 10. Needless to say, fashioning an international tax policy to further all of these goals is a formidable task.

This chapter has introduced the basic concepts and debates that inform the issues discussed throughout this book. Themes sounded here reverberate in the chapters that follow. The concepts of source and residence are fundamental to international taxation. The norms of CEN and CIN—and others—arise time and time again when assessing specific issues of international income taxation. A basic understanding of these concepts is essential for comprehending the policy debates in this field.

6. Nondiscrimination here generally refers to the principle that foreigners should be taxed the same as residents.

Chapter 2

Source of Income

2.1 Introduction

The source of income is a fundamental concept in international taxation for two reasons: It determines whether a foreign country will assert jurisdiction to tax a U.S. person, and it determines whether foreign persons will be subject to U.S. taxation. Generally when U.S. individuals or corporations have U.S. source income, they pay U.S. tax without regard to the international tax rules. On the other hand, the U.S. income tax typically does not apply when a foreign person has foreign source income. However, the U.S. does assert its taxing authority over a foreign person with U.S. source income. Likewise, when a U.S. person has foreign source income, the foreign country asserts its jurisdiction to tax that income. To mitigate the potential for double taxation, the U.S. allows a credit for the resulting foreign income taxes paid with the credit limited to ensure that the foreign taxes do not offset U.S. taxes on U.S. source income. In simplified terms, this limitation is based on the amount of U.S. tax owed on the taxpayer's foreign source income. Source is thus the determining factor in limiting the creditability of foreign taxes for a U.S. taxpayer. (The foreign tax credit is discussed in Chapter 4).

Our taxing system therefore depends critically on identifying the source of income. Unfortunately, current law performs this task poorly. Many of our source rules are open to substantial manipulation. In addition, while different countries often have similar rules for determining the source of income, these rules need not be the same and in fact typically vary in important ways. For instance in the U.S. and Canada, dividends are typically sourced to the country in which the corporation paying the dividend is resident, but Australia sources dividends to the location where the corporation earns its income.[1] Consequently, in the absence of a treaty harmonizing the tax treatment of each form of income, different source rules may create the potential for double or no taxation.[2]

1. Richard G. Tremblay, Foreign Tax Credit Planning, in Canadian Tax Foundation, Corporate Management Tax Conference 3:1, 3:18 (1993).

2. For example, absent a tax treaty, a dividend paid to a U.S. person holding shares in a Canadian corporation earning its income in Australia might be taxed by all three countries. Since both Canada and Australia would claim the income as domestic source income, neither would grant a foreign tax credit for taxes paid in the other.

2.2 U.S. Source Rules

Suppose a company manufactures and sells bicycles. Its owners live in Japan; its factory is in Mexico; its main offices are in Canada; its principal sales office is in the U.S., where most of its bicycles are sold; and it is incorporated in Bermuda. The geographical source of income from its bicycle sales is far from clear. On one hand, the Japanese owners supplied the capital to create the company, and the U.S. provides its principal market. But Mexico provides the bulk of its labor, Canada is the locus of its management, and Bermuda provides the legal arrangements enabling the company to exist.

Faced with this inherent complexity, the current methodology for determining the source of income is based upon a dizzying and frequently counter-intuitive array of rules, exceptions, and exceptions to exceptions. In order to determine the source of income one must first determine the type of income, then the residence of the parties involved (mindful that the definition of residence may be specific to the type of income), and finally ascertain whether any exceptions to the general rule for that type of income apply. As is often the case, in designing source rules there is an inherent tension between ensuring predictability on the one hand and preventing tax avoidance on the other. While bright line rules ensure that taxpayers and the IRS know the source of different items of income in advance, such rules also create opportunities for taxpayers to step over the line. By re-categorizing the form of income to one that receives more favorable sourcing and tax treatment, taxpayers may reduce their tax liability.

Like much of U.S. international tax law, the source rules are contained in the Internal Revenue Code and elaborated upon by the accompanying regulations. Here, as elsewhere, the Code and regulatory rules may be modified by treaty. The following chart provides a road map of the core source provisions, which are supplemented by numerous other sections throughout the Code that fill in particular details of the source regime.

Code Section	Rules
861	Basic source rules for U.S. source interest, dividends, rents, royalties, gains.
862	Basic source rules for foreign source income; mirror image to section 861.
863	Special rules on allocation of income/expense, income from multiple sources, transportation and communications income.
865	Source rules for sales of personal property other than inventory property.

When reading the following excerpts (and when reviewing Table 1 at the end of this section), all of which provide a partial summary of the most important source rules in the Code, consider the extent to which each source rule aims for clarity, identification of income's true economic source, or some other objective.

Hugh J. Ault & David F. Bradford, *Taxing International Income: An Analysis of the U.S. System and Its Economic Premises* 13–15 (from Taxation in the Global Economy) (Assaf Razin & Joel Slemrod eds., University of Chicago Press, 1990).

Source of Income Rules

The source rules are central to the taxing jurisdiction asserted over both U.S. and foreign persons. For foreign persons (including U.S.-owned foreign subsidiaries), the source rules define the U.S. tax base. For U.S. persons, the source rules control the operation of the foreign tax credit since they define the situations in which the United States is willing to give double-tax relief. In general, the same source rules apply in both situations, though there are some exceptions. The following are some of the most important source rules.

Interest

Interest received on an obligation issued by a U.S. resident (including the federal government) is U.S.-source income unless the payor has derived more than 80 percent of its income over the last three years from an active foreign trade or business. Interest paid by a foreign obligor in general has a foreign source, except that interest paid by a U.S. branch of a foreign corporation is U.S. source. * * *

Dividends

All dividends from U.S.-incorporated corporations are U.S.-source income regardless of the income composition of the corporation. Dividends paid by foreign corporations are in general foreign source unless the corporation has substantial U.S.-source business income, in which case the dividends are treated as partially from U.S. sources. As in the case of interest, a special rule preserves the U.S. source (for foreign tax credit purposes) of dividends paid by a U.S.-owned foreign corporation that itself has U.S.-source income.

Rents and Royalties and Services

Rents and royalties from leasing or licensing of tangible or intangible property have their source where the property is used. If a transaction involving intangible property is treated as a sale for tax purposes, the royalty source rule applies to the extent that any payments are contingent on productivity. Services income has its source where the services are performed.

Staff of the Joint Committee on Taxation, *Factors Affecting the International Competitiveness of the U.S.* 144–155 (JCS–6–91, MAY 30, 1991).

Insurance income

Underwriting income from issuing insurance or annuity contracts (that is, premiums earned on insurance contracts less losses incurred and expenses incurred) is sourced domestically if the contract is in connection with property in, liability arising out of an activity in, or lives or health of residents in the United States. * * * All underwriting income not treated as derived from U.S. sources under the above rules is treated as foreign source income.

Transportation income

Generally, 50 percent of income attributable to transportation which begins or ends in the United States is U.S. source. If the transportation both begins and ends in the United States, 100 percent of the transportation income is U.S. source. For this purpose, transportation income is income derived from, or in connection with, the use, or hiring or leasing for use, of a vessel or aircraft or the performance of services directly related to the use of such vessel or aircraft. Income from the performance of services attributable to transportation that begins and ends in the United States is fully U.S. source income, and income from the performance of services attributable to transportation between the United States and a U.S. possession is subject to the regular 50–50 rule for transportation income. However, any other income from the performance of services by seamen or airline employees for transportation that begins or ends in the United States, and not described above is not transportation income and is sourced as personal services income. * * *

Income from space or ocean activities or international communications

In the case of a U.S. person, income from an activity in space or on or under international waters generally is sourced domestically. International communications income is sourced 50 percent domestically and 50 percent foreign.

* * *

Dispositions of real property

Gains, profits, and income from the disposition of a United States real property interest are sourced domestically. Gains, profits and income from the sale or exchange of real property located outside the United States are sourced foreign.

Sales of personal property

In general

Subject to significant exceptions, income from the sale of personal property generally is sourced on the basis of the residence of the seller. Similarly, foreign currency gain or loss generally is sourced on the basis of the residence of the taxpayer. * * * [Following are some of the most important exceptions.]

Inventory property

Gains, profits and income derived from the purchase of inventory property within the United States and its sale or exchange without the United States are sourced foreign. Similarly, gains, profits, and income derived from the purchase of inventory property without the United States and its sale or exchange within the United States are sourced domestically. Income attributable to the marketing of inventory property by U.S. residents in other cases also has its source at the place of sale.

Title passage rule generally—The place of sale generally is the place where title to the property passes to the purchaser (the "title passage" rule). This title passage rule applies both to all income from the purchase and resale of inventory and to the marketing portion of income from the production of inventory property in the United States and marketing of that property abroad. Moreover, this rule applies regardless of whether the sale is to an unrelated purchaser or to a related person (for example, a foreign corporate subsidiary) that resells the property to an unrelated purchaser. * * *

Production/marketing split * * * Under Treasury regulations, 50 percent of * * * income [derived from the manufacture of products in the United States and their sale elsewhere] generally is attributed to the place of production (in this case, the United States), and 50 percent of the income is attributed to marketing activities and is sourced on the basis of the place of sale (determined under the title passage rule). Under certain circumstances, the division of the income between production and marketing activities must be made on the basis of an independent factory or production price, rather than on a 50–50 basis, where a taxpayer sells part of its output to wholly independent distributors or other selling concerns in such a way as to establish fairly the independent factor or production price unaffected by considerations of tax liability (Treas. Reg. sec. 1.863–3(b)(2), *Example (1)*). * * *

Income derived from the sale of depreciable personal property

Subject to a special rule, income derived from the sale of depreciable personal property, to the extent of prior depreciation deductions, is sourced under a recapture principle. Specifically, gain to the extent of prior depreciation deductions from the sale of depreciable personal property is sourced in the United States if the depreciation deductions giving rise to the gain were previously allocated against U.S. source income. If the deductions giving rise to the gain were previously allocated against foreign source income, gains from the sales (to the extent of prior deductions) is sourced foreign. Any gain in excess of prior depreciation deductions is sourced pursuant to the place-of-sale rule. * * *

Income attributable to an office or other fixed place of business

Another exception to the residence-of-the-seller rule applies to income derived from the sale of personal property when the sale is attributable to an office or other fixed place of business.

For U.S. residents, this office rule applies only if income is not already sourced as U.S. or foreign under the place-of-sale rule (which applies to inventory property, gain in excess of recapture income for certain depreciable personal property, and stock of certain affiliates), or the recapture rule for depreciable personal property. Under this office rule, U.S. residents that derive income from sales of personal property attributable to an office or other fixed place of business maintained in a foreign country generate foreign source income. However, the office rule only applies to U.S. residents, individual or otherwise, if an effective foreign income tax of 10 percent or more is paid to a foreign country on the income from the sale.

* * *

Income derived from the sale of stock in foreign affiliates

A place-of-sale rule applies to income derived from U.S. corporations from the sale of stock in certain foreign corporations. If a U.S. corporation sells stock of a foreign affiliate in the foreign country in which the affiliate derived from the active conduct of a trade or business more than 50 percent of its gross income for the 3–year period ending with the close of the affiliate's taxable year immediately preceding the year during which the sale occurs, any gain from the sale is foreign source. An affiliate, for this purpose, is any foreign corporation whose stock is at least 80 percent owned (by both voting power and value). A U.S. resident may for this purpose treat as one corporation an affiliate and all other corporations which are wholly owned by the affiliate.

Goodwill and other intangibles

Payments in consideration for the sale of goodwill are treated as from sources in the country in which the goodwill was generated. In the case of other intangibles, any gain in excess of amortized deductions (if any) are subject to the residence-of-the-seller rule only to the extent the payments in consideration of the sale are not contingent on the productivity, use, or disposition of the intangible. Payments that are so contingent are sourced as royalties. * * *

Allocation and apportionment of deductions

* * *

In general, the primary statutory authority for allocating and apportioning deductions between foreign and domestic income is that there shall be deducted from domestic and foreign source gross income, respectively, the expenses, losses, and other deductions "properly apportioned or allocated thereto" and "a ratable part of any expenses, losses, or other deductions which cannot definitely be allocated to some item or class of gross income" (secs. 861(b) and 862(b)). * * *

[D]eductions not definitely related to gross income (e.g., charitable deductions * * *) are apportioned on a pro rata basis between domestic and foreign source gross income. The regulations contemplate two other types of deductions: (1) deductions definitely related to all of the taxpayer's gross income, and (2) deductions definitely related to a subset or "class" of the taxpayer's gross income. * * * A deduction is considered definitely related to a class of gross income if it is incurred as a result of, or incident to, an activity or in connection with property from which that class of gross income is derived (Treas. Reg. sec. 1.861–8(b)(2)).

Once deductions are associated with the corresponding class of gross income (or all of gross income), an apportionment is made between the so-called "statutory grouping" of income in that class * * * and the so-called "residual grouping." * * *

The apportionment method is one which reflects to a reasonably close extent the factual relationship between the deduction and the groupings of gross income. In general, examples of bases and factors which should be considered include, but are not limited to: (1) comparison of units sold, (2) comparison of the amount of gross sales or receipts, (3) comparison of costs of good sold, (4) comparison of profit contribution, (5) comparison of expenses incurred, assets used, salaries paid, space utilized, and time spent which are attributable to the activities or properties giving rise to the class of gross income, and (6) comparison of the amount of gross income (Treas. Reg. sec. 1.861–8T(c)(1)).

* * *

As required by the 1986 Act, a tax-exempt asset and income from that asset are not taken into account for purposes of allocating and apportioning any deductible expense (Code sec. 864(e)(3); Treas. Reg. sec. 1.861–8T(d)(2)).

* * *

[T]he 1986 Act [also] requires that interest, and deductions other than interest which are not directly allocable or apportioned to any specific income producing activity, generally be allocated and apportioned as if all members of an affiliated group were a single corporation (sec. 864(e)(1) and (6)).

NOTES

1) *Details and More Details.* The previous excerpts omit some of the details of the source rules. For example, it may be unclear how the Code determines the place where intangible property is used and therefore the source of rents and royalties paid for its use. Typically the source of royalties paid for use of intangible property is the location providing the legal protections covering such property.[3] So if Company X receives royalties for licensing a U.S. patent or copyright, the royalties are U.S. source income. Such determinations are more difficult, however, when a company licenses intangible property for use in multiple countries, or when it receives royalty income for trade secrets, which are not legally protected by any particular nation.

2) *Compensation for Services.* Another wrinkle in the source rules lies in the sourcing of compensation for services. When an individual works partly in the U.S. and partly abroad, the source of her income is apportioned under a facts and circumstances test, often by the number of days she spends in each country.[4] However if the individual is a nonresident alien and earns less than $3,000 (or more under many

---

3. I.R.C. §§ 861(a)(4), 862(a)(4).
4. I.R.C. § 863(b)(1); Reg. § 1.861–4(b).

treaties) for services performed in the U.S., he may fall under a *de minimis* exception such that all of his compensation is foreign source.[5]

The following table provides a somewhat more comprehensive (but still incomplete) summary of the rules.

5. I.R.C. § 861(a)(3).

Table 1

Form of Income		Source Rules
Periodic Income from Capital	Interest	*Default rule*: Residence of debtor. *Exceptions that make income foreign source*: - Interest paid by foreign branch of U.S. bank. § 861(a)(1)(B). - Interest paid by U.S. resident alien individuals or domestic corporations with ≥ 80% gross income derived from foreign sources and attributable to active conduct of foreign trade or business is foreign source. § 861(a)(1)(A), (c). If paid to related person, only a portion is foreign source. § 861(c)(2)(A). *Exception that makes income U.S. source*: - Interest paid by U.S. trade or business of foreign corporation. § 884(f)(1)(A). *Other exceptions*: - Interest on notional principal contract sourced to country of residence of taxpayer. Reg. §§ 1.863-7(b)(1), 1.988-4(a).
	Dividends	*Default rule*: Country of incorporation of payor. § 861(a)(2)(A). *Exceptions that make income U.S. source*: - Dividends paid by foreign corporation with ≥ 25% gross income from sources effectively connected to U.S. trade or business. Then U.S. source to extent of that percentage. § 861(a)(2)(B). - Dividend paid by foreign corporation out of accumulated profits of predecessor U.S. corporation. §§ 861(a)(2)(C), 243(e).
	Rents & Royalties	*Default rule*: Location where property/rights used or physically located. For intangible property, usually location from which it derives legal protection. §§ 861(a)(4), 862(a)(4).
Personal Services	Compensation for Personal Services	*Default rule*: Location where services performed. If work partly in U.S. and partly abroad apportion under facts and circumstances, often by number of days in each country. §§ 861(a)(3), 862(a)(3), 863(b)(1); Reg. § 1.861-4(b). *Exceptions that make income foreign source*: - Compensation less than $3,000 paid to nonresident aliens in U.S. less than 90 days, and who did not work on behalf of foreign entity engaged in U.S. trade or business, or foreign branch of U.S. corporation. Compensation and time limit often higher under treaties. § 861(a)(3). - Compensation for member of crew of foreign vessel and in U.S. temporarily. *Id.*
	Sale of Real Property	*Default rule*: Location of property. §§ 861(a)(5), 862(a)(5).

Gain from Sale of Property	Sale of Personal Property	*Default rule*: Residence of seller. Exceptions tend to swallow rule so default applies mainly to sale of non-inventory stocks, bonds, works of art, and intangibles to the extent that income is not contingent on their productivity or use. *Exceptions*: - Sales of inventory sourced where title passes. §§ 861(a)(6), 862(a)(6), 865(b); Reg. § 1.861-7(c). - Sale of stock of foreign affiliate by U.S. person sourced where title passes if affiliate engaged in active conduct of trade or business, sale made in country where engaged in that business, and > 50% income derived from that business. § 865(f). *Exceptions that make income U.S. source*: - Depreciable or amortizable personal property to extent of such U.S. deductions taken. §§ 865(c)(2), 863(e)(1)(A). - Sale of property by foreign person attributable to U.S. office of fixed place of business. Exception does not apply when selling inventory for use outside the U.S. and foreign office materially participated in sale. § 865(e)(2)(B). *Exception that makes income foreign source*: - Sale of property by U.S. person attributable to foreign office if subject to at least 10% foreign tax and previous exceptions do not apply. § 865(e)(1).
	Manufacture & Sale of Personal Property	*Default rule*: Allocate: 1) 50% to manufacturing source, 50% to sales source, 2) in line with price charged in uncontrolled transaction (the "Independent Factory Price"), or 3) following taxpayer's accounting books. § 863(a), (b); Reg. § 1.863-3(b)(2).
Other	International Transportation or Communications Income	*Default rule*: 50/50 between country of origin and of destination. § 863(c)(2). *Exception that makes income U.S. source*: - International communications income attributable to U.S. fixed place of business of foreign person. § 863(e)(1)(B)(ii). *Exception that makes income foreign source*: - International communications income of foreign person not attributable to U.S. fixed place of business. § 863(e)(1)(B)(i).
	Space/Ocean Activities	*Default rule*: Residence of taxpayer. § 863(d).
	Foreign Exchange Income	*Default rule*: Residence of person realizing gain. § 988(a)(3)(A); Reg. § 1.988-4(a). *Exceptions*: - Income attributable to qualified business units, related party loans, currency gains from distributions of earnings and profits previously taxed under subpart F of passive foreign investment company provisions. § 988(a)(3)(B)(ii), (a)(3)(C); Reg. § 1.988-4(b), (e).
	Social Security Benefits	*Default rule*: U.S. source. § 861(a)(8).

2.3 POTENTIAL OBJECTIVES OF SOURCE RULES

Even a careful reading of the previous excerpts and Table 1 fails to illuminate a clear objective toward which the source rules are directed.

Some rules—such as the title passage rules for the sale of inventory property—seem to aim for simplicity and predictability while permitting great potential for manipulation. Others attempt to capture economic substance, but sometimes with arbitrary thresholds. For example, dividends paid by a foreign corporation whose income derives more than 25 percent from sources effectively connected to a U.S. trade or business are U.S. source to extent of that percentage, but dividends from companies with 24 percent of such income are foreign source entirely. Still others—such as the rule for income from space and ocean activities—paradoxically attempt to define the national source of income that derives from a commons outside of all nation-states. Finally, the source rules sometimes apply differently for mirror transactions by U.S. and foreign taxpayers, creating the potential for double taxation even when the foreign country employs the same rules.[6]

The current complexity and contradictions of the source rules are essentially due to the lack of a clear economic basis for what they should achieve. In fact, the previous suggestion to inquire whether the source rules reach the economic source of income may be a bit of a teaser. As the following paragraph illustrates, Hugh Ault and David Bradford argue that the source of income is not an economic concept, and they claim this is the essential problem in designing source rules:

> [An] income concept is not susceptible to characterization as to source at all. Income * * * attaches to someone or something that consumes and owns assets. Income does not come from some place, even though we may construct accounts to approximate it by keeping track of payments that have identifiable and perhaps locatable sources and destinations. To the extent that income describes an activity, it is not that of production but that of consumption and wealth accumulation, and its location is presumably the place of residence of the person doing the consuming and accumulating. * * * [L]arge changes in wealth occur continuously by virtue of changes that have no natural locational aspect. Examples [include] * * * simple changes in expectations and beliefs about the future, which can result in large changes in asset values. Attaching locations to these phenomena inevitably involves arbitrary line drawing, with its attendant controversy.[7]

6. For instance, there is no parallel provision granting foreign source status to dividends paid by a U.S. person to the extent that more than a quarter of their income is effectively connected to a foreign trade or business. Consequently, if a foreign country adopted the same source rules as the U.S., dividends paid by a U.S. company with 100% income effectively connected to a foreign business would be sourced to the U.S. by the U.S. and sourced to the foreign country by the foreign country.

7. Hugh J. Ault & David F. Bradford, U.S. Taxation of International Income, in TAXATION IN THE GLOBAL ECONOMY 30–31 (Assaf Razin & Joel Slemrod, eds., University of Chicago Press, 1990).

Ault and Bradford's argument is grounded in the Haig–Simons definition of income under which income is the sum of consumption and changes in wealth over a given period.[8] However other analysts regard the place of consumption as less important than Ault and Bradford suggest and contend that the source concept is intended to reflect the location where income is produced. For example, the *Eisner* definition of income as "the gain derived from capital, from labor, or from both combined," Eisner v. Macomber, 252 U.S. 189, 207 (1920), is somewhat more amenable to categorization by geographic source.

Putting aside this debate, there are at least four overarching purposes toward which a system of source rules might be directed: 1) allocating source-based taxation in proportion to the benefits provided to the taxpayer by different governments, 2) aligning source rules with the center(s) of economic activity producing income, 3) formulating source rules that maximize U.S. economic well-being, or 4) creating source rules that augment developing countries' taxing jurisdiction with the objective of redistributing to the poor internationally. We consider some potential implications of each objective.

The notion of allocating source in proportion to the benefits provided to taxpayers by different governments springs from the "benefits theory" of taxation.[9] Under the "benefits theory," tax burdens should be allocated in proportion to the relative benefits that each taxpayer receives from the government. While this theory has intuitive appeal, it is relatively rarely invoked today due to the difficulty of allocating specific government benefits to particular taxpayers. Even in the domestic context, for example, it would be hard to allocate tax burdens within a neighborhood based on the value of police protections provided to each person; it is difficult, if not impossible, to determine how much small business owners, renters and landlords each benefit from police protections relative to each other. Likewise, in the international context, it would be difficult, if not impossible, to value the relative benefits provided to one company by three countries if the first provides the infrastructure and less-skilled labor necessary for a manufacturing facility, the second provides the higher-skilled labor and intangible property rights protections necessary for sales and marketing operations, and the third provides a strong consumer market. It is reasonable, however, to assert that the company benefits from the services provided by each of the governments and therefore that each has some claim to tax the company. The benefits theory of taxation provides little latitude for addressing vertical equity (or redistributional) concerns.

A second goal of source rules is aligning source with the economic nexus of the activities generating income. Indeed, some argue this is the

---

8. MICHAEL J. GRAETZ & DEBORAH H. SCHENK, FEDERAL INCOME TAXATION 107 (Foundation Press, 3d ed., 1995).

9. For further discussion of this theory, see HARVEY S. ROSEN, PUBLIC FINANCE 315–18 (Irwin McGraw–Hill, 5th ed. 1999).

main objective driving the current source rules. As the Joint Committee on Taxation asserts: "Present law generally treats income as having a U.S. source when a reasonable economic nexus exists with the United States. For example, in the case of active business or service income, the location of the relevant economic activity generally determines nexus."[10] However, as will become increasingly apparent throughout this Chapter, many of the source rules perform this task poorly.

This should not be surprising, as countless real-world examples illustrate the potential difficulties and uncertainties associated with identifying economic nexus. For instance, the case of *Karrer v. United States*[11] grapples with the proper sourcing of income earned by a Swiss scientist who invented synthetic vitamin supplements for a Swiss-based corporation, which in turn manufactured the vitamins and sold them in the U.S. through its U.S. subsidiary. The Court of Claims held that the income was foreign under the source rules, since it was compensation for services that Karrer performed exclusively in Switzerland. It is far from clear, however, that this straightforward application of the source rule for personal services income adequately reflects the relevant economic activity giving rise to Karrer's income. As a Swiss resident, Karrer's ability to work was undoubtedly dependent upon Swiss education, employment, and infrastructure. Yet his income was also the product of the intellectual property protections, market infrastructure, and consumer buying power of the United States. Moreover, it would be inaccurate to attribute Karrer's skills and creativity entirely to Switzerland if he had ever studied abroad or learned from foreign textbooks. Ultimately, source rules fail to capture fully the complex economic interactions that constitute the value-added of global commerce.

In addition, it is often difficult to connect the objective of defining source as the economic center of activity giving rise to an item of income to the general economic objectives of international tax policy. Capital export neutrality (CEN),[12] for example, implies nothing about source rules. Since CEN aims solely to tax based on residence, it does not matter whether income is domestic or foreign. Likewise capital import neutrality (CIN) provides little insight in defining the geographic source of income. Because CIN seeks to impose identical tax rates on domestic and foreign persons doing business in the same country, CIN implies that a given country's source rules should not differ depending upon the taxpayer's residence. This may suggest, for example, that U.S. source income of foreigners should approximate the income of a U.S. taxpayer engaged in the same business with the same receipts and expenditures.

---

10. See JOINT COMMITTEE ON TAXATION, STUDY OF THE OVERALL STATE OF THE FEDERAL TAX SYSTEM AND RECOMMENDATIONS FOR SIMPLIFICATION 393 (JCS 3–01, Apr. 2001).

11. 152 F.Supp. 66 (Ct.Cl.1957).

12. See Chapter 1 for an explanation of the theoretical frameworks of Capital Export Neutrality (CEN) and Capital Import Neutrality (CIN).

Instead, since the inception of U.S. international taxation, the economic nexus approach has been connected to administrability concerns. As Thomas Adams, one of the architects of the modern system, argued: "[I]n agreements allocating tax sources for the purpose of preventing double taxation, the tax should not be assigned to a jurisdiction which cannot effectively administer and collect the tax."[13] Adams contends that every country will inevitably tax income whose economic nexus lies within that country, and on both normative and positive grounds, this power confers a right.[14]

As discussed in Chapter 1, the overarching goal of international tax policy need not be administrability or CEN or CIN.[15] Accordingly, a third potential objective in designing source rules is to create a system of internationally accepted source rules that maximize U.S. economic well-being and U.S. economic growth. A country operating in its own national interest will, from time to time, attempt to extend its ability to tax income, particularly of foreigners. This policy determination is sometimes effectuated through the enactment of more aggressive source rules. For example, in negotiations leading up to the League of Nations model treaty, Britain, as a capital exporter, doggedly tried to generate an international consensus that interest should be sourced by the residence of the lender as a way of increasing its share of the taxes from such transactions.[16]

There are two arguments one can make for broader U.S. taxing jurisdiction being in our national interest. First, it would strengthen our revenue return without raising rates, since our tax base would include more income formerly outside our jurisdiction. This in turn might increase our ability to satisfy other tax policy objectives, such as vertical equity goals, perhaps by financing tax relief for low-income families. Alternatively, a broader U.S. taxing jurisdiction might heighten our ability to attract investment by financing a lowering of tax rates. Since more income derived from both the U.S. and another country would be subject to U.S. tax, foreign and domestic taxpayers might be more sensitive to changes in U.S. taxation. On the other hand, one might counter that broader U.S. taxing jurisdiction might hinder economic growth depending on how other countries respond. The U.S. might be substantially worse off if the current consensus that facilitates international economic flows and growth were to break down.

13.   Thomas S. Adams, Interstate and International Double Taxation, in Lectures on Taxation 101, 112 (Roswell Magill ed., 1932), quoted in Graetz & O'Hear, The "Original Intent" of U.S. International Taxation, 46 Duke L. J. 1021, 1101 (1997).

14.   See id. at 1037.

15.   See generally Michael J. Graetz, The David R. Tillinghast Lecture: Taxing International Income: Inadequate Principles, Outdated Concepts, and Unsatisfactory Policies, 54 Tax L. Rev. 261, 270–316 (2001).

16.   Graetz & O'Hear, supra note 13, at 1071–72.

A final potential goal for source determinations might be redistributing to the poor internationally. For reasons similar to those that indicate that U.S.-biased source rules could benefit the U.S., developing countries could, in theory, benefit from source rules biased toward them. For instance, if sales of manufactured products were sourced to the country whose labor manufactured the products, the source-based taxes of developing countries might increase. This in turn might increase their ability to attract foreign direct investment, which is often associated with economic growth, if more affluent countries exempted their own residents' foreign source income from developing countries from taxation. Indeed, a number of industrialized nations have demonstrated a willingness to facilitate this redistributional policy by providing tax-sparing credits to their residents under tax treaties with developing countries.

Once again, however, closer inspection reveals that the predicted effects of such a regime may be more complicated. Like source rules designed to expand the U.S. tax base, the benefit of a set of source rules designed to favor developing countries may be contingent upon other countries going along. Even then the economic consequences are still uncertain. A small country may be better off not levying any source-based tax. Basing source determinations on certain factors may effectively create a tax on that factor.[17] Consequently, sourcing based on the supply of labor might in the long run suppress international demand for such labor and hence employment among the very people the policy intends to benefit.

2.4 THE UNRAVELING OF CURRENT U.S. SOURCE RULES AND THE EROSION OF U.S. SOURCE TAXATION

The previous discussion is intended to sketch only some of the normative concerns that may influence the formulation of source rules depending upon one's goals for international taxation. Regardless of the objectives of source rules, however, one should attempt to minimize the associated compliance and administrative costs. To this end, source rules should be as simple as feasible and difficult to circumvent. Otherwise taxpayers will incur wasteful tax planning costs. Unfortunately, the current source rules have not only been criticized for failing to articulate and pursue an overarching goal, but also for permitting widespread manipulation. Two prevalent types of source rule manipulation are the shifting of source within a particular category of income and the recharacterization of income into a different source category altogether. In each of these cases, taxpayers use the bright line tests for source to their advantage. Probably the most notable example of source shifting within an income category is the title passage rule for sales of inventory

---

17. KIRK J. STARK, THE QUIET REVOLUTION IN U.S. SUBNATIONAL CORPORATE INCOME TAXATION 15 (UCLA School of Law, Research Paper No. 01–9, 2001), citing Charles E. McLure, Jr., The State Corporate Income Tax: Lambs in Wolves' Clothing, in THE ECONOMICS OF TAXATION (H. Aaron & M. Boskin eds., 1980).

property, under which parties can elect a low-tax jurisdiction for title passage as a way to select the country of source of the income from a sale. The following excerpt discusses how U.S. persons benefit from such manipulation.

To provide some context for the excerpt, it may help to explain that U.S. taxpayers generally can benefit from manipulating the source of sales income if they have excess foreign tax credits in the "general limitation basket." As Chapter 4 describes, excess foreign tax credits arise because the U.S. provides U.S. taxpayers with a credit for foreign taxes paid but limits the credit to a level based on the U.S. tax rate to ensure that it does not offset U.S. tax on U.S. source income. Although the details of this limitation are complex, essentially they provide that for each of ten categories or "baskets" of foreign source income, the foreign tax credit cannot exceed the U.S. income tax that would be due on this income absent the credit. Income from the sale of inventory property falls in the residual or "general limitation" basket. If foreign taxes paid exceed the limit on this category, there will be "excess foreign tax credits" that cannot be used even if the taxpayer has low-taxed foreign source income in other baskets that might otherwise be offset by these credits. This creates an incentive for U.S. taxpayers to shift the source of inventory property sales to low or zero tax foreign countries, thus increasing their foreign income without increasing their foreign taxes and thereby allowing some of the "excess credits" to be used to reduce U.S. taxes. Depending on their sources of foreign income, a significant number of U.S. corporations might find themselves in such an excess credit position.

Dep't of the Treasury, *Report to the Congress on the Sales Source Rules* 7–10, 13–14 (1993).

The Source Rules for Sales of Inventory Property

* * *

The Code contains two source rules for the sale of inventory property that are of particular importance to U.S. exporters. One rule is for inventory property that the exporter purchases and sells; the other is for inventory property that the exporter produces and sells.

The Title–Passage Rule

The source of gross income derived from inventory property that is purchased by an exporter in the United States and sold outside the United States is determined under the "title passage" rule of section 862(a)(6), which treats such income as derived entirely from the country in which the sale occurs. Generally the regulations treat a sale as occurring when and where title passes. There are two exceptions to this rule. First, if a transaction is structured with tax avoidance as the primary purpose, then title is considered to pass when and where the substance of the sale occurs. Also, if bare legal title is retained by the seller, the regulations treat the sale as occurring when and where "beneficial ownership and risk of loss" are transferred.

Under conflict-of-law rules, foreign law sometimes may determine title passage in a cross-border sale. When U.S. law applies, however, the Uniform Commercial Code (U.C.C.) allows the parties to the sale to agree when and where title will pass, and, absent an agreement, make title pass upon performance of delivery. Thus under the Code and commercial law, parties to a transaction generally may determine the source of income from a sale of inventory property that is purchased for resale by their choice of the place and time for passage of title.

The Independent Factory Price Method and Related Rules

The source of income derived from the sale of property produced in the United States and sold outside the United States (or vice versa) is determined under section 863. Three examples set out in Treasury Regulations under that section govern this determination. The examples date back to regulations issued in 1922 to implement a predecessor of section 863.

Example (1) of the Regulations illustrates the independent factory price (IFP) method. * * * This method must be used whenever an independent factory price is available to the taxpayer. The second example illustrates the so-called 50–50 method, which determines the source of 50 percent of the income based on the location of the taxpayer's property held or used in the production or sale of the inventory, and the source of the other 50 percent based on the title-passage rule. Generally this method is used whenever an IFP is not available. The third example allows the source of income to be based on the allocation made on the taxpayer's books. This method may be used only with the IRS district director's consent.

* * *

In the past some U.S. exporters were uncertain whether, if they had sales that established an IFP, they were required to use the IFP method. In 1988 the Internal Revenue Service issued Rev. Ruling 88–73 which interprets Example (1) to require use of the IFP method, if an IFP exists. This interpretation was recently affirmed by the Tax Court in a reviewed opinion, *Phillips Petroleum Co. v. Commissioner*, 97 T.C. 30 (1991).

When an IFP does not exist, the 50–50 rule may be used to determine the source of income. Under the 50–50 rule an exporter's U.S. source gross income from exports equals:

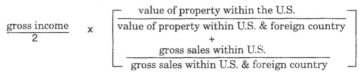

$$\frac{\text{gross income}}{2} \quad \times \quad \left[\frac{\text{value of property within the U.S.}}{\text{value of property within U.S. \& foreign country}} + \frac{\text{gross sales within U.S.}}{\text{gross sales within U.S. \& foreign country}} \right]$$

This rule generally permits an exporter to treat at least half of its export income as derived from foreign sources, because 50 percent of that income usually can be made foreign source by arranging for title to pass outside the United States. If a U.S. exporter has assets abroad that are held or used in the production or sale of the inventory property, the percentage of taxable income that is foreign source can be greater than 50 percent.

* * *

3.2   The Effect on Exports

* * *

The sales source rules benefit U.S. multinational exporters that have foreign tax credits in the general limitation category (either for the current year or that have been carried forward from prior years) that locate investment in the United States and export to foreign customers. The rules may create a cost advantage for these exporters leading them to export more to the extent that the rules treat all or a portion of export income as foreign source income and that income bears foreign income tax at a rate less than the U.S. exporter's U.S. income tax rate. When these conditions exist a U.S. exporter with excess foreign tax credits may average or cross-credit foreign income taxes in the general limitation category; i.e., effectively use taxes paid on foreign source income earned in a high-tax foreign country to cover some (or all) of the U.S. income tax liability on its export income. * * * In this way, the sales source rules can lower an exporter's marginal cost and lead to additional exports.

There are two cases, however, in which the sales source rules do not benefit a U.S. exporter with excess foreign tax credits. Both involve loss situations. First, if a U.S. exporter would have an overall U.S. source loss for the year under an activity-based rule, the sales source rules would create no benefit to the exporter. The domestic loss shelters both additional U.S. source and additional foreign source income from U.S. tax, so the source of additional income has no effect on tax liability.

The sales source rules also fail to benefit a U.S. exporter with an overall foreign loss under an activity-based rule. Additional foreign source income is sheltered from U.S. income tax by the foreign losses, not by excess foreign tax credits.

Finally, while they provide a tax savings, the sales source rules do not encourage exports by exporters that would have excess foreign tax credits under an activity-based source rule, but that have no excess foreign tax credits under the sales source rules. These exporters export more than enough to absorb all of their excess foreign tax credits, so they realize no tax saving from the last unit exported. If the last unit of exports was profitable without the tax saving, it is unlikely that the firm's total exports were affected by the tax saving. For these taxpayers, the sales source rules, however, make investment in a high-tax country more attractive, and thus provide an incentive to invest abroad.

NOTES

1) *Manipulation of Source Rules.* This Treasury report goes on to analyze the effects of the sales source rules and estimates that if the rules had been replaced with activity-based rules (such as allocating source based on the price charged to independent distributors in the U.S.), the U.S. income tax liability of multinational U.S. exporters would have increased by between $1.8 and $2.1 billion in 1990.[18] However, such a shift would also result in an estimated loss of approximately $1.7 billion in exports.[19] Since some economists believe exports benefit economies in general, one could argue that manipulation of the sales source rules is not necessarily a bad thing. On the other hand, it is unclear that tax-motivated exports are beneficial to an economy.[20] Moreover, the report also finds that in the long run any reduction in exports will be matched by a reduction in imports so a shift to activity-based rules might have little effect on the U.S. balance of payments.

2) *Innovations.* In 1999, the Clinton Administration proposed replacing the 50–50 source rule for the manufacture and sale of inventory property with one that allocated income between production and sales activities based on actual economic activity. The proposal stemmed from concern that U.S. exporters whose sale activities accounted for less than 50% of their income from production and sales were using the 50–50 rule to claim more foreign source income for Unites States tax purposes than was subject to foreign tax. Such U.S. exporters operating in high-tax

18. Dep't of the Treasury, Report to the Congress on the Sales Source Rules 2 (1993)
19. Id.
20. See, e.g., Gustav Ranis, Industrialization and Trade, in HANDBOOK OF DEVELOPMENT ECONOMICS 333 (Hollis B. Chenery & T.N. Srinivasan eds., 1989).

foreign countries could then credit foreign taxes in excess of the U.S. rate against their U.S. tax liability.[21] The proposal was not enacted.

———————

A second variety of manipulation of source rules involves re-categorizing the type of income to obtain tax-preferred sourcing. For example, royalties can be fairly easily characterized as compensation and vice versa. One famous case involves a German resident and conductor, Pierre Boulez, who contracted to direct the New York Philharmonic in several recordings for CBS Records.[22] Boulez argued that the payments he received—a percentage of the proceeds of record sales of these recordings—were royalties and therefore not subject to U.S. taxation. The IRS contended that the payments were compensation for services and thus taxable by the United States. Ultimately the IRS prevailed when the Tax Court held that the contract did not convey a property interest in the recordings to Boulez, a necessary condition for royalty income. Both the arguments by Boulez and the IRS seem plausible. *Boulez* therefore illustrates the inherent and long-standing difficulties in categorizing income.

Due to innovations in financial transactions that have now become commonplace, the unraveling of the source rules through re-categorizations of income has accelerated in recent years. The following excerpt discusses how financial innovations blur the line between gains from the sale of stock, dividends, and interest payments, thereby creating new opportunities for taxpayers to select their source of income and thereby minimize tax burdens through careful tax planning. Recall that interest and dividends are sourced based on the residence of the debtor and payor respectively, while gains on securities are sourced to the country of the seller's residence. As is discussed in Chapter 7, U.S. source portfolio interest income of foreign persons is generally exempt from U.S. taxation, while U.S. source dividend income of foreign persons is generally taxed. Further, as noted in Table 1, payments on notional principal contracts such as financial swaps are sourced to the residence of the taxpayer. Thus foreign persons face significant incentives to characterize dividends as interest, swap payments, or as gains on the sale of stock.

Jeffrey M. Colon, *Financial Products and Source Basis Taxation: U.S. International Tax Policy at the Crossroads*, 1999 U. Ill. L Rev. 775, 789–92, 798–800.

Foreign investors endeavoring to avoid U.S. taxes on FDAP

21. Testimony of Assistant Treasury Secretary Donald Lubick Before the Senate Finance Committee (Treasury News, Apr. 27, 1999), available at http://www.us-treas.gov/press/releases/pr3108.htm.

22. Boulez v. Commissioner, 83 T.C. 584 (1984).

income[23] can employ several strategies, such as trading around the record date, selling the dividend by contract, and creating synthetic equity and debt. With respect to U.S. source dividends, the simplest strategy involves trading around the record date. This strategy, explained in more detail below, has the effect of turning taxable dividends into nontaxable capital gain or return of capital. More complicated strategies use fundamental financial results to replicate equity returns, including dividends, through combinations of other financial instruments, such as forwards and options. Also, foreign investors may enter into transactions with financial intermediaries that permit avoidance of withholding tax on U.S. source interest. A foreign investor will want to avoid U.S. withholding tax whenever the investor is either tax exempt in its country of residence—a pension plan or a corporation incorporated in a tax haven—or the investor's country of residence will not credit (fully or partially) U.S. source basis taxes against residence basis taxes.
* * *

Trading Around the Record Date

One certain method to avoid withholding tax with respect to U.S. stock is to own only stocks that do not pay any dividends. There is evidence, however, that because dividends may be an important indicator of future performance, an investor may do herself a disservice by excluding dividend paying stocks from her portfolio.

Assume a foreign investor holds stock of a publicly traded U.S. corporation that has declared a $1 per share dividend, which will be subject to tax at either thirty percent or a reduced treaty rate. On the date the stock begins to trade ex-dividend, the price of the stock will normally drop by an amount approximately equal to the dividend. To capture the economic benefit of the $1 per share dividend, but not suffer any withholding tax on the $1 dividend, the foreign investor can sell the stock immediately prior to the ex-dividend date. By selling the stock cum-dividend, the foreign investor has been able to convert taxable dividend income into a nontaxable capital return.

Now assume that the foreign investor likes the future prospects of the U.S. company and therefore wishes to continue to hold his long stock position. The foreign investor could sell the stock immediately prior to the ex-dividend date and repurchase it on the ex-dividend date. By selling the stock cum-dividend and repurchasing ex-dividend, the investor has suc-

---

23.   FDAP income is fixed, determinable, annual or periodical income typically subject to a fixed gross-basis final "withholding" tax at a rate that depends on its character. The taxation of FDAP income is taken up in Chapter 7.

ceeded once again in converting taxable dividend income into a nontaxable capital return.

The foreign investor is exposed, however, to market risk between the time of sale and repurchase; because new information continuously arrives at the market, the price of the stock could increase during the time the investor does not own the stock. This risk, however, can be almost entirely eliminated by reducing the period during which the foreign investor is not long the stock. If the period between the sale and repurchase of the stock is extremely short, e.g., five minutes, the difference between the sale and repurchase price will be approximately the amount of the dividend. * * *

It is not entirely clear how much time must elapse between the sale and repurchase of a share of stock for the sale to constitute a realization event. Under Treasury regulations, the conversion of property into cash is a per se realization event. Any sale of stock on an exchange should thus be a realization event, regardless of the repurchase price, even though the cash received is being exchanged almost immediately back into identical stock. Once a sell order has been placed, there is no guarantee that the stock can be repurchased at the sales price (or any price), and the seller is therefore exposed to market risk. If both legs of the trade, however, do not occur at market prices, i.e., the trade is executed at prearranged prices so that the buyer/repurchaser has no risk of loss, the transaction could be treated as sale/repurchase transaction (repo). In such case, the transaction would not constitute a realization event, and the seller would be treated as the continuous owner of the stock.

In executing this strategy, a foreign investor faces the risk of unexpected market volatility and transaction costs such as trading commissions and the bid-asked spread. These costs are an implicit tax, and the transaction will be viable only if the U.S. tax avoided exceeds these costs. Because of these costs, the sale/repurchase strategy is viable only for large investors who face low transaction costs or with respect to a stock that is paying a significant dividend. * * *

Creating Equity with Swaps and Debt

[Another method for avoiding taxation on U.S. dividends is through an equity swap.] A swap is a contractual agreement between two parties to exchange cash flows in the future based on two or more different financial prices, e.g., dividends, equities, interest rates, commodities, or currency rates, and a notional principal amount that determines the magnitude of the payments. In tax parlance, swaps are part of the family of notional principal contracts. There is virtually no limit as to the cash flows that can be swapped. Common types of swaps include equity swaps and interest rate swaps.

When initiated, an on-market swap has zero value to both parties at initiation, and, consequently, no money changes hands. Payments can be swapped at any time during the life of the swap agreement and are generally netted. The more frequently payments are swapped, the less counterparty risk there is for the party for whom the swap has positive value. If the value of the swap swings significantly one way or the other, the swap may be marked to market, so as to reduce the risk of counterparty nonperformance.

To illustrate the payoffs to a foreign investor from using U.S. based equity swaps and debt to create synthetic equity returns, assume that a foreign investor enters into a total return equity swap with respect to 10,000 shares of USCO and the spot price of USCO is $100, the swap term is one year, the expected dividend is $4, and LIBOR[24] is six percent. The foreign investor also purchases a one-year zero coupon bond for $1,000,000 that will earn LIBOR. Under the swap, the foreign investor will receive from the counterparty, e.g., a U.S. investment bank, a payment consisting of any appreciation in the value of 10,000 shares of USCO over a one-year period and any dividends paid with respect to these shares. The foreign investor, in turn, is obligated to make a payment equal to the decrease, if any, in the value of 10,000 shares. Furthermore, the foreign investor is obligated to make an interest-like payment, e.g., LIBOR, based on the value of the USCO stock at initiation of the swap. The bond interest will fund the foreign investor's LIBOR obligations. * * *

To demonstrate that the payoffs from this strategy ensure that the foreign investor will receive payoffs equal to those had the investor actually purchased the USCO stock at initiation of the swap, received the dividends, and sold it at swap termination, assume that the stock can take one of two terminal values, $150 or $50, and that the $4 dividend is paid at swap termination. Purchasing the stock and receiving the dividend produces gain of $540,000 [$500,000 (10,000 × (150 − 100)) + $40,000 (dividend)] or loss of $460,000 [−$500,000 (10,000 × (100 − 150)) + $40,000]. Entering into the swap and buying the bond generates identical gain of $540,000 [$500,000 (appreciation) + $40,000 (dividend) − $60,000 (LIBOR) + $60,000 (bond interest)] or loss of $460,000 [$40,000 (dividend) − $500,000 (depreciation) − $60,000 (dividend payment) + $60,000 (interest)].

24. The LIBOR is the interest rate.

Although the two different investment strategies generate identical payoffs, the U.S. tax results differ. If the investor actually held the stock, the dividends would be subject to U.S. withholding tax and the gains or losses and cost of carry associated with the stock purchase and sale would not affect U.S. tax liability. By entering into the swap agreement, the foreign investor receives untaxed foreign source income.

One reason for the counterparty—most likely a swap dealer—to enter into the transaction is that it may be long on USCO, either because of other swap agreements or its investment holdings, and wishes to transform its equity position into an interest-like instrument.[25] Swap users, however, face risks that equity holders do not. Like forward contracts, swaps are credit agreements, and users face risk of counterparty default. Accordingly, their use is limited to financially secure investors.

* * *

Summary

These examples have shown that foreign investors can employ many strategies to avoid U.S. tax on U.S. source investment income. The effectiveness of the strategies described above is due generally to the combination of three different factors: (1) the United States taxes different cash flows differently; (2) foreigners are subject to U.S. tax on very limited categories of cash flows from the United States; and (3) the expected (and sometimes actual) values of cash flows that are subject to U.S. taxation can be recreated from combinations of other nontaxed cash flows. It is therefore evident that in some circumstances U.S. source basis taxation has become elective.

NOTE

Give up Source Based Taxation? In the remainder of his article, Colon considers whether the U.S. should even attempt to tax the U.S. source income of foreign investors given that the distinction between U.S. and foreign source income is increasingly a leaky bucket. In fact, as discussed in Chapter 7, this is the direction in which U.S. international tax may be headed. In general, foreign persons face far lower U.S. effective tax rates on U.S. source investment income than do U.S. taxpayers, in part due to the ease with which foreign persons can re-categorize U.S. source income as foreign source and therefore escape U.S. taxation altogether. This steady erosion of U.S. source jurisdiction has been compounded by tax treaties that exempt foreign persons, in whole or in part, from taxation on certain categories of their U.S. source income. See Chapter 7.

---

25. Another reason the counterparty may enter into the transaction is that it is tax-exempt.

2.5 DOUBLE OR ZERO TAXATION UNDER THE CURRENT SOURCE RULES

Just as most analysts agree that, regardless of their normative objectives, source rules should limit manipulation, most also agree that the source rules should prevent double taxation. Indeed this was a central rationale for the international tax system dividing up primary taxing jurisdiction by distinguishing between domestic and foreign source income in the first place. However, some of the current source rules—such as those allocating interest deductions—occasionally impose double taxation upon taxpayers unable to structure their business in a tax-preferred manner. The interest allocation rules are analyzed in Chapter 4.

Other forms of double taxation under the current source rules, especially those involving financial instruments, may involve interactions between the source rules and other relatively inflexible provisions of the Code. The following excerpt describes the arbitrary and sometimes harsh tax results that may occur for U.S. multinational companies engaged in internal risk-shifting, relative to taxation based on the actual economic substance of a transaction. A company that internally hedges may, however, escape U.S. taxes on U.S. source income through the same mechanisms, and thus the arbitrary interaction of the rules also presents an opportunity for tax avoidance through source rule manipulation.

Diane M. Ring, *Risk-Shifting Within a Multinational Corporation: The Incoherence of the U.S. Tax Regime*, 38 B.C. L. REV. 667, 667–69 (1997).

As multinational corporations play a growing role in the global economy, sensible taxation of their cross-border transactions becomes increasingly important. However, U.S. taxation of risk-shifting within a single multinational corporation produces arbitrary results that are at odds with the underlying economic relationships. For example, a U.S. corporation with debt payable in a foreign currency might hedge its exchange rate risk through a currency swap with a foreign branch, which in turn could hedge the risk with a foreign third party. Through these transactions, the U.S. corporation would successfully eliminate its currency risk and the transactions would net to zero. But despite the net zero economic impact of the debt and hedging, the transactions would have an important and often unpredictable effect on the corporation's U.S. tax liability.

This effect arises because the U.S. corporation's two third-party positions will have a different "source" for tax purposes, which in turn will affect the amount of foreign taxes that can be used to reduce U.S. tax liability. The foreign currency gain (or loss) on the U.S. corporation's debt will be U.S. source, but the foreign currency loss (or gain) on the foreign branch's third-party swap will be foreign source. These will be the only two contracts recognized because the United States does not recognize a contract made by a U.S. company with its own foreign branch.

The source of a U.S. corporation's income is critical in determining the amount of foreign tax credits that may be used to reduce U.S. income tax owed. The larger the portion of a taxpayer's income that is foreign source, the larger the amount of foreign tax credits that might be used. Thus, if the corporation's U.S. source income is increased (due to a foreign currency gain on the third-party debt) and foreign source income is correspondingly decreased (due to a parallel foreign currency loss on the foreign branch's third-party swap), then the taxpayer faces the possibility that it can use fewer foreign tax credits than it could in the absence of this economically net zero transaction. The reason is that the "foreign loss" reduces foreign source income, which otherwise might have carried additional foreign tax credits. Alternatively, if U.S. source income is decreased (due to a loss on the third-party debt) and foreign source income is increased (due to a gain on the branch's third-party swap), then this net zero transaction might enable the taxpayer to use more foreign tax credits than otherwise possible.

In either case, the amount of foreign tax credits that the taxpayer can use (and ultimately the tax owed to the United States) depends on a transaction which has no economic effect. Whether the taxpayer or the U.S. fisc will be the winner or loser in any particular case is not predictable. Nonetheless, such a result should be unappealing to a tax system that is designed to accurately reflect the income of each taxpayer and that seeks to prevent taxes from being impacted by transactions that produce no net non-tax effect. Moreover, this result, which occurs in various cases of risk-shifting within a corporation, is both arbitrary and inconsistent with the U.S. tax treatment of risk-shifting within a multinational group of related corporations.

This drastic divergence between economic substance and taxation derives from the U.S. tax treatment of internal risk-shifting. Unlike other major industrialized nations, the United States does not recognize risk-shifting within a multinational corporation, on the conceptual grounds that a party cannot contract with itself. Recognition of the interbranch contract between the home office and the foreign branch would result in four (instead of two) transaction legs to consider: (1) the home office's foreign currency debt, (2) the home office's position in the interbranch swap, (3) the foreign branch's position in the interbranch swap, and (4) the foreign branch's position in the third-party swap. If the interbranch swap were recognized for tax purposes, then the home office's gain (or loss) on its third-party debt would be U.S. source and would be offset by the home office's U.S. source loss (or gain) on the interbranch contract. Correspondingly, the branch's gain (or loss) on the interbranch contract and loss (or gain) on its third-party contract would both be foreign source and would offset each other. Recognition of the interbranch contract produces a tax result consistent with the underlying economic activity; a net zero transaction should not change a corporation's tax treatment and, with recognition of the interbranch contract, it does not.

2.6 FORMULARY APPORTIONMENT AS A POTENTIAL RESPONSE

Given taxpayers' increasing ability to manipulate the source rules and the resultant erosion of U.S source taxation, one option, which Colon suggests, is to exempt foreign persons from tax on U.S. source investment income altogether. Several commentators, including Ault and Bradford, have likewise called for discarding source taxation in favor of an exclusively residence-based system, citing the arbitrariness and lack of substance of the source-of-income concept. Leaving aside that residence also carries its own definitional challenges—an issue discussed in Chapter 3—these proposals overlook both the inevitability and normative validity of source-based taxation.

As a practical matter, source countries will almost always impose taxes on nonresident businesses in order to keep their domestic companies from crying "foul." In the words of Thomas Adams, "[c]very state insists upon taxing the nonresident alien who derives income from source within that country, and rightly so, at least inevitably so."[26] Domestic constituencies can always be expected to demand that their governments exercise source-based taxing jurisdiction for reasons of perceived fairness and competitiveness vis-à-vis nonresident businesses. Political realities dictate that foreign businesses, which lack representation in the legislature, must in turn concede to such jurisdiction if they seek to operate internationally. In any event, it is far easier for them to obtain relief in the form of an exemption or tax credit from their resident countries.

There is also a persistent normative basis for retaining source as a guideline for allocating international taxing authority. While the present source rules are certainly outdated and often lack economic coherence, it does not necessarily follow that source is a meaningless concept with respect to income. There are numerous indicia that point to the geographical location or locations where an economic activity is conducted. Each of these factors, in turn, represents a concrete justification for a

26. Thomas S. Adams, supra note 13, at 197.

state to exercise taxing jurisdiction over some portion of the income generated by the activity. As illustrated in previously discussed examples, these indications of source turn on where capital, labor and customers are located. Though allocation of income in accordance with these factors can often be ambiguous and complex, it does offer a baseline for aligning taxing authority with the economic origins of income.

Recognizing the inherent normative appeal of taxing income at its source, Stephen Shay, Clifton Fleming Jr. and Robert Peroni attribute much of the capriciousness of source rules to their failure to satisfy this norm:

> Where it is necessary to assign net income to specific time periods, the tax system relies on tax accounting methods, principally the cash and accrual methods. Unfortunately, there is no analogue to the cash method's constructive receipt doctrine or the accrual method's "all events" test to assign income to a geographical source. Instead, the United States resorts to a series of discrete source rules based on the categorization of the item of income. These rules are often arbitrary.
>
> An example illustrates the point. Suppose that a U.S. resident lawyer, who is educated in the United States and practices patent law in Boston for 20 years, spends over six months at an office in Paris rendering advice. Assuming that France asserts jurisdiction to tax the lawyer's entire related income, the United States treats the income as having its source wholly in France and, under the primacy-of-source rule, the United States contents itself with collecting a residual tax after allowing a credit for France's tax on 100% of this income. Yet, the intellectual capital that underlies the advice was developed entirely in the United States. While we acknowledge the administrative reasons for giving this income a single source, surely an objective observer would say there is an economic basis for attributing some of the income to the United States and freeing it pro tanto from French source taxation.[27]

The solution to the current inadequacies of source rules, according to Shay et al, is to formulate new rules based on principled decisions regarding the appropriate scope of both source and residence taxation.[28] To this end, one alternative regime that is gaining increasing attention in tax scholarship is formulary apportionment.

Under a formulary apportionment system, a person's or affiliated group's worldwide income is calculated without regard to the type of income, and then authority to tax that income is allocated to different countries based on a formula. The U.S. states employ formulary appor-

---

27. Stephen Shay et al., "What's Source Got to Do With It?" Source Rules and U.S. Taxation, 56 Tax L. Rev. 301, 357 (2002).

28. Id. at 358–59.

tionment in determining their taxing jurisdiction over corporations that operate in multiple states. The traditional state formula is one that allocates taxing jurisdiction based on the average of the percentages of sales, payroll and property of a firm in each state, although different states vary in the weights they assign to these factors.[29] Formulary apportionment addresses the pervasive dilemma in international taxation of pricing cross-border sales of goods and services between related persons. Left to their own discretion, multinational corporate groups can manipulate prices charged among subsidiaries in order to source income to low-tax jurisdictions. The current U.S. regime for dealing with this "transfer pricing" problem is discussed in Chapter 9, along with a more detailed analysis of the formulary apportionment alternative.

The following excerpt by David Noren provides some justifications for formulary apportionment as a way to determine the source of business income internationally and outlines which formulas may best benefit the U.S. national interest. Noren assumes that the U.S. national interest is to maximize the U.S. source-based taxing jurisdiction, and thus he does not consider what formula would be implied by other norms. Also, when this excerpt refers to an exemption system, it does not mean exempting foreign persons from taxation on U.S. source income, but rather the U.S. exempting businesses from taxation on their foreign source business income. (An exemption alternative to the foreign tax credit is considered in Chapter 5.)

David G. Noren, *The U.S. National Interest in International Tax Policy*, 54 Tax L. Rev. 337, 339–47 (2001).[30]

The Context of U.S. International Tax Policy

A.   The International Business Environment

With globalization, technological innovation, and particularly electronic commerce on the rise, much of the economic activity that the governments of the world will seek to tax will become more and more mobile. Traditionally, we are accustomed to thinking of portfolio capital as highly mobile, active direct investment of corporations as somewhat mobile, and labor as relatively immobile. Increasingly, however, all of these factors and activities are becoming more mobile, and thus more likely to move in response to tax rules. With an ever-greater share of the world's economic activity not necessarily tied down to any particular jurisdiction as a functional matter, govern-

---

29. Kirk J. Stark, The Quiet Revolution in U.S. Subnational Corporate Income Taxation 10–11 (UCLA School of Law Research Paper No. 01–9).

30. This article is a commentary on Michael J. Graetz, Taxing International Income: Inadequate Principles, Outdated Concepts, and Unsatisfactory Policies, 54 Tax L. Rev. 261 (2001).

ments will have to compete to attract and retain these activities within their borders. This means more regulatory competition, including tax competition. The United States, while a large and powerful country with many advantages to offer aside from whatever its regulatory and tax regimes may provide, will not be exempt from this competition.

This increased mobility and the resulting regulatory and tax competition mean that multinational business enterprises of all sizes will enjoy an unprecedented array of choices of regulatory and tax regimes, as well as unprecedented flexibility to take advantage of these choices without significantly altering or compromising their business plans. The nightmare scenario for tax collectors would be that the computer geniuses of the world move to tax havens, incorporate their businesses in tax havens, and do everything that they need to do to make lots of money all over the world, without establishing any taxable presence in the major countries into which they sell—the world's big industrial democracies. This would lead to erosion of the tax bases in the big industrial democracies, and eventually, to take the nightmare all the way, to the collapse of the modern welfare state in the digital age. Whatever one thinks of the severity and immediacy of this problem, it seems clear that some combination of tax and regulatory carrots and sticks will have to be deployed to keep this business activity and the tax dollars therefrom connected with major destination markets like the European Union and the United States.

Compounding the challenges posed by greater mobility of factors of production generally, the world's largest multinational corporations (MNCs) will continue to get bigger, more powerful, and more truly multinational in their operations and revenue sources—that is, lacking any true "residence" in the traditional sense. These MNCs will be (and to a significant extent already are) managed as global, integrated enterprises, making attempts to tax them on a nation-by-nation, or subsidiary-by-subsidiary basis increasingly challenging and artificial.
* * *

At the same time, although the largest MNCs will dominate world trade in terms of volume, smaller players will become involved in increasing numbers. * * * For example, as Graetz notes, large numbers of ordinary middle-class individuals trading online in their homes now find themselves dealing with the foreign tax credit rules. * * * So while the big MNCs will dominate international trade in terms of sheer amount, more and more individuals and small business enterprises for the first time will be coming into direct contact with the exceedingly complicated rules of international tax, which certainly were not designed with them in mind.

B.   The U.S. "Country Profile"

What traits set the United States apart from other countries in ways relevant to determining its international tax interest in this new business environment? In the old days, we spoke of countries as net capital exporters and net capital importers. Rich countries like the United States were net capital exporters, and their status as such told us a lot about what kinds of international tax policies they would prefer—residence-based taxation of investment income, for example. Now the capital export-import issue is pretty much a wash for the United States—we do a whole lot of both, and speaking simply of exporting or importing capital fails to capture the traits that are truly important to determining the country's national interest in the international tax area going forward.

Instead, two other defining characteristics will stand out as most relevant. First, the United States is at the forefront of technological innovation and e-commerce. Put another way, the nation is a net exporter of technology. Recognizing the increasing relevance of this criterion (and putting an even finer point on it), some commentators have begun referring to countries as e-commerce exporters or importers, with the United States of course as the main (if not the only) net e-commerce exporter. More broadly, the U.S. economy is in the process of moving further and further toward a specialization in services, ideas, and intellectual property, and away from traditional manufacturing. The United States appears destined to be a net exporter of services, ideas, and intangibles to the rest of the world, and a net importer of tangible "stuff" from the rest of the world. This characteristic surely will prove more relevant to the nation's interest in international tax policy than any tallying of overall capital inflows and outflows.

That takes us to the second trait. The United States stands out in the world as a heavily consumerist culture—there are an awful lot of us, we have a lot of money, and we have a voracious appetite for "stuff." MNCs may be increasingly large, powerful relative to national governments, and nationless, but for the foreseeable future they will continue to value the ability to sell into the U.S. market—to get those dollars from the consumption-crazed folks who live within the borders of this country. This enthusiasm for consumption, every bit as much as leadership in technological innovation, services, and ideas, will define the U.S. role in the world economy and will factor into any informed determination of the country's national interest in international tax matters. * * *

What International Tax Policies May Advance the U.S. National Interest in the Years to Come?

With all this in mind, what international tax policies will best serve the U.S. national interest? If the discussion in the previous Section accurately describes what the international business environment and the United States will look like, what should tax policymakers do to best serve the interests of the U.S. people?

A.   Source–Based Taxation?

Graetz notes that corporate residence is an increasingly meaningless and futile fiction to attempt to enforce with respect to MNCs, and this is one reason that he proposes an exemption system for active foreign source business income. If the concept of corporate residence makes no sense, then tax results should not be made to depend on it. An exemption system like the one described by Graetz would have the advantage of minimizing the relevance of corporate residence, since a U.S.-resident MNC would not face U.S. tax on its active foreign source business income. This would seem to make good sense, in that it would reduce the practical significance of a deeply flawed concept, but how does it square with the U.S. national interest in light of the discussion in Section II?

* * *

Graetz's proposal to move further in the direction of source-based taxation and away from residence-based concepts makes good sense and seems likely to be implemented in one form or another at some point in the future.

* * *

The main difficulty is that source itself is a deeply flawed concept in these days of high technology and e-commerce, and a premature shift to an exemption system, which would place even greater reliance on source than the current system does, would place further pressure on these inadequate rules and concepts. Source is not as hopeless as corporate residence—it is not inevitably an attempt "to put flesh into fiction," to use Graetz's words—but the source concepts currently in place clearly do not make sense in the e-commerce context, in which it becomes much more difficult to associate items of income with particular geographic locations. Moreover, the traditional source categories are outdated. Trying to make distinctions between sales of copyrighted articles versus sales or licenses of intangible property versus the provision of services, as the computer software sourcing regulations do, seems increasingly futile and highly prone to manipulation—many e-commerce activities can be plausibly analogized to any of these three categories, with different tax results. The categories were developed for a different time, and it makes little sense to force these new activities into one old category or another. With e-commerce, the labor can physically occur anywhere, the computer servers can be physically located anywhere, and the product may even be entirely electronic itself. The activity travels through cyberspace, and the product may reach its destination—a consumer living in a major industrial democracy, for example—without any income being sourced or taxed in a non-tax-haven jurisdiction under the current rules. So we cannot rely as heavily as we currently do on where transactions occur, where assets are located, or where labor occurs, and we cannot continue to break transactions down into categories like sales of property versus licenses of intellectual property versus services. Increasingly, none of these concepts will have much meaning. So what can we do to update source concepts, and adapt them to the greater role that they may be called upon to play in the future?

Reuven Avi–Yonah has proposed moving toward sales-based concepts of both source and permanent establishment (PE). In other words, if the consumer of the goods or services is located within the United States, the seller generally will be deemed to have a PE in the United States, and the income will be sourced in the United States. Moving toward some system along these lines probably makes sense and certainly warrants further investigation, if for no other reason than that the alternatives are so flawed. In a business environment in which the increasing mobility of factors of production presents a major challenge to tax administration, such a system would have the great virtue of determining tax results by reference to the least mobile factor in the whole equation—the location of the consumers. Moreover, a relatively simple focus on the location of the consumer would eliminate the need to provide different rules for royalties, sales, or services, for example. The system thus would sidestep the increasingly tricky classification issues that arise under the current source rules. In light of the status of the United States as the world's premier consumer, the system also would serve the interest of protecting the U.S. tax base from erosion. As long as the U.S. people for the most part still prefer to actually live in the United States and continue to have a voracious appetite for consumption, companies will always want to tap into this base of consumers. By focusing on the location of the consumer, the system would help ensure that the U.S. tax base is safe in the new environment.

At the same time, many U.S.-incorporated MNCs would benefit from an exemption system, as they would fully enjoy the advantage conferred by low rates in other source jurisdictions, which they generally do not under the current system of residence taxation with a limited foreign tax credit. This is really the major difference between an exemption and a credit system. So this system would help to keep the United States competitive as a place to incorporate, arguably helping to preserve to the country various spillover benefits that arise from headquarters operations and research and development activities, for example, which (if history is any guide, which it may or may not be) tend to concentrate in the country of incorporation.

NOTES

1) *Formulary Apportionment and Development.* The type of formulary apportionment that Noren discusses would allocate taxing jurisdiction over corporations solely based on the relative level of sales in different countries. As one may infer from his discussion of the objectives and consequences of such a source rule, developing countries are likely to oppose such a proposal vociferously given their relatively small consumer markets. One alternative is to place stronger weight on labor costs in the formula. However, the experience of the U.S. states with formulary apportionment suggests that this would be an unstable solution. Originally most states adopted a formula that equally weights property, payroll and sales.[31] But over the past quarter century, 33 states have increased the importance of sales in their formulas in response to competitive pressures in attracting corporate investment.[32] By eliminating the property and payroll factors from their formulary apportionment equation when other states retained the equally weighted formula, a state could effectively subsidize companies that moved their property and payroll to that state.[33] Thus, in the long run, international competition for jobs and investment might drive most nations toward a sales-based formula unless a large group of nations agree to some other methodology and bar unilateral defection from the agreement. The major drawback of a sales-based formula is that it tends to operate much like a tariff on imports.[34]

2) *Redefining Source Income.* David Noren suggests that U.S. economic well-being might be enhanced by exempting U.S. corporations from U.S. taxation on their active foreign source business income and redefining the source of income as the location of consumption. However, others contend that these objectives could be better realized by substituting a

31. STARK, supra note 17, at 8.

32. Id. at 21.

33. Id. at 20.

34. Charles E. McLure, Jr. and Walter Hellerstein, Does Sales-only Apportionment of Corporate Income Violate International Trade Rules? (forthcoming).

destination-based value-added tax (VAT) for some or all of the income tax. The VAT is a consumption tax. Typically each sale within the production process is taxed and the seller receives a credit for previous taxes paid on its inputs. Under a destination-based VAT, sales abroad are exempt from tax and, as a result, imports and sales of domestically-produced goods are taxed while exports are not. Like Noren's proposal, a destination-based VAT could reduce incentives for U.S. corporations to invest abroad in low-tax jurisdictions because the location of investment would have no effect on U.S. taxes paid. For further discussion of value-added taxes, see Liam Ebrill et al., THE MODERN VAT 176–88 (International Monetary Fund, 2001) and Staff of the Joint Committee on Taxation, *Background Materials on Business Tax Issues Prepared for the House Committee on Ways and Means Tax Policy Discussion Series* 68–74 (JCX–23–02, Apr. 4, 2002).

Chapter 3

Residence

3.1 INTRODUCTION

Source and residence are fundamental concepts of international income taxation. A principal focus of international tax policy is the allocation of income tax between countries of residence and countries of source. As Chapter 2 discussed, source rules generally attempt to identify the geographic locus of the economic activities or financial arrangements that generate income. Residence rules derive from nations' exercises of sovereignty and jurisdiction over their residents and citizens. The United States and other countries use a combination of both source and residence-based income taxation.

Many countries assert jurisdiction to tax their residents on their worldwide profits. The United States exercises its tax jurisdiction over its citizens, residents, and companies incorporated in the United States, regardless of where their income is earned. Certain other countries, such as the Netherlands, are often said not to tax their residents on a worldwide basis. Rather, these countries exempt most foreign income from domestic tax. This is often called a "territorial" system. Other countries have adopted an explicitly hybrid approach in which active business income in foreign countries is exempt from taxation, while passive investment income is taxed to residents when it is earned. Indeed, most countries employ some hybrid approach, in effect, taxing their residents on some of their worldwide income, while also conceding the primary right to tax certain income to the country of source. Regardless of what approach a nation embraces, an income tax must satisfy the claims both of source and resident countries.

Nations have found ample justification to tax their residents on both legal and political grounds. International and national laws strongly support the ability and authority of a nation to tax the income of its citizens and residents. Political ideas such as sovereignty, responsibilities in return for rights, and equality as well as public policy objectives are also advanced as providing such authority. The excerpts by Peggy B. Musgrave in Chapter 1 briefly explore these justifications.

This chapter describes and assesses residence-based taxation, looking at the existing framework of national rules and international norms pertaining to both individual and corporate residence. The first part of this chapter (Sections 3.2–3.5) explores residency rules as they pertain to individuals; the second part (Sections 3.6–3.10) addresses the special problems of residence-based corporate taxation.

3.2 DETERMINATION OF INDIVIDUAL RESIDENCE

The United States imposes tax on the worldwide income of U.S. citizens, regardless of where they reside or are domiciled. Likewise, non-citizen individuals who are classified as resident aliens under the U.S. tax code are also subject to tax on their worldwide income. The United States is virtually alone in its practice of subjecting its citizens to worldwide taxation. The vast majority of other countries treat non resident citizens the same way they treat nonresident aliens, taxing both groups only on their domestic-source income.

The following excerpt outlines how several OECD countries approach the problem of determining individual residence. It is followed by an excerpt from an article by David Tillinghast, which delineates the U.S. rules of individual residence and reflects on the policies underlying the "domestic" versus "foreign" distinction.

HUGH J. AULT, COMPARATIVE INCOME TAXATION: A STRUCTURAL ANALYSIS 369–71 (1997).

Personal taxing jurisdiction over individuals is typically asserted on the basis of "residence" and is often referred to as residence jurisdiction. The determination of residence often rests on a facts-and-circumstances test which looks at the various social and economic connections the taxpayer has to the taxing jurisdiction as well as the taxpayer's intent with regard to his stay and his connections to other jurisdictions. This general test is frequently supplemented with a mechanical test based on the number of days present in the jurisdiction. Residence for tax purposes may or may not be connected with residence in terms of immigration status.

The *United States* approach combines objective and facts-and-circumstances tests. A person is a resident for tax purposes if he possesses the right to permanent entry to the United States under the immigration laws (a so-called "green-card" test) or if he is physically present in the jurisdiction for 183 days or more during the taxable year. In addition, he may be treated as a resident if he is present in the jurisdiction thirty-one days or more and meets a cumulative presence test which looks to the days present in the current year and in the past two years. If the total days in the present year and the weighted days for the past two years is 183 or more, the individual will be a resident for tax purposes unless he can establish that his "tax home," usually his principal place of business, is in another country, and he has a "closer connection" to that country than to the United States. The factors in establishing the "closer connection" are those which are typically used in a residence determination. Special rules apply for students and diplomats which allow them to be present in the country without triggering the mechanical physical presence tests.

Unlike other jurisdictions, the United States also asserts personal jurisdiction based on citizenship. United States citizens are, in principle, taxable on their worldwide income regardless of where they are resident. This basis for personal jurisdiction increases the possibility of overlapping claims for worldwide taxation, an issue that is frequently dealt with in U.S. tax treaties.

In *Canada*, residence is, in general, determined on a case-by-case basis, applying a case-law-developed set of factors including the availability of a dwelling in Canada, the residence of family members, physical presence, and social and economic ties. Once residence is established, the intention to return to Canada is relevant in cases where the taxpayer has left the jurisdiction. In addition, a specific statutory provision deems a person resident of Canada if he "sojourns" there for 183 days during the taxable period. The meaning of the term "sojourn" is not entirely clear but it is not synonymous with physical presence; for example, if a person is resident in Canada for part of the year, he is not "sojourning" in Canada.

Australia also applies a facts-and-circumstances test which turns on being "domiciled" in Australia and having no "permanent place of abode" outside the country. Physical presence for more than one-half of the tax year also constitutes residence unless the taxpayer can establish that his usual place of abode is abroad and he does not have the intent of taking up residence in Australia. * * *

Germany treats an individual as resident for tax purposes if he has either his residence or habitual place of abode in the jurisdiction. * * * Residence is based on the availability to the taxpayer of a home (house, apartment, etc.) which he intends to retain and use. There is a highly developed case law applying this facts-and-circumstances test, Some of the factors considered are the period of time during which the home is used and regularity and frequency of the use. "Habitual abode" is established by presence in Germany indicating an intention to stay more than temporarily. In practice, a continuous stay of six months (even if spanning two calendar years) will constitute a habitual abode, though there are nuances in the rules.

The *French* system has an extensive statutory definition of residence. Individuals are resident for tax purposes if they have their permanent home in France, or, if their permanent home cannot be determined, if they are physically present in the jurisdiction for over 183 days. In addition, professional or employment activity in France will lead to resident treatment unless the taxpayer can establish that the activity is secondary to activities performed elsewhere. Finally, if the taxpayer has his "center of economic interest" in France, he will be treated as resident regardless of the nature of the activity.

The focus in the *Japanese* statute is on both domicile, defined as the base of personal operations, and more than a year of residence, defined as the place of day-to-day living. An administrative regulation provides that if a person is engaged in a business that ordinarily requires living in the country for one year, he will be treated, unless otherwise provided, as domiciled in Japan for tax purposes when he arrives in the country. However, if personal connections to Japan are significant, domicile will be present even if business activities are conducted outside Japan for significant periods of time. * * *

Japan also distinguishes between ordinary residents and "short-term" residents. A short-term resident is one who meets the normal residence test but does not intend to remain permanently in Japan and has not maintained a residence for five years. Short-term residents are only taxed on domestic source income and foreign source income which is remitted to Japan.

David Tillinghast, *A Matter of Definition: "Foreign" and "Domestic" Taxpayers*, 2 INT'L TAX & BUS. LAW. 239, 239–49 (1984).

Nothing is more fundamental under the federal income tax system than determining whether an individual is a domestic or a foreign taxpayer. Accordingly, the statutory rules that determine when an alien individual is a resident of the United States are worthy of critical evaluation. * * * Once the decision to distinguish domestic taxpayers from foreign taxpayers is made, as it has been in virtually all of the nations of the world, there is widespread agreement both within the United States and abroad on two fundamental principles:

(1) Taxpayers with a sufficiently close nexus to the jurisdiction to be considered 'domestic' should be taxed on their world-wide income; and

(2) Taxpayers without such close connections to the jurisdiction should be considered 'foreign' and taxed only on

income that is derived from or connected with the jurisdiction. * * *

As a broad foundation for discussing particular distinctions between 'foreign' and 'domestic' status, it may also be useful to reflect briefly on some of the policies which may underlie these distinctions.

First, choosing one status over the other, or changing from one to the other, should, to the greatest extent possible, involve a real choice (or change) of position. The choice should be consequential in the real world, whether the taxpayer is an individual, a corporation, a trust, an estate, or simply a tax-significant entity such as a partnership. Thus, a first step should be to identify the real connections of people and legal entities to particular countries, so that the definitions of domestic and foreign taxpayers can be based on consequential choices. Despite the difficulty in identifying the real life consequences of certain choices for legal entities, as compared with individual taxpayers, the issue of choice looms large as a criterion of domestic or foreign status. * * *

If a taxpayer's individual choices are to be the principal basis for imposing a tax, then, to the greatest extent possible, the taxpayer should neither benefit nor be harmed by separate choices made by other taxpayers to which or to whom the first taxpayer is in some way connected.

Another possible policy consideration is that the definitions of domestic and foreign taxpayers might be shaped and applied in a manner which would overall yield the most revenue. Tax-haven countries have made the conscious decision that they can garner more revenue by extending favorable terms to some taxpayers than they could by applying stringent standards. It is quite possible that a more liberal definition of 'foreign' taxpayers, and, particularly, non-resident aliens, would result in an influx of substantial additional foreign capital to the United States, and that the benefits of this foreign capital would outweigh the loss of tax revenues resulting from extension of foreign or non-resident alien status to some taxpayers currently classified as domestic. * * *

I.   DETERMINING THE STATUS OF INDIVIDUALS

A.   General Considerations

U.S. Citizens. From the beginning of the federal income tax system, an individual who is a citizen of the United States has been deemed a domestic taxpayer, subject to tax on world-wide income regardless of the individual's residence or domicile. The Supreme Court quickly held this rule to be constitutional and in practice the rule seems to have raised few problems of interpretation.

The force of the United States' claim on the world-wide income of even its non-resident citizens is demonstrated by the Rexach cases, a lengthy series of litigation involving deficiency assessments against Felix Benitez Rexach and his wife, Lucienne D'Hotelle de Benitez Rexach. Mr. Rexach renounced his American citizenship in 1958 before a U.S. consulate official in the Dominican Republic and a certificate of loss of nationality was approved by the Department of State. In 1962, however, he claimed that his renunciation of citizenship was not voluntary but had been compelled by economic pressure and physical threats. This argument was accepted and his certificate of loss of nationality was cancelled. Thereafter, the Internal Revenue Service (IRS) assessed taxes on Mr. Rexach's income for the period from 1958 through 1962. Mr. Rexach objected, claiming that since he was 'owed' no benefits during this period, he 'owed' no taxes. The First Circuit rejected the argument, stating that 'we will not hold that assessment of benefits is a prerequisite to assessment of taxes.'

Mrs. Rexach encountered a somewhat different problem. Mrs. Rexach, a native of France, was naturalized as a U.S. citizen in 1942. In 1946, she established residence in France, and, under a statute then in existence, forfeited her American citizenship in 1949 for having resided in the country of her birth for three years following naturalization. Nevertheless, the Governor of Puerto Rico extended Mrs. Rexach's U.S. passport, and she continued to enjoy the benefits of U.S. citizenship until 1952, when the passport was confiscated and a certificate of loss of nationality was issued. Mrs. Rexach's executor contended that she should not be taxed as a citizen for the period 1949 to 1952, when she was not, under law, entitled to citizenship. The argument failed because the Court held that 'fairness' and the fact that Mrs. Rexach 'received the protection of the United States government' warranted imposition of the tax.

In sum, the Rexach cases establish that an individual will be taxed as a citizen on his world-wide income, not only when he is and knows that he is a U.S. citizen, but also when, as in the case of Mr. Rexach, he is in fact a citizen, even though he thinks he is not or when, as in the case of Mrs. Rexach, she thinks she is a citizen, even though, in fact, she is not.

Presumably, the imposition of tax on world-wide income should be related in some reasonable way to the scope of the governmental services the taxing country may fairly be presumed to be extending to the taxpayer. While the range of governmental services enjoyed by a resident no doubt exceeds that extended to the nonresident citizen, there is equally no doubt that the latter enjoys substantial legal and practical protections by reason of his nationality, not the least of which is the right of reentry into the United States at will. * * *

When the United States taxes its non-resident citizens, it naturally increases the number of cases in which the world-wide income of an individual is taxed twice. As long as the United States continues to allow a foreign tax credit, limited only to the U.S. tax on the taxpayer's overall income, however, duplicative taxation can be eliminated in many cases. Since the tax imposed by the foreign country of residence on income from third countries, as well as income derived within its borders, can be credited against U.S. tax liability, the only significant problems arise from taxation of U.S.-source income by the foreign country of residence. In such cases, given the general international recognition of residence as the primary basis for the taxation of world-wide income, the United States should in fairness assure a full credit for the foreign tax imposed. This result can be achieved, however, without foregoing U.S. citizenship as a basis for general taxation of world-wide income.

Resident and Non–Resident Aliens. An alien who is a resident of the United States is taxed on world-wide income in substantially the same manner as a U.S. citizen. There is no doubt that this principle of taxation is fair and in accordance with internationally accepted standards. If reasonably applied, a residence rule reflects a real life connection to the United States and an exercise of choice by the affected individual, that is, coming to live in the United States. Since this principle is practically certain to remain part of our system, the question is not whether to adopt the principle itself but rather how to determine residence status and, depending upon the resolution of that issue, whether to adopt collateral rules to assure that harsh or distortive consequences do not flow from a finding of U.S. residence.

B.   The New Objective Test

Historically, residence in the United States for federal income tax purposes was determined on the basis of a generalized 'all of the facts and circumstances' test. * * * The Deficit Reduction Act of 1984 (hereinafter the 1984 Act) establishes an objective statutory test of residence. * * * Under the enacted version of the bill, three tests are established; an alien meeting any one of them is deemed to be a resident for income tax purposes.

Under the first test, an alien who has acquired the status of permanent resident under the immigration laws is deemed to be a resident for tax purposes from the first time he is physically present in the United States. Under the second test, an alien is deemed to be a resident if physically present in the United States for at least 183 days in the taxable year, with exceptions for personnel of foreign governments and international organizations, teachers, trainees, students, and those medically unable to leave the country.

If neither of these tests is met, the alien nevertheless will be presumed to be a resident if he is physically present: (i) for at least 31 days in the current taxable year; and (ii) for at least 183 days during the current and the preceding two years, counting each day in the preceding year as 1/3 of a day and each day in the second preceding year as 1/6 of a day. The effect is, for example, that an alien present in the United States for at least 122 days in every year would be presumed to be a resident in all years. The exceptions for employees of foreign governments and international organizations, teachers, trainees, students, and those medically unable to leave the country apply here also. In addition, the presumptive determination of residence will be overcome for a particular year if the alien established that he or she: (1) has a 'tax home' in a foreign country; (2) has a closer connection to such foreign country than to the United States; and (3) has not applied for or taken other steps looking toward the acquisition of permanent resident status under the immigration laws.

Under the so-called 'non-lapse' rules, if an individual who is a resident at any time in one year becomes a resident at any time in the next year, resident status continues in the intervening period. Moreover, if an individual, having been a resident for three consecutive years, again becomes a resident within the three succeeding years, U.S.-related income (but not foreign income) derived during the interval remains taxable on an ordinary net income basis and at individual progressive rates, regardless of whether it would normally be so taxed in the hands of a non-resident alien.

* * *

Whether the precise tests set forth in the 1984 Act represent the proper rules for determining U.S. residence depends, among other things, on how assertive the United States wishes to be as a matter of policy. Obviously, tougher residence rules may deter the free flow of individuals to the United States, but they also will assure the payment of a full tax by those availing themselves of substantial benefits of the government or its laws.

It seems fair to say that the rules adopted by the 1984 legislation are assertive, in the sense that they go beyond the kinds of rules which are applied by most countries of the world. For example, * * * a person holding a U.S. 'green card' will be considered a resident if he sets foot in the U.S. for just one day, or, indeed, if he never sets foot in the U.S. but holds a 'green card' throughout the year. * * *

Problems of Dual Residence. The United States may consider an alien to be a resident for income tax purposes even though he is simultaneously so considered by another country. * * * To the extent that the proposed objective test tightens the residence definition, * * * it may increase the number of instances in which this duality actually occurs. Many such dual residence cases will be dealt with by the United States' income tax treaties. * * * Moreover, many of the newer treaties contain a provision similar to article 4 of the OECD Model Double Taxation Convention, which is designed to prevent double taxation when both of the Contracting States consider an individual to be a resident taxpayer under their internal laws. This 'tie-breaker' provision looks first to the jurisdiction in which the person has a permanent home 'available', and if one is available in both jurisdictions, then to the country in which the person has his 'center of vital interests.' If these factors are not decisive or cannot be determined, then the provision looks to the jurisdiction in which the individual has his 'habitual abode'.

These provisions, as can be seen, operate on the basis of criteria wholly different from those utilized in the proposed legislative definition. Legal immigrant status is not relevant. The length of time present in the jurisdiction is not relevant, except to the unspecified extent that it may contribute to the identification of an 'habitual abode'. Only in the third level test under the 1984 Act, where the United States' definition of residence depends on whether the individual has a 'tax home' in and a 'closer connection' to another foreign country, do the factors set forth in the tax treaties seem to come into play.

It seems inevitable that a substantial number of cases will arise in which persons considered resident by the United States under the proposed statutory definition will also be considered by treaty partners to be resident in their countries. It seems inevitable, as well, that the 'tie-breaker' articles will result in many of these people being found to be residents of the foreign treaty partner, rather than the United States. To this substantial extent, the new statutory definition will not remove the detriments of the 'all of the facts and circumstances' test but will merely shift the focus of the determination to the particu-

lar, although still vague, factors referred to in the treaty articles.

3.3 ADVANTAGES OF RESIDENCY-BASED TAXATION

The following excerpts by Reuven S. Avi–Yonah and Peggy Musgrave discuss the advantages of residency-based income taxation as
compared to source-based taxation. The articles discuss a wide variety of
issues including national economic interests, political allegiance, capital
export neutrality, and horizontal and vertical equity. Reuven Avi–Yonah
provides an introduction to these issues, and Peggy Musgrave addresses
the effect on the international distribution of resources of taxation based
on residence and source. Residency-based taxation appears to be quite
appropriate for individuals. When corporations are considered, however,
residence no longer seems so compelling. This distinction is explored
further in the second part of this chapter.

Reuven S. Avi–Yonah, *The Structure of International Taxation: A Proposal for Simplification*, 74 TEX. L. REV. 1301, 1311–1314 (1996).

There appear * * * to be several solid grounds for prefer-
ring residence over source taxation for individuals. The first is a
pragmatic ground: individuals can only be in one place at any
given time. Thus, residence for individuals is a relatively easy
concept to establish, and in fact, it is possible to set down
bright-line rules for determining the fiscal residence of individuals. On the other hand, determining the source of income is a
highly problematic endeavor, and in most cases, income will
have more than one source. Thus, if one jurisdiction is to be
given the primary right to tax individuals, the residence jurisdiction is an obvious candidate.

Second, because most individuals have only one residence
jurisdiction and are part of only one society, distributional
concerns can be effectively addressed only in the country of
residence. If the personal income tax is to have a significant
redistributive function through progressive rates, it is necessary
to include all income (including foreign source income) in the
measurement of one's ability to pay. There may be no horizontal equity problem in taxing differently two equivalently situated taxpayers, only one of whom invests abroad and earns low-
taxed income there, as long as the other has the same choice of
investments open to her. There is, however, a significant vertical equity problem in taxing an investor with low domestic
earnings and high foreign earnings that are not taxed abroad in
the same way that a person with only low domestic earnings is
taxed. This problem can be resolved if the residence jurisdiction

is allowed to tax on a residual basis only foreign source income that is not taxed abroad (or is taxed at lower effective rates) and allows a credit for foreign taxes, but it is much simpler to address the issue if the residence jurisdiction is given the exclusive right to tax all income of its residents.

Third, the residence of individuals to some extent overlaps with their political allegiance. In democratic countries, it is considered important for individuals to have a right to partici-pate—through their representatives—in deciding how much tax they have to pay. The converse is even more significant: demo-cratic legislatures have a preference for raising taxes on foreign-ers precisely because they cannot vote. Thus, taxation based on residence is a useful, though far from perfect, proxy for taxation with representation.

Finally, economists have pointed out that residence-based taxation is compatible with the goal of capital export neutrality (CEN). This goal requires that the decision to invest in a given location not be affected by tax rates; otherwise, investments that yield the highest returns on a pretax basis will not be made because the after-tax return will be lower, causing global wel-fare (based on allocative efficiency) to be diminished. In a world with many taxing jurisdictions with varying rates, CEN is best achieved by taxing all investors at their residence country rate.
* * *

Why, then, not follow the path of pure residence-based taxation * * * ? There are two major reasons. The first is that to implement full residence-based taxation, it is necessary either to determine artificially the residence of corporations or to impute the earnings of publicly traded MNEs to their sharehold-ers. * * * The difficulty is that residence of corporations cannot be determined the way residence of individuals can be and imputation of earnings to shareholders is a very complex task, which may be administratively impossible.

The second objection to pure residence-based taxation is that it results in more revenue being collected by developed countries and less by developing countries. To illustrate this, it is convenient to refer to a model world made up of only three jurisdictions: a developed country (e.g., the United States), a developing country (e.g., India), and a tax haven (e.g., the Cayman Islands). The residents of the United States earn active income from the United States, earn passive income from in-vestments in the United States and in the Caymans, and earn passive income from investments in X, a MNE headquartered in the United States that does business in India. The residents of India earn active income from India, earn active income from working for X in India, and, in the case of the elite, earn investment income from the United States and the Caymans. X develops products in the United States, manufactures them in India, and sells them in the United States, but its profits arc, to a large extent, channeled to investments in the Caymans.

In this stylized world, if all taxation were based on residence, the United States would receive the taxes from the income of its residents (active and passive), as well as the entire taxes from X, either because X is headquartered there (if corporations are to have an artificial residence) or because all of X's shareholders are residents of the United States and none are residents of India. India, the developing country, would thus be left only with the taxation of the local income of its residents and the income of its elite from the United States and the Caymans, of which the latter is difficult for India to collect. This would likely be an insufficient amount of income for India, which would therefore refuse to cooperate in the residence-based system.

Peggy B. Musgrave, *Sovereignty, Entitlement, and Co-operation in International Taxation*, 26 BROOK. J. INT'L L. 1335, 1338–1341 (2001).

The choice by the country of residence (hereinafter referred to as R) of how to exercise its tax sovereignty is * * * largely a choice of how its own tax is to relate to the tax imposed by the country of source (hereinafter referred to as S). Acting unilaterally, in the absence of cooperation, the principal considerations in making that choice are equitable tax treatment for its residents/citizens and its national economic interests. Such interests include the level and growth of national income, the distribution of such income, and its balance of payments with the rest of the world; the latter bearing on its exchange rate and its terms of trade.

* * *

The basic consideration for the residence country is to preserve the integrity of its comprehensive income tax. Integrity of such a tax system requires the inclusion of all income earned abroad by R's residents in the tax base and subjecting it to national standards of tax equity. Without that basic provision, standards of both horizontal and vertical equity are violated. For individuals, the exercise of the residence entitlement suggests the use of a personalized income tax. * * * However, a rule for the equitable treatment of the foreign income taxes paid on that income is not clear cut, since a case can be made for either crediting, deducting, or even disregarding the foreign S tax. Full crediting for the foreign tax is called for if an "international" view of taxpayer equity is taken, with the foreign tax regarded as equivalent to, and substitutable for, the domestic tax. On the other hand, country R might define taxpayer equity in "national" terms. In this case, the S tax could be regarded as a cost to the taxpayer and, therefore, deducted from taxable foreign income, just as lower level domestic taxes usually are treated. Yet again, the definition of national equity might well disregard the foreign tax entirely, with R's tax applied to foreign income gross of the foreign tax with no allowance for the latter, on the ground that the standard of taxpayer equity should be applied to R's tax only and that the foreign tax is irrelevant in this regard. Which rule is followed, as in most other equity issues, has to be a matter of judgment by national consensus.

Although the concept of equity is more readily applied to individual taxpayers, the corporation is an essential halfway house for foreign income flowing to resident individual shareholders and similar principles should apply to its taxation. For resident corporations, these again call for a corporation tax which includes all income-foreign and domestic. For reasons familiar in the context of domestic taxation, both efficiency and equity call for taxation of corporations on an accrual basis without deferral until distribution. This applies to income earned abroad by the resident corporation, whether arising in a foreign affiliate or branch, or foreign-incorporated subsidiary form. But again on equity grounds, there is no definitive rule as to the treatment of foreign tax.

* * *

The transference of economic activity abroad may have a profound effect on the national economic interests of the residence country. None looms larger in this respect than overseas investment which affects the overall level and distribution of national income within the capital-exporting country. Consequently, tax policies which affect capital outflows are an important instrument of economic policy. Countries of residence can shape their tax policy to manipulate the size and type of capital outflow to their own advantage, rather than contribute to the worldwide gains obtained through a neutral tax policy, which promotes efficient international allocation of capital, or redistributional considerations calling for investment in the low-income countries.

Viewing the treatment of foreign taxes in national efficiency terms, it will be to R's advantage to maximize the contribution of investment made abroad to the national welfare. It then may seek to ensure that the national returns to investment made abroad are at least equal to those obtained on domestic investment. Since the foreign tax may be regarded as a subtraction from the national return, this goal of national efficiency is secured by allowing foreign income taxes as deductions from taxable income rather than as credits against the home country tax. Under this regime, investors will be inclined to invest abroad only if returns after foreign tax are equal to or greater than those obtainable before tax in the domestic economy. In this way, investment made abroad will be less than that called for on worldwide efficiency grounds, but will be consistent with a standard of national efficiency imposed by the country of residence.

There is a further national argument which can be made by R for the deduction treatment of foreign taxes. Provided that the combined effective tax rate of R and S on investment made abroad is similar to that on R's domestic investment, the net result will be an overall increase in the combined national income of R and S. However, the general assumption in neoclassical economics is that the decision of investors resident in country R, to invest R's savings in country S (the country of source of income), rather than in R, will raise the income of R's investors and S's labor, while lowering that of S's investors and R's labor. Thus, even if tax neutrality ensures efficiency with overall income gains, there will be redistributive effects in both R and S (presumably equalizing in S and the reverse in R). Furthermore, allowing for the tax take of country S in foreign investment earnings, there well may be a net income loss to the capital-exporting country R, with the presumption of larger income gains to S. Since direct investment abroad has powerful redistributive effects within and among participating countries, in terms of capital and labor earnings as well as sources of tax revenue, it is to be expected that the country of residence would wish to exercise some degree of control over such investment. Short run effects of capital outflow on the balance of payments may be a further concern for the home country R.

Thus, just as it generally is accepted that a country has the right to retain sovereignty over population immigration, it also is logical that sovereignty be exercised over the outflow of its capital. In the absence of direct capital controls, taxation is the favored instrument, and in particular the corporation income tax. Furthermore, it follows that pursuit of national interests generally will result in a tax penalty on investment made abroad by the country of residence.

3.4 The Special Problems of Students, Actors and Professional Athletes

International treaties seek to eliminate the problems of double taxation occurring when two countries assert jurisdiction over the same income. By recognizing the tax systems of two or more signatory countries, double taxation can usually be avoided. The following excerpts look at some of the special problems faced by international students, athletes, and artists, and the effects of treaties on the determination of their residence.

Ernest R. Larkins, *Coming to America: International Students Face a Labyrinth of Income Tax Issues,* **15 Conn. J. Int'l L. 47, 49–63 (2000).**

Most international students attending U.S. schools spend nine or more months in the United States each year. Absent some special provision, these students are considered U.S. residents under the substantial presence test * * * and, thus, subject to U.S. taxation on a worldwide basis. Notwithstanding their substantial U.S. presence, qualified students (defined below) are treated as nonresidents for a limited time by ignoring days of U.S. presence. In other words, students whose U.S. presence exceeds both the 31–day and 183–day thresholds may, nonetheless, be considered nonresidents and avoid U.S. income taxation on their foreign source incomes.

                                    * * *

To avoid U.S. residency treatment, a nonimmigrant (i.e., an alien without a green card) must be a student (or family member). A student is one who is: (1) temporarily present in the United States under an F, J, M, or Q visa and (2) substantially complying with all requirements of his or her visa * * * . Merely showing that one's visa has not been revoked is not determinative of substantial compliance. For tax purposes, the I.R.S. (rather than I.N.S.) must determine whether the visa holder is in compliance. International students on F–1 visas are not in compliance with visa requirements if they accept unauthorized employment or are not enrolled in an educational institution full time, even though the immigration authorities may be unaware of these violations and may not have revoked the students' visas. Based on the earlier discussion of visa requirements, attending an unapproved school also is noncompliance. Further, an international student who enters the United States on a temporary visa and, a short time later, applies for permanent residence might be considered noncompliant on the basis that his original intent was to remain in the United States permanently. In other words, such a position might be interpreted as inconsistent with the terms of his temporary visa since it suggests a preconceived intent to permanently remain in the United States. Finally, family members with F–2 visas are often precluded from U.S. employment and, thus, risk losing their nonresident status if they accept a job in the United States.

Students (and family members) meeting these requirements can avoid U.S. residency status for a portion or all of any five calendar years. The five calendar years need not be consecutive, neither must they be the immediately preceding calendar years. Thus, an alien individual who avoids U.S. residency status for any portion of 1990, 1991, 1992, and 1995 under the special rule for international students, has only one calendar year remaining to qualify as a nonresident under the student exception. Any prior calendar year for which the individual avoided U.S. residency status as a teacher or trainee, rather than as a student, counts as one of the five allowable years.

Beginning in the sixth calendar year, students (and family members) meeting the substantial presence test generally become U.S. residents and are subject to U.S. taxation on worldwide income. Nonetheless, if they can demonstrate (1) they have no intention of becoming permanent U.S. residents (i.e., obtaining green cards) and (2) they are still in substantial compliance with their visa requirements, students can continue to qualify as nonresidents beyond the fifth calendar year. Whether an alien individual intends to become a U.S. resident is based on the facts and circumstances, but two important considerations are: (1) whether the person has maintained a closer (i.e., more significant) connection with his home or another country than the United States and (2) whether the person has taken any affirmative steps to become a U.S. resident (e.g., by applying for a green card). The closer connection factor is itself based on the following facts and circumstances: (1) location of permanent home, (2) location of family, (3) location of personal belongings, (4) location of social, political, cultural, and religious organizations to which the individual belongs, (5) location of banking activities, (6) location of business activities, (7) location of the jurisdiction that authorized driver's license, (8) location where the individual votes, (9) country that the individual claims as residence on forms and documents, and (10) implications from the types of forms and documents that the individual files.

In many cases, tax treaties do not change the residency status of international students. For example, when the statutory rules * * * indicate that a student is a nonresident alien, a tax treaty with her home country does not affect such determination. With respect to the United States, she is treated as a nonresident alien in applying either statutory rules or treaty provisions. Similarly, when the statutory rules indicate that an international student is a U.S. resident but the student is not a resident of her home country under its domestic law, she is considered a U.S. resident in determining her U.S. tax liability.

A tax treaty changes an international student's U.S. residency status only if three conditions exist. First, the individual is a U.S. resident under the Code. Second, the student is a resident of her home country under its domestic law. Satisfying the first two conditions causes her to be a "dual resident." Third, the hierarchical tie-breaker provisions under the U.S. treaty with her home country classify her as a nonresident alien for U.S. tax purposes. In other words, a treaty's tie-breaker rules can classify a dual resident (U.S. resident under the Code) as a nonresident alien and, thus, override the Code.

Under most U.S. income tax treaties, a set of tie-breaker rules determine whether a dual resident is (1) a U.S. resident or (2) a resident of the home country (and, thus, a nonresident alien under most Code provisions). The tie-breaker rules in the U.S. Model Treaty are similar to those in other U.S. treaties and, since they sufficiently illustrate the classification process, are explained below. The rules are applied in order; the first rule to classify the dual resident completes the classification process.

If an individual student has a permanent home in one of the two treaty countries, but not both, her residency follows the permanent home. A student with permanent homes in both countries determines her residency according to the location of her personal and economic contacts or vital interests. A person's residency follows her habitual abode if either: (1) a permanent home exists in neither country or (2) permanent homes exist in both countries but the location of the vital interests is unclear. When the student has a habitual abode in both countries or neither country, her citizenship or nationality establishes residency. Competent authorities (i.e., the Internal Revenue Service and their foreign counterparts) classify persons who are citizens of both countries or neither country through a mutual agreement procedure.

U.S. income tax treaties with Barbados, Hungary, and Jamaica allow students to elect treatment as U.S. residents notwithstanding that they are otherwise classified as nonresidents. Under these elective provisions, international students (classified as nonresidents under either the Code or the treaty's tie-breaker rules) can choose to be taxed as U.S. residents. In contrast to nonresident aliens, U.S. residents are entitled to (1) file jointly with a spouse and, thus, benefit from lower tax rates, (2) deduct exemptions for spouses, children, and other dependents, and (3) claim the standard deduction. Thus, some Barbadian, Hungarian, and Jamaican students with small or moderate amounts of worldwide income can reduce or eliminate their U.S. tax liabilities through this special election. Individuals with large amounts of foreign source income generally should not make the election since it would cause such amounts to be taxable in the United States. However, once made, the election applies to the current and all subsequent years until the competent authorities (i.e., the Internal Revenue Service) are petitioned and agree to a revocation.

Carole C. Berry, *Taxation of U.S. Athletes Playing in Foreign Countries*, 13 MARQ. SPORTS L. REV. 1, 30–34 (2002).

[T]he U.S. and most of its trading partners have treaties to deal with the finer points of double taxation. Indeed, recent treaties between the U.S. and foreign nations contain specific provisions that relate to the taxation of athletes' income. In both the U.S and OECD Models, article 17, entitled Artistes and Sportsmen, covers the issue. There are four main requirements for article 17 to apply: (1) the individual is a sportsman; (2) the U.S. athlete is playing in a country that has a bilateral treaty with the U.S.; (3) the income falls within article 17; and (4) assuming there is a bilateral treaty, it contains an article 17 that covers the income in question. * * *

Article 17 is an outgrowth of large revenue losses by host countries involving performers and athletes who enter a host country, stay for a short period of time, make enormous amounts of money, and pay no taxes. One authority summarized the problem: "If they are (or make themselves) residents of a country connected to others through a useful network of treaties, and not itself given to fierce taxation, performers and athletes could enjoy virtual exemption from taxation under standard treaty provisions governing the performance of services."

To prevent the escape of taxation by high earning performers and athletes, both the U.S. Model Treaty and the OECD Model Treaty contain an article that deals specifically with that contingency. The U.S. Model Treaty states:

Income derived by a resident of a Contracting State as an entertainer, such as a theater, motion picture, radio, or television artiste, or a musician, or as a sportsman, from his personal activities as such exercised in the other Contracting State, which income would be exempt from tax in that other Contracting State [under the provisions of Articles 14 and 15] may be taxed in that other State, except where the amount of the gross receipts derived by such entertainer or sportsman, including expenses reimbursed to him or borne on his behalf, from such activities does not exceed twenty thousand United States dollars ($20,000) or its equivalent * * * for the taxable year concerned.

Simply put, if a non-resident entertainer or athlete makes more than $20,000 in any given year, the country of source may tax the income even when it normally would not be able to do so. * * *

If the performer exceeds the $20,000 threshold, which includes "expenses reimbursed to the [individual] or borne on his behalf," all amounts may be taxed in the State of performance. This means that if the gross receipts exceed $20,000 (or its equivalent in the currency of the other contracting state), the full amount of the monies received may be taxed—not just the excess over $20,000.

The OECD Model provides for taxation by the country of performance but begins negotiations with no dollar or time threshold. As a result, many treaties negotiated between the U.S. and its treaty partners have significantly different provisions. Many specify dollar amounts and time present in the country. For example, the French treaty provides for a $10,000 limit on monies earned but no time-in-country limit. On the other hand, the Japanese treaty with the U.S. provides that compensation of entertainers and athletes are taxed in the country of source, unless the dollar amount is less than $3,000 and the performer is present in the country for ninety days or less.

The threshold question of whether the income falls within article 17 relates to the very nature of the income. If the income is predominantly attributable to the performance or athletic event, article 17 will usually prevail, and the source state will tax the income. If the activity is attributable to other endeavors, different provisions will apply. For example, if a fee is paid to the entertainer or athlete to promote a specific performance in which the individual is involved, his or her participation will be considered to be closely associated with the performance itself and will fall within the purview of article 17. However, if the income is earned by the endorsement of a product used in the event or general promotion of events of the nature in which the entertainer or athlete performs, the income will probably fall outside article 17. Interestingly, a cancellation fee for a performance or event does not fall within article 17, but rather is considered either article 7, 14 or 15 income.

Paragraph 2 of both the OECD Model and the U.S. Model is aimed at the abusive "loan-out" companies that were developed to by-pass source country taxation. Both provide that income received from professional activities of the entertainer or sportsman, which accrue to another person, may be taxed to that person, notwithstanding the provisions of articles 7 (Business Profits) and 14 (Independent Personal Services), in the contracting state in which the activities are performed.

In one notable case, in an effort to qualify for favorable tax treatment, the boxer Ingemar Johansson, who was a citizen of Sweden, established "residence" in Switzerland and created a Swiss corporation. The corporation "employed" him to fight in a championship bout against Floyd Patterson. After the fight, the Swiss corporation (Johansson was its only client) paid him its entire receipts that resulted from the boxing match. Claiming treaty benefits between the U.S. and Switzerland, Johansson paid no tax to either country. The U.S. took umbrage with the arrangement, sued Johansson, and ultimately prevailed in court. The Fifth Circuit found that the Swiss company had no independent identity except to provide Mr. Johansson with employment. Nevertheless, language in the opinion set the stage for others to establish "loan-out" companies literally to avoid all worldwide taxation. Properly structured, the loan-out company accomplished this feat, at least for a time. However, at present, the second paragraph of both the U.S. Model Treaty and the OECD Model Treaty attempts to eliminate these types of arrangements.

Joel Nitikman, *Article 17: An Argument for Repeal*, INT'L TAX REV., June 1, 2001, at 45.

Does article 17 of the OECD model convention have its basis in outdated and discriminatory assumptions about artistes and athletes? Hold on to your hats for a whistle stop tour of its development, its lack of fit with the modern world and reasons for its repeal.

In the early 1930s, the Fiscal Committee of the League of Nations adopted the following idea: where an enterprise carries on business in its home (residence) jurisdiction and in a foreign (source) jurisdiction, the source jurisdiction should be able to tax the enterprise only if the enterprise carries on business in the source jurisdiction through a permanent establishment (PE), and then only to the extent the taxable profits of the enterprise in the source jurisdiction are equal to the profits the PE would have earned had it been a separate person acting at arm's length with the enterprise. While the relevance of the PE concept, now embodied in article 7 of the OECD model income tax treaty, has been questioned in the electronic age, both older and more recent cases show that the concept is still valid today.

However, there is one exception to the PE concept * * * : according to article 17 of the OECD model, artistes and athletes may be taxed by the source jurisdiction even in the absence of a PE in that jurisdiction. This article considers the history of this strange exception, and argues that the OECD should repeal it.

A review of the history of article 17 reveals that it was inserted in the OECD model treaty because it was believed that artistes and athletes would have a tendency not to report income earned in the source country to their country of residence. Accordingly, it was thought preferable to allow the source country to tax the income even in the absence of a PE, to ensure that at least some tax was paid on the income.

The forerunner to article 17 was inserted in a model treaty for the first time by the OEEC (the forerunner of the OECD) in 1959. The commentary * * * put forward by the OEEC as a rationale for adopting this type of article states that it is based on the "practical difficulties" of taxing artistes and athletes on source jurisdiction income. Translation: it was thought that such taxpayers might not report the source country income to the residence jurisdiction.

The OECD published a comprehensive study in 1987 that in essence adopted the OEEC's rationale for article 17. The present OECD commentary on article 17 adopts the 1987 report. Many portions of the 1987 report evidence the suspicion with which its drafters viewed artistes and athletes. Indeed, the very premise of the 1987 report, as stated in paragraph 3, is that these types of taxpayers represent a "problem" that must be overcome; this signifies a discriminatory attitude. Paragraphs 6 and 7 of the 1987 report state that low-level artistes frequently under-report their income, while high-level performers "frequently" employ "sophisticated tax avoidance schemes" involving tax havens. Paragraphs 16 and 17 of the 1987 report repeat the 1959 assertion that article 17 is justified by the practical difficulties encountered by the residence jurisdiction in taxing source country income earned by such taxpayers.

The policy behind article 17, as set forth in the 1987 report, was summarized in a recent US Internal Revenue Service (IRS) publication (Chief Counsel Advice 199938031) as follows:

The theory behind this rule is that artistes and sportsmen are often paid very large sums of money for very short periods of activity and physical presence in a host country. While such income is normally taxable in the individual's country of residence, it may be difficult for the home country to find out about the activities and income of its residents while they are abroad. These practical difficulties may lead to a general tax climate wherein well-known taxpayers are perceived to be avoiding the payment of taxes. Therefore, it is appropriate for the host country, which presumably has greater access to the relevant information, to have primary jurisdiction to tax the income.

What is not discussed in the 1959 commentary or the 1987 report is why it was thought that artistes and athletes are more of a risk to underreport source country income than other taxpayers. The 1987 report refers to a Canadian study on the matter but no details are given. There is essentially zero statistical data presented to prove the very assertion on which the 1987 report is based, and at most the 1987 report seems to be based on anecdotal rather than empirical evidence.

* * *

The clear picture that emerges is that article 17 assumes that artistes (and athletes) as a group are less likely than anyone else to report their source country income to their country of residence. * * *

The issue of how [this article] impacts * * * US actors working in Canada has simmered for many years. * * * In late 2000 the CCRA [Canada Customs and Revenue Agency] announced that, starting January 1 2001, [previously unenforced] requirements would be enforced. After intense lobbying by a number of groups, the Canadian Department of Finance issued proposed legislation to change the way in which some (but not all) foreign actors are taxed in Canada * * * .

Under the new regime, a non-Canadian resident actor working on a film or video in Canada is subject to a 23% tax on the gross payments received by him or her for services performed in Canada. If the actor provides the services through a corporation, the corporation is subject to the 23% tax and any payments made by the corporation to the actor are not subject to the 23% tax except to the extent that the payments to the actor exceed the payments to the corporation * * * . The minister of national revenue is given the authority to reduce the withholding if there is "undue hardship".

If the actor is subject to the 23% withholding tax, * * *
[t]he effect * * * is to eliminate the requirement to file a tax
return * * * . Similarly, if the actor works through a loan-out
corporation, any payment made by the corporation to the actor
that is not subject to the 23% tax * * * is excluded from the
actor's income * * *, so again, no return need be filed unless
the actor has other income that would otherwise be taxable in
Canada.

   * * * [T]he actor can elect to forgo the 23% gross withholding tax by electing to be taxed * * * on his or her net taxable
income earned in Canada. If there is some withholding tax
deducted prior to the election being filed, the withholding tax is
credited towards any tax eventually owing under the net election. Where a loan-out corporation makes the * * * election, the
actor is deemed to make the same election.

   These proposed amendments will go a long way towards
resolving many of the difficulties foreign actors have had in
Canada, but it is notable that they apply only to film or video
presentations. They do not apply to any other type of acting
services or to athletes. For them, article 17 of the model treaty
still very much applies * * * .

NOTES

1) *Collecting Taxes Is Not Easy.* Two concerns appear to have motivated
the special source-based taxation of athletes and entertainers. The first
is a concern that the residence country will not be able to acquire
sufficient information about the income to prevent under-reporting by
the performer. This is not a problem unique to these circumstances. As
Chapter 8 describes, similar enforcement difficulties plague the enforcement of residence-based taxes on investment income. That chapter
considers in detail whether improved information reporting might address this problem. Similar issues arise here.

   Second, there is some concern that artists and athletes, who earn
large incomes, might move their residence to low-tax countries. It is no
accident that many famous actors and athletes, and more than a few
other wealthy people, such as Boris Becker, Ringo Starr, Roger Moore,
Placido Domingo, Michael Jackson, and Ivana Trump reside in Monte
Carlo, which imposes no income tax on individuals. This problem, of
course, is also not unique to artists and athletes.

2) *Working in More Than One Country.* The movement of workers
across borders is not confined to students, athletes and artists. Many
more workers than in the past now earn income in more than one
country. This is particularly common in the European Union, where the
Treaty of Rome requires "free movement of labour" and prohibits
discriminatory taxation of nonresidents. Kees Van Raad has offered a

general proposal for non-discriminatory income taxation of nonresidents. In general this proposal would require nations, from which a non-resident individual derives income, to treat income on the same footing as income of a resident taxpayer. He also proposes that the residence state should restrict the individual's right to personal deductions to a fraction equal to the aggregate amount of income derived from sources in his residence state divided by worldwide income. See Chapter 10 for this proposal.

3.5 EXPATRIATION BY INDIVIDUALS

Because the taxation of individuals is usually determined by their country of residence, some taxpayers with substantial incomes seek to become residents of countries with low income tax. This problem has gained attention both in the United States and abroad when high profile taxpayers move their residences to low-taxation countries such as Belize and Monaco. In response, the United States Congress has passed legislation attempting to address this problem. In the following excerpt Michael Graetz describes the problem. The subsequent excerpt from a report by the Joint Committee on Taxation evaluates the congressional response and demonstrates how crucial effective enforcement is, if legislation is to fulfill its promises.

Michael J. Graetz, THE U.S. INCOME TAX 272 (1999).

In 1995, Congress became concerned with loopholes in the existing income and estate taxes that allow people to avoid paying large amounts of U.S. taxes by renouncing their citizenship and moving abroad. The president and the Congress proposed so-called Benedict Arnold amendments to eliminate the practice. The most notorious case involved a billionaire Kenneth Dart, president of Dart Container Corporation, a Styrofoam cup manufacturer. Mr. Dart in 1993 renounced his American citizenship and left his home in Sarasota, Florida, darting to the Central American nation of Belize (formerly British Honduras, south of Mexico on the Caribbean Sea), in the process saving millions of dollars in U.S. taxes. In 1995, the Belize government urged the U.S. State Department to allow it to open a consulate in Sarasota, Florida, where Mr. Dart's wife, children, and other relatives lived. Kenneth Dart apparently was to be appointed counsel to the United States from Belize and thereby, as a diplomat, would become free to come and go as he pleases, freeing him from a restriction that limits him to 120 days a year in this country. Dan Miller, Sarasota Republican congressman, said, "The Sarasota area is not known for its concentration of Belizean nationals," and speculated that the choice of location for the consulate where Mr. Dart's family lives was no coincidence. Florida's representative on the House Ways and Means

Committee, Sam Gibbons of Tampa, a Democrat, was only a bit more forgiving: "I do believe that Dart ought to be allowed to live with his family. But I also think he should pay taxes in order to do so." In 1996 Congress passed legislation to restrict somewhat such tax avoidance opportunities.

Staff of the Joint Committee on Taxation, *Review of the Present–Law Tax and Immigration Treatment of Relinquishment of Citizenship and Termination of Long–Term Residency*, JCS–2–03 (FEB. 2003).

U.S. citizens and noncitizens who are U.S. residents generally are subject to U.S. tax on a worldwide basis for U.S. Federal income, estate, and gift tax purposes. On the other hand, noncitizens who are nonresidents generally are subject to U.S. tax only on income from U.S. sources and income effectively connected with the conduct of a trade or business within the United States. In addition, noncitizens who are nonresidents generally are subject to U.S. estate and gift tax only with respect to U.S.-situated property. Bilateral tax treaties may modify the treatment under these general tax rules.

Since 1966, special tax rules have applied to a U.S. citizen who relinquishes U.S. citizenship with a principal purpose of avoiding U.S. taxes. These rules are referred to as the "alternative tax regime." Under the alternative tax regime enacted in 1966, a former citizen is subject to an alternative method of income taxation for 10 years following citizenship relinquishment. The alternative tax regime is a hybrid of the tax treatment of a U.S. citizen and a noncitizen who is a nonresident. For the 10–year period following citizenship relinquishment, the former citizen is subject to tax only on U.S.-source income at the rates applicable to U.S. citizens, rather than the rates applicable to noncitizens who are nonresidents. However, for this purpose, U.S.-source income has a broader scope than it does for normal U.S. Federal tax purposes and includes, for example, gain from the sale of U.S. corporate stock or debt obligations. The alternative tax regime applies only if it results in a higher U.S. tax liability than the liability that would result if the individual were taxed as a noncitizen who is a nonresident.

In addition, since 1966, the alternative tax regime has included special estate and gift tax rules. * * *

In 1996, several significant changes were made to the alternative tax regime. These amendments followed press reports and Congressional hearings indicating that a small number of very wealthy individuals had relinquished their U.S.

citizenship to avoid U.S. income, estate, and gift taxes, while nevertheless maintaining significant contacts with the United States. First, the 1996 amendments extended the application of the alternative tax regime to certain long-term residents who terminate their U.S. residency. Thus, under the 1996 amendments, the alternative tax regime applies both to U.S. citizens who relinquish citizenship and long-term residents who terminate residency with a principal purpose of avoiding U.S. taxes.

Under the 1996 amendments, a U.S. citizen who relinquishes citizenship or a long-term resident who terminates residency is treated as having done so with a principal purpose of tax avoidance (and, thus, generally is subject to the alternative tax regime) if: (1) the individual's average annual U.S. Federal income tax liability for the five taxable years preceding citizenship relinquishment or residency termination exceeds $100,000; or (2) the individual's net worth on the date of citizenship relinquishment or residency termination equals or exceeds $500,000. These amounts are adjusted annually for inflation. Certain categories of individuals can avoid being deemed to have a tax avoidance purpose for relinquishing citizenship or terminating residency by submitting a ruling request to the Internal Revenue Service ("IRS") regarding whether the individual relinquished citizenship or terminated residency principally for tax reasons.

* * *

The Illegal Immigration Reform and Immigrant Responsibility Act of 1996 prohibited individuals who renounce U.S. citizenship for purposes of avoiding taxation from entering the United States: Any alien who is a former citizen of the United States who officially renounces United States citizenship and who is determined by the Attorney General to have renounced United States citizenship for the purpose of avoiding taxation by the United States is inadmissible. * * *

An example of a wealthy individual who had renounced citizenship but desired to continue residing in the United States was used to illustrate the problem the amendment sought to address. It was noted that such individual had convinced a foreign government to appoint, or propose to appoint, the individual as a representative to the United States. In discussing the amendment, it was noted that "[t]he government of the United States should not reward those that renounce citizenship by granting them the privileges of residency."

Opponents criticized the measure on three grounds. First, opponents found the amendment too punitive. Second, it was noted that it would be difficult to ascertain precisely why someone renounced citizenship. Finally, opponents believed the measure gave too much discretion to the Attorney General to determine whether the renunciation was for tax avoidance.

Despite this criticism, the amendment * * * ultimately became part of the Immigration and Nationality Act at section 212(a)(10)(E), 8 U.S.C sec. 1182(a)(10)(E).

* * *

Based on the GAO and Joint Committee staff review of the various Federal agencies' administrative procedures, the Joint Committee staff concludes that there is little or no enforcement of the special tax and immigration rules applicable to tax-motivated citizenship relinquishment and residency termination. The GAO stated in their 2000 report that the IRS does not yet have a systematic compliance effort in place to enforce the present-law alternative tax regime. Since that time the IRS generally has ceased all compliance efforts directly relating to the income, estate, and gift tax obligations of former citizens and former long-term residents under the alternative tax regime, other than compiling a Certificate of Loss of Nationality ("CLN") database for such individuals and publishing their names in the *Federal Register* as required by section 6039G. In addition, the INS and the Department of State have not denied reentry into the United States to a single former citizen under the 1996 special immigration rule.

While the Joint Committee staff is aware that the INS has begun drafting guidelines to implement the immigration provision, it is unclear whether the guidelines will have any significant effect on enforcement. The Joint Committee staff believes that a key reason for inadequate enforcement of the alternative tax regime is the inability to obtain necessary information from individuals: (1) at the time of citizenship relinquishment or residency termination; and (2) during the 10–year period following citizenship relinquishment or residency termination, for those individuals who are subject to the alternative tax regime. These enforcement difficulties begin at the time individuals notify the Department of State of their intent to relinquish citizenship. * * *

The Joint Committee staff recognizes that monitoring the activities of individuals who no longer reside in the United States is inherently difficult, and that the need to do so poses serious challenges in enforcing these rules. At a minimum, an effective system for collecting and processing timely information relating to individuals who relinquish citizenship or terminate residency is a prerequisite to enforcing the rules. Enforcement of the immigration provision also is hindered by several factors, specifically lack of access by the Attorney General to the IRS records to identify former citizens who renounce citizenship for tax reasons, lack of access by the IRS to INS databases, differing interpretations between the INS and the Department of State as to what it means to officially renounce U.S. citizenship, and the lack of coordination between the tax rules and the immigration rules relating to individuals who relinquish citizenship or terminate their residency.

The Joint Committee staff also believes that inadequate enforcement of the alternative tax regime and the related immigration rules may be due in part to a low priority assigned to the enforcement of these rules by the Federal agencies involved. As indicated above, in 2000, the IRS generally ceased compliance efforts directed at former citizens and former long-term residents under the alternative tax regime. The IRS, therefore, cannot determine whether such individuals are meeting their tax return filing requirements under the alternative tax regime. Moreover, the GAO stated in its 2000 report that the IRS has never pursued an audit or otherwise examined those former citizens or former long-term residents who were determined in the ruling process to have a principal purpose of tax avoidance.

* * *

[T]he Joint Committee staff believes that certain of the problems inherent in present law can be addressed through modifications that would provide: (1) objective standards for determining whether former citizens or former long term residents are subject to the alternative tax regime; (2) tax-based (instead of immigration based) rules for determining when an individual is no longer a U.S. citizen or long-term resident for U.S. Federal tax purposes; (3) a sanction for individuals who are subject to the alternative tax regime and who return to the United States for extended periods; (4) imposition of U.S. gift tax on gifts of certain closely-held stock of foreign corporations that hold U.S.-situated property; and (5) an annual return-filing requirement for individuals who are subject to the alternative tax regime, for each of the 10 years following citizenship relinquishment or residency termination.

The Joint Committee staff also believes that certain changes to the present-law immigration provisions are necessary to improve the administrability of the special immigration rule relating to tax avoidance. These changes would promote greater coordination and information-sharing between the IRS and the agencies responsible for the immigration laws and would resolve certain inconsistencies between the tax and immigration provisions of present law.

* * *

While the Joint Committee staff believes that its recommendations would improve the effectiveness and administration of the present-law rules, it should be noted that, even if the Congress were to enact the Joint Committee staff recommendations, tax incentives for citizenship relinquishment and residency termination would remain. An alternative tax regime that is limited to U.S.-source income and, in the case of the estate and gift taxes, to U.S.-situated assets (albeit with expanded definitions of such income and assets) cannot eliminate the tax incentives to relinquish citizenship or terminate residency in cases in which an individual owns significant foreign-situated property. Similarly, an alternative tax regime that applies for a 10–year period following citizenship relinquishment or residency termination will not be effective with respect to individuals who are willing to wait the 10–year period prior to disposing of assets that would be subject to tax under the alternative tax regime. Perhaps most fundamentally, any tax regime applicable to individuals who are no longer physically present in the country, and whose assets may no longer be situated in the country or under the control of any U.S. person, inevitably faces serious challenges of enforcement as a practical matter. This enforcement effort requires significant resources to be devoted to the few individuals who are subject to the alternative tax regime. Accordingly, the Joint Committee staff believes that careful consideration should be given as to whether the alternative tax regime and related immigration rules, even as modified by the recommendations set forth * * *, can fully achieve the goals that the Congress intends to accomplish.

NOTE

Enforcement Priorities? The excerpt above makes clear the inability (or unwillingness) of the IRS to enforce provisions to limit expatriation to avoid tax. It is no wonder that the IRS is unable to track these tax evaders. Janet Novack's April 14, 2003 article in *Forbes Magazine*, "The IRS Wants You to Fess Up," reports that the IRS did face-to-face income tax audits of only one in 631 tax returns in 2001 and that the audit rate for those earning more than $100,000 fell 73% between 1996 and 2002. In an IRS effort to crack down on tax shelters, the Service has obtained client lists from tax shelter promoters. Obviously this is a higher priority than chasing individuals who expatriate. See also Chapter 8 for a more extensive discussion of enforcement issues.

In May 2003, after deciding that the current rules were ineffective, the Senate adopted legislation that would tax citizens who relinquish their U.S. citizenship and certain long-term residents who terminate their U.S. residency on the net unrealized gain on their property as if the property had been sold on the day before expatriation or termination of residency. Only gain in excess of $600,000 per person is subject to this tax. Special rules are provided for interests in qualified retirement plans. Payment of the tax may be deferred if the individual provides adequate security and agrees to pay a relatively high rate of interest. This legislation would remove the current penalty under immigration law that denies visas to individuals who have expatriated for tax reasons and replaces it with restrictions on those who do not fulfill their tax obligations under the new provisions. This provision was dropped by the House–Senate Conference on the 2003 legislation, but it seems likely to return soon to the congressional agenda.

3.6 Determination of Corporate Residence

Like United States individual citizens and resident aliens, U.S. corporations are (at least ostensibly) subject to U.S. income taxation on their worldwide income. Jurisdiction again stems from the residence principle; however, the application of that principle to corporations is far from straightforward. Imagine, for example, that several Italian citizens and residents own a corporation that has property and operates only in Spain, employs only Spanish nationals and sells products only in Spain. If the company's incorporation papers were filed in Delaware, the corporation would be a U.S. corporation subject to U.S. taxation on its worldwide income (with foreign tax credits allowed for other nations' income taxes). The United States is not alone in using a "place of incorporation" test for corporate residence, but many other jurisdictions also use a "place of management" test.

The following excerpt by Hugh Ault presents an overview of our major trading partners' approaches to the issue of corporate residence. Next David Tillinghast discusses the rationale for applying the residency principle to corporations and the problems it creates.

Hugh J. Ault, Comparative Income Taxation: A Structural Analysis 371–373 (1997).

Two basic approaches are used in establishing a personal jurisdictional connection for corporations. One is to focus on some formal legal connection to the jurisdiction such as incorporation or registry in the commercial register. The other is to select some economic or commercial connection such as the place of management, principal business location, or less frequently, residence of shareholders. Many jurisdictions combine these approaches, treating a corporation as resident if either test is satisfied. In some cases, the test of place of management becomes in effect a formal test by focusing on easily controlled events like the place at which the board of directors meets, rather than the situs of day-to-day management decisions.

The *United States* is an example of a jurisdiction which relies on a purely formal test. All corporations organized under the laws of the United States or one of the Federal States are treated as "domestic," i.e., resident, corporations, regardless of any other connection to the jurisdiction. Conversely, all other corporations are "foreign," i.e., non-resident, corporations, even if all of their commercial and economic activities are linked to the U.S. *Japan* also has a formal test, though the technical structure of the rule is somewhat different. Under the statutory definition of resident corporations, a corporation is a resident is its "headquarters" or "principal office" is located in Japan. However, these concepts are derived from civil law and commercial law and under these provisions, all corporations incorporated in Japan must have either a registered headquarters (Commercial Code) or a registered principal office (Civil Code) in Japan, thus in effect turning the test into one of incorporation in the case of domestically-organized corporations. On the other hand, a corporation organized in a foreign country can have a registered principal office or headquarters in Japan (if that is possible under the laws of the incorporating jurisdiction) and will also be treated by Japan as a resident corporation.

Sweden also has a formal test which turns on formation and registration under Swedish corporate law.

The *Commonwealth* countries, which traditionally focused on the place of central management and control to determine corporate residence, now combine that test with a test based on formal incorporation. Thus, in the *United Kingdom* prior to 1988, the only test was the factual one of central management and control of the company's business, which was generally, though not conclusively, where the board of directors met. In 1988, this test was supplemented by an incorporation rule which made companies incorporated in the U.K. resident there but left companies incorporated elsewhere to be liable to U.K. resident status under the old rule.

The *Canadian* rules follow the U.K. pattern. Either incorporation or place of management in Canada will result in resident treatment. The case law has focused primarily on the place of the meeting of the board of directors, thus giving the test a formal character, though in some situations the courts have examined the question of actual day-to-day control.

Australia has a similar approach. Formal incorporation under Australian law will cause the corporation to be treated as resident. In addition, if the corporation is doing business in Australia and has its place of central management in Australia, it is likewise resident. Since having management in Australia is deemed to constitute doing business there, the test is effectively based on the second factor. The Australian rules also take into consideration the residence of the shareholders. If a corporation is doing business in Australia and a majority of voting power is held by Australian residents, the corporation will be viewed as resident. However, the shareholder test is applied without attributing share ownership through interposed companies and can be avoided by interposing a nonresident entity between the corporation and the ultimate Australian shareholders.

Both *Germany* and *The Netherlands* combine incorporation and management tests. In Germany, a corporation is resident if it has its "statutory seat" in Germany. Since all corporations formed under German corporate law are required to designate a statutory seat in the jurisdiction, they are automatically treated as resident. In addition, if a corporation organized under foreign law has its place of management in Germany, it is treated as a resident taxpayer. The focus is on the activities of day-to-day management and not on the supervisory activities of the legal organ roughly equivalent to the (outside) board of directors.

The Netherlands similarly used both formal incorporation and, as with individuals, a determination "according to the circumstances." Case law gives great weight to the place of effective management, i.e. where the day-to-day management takes place. In this regard factors such as residence of directors, and location of board meetings, business and head office may be considered relevant circumstances. In *France*, a corporation formed under French law and having its registered office in France is treated as a resident. However, since France applies the territorial system to corporations, the law on corporate residence is not highly developed as to, for example, the extent to which a corporation must have its place of actual management in France in connection with its registered office.

David R. Tillinghast, *A Matter of Definition: "Foreign" and "Domestic" Taxpayers*, 2 INT'L TAX & BUS. LAW. 239, 252–72 (1984).

Entities are not people. One needs to recognize this fundamental difference at the outset of any search for the most acceptable rule or rules for determining the domestic or foreign nature of legal entities. Both tax laws and tax lawyers tend to attach to these entities the same labels used to describe the connections between individuals and taxing jurisdictions. For instance, the English courts have struggled to analogize the 'residence' of a company to that of an individual. There are common threads in the two situations, but each case is different and requires separate consideration.

It is reasonable and appropriate for a country to tax a legal entity on income which originates within its borders. The question then is what kind of 'ligatures', to use Ralf Dahrendorf's coinage, between the entity and the country justify going beyond this simple rule to tax income of the entity which is conceded to have its source elsewhere. Each kind of entity must be considered separately, for on empirical and, perhaps, theoretical grounds there may be significant differences among them. The fact that a partnership is not a taxable entity whereas a corporation is a taxable entity may, for example, have an effect on the outcome. And the fact that an estate is intimately identified with the personal affairs of the decedent may suggest treatment different from that of a corporation, even if the corporation is owned by a single individual.

Although the rationale for the 'place of incorporation' test has seldom been articulated, the test seems to rely on the notion that a corporation is able to earn income by virtue of being a juridical entity, in that it derives its income-earning capacity from the granting of its charter. The jurisdiction granting the charter and investing the entity with the legal capacity to earn income then has the right to tax that income when it arises. Taxing a corporation based on its place of incorporation is analogous to taxing an individual on the basis of citizenship because both focus on the grant of legal status to the taxpayer by the taxing country. Broadly stated, the policy of existing law is to allow a corporation to freely choose domestic or foreign status, including the status of an existing subsidiary, but to impose a consistency requirement. After the first free chance, a mid-life shift in a corporation's status may be achieved only at the price of 'killing' the old corporation and 'creating' a new one, with consequent tax effects under such recognition provisions as Code sections 367, 1491, and 1248.

The 'place of incorporation' test has one distinct advantage and one serious drawback. Its advantage lies in the certainty which arises from its application. If the test is applied by reference solely to the jurisdiction in which the corporation's charter is filed and by whose laws, therefore, the relations among its shareholders are governed, there can be no doubt as to what is a domestic and what is a foreign corporation. The drawback of the 'place of incorporation' test is that a corporation is by nature androgynous; it can and does autonomously create progeny. In this characteristic lies the important difference between the corporation and the individual. While there are some factors which may strongly influence the decision to incorporate a business in the United States rather than abroad, it is unlikely that a business such as IBM would have been incorporated outside the United States under any circumstances. Once the decision to incorporate in the United States is made, there are tax restraints on changing the decision and reincorporating abroad. There are far fewer restraints, however, on the ability of a U.S. corporation simply to incorporate a subsidiary abroad, thus creating another taxpayer having a different status.

There is little question that the place of incorporation is a crude, if not naive, criterion of domestic corporate status. The question really is whether there exists a more rational and workable alternative. Some of the alternative tests that have been devised seem workable, but they do not address the central problem of U.S.-connected entities deriving entirely foreign income. For example, the United States might provide, as is done in Pakistan, that any corporation which has more than half of its gross income for a requisite period effectively connected with the conduct of a trade or business in the United States is a U.S. corporation. Such a rule would accomplish relatively little, however, as the effectively connected income of even a foreign corporation is already taxable under the Code. Thus, any increase in taxability under U.S. laws would be only on the remaining income of the corporation.

Moreover, a change of this kind could be made effective only by overriding the provisions of existing income tax treaties. The reaction of trading partners to actions which depart this far from traditional international tax conceptions [will be] outcry * * * [and] resentment * * * . Here the gain does not seem worth the stakes. The same is true of similar rules which base the domestic status of a corporation on the conduct of business within the jurisdiction, in combination with other factors relating to ownership and control.

The obvious and more responsive possibility would be to fashion a test under which a corporation would be considered a U.S. person on the basis of what is popularly known as its 'residence'. The test might be cast in any of several ways, including reference to the place of the corporation's central management and control, the place of its effective management, or the place in which its business is principally transacted. Although the particular factors to be taken into account would vary according to the exact formulation of the test, the concept

would be to identify, not the jurisdiction which gives the corporation its legal life, but rather the jurisdiction in which its
economic life is centered, focusing on inputs such as the capital,
technology, and management skills which give the corporation
the economic ability to earn income. This jurisdiction may be
easier to identify in concept than in practice, however.

England and the other Commonwealth countries provide a
good example of the problems associated with the 'residence'
test. In these countries, the residence of a company is a matter
of common law. The courts have for many years followed, or
purported to follow, the landmark decision in the de Beers case.
De Beers enunciated the test that the residence of a company,
while a question of fact, depends upon the location of the
'central management and control' of the company. The most
important factor in determining the location of the central
management and control is the location at which the company's
Board of Directors meets or otherwise discharges its functions.
At least one leading case suggests that this factor is decisive
and, in the broad range of cases, the law has in fact been so
applied.

The English reports are littered, however, with more disturbing opinions. One case, for example, holds that an English
company was resident in England although all of its Board of
Directors meetings were held and its entire business was carried
on in Sweden. Another case states that a company may be
simultaneously resident in two countries because parts of its
management process are carried on in each. An opinion in this
case further maintains that when a company engages in more
than two businesses, each business may have a different place of
management and control. Although the case did not specify this
result, presumably this view requires either that the world-wide
income of the company be taxed in full by both jurisdictions, or
that the two businesses be separated and the separate income of
each be taxed by the country of its domicile.

This uncertain state of affairs seems highly unsatisfactory
for several reasons. First, even if the place where the Board of
Directors discharges its functions is held to be decisive, in the
modern world this location may not be easy to determine. Many
corporations rotate their Board meetings from one country to
another. Directors are often of differing residence and nationality. With increasing frequency, Board actions are taken by written consent or in telephonic meetings. Directors waive their
participation or give proxies to other directors. Management
functions of large corporations are, moreover, often shared by
the Board and its committees, which may, of course, meet at
different places or by different means. Even if this process is

correctly stage-managed, companies are always at risk that a different finding will be made. Under the English practice, such factual findings are made by Commissioners, who are employees of the Inland Revenue and the courts have reviewed the findings of the Commissioners with the utmost deference. * * *

The conclusion which emerges is that domestic or foreign status will remain in effect elective over a broad range of cases under any rule which is likely to be adopted. Big companies with a range of choices concerning the deployment of personnel and access to good legal advice will normally be able to qualify for foreign status, even under standards more stringent than the place of incorporation test. An attempt to impose more stringent standards is likely to weigh particularly heavily on smaller enterprises or those which for one reason or another do not have the range of flexibility that most multinationals have. Under these circumstances, the case seems persuasive for continuing the approach of current law, making domestic or foreign status effectively elective under the place of incorporation test and utilizing Subpart F to tax through to U.S. shareholders their shares of the income of foreign corporations whose activities are not sufficiently enmeshed in the economies of foreign countries to justify, in the Congress' view, tax deferral.

The logic of this conclusion leads to another view so radical that it has not even been whispered for twenty years, that U.S. persons might be given the election to treat a U.S. incorporated entity as a foreign one. Experience that few purchasers are willing to pay full federal income tax as the price for access to the law of Delaware as governing law and prefer, if it comes to that, the laws of Canada, Bermuda, or other jurisdictions whose prices for nearly identical goods are more reasonable. The object of allowing such an election would be the rationalization of this recognized electivity, and nothing more. The proposal is senseless if an attempt is made to attach conditions to such an election that do not attach to owning a foreign corporation. On the other hand, all of the effects of 'foreignness', such as the application of Code sections 367 and 1248, as well as Subpart F, must flow from the election, lest unintended benefits arise.

NOTE

Multinationals. The foregoing articles make clear the difficulties inherent in attempting to interject economic substance into the concept of corporate residence. We don't call them multinationals for nothing.

3.7 CORPORATE EXPATRIATION AND INVERSIONS

Corporations, like many individuals, often search for opportunities to minimize their taxes. One avenue is through incorporation in a country with lower taxation. Inversions are largely paper transactions where a U.S. corporation first creates a foreign subsidiary that may be little more than a post office box in a foreign tax haven. Corporate ownership is then "inverted" by turning the foreign subsidiary into the parent company in an effort to avoid U.S. taxation on income earned abroad. In addition, the new parent company can supply inter-company debt to the U.S. subsidiary, thereby providing interest deductions, which will have the effect of reducing the U.S. source taxable income and taxes payable to the United States.

The following excerpt from *The New Yorker* offers some examples of inversion schemes and describes the general climate in which have they occurred.

James Surowiecki, *Tax Cheat, Inc.*, THE NEW YORKER, Apr. 22, 2002, at 62.

If you want to avoid taxes with impunity, hide millions in offshore banks, and contentedly snub the tax authorities of your home country, you need to be something more than an ordinary citizen. You need to be a corporation. You need to be, say, Ingersoll–Rand.

Ingersoll–Rand, the venerable machinery manufacturer, has been an American company since its founding, a century ago. It made the jackhammers that made Mt. Rushmore. It has major contracts with the federal government. (It's currently trying to sell the feds new airport screening machines.) Yet, when it comes to paying taxes, Ingersoll–Rand is not an American company. It's Bermudan. Last December, Ingersoll reincorporated itself in Bermuda, where there are no corporate income taxes. The company has no operations on the island—just a small office, with no employees, that's little more than a mail drop. But this is enough to save the company forty million dollars a year.

Ingersoll–Rand is not alone. Among the many U.S. firms that, since 1994, have decided to reincorporate in Bermuda are the giant conglomerate Tyco, the electrical-parts manufacturer Cooper Industries, and the hardware maker Stanley Works. They're * * * using paper transactions to shift income abroad in order to avoid taxes.

If Ingersoll actually wants to leave the United States and set up shop in Bermuda, so be it. Lovely golf courses, and all that. For that matter, if Toyota wanted to move to Michigan it would be more than welcome. But Ingersoll–Rand doesn't want to leave. Its executive offices are in Woodcliff Lake, New Jersey. Its C.E.O. and all its top officers live here in the States. It wants the benefits of U.S. citizenship; it just doesn't want to pay for them.

Someone who spends a hundred and eighty-three days a year in the United States is an American, as far as the tax man is concerned. So why should corporations, which, after all, are deemed "persons" in legal terms, enjoy the benefits of drop-box citizenship while human beings, who are also persons, sweat over their 1040s? It's not that complicated. If, say, the people who run a company live and work in northern New Jersey, let's agree that the company is American. Until Herbert Henkel, Ingersoll–Rand's C.E.O., moves his family, his desk, and his executive corps to Bermuda the firm's tax address there is just a joke.

And the joke's on us, because Ingersoll is simply doing what the law allows. So maybe there ought to be another law. Senator Charles Grassley, a solid Republican and an avid tax-cutter, introduced legislation last week that would discourage reincorporations like Ingersoll's, but the bill is sure to run into stiff opposition from House Republicans, who, cajoled by industry lobbyists, tend to equate the closing of any tax loophole with a tax hike. "We want to get at those cases where there's no legitimate business purpose behind the move, where companies have nothing more offshore than a piece of paper and a filing cabinet," Grassley says. Watch to see which way your congressman jumps.

The billions of dollars in tax revenue lost to corporate tax shelters is bad enough. But the real problem with the proliferation of shelters is that they sour the average American on one of the obligations of citizenship. "The more people think that the tax system is operating unfairly and arbitrarily, giving some special breaks, the more they'll look for a way not to pay taxes," Michael Graetz, a Yale law professor, says. The system depends on people's being what the political scientist Margaret Levi calls "contingent cooperators." Most Americans pay their taxes willingly—if grudgingly—even though in purely economic terms it's rational not to, given that the chances of getting audited are so slim. But people are willing to pay only as long as they think that everyone else is paying, too, and as long as they believe that tax dodgers will get their due. Big-name corporate tax scamps, like Ingersoll–Rand, are helping to corrode the very system that makes America work. They might as well take a jackhammer to Mt. Rushmore.

NOTE

A Mega-trend? The *New York Times* reporter David Cay Johnston reported in 2002 that incorporation in Bermuda was becoming a "mega-trend" due to the tax advantages and ease of access from the United States.[1] Companies, such as Ingersoll–Rand, continue to have their main offices in the United States, benefiting from the security provided by the U.S. government and our legal system, while avoiding U.S. taxes. In addition to avoiding U.S. tax on foreign-source income, the American company may borrow from its Bermuda parent company; this loan creates a deduction for interest paid to the parent that will reduce U.S. income taxes in circumstances where Bermuda will impose no tax on the income of the parent company. Professor Samuel Thompson, whose article is excerpted below, claims that "[t]here is a substantial incentive for virtually every U.S. corporation with significant foreign operations to consider making the move to Bermuda or another tax haven jurisdiction."[2] The potential pervasiveness of inversion transactions has become an important policy issue facing the U.S. government. The Code attempts to thwart these efforts by requiring that shareholders pay taxes on any increase in the value of their shares between the date they bought them and the date the company expatriated—whether or not they sell their shares.

In the following excerpt, Mihir Desai and James Hines look at the mechanics of inversion transactions and the incentive for companies to engage in such transactions. They take a hard look at the planned inversion in 2002 of Stanley Works, a Connecticut company.

Mihir A. Desai and James R. Hines, *Expectations and Expatriations: Tracing the Causes and Consequences of Corporate Inversions*, Working Paper No. 9057. Cambridge, Mass.: National Bureau of Economic Research, July 2002.

Expatriation mechanics. An expatriation is accomplished by removing foreign assets and foreign business activity from ownership by an American corporation, thereby effectively eliminating U.S. taxes on any income they generate. * * * Prior to inverting, dividends from foreign operations are received by the American parent company, while subsequent to the inversion, dividends from foreign operations, as well as those from American operations, are received by [for example] the Bermuda parent company. This structure is beneficial as long as any withholding taxes or other costs associated with dividend payments to Bermuda (which has no corporate income tax) are less than the costs associated with U.S. taxation of foreign income.

1. David Cay Johnston, U.S. Companies Are Using Bermuda to Slash Tax Bills, *New York Times*, Feb. 18, 2002.

2. Samuel C. Thompson, Section 367: A 'Wimp' for Inversions And a 'Bully' for Real Cross–Border Acquisitions, 94 Tax Notes 1505, 1506 (Mar. 18, 2002).

U.S. law generally requires foreign inversions to be recognition events for capital gains tax purposes, meaning that taxpayers will incur capital gains tax liabilities for any previously unrecognized gains. The nature of the capital gains taxes triggered by inversions depends on the way in which the inversion is structured; there are several possibilities, falling into two general categories * * * . In a taxable stock transfer, the new foreign parent company effectively exchanges its own shares for shares of the American company, a transaction that requires individual and other shareholders to recognize capital gains equal to the difference between fair market values of the shares and tax basis. At the conclusion of such a transfer, shareholders own stakes in the new foreign parent company, and the American operations are typically organized as a subsidiary of the new foreign parent. In an asset transaction, the new foreign parent company acquires an American firm's assets, thereby triggering taxes on capital gains at the corporate level equal to the difference between fair market value and basis. There are variants, including drop down transactions, that entail a combination of these two transactions, and associated capital gains tax liabilities at both the individual shareholder and U.S. corporate level. * * *

Incentives to expatriate. Firms that expatriate remain subject to U.S. taxation of their U.S. income, since the American subsidiary under the new corporate structure is taxed as a U.S. corporation. The tax incentives for an American firm to expatriate can therefore be organized around *(i)* the tax consequences that arise from no longer being subject to rules arising from the U.S. treatment of foreign source income, *(ii)* the tax consequences that arise from triggering capital gains at the firm level or shareholder level, and *(iii)* the tax consequences that arise from enhanced opportunities to relocate profits worldwide in a tax-advantaged way after an expatriation.

The tax benefits of expatriating that relate to the U.S. treatment of foreign source income can be construed to have two distinct components. First, repatriation taxes, and costly actions taken to avoid repatriation taxes, would be avoided upon expatriation. These savings, and the restructuring of worldwide operations such that non-U.S. operations would avoid repatriation taxes and the encumbrances associated with Subpart F, are the most widely cited reasons for expatriating. Separately, and as highlighted above, expense allocation rules, including those related to the allocation of interest expense to foreign source income, can provide incentives to expatriate. By expatriating in a way that removes foreign assets from U.S. ownership, it is possible to receive the full benefits of tax shields associated with interest expenses that might not be as valuable currently * * * .

Many * * * expatriations * * * are also characterized by a realization event whereby capital gains are recognized at the shareholder or firm level. A primary tax cost associated with such expatriations is the capital gains tax liability that would otherwise have been deferred or possibly avoided altogether. Given that most expatriations are structured as taxable stock transfers that trigger liabilities at the shareholder level, the price path of a firm's stock would determine the tax costs shareholders incur as a result of expatriating. A second potential tax cost associated with expatriating is withholding taxes on subsequent payments to the new foreign parent company, the avoidance of which requires careful choice of new corporate home.

Finally, an expatriating firm and its shareholders may perceive gains from increased flexibility with respect to the worldwide allocation of taxable profits. This increased flexibility pertains to the location of profits within foreign and domestic operations. Within their foreign operations, the foreign tax credit and the potential repatriation taxes a firm faces when bringing income home to the United States limits the returns to relocating profits from high-tax to low-tax jurisdictions. Given that this barrier is removed, and an expatriating firm therefore no longer faces a residual repatriation tax, incentives to be more aggressive in their structuring of worldwide operations would also increase, possibly resulting in increased after-tax cash flows. Similarly, an expatriating firm may become more aggressive with respect to relocating its U.S. income to the tax haven to which they are expatriating. While limits on such activity exist in U.S. tax law, the structuring of debt contracts with the new parents in tax haven countries may allow for reduced domestic tax obligations—sometimes referred to as interest stripping. Interest stripping entails financing a tax haven parent company's ownership of its American subsidiary largely with debt, thereby generating interest deductions against U.S. taxable income. The resulting interest income is untaxed (or taxed very lightly) by the tax haven, and is not taxed by the United States under Subpart F, since the interest recipient is no longer owned by the American company.

Stanley Works: An examination of an expatriation in process. A close examination of one corporate expatriation offers the opportunity for a detailed analysis of the stock market's reaction. In particular, market value changes can be mapped to projected tax savings arising from sources explored in the previous section. Recent developments surrounding the announced expatriation of Stanley Works have received widespread attention, affording the opportunity to interpret stock market reactions to favorable and unfavorable expatriation events through the lens of tax opportunities.

Background and chronology. Founded in 1843 by Frederick T. Stanley, The Stanley Works ("Stanley") has grown to nearly 15,000 employees, is part of the Standard & Poor's 500 Index, and is the leading toolmaker in the United States with sales of $2.6 billion by 2001. Its operations are divided into two groups, Tools (77 percent of sales) and Doors (23 percent of sales). The Tools Group manufactures hand tools for consumer and professional use, mechanics' tools for industrial uses, and pneumatic and hydraulic tools. Hand tools are distributed directly to retail outlets such as home centers and indirectly to end users through third party distributors. Ultimately the products are used for everything from simple around-the-home fix-it jobs to major construction projects ranging from buildings to utilities to railroads. The more sophisticated products find their way onto assembly line equipment at major vehicle makers. The Doors division manufactures a full range of door systems, from ordinary doors for use in residential homes to reinforced commercial systems such as automatic and revolving doors. Door products are sold under a variety of brand names through both direct and indirect sales channels. Much of Stanley's sales are concentrated in a few mass-market home centers—Home Depot, Sears, and Wal–Mart, for example—with Home Depot alone accounting for approximately 18 percent of 2001 revenues.

On February 8, 2002, Stanley announced its intention to expatriate, and the accompanying press release provided a general outline of its motivation. Stanley would become a Bermuda corporation, which in turn would own the former American parent company. Stanley's foreign operations remain the property of the American company, but would presumably be quickly sold to the Bermuda corporation, thereby removing them from American ownership. The Bermuda corporation would be managed and controlled in Barbados in order to benefit from reduced withholding tax rates provided in the U.S.–Barbados tax treaty. Chairman and Chief Executive John Trani cited both increased operational flexibility and improved tax efficiency as strategic motivations for implementing the restructuring. Specifically, Trani projected that Stanley's effective income tax rate would fall by 7 to 9 percentage points from its current level of 32 percent. He also clarified that the new future foreign entity would continue to be managed out of Stanley's New Britain, CT headquarters and that its then current ownership structure would not change.* * * On the date of the announcement, the market value of Stanley equity increased by $199 million. In the subsequent weeks several developments associated with the operations of Stanley caused substantial movements in the stock price, including a strategic alliance with Home Depot and changed expectations associated with earnings not related to tax obligations. Two expatriation-related events did cause additional, significant, price movements in the following weeks. The announcement of proposed legislation to limit expatriations on April 11 resulted in a price drop. Finally, on May 10 a shareholder vote on the expatriation passed very narrowly but was challenged by the Connecticut Attorney General, who suggested that "the meeting was rife with voting irregularities." On that day, the market value of Stanley dropped by $252 million.

Given the extraordinary volume and dramatic price movements on both February 8, 2002 and May 10, 2002, it is safe to assume that the value changes on those days were associated with changed assessments of future cash flows associated with tax savings stemming from the proposed expatriation. Given that the announcement of the expatriation, as well as the difficulties associated with the shareholder vote, did not involve certain or guaranteed changes in tax savings, it is also safe to assume that the market's evaluation of the aggregate present value of the impact of the expatriation is at least $250 million. The actual market assessment of the present value gains associated with expatriation could be considerably higher if these events simply resulted in revised probabilities of realizing those tax savings.

NOTE

Stanley Works Retreats. In August of 2002 due to intense pressure from lawmakers, Stanley Works called off its plans to reincorporate in Bermuda. Prior to abandoning the idea, Stanley Works had predicted that a move to Bermuda would have saved the company $30 million a year in taxes. Considering that the company paid only $7 million on its foreign income in 2001, the clear implication is that more than three-fourths of the tax savings would have come from reducing U.S. taxes on U.S. profits.

The following excerpt by Willard Taylor explores the reasons for and against corporate expatriation. Taylor points to corporations' dissatisfaction with subpart F of the Internal Revenue Code (which Congress is considering loosening, see Chapter 5) and attempts to debunk some of the concerns about corporate expatriations.

Willard Taylor, *Corporate Expatriations—Why Not?*, TAXES, March 2000, at 146, 156–57.

Why Expatriate? * * * U.S. corporations are generally dissatisfied with the U.S. rules relating to taxation of foreign income—specifically, subpart F, Code Sec. 956 and the effect of the interest allocation regulations on allowable foreign tax credits. The U.S. tax reasons for expatriation that are given in the proxy materials soliciting shareholder approval for such transactions make the same points.

In fairness to the U.S. tax rules that apply to the foreign income of U.S. corporations, however, there are other considerations:

(a) The same impulse that drives U.S. corporations to enter into questionable tax-motivated transactions—the desire to manage income tax expense—favors expatriation. If an expatriation can be effected on a tax-efficient basis, isn't this a home run for a business that has the right kind of income?

To this should be added a general disbelief on the part of many in the IRS's ability to enforce the rules which prevent foreign corporations from shifting income away from the United States—that is, the Code Sec. 311 and Code Sec. 367 rules that apply to transfers of intangible value, the arm's length pricing rules of Code Sec. 482 and the rules with respect to effectively connected income. High priced valuation and pricing studies (often mischaracterizing the issues) are part of this. This disbelief—no different from the disbelief that the IRS can deal with corporate tax shelters—is central to the expatriation phenomenon. The ability to shift income without materially adverse tax consequences was the premise of many of the * * * recent expatriation transactions.

(b) The increased economic importance of income, which, because the "source" of income and "engaged in a trade or business in the United States" rules, can avoid U.S. (and possibly all) tax if it is earned by a foreign corporation organized in a tax haven country. The effective absence of any tax on this income creates an important opportunity.

David Tillinghast has persuasively made the case that the source and effectively connected rules (relying as they do on the classification of income as sales income, rental income or royalties and on whether property is manufactured or produced) are sufficiently unclear that a foreign corporation which is engaged in the development and exploitation of software may pay relatively little U.S. tax, notwithstanding that much of the software development is undertaken in the United States and many of the users are here. The same analysis can be applied to other businesses, such as internet-selling, investment advice, international communication, cruise lines and insurance.

The presence of income which is taxed in the United States only because place of incorporation was an essential feature of * * * complete or partial expatriation transactions. But it is hardly a novel, distinguishing characteristic of these transactions—any business that operates internationally will have income that is not effectively connected with a U.S. trade or business (or is foreign source income that would not be taxed even if it was effectively connected) and therefore potentially not subject to U.S. tax. The less than comprehensive source of income rules set out in the Internal Revenue Code simply compound the problem.

(c) * * * One of the drivers in structuring a cross-border transaction is the accommodation of shareholders in many countries * * * . Depending on the source of its income, a tax haven corporation may well be better from that point of view than a U.S. corporation.

Why Not Expatriate? The obstacles to expatriation are reasonably clear. While the reincorporation can be a tax-free reorganization (or a tax-free transfer to a controlled corporation under Code Sec. 351), an exit tax will generally be imposed by the Code Sec. 367 regulations on the shareholders and/or the corporation * * * . Post-expatriation, U.S. tax will be paid on the income of any U.S. corporation in the group or on any effectively connected income of a foreign member of the group, and it is likely (since expatriation will normally be to a tax haven) that U.S. withholding (or branch profits) tax will be paid at a 30 percent non-treaty rate on repatriated earnings of the U.S. business. The prize, of course, will be the absence of U.S. tax (and possibly any tax) on non-effectively connected and/or foreign source income and the absence of U.S. withholding tax on distributions to foreign shareholders. The issue is whether the costs can be managed so they are worth the prize, and this will obviously depend on the particular facts.

In the "real" world, such as it is, the obstacles may not be insurmountable, and the prize may be substantial.

In the following excerpt, Samuel Thompson examines Section 367 of the Internal Revenue Code, which was supposed to address the problem raised by these inversion transactions. He argues that it is simultaneously inadequate to address inversion transactions and unduly inhibits cross-border transactions. Thompson also analyzes one proposed remedy: a bill labeled Reversing the Expatriation of Profits Offshore (REPO).

Samuel C. Thompson, *Analysis of the Non–Wimpy Grassley/Baucus Inversion Bill*, 26 TAX NOTES INT'L 741, 741–46 (May 13, 2002).

Identification of the Problem. The U.S. Congress is concerned with the growing number of inversion transactions in which American companies, including Stanley Works, Tyco, and Coopers Industries, are relocating to Bermuda or other tax haven jurisdictions to lower their corporate taxes by avoiding the controlled foreign corporation (CFC) provisions of the U.S. Internal Revenue Code. * * *

To bring an end to these and related transactions, on 11 April 2002, Senator Charles E. Grassley, R–Iowa, the ranking minority member of the Senate Finance Committee, and Senator Max Baucus, D-Montana, the chairman of the committee, introduced the Reversing the Expatriation of Profits Offshore (REPO) bill (S. 2119). * * *

Inversion and similar transactions are, for the reasons I will outline below, indefensible on tax policy grounds, and the Grassley–Baucus REPO bill provides what appears to be an effective approach for addressing these problems. Congress should quickly enact the REPO bill or some other approach to bring an end to these abusive transactions.

To illustrate the inversion problem and the effect of the REPO bill, this article first examines a prototypical inversion transaction and then applies the concepts in the REPO bill to this transaction and to various modifications thereof. The currently proposed inversion transaction of Coopers Industries Inc. provides a good prototypical inversion.

Illustration of the Problem: Coopers Industries Transaction. Coopers Industries is a corporation listed on the New York Stock Exchange that is incorporated in Ohio with its head office in Houston. Through the use of a reverse subsidiary merger that would otherwise qualify as a tax-free reorganization under section 368(a)(2)(E) of the code, Coopers Ohio will become a subsidiary of a newly formed publicly held Bermuda holding company (Coopers Bermuda). In this transaction, the public shareholders of Coopers Ohio will become public shareholders of Coopers Bermuda, holding the class A stock of Coopers Bermuda. The Coopers Ohio shareholders will have the same proportionate interests in Coopers Bermuda that they now have in Coopers Ohio. The operating headquarters of Coopers Ohio will continue to be located in Houston, and the shares of Coopers Bermuda will be listed on the New York Stock Exchange.

Similar transactions can occur on the formation of a tax haven holding company in an initial public offering of a U.S. corporation. This method was followed in the organization in 1999 of Accenture Ltd., the former consulting arm of Arthur Andersen, as a Bermuda holding company.

Reason for Benefits From Pure Inversion Transactions. The benefits from the pure inversion and related transactions arise principally from the avoidance of the CFC provisions. The avoidance is achieved when the U.S. corporation that is ac- quired in the inversion transaction (Coopers Ohio) transfers the stock of its foreign subsidiaries to the foreign acquirer (Coopers Bermuda). Coopers Ohio will receive class B stock of Coopers Bermuda in exchange for the stock of its foreign subsidiaries. Although these foreign subsidiaries are CFCs in the hands of Coopers Ohio, in the hands of Coopers Bermuda, which as a public corporation is not a CFC, these subsidiaries are not CFCs. Consequently, the passive income and other subpart F income of these foreign subsidiaries will no longer be subject to [U.S. taxation] under the CFC rules. Thus, even though Coopers Ohio will continue to be subject to taxation in the United States on its U.S. operations, it will have avoided future taxation under the CFC provisions with respect to its former foreign subsidiar- ies. [These provisions are taken up in Chapter 5–ed.]

On the transfer of the stock of the foreign subsidiaries, Coopers Ohio will be able to offset the gain with foreign tax credits allowed under sections 1248 and 902, and this will reduce the tax cost of the transfers.

Benefits Also From Stripping Income Through Interest Pay- ments. In addition to avoiding the subpart F inclusion rules under the CFC provisions, inversions can be used to strip or divert U.S. taxable income from the inverted U.S. corporation to a related foreign corporation. This can be accomplished by having the inverted corporation (Coopers Ohio) pay interest on its debt that is held by a related corporation that is not subject to U.S. withholding tax on the interest (a Luxembourg sub of Coopers Bermuda). With this interest stripping, income tax on U.S. earnings is avoided by merely shifting income from the U.S. corporate pocket to a related foreign corporate pocket.

Parking of Passive Income. Further, the earnings of the non-CFCs could be invested in assets producing passive income, and there will be no [U.S. taxation] of the passive income as long as such investments do not cause the foreign holding company (Coopers Bermuda) to become a passive foreign investment company. Thus, the inversion transaction offers a way of parking passive income offshore without any current taxation.

Aggressive Transfer Pricing. In addition, these non-CFCs could engage in aggressive transactions with the U.S. corporation that would otherwise create foreign base company sales income under the subpart F rules, thereby putting additional pressure on the already overloaded transfer pricing rules under the code.

Expected Tax Savings in the Coopers Transaction. Coopers has estimated that after the reorganization, its worldwide effective tax rate will be reduced from approximately 32 percent to approximately 20 percent to 25 percent, which translates into an annual tax savings of approximately US $55 million.

Section 367 Is a Wimp in Dealing With Inversion Transactions. The purpose of section 367 is to protect the integrity of the U.S. system of worldwide taxation by deterring these inversion and other similar transactions. Under the regulations under section 367, because the U.S. shareholders end up with over 50 percent of the stock of the foreign acquirer in these inversion transactions, the U.S. shareholders are subject to tax on their gains realized on the exchange. Thus, even though the transaction would otherwise qualify for tax-free treatment for the shareholders under section 354 because the transaction qualifies as a reorganization, under the section 367 regulations, the shareholders are subject to tax on their gains. As demonstrated by the recent stream of inversion transactions, this tax under section 367 is not a sufficient deterrent to the effectuation of such transactions. Thus, as I have argued, section 367 is a "wimp" in dealing with pure inversion transactions. * * *

The 'Non–Wimpy' Grassley–Baucus REPO Bill. Introduction. The REPO bill, which would add section 7874 to the code, deals with pure inversions and limited inversions. In pure inversion transactions, the foreign acquirer is treated as a domestic corporation, thereby eliminating the avoidance of the CFC rules. In a limited inversion, the foreign acquirer is not treated as a domestic corporation, but certain transactions between the U.S. corporation and the foreign acquirer or other foreign members of the group are subject to: (1) a special penalty tax on "inversion gains," and (2) a special IRS approval process for interest stripping and other similar transactions. * * *

Pure Inversions Under the REPO Bill. In General. The REPO bill treats certain foreign acquiring corporations (Foreign Incorporated Entities) as "Inverted Domestic Corporations," which are treated for all purposes of the code as domestic corporations. (Section 7874(a)) Under section 7874(a)(2), if "pursuant to a plan (or series of related transactions)" the following three conditions are satisfied, a Foreign Incorporated Entity is treated as an Inverted Domestic Corporation:

First, the Foreign Incorporated Entity must acquire directly or indirectly substantially all the properties held directly or indirectly by a U.S. corporation (or substantially all the properties constituting a trade or business of a U.S. partnership; the focus here is on corporations). (Section 7874(a)(2)(A)) * * *

Second, the shareholders of the U.S. target (or partners of a U.S. partnership) must end up owning at least 80 percent of the stock (measured by vote or value) of the Foreign Incorporated Entity. (Section 7874(a)(2)(B))

Third, the "expanded affiliated group" of the Foreign Incorporated Entity (using a more than 50 percent test for affiliation and including foreign corporations, section 7874(e)(2)) does not have "substantial business activities" in the country of incorporation of the Foreign Incorporated Entity, "when compared to the total business activities of such expanded affiliated group" (the Substantial Business Activities Test). (Section 7874(a)(2)(C))

Although an Inverted Domestic Corporation is on paper a foreign corporation, it is treated as a domestic corporation for purposes of the code, thereby eliminating the benefits of the inversion transaction that would otherwise come from the avoidance of the CFC rules. (Section 7874(a)(1))

* * *

Comments on the REPO Bill. The REPO bill seems to address the basic concern with standard inversion transactions like the Coopers Industries transaction.

NOTE

Where Is the REPO Bill Now? On May 16, 2003 legislation passed the Senate which would inhibit corporate inversions. As described by Sam Thompson, the "Jobs and Growth Tax Relief Reconciliation Act of 2003" adds a new section 7874 to the Code. This provision for corporate inversions considers two structures: those in which the former shareholders of the U.S. company hold eighty percent or more of the stock in the foreign-incorporated entity after the transaction, and those in which between fifty and eighty percent of the stock in the foreign-incorporated company is held by the former shareholders of the U.S. entity. The new provisions deny the intended tax benefit of this type of inversion to the first structure (with some exceptions) by deeming the top-tier foreign corporation to be a domestic corporation for U.S. tax purposes. The second structure receives heightened scrutiny resulting in a limitation of tax benefits. As promised by Senators Grassley and Baucus, the new legislation applies to any inversion transactions completed after March 20, 2002. In addition, the legislation imposes a 20 percent excise tax on stock options and other stock-based compensation of executives whose companies engage in inversion transactions. These provisions were dropped from the 2003 legislation in conference, but seem likely to reappear in subsequent legislation.

3.8 ELECTRONIC COMMERCE

The rise of electronic commerce has put new pressure on both source and residence-based taxation of corporate income, raising the question where, or whether, income from such transactions will be taxed. The essential problem is that e-commerce "does not rely upon the traditional concepts of geographical boundaries or physical location for source, residency and permanent establishment determinations."[3]

A brief glance at typical e-commerce activities reveals the difficulty of applying longstanding international tax concepts to Internet businesses. The main problem lies in the general configuration of the Internet; a virtual store can be present everywhere: "There is no central, worldwide, technical control point, and it is difficult to assign a physical location for taxation purposes to the component parts of electronic transactions or the digital bits associated therewith, and thus, by extension to the companies doing business via the Internet."[4] The way information—and sometimes products—pass through cyberspace is a further complication: "Users of the Internet have no control over, and usually no specific knowledge of, the path that is traveled by the information they seek or publish."[5] Businesses operating on the Internet, therefore, cannot know whether or when they will fall within any country's jurisdiction for taxation purposes, thus leaving them open to international double taxation and creating the possibility of no taxation.[6] "[C]ompanies selling information over the Internet can call any place home, and the savvy ones are choosing jurisdictions with low or no taxes, financial privacy, governmental stability, and decent communications systems."[7] As e-commerce evolves, it will be necessary to decide whether "a server, internet service provider, user, web page, cables, terminal, or

---

3. Adrian J. Sawyer, Electronic Commerce: International Policy Implications for Revenue Authorities and Governments, 19 Va. Tax Rev. 73, 87 (1999).

4. Kyrie E. Thorpe, International Taxation of Electronic Commerce: Is the Internet Age Rendering the Concept of Permanent Establishment Obsolete? 11 Emory Int'l L. Rev. 633, 637 (1997).

5. Id.

6. Id.

7. M. Murphy, Cooling the Net Hype, *Wired*, Sept. 1996, at 86.

any other related item satisfies the requirements for residence or permanent establishment."[8]

In 1996 the United States Treasury Department released a report—a "White Paper"—on the income tax implications of e-commerce, which immediately became the foundation for much of the discussion that followed. Though now a bit dated, the following excerpt from this report delineates its most important contentions. The subsequent excerpts by Arthur J. Cockfield and Reuven S. Avi–Yonah address the difficulties in determining the source of income in e-commerce, but question the Treasury Department's judgment that e-commerce will breathe new life into the residence principle for corporations. (See Chapter 6 for discussion of the problem of e-commerce in relation to the treaty concept of permanent establishment. The concept of permanent establishment does not translate easily to today's Internet-based businesses.)

U.S. Treasury Department Office of Tax Policy, *Selected Tax Policy Implications of Global Electronic Commerce* AT 27–36 (NOVEMBER 1996).

The growth of new communications technologies and electronic commerce will likely require that principles of residence-based taxation assume even greater importance. In the world of cyberspace, it is often difficult, if not impossible, to apply traditional source concepts to link an item of income with a specific geographical location. Therefore, source based taxation could lose its rationale and be rendered obsolete by electronic commerce. By contrast, almost all taxpayers are resident somewhere. An individual is almost always a citizen or resident of a given country and, at least under U.S. law, all corporations must be established under the laws of a given jurisdiction. However, a review of current residency definitions and taxation rules may be appropriate.

In situations where traditional source concepts have already been rendered too difficult to apply effectively, the residence of the taxpayer has been the most likely means to identify the jurisdiction where the economic activities that created the income took place, and thus the jurisdiction that should have the primary right to tax such income. * * * In the case of certain sales of personal property, the residence of the seller was thought to best represent the location where the underlying economic activity occurred. Similar rules were adopted for certain space and ocean activities. Therefore, United States tax policy has already recognized that as traditional source principles lose their significance, residence-based taxation can step in and take their place. This trend will be accelerated by develop-

8. Thorpe, supra note 4 at 637.

ments in electronic commerce where principles of residence-based taxation will also play a major role.

Taxation of non-resident aliens and foreign corporations. Non-resident aliens and foreign corporations are generally only subject to tax on their U.S. source income, including income derived from the performance of personal services in the United States, and certain foreign source income that is attributable to a U.S. trade or business. Unless a treaty applies, non-resident aliens and foreign corporations are taxed at ordinary graduated rates on their net income effectively connected with a trade or business in the United States, and are taxed at a flat rate on the gross amount of their U.S. source "fixed or determinable annual or periodical gains, profits and income." A U.S. trade or business includes the performance of personal services within the United States. Therefore being engaged in a trade or business *in the United States* is a threshold requirement for the taxation of active business income earned by foreign persons.

"In the United States." In many cases, it is clear that a foreign person is engaged in a trade or business but it is not clear whether they are so engaged "in the United States." However, a foreign person not physically present in the United States who merely solicits orders from within the United States only through advertising and then sends tangible goods to the United States in satisfaction of the orders is unlikely to be engaged in a trade or business in the United States even though such a person is clearly engaged in a trade or business. A person who is not directly engaged in a U.S. trade or business may nevertheless be deemed to be engaged in a U.S. trade or business as the result of the activities of an agent.

Impact of tax treaties: Permanent establishment concept. Tax treaties adopt a different and generally higher threshold for source basis taxation of active income. U.S. source active income ("business profits") of non-resident aliens and foreign corporations who are entitled to benefits under a U.S. income tax treaty is only subject to U.S. tax if the income is attributable to a permanent establishment located in the United States. A permanent establishment is a fixed place of business through which the business of an enterprise is wholly or partly carried on. "[I]t has come to be accepted in international fiscal matters that until an enterprise of one State sets up a permanent establishment in another State it should not properly be regarded as participating in the economic life of that other State to such an extent that it comes within the jurisdiction of that other State's taxing rights." Therefore, a foreign person who is entitled to benefits under a tax treaty with the United States will not be subject to U.S. tax on the income arising from a trade or business in the United States if the income is not attributable to a permanent establishment in the United States.

U.S. tax jurisdiction in the context of electronic commerce. U.S. trade or business. The concept of a U.S. trade or business was developed in the context of conventional types of commerce, which generally are conducted through identifiable physical locations. Electronic commerce, on the other hand, may be conducted without regard to national boundaries and may dissolve the link between an income-producing activity and a specific location. From a certain perspective, electronic commerce doesn't seem to occur in any physical location but instead takes place in the nebulous world of "cyberspace." Persons engaged in electronic commerce could be located anywhere in the world and their customers will be ignorant of, or indifferent to, their location. Indeed, this is an important advantage of electronic commerce in that it gives small businesses the potential to reach customers all over the world.

Electronic commerce permits a foreign person to engage in extensive transactions with U.S. customers without entering the United States. Although such a person is clearly engaged in a trade or business, questions will arise as to whether he is engaged in a trade or business in the United States or has a permanent establishment in the United States. Therefore, it is necessary to clarify the application of the U.S. trade or business and permanent establishment concepts to persons engaged in electronic commerce. In developing principles to classify these activities, it will be important to consider the extent to which electronic commerce simply represents an extension of current means of doing business, the tax consequences of which are understood. For example, to the extent that the activities of a person engaged in electronic commerce are equivalent to the mere solicitation of orders from U.S. customers, without any other U.S. activity, it may not be appropriate to treat such activities as a U.S. trade or business. It will also be necessary to consider whether it is appropriate or practical to treat foreign persons engaged in electronic commerce with U.S. customers as being engaged in a U.S. trade or business if they are physically located outside the United States.

Another example is the treatment of foreign persons who maintain or utilize a computer server in the United States. Computer servers can be located anywhere in the world and their users are indifferent to their location. It is possible that such a server, or similar equipment, is not a sufficiently significant element in the creation of certain types of income to be taken into account for purposes of determining whether a U.S. trade or business exists. It is also possible that if the existence of a U.S.-based server is taken into account for this purpose, foreign persons will simply utilize servers located outside the United States since the server's location is irrelevant.

Finally, consideration may also be given to the role other activities should play in determining whether a U.S. trade or business exists. For example, it may ultimately be decided that a foreign person who operates a computerized research service through computers located outside of the United States might not be engaged in a U.S. trade or business unless other U.S. situs activities exist. However, U.S.-based individuals engaged in providing marketing and support services for a foreign-based provider of computerized research may create a U.S. trade or business for the foreign person even if the computer servers and other activities are located outside the United States.

Arthur J. Cockfield, *Balancing National Interests in the Taxation of Electronic Commerce Business Profits*, 74 TUL. L. REV. 133, 169–72, 216 (1999).

The emergence of new communications technologies, the rise of e-commerce, the globalization of business, and the movement in many countries toward service and information-oriented industries have created a number of challenges to the international income tax regime. With respect to e-commerce, perhaps the greatest challenge to this regime is the inability to identify the source of many direct e-commerce transactions where the good or service may never assume a tangible form. The current method of allocating source-state taxing authority over income arising from permanent establishments seems particularly fruitless when applied to this new form of commerce. Nevertheless, states, international organizations, and many commentators have generally asserted a preference for maintaining traditional international tax rules and practices to meet these challenges.

* * *

The Treasury Department indicates [that] the growth of new communications technologies and electronic commerce will likely require that principles of residence-based taxation assume even greater importance. In the world of cyberspace, it is often difficult, if not impossible, to apply traditional source concepts to link an item of income with a specific geographical location. Therefore, source based taxation could lose its rationale and be rendered obsolete by electronic commerce. By contrast, almost all taxpayers are resident somewhere.

As a result, the Treasury Department suggests that residence-based taxation of e-commerce may be the appropriate solution.

Other commentators have also favored moving toward a purely residence-based system of taxing business profits derived from e-commerce. * * * Proponents of a purely residence-based system are often concerned that e-commerce will escape taxation altogether unless the resident is taxed.

And yet a residence-based system raises a number of difficult issues. For example, it is often difficult to identify where the taxpayer is a resident. This problem will only be exacerbated by the new technologies that make e-commerce possible.

* * *

[The place of central management and control] test normally involves looking to the location of a company's head office or the board of directors' regular meetings. The Australian Taxation Office suggests that the development of new technologies presents a number of challenges to this test because it is often difficult to establish the place of management and control. Commentators have also noted that the development of video-conferencing, which allows directors or upper-level corporate officers to maintain residences in different jurisdictions, poses a challenge to the place of central management and control test.

* * *

If a purely residence-based system were implemented, companies would be given an incentive to relocate their e-commerce base of operations to low or nil tax jurisdictions like tax havens. In general, profits from these e-commerce transactions would not be taxed by the residence country until they were distributed back to the parent company. Taxes would thus be deferred or possibly avoided altogether. The Treasury Department recognizes this issue and indicates:

> If [controlled foreign corporations] can engage in extensive commerce in information and services through Web sites or computer networks located in a tax haven, it may become increasingly difficult to enforce [rules governing the taxation of their profits]. Some persons engaged in electronic commerce may already be locating their businesses offshore. * * * [T]his presents enforcement problems because it may be difficult to verify the identity of the taxpayer to whom foreign base company sales income accrues and the amount of such income.

However, a revision of tax rules to ensure that undistributed earnings are taxed by the residence country will not do anything to prevent start-up e-commerce companies from locating their operations within tax havens in order to avoid paying taxes. A company that is initially a resident within one of these countries may never pay any tax on its e-commerce profits under a purely residence-based approach. There are already indications that e-commerce businesses are responding to this tax incentive. For example, most e-commerce pornography operations are situated within Guyana. And most of the world's on-line gambling takes place on sites located within Grenada, home of Sports International.

Movement toward a residence-based system would invariably favor countries that are net exporters of e-commerce goods and services. The greatest beneficiary of this system would likely be the United States since it currently leads the world in the production and export of these goods and services. This leads to perhaps the most serious drawback of the proposal: a residence-based system would dramatically affect the current allocation of tax revenues. * * *

* * * [T]he guiding principles in the taxation of e-commerce include the need for international cooperation in resolving the challenges presented by this new form of commerce. It is unlikely that many, if not most, countries in the world would support a move toward pure residence-based taxation since their future tax revenue streams would be adversely affected. Proposals to move toward a purely residence-based system of taxation would thus not likely attract the requisite international consensus and may not resolve a number of additional challenges confronting the taxation of e-commerce business profits.

Reuven S. Avi–Yonah, *International Taxation of Electronic Commerce*, 52 TAX L. REV. 507, 525–26 (1997).

[Taxing active business] income * * * primarily or exclusively on a residence basis is inconsistent with the generally accepted international consensus, as embodied in tax treaties and in the U.S. international tax regime. * * * [T]hat consensus is based on the Benefits Principle, which reflects a compromise reached in the 1920's on dividing the tax base between residence and source jurisdictions, allocating the right to tax active income primarily to the source jurisdiction.

As noted by O'Hear and Professor Graetz, the "original intent" underlying U.S. international tax policy was based on a preference for source-based taxation of active income. Moreover, it is hard to detect a trend toward more residence-based taxation in recent U.S. tax policy, despite the suggestion to the contrary in the [Treasury's 1996] White Paper. As far as the U.S.'s own claims to source-based taxation of active income, the U.S. trade or business threshold has always been quite low, and there is no indication that it or the permanent establishment threshold has been raised recently. To the contrary, as the United States enters into more tax treaties with developing countries, the latter threshold tends to be lower.

     * * * [T]he international consensus reflects the Benefits Principle, which has a policy rationale behind it. Most active business income from international transactions is earned by multinational corporations, and it is not at all clear what residence means in the case of a multinational, especially now that the shareholder base, sources of capital, and location of business activities of multinationals may all be dispersed over many taxing jurisdictions. Even the White Paper admits that "a review of current residency definitions and taxation rules may be appropriate" in light of electronic commerce.

3.9 TREATY SHOPPING

Treaty shopping refers to attempts by individuals to obtain benefits from bilateral treaties even though they are not residents of either country that is a party to the treaty. The nonresident who wants to obtain benefits otherwise not available typically begins by creating a corporation in one of the treaty countries. The basic idea is to reroute income through a treaty country to take advantage of tax reductions provided by the treaty. Commentators disagree as to whether or not treaty shopping is a problem worthy of the attention it has gained. Some would excuse it as a legitimate and legal practice of minimizing taxes; others view it as undermining the very purpose of the treaty being exploited.

In March 2003 the United States Senate ratified updated bilateral tax agreements between the United States and the United Kingdom, and protocols with Australia and Mexico. These treaties, among other things, encourage investment by exempting from withholding taxation by the source country most dividends received by a parent company from an overseas subsidiary. As with all prior treaties signed by the United States in the past two decades, the treaty attempts to limit "treaty shopping" by residents of third countries who may establish entities in a treaty country, for example, to take advantage of the zero withholding rates on dividends provided by the treaty.

Article 22, the Limitation on Benefits (treaty shopping) provision of the United States Model Treaty, is set forth below.[9]

---

9. United States Model Income Tax Convention, September 20, 1996 available at http://www.ustreas.gov/offices/tax-policy/library/model996.pdf.

Article 22, U.S. Model Treaty

1. A resident of a Contracting State shall be entitled to benefits otherwise accorded to residents of a Contracting State by this Convention only to the extent provided in this Article.

2. A resident of a Contracting State shall be entitled to all the benefits of this Convention if the resident is:

   a) an individual;

   b) a qualified governmental entity;

   c) a company, if

       i. all the shares in the class or classes of shares representing more than 50 percent of the voting power and value of the company are regularly traded on a recognized stock exchange, or

       ii. at least 50 percent of each class of shares in the company is owned directly or indirectly by companies entitled to benefits under clause i), provided that in the case of indirect ownership, each intermediate owner is a person entitled to benefits of the Convention under this paragraph;

   d) described in subparagraph 1(b)(i) of Article 4 (Residence);

   e) described in subparagraph 1(b)(ii) of Article 4 (Residence), provided that more than 50 percent of the person's beneficiaries, members or participants are individuals resident in either Contracting State; or

   f) a person other than an individual, if:

       i. On at least half the days of the taxable year persons described in subparagraphs a), b), c), d) or e) own, directly or indirectly (through a chain of ownership in which each person is entitled to benefits of the Convention under this paragraph), at least 50 percent of each class of shares or other beneficial interests in the person, and

       ii. less than 50 percent of the person's gross income for the taxable year is paid or accrued, directly or indirectly, to persons who are not residents of either Contracting State (unless the payment is attributable to a permanent establishment situated in either State), in the form of payments that are deductible for income tax purposes in the person's State of residence.

3.

   a) A resident of a Contracting State not otherwise entitled to benefits shall be entitled to the benefits of this Convention with respect to an item of income derived from the other State, if:

    i.   the resident is engaged in the active conduct of a trade or business in the first-mentioned State,

    ii.   the income is connected with or incidental to the trade or business, and

    iii.   the trade or business is substantial in relation to the activity in the other State generating the income.

b) For purposes of this paragraph, the business of making or managing investments will not be considered an active trade or business unless the activity is banking, insurance or securities activity conducted by a bank, insurance company or registered securities dealer.

c) Whether a trade or business is substantial for purposes of this paragraph will be determined based on all the facts and circumstances. In any case, however, a trade or business will be deemed substantial if, for the preceding taxable year, or for the average of the three preceding taxable years, the asset value, the gross income, and the payroll expense that are related to the trade or business in the first-mentioned State equal at least 7.5 percent of the resident's (and any related parties') proportionate share of the asset value, gross income and payroll expense, respectively, that are related to the activity that generated the income in the other State, and the average of the three ratios exceeds 10 percent.

d) Income is derived in connection with a trade or business if the activity in the other State generating the income is a line of business that forms a part of or is complementary to the trade or business. Income is incidental to a trade or business if it facilitates the conduct of the trade or business in the other State.

4.   A resident of a Contracting State not otherwise entitled to benefits may be granted benefits of the Convention if the competent authority of the State from which benefits are claimed so determines.

NOTE

Aiken Industries. The absence of an explicit anti-treaty shopping clause, such as the one above, does not mean that the practice is permitted. Domestic law may be used to preclude abuse even when treaty shopping is not explicitly curbed in the treaty. The seminal case on this point is *Aiken Industries Inc. v. Commissioner,* 56 T.C. 925 (1971). *Aiken Industries* involved three related companies in Ecuador, Honduras, and the

United States. The company in Ecuador loaned money to the Honduran company which in turn loaned the same amount to a U.S. company. The issue was whether the interest payments that the U.S. company paid to the Honduran company were subject to U.S. taxation and withholding even though interest payments between U.S. and Honduran parties were exempt under the bilateral treaty then in effect between the two countries. No treaty existed between the United States and Ecuador. The Tax Court held that the interest income in question was in substance received by the Ecuadoran, not the Honduran company, denying the treaty benefit based on a substance-over-form interpretation of the treaty language. The interest income was subject to withholding tax under the U.S. code.

In the two excerpts that follow, Simone M. Haug details the reasons why treaty countries consider it necessary to protect themselves against treaty shopping and Richard L. Reinhold offers a detailed critique of treaty shopping. Consider whether the Limitation on Benefits provisions of the U.S. Model Treaty provision would preclude transactions such as those discussed in these excerpts.

Simone M. Haug, *The United States Policy of Stringent Anti–Treaty–Shopping Provisions: A Comparative Analysis,* 29 VAND. J. TRANSNAT'L L. 191, 195–220 (1996).

Over the last fifteen years, treaty shopping has become a highly sensitive problem in the context of tax avoidance and evasion. Intergovernmental organizations like the Organization for Economic Cooperation and Development (OECD) and the United Nations (U.N.) developed official commentaries on the topic. In addition, the United States inserted anti-treaty-shopping clauses into its model treaty and domestic law. The practical solution to treaty shopping is the subject of many controversies among OECD member states, tax practitioners, and commentators.

* * *

The United States is a leader in setting policies to prevent treaty shopping, not only in substantive treaty provisions, but also in domestic law. * * * Since 1981, a limitation-on-benefits article has been inserted into every newly negotiated or renegotiated U.S. tax treaty. These measures, however, were not deemed sufficient to combat treaty shopping, especially in connection with the changes to U.S. domestic law made by the 1986 Tax Reform Act. The United States enacted, as part of its domestic law, a safeguard against the possibility of obtaining treaty relief from the newly introduced branch profits tax by anyone other than a "qualified resident" of a treaty partner.

This elaborate domestic anti-treaty-shopping law, however, was surpassed in its sophistication by the anti-abuse provisions in the recent treaties the United States has made with Germany, Mexico, and, in particular, the Netherlands. This high level of sophistication has led some experts to complain about the complexity of the limitation-on-benefits articles contained in those tax treaties and those expected to be included in a new version of the U.S. Model Income Tax Treaty.

The elaborate limitation-on-benefits provisions in U.S. treaties and domestic law have caused officials in other countries, as well as practitioners in the United States, to characterize U.S. officials as paranoid concerning the issue of treaty shopping. For example, former International Tax Counsel, David Rosenbloom, coined the expression that "anything worth doing is worth overdoing" when describing the U.S. attitude toward treaty shopping.

* * *

Treaty shopping is often referred to as "treaty abuse" or "tax avoidance," however, it has long been regarded as a legitimate instrument of international tax planning. There is a general understanding that taxpayers are free to structure their economic actions in ways they deem most beneficial so long as they do not go beyond a tolerable point. At what point legitimate tax planning ends and tax avoidance or abuse begins, however, is often a matter of interpretation.

In the international context, a taxpayer will always seek to diminish worldwide tax liability. While this is also true for business activities conducted in a single jurisdiction, there seems to be a much higher level of awareness of the tax consequences in international transactions. There are two underlying reasons for this phenomenon. First, a taxpayer considering an investment abroad must find out whether he or she will be subject to double taxation resulting from an overlap of concurring residence and source taxation. For reasons of competitiveness, a taxpayer may be obliged to find means of avoiding double taxation. For example, the taxpayer might take advantage of the source tax relief granted by a tax treaty. Second, differences in the taxation of a certain type of income at diverging tax rates in the international community provide many more possibilities to reduce the overall tax burden than when a business is conducted in a single jurisdiction. The international investor may be able to minimize tax liability by basing the business in a low-tax jurisdiction by routing the investment through other jurisdictions, or by modifying the form of the investment.

* * *

The opportunity for taxpayers to take advantage of source tax relief granted by the existence of a treaty arises from the dissimilarities among domestic international tax systems. These dissimilarities are exacerbated when states seek to gain an advantage by creating a favorable tax environment in order to attract foreign capital.

While the location of direct investment is partly restricted by such factors as work-force quality, production costs, and infrastructure, growing internationalization is creating greater mobility of persons and products. The growing mobility of capital coupled with the flexibility to choose a multinational's organizational structure may lead to an increasing influence of tax differentials in the determination of investment location. As the economic integration of the world economy proceeds and the non-tax barriers to cross-border investment vanish with growing internationalization, investment decisions are increasingly influenced by tax considerations.

* * *

Definition. Treaty shopping occurs when a taxpayer, residing in a third country, takes advantage of the benefits of a treaty that would not normally be available to the taxpayer. The treaty shopper does so by creating a corporation in a country that has a favorable tax treaty with the target country. In other words, treaty shopping is the practice of rerouting income through one or more artificial entities in different countries for the main or sole purpose of obtaining treaty benefits that are not directly available to the true earner of income. From the United States and OECD points of view, treaty shopping occurs when a third country resident takes advantage of a bilateral treaty that is intended to benefit only residents of the contracting states. In other countries, however, the term may be used more broadly, not necessarily involving a triangular arrangement.

The Basic Situations. The Commentaries on the 1995 OECD Model Convention mention two principal means by which treaty benefits may be obtained: (1) the direct conduit method and (2) the stepping stone structure. The direct conduit method is a way of shifting income through an interposed corporation in a country that has an advantageous tax treaty. For example, assume countries A and B have entered into a tax treaty that entitles their residents, including companies organized under their laws, to benefits with regard to income derived from the other country. Country C has no or a less favorable treaty with country A, but does have a favorable treaty with country B. When a resident of country C forms a corporation in country B, this conduit company, being a resident of country B, is entitled to benefits under the bilateral A–B treaty. In addition, the income of the conduit company enjoys a special tax exemption under the domestic laws of country B (e.g., a branch exemption in a parent-subsidiary relationship). The conduit company is thereby able to distribute its profits to the resident of country C under beneficial circumstances.

The stepping-stone structure is similar to the direct conduit method. The difference is that the corporation in country B, a high tax country, is fully subject to tax and thus must pay tax on its interest, dividend, and royalty income. Since expenses are deductible in country B, however, the corporation avoids having substantial net income by paying out large amounts of interest, commissions, service fees, and similar expenses to a related company in a low-tax jurisdiction (e.g., country C). The income from country A is thereby channeled from country A to country C at almost no tax cost due to the tax treaty between the high-tax countries, A and B, and the base reduction practiced by the conduit company in country B.

The essential difference between the direct conduit method and the stepping stone is that the direct conduit makes use of an exemption from tax in the intermediary country, while the stepping stone reduces the tax liability in the intermediary country by means of a counterbalancing expense. Stepping stone companies profit from three important elements: (1) the stepping stone company can deduct all of its expenses against its receipts; (2) the stepping stone country does not impose a significant withholding tax on the outbound payments; and (3) the stepping stone company's receipts must be received free of host-country withholding tax (or subject to significantly reduced withholding tax) by virtue of an existing tax treaty.

As these examples illustrate, there are a great variety of arrangements that can yield tax treaty benefits. There is the potential to channel funds tax-free or tax-reduced through several intermediary countries by using different forms of interposed entities (e.g., partnerships, trusts, etc.). The income involved may change its character several times during the transfer (e.g., from dividend to interest income, or vice versa).

The described treaty shopping structures have three common characteristics. First, the beneficial owner or owners of the treaty shopping entity are not residents of the country where the entity is created. Second, little, if any, real economic contact with or presence in the jurisdiction of the interposed entity exists. Finally, either the legal entities or the income involved is subject to little or no tax in the treaty jurisdiction of their residence.

The Problems of Treaty Shopping. * * * It can be argued that it is not treaty shopping, but rather the dissimilarity of tax systems, the overlapping tax jurisdictions leading to double taxation, and intergovernmental tax competition that are primarily responsible for the distortion of the economic flows. Thus, the investor, in order to preserve competitiveness, must find ways to deal with the discontinuities among national tax regimes, and does so by using tax treaties to reduce source country tax. Since the main objective of tax treaties is to provide free flows of international trade and investment, some commentators argue that it does not matter whether the desirable result is achieved by the direct or indirect use of tax treaties. While this view may seem reasonable to investors, it does not take into account the interests of the source country.

Revenue Loss. Treaty shopping results in tremendous revenue losses for the source country. * * * The fact that, in 1981, sixty-eight percent of U.S. source income flowed to only five U.S. treaty countries, three of which were considered tax havens, indicates that many third-country investors took advantage of an existing treaty network for their investments in the United States. The assumed revenue loss is a significant amount that a state cannot afford to ignore. Furthermore, if no efficient safeguards for the same country were inserted into the respective treaties, the revenue loss would increase with the growing trade and investment volume, leaving a far larger tax deficiency for the United States.

The Impediment of the Principle of Reciprocity. The underlying principle of all bilateral tax treaties, the principle of reciprocity, is impeded when a third-country resident derives benefits from a treaty intended to serve only the interests of residents of the contracting states. This deficiency in reciprocity results when a third-country resident derives benefits through the interposition of a treaty-protected entity, while the source country's residents are not necessarily able to obtain similar benefits from the third country. This may have an adverse effect on both the source country's government and its resident investors.

In general, both parties to a tax treaty make concessions on their source based tax. The source country fully or partially relinquishes its right to tax domestic source income earned by residents of the other party and reciprocally obtains the same concessions for its own residents. * * *

One state's renunciation of the right to tax a certain type of income in a tax treaty is usually based on the right to tax such income by the other party to the treaty. Thus, the purpose of the treaty is to alleviate double taxation when a beneficiary of one contracting state derives income from sources within the other state. In circumstances where unintended beneficiaries are free to choose the location of the intermediary entity, however, treaties designed to eliminate double taxation are frequently being utilized to eliminate taxation altogether. This is especially true in combination with tax haven situations. This result goes beyond the treaty's purpose.

* * * In addition, any deviation from provisions of the source country's domestic tax law should be limited to the intended beneficiaries, otherwise the objective of the legislation enacting such provisions is subverted.

* * *

Reduction of the Incentive to Conclude Tax Treaties. If residents of third countries that have no tax treaty or a less favorable tax treaty with the source country can still obtain source basis tax benefits, these third countries will be under less pressure to enter into a treaty with the source country. They will lack motivation to form their own treaties, since their residents are able to shop for benefits in the existing treaty network at minimal cost and without the third country having to grant any reciprocal rights. Undoubtedly such incentives would have a detrimental effect on the source country, especially with regard to its ability to expand its income tax treaty network and its ability to renegotiate its existing treaties on more favorable terms.

* * *

If a third country, whose residents are able to treaty shop, is nonetheless willing to enter into treaty negotiations, the third country's bargaining position is generally enhanced, making it difficult for the source country to obtain concessions in negotiations. Since the third country is accustomed to having the most favorable benefits under another treaty for its investors, it will want to be granted the most advantageous provisions for its treaty or otherwise refuse to conclude one. It is not always possible, however, to make the same concessions to every country, since the outcome of the negotiations largely depends on the specific situation between the negotiating countries.

Besides eliminating double taxation and thus providing a more favorable investment environment for the residents of contracting states, treaties are designed to provide an exchange of information. The possibility for a taxpayer involved in cross-border transactions to engage in tax avoidance or evasion is substantially diminished when a mutual exchange of information is provided. Therefore, one important aspect of tax treaties is to assist the tax authorities in dealing with international auditing problems. In this respect, the expansion of a country's treaty network is indispensable, but may be inhibited by treaty shopping.

Taking all these factors into account, it is clear that treaty shopping has a detrimental effect on the source country's revenue, as well as its position within the international community. In the last two decades, treaty shopping has become a widely employed tax-planning device with significant economic impact. It is understandable, therefore, that a source country would fight treaty shopping with all possible means at its disposal.

Richard L. Reinhold, *What is Treaty Abuse? (Is Treaty Shopping an Outdated Concept?)*, 53 TAX LAWYER 663, 664, 672–683 (2000).

This paper represents an effort to re-examine the principal measures that have been developed to curb certain practices that have been labeled "tax treaty abuse." Much attention has been devoted to this subject—both on the part of government as well as the private sector—since the 1970s, when the problem first received significant attention. However, the commercial landscape has changed dramatically in the intervening years, and the pertinent legal concepts, including those that have been adopted to combat treaty abuse, have also evolved. This Article attempts to take stock of some of the current treaty-abuse measures in light of these changes, and reaches the following conclusions:

1. The 1970s saw a proliferation of tax avoidance strategies involving third-country nationals' use of tax-haven entities to gain advantages under tax treaties between the United States and the tax-haven jurisdictions. To curb this practice—referred to as "treaty shopping"—the United States insisted on inclusion of detailed "limitation on benefits" ("LOB") provisions in tax treaties; these LOB provisions generally restrict treaty benefits to entities (1) that are owned to a sufficient degree by residents of treaty jurisdictions and (2) that do not erode their residence country tax base through deductible payments to persons outside the treaty jurisdictions.

2. Significant changes in applicable tax rules and the general elimination of tax treaties between the United

States and tax-haven jurisdictions call into question the need for LOB provisions: with relatively few exceptions, it seems unnecessary to restrict treaty benefits in the case of companies formed in the industrialized jurisdictions that are the main trading partners of the United States.

3. In recent years, treaty LOB provisions have become increasingly complex and detailed, and in some cases quite restrictive. At the same time, some features of the provisions—particularly the exemption for public companies and so-called "derivative benefits" provisions—create potential gaps in the coverage of LOB rules. In circumstances in which LOB provisions might properly apply, it would seem that their functioning could be improved.

4. Separately, the issue arises as to entitlement to tax treaty benefits resulting from particular transactions entered into for a principal purpose of obtaining such benefits. Recently-signed treaties with Italy and Slovenia contain so-called "main purpose" provisions targeted at these transactions. While the provisions may duplicate principles already present in U.S. common law—business purpose, step transaction, economic substance, etc.—there may be a benefit to including these provisions in tax treaties.

* * *

Policy Background. * * * Treaty drafters have employed two types of measures to limit tax treaty benefits to their intended beneficiaries. The first * * * inquires as to the appropriateness of making the benefits of a particular treaty available to a given person. Tax treaties generally operate for the benefit of the "residents" of the other Contracting State. The LOB provisions that have been included in tax treaties effectively embellish on the definition of the term resident and, in general, function as a gatekeeper to deny treaty benefits to entities of third-country owners without adequate linkage to the residence jurisdiction.

The second type of limitation functions on the premise that the party seeking treaty benefits is a resident and satisfies the LOB criteria, but then inquires whether a particular income item is appropriately the subject of tax treaty benefits. Restrictions of this second type, utilized to a greater extent in older treaties, take into account such factors as non-tax business purpose in determining qualification for treaty benefits.

* * *

[T]reaty drafters limit the benefit of source tax reductions to persons who are subject to the personal taxing jurisdiction of the other treaty partner. Persons subject to the personal taxing jurisdiction are, after all, potentially subject to double taxation by reason of source taxation, and the elimination of double taxation is a prime objective of tax treaties. Tax treaties thus confine most treaty benefits to the class of persons who or which qualify as a "resident" of the other jurisdiction.

Article 4(1) of the U.S. Model Tax Treaty defines a "resident of a Contracting State" as a "person who, under the laws of that State, is liable to tax therein by reason of his residence, citizenship, place of management, place of incorporation, or any other criterion of a similar nature." Except with regard to the treatment of non-resident citizens of the United States, the U.S. Model Tax Treaty is typical of U.S. tax treaties in force.

But the mere fact of an entity's satisfying the definition of "resident" does not necessarily allay policy concerns regarding third-country persons' use of a treaty to avoid source taxation. Several issues arise:

(i) *Really a Resident?* Courts have considered situations involving the appearance of residency without the substance of residence. * * * Interesting, however, is the extent to which the opinions are informed by the policy underlying the treaty in reaching their conclusions. For example, in *Johansson*, Johansson, a heavy-weight boxer, claimed to have established residency in Switzerland and thereby to have become entitled to the benefits of Article X(1) of the Swiss treaty then in effect—the so-called "commercial traveler" provision—in order to avoid U.S. tax on his income from prize fights in the United States. The record supporting Swiss residence was thin: the critical element, according to the taxpayer, was a determination by the Swiss authorities of his Swiss residence, which, in turn, seems to have been based primarily on the taxpayer's (self-serving) declaration to that effect. The court stated that residence status could not be evaluated in the abstract and quoted from the decision of the Supreme Court in *Maximov v. United States*: "[T]o give the specific words of a treaty a meaning consistent with the genuine shared expectations of the contracting parties, it is necessary to examine not only the language, but the entire context of agreement." The court then went on to make a detailed analysis of the objectives of tax treaty arrangements; the basis upon which the jurisdiction to tax is apportioned by tax treaties—as relevant here, the locus of the "economic impact" of the income-producing activity; and the basis for so-called commercial traveler provisions in tax treaties. In light of this policy background, the court concluded that "[w]hile Johansson may have brought himself within the words of the Swiss treaty by his 'residence' in Switzerland and his 'employment' by a 'Swiss corporation,' he has failed to establish any substantial reasons for deviating from the treaty's basic rule that income from services is taxable where the services were rendered."

* * *

(ii) *A Resident in Form but Not in Tax Substance?* Assume Nemo Ltd., a Country X corporation, is one-hundred-percent owned by individual residents of Country X. The Company's residence status and local ownership would prima facie entitle it to the benefit of the U.S.-X treaty. Assume further, however, that Nemo earned $100 of U.S.-source interest income, its only income for the year, and that it paid $51 on a tax-deductible basis to a person who is not a resident of Country X or the United States. Because Nemo's base of income subject to tax by Country X is substantially eroded through a deductible payment and no counterbalancing tax has been imposed by Country X or the United States (or other qualifying jurisdiction), Nemo's status as a person subject to tax by Country X on a residence basis has been undermined. Outside the setting of publicly-traded entities, U.S. tax policy firmly establishes that U.S.-source taxes should not be reduced in a situation such as this involving the erosion of the Country X tax base. * * * Note that deductible payments by individuals do not jeopardize their ability to claim tax treaty benefits. The seeming tax-shelter opportunity is doubtless outweighed by the non-tax significance of residence status in a particular place by an individual.

(iii) *Owned by a Resident?* If Naught Ltd., a Country Y corporation, is one-hundred-percent owned by Q, a third-country citizen and resident, should the company be treated as a "resident" of Country Y for purposes of the U.S.-Y tax treaty? For purposes of this question, assume that, although Naught carries on a business in Country Y, the U.S.-source income that it earns is derived from a separate line of business that is not connected with or incidental to the Country Y business. Further assume that Naught does not violate any base erosion test. Since at least 1981, policy-makers at Treasury and in Congress have taken the view that a company in Naught's position is treaty shopping and therefore is not entitled to tax treaty benefits. This result obtains notwithstanding that (1) Naught may be fully subject to Country Y tax on its income, and (2) either (a) shareholder taxes may also be imposed by Country Y on remittances to Q, or (b) if Country Y maintains an integrated corporation-shareholder tax regime, it may be the case that no additional shareholder-level tax would fall due when corporate earnings are distributed.

* * *

[I]t must be regarded as settled at this point that Naught will not be afforded tax treaty relief from U.S.-source-basis taxes, irrespective of the level of the tax to which Naught (or Q) is subject by Country X or Q's home jurisdiction.

There is apparent recognition of the possible harshness of this approach in the business nexus rule, as well as in the exception for headquarters companies of multinational groups in the treaties with France and the Netherlands. Both provisions rely on activities within the residence jurisdiction and apparent liability for tax therein as a condition to their application, but they impose no requirement regarding the ownership of the entity.

* * *

Residence Tax Policy Issues. The foregoing issues of tax treaty abuse relate to a country's interest in protecting its source tax base. However, countries also have a substantial residence tax interest to protect, and positions adopted to protect a residence tax interest will often conflict with the country's source tax interest. To illustrate, Country A insists on a strict LOB test in its tax treaty with Country B to prevent non-B persons from obtaining an improper reduction in A-source taxes. But what if the restrictive LOB clause has the effect—based on prevailing patterns of business ownership in Country A—of denying some significant number of Country A residents a reduced level of Country B source taxes? From the point of view of the United States and its taxpayers, overly-restrictive LOB provisions could mean increased foreign-source-based taxes being imposed on U.S. persons making outbound investments, and, on a net basis, an increased tax burden on those U.S. investors, because the incremental foreign taxes are less likely to be creditable in the United States.

There are many reasons why companies with no indicia of treaty shopping may fail to satisfy LOB criteria. These include placement of equity with third country nationals; acquisition transactions—the degree of cross-border activity having increased significantly in recent years; and joint venture transactions with third-country nationals. Although the foregoing concerns have been voiced by the ALI and others, it seems fair to conclude that the United States continues to place protection of source taxes ahead of residency tax concerns. It is possible that the broad relief for publicly-traded entities in LOB provisions contained in existing treaties, especially in conjunction with the so-called derivative benefits test, affords a measure of protection against inappropriate denial of source taxation relief for U.S.-resident companies. * * *

Conclusions Regarding Tax Policy Issues. A treaty drafter must strike a balance among a series of competing interests. First, relief from source taxation must be limited to persons who are bona fide subject to residency-based taxation by the treaty partner. Under present U.S. tax policy, an investor's bona fides will be in question if it is owned disproportionately by third-country nationals, although a complete denial of treaty benefits in such a case is probably too restrictive, and the relief provisions based on business nexus and headquarter company structures appear to recognize this shortcoming. Second, relief from source taxation should never be afforded to tax-haven investors * * * .

Third, the United States plainly has a host-country interest, in addition to its residence-country interest, and the significance of its status as a host country is increasing. With regard to U.S.-source income, the present thirty-percent withholding tax rate on FDAP is quite high relative to present international norms. A 30–percent tax on gross income would seem high even when prevailing rates on net income are in the range of 45 percent to 50 percent; such a rate is simply out of step with today's 39.6 percent and 35 percent individual and corporate tax rates. A general withholding tax rate of fifteen percent, possibly ten percent, would seem sensible to me. * * *

Fourth, residency-based concerns create a bias in favor of loose restrictions on source-based reductions, and conflict directly with the desire to avoid benefiting tax-haven investors.

3.10 TAX ARBITRAGE: DUAL RESIDENCE

"Double dipping" and "international tax arbitrage" are labels for the exploitation of inconsistent tax rules in two (or more) countries. Countries frequently differ in many rules of tax law. One important instance is their methods of determining corporate residence. Since taxpayers will try to minimize their tax burdens, those engaged in cross-border commerce will seek to turn conflicting rules of individual countries to their advantage. This manipulation of legal differences among countries has produced an uneasiness among U.S. tax policymakers.

"Dual resident companies" (DRCs) provide one example of international tax arbitrage. DRCs have been defined as "corporations whose losses might be used simultaneously to reduce taxable income of a related U.S. corporation and another related corporation in another country."[10] In the excerpt below, David Rosenbloom questions whether the United States government has any legitimate interest in attacking benefits received by taxpayers through this type of tax planning. A contrary view is offered in the next excerpt by Diane Ring. She contends that different types of tax arbitrage pose different problems for efficiency and equity in international taxation and is concerned that government intervention results in high administrative costs and risks to both sovereignty and diversity. She claims that any attempt to intervene must balance these competing goals.

H. David Rosenbloom, *International Tax Arbitrage and the "International Tax System,"* 53 TAX L. REV. 137, 141–66 (2000).

The implications of differences among country tax systems have come into sharp focus in recent years. * * * In part, this is because * * * several of the principal landmarks in planning for a U.S. multinational company * * * have been tightened and refined, so that home-grown solutions for problems encountered abroad have become scarcer.

* * *

One result has been increasing taxpayer interest in "international tax arbitrage"—a lofty term that refers to taking advantage of differences among country tax systems, usually differences in addressing a common tax question. * * * The result is not a breach of U.S. rules, for there is no such breach (although the effort to meet foreign requirements may require massaging of facts, and in that process the application of U.S. law may pass from clear to arguable). The goal is to adhere, insofar as possible, to those rules while structuring the situation so as to meet the entirely different rules that obtain in the other country or countries. If the effort is successful, tax benefits will flow in the United States and at least one other country. * * *

In its purest sense, the technique may be used to duplicate (in some cases, triplicate) tax benefits. The dual resident company [for example] * * * permit[s] deductions to be claimed in more than one country. The unrelated income against which the deductions are applied is subject to tax in just one country; thus, a single transaction or arrangement gives rise to independent benefits in two or more countries. The same goal can be attained with * * * foreign tax credits, which the laws of two or

---

10. H. David Rosenbloom, International Tax Arbitrage and the "International Tax System," 53 Tax L. Rev. 137, 137 (2000).

more countries may permit to be claimed independently in each country. In some cases, a different view regarding the nature of an instrument, and consequently, a payment, may allow different treatment in different tax jurisdictions; this is the case involving the dividend that another country perceives as an interest payment.

* * *

There is an undeniable elegance to these arrangements. But elegance by itself is not a satisfactory reason for singling out these examples of tax arbitrage from other, more traditional forms of planning. If a foreign country allows a resident parent corporation to borrow and pay deductible interest, to use the borrowed funds to capitalize a subsidiary in a low-tax jurisdiction, and to have that subsidiary lend funds to a U.S. enterprise with no consequences in the home country of the parent (thus generating two interest deductions and only a single income inclusion, and that subject to a low tax rate), the effect would appear to be no different in substance from the dual resident company ["DRC"]. More broadly, as long as the arbitrage hews to the rules in each affected country, it is hard to identify the difference between the more elegant examples and any situation in which a foreign country simply allows a tax benefit that the United States does not.

* * *

The Senate Finance Committee, which initiated the congressional action in 1986, described the DRC issue as follows:

[A] corporation may be at the same time a U.S. resident and a resident of another country. Such companies are sometimes referred to as "dual resident companies." A dual resident company is taxable in both countries on its worldwide income (or it can deduct its worldwide losses). In addition, if the company is a resident of both the United States and either the United Kingdom or Australia, it is able, in effect, to use its losses to offset the income of commonly owned corporate residents in the two countries. (The committee is aware of the ability to share losses in this way only in the case of Australia and the United Kingdom; this ability may occur in other cases as well.) In general, neither of these countries taxes the active business income of foreign corporations that operate solely abroad.

Corporate groups attempt to isolate expenses in dual resident companies so that, viewed in isolation, the dual resident company is losing money for tax purposes. This isolation of expenses allows, in effect, the consolidation of tax results of one money-losing dual resident corporation with two profitable companies, one in each of two countries. This use of one deduction by two different corporate groups is sometimes referred to as "double dipping." The profitable companies report their income to only one country.

* * *

The Committee accordingly proposed that losses of a foreign-owned DRC not be allowed to reduce the income of other U.S. members of the affiliated group. Obviously, the focus here was inbound investment, and the potential for competition between foreign investors and similarly situated U.S. persons. In fact, competition concerns represent a common thread of U.S. tax policy affecting U.S. investment by foreign persons. Such concerns undeniably have informed the tax regime applicable to foreign persons engaged in a U.S. trade or business or deemed to be so engaged.

In conference, however, the statutory remedy for DRCs (changed in various technical respects) was broadened to reach outbound investment—companies ultimately owed by U.S. persons. The conferees made this change because they believed it was fair: "[T]he conferees are not aware of a case where the use of one company's deduction by two other companies in two tax jurisdictions makes sense as a matter of tax policy." In addition, the conferees took note of the arguments that the Senate provision "discriminated against foreign-owned U.S. corporations." The statute as amended by the conference would restrict the use of losses in the United States when those losses are "shared with foreign corporations whose earnings will be subject to U.S. tax (which are typically U.S.-controlled) and not only to losses shared with foreign corporations whose earnings are never subject to U.S. tax (which are typically foreign-controlled)."

* * *

Lost in the debate were two questions that seemed reasonably important at the time and that have grown considerably in importance in the ensuing * * * years: (1) Are DRCs relevantly different from other techniques for taking advantage of differing tax rules in different countries? (2) What tax policy justifies the elimination of otherwise available U.S. tax benefits for the sole reason that the person claiming such benefits (or an economically related person) also enjoys benefits, tax or otherwise, in another country?

* * *

The DRC represents a clear-cut example of deliberate, direct, transactional arbitrage. A duplication of tax benefits is obtained through the intentional use of a corporation organized in the United States and therefore resident in the United States for U.S. tax purposes but managed and controlled in another country and therefore resident in that country under its tax law. Through borrowings or otherwise, the corporation is placed in a loss position and the loss is claimed, through the consolidation and grouping rules of each country, as an offset to positive income in each country. There is nothing diffuse, indirect, or accidental about this planning, which generally is undertaken for a specific purpose such as the acquisition of a U.S. business. From the U.S. point of view, the planning produces a U.S. deduction that may be used to reduce the tax on purely U.S. income of related corporations, while also producing a parallel deduction in the United Kingdom (or Australia).

* * *

It is not a full or satisfactory response * * * that it may be relatively simple to identify the "duplication" of benefits in the case of a DRC. That response does not explain why the identified cases are different in substance from DRCs, or why, on policy grounds, any of these situations should result in a reduction or elimination of U.S. tax benefits—why the United States should even consider altering the available U.S. interest deduction because Japan has lowered its corporate tax rate or Canada (for example) has adopted particularly beneficial rules for foreign investment by Canadian insurance companies. These cases merely involve taxpayers taking advantage of the national tax laws of different nations. It seems appropriate to link the denial of U.S. tax benefits to benefits available under the laws of other countries only if we conclude that the United States has a policy interest that tax be imposed by those countries at some minimum level on income not subject to U.S. taxation. What is that policy interest? The direct correspondence—parallelism—of benefits in some cases but not others may come into play as a way of easing administration only after a reason for concern in the most administrable of situations has been identified.

The DRC is surely an administrable case * * * . And it may be noted that the combination of benefits was unforeseen—apparently not intended—by any single country, and the taxpayer would not have engaged in the planning but for the availability of duplicate tax benefits. In all probability, neither the United Kingdom nor Australia adopted residence and grouping rules with the intention that taxpayers take advantage of the juxtaposition of these rules with those of the United States to obtain benefits in both countries. It doubtless can be stipulated, moreover, that most taxpayers would not have engaged in the formation and use of DRCs if benefits were limited to one country. Still, from the standpoint of any one country, including the United States, it is not clear what, if anything, flows from these observations. The taxpayer obviously has engaged in tax planning. But that, by itself, is not normally cause for a loss of tax benefits, as long as the result is a real transaction in which substance and form coincide. As noted above, country rules regarding taxation inevitably will differ in many respects, and the well-advised taxpayer will pay attention to, and seek to derive advantage from, the differences. It is hard to see why such fully anticipated behavior of the taxpayer should be the target of legislative pique in any country.

If there is any justification for this pique, it must lie in the area of competitiveness—specifically, the relationship between the combination of benefits achieved through arbitrage and the solitary (U.S.) benefit available to the U.S. person who is unable to put itself in a position to take advantage of arbitrage possibilities. This is the rationale that the Senate Finance Committee invoked * * * and perhaps this is the policy underpinning of the "international tax system" to which the Committee referred. But consider the point in stark terms: It implies that the United States would have an interest in the level of French tax on French income of a French resident assuming that the French resident was also, or became, a U.S. taxpayer, or, perhaps, invested in a U.S. taxpayer. Line-drawing concerns might dictate that the policy not be pursued in all conceivable situations, but line-drawing concerns are conceptually independent of the policy itself.

An attempt to "level the playing field" by mandating that foreign persons directly or indirectly entering the U.S. tax system must pay tax at some acceptable level on non-U.S. income is inconsistent with the practical nature of taxation. Certainly there are better and worse tax systems. But the overriding justification of taxation is that it represents a way for government to fund itself on a periodic basis. There is no time for perfection, only for improvement. And there is no clear reason to seek through the tax system an ideal of egalitarianism not pursued in other aspects of national life.

* * *

For these reasons, competitiveness and nondiscrimination represent shaky foundations for the assault on DRCs, much less for a more general attack on international tax arbitrage. And deliberate international duplication of tax benefits not foreseen by any one country plainly extends beyond DRCs. The main point at issue, in the case of such companies, is the rule for determining an entity's residence: The United States looks to place of incorporation, while the United Kingdom and Australia look to place of management and control. If there is any cause for objection here, it should apply [elsewhere] as well * * * . As noted previously, the field of arbitrage and arbitrage possibilities not anticipated by any country is large indeed.

* * *

What to do? A starting point might be for Congress to attempt once again to answer the underlying questions, raised but admittedly not disposed of in this essay, of whether we care about arbitrage and why. The exercise might enable tax policy-makers either to press beyond DRCs into other specific areas or to make a thoughtful, and forthright, retreat. The shape of a sensible statutory provision in this area is not going to become clear unless and until there has been an intelligent explanation of purpose.

Conclusion. International tax arbitrage, the deliberate exploitation of differences in national tax systems, is the planning focus of the future. This is not a passing fad, not a minor phenomenon. Thanks in large part to the tutelage of U.S. professionals, taxpayers throughout the world have become conscious of the many benefits of threading a course among domestic tax laws.

The question this essay asks is: So what? The policy response the United States has offered so far calls to mind a deer caught in headlights. If we have a legitimate concern about benefits obtained by taxpayers on income or activities not subject to U.S. jurisdiction, we should endeavor to explain coherently what that interest is. Invoking the international tax system does not constitute an explanation, since that system appears to be imaginary. Whether it would be desirable is a different question—but one bearing only marginally on the intensely practical world of international tax policy.

Diane M. Ring, *One Nation Among Many: Policy Implications of Cross–Border Tax Arbitrage*, 44 B.C.L. REV. 79, 79–85 (2002).

The central challenge in international tax is navigating the relationship between an individual country's tax system and the rest of the world—a question of how nations should balance competing demands of revenue, domestic policy, retaliation, and global goals. The question grows more pressing as the pace of intersections among tax regimes escalates. The difficulty of this exercise manifests itself quite clearly in the emerging questions about cross-border tax arbitrage. Does cross-border tax arbitrage represent egregious abuse of the tax system? Is it the natural outcome of a multi-jurisdictional world? What is the proper view of cross-border tax arbitrage and how should its analysis be framed?

In its simplest terms, cross-border tax arbitrage refers to a situation in which a taxpayer or taxpayers rely on conflicts or differences between two countries' tax rules to structure a transaction or entity with the goal of obtaining tax benefits (for example, reduced or no taxation) overall. Had the structure or transactions taken place entirely domestically, the net tax benefit (which was created by the conflict between the two countries) would not exist. Thus, taxpayers in the arbitrage transaction or structure exploit the intersection of the two countries' tax systems to eliminate or reduce substantially their income tax. Particular areas of tax law can prove to be especially fertile "breeding ground[s] for arbitrage," either because one country's tax rule is rather unique or because it is difficult to apply predictably.

The starting point for analysis of cross-border tax arbitrage, as with most other international tax analyses, is recognition of the power of globalization. The international scope of business, along with related changes in communication, cash flow restrictions, and regulatory practices, has increased the ease and volume of cross-border activity. The reality of these changes helps shape international taxation as a topic, and has contributed to the burgeoning growth of arbitrage.

The opportunity for cross-border tax arbitrage arises where transactions are subject to two or more countries' tax regimes. This regulatory intersection between two countries presents the potential for conflicting rules. Despite many common features in our trading partners' tax systems, the multitude of factors that produce tax law, including social policy, administrative constraints, and political compromise render conflicting rules a likely possibility. Conflict in rules produces one of two results: taxation by both countries (double taxation) or taxation by neither (nontaxation). Domestic tax laws and bilateral treaties include mechanisms for limiting double taxation, which is generally viewed as a barrier to cross-border activity. Where the conflict in rules leads to nontaxation, taxpayers (and governments, perhaps because of reduced taxpayer advocacy on the issue) have traditionally paid less attention. The internationalization of the economy, however, combined with developments in technology, has fueled taxpayer recognition of these tax-law conflicts as an opportunity for profitable tax planning. Tax

differences exploited by taxpayers to achieve nontaxation produce cross-border tax arbitrage.

What should be the federal government's response to such
arbitrage? At the end of the 1990s, the U.S. Treasury Department ("Treasury") identified cross-border arbitrage issues as a
high priority; the international community is now displaying a
growing interest. When exploring these issues, it is critical to
specify precisely what is included in and what is excluded from
the concept of cross-border tax arbitrage. As noted above, arbitrage is generally considered the "exploit[ation of] differences
between the tax system[s] of two different jurisdictions to
minimize the taxes paid to either or both." What is excluded
from the concept here are those transactions that can be characterized as cross-border "shelters." Such transactions already
face scrutiny and examination under the developing shelter
rules. The arbitrage question differs because it confronts those
transactions that are benefiting from inconsistent treatment
across jurisdictions, but presumably have more substance than
shelters. * * *

The core tax policy issues for cross-border tax arbitrage can
be separated into two discrete sets of questions: (1) why and
when is the arbitrage problematic; and (2) whether and how a
country, in this case the United States, should respond. Answering these questions demands a comprehensive consideration of
tax policy goals, competing values, and practical constraints.
Two rather polar responses can be readily imagined. The first,
favored by many taxpayers, argues that the United States has
no legitimate interest in whether and how much tax is paid to a
foreign country. If the U.S. tax rules are followed (and the
transaction is not otherwise challenged as a shelter), then no
further government action or response is appropriate. In fact,
the United States should be quite satisfied that domestic taxpayers might be able to reduce their foreign tax burden. The
second response, evident in the U.S. government's effort in the
late 1990s to eliminate certain arbitrage opportunities, reflects a
generalized but not fully articulated sense that it can be inappropriate to manipulate the differences between countries' tax
rules to reduce or eliminate tax.

The very source of conflict between these positions is the
reason that neither constitutes an adequate response. Both
positions, at least in their extreme form, grant paramount
priority to one of the tax system's goals without adequate
acknowledgment of the validity of the others. The view that no
action is warranted where U.S. rules have been followed gives
dominant weight to national regulatory independence, and perhaps implicitly to administrability, while giving seemingly no
weight to the economic distortions and equity harms generated.

Conversely, a blanket desire to eradicate cross-border tax arbitrage elevates the elimination of distortions at the expense of other factors, including administrability and domestic policy. A comprehensive policy for cross-border tax arbitrage must integrate and balance all competing goals. As a result, however, any resolution reached here will inevitably have an air of compromise. It will neither seek full elimination nor full acceptance of cross-border tax arbitrage. Steps taken to control arbitrage will reduce domestic autonomy and increase harmonization, but these steps will not fully curb arbitrage. Despite these limitations, the analysis of the arbitrage question should be undertaken in a principled manner and proposals measured against established tax criteria.

Ultimately, this Article contends that the government can legitimately respond to some instances of arbitrage but that the continued existence of many more will be an ineluctable feature of a multi-jurisdictional business environment. The conclusion is not surprising; it acknowledges the strengths behind the polar positions articulated above. More specification, however, is needed to translate this broad determination into policy guidance. This Article proposes a balancing test that identifies and evaluates the competing goals in each arbitrage case to derive an appropriate response. In addition, this Article offers insights as to the factors that are most likely to be salient and the types of risks that are most likely to arise with particular anti-arbitrage policies.

It is important to be quite clear about the value and the limits of this analytical framework. First, it provides a structure for discussion of arbitrage that targets the core issues. Second, it weaves the divergent strands of the arbitrage argument into a single debate by fostering recognition of the multiplicity of national and international goals. Third, it offers an approach for the policymaker attempting to answer, in a coherent and reasonably uniform manner, the question of whether to intervene and, if so, how. The balancing test, however, is not self-applying. There will continue to be very significant questions of policy to debate. That outcome is not a failing of the framework but rather a reflection of the nature of the endeavor, which demands the accommodation of a variety of competing policy goals in a wide range of circumstances. Furthermore, evaluating the examples under the balancing test is not a static exercise; it may change as tax rules, policy goals, or other features of the tax system change. The balancing test, however, should enable comprehensive consideration of arbitrage without reliance on ad hoc case assessments, along with the development of a sophisticated understanding of the arbitrage problem and the responses that can be crafted.

Through the detailed investigation of this major example of an international regulatory clash (cross-border tax arbitrage), the fundamental question of all global regulatory systems can be clarified and distilled: What vision of international regulatory relations should animate government policy? In making regulatory decisions in the absence of full information, countries must determine the nature of the relationship between and among nationally based regulatory regimes. A nationalist-driven perspective emphasizes competition; a more global perspective encourages cooperation. In reality, neither approach likely serves national or international interests because neither nationalism nor globalism constitutes a defensible, definable goal. The real question is whose interests are to be taken into account in making a policy decision and what outcomes will serve those interests. In tax matters, nations are the dominant actors and can be expected (at least loosely) to promote national interests. The paths most likely to advance these interests will vary by time and context, and may include a range of more or less cooperative behaviors. It is through the detailed investigation of cross-border tax arbitrage that we can gain more insight into this universal regulatory question.

NOTE

A Balancing Act. Diane Ring weighs the criteria of efficiency, equity, political accountability, and revenue impact in her assessment of responses to different forms of tax arbitrage. She acknowledges that the results of her balancing test are not static and will change with the policy goals of the United States government. Specifically in regard to the United States legislation addressing DRCs, Ring uses her balancing test to suggest that:

> The U.S. course of action raises the question of why Congress felt compelled to act in a case in which the balancing test suggests it may not have been advisable to do so unilaterally. Based on the legislative history and commentary surrounding the arbitrage, the most likely answer is a combination of strong pressure from U.S. corporations and a powerful sense of outrage at what seemed an insultingly blatant thwarting of the single-tax principle. In addition, unilateral action was available to Congress whereas multilateral action would typically require the administration's involvement.

Professor Ring concludes with her opinion that a combination of harmonization and competition/independence is the most desirable outcome in cross-border tax regulation. She states, however, that there are multiple ways in which these goals can be achieved and that they need to be considered within the context of the complicated relationships between the relevant countries. For further discussion of tax competition and harmonization, see Chapter 11.

Chapter 4

The Foreign Tax Credit

4.1 INTRODUCTION

The U.S. allows income taxes imposed by nations where U.S. citizens or residents earn foreign-source income to be credited against the income taxes that would otherwise be imposed by the United States. Technically, U.S. citizens and residents are subject to U.S. taxation of their worldwide income regardless of its source and therefore need tax relief in order to reduce or eliminate "double taxation." A foreign tax credit ("FTC") is a means of relieving international taxpayers from the burden of paying taxes twice on the same income: once to the country of source, where the income is earned, and again to the country where the taxpayer resides. This system of crediting foreign income taxes first entered the U.S. income tax law in 1918. In 1921 Congress limited the foreign tax credit to the amount of U.S. tax that would have been imposed on the foreign source income. The foreign tax credit has served as the cornerstone of U.S. international tax policy ever since.

There are traditionally three ways by which the country of residence may afford relief: (1) by allowing a deduction of source-country taxes; (2) by exempting source-country income from residence-country taxation; and (3) by crediting source-country taxes against residence-country taxes. The deduction system is the least generous, since the relief is limited to the foreign tax times the taxpayer's domestic marginal tax rate. Exemption is the most generous, subjecting the foreign-source income only to foreign taxation, no matter how low the foreign rate. A credit may offer dollar-for-dollar relief against residence-country taxation. The following table illustrates these three different methods. Assume the U.S. taxpayer's foreign operations generate $100 of taxable income, subject to a foreign tax rate of 30%, and its domestic operations generate $100 of taxable income, subject to the U.S. tax rate of 35%.

Method	Foreign tax	Total U.S. tax (on both domestic and foreign income)	U.S. tax on foreign income	Total tax on foreign income (U.S. tax + foreign tax)
Deduct foreign taxes	$30	$59.50 ($200 − $30) = $170 × .35	$24.50 ($59.50 − $35) [Total U.S. tax	$54.50

		[Total income minus foreign tax multiplied by U.S. tax rate of 35%]	minus U.S. tax on U.S. source income]	
Exempt foreign income	$30	$35 ($100 × .35) [No U.S. tax on foreign income]	$0	$30
Credit foreign income taxes	$30 [U.S. tax on worldwide income ($70) minus foreign tax ($30)]	$40 ($70 − $30) [$70 (U.S. tax on worldwide income) minus $30 (the foreign tax credited)]	$5 ($40 − $35)	$35

For the first five years after the Sixteenth Amendment took effect in 1913, the Treasury allowed only a deduction for foreign taxes paid. In 1918 the United States unilaterally instituted a foreign tax credit at the suggestion of T.S. Adams, an economist who was the key Treasury tax advisor during the period when the policy regarding international taxation was being formulated.

When a foreign tax credit is adopted, various issues arise that inevitably complicate the computation of tax. First is the limitation on the credit. If the residence country were to credit fully foreign taxes imposed on foreign-source income at a higher tax rate than the residence country's rate, the residence country would reduce the tax otherwise collected on income earned in its own jurisdiction, in effect benefiting the foreign treasury at the expense of its own fisc. A limitation on the foreign tax credit is essential if the U.S. is to collect its income tax on U.S. source income.

For example, in the preceding example, if the foreign tax rate were 50%, and the United States allowed a full foreign tax credit without limitation, the United States would collect a *total* U.S. tax of only $20 ($70 − $50 FTC). In that case, the foreign tax credit would effectively reduce U.S. tax on *U.S. income* by $15. A limitation is thus necessary to protect the integrity of the residence country's own revenue system. In 1921 Congress enacted a limitation on the foreign tax credit to prevent crediting higher-rate foreign taxes against U.S. taxes on U.S.–source income. The foreign tax credit limitation rules provide, in essence, that the foreign tax credit cannot exceed the tax at the U.S. rate on the foreign income—in the example above, $35.

The policy rationale for the limitation has remained unchanged, but the method of determining the limitation has changed over time. First, Congress has vacillated about whether to group all foreign income and taxes together, regardless of foreign tax rates, in computing the limitation, or whether to calculate the credit and limitation separately for each foreign jurisdiction. These methods are called the "overall limitation" and the "per-country limitation," respectively. Originally, in 1921 Congress enacted an overall limitation. In 1932 Congress required taxpayers to use the lesser of an overall or per-country limitation. The overall limitation was repealed in 1954 in favor of a per-country limitation. In 1960 Congress restored the overall limitation and allowed taxpayers to choose the more advantageous of the per-country or overall limitation. In 1976 Congress repealed the per-country limitation, and taxpayers were back to the overall limitation first adopted in 1921.

An overall limitation gives corporate taxpayers earning income in more than one foreign jurisdiction the ability to average foreign tax rates. In principle, taxes paid to countries with rates higher than the United States's are not fully creditable because of the Treasury's concern that foreign taxes not diminish taxes due on U.S.–source income. Under an overall limitation, however, taxes paid to jurisdictions with higher rates are averaged with those paid to jurisdictions with lower rates, in effect cross-crediting the higher and lower taxes. The averaging of foreign tax rates under an overall limitation maintains the integrity of the U.S. tax on U.S. source income but is often sufficiently advantageous that it may affect corporate taxpayers' decisions about where to locate their investments.[1] The following simple example illustrates how overall and per-country limitations might work:

Source country	Qatar	Ireland	U.S.
Income	$100	$100	$100
Income tax rate	90%	10%	50%
Foreign taxes paid	$90	$10	?

The U.S. taxpayer has worldwide income of $300, on which it owes (.50 × $300 =) $150 in U.S. income taxes before the allowance of the foreign tax credit. Under an overall limitation, the taxes paid to Qatar and Ireland could be added together to determine the foreign tax credit limitation. Thus, when the limitation fraction of 2/3 ($200 foreign income/$300 worldwide income) is multiplied by the U.S. pre-credit tax of $150, the creditable amount would be $100, and the entire amount paid to both foreign jurisdictions would be creditable. Under a per-country limitation, on the other hand, the limitation fraction would be 1/3 for each of the two foreign countries ($100 per country income/$300 worldwide income), and thus only $50 would be creditable of each of the discrete amounts of income tax paid to Qatar and Ireland. This more than covers the Irish taxes, which are fully creditable, but disallows credits for $40 of the Qatar taxes, which may be carried over to subsequent years. The foreign tax credit would thus be limited to a total

---

   1. The per-country limitation was more favorable in circumstances where the taxpayer had losses in one country and income in another. The foreign taxes on the income were creditable without any reduction for the losses, whereas under an overall limitation foreign losses may offset foreign income and reduce the total creditable foreign taxes.

of $60 ($50 of Qatar taxes and all $10 of Ireland's taxes). When a per-country limitation was in force, taxpayers found ways through tax planning to achieve averaging in many circumstances. For example, patent rights might be transferred to a corporation located in a low-tax country, which would in turn license its use to a related corporation in a high-tax country, producing deductions in the high-tax country and income in the low-tax country. A simple example makes a per-country limitation look as if it works well, but in practice it did not.

The second significant structural development in the foreign tax credit limitation has been to distinguish among various categories of income in an effort to ensure that taxes paid on highly mobile forms of income cannot be averaged with taxes paid on income earned in the active conduct of a business. Separate foreign tax credit income "baskets" were first created in 1962 and greatly expanded in 1986. They are intended to prevent companies from transferring mobile investments to a foreign country principally to earn foreign tax credits. Currently there are ten baskets: (1) passive income; (2) high withholding tax interest; (3) financial services income; (4) shipping income; (5) dividends from noncontrolled section 902 corporations; (6) dividends from a domestic international sales corporation (DISC) or former DISC, to the extent dividends are treated as from foreign sources; (7) taxable income attributable to foreign trade income; (8) certain distributions from a foreign sales corporation (FSC) or former FSC; (9) foreign oil and gas extraction income; and (10) the largest single basket, the residual category called "other income."[2] The residual basket contains active foreign business income earned directly by the taxpayer or from U.S.–controlled foreign subsidiaries, no matter where located, and, thus, permits considerable averaging between high- and low-tax countries. (The baskets are described in more detail in Section 4.3 of this chapter, where they are also summarized in a table.) Excess credits from any given year may be carried back two years and forward five, beginning with the earliest year.

How the limitation should work remains a major source of controversy, because it determines the extent to which corporations may take advantage of averaging high and low foreign taxes, or cross-crediting. When the residence country has the highest tax rate, cross-crediting is much less important because corporations should always owe some residual tax on foreign-source income.

Another important feature of the foreign tax credit system is the so-called "indirect foreign tax credit" of section 902. The indirect foreign

---

2. Until 2003 income from each noncontrolled section 902 corporation—a corporation in which U.S. persons own at least 10 percent but not a majority of the voting stock—had to be put in a separate basket, making the number of baskets proliferate, but after 2003 separate baskets are not required for each noncontrolled corporation. The taxation of dividends paid from pre–2003 earnings and profits is, however, treated differently than dividends from post–2003 earnings and profits. See Section 4.3 for a more detailed explanation.

tax credit was instituted in 1918 to produce greater parity between U.S. corporations operating through branches in foreign jurisdictions and those operating through foreign subsidiaries. The income earned by foreign branches of U.S. corporations is subject to immediate U.S. taxation offset by the foreign tax credit, but the income of foreign subsidiaries is taxed only when earnings are repatriated in the form of dividends to the U.S. parent corporations. (See Chapter 5.) Subsidiaries typically, however, also pay income taxes to foreign jurisdictions, an expense that will reduce the amount of dividends that can be repatriated to the U.S. parent corporation. In the absence of an indirect foreign tax credit, the share of the foreign taxes paid by the subsidiary would not be creditable by the parent and would thus be subject to double taxation. Thus, section 902 of the Code allows an indirect foreign tax credit—a credit for foreign income taxes attributable to the dividend received from the foreign subsidiary. The foreign tax is "deemed paid" by the domestic parent, which is why this provision is sometimes referred to as the "deemed paid" foreign tax credit. It is allowable only to a domestic corporation which owns 10 percent or more of the voting stock of the foreign corporation. The trick when calculating the indirect foreign tax credit is that the repatriated dividend is grossed up by the amount of the foreign taxes paid.[3] Otherwise, the U.S. parent corporation would receive a deduction as well as a credit. Thus, if a foreign subsidiary earns $100, pays foreign income taxes of $25 and pays a $75 dividend to its parent, the parent will include $100 in income and receive an indirect foreign tax credit of $25. See § 78 of the Code.

In discussions of how to design a foreign tax credit—or even whether to have one at all—a group of familiar normative arguments continually appear. These theories can be divided roughly into two overlapping types: economic theories and theories of equity. H. David Rosenbloom describes the theories as follows:

H. David Rosenbloom, *From the Bottom Up: Taxing the Income of Foreign Controlled Corporations*, 26 BROOK. J. INT'L L. 1525, 1526–27 (2001).

Since most countries impose taxes upon some form of economic activity, and since a rational nation has an interest in supporting economic activity of persons subject to its taxing jurisdiction, the nation generally will wish to impose its tax with as much care as possible to preserve maximum room for that activity, given the necessity of the tax. This may be difficult in particular situations, but the general directive is clear: As between two taxes having the same effect, the one that inter-

---

3. I.R.C. § 78 allows a domestic corporation, choosing the FTC, to treat amounts paid under § 902(a) (relating to credit for corporate stockholder in foreign corporation) or under § 960(a)(1) (relating to taxes paid by a foreign corporation) as dividends received from the foreign corporation.

feres less with economic freedom is to be preferred. More broadly, it could be argued that general freedom of decision-making is a "good" meriting government protection, and taxes therefore should be imposed with as much leeway as possible for such freedom. Such considerations are commonly referred to as "efficiency." Professor Gergen invokes instead, and probably more fittingly, "the natural law of the parasite: Do the least damage to the host in extracting sustenance from it."

A second desirable feature in a tax system, no less important than efficiency, is what some refer to as "equity." This condition obtains when persons who stand in the same place insofar as the relevant target of tax is concerned are treated similarly by the tax regime. The point is important because tax systems in countries that are not totalitarian ultimately depend, to a large extent, upon the (sometimes grudging) consent of the taxed. If the system does not operate in an equitable way, that consent is difficult to acquire and more difficult to retain, with the result that those subject to the system will devote greater energy to frustrating, avoiding, or evading it. Such actions, in turn, render the system more difficult to administer and enforce in an equitable way which, in turn, only will add to the frustration of persons subject to the regime. For this reason, equity is needed in a tax system for the most pragmatic of reasons, to permit the system to function.

NOTE

Efficiency and Equity. The two theoretical goals, efficiency and equity, sometimes overlap with each other. For example, the Treasury sometimes claims it is both efficient and equitable for a U.S. taxpayer doing business abroad to be taxed at the same rate as its competitors in the U.S. Companies sometimes counter that equity and efficiency demand that they pay the same tax as their competitors in the foreign country where they operate. On the other hand, equity and efficiency are often thought to conflict. The classic example is the claim that equity demands the taxation of income from capital, while efficiency suggests it should go untaxed.

4.2 ORIGINS OF THE FOREIGN TAX CREDIT AND THE FOREIGN TAX CREDIT LIMITATION

The History of the Foreign Tax Credit

Michael J. Graetz & Michael M. O'Hear, *The "Original Intent" of U.S. International Taxation*, 46 DUKE L.J. 1021, 1043–56 (1997).

Just as the enactment of a deduction for foreign taxes occurred in 1913 without any talk of "national neutrality," the move away from this deduction to a foreign tax credit in the 1918 Act took place without any political decision to shift U.S. tax policy to favor "worldwide efficiency" or "capital export neutrality." The Sixteenth Amendment permitting a federal income tax had recently been sold to the American people on fairness grounds, and, in 1918, arguments grounded in tax equity remained far more persuasive politically than notions of promoting more economically efficient investments. T.S. Adams was then just beginning to create the institutional capacity within the Treasury and Internal Revenue Service to analyze the social and economic consequences of fiscal and monetary policies. A politically persuasive case for free trade policies loomed only in a distant future. Throughout the early part of this century, America's trade policy viewed imports unfavorably, and Congress was soon to raise its already substantial protective tariffs.

Then, as now, international tax policy was "something of a stepchild" in the tax legislative process. The big issue before the Congress was finding the means to finance [World War I], in particular the question whether to impose a war profits or excess profits tax. Indeed, Adams initially joined the Treasury Department to assist with the massive tax increases that would be necessary to fund the United States war effort.

This tax-raising occasion was an odd time for Adams to succeed in making the foreign tax credit (FTC) his first enduring contribution to international tax policy. But, because the United States insisted on taxing the worldwide income of its citizens, the pre–1918 arrangement permitted a form of double taxation, with foreign-source income being fully subject to taxation both at home and abroad. In 1913, when the American income tax was first implemented, tax rates were low and this double taxation may have been a comparatively minor nuisance. In 1918, however, with the world at war and tax rates inflating rapidly around the globe, international double taxation was becoming a far more serious burden on Americans doing business or investing abroad. The top marginal rates on individuals in the United States reached 77 percent, and although the basic corporate rate was only 10 percent, an excess profits tax at rates from 8 to 60 percent also applied to many large companies. In such circumstances, additional layers of taxation from other nations were potentially confiscatory. Relief became a matter of some urgency.

In this context, Adams presented an extraordinary proposal: the foreign tax credit, which he described as "one of the most striking departures" in the 1918 Act. Under the FTC, Americans could claim a credit against their American taxes for taxes paid to other countries; taxes paid abroad would reduce American tax revenue dollar for dollar. The FTC represented what was an extraordinarily generous measure for its time: the United States was assuming sole responsibility for the costs of reducing the double taxation of its residents and citizens. * * * In so doing, the U.S. unilaterally renounced a potentially important bargaining chip in convincing other nations to forego taxing their residents on U.S. source income. * * *

Such generosity was virtually unprecedented. Great Britain, for example, limited its relief from double taxation, also a foreign tax credit, to taxation within the British Empire and, in legislation in 1920, the British further limited its FTC to a maximum of one-half of the British taxes on the foreign income. Yet Adams pursued his scheme because he felt that "it touched the equitable chord or sense, and because double taxation under the heavy war rates might not only cause injustice but the actual bankruptcy of the taxpayer."

To Adams' surprise, the FTC provoked little opposition (or indeed notice) and became law in 1919. Adams attributed the success of his proposal to the fact that legislators are particularly sensitive to the charge of double taxation. Adams later observed, "In my experience with legislative bodies I have found that you can accomplish more for equity and justice in taxation in the name of eliminating or preventing double taxation, than with any other slogan or appeal." * * *

Adams framed the problem of double taxation not as an issue of economic efficiency, but as a matter of invidious discrimination.

Adams identified the ultimate culprit causing this discrimination as the nation of residence: "More double taxation of the unjust variety is inflicted upon the taxpayer by his own government than by foreign governments." He elaborated:

> Every state insists upon taxing the non-resident alien who derives income from sources within that country, and rightly so, at least inevitably so. Now, then, in due course of time, citizens of the home state inevitably invest abroad and derive income from foreign sources. The average state refuses to acknowledge in this situation the right of its own citizen to a proper exemption on income derived from foreign sources. It * * * refuses to recognize when one of its own citizens or nationals gets income from a foreign source that he inevitably will be taxed abroad.

Given the predictability and the justness of taxation abroad, in Adams' view, the nation of residence wronged its taxpayers by levying an additional tax upon foreign-source income, thereby discriminating unfairly against residents who happened to earn their income abroad.

Though Adams felt, as a matter of principle, that nations should work to alleviate the double taxation of their residents, and, during the limited discussion of the measure, members of Congress focused on the great burden of double taxation and the urgency of relieving it given wartime tax rates, other factors also played a role. In particular, there was a growing recognition of a need to encourage private investments by Americans in Europe. Adams also believed that the United States would reap practical benefits from providing relief to its own taxpayers; he was convinced that a discriminatory tax system that imposed unconscionably high rates on some taxpayers would ultimately prove to be unenforceable.

Moreover, Adams generally shared the sentiments about business of the Administrations for which he worked; he believed American prosperity depended in large measure on the competitiveness of American business abroad. Certain members of Congress also depicted the FTC "as a method to encourage foreign trade and to prevent revenue loss through incorporation of foreign subsidiaries or expatriation." Trade abroad was considered crucial to the nation's economic well-being and was thought to require appropriate support from the government. Relief from double taxation constituted just such appropriate support. And there is some evidence that Adams had this policy in mind in his international tax efforts. * * *

By the end of 1918, the United States had another reason to favor relief for Americans investing abroad: A variety of American economic and diplomatic interests required that a substantial quantity of American capital be channeled to rebuild post-war Europe. The United States was owed eleven billion dollars by allied governments for wartime loans; somehow Europe would need access to American dollars to pay off this debt. Europe would also need American dollars to purchase American exports—a central goal of American economic policy. Given the U.S. antipathy to imports and its high tariffs, it was difficult for Europeans to sell goods to the United States. Moreover, the wartime devastation of Europe's human, physical, and financial capital made serious competition in American markets unlikely. If dollars could not be raised through sales, another possibility was loan forgiveness or other public financing of European recovery by the American government. However, domestic politics in the United States were very different after World War I than after World War II. Americans wanted smaller government, lower taxes, and fewer international entanglements. Americans would not tolerate loan forgiveness, much less a

Marshall Plan, to aid Europe at a time when the United States government was itself sagging beneath what it considered an enormous wartime debt. In sum, if Europe was going to get the dollars necessary for the repayment of its debts, the purchase of American exports, and the economic stability necessary for peace, the source would have to be private investment. * * *

B.   The 1921 Act—Limiting the FTC and Enacting Specific Source Rules

With the FTC, Congress put into place the centerpiece of an American international tax scheme that persists to this day: the United States taxes non-residents on U.S.–source income, and residents and citizens on world-wide income, but allows the latter to offset their U.S. tax liability with a credit for income taxes paid abroad to alleviate double taxation. Though the Revenue Act of 1921 retained this basic structure, Adams returned to Capitol Hill once again as spokesman for the Treasury Department to urge a number of significant refinements to the mechanism.

The most important of these reforms was a limitation on the FTC. As originally devised, the FTC could be used to offset up to the full amount of any U.S. "income, war profits and excess-profits taxes" owed by an American taxpayer. Thus, an American with substantial investments abroad, particularly if made in a high-tax nation (or nations), might eliminate his entire tax bill to the United States. Such an unlimited feature of a foreign tax credit in fact furthers the principle of capital export neutrality because, under such a regime, decisions about where to make investments turn only on comparing pre-tax rates of return even when the foreign tax rate is higher than the domestic tax rate. But neither Adams nor Congress was thinking about achieving such neutrality during this period, and both regarded the limitless FTC in 1921 as creating the potential for "abuse." With the high U.S. tax rates obtaining in 1918 and 1919, the ability of the FTC to erase U.S. tax liability was not readily apparent. By 1921, however, U.S. rates had fallen considerably and were in the process of being reduced further. Meanwhile, European nations maintained their higher rates. For instance, in 1921 the "normal tax" (i.e., the base rate applied to the lowest income categories) was 10 percent in the United States, but 30 percent in Great Britain. Under such circumstances, an American investing in Great Britain might easily wipe out his entire U.S. tax liability even though the lion's share of his income was from U.S. sources. * * *

Specifically, Adams requested and Congress enacted what we now call an "overall limitation": the amount of FTC available to any given taxpayer was limited to a proportion of the taxpayer's overall U.S. tax liability equal to the proportion of the taxpayer's global income derived from foreign sources. For instance, an American obtaining 10 percent of his income from foreign sources could use the FTC to offset a maximum of 10% of his total U.S. tax liability on his worldwide income; the taxpayer would thus have to bear an increased tax burden for investing in foreign countries with higher average taxes than the United States. To the Senate Finance Committee, the case for such a limitation was so strong that there was no need even to discuss the proposal. The repeal of the U.S. excess profits tax in 1921 made such a limit even more compelling. Contemporary critics derided the limitless FTC as an instance of unjustified "prodigality" on the part of the American government.

The fundamental purpose of the 1921 foreign tax credit limitation was to protect the ability of the U.S. to collect tax on U.S. source income, but the limitation on the foreign tax credit also has had a number of effects on the investment decisions of U.S. residents. Generally, under such a limitation, if a foreign country's tax rate is higher than the U.S. rate, a U.S. investor will prefer a domestic investment to a foreign investment with an identical pre-tax rate of return. For an investor who has already made some foreign investments, however, the limitation's averaging of foreign taxes of high-tax and low-tax countries might create advantages for investments in low-tax countries (to average against the high-tax foreign country's taxes as a way of offsetting U.S. tax) or indifference about investments in high tax countries (because, due to investments in low tax countries, the limitation may not be reached). The limitation enacted in 1921 clearly eliminated the pure neutrality as between foreign and domestic investments with the same pre-tax rates of returns that had existed under the unlimited earlier version of the FTC.

NOTES

1) *Adams's Outlook.* In the article excerpted above, Michael Graetz and Michael O'Hear look closely at T.S. Adams's papers and determine that the principal theories influencing the discussion of international tax policy since that time—theories of worldwide and national economic efficiency—were not the ones that motivated Adams when he proposed the foreign tax credit. Much of the discussion in Adams's time (and since) has been about the primacy of source-country as opposed to residence-country jurisdiction over business income. The "benefit" theory supporting source-based taxation is expressed in Adams's statement that business "ought to be taxed because it costs money to maintain a market and those costs should in some way be distributed over all the

beneficiaries of that market."[4] As a practical matter, he also argued, "[i]n the long run the business unit or source will yield more revenue to the public treasury than the individual; and the place where the income is earned will derive larger revenues than the jurisdiction of the person."[5] Although Adams believed in the primacy of source-based taxation, he also regarded residence-based taxation as a necessary backstop in international taxation.

2) *Practice and Theory.* T.S. Adams had seen in his earlier work with Wisconsin's income tax how inequities in taxation could result from a tax system that was not enforceable. Such inequities might undercut the very legitimacy of the government's power to tax income. Thus, he brought to his work for the U.S. Treasury as great a concern for practice as for theory. There are special concerns for legitimacy when taxation is a cooperative effort between otherwise competing sovereign states. As Graetz and O'Hear write:

> Adams had an additional reason for stressing enforceability in source rules: rules based on administrative practicability stood the best chance of gaining widespread international acceptance. Adams believed that nations would surrender tax jurisdiction only so long as they could do so without incurring significant financial harm. * * * Adams was sure that nations would most easily be swayed to surrender jurisdiction over income that they could not tax effectively anyway.[6]

3) *The Bumpy Road Ahead.* Graetz and O'Hear write:

> The United States retains a classical corporate tax, under which business income earned by a corporation is taxed twice: first when it is earned by the corporation, and again when it is distributed to shareholders as dividends. Many of our trading partners, however, have moved in recent years to eliminate or substantially reduce this double taxation. The international tax regime, however, is predicated on the existence of a double corporate tax. It generally allocates the corporate level tax to the country where the businesses' income is earned and the personal tax on dividends to the country where the recipients reside. A country's unilateral decision to eliminate either the corporate or individual level of tax upsets this equilibrium and demands fundamental reconsideration of the international consensus about how this income should be taxed.[7]

---

4. Michael J. Graetz & Michael M. O'Hear, The "Original Intent" of U.S. International Taxation, 46 Duke L.J. 1021, 1036 (1997).

5. Id. at 1038.

6. Id. at 1102.

7. Id. at 1025.

The Foreign Tax Credit Limitation

Elisabeth A. Owens's classic study of the foreign tax credit is more than four decades old, having been written before many legislative changes were adopted. In particular, her characterization of the United States as a country with a high-tax rate is now dated; the U.S. corporate tax rate is higher than that of some OECD nations, but lower than others. Nevertheless, her structural discussion of the FTC limitation remains current, as does her analysis of various forms of the limitation on fairness, incentives for foreign investments by U.S. persons, and revenue.

Elisabeth A. Owens, THE FOREIGN TAX CREDIT 295–311 (1961).

[I]f a country which taxes its nationals on income from all geographical sources decides to take unilateral action to relieve double taxation, it can do so only by allowing the country of source of the income the prior claim on that income. A complete shift to the principle of taxation only at source is unnecessary since the "burden" of double taxation under a tax credit system is deemed to be only the excess taxation occurring when the taxpayer is subjected, because it pays taxes to more than one country, to an aggregate tax rate which exceeds the generally applicable rate of the crediting country. Consequently, the tax credit system is based on two principles: first, that the place of source has the first claim on the taxpayer's income and second, that the crediting country, as the country of nationality, may properly impose an additional tax to the extent income has not already been taxed at its source at a rate as high as that of the crediting country.

Within this broad framework, there are several types of limitation which may be used. At one extreme, the crediting country, the United States, can use the limitation only to protect its right to tax as a country of source of income. Since a credit system is based on recognition of the claim of the country of source to tax income, the United States will at least retain its right to tax the domestic source income of its nationals. Some form of limitation is, therefore, inherent in the credit system. Application of an over-all limitation which allows foreign taxes to be credited up to the point at which any additional amount of credit in a given year would reduce the United States tax on United States source income protects the United States' right to tax as a country of source. If an over-all limitation is used, however, the United States either recognizes the right of a foreign country to assert jurisdiction over income from sources in all other countries except the United States, or allows a foreign country, because it has a tax rate higher than the United States tax rate, a claim prior to that of the United States on the income from all other countries except the United States. * * *

At the other extreme, the crediting country can, with equal logic, use the limitation for the purpose of allowing a credit for only that portion of the tax paid to any one foreign country which is imposed on income from sources within that country, since the superior claim of the foreign country is based only on its right to tax as a country of source. The per-country limitation appears to be based on this concept. If stringently applied, no carry-over of credit would be allowed. * * *

It is clear that the logic of a tax credit system itself does not indicate what is the proper form of limitation. Whether a crediting country, such as the United States which has a relatively high tax rate in comparison to that of many other countries, wishes to allow more credit by using an over-all limitation, or less credit by using a per-country limitation, depends upon other considerations. All the forms of limitation discussed here represent alternatives which have a practical consequence because the United States has a relatively high tax rate. If a crediting country has a very low tax rate relative to other countries, the operative effects are substantially the same whether it uses an over-all or a per-country limitation.

The function of the limitation as a part of the tax credit device for relieving international double taxation raises a problem basically because there are two types of equity involved; equity as between taxpayers of the crediting country and equity as between the countries involved. With respect to the first type, the right of the crediting country to impose a tax in addition to that imposed at the source of the income which will result in an aggregate tax rate equal to that in effect in the crediting country may be accepted as equitable treatment by taxpayers. By the same token, however, it will not appear to be equitable to use a form of limitation which will inevitably tend to result in a higher aggregate tax rate than that in effect in the crediting country. Only the most liberal form of limitation is satisfactory from this point of view, since that form will tend to approximate neutral taxation, i.e., taxation at the same rate whether foreign or domestic income is earned, for the greatest number of taxpayers in the greatest number of cases. A limitation operating on an annual or country-by-country basis will inevitably subject taxpayers to a rate higher than the United States rate if the taxpayer pays taxes in any year or to any foreign country at a rate higher than the United States rate. Insofar as the credit system is a means of producing tax neutrality as between those taxpayers who engage in foreign activities and those who do not, to the extent it is within the power of the United States to provide such neutrality unilaterally, it is natural that the more restrictive forms of limitation will be subject to criticism on the ground that they do not produce neutrality. It is true that any form of limitation is an obstacle to achieving neutrality, as is the fact that the United States does not compensate taxpayers by a refund for foreign tax paid at a rate which is higher than the United States rate. Generally, however, neither entire elimination of the limitation nor refunds have been advocated as practicably acceptable alternatives. The policy of tax neutrality is probably the taxpayer's strongest argument in favor of liberalizing the form of limitation. * * *

From the standpoint of equity as between countries, however, the crediting country is not solely responsible for providing relief from excessive taxation resulting from international contacts. One justification for a more restrictive form of limitation lies in the view that the responsibility is not solely that of the United States but is to some extent shared by other countries which also secure some of the benefits of freeing international trade and investment from a repressive burden of taxation. In other words, the credit system can be viewed in the light of desirable tax relations between the countries involved—equity as between countries—rather than solely from the standpoint of relieving the burden of taxation on United States nationals—equity as between United States taxpayers. There is no doubt that the solution to the problem of double taxation is the responsibility of all countries involved and that the necessary sacrifice of tax revenues should be shared in some reasonable manner. It can also readily be seen why a restrictive form of limitation may seem reasonable to the government of a crediting country. The crediting country starts from the premise that its tax jurisdiction over its nationals is unlimited and is at least equally as well-founded as the asserted jurisdiction of other countries. In using a tax credit system, even with the most restrictive form of limitation theoretically compatible with the system, the crediting country may feel that it has assumed the greatest share of responsibility for excessive tax rates on international transactions and has relinquished the maximum amount of revenue which could reasonably be expected of it.

* * *

Concepts of Double Taxation

The form of limitation used may be subject to criticism because it is alleged to cause double taxation. There are two aspects to this problem. First, the type of limitation applied may be criticized because of the concept of double taxation embodied in the limitation. Each form of limitation involves a different concept and the concept itself may seem to be more or less valid. Second, a type of limitation may be analyzed in terms of the extent to which the type of double taxation relief inherently involved in that type of limitation is achieved.

The narrowest concept of double taxation is involved in the per-country limitation (without provision for carry-over of excess credit); that limitation will be discussed first.

Per-country Limitation

The concept of double taxation embodied in the per-country limitation is taxation both by the United States and a foreign country of a taxpayer's annual income derived from sources in a foreign country as that income is calculated under United States law. This concept is narrower than that involved in the over-all limitation because the "income" deemed to be subject to double taxation under the per-country limitation is income from one foreign country rather than income from all foreign sources; it is also narrower than that involved in any provision for carry-over of credit because the "income" is the income of one year rather than several years. It is by no means, however, the narrowest concept that could reasonably be used. * * *

When the per-country limitation does not reduce the amount of creditable tax, double taxation as defined above is eliminated because, although a tax is paid to both the United States and the foreign country, the tax rate is the United States tax rate. The tax is the same as if only the United States imposed a tax. When the limitation is operative to reduce the amount of creditable tax, double taxation as defined above may or may not be eliminated, depending on the reason for the loss of credit. If the reason is that the foreign statutory tax rate is higher than the United States rate, double taxation is eliminated. Both countries tax the same income, but the credit cancels out the United States tax and a tax is paid only to the foreign country. Similarly, if the reason is that the foreign country has a broader tax base than the United States as where it allows fewer deductions or taxes additional kinds of receipts, double taxation in any year as between the United States and the foreign country is eliminated because the excess amount of income taxed in the foreign country is not taxed at all by the United States.

If, however, the excess tax for which credit is not given is a tax on income which is also taxed by the United States, and the excess tax does not arise out of a higher foreign statutory rate, then double taxation does occur when the limitation is operative. This may happen * * * in several kinds of situations: (1) when the foreign country taxes the world-wide income of United States nationals, (2) when the source rules of the foreign country are different from the source rules of the United States, (3) when a divergence between the characterization of income in a foreign country and in the United States results in the application of different source rules to the same receipts, and (4) when the foreign tax is credited against a United States tax on a different year's income. * * *

Although there are thus several circumstances in which double taxation of the kind implied in the per-country limitation may arise, its actual incidence is probably not very great since it depends both upon the per-country limitation becoming operative and upon relatively uncommon conditions. Generally, for example, the source rules and concepts of taxable income in a foreign country are not very different from those of the United States, and generally the foreign tax is applied against the United States tax on the same year's income. Moreover, except in the relatively rare situation in which a taxpayer has no taxable income from a foreign country in a given year under United States source rules and concepts of taxable income, the existence of these theoretical limits to the effective operation of the credit system will not often result in a loss of credit. This is because the United States tax rate is relatively high as compared to the rates of many foreign countries and the entire foreign tax will be creditable despite discrepancies in source rules, etc. Double taxation which does occur under the per-country limitation can be eliminated or mitigated by allowing excess tax over and above the amount of limitation to be credited through use of a carry-over limitation or an over-all limitation. Such relief goes beyond the need, however, in the sense that it allows excess tax to be credited regardless of the circumstances which cause the per-country limitation to become operative; or to state it another way, it involves shifting to a broader concept of double taxation. Double taxation can also be relieved in many instances on an ad hoc basis, as for example, by obtaining a change in source principles in a foreign country through income tax treaties or by the formulation of United States rules which will consistently result in the application of a foreign tax against the United States tax on the same year's income.

Over-all Limitation

The concept of double taxation embodied in the over-all limitation on the credit is the taxation by the United States, on the one hand, and all foreign countries, on the other, of annual income derived from all foreign sources, as that income is calculated under United States law. The income conceived to be subject to double taxation is aggregate foreign source income as compared to income derived from a particular country under the per-country limitation. * * *

Double taxation of foreign source income in the aggregate can occur under an over-all limitation just as double taxation of the income from one country can occur under the per-country limitation. But as the concept of double taxation embodied in the law is broadened the incidence of double taxation naturally tends to decrease. In a conceptual sense, this is because double taxation will not occur merely because a foreign country taxes income derived from sources in other foreign countries. This decrease is also due to the fact that the limitation must be operative and thus reduce the amount of creditable tax in order for double taxation to arise and the averaging effect of the over-all limitation will lessen the number of instances in which the limitation becomes operative.

Carry-over Limitation

A carry-over of excess credit from one year to other years in a carry-over period can be applied in conjunction with either a per-country or an over-all limitation. It broadens the concept of double taxation by enlarging the "income" deemed to be subject to double taxation from income measured on an annual basis to income measured over a period of years. * * *

Evaluation of Concepts of Double Taxation Inherent in Forms of Limitation

It is clear that the concept of what constitutes double taxation, even as that term is understood in connection with a tax credit system, is flexible. Clarification of the various concepts involved is useful in assessing criticisms based on whether a particular form of limitation does or does not tend to eliminate double taxation. Analysis in these terms, however, cannot determine any one proper form of limitation. Legislative history indicates that other considerations—the problem of providing fair treatment to differently situated taxpayers, the prevailing attitude towards providing more or less encouragement to foreign trade and investment, and current revenue needs—have been the determinants of the form of limitation. The concept of double taxation involved has been more the result than the cause of the form of limitation adopted. * * *

Incentive Effect

The changes which have been made in the character of the limitation probably reflect more than anything else changes in policy with respect to the encouragement of foreign trade and investment. * * * [I]t can be assumed that the greater the amount of credit allowed and the lower the aggregate tax rate on foreign source income, the greater the encouragement to foreign trade and investment. This kind of approach to the selection of the form of limitation suffers from the defect that it is impossible to ascertain pragmatically the quantitative effect on the amount of foreign trade and investment resulting from a more or less restrictive form of limitation. While it can be taken for granted that there will be more foreign trade and investment if a tax credit is available than if it is not, it cannot be so readily assumed that the relatively minor differences in the effects of various forms of limitation will appreciably encourage or discourage international business operations. The revenue effects must also, of course, be taken into account. Since it is difficult to estimate either the short-run costs of a liberalization, before it has stimulated increased investment, or the long-run costs, after the expected increase has occurred, both the cost and the benefit are problematical. This difficulty, however, is intrinsic in considering any tax provision in terms of its incentive effect, and its probable effects on foreign trade and investment are, nevertheless, perhaps the most crucial consideration in deciding upon the form of the limitation on the credit.

The alternative forms of limitation used in the past and the forms which have been proposed can be listed, with a fair presumption of accuracy, in order of the degree to which they will result in the payment of less United States tax and, therefore, a greater amount of encouragement to foreign trade and investment. In ascending order of encouragement, they are as follows:

1. Application of lesser of per-country or over-all limitation.
2. Per-country limitation.
3. Per-country limitation with carry-over of excess credit.
4. Over-all limitation.
5. Application of greater of per-country or over-all limitation, i.e., annual election by taxpayer.
6. Over-all limitation with carry-over of excess credit.
7. Application of greater of per-country or over-all limitation, i.e., election by taxpayer, plus carry-over of excess credit.

NOTES

1) *Efficiency*. For an economic analysis of the efficiency of separate limitations based on type or source of income versus an overall limitation

aggregating the limitation across all foreign income, see Andrew B.
Lyon & Matthew Haag, Optimality of the Foreign Tax Credit System:
Separate vs. Overall Limitations (2000), available at http://
www.bsos.umd.edu/econ/lyon. This paper is also summarized in 1 NA-
TIONAL FOREIGN TRADE COUNCIL, INC., THE NFTC FOREIGN INCOME PROJECT:
INTERNATIONAL TAX POLICY FOR THE 21ST CENTURY 293–97 (2001). Lyon and
Haag contend that the economic efficiency of a per-country versus
overall limitation turns on the relationship of the residence country's tax
rate to rates elsewhere in the world. They argue that at current U.S.
rates as compared with generally lower foreign tax rates, an overall
limitation best serves efficiency goals.

2) *A Corporate Practitioner's Outlook.* Charles I. Kingson, in *The Foreign Tax Credit and Its Critics*, provides a practitioner's look at the
inconsistencies that legislative compromises have wrought in the development of the foreign tax credit. He concludes that the "credit's technical flaws are minor. Its major ones are political—the result of interlock-
ing choices (here and abroad) that reject equity for advantage. The
present credit embodies skill and principle in the face of significant
pressure; and it breathes just a whisper that when President Carter
called the Code a disgrace to the human race, he got it backwards."[8]

The Indirect Foreign Tax Credit

The excerpt below discusses the history of the indirect foreign tax
credit, § 902, enacted to protect U.S. companies with foreign subsidiaries
from double taxation. Critics of the indirect foreign tax credit charge
that it places domestic companies with foreign branch operations at a tax
disadvantage compared to those with foreign subsidiaries.

Jonathan Davis, *The Foreign Tax Credit: History and Evolution* 11–18, 42–44 (MARCH 8, 1995) (UNPUBLISHED MANUSCRIPT, ON FILE WITH THE AUTHOR).

The Indirect Foreign Tax Credit

The direct foreign tax credit did not fully address the issue
of double taxation. In addition, the 1918 act created the indirect
foreign tax credit, which allowed American companies to get
credit for taxes paid by their wholly owned foreign subsidiaries.
* * *

Many American companies operate abroad through subsidiaries incorporated in foreign countries. This can create a tax
advantage, because the United States respects the form of the
entity and treats the subsidiary as a foreign entity that is not
subject to United States taxation. Prior to 1918, however, own-

---

8. Charles I. Kingson, The Foreign Tax Credit and Its Critics, 9 AM. J. TAX POL'Y 1 at
57 (1991).

ership of foreign subsidiaries could also create a tax penalty because of double taxation. The double taxation occurred when the money was repatriated to the American parent in the form of a dividend. For example, assume company A, an American company, has a subsidiary, little A, which is incorporated and operates in country Y. If little A makes $1000, $500 will be paid in taxes to country Y, which has a 50% tax rate. Assume that the rest is repatriated to company A in the form of a $500 dividend. Prior to 1921, this $500 dividend was taxed at the United States ordinary corporate rate with no credit. As a result, assuming a 25% United States tax rate, company A would pay an additional $125 tax and would be left with $375. In this example, the effective tax rate based on the combination of taxes paid to country Y and the United States would be 62.5%. If company A had invested directly in country Y, it would have received * * * a credit after 1918 for its foreign taxes paid. [This] would have the effect of eliminating the United States tax leaving company A with the full $500 dividend.

Congress did not perceive any reason to tax a company operating through a subsidiary differently than a company operating through a branch. The indirect credit was meant to simulate the direct credit that the company operating through a branch would receive. * * *

In addition to equalizing treatment between subsidiaries and branches, Congress also wanted to equalize treatment for receipt of dividends from domestic and foreign corporations. Corporations are subject to a two-tiered tax system. The corporation pays tax on its income, and the shareholder pays tax on the dividends issued. If a corporation were a shareholder, this would create a three-tiered tax system as the same income would be taxed when earned, when issued to the shareholder corporation as a dividend, and when issued to the ultimate individual shareholder. Section 234 of the Revenue Act of 1918 created the dividends received deduction. This allowed a corporation a deduction for any dividends received from another domestic corporation. The indirect credit exempted dividends from foreign corporations which were at least 50% owned by American corporations.

It appears that two purposes were solved by separating the indirect tax credit from the dividends received deduction. First, the credit was more restrictive. Corporations received the dividends received deduction even if they only own one share of the domestic corporation issuing the dividend, while the indirect credit was only available if the parent owned at least 50% of the stock of the foreign corporation issuing the dividend. [Now 10%- ed.] Secondly, the indirect credit protects the direct tax credit. If a dividends received deduction were allowed from foreign corpo- rations, then a corporation could avoid being taxed on its foreign income. The corporation would set up a foreign subsid- iary and have all profits remitted to the parent through a dividend. The parent would get a full dividends received deduc- tion and pay no tax on the money earned. If the money was originally earned in a jurisdiction with no corporate tax, then the corporate tax could be avoided completely.

As stated above, in addition to creating parity with the dividends received deduction, the indirect tax credit was created so that income from foreign subsidiaries would have the same tax treatment as income from foreign branch operations. This goal was not achieved. Instead, the credit actually created tax incentives for a company to operate through a foreign subsid- iary instead of a foreign branch. The subsidiary has two main advantages: first the indirect credit was technically flawed [as originally enacted] in that it gave a tax subsidy to subsidiaries incorporated in low tax countries; and secondly, subsidiaries always could avoid or at least delay the payment of United States taxes by not issuing dividends, so that the money would not be subject to American tax jurisdiction.

* * *

The second criticism of the indirect tax credit involves the issue of deferral. It is a basic tax concept that it is better to pay taxes later rather than sooner. By operating through a foreign subsidiary, company A can defer paying taxes on its earnings by deferring the payment of a dividend. * * *

President Kennedy was the first Democratic president to address the foreign tax credit since the Wilson administration first enacted the foreign tax credit in 1918. In 1962, Kennedy was able to get some changes through Congress aimed at eliminating some of the perceived unfair aspects of both the direct and the indirect credit. * * *

Congress * * * attacked [an] aspect of the indirect credit that [gave] incentives to operate through a foreign subsidiary instead of a foreign branch. Congress added gross-up rules in computing the indirect tax credit. * * *

The gross-up rules corrected the technical problem with the indirect credit * * * . Under the old system, a parent operating through a subsidiary could get as much as a 7% lower effective tax rate than a company operating through a branch even before considering deferral. The gross-up rules eliminated this loophole. For illustration, assume that company A has incorpo- rated little A in country X, which has a 10% tax rate. Assume that the U.S. has a 25% tax rate. Further assume that little A makes $1000 of country X source income, pays $100 in tax and repatriates the other $900 to company A in the form of a dividend. Under the old rule, company X has tax liability of $225 and deemed paid credit of $90, so it pays tax of $135 to the United States for total tax liability of $235. The gross-up rules state that company A is deemed to have received the full dividend of $1000 and receives credit for the full $100. Thus, company A's United States tax liability is $150 and its total liability is $250 or 25 percent. If little A paid only a $600 dividend and reinvested the other $300, then company A would be deemed to have received a dividend of $667 and would receive a credit for $67 in taxes paid to country X. The other $33 in tax would be available as a credit when the remaining $300 of little A's earnings and profits were remitted to company A.

NOTE

More about the Indirect Credit. For more extensive analysis of the indirect foreign tax credit, see ELISABETH A. OWENS & GERALD T. BALL, THE INDIRECT CREDIT at pages 3–30 (1979) (on the function and rules of the indirect foreign tax credit) and at pages 329–33 (discussing the relevant policy issues).

4.3 MECHANICS AND STRUCTURAL PROBLEMS

The Basket System

As discussed above, since 1921 the Treasury has limited the foreign tax credit to restrict the crediting of taxes paid on foreign-source income earned in countries with higher tax rates than the U.S. This prevents offsetting foreign taxes against U.S. taxes on U.S.-source income. With an overall limitation, however, it is still possible to cross-credit taxes on income sourced to foreign countries with higher-than-U.S. tax rates against taxes on income sourced to foreign countries with lower-than-U.S. tax rates. In 1976 Congress repealed the per-country limitation and reverted to the overall limitation. To restrict cross-crediting, or "averaging," under the overall limitation, Congress in 1986 enacted a complex "basket" system. Separate basket limitations, related to the total amount of foreign-source taxable income included in each of the baskets, apply to the total of direct foreign tax credits under sections 901 and 903 and to indirect foreign tax credits under sections 902 and 960.

Under the basket system, the foreign tax credit limitation of section 904(a) must be applied separately to nine categories of foreign-source income. The categories are listed in section 904(d)(1)(A) through (I). (Under section 907, foreign oil and gas income are subjected to a separate but similar limitation process.) The limitation for the separate categories is calculated with the following formula:

$$\frac{\text{Foreign-source taxable income in relevant basket}}{\text{Worldwide taxable income}} \quad X \quad \begin{array}{c}\text{U.S. tax on} \\ \text{worldwide} \\ \text{income}\end{array} \quad = \quad \begin{array}{c}\text{Limitation applicable} \\ \text{to income in that} \\ \text{basket}\end{array}$$

Because the ratio is multiplied by the U.S. tax rate on worldwide income, the limitation for foreign taxes on income in any basket cannot exceed the U.S. tax rate on that income.

To figure out the amount of foreign-source taxable income in each basket, a taxpayer must first determine the amount of gross income in the basket; then allocate deductions to obtain taxable income in the basket; finally, the taxpayer must ascertain all direct and indirect foreign tax credits attributable to the taxable income in the basket. Section 904(d)(3) provides look-through rules for interest, rents, royalties, and dividends from controlled foreign corporations (CFCs). This means that a U.S. taxpayer owning at least 10 percent of the voting stock of a CFC must "look through" any dividend to the distributing corporation's underlying income in order to determine the character of the income and its appropriate basket. (This is where the anti-deferral regime of Subpart F, discussed in Chapter 5, flows into the foreign tax credit limitation regime.) Finally, a taxpayer may have to apply the section 904(c) rules for carrying excess foreign tax credits back two years and forward five.

The nine baskets under Section 904 are:

1:   904(d)(1)(A): Passive Income

This basket includes income that would be foreign personal holding company income under section 954(c) if it were received by a controlled foreign corporation (one way in which the foreign tax credit limitation and Subpart F run on parallel tracks). Such income generally includes dividends, interest, royalties, and rents (with exceptions noted below). It also includes gains from the sale or exchange of property (other than inventory) that produce foreign personal holding company income or that produce no income (e.g., diamonds). The guiding idea here is to isolate easily relocated types of investment income, often subject to low rates of tax abroad, so that they cannot be used for averaging against foreign business income more likely to be subject to higher foreign tax rates.

There are some important exceptions. Passive income here does not usually include royalties or rents from unrelated persons earned in the active conduct of a trade or business. For export promotion reasons, the FTC limitation on passive income does not include export financing interest. Neither does it include high-taxed income. This last category of income is subject to the "high-tax kickout" that applies to passive income taxed at a rate higher than the highest rate of U.S. individual or corporate tax. This distinction is intended to prevent cross-crediting *within* the passive income basket. High-tax passive income is kicked out to the residual (or general limitation) basket.

2: 904(d)(1)(B): High Withholding Tax Interest

This basket includes interest payments on which a foreign withholding tax of at least five percent has been imposed on a gross basis. This income goes into a separate basket because a five percent tax on gross interest income might well represent a much higher rate on a net basis (considering the high percentage of expenses in the income of financial intermediaries) and would therefore enable cross-crediting against low-taxed income if it were placed in the passive income basket. For export promotion reasons, export financing interest is excluded from the high withholding tax interest basket and put in the general limitation basket.

3: 904(d)(1)(C): Financial Services Income

This basket includes income of a "financial services entity," i.e., an entity "predominantly engaged in the active conduct of a banking, insurance, financing or similar business" (as defined in section 904(d)(2)(C)(i); Reg. § 1.904–4(e)(3)(i) tells us that "predominantly" means that at least 80 percent of the entity's gross income must come from "active financing income"). The point here is to prevent U.S. corporations from setting up banking and financing subsidiaries in tax havens in order to cross-credit low-taxed financial services income against other high-taxed active business income. This income includes: (1) income from an active banking or financing business; (2) income from the investment by an insurance company of its unearned premiums or reserves; (3) passive income, even if it would be excluded from the passive income basket for another reason; and (4) export financing interest that would be high withholding tax interest.

High withholding tax interest and export financing interest that does not come under the definition of high withholding tax interest are excepted. This basket takes priority over the passive income and shipping income baskets.

4: 904(d)(1)(D): Shipping Income

Foreign jurisdictions often tax shipping income at low rates, if at all. Such income would thus be valuable for averaging against active business income by corporations in excess foreign tax credit positions if it were not put into a separate basket.

5: 904(d)(1)(E): Dividends from Each Noncontrolled Section 902 Corporation

Unlike the case with CFCs, Congress does not try to equalize the treatment of *non*controlled foreign corporations and foreign branches. This basket applies only to corporate taxpayers receiving a dividend from a foreign corporation in which it owns at least 10 percent, but not a majority, of the voting stock (a so-called "10/50" foreign corporation). In this more stringent regime, prior to 2003, the dividends from each noncontrolled section 902 corporation were put into a separate basket, allowing no cross-crediting against income of any other type or of any other noncontrolled corporation. In addition, prior to January 2003, the look-through rules did not apply to noncontrolled foreign corporations as they do to CFCs. These rules have changed as of January 2003. Dividends paid out of pre–2003 earnings and profits go into one basket. Dividends paid out of subsequent earnings and profits will generally be treated as income in a separate basket based on the amount of the underlying earnings and profits being dispersed, i.e., on a look-through basis (see § 904(d)(2)(E)(4)). The IRS issued Notice 2003–5 to explain how the credit limitation under section 904 applies to dividends distributed by a 10/50 foreign corporation in post–2002 tax years. This change is intended to simplify the system by not requiring the taxpayer to compute a separate FTC limitation for dividends received from each 10/50 corporation and is generally favorable to taxpayers. For a more in-depth discussion of the new rules, see Carol D. Klein & Lisa A. Felix, Putting All Your Eggs in a Single 10/50 Basket: Here's How, 98 Tax Notes 2015 (2003).

> *6:   904(d)(1)(F): Dividends from a DISC or Former DISC (as Defined in Section 992(a)) (to the Extent Such Dividends Are Treated as Income from Sources Without the U.S.)*

Foreign-source dividends from DISCs, or domestic international sales corporations, are often untaxed by foreign jurisdictions and so are put in their own basket to prevent cross-crediting against high-taxed income. (In 1976, a GATT (General Agreement on Trade and Tariffs) panel determined that the DISC rules constituted a prohibited export subsidy; the DISC was then replaced with the FSC (foreign sales corporation).)

> *7:   904(d)(1)(G): Foreign Trade Income*

Foreign trade income refers to gross income attributable to foreign trading receipts of a foreign sales corporation (FSC). See below.

> *8:   904(d)(1)(H): Distributions from a FSC (or Former FSC) out of Earnings and Profits Attributable to Foreign Trade Income, Etc.*

In 1999, a World Trade Organization (WTO) panel agreed with a complaint from the European Union that the FSC regime (which had replaced the DISC regime) constituted a prohibited export subsidy under the relevant WTO agreements. In early 2000 a WTO Appellate Body upheld that finding. In an effort to avoid the impact of these rulings, Congress in late 2000 repealed the FSC regime and enacted the "ETI" (Extraterritorial Income) regime.[9] The ETI system met the same fate in the WTO in 2002. Congress now seems to have given up on sustaining any similar export subsidy regime. The FSC provisions referred to in

---

9.   I.R.C. § 114.

Section 904(d)(1)(G) and (H) were repealed, but this basket still applies to income distributed by corporations that qualified as FSC income when that provision was in force.

9: 904(d)(1)(I). General Limitation Basket

This basket is the residual category under section 904(d), and thus it includes all income not caught in one of the previous eight baskets. This basket includes most foreign-source income earned in the active conduct of a business, the obvious exceptions being financial services income and shipping income. Although structurally this is the "residual" basket, in practice it is the basket into which most foreign-source income earned by U.S. corporations falls. Thus, many opportunities for averaging of high- and low-taxed income still exist. The critical policy question is whether the compliance costs of corporations and enforcement expenses of the Treasury due to the staggering complexity of the basket system are worth the supposed benefits it achieves. A number of proposals to simplify the regime are now before Congress.

The following table summarizes the rules:

Basket	Income Source(s)
Passive Income § 904(d)(1)(A)	1. Dividends and interest. 2. Rents and royalties (unless derived in the active conduct of a trade or business and received from an unrelated person). 3. Excess of gains over losses from stock, bond, and property sales and exchanges that produce rent, royalty, or no income. *Exceptions:* 1. Income included within any of the other baskets. 2. Export financing interest. 3. High-taxed income (high-tax kick-out).
High Withholding Tax Interest § 904(d)(1)(B)	Interest payments on which a foreign withholding tax of at least 5% is imposed on a gross basis. *Exception:* Export financing interest.
Financial Services Income § 904(d)(1)(C)	1. Active banking or financing income (if it makes up at least 80% of the entity's gross income). 2. Income from the investment by an insurance company of its unearned premiums or reserves. 3. Passive income (even if it would be excluded from passive income basket). 4. Export financing interest that would be high withholding tax interest.

Basket	Income Source(s)
	Exceptions: High withholding tax interest and export financing interest that do not come under the definition of high withholding tax interest.
Shipping Income § 904(d)(1)(D)	1. Income from the use of a vessel or aircraft in foreign commerce. 2. Income from leasing or hiring a vessel or aircraft for such use. 3. Income from the performance of service in connection with such use. *Exception:* Financial services income of a financial service entity (see immediately above).
Dividends from Each Noncontrolled Section 902 Corporation § 904(d)(1)(E)	Pre–2003 dividends from a foreign corporation in which the taxpayers owns at least 10%, but not a majority, of the voting stock will be treated as income in the single 10/50 basket. Post–2002, dividends paid out of earnings are generally treated on a look-through basis.
Dividends from a DISC or Former DISC § 904(d)(1)(F)	Foreign-source dividends from DISCs.
Foreign Trade Income § 904(d)(1)(G)	Distributions from earning and profits of a FSC attributable to foreign trade income.
Distributions from a FSC or Former FSC § 904(d)(1)(H)	Gross income attributable to a FSC.
Oil & Gas § 907	1. Foreign oil and gas extraction income (FOGEI), which is income derived from foreign sources from extraction of minerals from oil or gas wells or the sale or exchange of assets used by the taxpayer in this type trade or business. 2. Foreign oil related income (FORI), which is taxable income derived from foreign sources from the processing of minerals from oil or gas wells into their primary products, transportation or distribution of such minerals or products, disposition of assets used in the trade or business, and the performance of any other related service. *Exception:* Dividend or interest income that is passive income.

Basket	Income Source(s)
General Limitation § 904(d)(1)(I)	All residual income including most foreign-source income earned in the active conduct of business. *Exceptions:* 1. Financial services income. 2. Shipping income.

NOTE

The Effect of a Reduction in Rates. When the basket system was expanded in 1986, the U.S. had also reduced its corporate tax rate to 35%, giving the U.S. the lowest rate among its principal trading partners. This tended to put most U.S. multinational corporations in a position of having more foreign tax credits than they could use given the FTC limitation—a so-called excess credit position. Thus, cross-crediting became more important for those corporations—and more of a concern for the Treasury. Since the enactment of the current basket system in 1986, many other OECD countries have also lowered their corporate tax rates, and they are now generally closer to the U.S. rate and in some cases lower. Thus, the 1986 situation no longer exists, raising the question of whether such an elaborate defense against cross-crediting remains worthwhile, given its complexity and costs.

Unintended Consequences

Foreign Tax Credit Manipulation. Taxpayers have sometimes traded shares around the record date for dividends in an effort to shelter U.S. source income from U.S. taxation. For instance in *Compaq Computer Corp. v. Commissioner*, Compaq received a large capital gain in 1992 and sought to offset the U.S. tax on that gain with capital losses while it shielded dividend income with foreign tax credits.[10] To do so it purchased shares cum-dividend in Royal Dutch Petroleum, which had announced but not yet paid a dividend that was going to be subject to Netherlands withholding tax and thus carry substantial foreign tax credits. Compaq then resold all the shares within an hour at the lower ex-dividend price.[11] By that time the price had fallen by the amount of the dividend minus the Netherlands withholding tax. As a result, Compaq suffered a capital loss that was almost precisely offset by the dividend after withholding, but it also received large foreign tax credits. In effect Compaq purchased foreign tax credits for the price of relatively minor transaction costs. The validity of such transactions trading around the record date was challenged by the IRS in the courts. The Tax Court denied the foreign tax credits in *Compaq* on the grounds that the transaction lacked economic substance and any business purpose, but the Fifth Circuit reversed.[12] The following excerpt criticizes the appellate court's decision.

10. Compaq Computer Corp. v. Commissioner, 113 T.C. 214, 215 (1999), rev'd 277 F.3d 778 (2001).

11. 113 T.C. at 217–18.

12. Compaq Computer Corp. v. Commissioner, 277 F.3d 778, 787 (5th Cir.2001).

Daniel N. Shaviro & David A. Weisbach, *The Fifth Circuit Gets It Wrong in Compaq v. Commissioner*, 94 TAX NOTES 511, 513–14 (Jan. 28, 2002).

Historically, most tax shelters have involved the use of tax arbitrage to create losses that can be used to shelter other income from tax. However, shelters can work just as well * * * by arbitraging credits, such as the foreign tax credit, against phantom taxable income, with the aim of sheltering other foreign-source income from U.S. tax.

To illustrate a basic tax planning opportunity associated with foreign tax credits, suppose a U.S. multinational [is excess limit, i.e., the foreign tax rate on its existing foreign source income is lower than the U.S. tax rate so it could receive more foreign tax credits if it "paid" more foreign taxes without hitting the foreign tax credit limitation. It] makes a new investment abroad, earning $100 that does not qualify for deferral and paying $35 of foreign tax. This is a wash from a U.S. tax standpoint, since the credit equals the U.S. tax liability on the pre-foreign-tax income. Suppose, however, that the multinational could arrange instead to earn an extra $1,000 from a foreign business partner or counterparty, with the entire $1,000 then being taxed away by the foreign government. (The business partner or counterparty that paid it the extra $1,000 might, for example, be informally controlled or secretly compensated by the government that got the money back in tax revenues.)

All of a sudden, the American company would be clearing the same $65 in pre-tax cash as previously. However, it would also be reducing its U.S. tax bill by $650 (the $1,000 of foreign tax credits minus the $350 U.S. tax on the extra phantom income created by not deducting the foreign taxes). Any sophisticated observer would realize that this was a tax arbitrage, * * * even though it arbitraged tax credits against phantom income rather than current deductions against deferred gain. * * * [H]owever, the Fifth Circuit in Compaq would completely misunderstand this. Look at the big enhancement to the pre-tax profit (it would evidently say)—obviously this is a business deal, not a tax deal! [Compaq made a profit on the transaction if one measured profit before the Netherlands withholding tax *and* the U.S. tax because the post-dividend decline in the price of the Royal Dutch Petroleum stock accounted for the withholding tax. If one measured profit after the withholding tax but before the U.S. tax, however, the transaction was unprofitable. When the Fifth Circuit examined the transaction, it adopted the former analysis.]

NOTE

Congress Acts. Ultimately Congress responded to this particular scheme by enacting § 901(k), which disallows credits for withholding taxes on dividends when the dividend-paying stock is held for less than 15 days during the 30–day period beginning on the date which is 15 days before the date on which such share becomes ex-dividend. This rule renders transactions like Compaq's invalid. However, the Fifth Circuit's decision illustrates that the courts are not always quick to disallow such manipulations.

Allocation of Deductions

The foreign tax credit limitation requires that taxpayers compute both U.S. and foreign source income. In doing so, some judgment must be made whether deductions offset foreign or domestic income. In answering this question, it is not enough simply to ask in what country was the money giving rise to the deduction spent. The regulations require an allocation of deductions between domestic and foreign source income. As the following two excerpts illustrate, interest and research and development expenses have proved the most troublesome issues. See § 864 (e) and (f).

Martin A. Sullivan, *Interest Allocation Reform: Time To Talk or Time To Act?* 84 TAX NOTES 1223, 1223–25 (1999).

Under the U.S. system of international taxation, the worldwide income of U.S. corporations is subject to U.S. tax. To prevent double taxation, a credit is allowed against U.S. income taxes for foreign income taxes. But there is a limit on how much foreign tax credit any corporation can claim. The limit is equal to the amount of U.S. tax allocable to foreign-source income. If U.S. corporations pay relatively low foreign income taxes, the limit is not binding. These corporations—called "excess limit" corporations—do not worry too much about how their foreign-source income is calculated for U.S. tax purposes.

But for firms with foreign income taxes in excess of the foreign tax credit limitation—so-called "excess credit" corporations—maximizing foreign-source income is the name of the game. Therefore, the tax directors of firms with excess credits would like to be able to shift as much interest expenses as possible from foreign-source income to domestic-source income so that those expenses don't reduce foreign-source income.

Before passage of the Tax Reform Act of 1986, U.S. corporations could minimize interest expense allocated to foreign-source income by allocating expenses on a separate company basis, and interest expense incurred in the United States would be allocated entirely to U.S.-source income. It was possible for U.S. corporations to borrow in the United States, use the funds to invest in foreign operations, but not have any interest expenses allocated to foreign-source income. In the words of the Joint Committee on Taxation, this type of behavior resulted in "an unwarranted amount of foreign tax credits" to U.S. multinationals operating abroad.

The 1986 Act put an end to the most lucrative planning techniques. But it did not stop there. In the need for additional revenue, the Act installed rules that routinely result in an over-allocation of interest to foreign-source income.

The general theory behind the change was that money is fungible. According to the fungibility concept, interest expense—no matter where or for what purpose it is incurred—supports worldwide operations. But the 1986 act did not remain true to the fungibility concept. Interest incurred by foreign subsidiaries of U.S. multinationals simply was excluded from the allocation of interest expense between foreign and domestic income. So, if an affiliated group consists of two identical corporations—one domestic and one foreign—and each corporation incurs equal interest expense, three-quarters of the interest expense of the entire group is allocated to foreign-source income. [All of the foreign corporation's interest expense plus one-half of the U.S. corporation's interest expense.—ed.] This has become known as "water's edge fungibility."

The alternative to water's edge fungibility—and the starting point for efforts to reform current law—is "worldwide fungibility." Under this principle, the interest expenses of foreign members of an affiliated group are not automatically allocated to foreign-source income. Instead, they are put on equal footing with domestic interest and allocated worldwide on the basis of the ratio of domestic to foreign assets. By reducing interest allocated to foreign-source income, this rule increases foreign tax credits for excess credit taxpayers. The interest allocation rules included in the Senate version of the Tax Reform Act of 1986 adopted the principle of worldwide fungibility, but to save revenue it was dropped in conference from the final bill.

ECONOMIC DISTORTIONS

Under current law, borrowing by a U.S. parent and its U.S. subsidiaries reduces the foreign tax credit limitation. Borrowing by foreign entities, however, has no direct impact on the foreign tax credit limitation. This over-allocation of interest expense is more than just "unfair" to U.S. multinationals, it gives rise to a variety of economic distortions.

As is the case for any restrictions on the foreign tax credit limitation, current interest allocation rules increase the taxation on outbound investment by U.S. multinational corporations. In the simplest case, an excess credit corporation has excess credits because its foreign operations are subject to higher rates of tax abroad than in the United States. If the foreign tax credit limitation worked correctly, it would give the U.S. corporation foreign tax credits equal to the U.S. tax rate times its foreign-source income. In that case no U.S. tax—just the high rate of foreign tax—would be paid on the foreign income. But because interest allocation rules can artificially reduce foreign-source income, U.S. multinationals in effect must pay U.S. tax on foreign-source income in addition to the high rate of tax paid to the host government.

Of course, this makes it harder for U.S. corporations to compete abroad. And, as can be expected, U.S. corporations have unendingly criticized the current interest allocation rules. But interest allocation rules do more than violate the principles of competitiveness. They clearly penalize foreign investment and thereby violate the principle of economic neutrality—the principle that Treasury has often cited as a guiding principle of its tax policy.

The interest allocation rules also operate in a manner that discourages investment in the United States. If a U.S. multinational is in an excess credit position, any investment in plant and equipment in the United States financed with debt reduces foreign tax credits. Thus, the interest allocation rules increase the cost of capital on U.S. investment. This in particular has been a problem for highly leveraged U.S. public utilities investing abroad. * * *

Finally, the U.S. interest allocation rules distort financing decisions by U.S. multinational corporations. To mitigate the damaging effects of the current interest allocation rules, U.S. companies avoid borrowing in the United States and instead borrow abroad where they can get a deduction under foreign law without any reduction in their U.S. foreign tax credit limit. * * *

Two economic studies have estimated that the empirical effects of the interest allocation rules have some effect on the investment and financial behavior of U.S. multinationals. * * *

Despite all these problems, it is important to put the interest allocation rules in perspective. No doubt there are many situations in which the current rules result in rough justice for U.S. multinational corporations. But other provisions of U.S. tax law—particularly the ability to defer U.S. tax until income is repatriated as dividends—mitigate the negative impact of the interest allocation rules. In the aggregate, it does not appear as though double taxation of foreign-source income is a widespread problem. Data from the IRS Statistics of Income Division show that in 1994 * * * $26.5 billion in foreign taxes were paid by U.S. corporations and were offset by $25.4 billion in U.S. foreign tax credits.

Karen B. Brown, *Neutral International Tax Rules Allocating Costs: Successful Formula for U.S. Research and Development*, 1 FLA. TAX REV. 333, 334–53 (1993).

One example of important tax rules for U.S. businesses is the rules governing the allocation and apportionment of research and development expenses to domestic or foreign source income. Research cost allocation is a crucial determinant of the allowable foreign tax credit for multinational businesses. * * * Because the credit against U.S. tax liability is limited to a tax computed at U.S. rates on foreign source taxable income, the Internal Revenue Code rewards the allocation of research expenses to domestic source income, which results in a corresponding increase in foreign source taxable income as a proportionate part of worldwide taxable income. In the past, Congress has employed international tax policy to stimulate U.S.-based research by enacting rules that favor U.S.-based research. Those rules were promulgated in response to complaints by the U.S. business community that the 1977 regulations resulted in an inappropriate allocation of research expenses to foreign source income, which resulted in an inability to obtain full credit against U.S. tax liability for taxes paid abroad. President Clinton * * * [proposed] allocation of all U.S.-based research costs to domestic source income. This article contends that tax rules should not provide an incentive for U.S.-based research. Accordingly, this article supports neutral tax rules that apportion research costs on the basis of income expected to be derived from those activities.

II.   ORIGIN OF CURRENT RESEARCH AND DEVELOPMENT ALLOCATION RULES

Section 174(a) of the Code permits a deduction for research or experimental expenditures made in connection with a trade or business. Research or experimental expenditures are those "incurred in connection with a trade or business which represent research and development costs in the experimental or laboratory sense." U.S. multinational businesses must determine the proper method for allocating and apportioning those expenses to domestic or foreign source income in order to compute foreign tax credit. Because of the foreign tax credit limitation, U.S. taxpayers prefer to allocate most research costs to domestic source income. Allocation of expenses to domestic source income will result in higher foreign source taxable income and increase the credit for foreign income taxes paid.

The current research allocation and apportionment rules derive from regulations promulgated by the Treasury Department in 1977. [Discussion of the details of the 1977 Regulations and Congressional moratoriums on their implementation in 1981, 1983, and 1985 and changes in 1986 have been omitted–ed.]

In 1988, Congress enacted new research expense allocation rules. The new rules retained the former government requirements rule of the regulations, which in general required allocation of research expenses to the geographical location of the political entity imposing legal requirements that necessitate the conduct of research. For all other research expenses, the rules allocated sixty-four percent of expenditures for research conducted in the United States to U.S. source income and sixty-four percent of expenditures for research conducted outside the United States to foreign source income. The remainder was apportioned at the taxpayer's election on the basis of either gross sales or gross income. Special provisions governed expenditures attributable to activities conducted in space and activities of affiliated groups. The rules were a stop-gap measure that applied for only four months of the taxable year beginning after August 1, 1987. The 1977 regulations applied to the balance of the year.

In 1989, Congress enacted Code section 864(f) to deal with the allocation question and to eliminate the necessity for periodic modifications of the 1977 regulations. The provisions contained in the new Code section were identical to those enacted in 1988. The rules adopted were not permanent, however, as they were effective only for taxable years beginning after August 1, 1989 and before August 2, 1990. * * *

Congress extended section 864(f) in 1990 and again in 1991, but failed to extend the provision in 1992. Consequently, those rules expired on June 30, 1992 for calendar year taxpayers. Commentators concluded that on expiration of section 864(f) the 1977 regulations regained control over the allocation of research deductions by U.S. businesses. In July 1992, however, the Service issued *Revenue Procedure 92–56*, which permitted U.S. taxpayers to elect to apply rules substantially similar to those contained in section 864(f) rules for eighteen months.

Eventually these rules will be replaced by permanent rules promulgated by the Treasury Department or enacted by Congress.

A recent proposal by the Clinton administration * * * offers two permanent proposals that affect research cost allocation rules. First, all expenses for U.S.-based research would be directly allocated to domestic source income, and all expenses for foreign-based research would be allocated on the basis of gross sales. Second, the tax credit for increases in qualified research expenditures for U.S.-based activities would be extended. * * *

III. U.S. TAX RULES SHOULD NOT FAVOR U.S.-BASED RESEARCH

* * *

In general, one must distinguish between the rules set forth in the regulations that applied before the effective date of section 864(f), the pre-moratorium regulations, and the rules set forth in new Code section 864(f), the post-moratorium rules. The pre-moratorium regulations provided a complex allocation and apportionment formula to be used by domestic and foreign multinational businesses. A fixed portion (thirty percent) of research and development costs was apportioned to income derived from the location of research activities. Under the post-moratorium rules of section 864(f), sixty-four percent of research costs was allocated to income derived from the location of research activities. * * *

Research and development is a valuable business activity. Government action to encourage that activity—by direct subsidy of research ventures—is appropriate and increasingly necessary in the competitive international business arena. Favorable tax rules allocating research costs also may influence research strategies for multinational businesses. The enactment of such rules, however, is not a valid means of stimulating research and development. The development of sound tax policy is informed by three important goals—maximization of revenue, fairness and efficiency. These goals have been neglected by Congress and the executive branch in the formulation of research and development tax rules. These goals are not and cannot be served by tax rules that encourage U.S.-based research.

This article advocates adoption of neutral research expense allocation rules that address these three goals. The expired rules described above failed because they resulted in an unnecessary loss of U.S. revenue, treated foreign and domestic taxpayers differently, did not respond to the needs of multinational businesses and ignored recent trends in the global marketplace. * * *

A tax policy that encourages the conduct of research activities in the United States represents mere chauvinism. Such a policy is misplaced because it ignores the growing trend of internationalization of industrial research and development. U.S. tax policy should permit U.S. businesses to secure the most efficient research and development opportunities whether they are in or outside of the United States. It should also support collaboration among U.S. and foreign businesses and academic institutions. * * *

Tax rules that favor U.S.-based research derive, in part, from an inaccurate idea that such activities will produce products that will wipe out the burgeoning U.S. trade deficit. However, despite the enactment since 1981 of a series of tax rules encouraging research in the United States, domestic research has declined and international research ventures have proliferated. Moreover, since 1981, the U.S. trade imbalance has steadily accelerated. The government has demonstrated no connection between exports of U.S. products and the location of research activities (United States versus foreign locations) by U.S. taxpayers. Finally, there is no nexus between the measurement of income appropriately taxed and the expired U.S. tax rules that set up a preference for location of the activities in the United States. Consequently, failure to encourage international collaboration places the United States in the unfortunate position of exalting a weak national interest (pride in U.S. ingenuity) over stronger international (efficiency and collaboration) and national (revenue and rational tax rules) interests. * * *

IV. RESEARCH ALLOCATION RULES SHOULD BE NEUTRAL

Congress failed to extend section 864(f) or to provide permanent allocation rules because it believed that the executive branch should adopt acceptable rules that appropriately balance concerns of both government and business. Some believe that Congress abdicated its responsibility to legislate * * * .

One may speculate whether Congress's failure to provide research expense allocation rules resulted from its concern about the revenue impact or its genuine belief that such rules are more appropriately promulgated by the Treasury Department, which is charged with the responsibility to investigate and propose a solution in this area. Congressional inaction in 1992, provides an opportunity to examine the failure of any branch of the federal government to develop effective tax policy. Examination suggests two needs: promulgation of permanent research cost allocation and apportionment rules that fairly link research costs to the sources of income generated and elimination of arbitrary location-based allocation provisions.

A fair measurement of income derived by multinational businesses that conduct substantial research and development requires the apportionment of research costs to gross income, gross sales or assets of the enterprise. * * * A rational tax system would allocate and apportion deductions on the basis of fair measurement of income * * * .

[My] proposal is that the rules eliminate allocation and apportionment of research costs based on the location of research activities. The allocation provisions should attempt to measure income of all multinational businesses, whether domestic or foreign, by attributing research expenses to gross income or gross sales of the business. Unlike the 1977 regulations, the proposal would permit allocation on the basis of gross sales or gross income without limitation. An alternative basis for allocation * * * would be the asset method employed under the current rules in which a taxpayer allocates interest expense to the source of income derived from the location of its assets (determined on the basis of asset or book value). That method of allocation is based upon a belief that research expense is fungible—attributable to all activities and property regardless of location.

NOTE

The Business Community's Perspective on Interest and R & D Deduction Allocation. Needless to say, U.S. multinationals agree with Martin Sullivan's recommendation for "worldwide fungibility" in allocating interest expenses, but they are not enamored with Karen Brown's suggestion that research and development expenditures be allocated on a worldwide basis relative to sales or assets. As discussed in the Karen Brown excerpt, President Clinton in 1992 proposed that U.S.-based research costs should be allocated to domestic source income. This would have provided an incentive to companies to perform research in the U.S. The American business community supported the proposal because—at least for companies with excess foreign tax credits—it would have lowered the cost of U.S.-based research. Under the proposal, this benefit would have been available only to domestic taxpayers. The Clinton Administration hoped to encourage U.S.-based research by U.S. companies in order to assist a proposed shift in military research activities to the private sector and to help U.S. companies competing in the burgeoning technology sector. In 1993, Congress rejected Clinton's proposed 100% allocation of U.S.-based research costs to domestic source income instead permitting only a 50% allocation. See § 864 (f).

4.4 POLICY DIRECTIONS

The following excerpt suggests that changes in economic circumstances may imply revisions of the U.S. rules for taxing business income abroad.

Council of Economic Advisers, ECONOMIC REPORT OF THE PRESIDENT 208–10 (Feb. 2003).

International Tax Considerations

The U.S. economy is increasingly linked to the world economy through trade and investment. Domestically based multinational businesses and their foreign investment help bring the benefits of global markets back to the United States by providing jobs and income. Like all firms, multinationals face a number of business decisions, including how much to invest and where. Because multinationals by definition operate in a number of countries, they also have to decide in which country to locate their headquarters, and their decisions in turn affect which countries reap the majority of benefits from the multinationals' operations.

In the context of tax reform, it is important to consider how changes in the international taxation of income would change the incentives for companies to locate production, intangible assets, and research and development in one country rather than another. Reform can have important effects on these business decisions and on the efficient use of the Nation's economic resources, affecting employment and the competitiveness of workers in the United States.

* * *

The rules surrounding deferral are the source of considerable complexity, involving a bewildering assortment of definitions and rules. Deferral is extended to income from active business operations abroad in order to provide an equal footing with other operating businesses in the same foreign country. Deferral of U.S. tax is not extended to income from portfolio investments and other income viewed as highly mobile. Consequently, certain income from portfolio-type foreign investments (for example, interest, dividends, and royalties) is "deemed distributed" and is subject to current U.S. tax. However, such income also includes various categories that are more active than passive, such as foreign base company sales and services income, income from shipping, and certain income from oil activities. [For more on deferral, see Chapter 5—ed.]

The foreign tax credit requires companies to make complex calculations in order to claim the credit against the U.S. tax on repatriated dividends. The foreign tax credit is calculated by "basket" or type of income (for example, passive, financial services, and general active income) so that excess credits generated on highly taxed active foreign business income cannot be used to reduce the U.S. tax on lower taxed foreign income such as passive interest. Over the past 30 years, U.S. companies have repatriated roughly half of the after-tax income earned by their foreign subsidiaries.

The U.S. system of taxing international income dates back to the 1960s, when the United States was the source of half of all multinational investment worldwide, produced 40 percent of the world's output, and was the world's largest capital exporter. From this perspective it was appealing to construct a tax system that was viewed as neutral with respect to the location of foreign investment by taxing all income and taxing it all at the same rate. However, this system is based on the idea that investment abroad is a substitute for domestic investment and on the assumption of perfectly competitive markets in a world with aggressive pricing and ease of entry, and with no brand-name loyalty, economies of scale, or other sources of extraordinary profits.

The underpinnings of the worldwide system have shifted, however. It is now recognized that most multinational corporations produce differentiated products and compete in industries characterized by economies of scale, thereby undermining the perfect competition model of the past. There is some evidence that returns on foreign investment surpass those on domestic investment and exhibit above-normal returns because of factors such as intangibles (brands, patents, and the like). Moreover, the United States is now the world's largest importer of capital and no longer dominates foreign markets. For example, in 1960, 18 of the world's 20 largest companies (ranked by sales) were located in the United States, but by the mid–1990s that number had fallen to 8. Companies can choose where to locate, and, under the worldwide system of taxation, unless the domestic tax rate is the same in all countries in which a company operates, the decision where to locate the company's headquarters will be affected by the countries' tax systems.

There is some concern that the United States has become a less attractive location for the headquarters of multinational corporations. Although multinationals operate in a number of countries, the Department of Commerce reports that the bulk of the revenue, investment, and employment of domestic multinational companies is located in the United States. In 1999 U.S.

parent companies accounted for about three-fourths of U.S.-based multinationals' sales, capital expenditure, and employment. Therefore, where a firm chooses to place its headquarters will have a large influence on how much that country benefits from its domestic and international operations.

———

In the following excerpt, a tax practitioner addresses the averaging of foreign tax credits. This article was written just before the expansion of baskets and tax rate reductions of the 1986 Act. Thus the tax rates described are higher than those now in effect.

Alan W. Granwell, *Calculating the Foreign Tax Credit Limitation on a Per Country Basis*, 27 TAX NOTES 567, 573–75 (1985).

The Conceptual Soundness of the Overall Limitation

One effect of the overall limitation is to permit averaging of taxes paid in high-tax countries with those in low-tax countries. Although the Administration may regard averaging as a potential abuse, averaging of bona fide foreign taxes imposed on foreign source income is a proper attribute of a foreign tax credit for the following reasons: * * *

1. Averaging is consistent with the conduct of a global business. In 1960, when Congress reintroduced the overall method as an alternative to per country, the Ways and Means Committee specifically recognized the appropriateness of averaging. The Ways and Means Committee then endorsed averaging as being consistent with economic reality:

> In most cases American firms operating abroad think of their foreign business as a single organization and in fact it is understood that many of them set up their organizations on this basis. It appears appropriate in such cases to permit the taxpayer to treat his domestic business as one operation and all of his foreign business as another and to average together the high and low taxes of the various countries in which he may be operating by using the overall limitation.

This same view was espoused in 1977 by the Ways and Means Committee Task Force on Foreign Source Income which recommended retention of the overall method adopted in the Tax Reform Act of 1976:

> In many instances * * * averaging of foreign taxes would appear to be appropriate. Many businesses do not

have separate operations in each foreign country but have an integrated structure that covers an entire region (such as Western Europe). In these instances a good case can be made for allowing the taxes paid to the various countries within the region to be added together for purposes of the tax credit limitation.

There is no inherent justification for regarding a country-by-country assignment of income as a more theoretically correct measure of foreign income-producing activity. As Congress has correctly observed (and the Administration concedes), companies do not organize strictly on a country-by-country basis. For example, a German manufacturing subsidiary of a U.S. company may well develop technology that it licenses to a Dutch or Japanese enterprise and may sell its products throughout Europe, Africa and perhaps elsewhere through branches or subsidiaries. The averaging effect of the overall method is consistent with the approach normally taken by U.S. businesses in making investments abroad—to serve broad geographic markets which may involve production, transportation and marketing facilities in several different countries.

Moreover, the rationale for the per country proposal does not necessarily reflect the international norm for those countries that utilize a credit system to avoid international double taxation. In addition, the complex tracing required in the per country computations has no parallel in any other jurisdiction's per country method. Thus, it represents a completely untested mechanism.

2.   Averaging permitted under per country limit. Averaging, in effect, has been permitted under the per country limitations previously enacted by Congress. In fact, this was one of the reasons Congress adopted the overall method as an alternative to per country in 1960. In that regard, the Ways and Means Committee noted,

> In addition, making the overall limitation generally available for foreign operations only provides treatment which is already available in the case of the so-called foreign base corporation, or foreign subsidiary serving as a holding company for its subsidiaries carrying on active business enterprises. In the case of a foreign base corporation the Treasury regulations provide that the taxes paid by its subsidiaries are to be treated as if they were paid to the foreign country where the foreign base company is incorporated, and thus aggregated for purposes of applying the limitation.

3. Averaging mitigates the disparity among different tax systems; the per country limitation increases the effective tax rate on foreign source income. The per country proposal will lead to an increase in the overall effective tax rate on foreign source income both because it will accentuate the mismatching of income, deductions and taxes and because of the difference in U.S. versus foreign tax rates.

Averaging mixes income from countries with statutory rates both higher and lower than the U.S. rate. U.S. tax rules have evolved by statute and regulation to accept averaging while denying credits for artificially high foreign levies or for certain types of income subject to manipulation for credit purposes.

Rather than just averaging differences in rates, however, the overall limitation additionally performs an inherently sensible role in adjusting the system under which a U.S. taxpayer operates to the infinite diversity of other tax systems. The averaging permitted under the overall method ameliorates differences that exist between the U.S. concept of foreign taxable income, upon which the credit limitation is computed, and the computation of the income tax base used by foreign countries. These differences often result in a mismatching of foreign tax credits with U.S. tax liability.

For example, if a foreign country grants a 100 percent cost recovery deduction for a certain class of capital property, the income base would be different for foreign and U.S. purposes and, assuming the foreign country's tax rates are equivalent to the U.S. rates, the taxpayer would initially have a lower effective foreign tax rate than for U.S. tax purposes. So too, a second foreign country may have cost recovery rules that create an initially higher foreign effective tax rate than the United States in the early years. Because of the differences in these rules, the timing of the imposition of foreign and U.S. tax will differ, thus creating the mismatching of income and resultant credits. Similarly, a transaction that is tax free in one foreign jurisdiction may be taxable in another jurisdiction. In these cases (and others) averaging minimizes the mismatching of income and taxes for the U.S. company on its aggregate foreign business.

The overall foreign tax credit limitation, through its averaging mechanism, permits the U.S. taxpayer to pay an overall rate of tax equivalent to 46 percent [now 35 percent—ed]. A per country limitation, however, may cause excess foreign tax credits. This could arise because of the way the United States determines its foreign tax credit limitation, i.e., by computing the limitation with reference to net foreign source income (gross income less deductions). For example, the United States has negotiated tax treaties permitting foreign withholding taxes on gross income (income without reduction by expenses). Indeed, in some important instances, * * * the Treasury Department has failed to obtain a concession reducing the excessively high foreign corporate and withholding taxes in a country in which there is a substantial amount of U.S. foreign investment. This discrepancy can cause inequities even under the overall limitation, but the overall limitation mitigates the harm because foreign tax credits generated in one country may be taken against income generated in another country (one in which, perhaps, little if any foreign tax is paid). Under the per country method, the foreign withholding tax (based on gross income) may well exceed 100 percent of the net income determined after applying Reg. section 1.861–8, and thereby create excess foreign tax credits. * * *

4. Averaging does not reduce U.S. tax on U.S. income. The overall limitation does not cause foreign income tax to offset U.S. tax on U.S. source income. Mathematically, that simply is not the case.

Example. Assume that a U.S. corporation has $100 of U.S. income and $100 in income from each of Countries X and Y. The applicable tax rates are 46 percent in the United States, 60 percent in Country X and 40 percent in Country Y. Worldwide income is $300 and U.S. tax before credit is $138 ($300 × .46). Foreign taxes would be $100 ($60 plus $40). Under the overall method the tax credit would be limited to $92, calculated as follows:

$$\$138 \ \times \ \frac{\$200 \text{ (foreign source taxable income)}}{\$300 \text{ (worldwide taxable income)}} \ = \ \$92$$

The U.S. tax liability is $46 ($138 − $92), which is precisely the U.S. tax due on the U.S. source income. The U.S. taxpayer has excess foreign tax credits of $8.

The present overall limitation thus prevents the credit from reducing U.S. tax on domestic source income and need not be changed. So, too, the per country limitation prevents foreign income tax from offsetting U.S. tax on U.S. source income. Thus, both limitations, in this regard, work as Congress intended.

NOTE

Schizophrenic Attitude Toward Averaging. As this chapter has noted, U.S. tax policy toward averaging of foreign taxes from different countries has swung from the overall to the per-country limitation and back again. The basket system, put in effect to limit averaging of income taxed at high foreign rates against income earned at lower rates is a major cause of complexity in the foreign tax credit limitation. In 1985, when Alan Granwell wrote this article, the Administration had proposed to curtail averaging by returning to the per-country limitation. In his introduction, not included here, Granwell states, "The basic premise of the [Administration's] proposal is faulty—namely, that the averaging effect of the overall limitation leads to distorted investment decisions. On the contrary, the overall limitation is the correct approach because businesses operate on a global rather than on a country-by-country basis."[13] This is, of course, an empirical claim, which doesn't directly address, or rule out, the possibility that corporate decisions about the location of business activities might be distorted by differences in tax rates from country to country, an issue discussed in the following excerpt.

Robert J. Peroni, J. Clifton Fleming, Jr. & Stephen E. Shay, Reform and Simplification of the Foreign Tax Credit Rules (July 6, 2003) (forthcoming).

In seeking to simplify and reform the foreign tax credit rules, it is helpful to identify the major sources of complexity. We believe that there are five fundamental reasons for the complexity of the current foreign tax credit rules.

First, the design of the foreign tax credit rules is not always tied to the fundamental purpose of the foreign tax credit. As stated by one of the authors in an earlier article:

> * * * The purpose of the foreign tax credit is to mitigate international double taxation and prevent such double taxation from discouraging efficiency enhancing cross-border transactions from taking place. Its function is not, and should not be: to provide a subsidy for foreign investment by U.S. persons, to favor foreign investment over domestic investment or vice versa, or to favor any particular type of foreign investment over any other type of foreign investment.

> Arguments by some multinational corporations and their tax advisers that the foreign tax credit provisions should be designed to promote the "competitiveness" of U.S. multinationals in the global economy are essentially claims that the U.S. tax system should subsidize foreign-source income by taxing it more lightly than it does domestic-source income. Those arguments have little to do with the fundamental purpose of the foreign tax credit provisions, which is to

---

13. Alan W. Granwell, Calculating the Foreign Tax Credit Limitation on a Per Country Basis, 27 Tax Notes 567, 568 (1985).

provide unilateral double taxation relief by the residence country. Moreover, these arguments in favor of skewing the foreign tax credit provisions in favor of "competitiveness" are often made with rather unconvincing empirical support for the claim that the foreign tax credit provisions of current law in fact are causing any competitive harm to U.S. multinationals. * * *

Second, we lack general agreement on which economic model (capital export neutrality, capital import neutrality/competitiveness, national neutrality, or some other approach) should drive the formation of the U.S. international tax rules. Therefore, in designing a particular international tax rule (including the foreign tax credit rules), we often make a compromise between, for example, a rule that effectuates capital export neutrality and a rule that effectuates capital import neutrality. Such compromises often result in the adoption of rules that are more complex, less coherent, and less effective than rules exclusively reflecting one economic model or the other. Unsurprisingly, the current rules reflect a schizophrenia in the tax system caused by the fact that the U.S. tax system reflects all three economic models and, therefore, contains examples of rules that in fact effectuate each of the three divergent economic models. * * *

Third, to a certain extent, complexity in the rules for taxing the foreign-source income of U.S. persons is a result of attempts to make the tax system fairer, more precise, and more economically efficient. In other words, in this as in other areas of taxation, additional complexity is the price we have to pay for greater certainty and equity and more economically efficient tax rules. For example, we could markedly reduce the complexity of the foreign tax credit limit by eliminating the current basket limit system and the current law rules for allocating and apportioning deductions for foreign tax credit limit purposes and by substituting in their place a foreign tax credit limit based on a specified percentage (e.g., 10 percent) of the taxpayer's foreign-source gross income. Such an approach, however, would rank low in an evaluation based on equity and efficiency criteria. As another example, the goal of simplification implies a reduction in the number of separate foreign tax credit limit categories but economic efficiency concerns push the system in the direction of tightening the foreign tax credit limit to prevent cross-crediting, thereby removing an incentive for taxpayers with high-taxed foreign-source income to divert other income to a low tax foreign country. Thus, reducing complexity cannot be the sole objective of any sensible tax reform legislation, but to achieve any significant degree of simplification we have to reduce the emphasis we place on other tax policy criteria such as fairness and efficiency.

Fourth, cross-border transactions themselves are very complicated and, because they transcend the borders of any particular country, such transactions implicate the tax systems of two or more countries. In addition, sophisticated practitioners in the international tax arena will design these cross-border transactions to take advantage of inconsistencies in the tax treatment of a particular transaction among countries, resulting in cross-border tax arbitrage. * * * The tax rules formulated to deal with such complicated transactions, * * * are not likely to be simple.

Finally, complexity results from the inconsistent conceptual foundations that underlie the U.S. tax rules relating to outbound cross-border investment. As one important example, the Code has two inconsistent approaches for how it views a U.S. corporation that owns stock in a foreign corporation. Thus, in some instances, under the deferral privilege, a U.S. shareholder is allowed to avoid U.S. tax on the profits of a foreign corporation until they are repatriated, thus treating the U.S. shareholder as the owner of stock in the foreign corporation and the foreign corporation as an entity distinct from its U.S. shareholder. By contrast, other Code rules, such as the indirect foreign tax credit allowed by Sections 902 and 960 and the look-through rules in Sections 904(d)(3) and (d)(4), treat a U.S. corporate shareholder that owns at least 10 percent of the voting stock as equivalent to operating a foreign branch operation and, thus, as, in effect, the owner of the foreign corporation's underlying assets and income. These inconsistencies lead to an incoherent tax system that is tremendously complex. The tax system would be much less complex if one consistent conceptual approach were used.

Radical Alternatives to the Current Foreign Tax Credit System and Its Overall Limit With Baskets

One way to think about simplifying the foreign tax credit provisions is to consider alternatives to our current approach for mitigating double taxation of foreign-source income. The current law contains an overall limit with separate baskets that reduce, but certainly do not eliminate, the ability of taxpayers to average high foreign taxes on one item of foreign-source income with low foreign taxes on another item of foreign-source income.

One alternative would be to eliminate the elective foreign tax credit of current law and replace it with only a deduction for foreign taxes paid or accrued. As mentioned above, allowing only a deduction for foreign taxes would move the tax system markedly in the direction of the highly distortive national neutrality economic model. U.S. taxpayers who engaged in foreign activities would end up bearing more total tax (U.S. and foreign) on their foreign-source income than on their U.S.-source income, except for income earned in foreign countries that did not impose any source tax on the income by statute or treaty exemption. Such an approach would, nevertheless, rank high on the simplicity scale. The degree of possible simplification can be quickly appreciated by comparing the Code provisions and regulations dealing with the foreign tax credit to the much more limited Code provisions and regulations relating to the Section 164 deduction for state, local, and foreign taxes. To be specific, replacing the foreign tax credit with a deduction for foreign taxes would:

(1) eliminate the need to determine whether foreign taxes imposed were income taxes in the U.S. sense or "in lieu of" taxes;

(2) eliminate the need for any indirect credit since only a foreign corporation's income net of foreign taxes would be taxable as a dividend to a U.S. corporation holding stock in the foreign corporation (i.e., the foreign taxes paid by the foreign corporation would reduce the amount available to be paid as a dividend to the U.S. corporation);

(3) allow the elimination of the foreign tax credit limit in any form and, hence, the elimination of the need to separate a U.S. taxpayer's gross income, deductions, and foreign taxes into various categories or baskets;

(4) vastly reduce the importance of the source rules for income items and the allocation and apportionment rules for deduction items, thus eliminating a major source of complexity in our current system; and

(5) reduce the pressure on the transfer pricing rules (at least from the perspective of U.S. taxation of outbound activity), thus simplifying compliance for taxpayers and administration for the IRS.

In addition, one could argue that a deduction for foreign taxes has more theoretical consistency with a * * * pure income tax system than does a foreign tax credit; although some other commentators vigorously argue that fairness concerns strongly support using a foreign tax credit as the means for remedying international double taxation. So if simplification were our only criterion for designing the U.S. international tax system, allowing a deduction for foreign taxes would be the way to go.

However, changing from a credit system to a deduction system would have serious negative consequences that more than offset any simplification gains from such a drastic change. Such a move would be viewed by foreign countries, properly so in our opinion, as the tax equivalent of trade protectionism because it would almost certainly (at least at the margin) discourage U.S. persons from engaging in foreign investment and business activities. Furthermore, such a move would not comport with internationally accepted norms for avoiding international double taxation and would require a revision or termination of our current tax treaties. Accordingly, those who argue that simplification concerns should trump all other tax policy criteria and dictate the shape of the international tax rules for double taxation relief cannot mean what they say.

Another alternative would be to eliminate the foreign tax credit and replace it with a system of exempting foreign-source income from U.S. tax. Such an approach would move the tax system toward the model of capital import neutrality and, at least on paper, would be simpler than the current system. Opponents of such an approach, however, would argue that such a system creates a tax bias in favor of foreign investment and the transfer of business activities and investment abroad to lower-tax foreign jurisdictions. * * * [T]o reduce the incentive to transfer easily movable capital abroad, separate treatment of passive income would be necessary (i.e., taxing foreign passive income, but allowing a foreign tax credit for foreign taxes paid on passive income). Any distinct treatment of passive income would reduce simplicity gains from moving to an exemption system. * * *

Yet another alternative would be to follow pure export neutrality and allow an unlimited foreign tax credit. Such an approach would be simple because all that would be required would be to determine the amount of the taxpayer's creditable foreign taxes. The source of the taxpayer's income and deductions would be irrelevant since an unlimited credit would be allowed without regard to whether the foreign tax exceeded the U.S. rate on the taxpayer's foreign-source income. Of course, such an approach would result in the United States ceding its taxing authority over even U.S.-source income to high-tax foreign countries (to the extent of the excess of the foreign tax credit over the taxpayer's U.S. tax on foreign-source income) and, thus, could lead to a substantial erosion of the U.S. tax base. The United States would, in effect, be subsidizing the public sectors of high-tax foreign countries, which could impose tax rates in excess of the U.S. tax rate without suffering any loss of U.S. investment * * * . [S]uch an unlimited foreign tax credit would be fully refundable and result in a substantial diversion of funds from the U.S. Treasury to the treasuries of foreign countries. No country to our knowledge has adopted an unlimited foreign tax credit and no country (including the United States) is likely to do so. * * *

Finally, another alternative to our current system would be a system that attempts to prevent any cross-crediting or averaging to any extent in order to minimize the effect of the foreign tax credit system on economic behavior. In theory, if this approach were strictly adhered to, a foreign tax credit should be allowed only to the extent that allowance of the credit does not induce a change in the behavior of U.S. persons to move business or investment activities abroad. Such a theoretically pure approach would require that we treat net income from each transaction (or narrow groupings of transactions) separately for foreign tax credit purposes and allow a foreign tax credit only for the foreign taxes paid or accrued on such income up to the amount of U.S. tax on such income. Any departure from this strict item-by-item approach allows a taxpayer leeway for averaging high foreign taxes on the income from some transactions with low foreign taxes on the income from other transactions and, thus, creates some incentive for U.S. persons to move business or investment activities abroad to low-tax countries.

Nevertheless, an item-by-item approach is probably not administratively feasible at any acceptable cost. Accordingly, some averaging of high and low foreign taxes will be tolerated; the issue is how and where to draw the limits on such averaging. * * * We recommend below that a per-country limitation be enacted, which will substantially reduce cross-crediting opportunities. * * *

Per–Country Limit

Under a per-country limit, a taxpayer separately computes the creditable foreign taxes paid or deemed paid with respect to each foreign country and computes the limit based on its taxable income in each country. Under a pure per-country limit, with no basket limitations within each country, no attempt is made to segregate the various types of income received within the same country and the cross-crediting of high and low foreign taxes on different types of income within the same country is allowed.

Because this limit prevents a taxpayer from cross-crediting the high rates of foreign tax in one foreign country against the low rates or no taxes in other foreign countries, it comes closer to achieving the objective of the theoretically ideal item-by-item limit than does the overall limit. Moreover, at a time when nominal U.S. income tax rates are lower than the nominal rates in many foreign countries, the per-country limit promotes economic efficiency by significantly reducing the incentive for taxpayers with high-taxed foreign income to move capital to low-tax foreign jurisdictions.

One disadvantage of the per-country limit is that it engenders significant complexity by requiring a taxpayer with operations in many foreign countries to make a large number of separate limitation computations. This limit may require a taxpayer to allocate income and deductions from integrated business activities, parts of which arise in several foreign countries, among the various countries. Thus, opponents of the per-country limit argue that it exacerbates the artificial distinctions made in any system of dividing income and deductions from a single business activity among several jurisdictions.

Furthermore to prevent a U.S. person from routing U.S.-source income through a foreign corporation to change the source of the income, a rule similar to Section 904(g) would be needed to look through dividends, interest, and royalties as to geographical source. Obviously, such a rule would be complicated in application, although probably not measurably more complicated than current law.

Under a per-country limit, a serious technical problem arises when a taxpayer's foreign-source income is taxed by more than one foreign country. The per-country limit may prevent the taxpayer from crediting foreign taxes imposed by a foreign country other than the source country. One solution to this problem is to apply a special source rule under which income having its source in one country but taxed in another country retains its geographical source, but any foreign tax imposed by it is considered a tax imposed by the source country. Needless to say, however, application of such a rule would be complex.

* * *

Another technical defect in the per-country limit is that it allows a taxpayer with losses in one foreign country to use those losses to reduce U.S.-source income while at the same time crediting foreign taxes on foreign-source income in other foreign countries against the taxpayer's U.S. tax liability. This problem was one of the major reasons that Congress repealed the elective per-country limit in 1976. This defect can be cured by adopting a rule similar to Section 904(f)(5) of current law that would allocate the loss from one country proportionately among all of the countries (including the United States) in which the taxpayer has positive amounts of taxable income. Such an allocation rule, of course, would not be simple in operation. Alternatively, a simpler way of mitigating this problem is to adopt an unlimited foreign loss carryforward with excess losses being usable only against income generated in the country where the losses arose.

The per-country limit does not eliminate the incentive for a taxpayer to shift passive investment capital to a foreign country provided that the investment produces low-taxed income sourced in the same foreign country in which the taxpayer has earned the high-taxed foreign-source income. To ameliorate this problem, we propose that the per-country limit be combined with a separate basket category for passive income from each foreign country. This limit approach comes the closest of all of these alternatives to the theoretical ideal of actual item-by-item approach to limiting the foreign tax credit.

* * *

[P]erhaps the complexity of the per-country limitation could be reduced by treating countries with which the United States has a modern tax treaty and which have substantial income tax systems as a single country for purposes of this limitation. Under this modified per-country limitation approach, a separate limitation would be computed for each other country not qualifying for this aggregation rule.

NOTE

A Response. John Steines, a NYU law professor, has responded to this suggestion of a per-country limitation. He contends that there are ownership structure techniques which corporations could employ to enable cross-country averaging, effectively skirting the intent behind the per-country system proposal. Therefore, Steines believes that such a system would likely add "complexity to the foreign tax credit limitation system and to the transactions it governs without meaningfully curtailing cross-crediting."[14]

In the following excerpt, David Tillinghast rejects a per-country limitation and instead contends that the foreign tax credit limitation could be simplified by streamlining the basket system.

David R. Tillinghast, *International Tax Simplification*, 8 Am. J. Tax Pol'y 187, 215–31 (1990).

Simplifying the Limitation Rules

Certainly the place to start in simplifying the foreign tax credit is at the point of its greatest complexity—the multiple

---

14. John P. Steines, Jr., Foreign Tax Credit Reform (Feb. 27, 2003) (unpublished manuscript).

limitation baskets that have been applied since the Tax Reform Act of 1986. In appraising how these might be restructured, it is well to remember why they are there in the first place.

Unless the foreign tax credit is applied strictly on an item-by-item basis, a high rate of foreign tax on one item of foreign source income may be averaged against the low rate of foreign tax imposed on another. In effect, the residual U.S. tax which would be imposed on the lightly taxed income is offset by the excess foreign tax imposed on the heavily taxed income. Philosophically, this seems inappropriate to some but not to others. In practical terms, however, the different schools of thought converge on a couple of points. The first is that a strict item-by-item matching of foreign taxes paid against U.S. tax is unadministrable. The second is that, as long as the U.S. rate remains relatively low compared with foreign rates, some sort of limitation on the cross-crediting of foreign taxes seems necessary. The U.S. taxpayer already deriving heavily taxed foreign income will prefer to earn lightly taxed foreign income, rather than U.S. source income, if he can average his foreign tax credits, since that foreign income can be derived tax free (or at a lower effective rate). Thus, the U.S. government sees multiple limitations as serving a need to protect its revenue base from erosion.

There are two readily apparent ways to deal with the government's concern, short of a full item-by-item matching of credits and U.S. tax. The first is to segregate all of the items of income that bear high foreign taxes from those that bear low foreign taxes. The other is to group items of income into categories based on their character, allowing taxes on like-kind items to be cross-credited but not against other kinds of income. The limitation system we now have, employing multiple baskets of income, represents one version of the second method. The discussion here will first turn to the simplification issues arising in this context and then will return to the issue of whether a high-tax/low-tax system would be preferable. * * *

Simplifying the Basket System

Since we now have a system based on limitation baskets and since for present purposes the system is by definition too complex, one obvious goal would be to reduce the number of baskets. The way to go about this, it seems, is simply to identify what features of the regime we consider most essential and which we consider most dispensable, retaining the first and discarding the latter until we reach the point at which other policy objectives argue more strongly than simplification for keeping what is left.

Before detailed consideration of basket simplification issues, it may be well briefly to consider—and reject—a return to the per-country limitation. Under this system, the limitation on the credit for a tax imposed by a particular foreign country was computed by aggregating all taxes paid to that country and all income derived from within its territory. There are several reasons why this system works badly.

To begin with, given the number of countries there are in the world, the per-country system can involve the computation of a very large number of limitations, at least for substantial numbers of taxpayers. To avoid simple manipulative techniques, dividends (and perhaps interest and royalties) received from a foreign corporation would have to be looked through as to geographical source; and it is not easy to make these rules come out right. Under the per-country limitation system, losses in a particular country reduce U.S. source income rather than for-eign source income from other countries, thus reducing U.S. tax overall while leaving credits for other countries' taxes unaffect-ed. And finally, grouping income by geographical source alone does not adequately prevent erosion of the U.S. tax base, since it is relatively easy for a taxpayer deriving income in a high-tax country (say, Germany) to create income from sources within the country that bears little or no tax (interest exempt under treaty, for example). Accordingly, even when the Reagan admin-istration proposed a per-country system, it also proposed to segregate the income from each country into baskets according to its character. The potential complexity of this proposal was staggering, and it was abandoned.

Assuming, therefore, that we are talking about worldwide categories of income, let us return to consider, first, some fundamentals of the basket system. As indicated above, two features seem essential. First, there must be a rule like the section 904(g) rule (although not necessarily that particular one) to prevent the routing of income through a foreign corpora-tion from converting U.S. source items into foreign source dividend or interest payments. Furthermore, we must be pre-pared to apply this rule—as well as any other hereafter adopted—to all foreign corporations at all tiers of ownership. Thus armed, we may start the process of elimination.

(i) Passive Income

Almost everyone's first choice to maintain as a separate limitation basket has to be the passive income basket. Of all of the things that can be done to generate lightly taxed foreign source income, none approaches the ease of diverting passive investments to earn income abroad. Not only is such income typically subject only to withholding taxes, frequently reduced or eliminated by treaty or unilateral enactment, but it also can relatively easily he derived in jurisdictions that have no income tax at all. A first priority, then, is to cordon passive income off from "business income," as the rest of the income world may be called. Once this is said, however, further consideration needs to be given to simplifying the contours of the passive income basket itself.

* * *

(A) The High–Tax Kick–Out

[T]he most promising simplification would be to eliminate the so-called high tax kick-out. Under this provision, income which is otherwise characterized as passive income is kicked out of the passive income limitation category, into the residual or business income category if the rate of foreign tax imposed on the income equals or exceeds the U.S. rate. The provision creates enormous complexity. * * * Under the high-tax kick-out it is necessary to identity income items (and provide rules for grouping them, if the test is not to be applied on a strictly item-by-item basis, which is an administrative nightmare), allocate and apportion taxes and expenses to them, determine the effective rates of foreign tax that result, and compare this to the applicable U.S. rate. A review of the existing regulation, which consists of several pages of text and examples, will indicate some of the difficulties involved.

That it is necessary to have the high-tax kick-out is far from clear. As discussed above, there is an identifiable rationale for preventing a U.S. taxpayer already paying high foreign taxes from affecting the foreign tax credit computation by the relatively simple gambit of generating low-taxed passive income abroad. But a taxpayer has no comparable incentive to generate passive income taxed at a rate in excess of the U.S. rate; in fact, it would be preferable to derive U.S. source income and bear only the U.S. rate. It therefore does not seem necessary to purge such income from the passive income basket to prevent the creation of revenue eroding incentives.

* * * Passive income is, above all things, highly moveable; the international portfolio investor seeks out situations in which withholding or other source-based taxes will be low or nonexistent. (The United States' own portfolio interest exemption is a testament to this.) Moreover, if the taxpayer in fact earns both high-taxed and low-taxed passive income, the rationale for disallowing cross-crediting within this particular category of income, while allowing it in other categories, is far from clear.

* * *

(B) Export Financing Interest

Under a special exception, export financing interest is carried out of the passive income category (as well as the high withholding tax interest category discussed below). While this rule has the stated purpose of assuring that the 1986 changes did not have "a negative impact on the volume of exports," its importance in achieving this end seems dubious at best. It applies, to begin with, only to interest derived from financing exports produced by the taxpayer itself or a related party. * * * [I]t is at least questionable how seriously exports would be depressed if the exception were eliminated. Alternatively, a broader and simpler exception rule could undoubtedly be designed, if the foreign tax credit treatment of interest on export financing were really considered a critical stimulus to that desired activity.

(C) High Withholding Tax Interest

High withholding tax interest, defined as any interest on which a foreign withholding (or other gross basis) tax is imposed at a rate of five percent or more, is carved out of the passive income category (as well as every other limitation category) and separately treated. This has a special significance for financial institutions, and this is discussed below. For other taxpayers, the effect is like the high-tax kick-out discussed above, except that the income which is kicked out does not go into the residual or business income limitation category but into a separate category of its own.

* * * For portfolio investors, however, that—unlike the financial institutions—presumptively are not relenders of borrowed money, five percent and higher rates of withholding tax do not seem like high rates; and in any event, the reasons for thinking that it might be feasible to eliminate the high-tax kick-out would apply in this case as well.

(ii) Elimination of the "10–50" Baskets

In general, when a U.S. corporation receives a dividend, interest, rents, or royalties from a controlled foreign corporation in which it is a U.S. shareholder (that is, an owner of 10 percent or more of the stock), the income item is not itself assigned to a limitation category. Rather under a lookthrough rule, the income is categorized according to the nature of the underlying income of the payor corporation.

On the other hand, a U.S. corporation which owns 10 percent or more of the voting stock of a foreign corporation that is not a controlled foreign corporation, as defined in section 957, does not (generally) apply the look through rule to such corporation but must segregate any dividends received from that corporation into a separate basket. A U.S. corporation owning non-controlling interests in many foreign corporations thus must create a very large number of separate baskets. This of course wholly precludes cross-crediting of foreign taxes on such income and contributes very substantially to the complexity problem.

This is of far more than academic concern. The principal impact is on U.S. foreign joint ventures. A lot of effort is consumed in attempting to transform plain vanilla 50–50 joint venture corporations into controlled foreign corporations * * * .

In many cases, however, these techniques do not work. * * *

The policy premises for the "10–50" separate baskets are hard to understand. [Congress in 1997 adopted a provision providing look-through rules and enabling companies to group all 10–50 corporations into one basket, effective January 2003– ed.]

* * *

(iii) Limitations on the Pooling of Business Income

While it is common to refer to a residual limitation basket into which a taxpayer's business income falls, in fact there are three such baskets, and these may be further intersected by a special basket. Depending upon the nature of the business or businesses in which the taxpayer is engaged, residual income may constitute: (a) foreign oil and gas extraction income (FO-GEI), which is in effect segregated under separate rules; (b) financial services income, which has its own limitation; or (c) income not described in any of the other limitation categories— the true residual income category, into which falls income from business activities such as the manufacturing and sale of goods, performance of nonfinancial services, active real estate income and the like.

It is at least highly debatable whether the segregation of FOGEI continues to be justified. The regime was originally adopted because of Congressional concern that the sometimes very high rates of income taxes paid by companies engaged in foreign extractive activities might in substance constitute economic rent (royalties) paid to foreign governments that owned the underlying minerals, as well as imposing taxes in their sovereign capacities. It was deemed prudent to remove these taxes from the overall pot, lest the petroleum companies (in particular) be given an irresistible incentive to utilize the massive excess foreign tax credits arising from their extractive operations by buying up unrelated foreign businesses bearing low rates of foreign tax.

This segregation of high-tax operations from (potential) low-tax operations is of course not the rule for the residual basket generally: a manufacturing company subject to very high rates of tax in, say, India, can still cross-credit Indian taxes with lower taxes paid on its operations elsewhere. The royalty aspects of taxes on extractive activities may have been thought to present unique problems at the time. Subsequently, however, regulations were issued under section 901 to deal with the royalty vs. income lax issue in the context of defining what (and how much) constitutes a creditable tax. With this protection in place, it is at least highly questionable whether the additional complexity of the section 907(c) segregation is necessary.

The idea of segregating financial services income from other types of business income apparently proceeds again from a concern about incentives to average income taxed at high rates with income taxed at low rates. Whereas the FOGEI rules focus on excessively taxed income, the financial services rule focuses on the fact that at least a great deal of financial services income is moveable, in the sense that a taxpayer has wide latitude in deciding the jurisdiction in which it will be earned, and therefore is often taxed abroad at very low rates. The volume of bank lending which has been routed in the past through Bermuda, the Bahamas, and the Cayman Islands, as well as the formerly explosive growth of tax haven insurance (and even more important, reinsurance) operations, can be traced to this circumstance. The Congress felt that permitting cross-crediting of taxes on income from these kinds of activities with taxes from manufacturing and other, more site-specific, business activities might give undesirable incentives for the combination of financial services businesses with other types of business operations.

The author is in no position to argue the economic merits of this decision. Obviously, the foreign tax credit would be simpler if the separate financial services income category were dropped from the limitation scheme. On the other hand, in the vast majority of cases, the financial services limitation will apply to all of the residual income, *i.e.*, income not subject to specific limitation categories, of an affected entity; in other words, most entities will not have income in the financial services income limitation and also in the general business income limitation category, although of course entities within the same controlled group will often fall on different sides of the blanket.

If the financial services income category is retained, however, serious consideration should be given to repealing the rule under which high withholding tax interest is kicked out of this category into a separate one. * * *

(iv) Pooling Low–Taxed Income Categories

The existing statute creates separate limitation categories not only for passive income, as described above, but also for: (a) shipping income; (b) income representing distributions from a Domestic International Sales Corporation (DISC) or from a former DISC; (c) foreign trade income derived by a Foreign Sales Corporation (FSC); and (d) distributions made by an FSC or former FSC out of foreign trade income. Although the legislative history is not illuminating, it seems clear that each of these categories was cordoned off from income in the residual category because it was thought likely to bear little or no foreign tax. What is not so clear is why it was felt necessary to separate each of these categories from each other. For the reasons discussed above; it seems highly unlikely that a taxpayer would go out of his way to create highly taxed income in these categories— voluntarily to subject an FSC, for example, to substantial foreign taxes (which would completely destroy the purpose of the special purpose corporation). Accordingly, there is no apparent reason why income in all of these categories could not simply be combined in a single limitation basket.

The only possible reservation relates to shipping income. In the author's experience, this is characteristically low-taxed income. But in principle investors might go into high-taxed shipping operations for autonomous business-related reasons; moreover, income that falls in the shipping category sometimes can be structured to produce early year losses, as in the case of aircraft leases. There may, therefore, be reasons not to permit such income to be pooled with the other categories of low-taxed income referred to above.

(v) Summary

If all of the changes discussed in this part were adopted, the limitation baskets would include only:

(1) Passive Income (including DISC and FSC related income), regardless of the rate of foreign taxes borne;

(2) possibly, shipping income;

(3) financial services income;

(4) all other income.

The passthrough rules would continue to apply, as would section 904(g). Income received by a corporation from a noncontrolled section 902 foreign corporation would generally be subject to the pass-through rules, but could be kicked out into the passive basket (with a cap on the related credit) if the taxpayer could not supply the Service with information sufficient to verify the passthrough computations.

This would not be a model of simplicity, but it would certainly be far less complex than the existing law.

NOTE

NFTC Proposals. The National Foreign Trade Council (NFTC) has also put forth foreign tax credit legislative recommendations. One example is the adoption of an approach in which U.S. interest expense would be applied against foreign-source income only when the debt-to-asset ratio is higher for U.S. investments. Another recommendation addressing the asymmetry caused by the recapture of foreign losses but not domestic losses allows domestic losses to be recaptured for multinationals unable to credit foreign taxes paid. Primarily, the NFTC calls for simplification. For example, like David Tillinghast, the NFTC recommends repealing the high-tax kick-out from the separate limitation for passive income, combining low-tax baskets such as passive, DISC, FSC and shipping baskets, and repealing the separate limitation for high withholding tax interest. See II THE NFTC FOREIGN INCOME PROJECT: INTERNATIONAL TAX POLICY FOR THE 21ST CENTURY 49–60 (2001) for a complete discussion of these legislative proposals. For another take on the foreign tax credit, see Chapter 5, which discusses an exemption alternative.

Chapter 5

Deferral and Controlled Foreign Corporations

5.1 INTRODUCTION

Taxation of profits earned by U.S. individuals and corporations from their ownership interests in foreign corporations is generally deferred until the earnings are repatriated to the U.S. shareholders in the form of a dividend or realized by U.S. shareholders as gain from the sale of shares. This postponement of taxation, commonly referred to as deferral, is a natural corollary of two long-standing principles in U.S. international taxation: the decision to honor the distinct legal identity of foreign subsidiaries and the principle of not taxing the foreign earnings of foreign persons. Any corporation formed with a valid business purpose is treated as a separate entity for tax purposes. The U.S. income tax consequently regards all foreign-chartered corporations as foreign persons even if they are beneficially owned and controlled by U.S. persons. Since foreign persons are not taxed currently on their foreign-source income, profits attributable to U.S. shareholders escape U.S. tax for as long as they are reinvested outside of the United States. Deferral along these lines has always been a part of U.S. international income tax law and is a common practice throughout the world.

This so-called deferral privilege is very valuable to U.S. multinational corporations. By establishing a subsidiary in a low-tax foreign jurisdiction, a U.S. corporation can essentially remove income-generating assets from the immediate reach of U.S. taxation. Although income accumulated in a foreign subsidiary will eventually be subject to U.S. tax upon repatriation to the domestic parent, the effective rate of this tax is diminished due to the time value of money. Over a long enough period of time, the present value of this future tax approaches zero and the U.S. corporation obtains the benefit of any difference between the U.S. tax rate and that of the jurisdiction of the foreign subsidiary.

Because of the ease with which U.S. corporations can establish foreign subsidiaries and choose their country of residence, opportunities for deferral must be limited in order to preserve the U.S. tax base. Without constraints, the deferral privilege would be easy to abuse through artificial manipulations of income, for example, by moving highly mobile forms of income to foreign entities in order to postpone taxation or by having related foreign subsidiaries report income that should properly be attributed to the domestic parent. From as early as 1937, Congress recognized the need to limit deferral and moved to adopt anti-abuse measures. The earliest of these was a limitation on foreign personal holding companies, companies formed essentially to earn mobile passive income. The most important and complex anti-deferral regime is subpart F of the Code's foreign income subchapter—enacted in 1962. Subpart F taxes currently certain income earned by a foreign corporation that has been deemed a "controlled foreign corporation" (CFC). Generally speaking, a CFC is a foreign corporation that is majority owned by U.S. individuals or corporations, counting only those U.S. shareholders who hold 10% or more of the stock. Subpart F specifies several categories of CFC income that are subject to current U.S. income tax; these types of income have typically been singled out due to the relative ease with which they can be shifted to low-tax jurisdictions.

The Code's anti-deferral regimes are also designed to discourage U.S. corporations from shifting income to foreign "base" companies located in tax haven countries such as Bermuda, Switzerland, and the Bahamas. A typical transaction of this sort is the use of a foreign base company as a conduit for the overseas sales of U.S.-manufactured goods. A U.S. parent corporation intending to market and sell its goods in Germany might sell them first to its wholly owned subsidiary in Switzerland at a below-market price, thus minimizing any profit realized in the United States. The Swiss subsidiary might then sell the goods to the German subsidiary of the same U.S. parent at a price that is inflated so that little German income would be earned upon ultimate sale of the goods at retail. This transaction results in the deflection of income that is in substance associated with economic activity in the United States and Germany to a base company in a low-tax jurisdiction such as Switzerland.

In the absence of current taxation by Subpart F (or reallocation of the income to the proper country through transfer pricing mechanisms discussed in Chapter 9), this income could be reinvested indefinitely in other overseas ventures with the proceeds escaping current U.S. taxation. Moreover, foreign base companies might be utilized in numerous other types of transactions that, in the absence of measures limiting deferral, would have the same effect of diverting income from high-tax jurisdictions to a low-tax jurisdiction. These include ownership of passive investment assets, provision of services to the parent and other related entities within the U.S.-controlled business group, making loans within the controlled group, and holding intellectual property for licensing to related entities. The common strategy employed in all these transactions is the nominal transfer of a multinational corporation's assets, capital and know-how into a base company situated in a low-tax country. These resources are then licensed, loaned, or resold to affiliated corporations located in high-tax jurisdictions, thus accumulating profits in the foreign base company—profits that are shielded by the deferral privilege from current U.S. taxation. As with the example above involving the cross-border sale of manufactured goods, these foreign base company transactions effectively divert income into jurisdictions with only an artificial connection to the actual taxable economic activity.

Because of the ease with which certain highly mobile assets can be transferred abroad, the U.S. tax base would be significantly eroded without constraints on the default policy of deferral. This chapter traces the development of Subpart F and other anti-deferral regimes in the Code, examines the policy debates about the appropriate scope of the deferral privilege, and discusses a variety of proposals before Congress in this area of international tax policy.

5.2 HISTORY AND OVERVIEW OF SUBPART F

Deferral has long been controversial as a policy matter; it affects the revenue to the treasury, the competitiveness of U.S. versus foreign corporations, the use of tax havens to shelter tax, and the rewards from shifting the source of various kinds of income. The following excerpt chronicles the policy struggles that have produced the complex and varied anti-deferral regimes we have today.

Keith Engel, *Tax Neutrality to the Left, International Competitiveness to the Right, Stuck in the Middle With Subpart F*, 79 TEX. L. REV. 1525, 1526–1551 (2001).

From 1913 through the 1950s, U.S. multinational corporations operated free from current U.S. income tax to the extent that they conducted operations through foreign subsidiaries. U.S. income tax applied to foreign subsidiaries only when they repatriated income to the United States. As a result, a growing chorus of U.S. multinationals began to shift their operations offshore. In response to the growing erosion of the U.S. tax base, the Kennedy Administration introduced groundbreaking international taxation legislation.

Under the initial Kennedy Administration Proposal, foreign subsidiary activity was generally to trigger current U.S. income tax for the subsidiaries' U.S. multinational shareholders. The aim of this Proposal was simple—global tax neutrality. Thus, foreign activities of U.S. multinationals were to be taxed at the same rates imposed on wholly domestic U.S. enterprises, ensuring that wholly domestic enterprises would remain competitive with their U.S. multinational rivals.

The Kennedy Administration Proposal faced serious congressional opposition, primarily on the grounds of international competitiveness. The opposition believed that the Proposal would have subjected U.S.-owned foreign subsidiaries to higher overall taxes than the taxes imposed on their locally owned foreign competitors. Thus, they believed that foreign local neutrality was necessary to ensure that U.S.-owned foreign subsidiaries would remain competitive abroad.

Both sides soon came to a compromise. Under this compromise (known as "Subpart F"), U.S. multinationals are generally subject to current U.S. income tax to the extent their foreign subsidiaries receive disfavored forms of income. These disfavored forms of income include income from passive investments, such as portfolio stocks and bonds. Disfavored forms of business income are of a more limited nature, mainly involving structures that shift income outside a foreign subsidiary's place of incorporation without significant economic cost.

* * *

Historic Development of the Subpart F Compromise

From the earliest days of the Internal Revenue Code, U.S. taxpayers investing abroad faced the same basic choice that they face today. U.S. taxpayers could either invest through a foreign branch or through a foreign subsidiary. Both choices have never been tax neutral.

In the beginning, foreign subsidiaries existed fully outside U.S. taxing jurisdiction without any anti-deferral regimes. The U.S. tax system initially accounted for foreign subsidiary income only upon repatriation to U.S. owners. Repatriation created fully taxable income with foreign tax credit offsets.

Early Measures to Prevent Offshore Movements of Liquid Passive Assets

The initial 1913 failure to impose immediate U.S. tax on foreign subsidiary income soon gave rise to tax avoidance. In the 1930s, Congress responded to these offshore shifts by adopting anti-avoidance measures.

The primary avoidance technique involved the use of foreign subsidiaries as incorporated pocketbooks. Under this technique, U.S. persons would form foreign subsidiaries in tax havens that would simply hold liquid passive assets (such as stocks and securities), producing income outside U.S. taxing jurisdiction. The income produced by these passive assets was subject to little or no tax by the tax-haven country and was not taxed by the United States until repatriated.

Congress viewed this technique as problematic. Holding liquid passive assets in tax-haven subsidiaries as opposed to direct U.S. holdings was of no significant economic consequence for U.S. taxpayers, and yet this noneconomic distinction yielded substantial global tax savings. Congress responded by enacting the Foreign Personal Holding Company regime. The net effect of this regime was to pierce the corporate veil of foreign subsidiaries qualifying as foreign personal holding companies. U.S. owners are now subject to tax on certain forms of passive foreign subsidiary income during the same year the income accrues in the hands of the foreign subsidiary as if the U.S. owners earned the income directly.

The Foreign Personal Holding Company regime targets only a limited class of closely held foreign subsidiaries. In order to qualify as a foreign personal holding company, the foreign subsidiary has to satisfy stock-ownership and income-producing requirements: (i) the foreign subsidiary has to be owned, directly or indirectly, by five or fewer U.S. individuals; and (ii) at least sixty percent of the foreign subsidiary's gross income initially has to come from certain passive categories. Thus, this regime does not reach foreign subsidiaries owned by publicly held U.S. multinationals, nor does it reach foreign subsidiaries with a preponderance of active income.

In the end, the initial deferral landscape for foreign subsidiaries was left largely intact. No further restrictive action was taken in the foreign area until the early 1960s.

* * *

The Initial 1961 Kennedy Proposal

While the political climate largely favored liberalization until the late 1950s, conditions had changed by the early 1960s. The United States was running a large deficit for the first time in many years, and U.S. multinational investment in foreign subsidiaries was suddenly viewed by some as contributing to this deficit. Still worse, U.S. economic growth in terms of the gross national product had fallen to approximately two percent from a long-standing three percent average. Meanwhile, other industrialized countries had recovered from the ravages of World War II, generating double-and triple-digit growth; even the Soviet Union was reportedly growing at seven percent.

In order to combat this relative economic decline, the Kennedy Administration adopted a two-prong Proposal as part of its 1961 recommended budget. The first proposal was for Congress to adopt a new investment tax credit to stimulate purchases of plant, machinery, and equipment for domestic industries. The Kennedy Administration, with the guidance of Stanley Surrey as the Assistant Secretary of Tax Policy, also proposed that deferral for U.S.-owned foreign subsidiaries be largely eliminated so that domestic investment would receive full tax parity with foreign investment.

Even more problematic to the Kennedy Administration was the growing use of tax havens to divert business income. The base company mechanism * * * was no longer viewed as a favorable mechanism of promoting foreign investment, but instead as a malignant mechanism to avoid worldwide tax.

The first and most notable structures of concern to the Kennedy Administration involved the diversion of income from high-tax foreign countries to tax havens. The primary example of this structure cited by the Administration involved a U.S.-owned subsidiary in Germany, which had a fifty percent rate that diverted income to a related company in Switzerland, which had an eight percent rate. The Administration regarded this diversion to the lower Swiss rate as an implicit tax incentive for business investors to operate abroad.

However, the Administration generally appeared to view transactions diverting income from U.S. shores to tax havens as a secondary concern to the larger question of global tax neutrality. While U.S. tax revenue was lost, these diversions effectively lowered the tax of operating within U.S. shores, thereby removing the incentive for U.S. multinationals to divert their operations elsewhere.

In specific terms, the Kennedy Administration recommended the outright elimination of deferral for foreign subsidiaries operating within economically developed countries. Deferral would have continued only for foreign subsidiaries within developing countries (who were still in need of economic stimulus). Moreover, even foreign subsidiaries within developing countries would lose the benefit of deferral if those subsidiaries received their income through profit shifting and profit extraction, which the Administration generally viewed as lacking any economic nexus to the country of incorporation.

The Legislative Debate

The Kennedy Administration's antideferral Proposal faced stiff resistance in the House. Certain members of the House Ways and Means Committee questioned the constitutionality of the Administration's Proposal as well as its potential adverse impact on international competitiveness of U.S. businesses.

Similarly, witnesses from the U.S. international business community raised the banner of competitiveness in opposition to the Proposals. While conceding that most of their competitors were from high-tax industrialized nations, these witnesses argued that these foreign competitors were similarly using tax-haven devices to reduce their own foreign tax burdens. Therefore, if the Administration ended deferral as proposed, U.S. businesses would be unable to compete with their foreign counterparts who would continue to reduce their global tax burdens through the tax-haven device. * * *

The Structure of the 1962 Subpart F Regime

The Kennedy Administration's concerns regarding tax havens ultimately became the centerpiece of reform in 1962. Repeating President Kennedy's declaration, both the House and the Senate announced their intent to "eliminate the tax haven device anywhere in the world," viewing the tax-haven device as one that "exploits the multiplicity of foreign tax systems and international agreements in order to reduce sharply or eliminate completely their tax liabilities both at home and abroad." However, Congress stopped short of ending deferral for all U.S.-owned foreign subsidiary income. The 1961 hearings convinced Congress that the Administration's more generalized antideferral approach would have placed legitimate U.S.-owned businesses at a competitive disadvantage.

The modified 1962 Proposal targeted only "tax-haven" income earned by CFCs (hereinafter referred to as "Subpart F income"), leaving deferral intact for the remainder. Subpart F income generally includes income from liquid passive investments, income from diversionary transactions (e.g., profit extraction and profit shifting), and income from related parties that is deemed to be a mechanism for extending deferral; each type of income is discussed below.

a. Passive Income

One major category of Subpart F income involves income from liquid passive investments (referred to in the Code as "foreign personal holding company income"). This category includes dividends, interest, rents, and royalties arising from passive assets. This category also includes the sale or exchange of property that generates these forms of income, such as the sale or exchange of stock and securities.

Congress targeted passive income because it believed that no rationale existed for generally delaying the taxation of foreign subsidiary passive income because passive income failed to create competitive business concerns. Congress was also well aware that deferral created an irresistible temptation to shift liquid passive assets offshore because the underlying economic earnings from these assets remained the same regardless of location. Subpart F treatment for these items of passive income effectively levels the playing field for foreign subsidiaries owned by publicly held U.S. multinationals with those owned by closely held U.S. persons, the latter of which were already denied deferral under the Foreign Personal Holding Company regime. * * *

b. Diversionary Sales Income

A CFC's sale of personal property generally does not create Subpart F income (referred to by statute as "foreign base company sales income") unless the sale both involves a related party and lacks any economic nexus to the CFC's country of incorporation. Restated in technical terms, the sale of personal property by a CFC creates Subpart F income if: (i) the CFC purchases personal property from, or sells personal property to, a related party (the related-party requirement); and (ii) the CFC neither produces the property within its country of incorporation, nor is the property ultimately sold for use, consumption, or disposition within the CFC's country of incorporation (the lack-of-economic-nexus requirement).

The net effect of the Subpart F sales rule is to eliminate the diversionary sales arrangements initially identified by the Kennedy Administration. The related-party requirement targets artificial diversions among members of the same group because income diversions of this kind have no underlying economic meaning. * * *

c. Diversionary Services Income

Subpart F services income (referred to by statute as "foreign base company services income") operates in similar fashion to the Subpart F rules for related-party sales. Similar to Subpart F sales, CFC services do not create Subpart F income unless the services both involve a related party and lack any economic nexus to the country of incorporation. * * *

1963–1993: Gradual Tightening of Antideferral

The Subpart F compromise for U.S.-owned foreign subsidiaries has remained largely in place since its initial 1962 enactment. Subsequent legislative changes have been largely peripheral with most of the changes from 1963 through 1993 representing a gradual tightening of antideferral.

Changes to the Subpart F Income Categories

Congress has generally expanded the Subpart F income categories since its 1962 enactment. In addition to the creation of the foreign base company shipping and foreign base company oil related income categories, Congress has expanded the passive income category.

Congress extended the Subpart F passive income category to include additional identified forms of liquid passive items, such as income from commodity sales, currency transactions, interest equivalents, and notional principal contracts. Congress believed that these items had the same liquid nature (with the attendant avoidance potential) as the passive income identified in 1962.

* * *

The Mid–1990s: Reversing Course

By the mid–1990s, the political forces favoring international competition successfully pressed their case that antideferral had become too restrictive. This political effort provided CFCs with relief against passive asset accumulations and for active banking income.

NOTES

1) *Compromising Between CEN and CIN.* Because Subpart F originated as a policy compromise between the Kennedy Administration's worldwide efficiency goal and the business community's concerns over international competitiveness, debates over deferral often continue to be dominated by the ideological rift between CEN and CIN. From the standpoint of capital export neutrality, the deferral privilege ought to be eliminated entirely since it distorts investment decisions by creating an incentive to move capital overseas to low-tax countries. Capital import neutrality, on the other hand, favors the preservation of deferral in order to ensure that U.S. businesses receive the same tax treatment as their competitors when operating in foreign markets. Subpart F could thus be viewed as striking a balance between these two positions by eliminating deferral with respect to certain types of income while otherwise keeping the deferral privilege intact. Over time, the anti-deferral rules have been relaxed and tightened, perhaps reflecting Congress's ever-evolving balance between CEN and CIN.

Beyond the idea of striking a balance between these two theoretical poles of international tax policy, it is difficult to find any coherent policy underlying this unstable compromise on deferral. Much of the legislative history of Subpart F suggests that Congress in 1962 was motivated primarily by the pragmatic goal of preserving the U.S. tax base and not by any fundamental desire to implement worldwide efficiency in taxation. For instance, the House Ways and Means Committee's March 1962 report on the proposed Subpart F legislation stated four objectives: "(1) to prevent U.S. taxpayers from taking advantage of foreign tax systems to avoid taxation by the United States 'on what could ordinarily be expected to be U.S. income'; (2) to reach income retained abroad that was not used in the taxpayer's trade or business and not invested in an under-developed nation; (3) to prevent the repatriation of income to the United States in such ways that it would not be subject to U.S. taxation; and (4) to prevent taxpayers from using foreign tax systems to divert sales profits from goods manufactured by related parties either in the United States or abroad."[1]

2) *Transfer Pricing.* An additional anti-abuse tool that has existed since long before the inception of Subpart F is the transfer pricing regime, which is presently codified in section 482. This provision authorizes the Commissioner to restate the prices charged for goods and services sold between related business entities in order to prevent tax avoidance and more accurately reflect the income of such entities. Under this reallocation mechanism, the government may administratively reverse pricing manipulations used to shift income into tax havens in transactions with foreign base companies. For a more detailed discussion of the U.S. transfer pricing regime and its enforcement, see Chapter 9.

5.3   SUBPART F AND OTHER ANTI-DEFERRAL REGIMES

The ongoing policy compromises on deferral have produced a stifling array of complex rules making up the present version of Subpart F and the several other anti-deferral regimes still in existence. Ostensibly, the function of Subpart F remains distinguishing between the "good" deferral of active business income and the "bad" deferral of passive tax haven income, singling the latter out for current taxation. Rather than establishing a general standard aimed at determining a taxpayer's motive in any given transaction, Subpart F accomplishes this purpose using objective and mechanical rules designed to isolate income typically associated with tax avoidance. This is necessarily an imperfect endeavor, and, as is often the case with bright-line rules in the Code, anti-deferral provisions are constantly subject to tax planning strategies that circumvent the statutory purpose while maintaining literal compliance with the law. Much of the complexity of Subpart F stems from the perpetual legislative process of grafting layers of new rules onto the original statutory scheme in order to foreclose particular tax-reduction opportunities. The following excerpt provides a summary of the Code's anti-deferral regimes as they exist today, leaving out much of the formidable detail of the statutory and regulatory rules. Consider the extent to which these various mechanisms serve a discernible common objective.

STAFF OF THE JOINT COMMITTEE ON TAXATION, TECHNICAL EXPLANATION OF THE TAX SIMPLIFICATION ACT OF 1993, JCS–1–93 (Jan. 8, 1993).

Since 1937, the Code has set forth one or more regimes providing exceptions to the general rule deferring U.S. tax on income earned indirectly through a foreign corporation. Today the Code sets forth the following anti-deferral regimes: the

---

1.   H.R. Rep. No. 87–1447, at 58 (1962), quoted in 1 National Foreign Trade Council, Inc., The NFTC Foreign Income Project: International Tax Policy for the 21st Century, Report and Analysis 49 (2001).

controlled foreign corporation rules (secs. 951–964); the foreign personal holding company rules (secs. 551–558); passive foreign investment company (PFIC) rules (secs. 1291–1297); the personal holding company rules (secs. 541–547); the accumulated earnings tax (secs. 531–537); and rules for foreign investment companies (sec. 1246) and electing foreign investment companies (sec. 1247). The operation and application of these regimes are discussed in the following sections.

Controlled Foreign Corporations

General Definitions

A controlled foreign corporation is defined in the Code generally as any foreign corporation if U.S. persons own more than 50 percent of the corporation's stock (measured by vote or value), taking into account only those U.S. persons that own at least 10 percent of the stock (measured by vote only) (sec. 957). Stock ownership includes not only stock owned directly, but also all stock owned indirectly or constructively (sec. 958).

Deferral of U.S. tax on undistributed income of a controlled foreign corporation is not available for certain kinds of income (sometimes referred to as "subpart F income") under the Code's subpart F provisions. When a controlled foreign corporation earns subpart F income, the United States generally taxes the corporation's 10–percent U.S. shareholders currently on their pro rata share of the subpart F income. In effect, the Code treats those U.S. shareholders as having received a current distribution out of the subpart F income. In this case, also, the foreign tax credit may reduce the U.S. tax.

Subpart F income typically is income that is relatively movable from one taxing jurisdiction to another and that is subject to low rates of foreign tax. Subpart F income consists of foreign base company income (defined in sec. 954), insurance income (defined in sec. 953), and certain income relating to international boycotts and other violations of public policy (defined in sec. 952(a)(3)–(5)). Subpart F income does not include the foreign corporation's income that is effectively connected with the conduct of a trade or business within the United States, which income is subject to current tax in the United States (sec. 952(b)).

Foreign Base Company Income

In general.—Foreign base company income includes five categories of income: foreign personal holding company income, foreign base company sales income, foreign base company services income, foreign base company shipping income, and foreign base company oil-related income (sec. 954(a)). In computing foreign base company income, amounts of income in these five categories are reduced by allowable deductions (including taxes and interest) properly allocable, under regulations, to such amounts of income (sec. 954(b)(5)).

Foreign personal holding company income.—One category of foreign base company income is foreign personal holding company income (sec. 954(c)). For subpart F purposes, foreign personal holding company income generally includes interest, dividends, and annuities; some rents and royalties; related party factoring income; net commodities gains; net foreign currency gains; and net gains from sales or exchanges of certain other property.

This last category of net gains from sales of property generally includes the excess of gains over losses from sales and exchanges of non-income producing property and property that gives rise to interest, dividends, rents, royalties, and annuities. Thus, foreign personal holding company income includes gain on the sale of property that was held for investment purposes, but does not include gain on the sale of land, buildings, or equipment that was used by the seller in an active trade or business of the seller [Reg. sec. 4.954–2(e)(3).] Stock and securities gains generally are treated as foreign personal holding company income. * * *

Income received by a foreign insurance company, including income derived from its investments of funds, generally is subject to taxation under section 953. * * * Treasury regulations specify that taxation of an insurance company's income under section 953 takes precedence over taxation of that income as foreign personal holding company income under section 954 (Proposed Treas. Reg. sec. 1.953–6(g)). When dividends, interest, or securities gains derived by a controlled foreign insurance company are not taxed under section 953, they generally are taxed as foreign personal holding company income under section 954. * * *

Other categories of foreign base company income.—Foreign base company income also includes foreign base company sales and services income, consisting respectively of income attributable to related party purchases and sales routed through the income recipient's country if that country is neither the origin nor the destination of the goods, and income from services performed outside the country of the corporation's incorporation for or on behalf of related persons. Foreign base company income also includes foreign base company shipping income. Finally, foreign base company income generally includes "downstream" oil-related income, that is, foreign oil-related income other than extraction income.

* * *

Certain operating rules

Income inclusion.—When a controlled foreign corporation earns subpart F income, the United States generally taxes the corporation's U.S. shareholders currently on their pro rata share of the subpart F income (sec. 951). In the case of a corporation that is a controlled foreign corporation for its entire taxable year, and a U.S. shareholder that owns the same proportion of stock in the corporation throughout the corporation's taxable year, the U.S. shareholder's pro rata share of subpart F income is the amount that would have been distributed, with respect to the shareholder's stock if on the last day of the corporation's taxable year the controlled foreign corporation had distributed all of its subpart F income pro rata to all of its shareholders. The pro rata share definition provides for adjustments where the corporation is a controlled foreign corporation for less than the entire year or where actual distributions are made with respect to stock the shareholder owns for less than the entire year.

In addition, the United States generally taxes the corporation's U.S. shareholders currently on their pro rata share of the corporation's increase in earnings invested in U.S. property for the taxable year. * * *

Distributions of previously taxed income.—Earnings and profits of a controlled foreign corporation that are (or previously have been) included in the incomes of the U.S. shareholders are not taxed again when such earnings are actually distributed to the U.S. shareholders (sec. 959(a)(1)). * * *

Distributions by a controlled foreign corporation are allocated first to previously taxed income, then to other earnings and profits (sec. 959(c)). Therefore, a controlled foreign corporation may distribute its previously taxed income to its shareholders, resulting in no additional U.S. income taxation, before it makes any taxable dividend distributions of any current or accumulated non-subpart F earnings and profits.

Allowance of foreign tax credit.—U.S. corporate shareholders of a controlled foreign corporation who include subpart F income in their own gross incomes are also treated as having paid the foreign taxes actually paid by the controlled foreign corporation on that income, to the same general extent as if they had received a dividend distribution of that income (sec. 960). Therefore, the U.S. corporate shareholders may claim foreign tax credits for those taxes to the same general extent as if they had received a dividend. Actual distributions by a controlled foreign corporation are not treated as dividends, and thus generally do not carry further eligibility for deemed-paid foreign tax credits, to the extent that the distributions are of previously taxed income.

* * *

Gain from certain sales or exchanges of stock in certain foreign corporations

If a U.S. person sells or exchanges stock in a foreign corporation, or receives a distribution from a foreign corporation that is treated as an exchange of stock, and, at any time during the five-year period ending on the date of the sale or exchange, the foreign corporation was a controlled foreign corporation and the U.S. person was a 10-percent shareholder (counting stock owned directly, indirectly, and constructively), then the gain recognized on the sale or exchange is included in the shareholder's income as a dividend, to the extent of the earnings and profits of the foreign corporation which were accumulated during the period that the shareholder held stock while the corporation was a controlled foreign corporation (sec. 1248). * * *

Foreign personal holding companies

In general

Congress enacted the foreign personal holding company rules (secs. 551–558) to prevent U.S. taxpayers from accumulating income tax-free in foreign "incorporated pocketbooks." If five or fewer U.S. citizens or residents own, directly or indirectly, more than half of the outstanding stock (in vote or value) of a foreign corporation that has primarily foreign personal holding company income, that corporation will be a foreign personal holding company. In that case, all the foreign corporation's U.S. shareholders are subject to U.S. tax on their pro rata share of the corporation's undistributed foreign personal holding company income.

Operating rules

A foreign corporation is a foreign personal holding company if it satisfies both a stock ownership requirement (sec. 552(a)(2)) and a gross income requirement (sec. 552(a)(1)). The stock ownership requirement is satisfied if, at any time during the taxable year, more than 50 percent of either (1) the total combined voting power of all classes of stock of the corporation that are entitled to vote, or (2) the total value of the stock of the corporation, is owned (directly, indirectly, or constructively) by or for five or fewer individual citizens or residents of the United States. The gross income requirement is satisfied initially if at least 60 percent of the corporation's gross income is foreign personal holding company income. Once the corporation is a foreign personal holding company, however, the gross income threshold each year will be only 50 percent until the expiration of either one full taxable year during which the stock ownership requirement is not satisfied, or three consecutive taxable years for which the gross income requirement is not satisfied at the 50–percent threshold.

Foreign personal holding company income generally includes passive income such as dividends, interest, royalties (but not including active business royalties), and rents (if rental income does not amount to 50 percent of gross income) (sec. 553(a)). It also includes, among other things, gains (other than gains of dealers) from stock and securities transactions, commodities transactions, and amounts received with respect to certain personal services contracts. * * *

Passive foreign investment companies

The 1986 Act established an anti-deferral regime for passive foreign investment companies (PFICs) and established separate rules for each of two types of PFICs. One set of rules applies to PFICs that are "qualified electing funds," where electing U.S. shareholders include currently in gross income their respective shares of a PFIC's total earnings, with a separate election to defer payment of tax, subject to an interest charge, on income not currently received. The second set of rules applies to PFICs that are not qualified electing funds ("nonqualified funds"), whose U.S. shareholders pay tax on income realized from a PFIC and an interest charge which is attributable to the value of deferral.

NOTES

1) *Coordination of Anti–Deferral Regimes.* Foreign corporations that meet the definition of a CFC under section 957 cannot avoid the Subpart F rules by qualifying as entities covered under another anti-deferral regime. In the case of foreign personal holding companies, items of income that are currently taxable under both this regime and Subpart F are included only under the Subpart F rules. Income that is includible only under one of these regimes but not the other is taxed without regard to the other set of rules. Under 1998 amendments to the Code, a corporation that meets the definitions of both a CFC and a PFIC is in most cases not treated as a PFIC. The overlap between these two regimes has thus been minimized, with the PFIC regime now having

somewhat lesser significance in curtailing deferral. It might be worth-while to consider, however, the use of the PFIC interest charge method as a broader means for handling anti-deferral under Subpart F. Repatriation is already discretionary for multinationals, and there exist substantial disincentives for it. See Chapter 7 for discussion of the PFIC regime, along with other rules governing the taxation of foreign portfolio investments

2) *Defining CFCs.* Since Subpart F only applies to foreign corporations that meet the greater than 50% ownership requirement, tremendous pressure is placed on this definition of "control." While one can argue whether the requirement for majority control by U.S. shareholders is necessary, it was originally adopted out of concern for fairness. To demand current payments from shareholders before profits are repatriated—and thus before the shareholders are in a position to pay—seemed unfair. Congress thought that only with a majority of shareholders could those who owe tax compel repatriation of the foreign subsidiary's profits by voting a dividend to fund the tax.

In order to avoid Subpart F, many U.S. corporations have sought to structure their ownership of foreign subsidiaries in a manner that excludes them from the CFC definition while still maximizing their control of the subsidiaries' activities. The Treasury regulations under § 957 reflect the government's efforts to challenge certain abusive varieties of "decontrol" transactions fashioned for this purpose. They make clear that formal ownership arrangements will be disregarded if the original parent corporation has actually retained majority control over its foreign subsidiary. The typical technique is an express or implied arrangement under which the new shareholders agree not to exercise their voting power contrary to the parent's wishes.

5.4 THE CONTEMPORARY POLICY DEBATE OVER DEFERRAL

As the previous discussion illustrates, Subpart F reflects a political compromise that has satisfied no one. Moreover, its immense complexity has created costly compliance and enforcement challenges. Notwithstanding the contested policy considerations and empirical claims, the interplay of deferral with the foreign tax credit provisions gives corporations considerable leeway to game the taxation of income earned abroad. The foreign tax credit is allowed either where a corporation earns income itself or when it receives either an actual or statutorily deemed dividend from a subsidiary. Both of these direct and indirect foreign tax credits are filtered through the foreign tax credit's basket system, and interest and other deductions are allocated to the income on which the foreign taxes were paid. Subpart F requires that certain items of income are taxed currently, but as long as repatriation remains voluntary, a corporation can make dividend payments to offset the Subpart F income in the same basket. A corporation, for instance, may repatriate dividends out of high-taxed foreign business income to balance a low or zero-taxed royalty payment, taxed currently by way of Subpart F and caught in the general limitation basket. By cross-crediting the high-taxed income against the low-taxed income, the corporation may effectively reduce the U.S. tax on its total realized foreign income. This is but one straightforward example illustrating that even extremely elaborate anti-deferral systems do not prevent entirely the kind of behavior they were enacted to curb.

The following excerpt chronicles how perceived abuses of the deferral privilege by U.S. corporations have sparked renewed debate in recent years over the appropriate scope of Subpart F and whether the regime continues to fulfill its intended purposes.

Keith Engel, *Tax Neutrality to the Left, International Competitiveness to the Right, Stuck in the Middle with Subpart F*, 79 TEX. L. REV. 1525, 1552–1557 (2001).

The current dispute between tax practitioners and the Service over the proper role of Subpart F came into sharp focus when practitioners began forming hybrid branches after the Treasury issued the "Check-the-Box" regulations in the mid–1990s.[2] Under these regulations, a foreign entity can qualify as a corporation for foreign tax purposes but as a branch (i.e., generally disregarded) for U.S. tax purposes. The purpose of the hybrid branch structure is to utilize an intragroup note to shift income from a high-tax country to a tax haven while simultaneously avoiding Subpart F.

A typical hybrid branch structure involves three U.S.-owned foreign entities: (i) a foreign holding company, (ii) a foreign active company, and (iii) a foreign hybrid entity. The foreign holding company and the active company (as well as the active company's business) are located in the same high-tax country. The foreign holding company forms a hybrid branch in a tax haven with the hybrid qualifying as a corporation for foreign tax purposes but as a branch for U.S. tax purposes. The parties then establish a creditor-debtor relationship with the foreign active company paying interest to the hybrid branch.

If the structure works as designed, the hybrid structure has a twofold effect. First, the interest payments siphon foreign taxable income from the active (high-tax) company to the tax-haven hybrid because the hybrid qualifies as a separate corporation for foreign tax purposes. Second, the transaction arguably avoids Subpart F by virtue of the same-country exception for

---

2. The Check-the-Box regulations essentially allow taxpayers to freely elect their entity status for U.S. tax purposes. Treas. Reg. § 301.7701–2(a), –3(a) (1996). In the case of single-owner entities, such as the hybrid, the Check-the-Box regulations freely allow taxpayers to elect corporate subsidiary or branch status. § 301.7701–2(a).

related parties. Because the hybrid branch is generally ignored for U.S. tax purposes, the transaction is deemed a direct payment between the foreign holding and active companies located within the same country.

* * *

Service Challenge and Ensuing Debate

In early 1998, the Service issued temporary regulations that essentially reverse the hybrid's nonentity U.S. tax status.[3] These antihybrid regulations treat the hybrid as a corporation for Subpart F purposes. The hybrid's receipt of income thus qualifies as Subpart F income falling outside the same-country exception because the interest is deemed received by the hybrid, an entity located in a different country from that of the related payor.

The new antihybrid regulations soon faced heavy opposition. Practitioners seriously questioned whether the Service had the unilateral regulatory authority to prevent the tax-avoidance impact of the hybrid structure. Practitioners also contended that the Service's interpretation represents poor tax policy vis-à-vis the intended scope of Subpart F. They argued that the hybrid branch structure merely avoids foreign tax, which is not a concern to the U.S. fisc. Practitioners also believed that U.S. multinationals need the hybrid structure to maintain a level playing field with their foreign rivals who were similarly utilizing tax havens to reduce their global tax burdens.

The Service responded by arguing that the antihybrid regulations were needed to protect the integrity of Subpart F because Subpart F represents a balance between global tax neutrality and international competitiveness, which the hybrid structure upsets. Stated differently, the Service believed that Subpart F's mandate includes the prevention of the avoidance of worldwide tax, "otherwise, U.S. businesses striving to be competitive in the United States could have been disadvantaged by tax burdens higher than those imposed on their multinational counterparts that availed themselves of hybrid structures."

* * *

Congressional Response and Service Compromise

Recognizing that the Service was not going to yield, practitioners soon began an intensive congressional lobbying effort to terminate the antihybrid regulations. Congress responded by proposing legislation that would have postponed implementation of the antihybrid regulations for six months for further

---

3. Reg. § 1.954–9T.

study. To avoid congressional action, the Service reissued the antihybrid regulations in proposed form with a June 19, 1998 effective date as well as a limited grandfather provision for hybrid structures entered into before June 19, 1998. In face of a potential further congressional moratorium, the Service retreated again, delaying the effective date to no sooner than five years after the regulations are finalized (the latter of which will occur no sooner than July 1, 2000). [As of June 2003, these regulations have still not been finalized.—ed.]

The heated controversy over the proposed anti-hybrid regulations demonstrates that the policy discourse over deferral is still predominantly couched as a struggle between CEN and CIN. For its part, the Treasury Department reaffirmed its longstanding position that worldwide efficiency in investment incentives is one of the pivotal aims of Subpart F. The anti-hybrid regulations underscored the government's willingness to pursue this norm even where there is no immediate threat to the U.S. tax base. After delaying the implementation of its regulations in 1998, the Treasury Department announced that it would conduct a study of the rules contained in Subpart F. In this report, which follows, the Treasury discusses the challenges to Subpart F and evaluates criteria and options for reforming the system. At the outset, the report lists several goals that should form the basis of any potential reform: (1) meeting revenue needs in an equitable manner, (2) reducing complexity, (3) minimizing distortions in investment decisions, (4) conforming with international norms, and (5) preserving the competitiveness of U.S. businesses. The following excerpt, however, demonstrates that—at least as of the end of the year 2000—the Treasury remained committed to furthering a policy of capital export neutrality above all other objectives. The excerpt describes various factors—including, most notably, changes in the global economy—which hinder the effectiveness of Subpart F and summarizes the government's conclusions regarding possible solutions.

U.S. TREASURY DEPARTMENT, THE DEFERRAL OF INCOME EARNED THROUGH U.S. CONTROLLED FOREIGN CORPORATIONS: A POLICY STUDY 62–99 (Dec. 2000).

CHAPTER 5
AVOIDING THE RULES OF SUBPART F

I. General

* * *

The purpose of this chapter is to examine generally the effectiveness of the specific rules of subpart F in meeting [its intended] goals. Subpart F attempts to achieve its goals through specific rules that are intended to tax passive income on a current basis and to prevent the deflection of income to low-tax jurisdictions and other special tax regimes. This chapter considers two illustrative categories of transactions that avoid the application of those specific rules.

II.   Illustrations of Techniques to Avoid Subpart F

A.   Hybrid Entity Techniques

The rules of subpart F are largely premised on the assumption that for non-tax reasons business will be carried on in corporate form (e.g., to limit liability). Even if this assumption still holds true in the foreign context, it is no longer true in the United States. As a result, subpart F can be avoided by planning techniques that exploit both the corporate focus of the subpart F related party rules and the failure of subpart F to address directly inter-branch passive income payments. These tax avoidance techniques generally involve the use of hybrid entities. A hybrid entity is an entity that is classified differently for U.S. tax purposes than it is classified for foreign tax purposes.

* * *

B.   Manufacturing Exception to FBCSI

As previously noted, [foreign base company sales income (FBCSI)] is income of a CFC from the sale of personal property that is purchased from, or on behalf of, or sold to, or on behalf of, a related person where the property is both manufactured and sold for use outside the CFC's country of incorporation. * * * One weakness of the FBCSI rules is that they may not apply to some types of transactions through which income from the sale of goods manufactured in a high-tax jurisdiction can be diverted to a low-tax jurisdiction, such as certain transactions in which there are no purchases or sales involving related persons. These transactions are illustrated below.

1.   Contract Manufacturing

The first technique relies upon the focus in the FBCSI rules on the owner of the property being sold. Thus, if at all stages in the acquisition, production, and disposition of the property from or to unrelated persons, only one CFC holds title to the property (although others may be involved in manufacturing the property to be sold), then the FBCSI rules will never apply. This is because there will have been no sale to, from, or on behalf of a related person.

Assume CFC2, a contract manufacturer, is related to CFC1, the selling CFC. CFC1 holds title to raw materials that are being processed by CFC2, and CFC1 pays CFC2 for processing them. CFC2 is incorporated and has its operations in a high-tax jurisdiction, while CFC1 is incorporated and has its operations in a low tax jurisdiction. The processing takes place outside of CFC1's country of incorporation. CFC1 purchases the raw materials from an unrelated party and sells the finished goods to an unrelated party outside CFC1's country of incorporation. If CFC1 had instead sold raw materials to CFC2 and then repurchased the manufactured goods from CFC2, or if CFC1 had purchased finished goods from CFC2, CFC1's resulting sales income would have been FBCSI.

However, in this case, the taxpayer takes the position that subpart F does not apply to CFC1 because there has been no sale to, from or on behalf of a related person. This is despite the fact that the group of related corporations has managed to reduce income in a high-tax jurisdiction by splitting off the sales profit into CFC1 and reducing the manufacturer's profit in CFC2 (for example, to a small mark-up over costs). Thus, the sales profits have been diverted within the group to an entity (CFC1) in a low-tax jurisdiction, in the manner that the FBCSI rules were intended to prevent. The taxpayer might also take the position that the amounts paid to CFC2 are not foreign base company services income because the goods are manufactured (and hence the manufacturing services are performed) in the country where CFC2 is incorporated.

* * *

III. Is Subpart F Still Effective?

The examples in this chapter show that it may be possible to circumvent crucial provisions of subpart F. In these cases, subpart F may no longer effectively prevent deflection of income. The next chapter examines challenges that subpart F faces now and will face in the future.

CHAPTER 6

CHALLENGES TO SUBPART F: ENTITY CLASSIFICATION, SERVICES AND ELECTRONIC COMMERCE

I. Introduction

The last chapter described how parts of subpart F may now be avoided, particularly by the use of hybrid entities. The creation of these hybrid entities are facilitated by changes in the federal tax entity classification rules. However, changes in the entity classification rules are not the only changes that have challenged the current rules of subpart F. The nature of business is also changing. Subpart F was designed and enacted in

the 1960s when the foreign business paradigm was a manufacturing plant. Since that time, however, services activities have
grown significantly as a percentage of the overall U.S. economy,
and this growth appears likely to continue. The treatment of
services under subpart F is already posing a number of challenges to subpart F. Further, it is possible now to perceive some
of the challenges to subpart F that will be posed by electronic
commerce.

* * *

III.   Subpart F and Services

As noted above, services activities are a significantly greater
contributor to the overall U.S. economy today than when subpart F was originally enacted, and this growth in services
activities seems likely to continue. Subpart F was designed
principally to deal with manufacturing industries operating in
high-tax, developed countries, rather than with service industries. The treatment of services is already posing a number of
challenges to subpart F. One example of these challenges is
provided by the financial services exception to subpart F under
section 954.

A.   The Financial Services Exception as an Illustration

* * *

Financial services income is by its nature highly mobile,
and it is thus often hard to determine precisely where such
income is earned. The statute attempts to address this problem,
for example in the context of "qualified banking or financing
income," by providing that the income must be "treated as
earned by such corporation or unit in its home country for
purposes of such country's tax laws." This provision was intended to ensure that the income be reported as earned for tax
purposes in the country where it was actually earned as an
economic matter. One weakness in the provision, however, is
that, although it may ensure that the items are included in
gross taxable income where they are actually earned, it does not
prevent subsequent deflection of this income for foreign purposes by some of the hybrid transactions described above. Thus,
the amount may be included in gross taxable income but not in
the actual net amount on which tax is imposed.

Additionally, the statute prevents all active financial services income from constituting foreign base company services
income. As a result, to the extent that active financial services
income can be earned in a low-tax jurisdiction, such income

(unlike other types of services income) is insulated from treatment as foreign base company services income.

B.   Conclusion on the Potential Impact on Subpart F of a More Service–Based Economy

Subpart F does not deal with other service industries in anywhere near the level of detail of the financial services rules. Nevertheless, despite their level of detail, the financial services rules do not sufficiently address the mobility of business enterprises or of income, nor do they adequately distinguish active from passive businesses. However, even if changes were made to deal properly with services within the current structure of subpart F, the result would be more complexity. Industry specific lists of factors indicating when a business is active, for example, would need to be produced and then kept updated. Bright line rules would be replaced by subjective facts and circumstances tests. This complexity is disadvantageous for both taxpayers and the government. Complexity may require taxpayers to spend more on compliance (or may discourage them from complying). Government may also be required to devote more resources to administering the system, and the complex nature of the law may hinder uniform government enforcement.

IV.   The Challenges to Subpart F Posed by Electronic Commerce

A.   General

The previous section noted the difficulties of applying subpart F to the provision of services generally. The ability of taxpayers to provide services (as well as goods) over the Internet and through other electronic media will present further challenges to the current subpart F regime. None of these challenges is entirely new. The increased commercial use of the telephone, radio, television, and facsimile has contributed to a trend in which the physical location of the provider of goods and services is less significant and more difficult to determine.

* * *

Electronic commerce may present challenges to the subpart F rules to the extent that such rules look to where transactions or activities take place. For example, the technologies underlying electronic commerce make possible new sorts of services, such as Internet access, and make easier the remote provision of other services, such as remote database access, video conferencing and remote order processing. With respect to all such services, it is difficult to assign a place of performance, a factor that is relevant with respect to certain subpart F rules. Similarly, it may be difficult to ascertain a place of use, consumption or disposition (another factor relevant in the application of certain subpart F rules) with respect to the sale of digitizable products, such as images and computer software, delivered electronically.

New technologies increase opportunities for CFCs to be incorporated in low- or no-tax jurisdictions. These technologies increase the ease with which employees of a CFC can be located outside the CFC's jurisdiction of incorporation, and increase the ease with which certain products and services can be provided to a CFC. They also allow CFCs to provide services to customers located outside their jurisdiction of incorporation with relative ease. * * * [T]hese developments together increase opportunities for CFCs to earn income that may not be subpart F income.

* * *

As planning opportunities become more generally known, offshore companies may become the operating vehicles of choice for many newly formed electronic commerce companies. In addition, many U.S. electronic commerce companies are relatively new. Therefore, it may be possible for them to move offshore without incurring a significant tax liability. These developments, taken together, may pose greater challenges to subpart F in the future.

V.   Conclusions Relating to Challenges to Subpart F

* * * [S]ubpart F was intended to address a systemic problem in the U.S. tax system that created inequity and caused tax base erosion. Many of the specific rules of subpart F, however, may no longer operate effectively. In addition, weaknesses in these rules are exacerbated by the new entity classification rules, which have facilitated the creation of hybrid entities. The growth in service industries is creating new issues that may be difficult to resolve without adding considerable complexity to the subpart F rules. The challenges that will be posed by electronic commerce and the Internet are only just beginning to emerge. Thus, although the policies underlying subpart F may be as important (or more important) today as they were in 1962 (when subpart F was enacted), new developments are already challenging the effectiveness of subpart F, and these challenges seem likely to increase in the future.

* * *

CHAPTER 8
RESTATEMENT OF CONCLUSIONS
* * *

Competitiveness and the Taxation of Foreign Income

Chapter 4 considered the issue of multinational competitiveness. The chapter first noted that promoting multinational competitiveness may conflict with the goal of promoting economic welfare. It then attempted to evaluate the effect of subpart F on competitiveness and concluded that the available data do not provide a reliable basis for evaluating whether subpart F has had a significant effect on multinational competitiveness. Although some have attempted to use statistics selectively in an attempt to show a decline in U.S. competitiveness, there is no convincing evidence of such a decline, nor is there convincing evidence regarding what impact, if any, subpart F may have had on these figures. Further, there are many other statistics that appear to show, generally, that the U.S. economy is highly competitive.

* * *

Considering Options for Change

Chapter 7 discussed several options for the reform of subpart F. Although the chapter made no specific recommendations, it noted that any subsequent reform of subpart F should be guided by the fundamental goals of international tax policy as those goals were developed from the conclusions of this study. Thus, Chapter 7 concluded, generally, that to further the goal of equity, an anti-deferral regime should contribute to the even apportionment of the tax burden between income from domestic and foreign investment, it should tax passive income on a current basis, and it should avoid inappropriate distinctions between the conduct of business in corporate form and the conduct of business in non-corporate form. To promote the goal of economic efficiency, an anti-deferral regime generally should reduce the tax disparity between income from U.S. and foreign investment. To promote simplicity and administrability, an anti-deferral regime should provide a clear, simple and coherent distinction between passive and active income, and should use a more comprehensive approach in targeting income subject to the anti-deferral rules. To promote the goal of consistency with international norms, a broad range of anti-deferral regimes are possible, although any such regime should avoid rules that may lead to international double taxation or double non-taxation or that radically increase administrative burdens. Chapter 7 also noted that the impact of an anti-deferral regime on multinational competitiveness is a relevant factor but should not be considered in isolation, as it may conflict with the fundamental policy goals of equity and efficiency.

Summary of Conclusions

Subpart F was intended to address problems arising from incompatible features of U.S. tax law. These features are still incompatible and still in place. The problems they create still exist, and the need to address these problems is perhaps greater than ever. Because of changes in other areas of the law and changes in the nature of business, however, in significant ways subpart F may not effectively address these problems, and it may become less effective in the future.

A careful review of the economic literature reveals that capital export neutrality, which provides that U.S. and foreign income should be taxed at the same rates, is probably the best policy when the goal is to maximize economic welfare (although the foreign-to-foreign related party rules of subpart F may not be maximally efficient in all cases). Therefore, preventing significant tax disparity should remain an important goal.

An anti-deferral regime continues to be needed to prevent significant disparity between the rates of tax on U.S. and foreign income, thereby promoting efficiency, preserving the tax base and promoting equity.

NOTE

Continued Preeminence of CEN. As Chapter 8 of Treasury's Subpart F study makes clear, the Treasury Department dismisses multinational competitiveness as a guiding justification in Subpart F reform, and suggests that it might conflict with other policy goals. Indeed, most of the other stated goals are largely ignored by the study or conflated with the objectives of CEN. Equity, for example, is treated as identical to capital export neutrality, requiring that "the tax burden should be imposed equally on all income, without regard to its source," with Treasury noting that a "more detailed analysis of equity concepts in international taxation is beyond the scope of this study."[4] The report also places little emphasis on the goal of simplification, apart from claiming that an elimination of deferral would be simpler than the present regime.[5] Recognizing a goal of conforming with international norms, however, the Treasury stops short of proposing a complete repeal of the deferral privilege; none of the United States's trading partners has adopted such a strong anti-deferral policy.

As the following excerpt illustrates, some academic commentators have gone further than the Treasury Department in advocating an anti-deferral regime that conforms more closely to the precepts of CEN. They contend that eliminating deferral altogether would be the most effective solution to the problems plaguing Subpart F.

4. U.S. Treasury Department, The Deferral of Income Earned Through U.S. Controlled Foreign Corporations: A Policy Study at 82–83 n.3 (2000).

5. Id. at 90.

Robert J. Peroni, *Back to the Future: A Path to Progressive Reform of the U.S. International Income Tax Rules*, 51 U. Miami L. Rev. 975, 986–989 (1997).

The deferral principle is one of the most significant elements complicating the U.S. international tax system.* * * To combat abuse of that principle, the United States has enacted a series of extremely complex and somewhat overlapping anti-deferral regimes, which have provided much work for tax attorneys, accountants, and treatise authors * * * . Yet, despite this myriad of complex anti-deferral regimes, the basic principle of deferral remains, a principle that substantially undercuts the fairness and efficiency of the U.S. tax system.

The deferral principle undercuts tax fairness by allowing U.S. persons to avoid paying current U.S. tax on their economic income earned through foreign corporations conducting business operations in low-tax foreign countries, while U.S. persons with the same amounts of economic income earned directly through a branch operation abroad or through a business conducted in the United States must pay current U.S. tax on their income. Moreover, the deferral principle encourages U.S. persons to shift investments to low-tax foreign countries in violation of capital export neutrality, thereby reducing worldwide economic welfare.

The complicated web of anti-deferral regimes of current law represents a compromise between ending deferral altogether and allowing deferral of income earned through foreign corporations without limitation. Congress has tinkered with the anti-deferral regimes over the years by tightening up the definition of Subpart F income in the CFC provisions and adding new anti-deferral regimes, as in 1986 with the introduction of the PFIC regime. The tinkering, however, has only made the system more complex without significantly eliminating the problems caused by the deferral principle. As a result, a ridiculously complicated set of rules has evolved that makes deferral elective for the well-advised U.S. taxpayer and creates traps for the unwary. For example, a U.S. corporation is likely to elect branch status for a foreign entity with income earned in a high-tax foreign country where a foreign tax credit will offset any U.S. tax on the income. A U.S. corporation is also likely to elect branch status for a foreign entity with losses so that the losses can offset the U.S. corporation's income.

The elective nature of the deferral principle has been fortified and made more explicit by the Treasury Department's recent adoption of the so-called check-the-box entity classification system. Under this system, U.S. persons operating abroad through foreign entities other than per se foreign corporations, will more readily be able to elect deferral of U.S. tax on their foreign source income by choosing whether to have the foreign entities treated as corporations or partnerships (or branches in the case of an entity with a single owner) for tax purposes. This essentially elective deferral system is unacceptable from a policy point of view and needs to be changed in order to accomplish any significant reform of the U.S. international tax system.

Less radical proposals have been advanced to simplify the anti-deferral regimes by expanding the definition of Subpart F income in the CFC provisions and combining the other anti-deferral regimes aimed primarily at passive income into one or two unified regimes. These efforts might achieve some marginal improvement over the current law, but I believe that more radical reform of the anti-deferral regimes is necessary. At a minimum, it is time to repeal deferral for U.S. shareholders of CFCs and reformulate the PFIC provisions to constitute the only anti-deferral regime aimed primarily at passive income earned by U.S. persons through non-controlled foreign corporations.

Undoubtedly, U.S. multinationals and commentators who advocate the capital import neutrality standard would oppose any proposal to repeal deferral for CFCs on the ground that repealing deferral would substantially impair the international competitiveness of U.S. persons operating businesses abroad. They would argue that repeal of deferral would impose an extra cost (a current U.S. tax) on U.S. multinationals operating in low-tax foreign countries—a cost not borne by their competitors from countries which allow deferral or use a territorial system for taxing foreign source income—and, would, thus, erode their competitive position in the global economy. However, this argument assumes that firms from different countries have to pay the same tax rate in the host country for international investment to be allocated efficiently—an assumption that is incorrect. As stated by Jane Gravelle:

> [Arguments against further restricting deferral focus] on a vague term—"competitiveness"—when what should really be considered is efficiency. There is no reason that firms from different countries need to pay the same tax rate in a location for investment to be allocated efficiently; the important thing is for a firm to face the same tax rate wherever its location. If firms face the same tax rate in each location and earn the same after-tax return in each location, their pretax return on their marginal investments will be equal. The pretax return measures the true economic productivity of capital.

We are operating in a second-best world because other countries, like ourselves, do not tax currently the returns of their firms in foreign jurisdictions. All marginal investments by foreign firms in tax haven countries, therefore, tend to have lower pretax returns than investments in higher tax rate countries. Regardless of what these other firms do, it is more efficient for our firms to move some investment back to the United States, when tax rates are lower abroad, if they are earning a lower rate of pretax return tax in the tax haven and thus are less productive than an investment in the United States.

NOTE

U.S. Multinationals Weigh In. In sharp contrast to both the views of the Treasury Department expressed in its Subpart F report and of Professor Peroni, the U.S. multinational business community has lobbied aggressively for a liberalization of the Subpart F rules to broaden the deferral privilege. The argument for this policy direction is rooted in familiar notions of competitiveness and capital import neutrality. Responding to the Treasury's anti-hybrid regulations and Subpart F study, the National Foreign Trade Council (NFTC), an association of U.S. multinational corporations, released its own report on Subpart F reform in 2001. As with the Treasury study, the NFTC report acknowledges the worldwide economic changes that have occurred since the enactment of Subpart F and agrees that the present regime fails to accomplish its original purposes. Yet, as the following excerpt shows, the NFTC draws entirely different conclusions about the correct path for reforming U.S. anti-deferral policy.

1 NATIONAL FOREIGN TRADE COUNCIL, INC., THE NFTC FOREIGN INCOME PROJECT: INTERNATIONAL TAX POLICY FOR THE 21ST CENTURY, REPORT AND ANALYSIS 67–127 (2001).

Chapter 4

Other Countries' Approaches to Anti–Deferral Policy

This chapter compares selected portions of the anti-deferral regimes of Canada, France, Germany, Japan, the Netherlands, and the United Kingdom with that of the United States. * * * The comparison illustrates that, in several important areas, the U.S. controlled foreign corporation (CFC) provisions in subpart F are harsher than the rules in the foreign countries' comparable regimes. The comparison is important, not because it implies that the United States should join a "race to the bottom," but because it demonstrates that the rest of the developed world has not joined the United States in a "race to the top."

U.S. government officials, have increasingly criticized suggestions that U.S. taxation of international business be relaxed. Their criticism either directly or implicitly accuses proponents of such relaxation of advocating an unwarranted reaction to "harmful tax competition" by joining a race to the bottom. * * * The inference is unwarranted. The CFC regimes enacted by these countries all were enacted in response to and after several years of scrutiny of the U.S. subpart F regime. They reflect a careful study of the impact of subpart F and, in every case, include some significant refinements of the U.S. rules. Each regime has been in place long enough for each respective government to study its operation and to conclude whether it is either too harsh or too liberal. While each jurisdiction has approached CFC issues somewhat differently, each has adopted a regime that, in at least some important respects, is less harsh than subpart F. The proper inference to draw from this comparison is that the United States has tried to lead and, while many have followed, none has followed quite as far as the United States has gone. A relaxation of subpart F to the *highest* common denominator among other countries' CFC regimes would help redress the competitive imbalance created by subpart F without contributing to a race to the bottom. * * *

Some of these regimes may also, in fact, be stricter than the U.S. subpart F regime in certain respects. This chapter has not exhaustively examined each of the CFC regimes to identify all the differences between them and subpart F. * * * Nevertheless, this chapter reveals * * * that the U.S. regime is almost always the harshest, sometimes by a wide margin. * * *

Table 4–1a. Summary of Examples

Country	Active financial services income from unrelated parties	Active financial services income from related parties	Engaged in active business-dividend from subsidiary in another country	Holding company dividend from active subsidiary in another country
Canada	Deferred	Deferred	Deferred	Deferred
France	Deferred	Deferred	Deferred	Attributed, but gets 100% participation exemption
Germany	Deferred	Taxed currently	Deferred if holdings are commercially related to its own active business	Taxed currently unless it would have been exempt to parent

Country	Active financial services income from unrelated parties	Active financial services income from related parties	Engaged in active business-dividend from subsidiary in another country	Holding company dividend from active subsidiary in another country
Japan	Deferred	Taxed currently	Deferred	Taxed currently
Netherlands	Deferred	Deferred	Deferred	Deferred
United Kingdom	Not taxed currently	Taxed currently	Deferred	Deferred if CFC has a business establishment effectively managed there and 90% of its income is from companies in active business
United States	Taxed currently	Taxed currently	Taxed currently	Taxed currently

Table 4–1b. Summary of Examples

Country	Engaged in active business-interest from active subsidiary in another country	Holding company-interest from active subsidiary in another country	Active business-royalty payments from subsidiary in another country
Canada	Deferred	Deferred	Deferred
France	Deferred	Taxed currently	Deferred
Germany	Deferred if lent on a short-term basis or if funds are borrowed on foreign capital market and lent on a long-term basis	Deferred if funds are borrowed on foreign capital market and lent on a long-term basis	Deferred if used on R & D and no participation of related parties
Japan	Deferred	Taxed currently	Deferred if it meets non-related party or location criteria
Netherlands	Deferred	Deferred	Deferred
United Kingdom	Deferred	Deferred if CFC has a business establishment effectively managed there and 90% of its income is from companies in active business	Deferred
United States	Taxed currently	Taxed currently	Taxed currently

* * *

Chapter 5

The Economy Three Decades after Subpart F

* * *

In the decades since subpart F was enacted in 1962, the global economy has grown more rapidly than the U.S. economy. Concomitantly, U.S. companies have confronted both the rise of powerful foreign competitors and the growth of market opportunities abroad. By almost every measure—income, exports, or cross-border investment—the United States today represents a smaller share of the global market. At the same time, U.S. companies have increasingly focused on foreign markets for continued growth and prosperity. Over the last three decades, sales and income from foreign subsidiaries have increased much more rapidly than sales and income from domestic operations. To compete successfully both at home and abroad, U.S. companies have adopted global sourcing and distribution channels, as have their competitors.

These developments have a number of potential implications for tax policy. U.S. tax rules that are out of step with those of other major industrial countries are more likely to hamper the competitiveness of U.S. multinationals in today's global economy than was the case in the 1960s. The growing economic integration among nations—especially the formation of common markets and free trade areas—raises questions about the appropriateness of U.S. tax rules that treat foreign transactions that cross national borders differently from those that occur within the same country. The eclipsing of foreign direct investment by portfolio investment calls into question the ability of tax policy focused on foreign direct investment to influence the global allocation of capital. The adoption of flexible exchange rates has eliminated currency considerations as a rationale for using tax policy to discourage U.S. investment abroad. Indeed, as the world's largest debtor nation, the use of tax policy by the United States to discourage investment abroad is thoroughly antiquated.

Chapter 6

The Neutrality–Competitiveness Balance Reconsidered

* * *

U.S. international tax policy represents a balancing of two generally inconsistent economic principles—*competitiveness* and *capital export neutrality*. Subpart F, enacted in 1962, did not terminate deferral (as would be required to achieve capital export neutrality), but instead limited deferral in certain cases where opportunities for abuse were perceived to exist. In subsequent amendments to subpart F, the balance has generally shifted in favor of capital export neutrality and away from competitiveness.

As we approach the end of the 20th century, there are important reasons to re-examine the current balance point embodied in the subpart F rules:

- U.S. multinationals face much greater global competition than was the case when subpart F was first enacted.

- No country, including the United States, has adopted international tax rules that are consistent with capital export neutrality. None imposes current tax on all foreign-source income and none has an unlimited foreign tax credit. Indeed, half of the OECD countries *exempt* foreign source business income either by statute or treaty—these countries do not tax foreign-source income even when it is distributed.

- Annual foreign portfolio investment now exceeds foreign direct investment. With the growth in portfolio capital flows, imposition of capital export neutrality tax rules upon foreign direct investment does *not* necessarily improve international capital allocation, but does make it more difficult for U.S. multinationals to compete abroad.

- The theoretical link between current taxation of foreign-source income and efficient investment location depends crucially on a stylized view that treats foreign direct investment as indistinguishable from portfolio investment. Empirical evidence, however, suggests that this stylized view of foreign direct investment is incorrect. When more realistic assumptions are adopted, Professors Devereux and Hubbard find that deferral, rather than current taxation, is most consistent with national welfare maximization (for investments in low-tax foreign countries).

Both changes in the international economic environment and refinements in the theory of international taxation are consistent with a re-balancing of U.S. international tax policy towards competitiveness and away from capital export neutrality. This could be accomplished by narrowing the scope of subpart F to passive income. A secondary benefit from such a shift in policy would be a major simplification of U.S. tax rules, as the subpart F rules are a source of substantial complexity and tax controversy. Such a shift also would tend to harmonize

U.S. tax rules with those of other major industrial countries
that target their anti-deferral rules more narrowly on passive-
type income.

5.5   Proposed Reforms to Subpart F

Congress in 2003 seemed more inclined to agree with the arguments
of the multinational business community for loosening some of the
constrictions of Subpart F than with the academics who would tighten
them. A number of bills have been introduced in the Congress to
liberalize Subpart F. Some of these have been coupled with legislative
proposals to inhibit corporate inversions. As discussed in Chapter 3,
lawmakers have become increasingly concerned about the number of
U.S. corporations seeking to reincorporate abroad. Among the reasons
cited by multinational corporations for pursuing such transactions is the
desire to escape the broad reach of current taxation under Subpart F.
Whether or not the relative severity of Subpart F actually constitutes a
significant impetus for U.S. companies to shift their residence overseas,
Congress seems receptive to this argument as well as to the general
appeals for multinational competitiveness. A description of some recent
proposals before Congress for narrowing the scope of Subpart F follows.

**Staff of the Joint Committee on Taxation, Background
Materials on Business Tax Issues Prepared for the
House Committee on Ways and Means Tax Policy Discus-
sion Series, JCX–23–02 (Apr. 4, 2002).**

Incremental reform proposals relating to the subpart F anti-
deferral rules

Background

Generally, income earned indirectly by a U.S. person
through a foreign corporation is subject to U.S. tax only when
the income is distributed to the U.S. person. This deferral of
U.S. tax is limited by a number of anti-deferral regimes (e.g.,
"subpart F") that impose current U.S. tax on certain types of
income earned by certain corporations. Drawing the line between "good" income (active business income) and "tainted"
income (passive or highly mobile income) has proven contentious and has also engendered considerable complexity.

Exclusion of all active income from the scope of subpart F

Present law places the income from many sales, services,
shipping, and certain other activities conducted abroad on the
"tainted" side of the line (because such activities are thought to
be highly mobile and thus prone to tax-motivated manipulation), thus subjecting the income from such activities to current U.S. tax. Many U.S.-based multinationals complain that

these rules penalize the use of common, non-tax-motivated business structures (e.g., centralizing sales and services functions for a number of different foreign markets within a single foreign entity), thus placing U.S.-headquartered businesses at a competitive disadvantage in the normal conduct of their active business activities around the world. They argue that the scope of subpart F should be limited to passive income (e.g., dividends and interest) earned abroad, and that other rules (e.g., the arm's length transfer pricing rules of section 482) are sufficient to address any abuses involving the manipulation of active income streams. The proposal would eliminate certain subpart F active-income categories (the foreign base company sales, services, shipping, and oil-related income categories). This proposal arguably could exacerbate problems that may arise in taxing income from electronic-commerce transactions.

Permanent "active financing" exception

Passive income (e.g., interest) generally falls on the "tainted" side of the subpart F line, since such income can easily be shifted into low-tax jurisdictions. In the case of banking, financing, insurance, and similar businesses, however, this taint is arguably inappropriate, since these businesses earn this type of income in the active conduct of their core business activities. Subjecting this income to subpart F would arguably cause U.S.-based financial services companies to be treated more harshly than both U.S.-based manufacturing companies and foreign-based financial services companies. Accordingly, since 1997 a temporary exception from subpart F for "active financing income" has been provided. The exception under present law is set to expire after 2006. U.S.-based financial services companies argue that the temporary nature of the exception makes it difficult for them to engage in long-range business planning. The proposal would make the exception permanent.

Expansion of the "de minimis" exception

To avoid subjecting taxpayers to the complex rules of subpart F when a controlled foreign corporation earns incidental amounts of "tainted" income, subpart F provides a "de minimis" exception. Under this exception, a controlled foreign corporation's income is not treated as tainted as long as the tainted income constitutes less than the lesser of $1 million or 5% of the corporation's gross income. For example, a controlled foreign corporation that conducts an active business but also earns a trivial amount of interest on its working capital generally does not need to contend with subpart F, as long as the amount of the interest falls short of the de minimis threshold. U.S.-based multinational enterprises argue that this threshold is set too low to provide them any meaningful relief. For example, a controlled foreign corporation that earns only $1 million of interest income on its working capital is ineligible for the exception, even though $1 million may indeed represent an incidental amount in the context of a large foreign subsidiary of a U.S.-based multinational. The proposal would raise the dollar limit (or even eliminate it), and the percentage limit.

NOTE

The Influence of U.S. Multinationals. The influence of the NFTC report and its arguments are readily apparent in these proposals. Indeed, all three of the measures described above were specifically urged in the second volume of the NFTC's publication, which sets forth recommendations for the incremental reform of Subpart F.[6] If this is indicative of a prevailing legislative trend, the multinational business community seems likely to accomplish its agenda of reorienting the policy balance of Subpart F more toward competitiveness.

5.6 AN EXEMPTION OF FOREIGN SOURCE BUSINESS INCOME AS AN ALTERNATIVE TO THE FOREIGN TAX CREDIT

Another international tax reform proposal that has drawn growing attention from academics and lawmakers is the exemption of foreign source active business income. Several industrialized countries, including France, Germany and the Netherlands, utilize this sort of exemption regime. In practice, our present system of deferral complemented by a foreign tax credit already enables many U.S. corporations essentially to exclude foreign source business income from U.S. taxation by holding profits offshore and selectively repatriating dividends. In 1996, for example, the United States collected only about $1 billion of residual U.S. income tax on the foreign source income earned by U.S. corporations abroad.[7] An exemption of such income offers the potential of simplifying the U.S. international tax system, for example, by eliminating the foreign tax credit basket system. In addition, recent economic research suggests that moving to an exemption system might increase revenue to the U.S. treasury by over $9 billion annually.[8] The following excerpt examines how an exemption system might work in the U.S., concluding that any gains from simplification would depend heavily on the details of the exemption regime.

6. 2 National Foreign Trade Council, Inc., The NFTC Foreign Income Project: International Tax Policy for the 21st Century, Conclusions and Recommendations 37–57 (2001).

7. Harry Grubert, Enacting Dividend Exemption and Tax Revenue, 54 Nat'l Tax J. 811, 816–817 (2001).

8. Id.

Michael J. Graetz & Paul W. Oosterhuis, *Structuring an Exemption System for Foreign Income of U.S. Corporations*, 54 NAT'L TAX J. 771 (2001).

The OECD nations have split virtually evenly over the best structure for taxing foreign source business income earned by multinational corporations. About half the OECD countries provide a tax credit for foreign taxes; the other half exempt from domestic taxation active business income earned abroad. Discussions of international tax policy often treat this choice as grounded in different philosophies or normative judgments about international taxation. Foreign tax credit systems are frequently said to implement "worldwide" taxation or a "universality" principle, while exemption systems are described as "territorial" taxation. Likewise, tax credit systems supposedly implement "capital export neutrality" while exemption systems further "capital import neutrality". However, tax credit and exemption systems are far closer in practice than these dichotomies suggest. The OECD nations have all conceded that the country of source—the nation where income is earned—enjoys the primary right to tax active business income, with the residence country—the nation where the business is incorporated or managed—retaining at most a residual right to tax such income.

Since the enactment of the foreign tax credit in 1918, the United States has never seriously considered replacing it with an exemption system. In 2000, however, the U.S. Congress, in an apparently unsuccessful effort to thwart World Trade Organization disapproval of U.S. tax benefits for "foreign sales corporations," characterized as normal U.S. exemption of foreign business income. Issues under foreign trade agreements may push the United States to consider replacing the foreign tax credit with exemption. Recent analyses by economists suggest that moving to an exemption system for direct investment (with appropriate anti-abuse rules) could increase U.S. revenues without precipitating any substantial reallocation of capital by U.S. firms. Moreover, the existing U.S. foreign tax credit rules are extraordinarily complex, requiring U.S. companies doing business abroad to spend large and disproportionate amounts to comply. One study estimates that nearly 40 percent of the income tax compliance costs of U.S. multinationals is attributable to the taxation of foreign source income, even though foreign operations account for only about 20 percent of these companies' economic activity. Some analysts are now calling for the U.S. to take a serious look at exemption of foreign source business income, often on the grounds that an exemption system might be simpler than the existing credit system. To date, however, little work has been done in identifying the issues that must be resolved for exemption to be implemented and discussing the potential structure of an exemption system for the U.S. Such analysis is essential to assess the likelihood of accomplishing simplification goals. We undertake a preliminary foray into those questions here.

Implementing either a foreign tax credit or an exemption system for foreign source business income demands resolution of similar questions. Most of the issues raised by an exemption system parallel those that have been debated over the years under the current credit system. This is not surprising; both systems share the same general goal: avoiding international double taxation without stimulating U.S. taxpayers to shift operations, assets or earnings abroad. Domestic and foreign source income must be measured in both systems. Both systems must answer the question of what income qualifies for exemption or credit. Whether income earned abroad by a foreign corporation should be included currently in U.S. income or included only when repatriated as a dividend has long been debated under our foreign tax credit system. If not all foreign source income is exempt, this question remains important in an exemption system. And it is necessary to decide the appropriate treatment of foreign corporations with different levels of U.S. ownership. Likewise, transfer pricing issues are significant and difficult to resolve under either a credit or exemption system.

Detailed analysis and evaluation of each of these issues is not possible here. We start, therefore, by assuming that the political and economic determinations that have shaped current law will continue to exert great influence over the design of an exemption system. We also assume that if the U.S. were to adopt an exemption system, it would generally resemble exemption systems of other OECD nations that have used exemption rather than foreign tax credits. But, even with these constraints, investigating the potential structure of an exemption system spurs reconsideration of issues long taken for granted under our foreign tax credit regime. Our analysis illustrates that shifting to an exemption system might well afford an opportunity to simplify U.S. international income tax law, but only if simplification is made a priority in enacting such a change. Our discussion here also points to potential simplification of the rules governing international taxation of business, whether or not exemption is enacted. As a political matter, however, such simplification may be more likely when Congress is making a substantial change in the regime for taxing international business income. * * *

INCOME ELIGIBLE FOR EXEMPTION

Alternatives

The first issue in designing an exemption is deciding what foreign source income is exempt. Potentially such an exemption could apply broadly to all foreign source income or narrowly, for example, only to active business income that is subject to tax by a nation with which the U.S. has an income tax treaty or which taxes income at rates comparable to the U.S. rate. Some OECD countries limit their exemption systems to countries with which they have tax treaties or to income taxed at a certain level abroad; others do not. We consider first the potential structure an exemption system applicable generally to active business income without regard to whether the income is generated in a treaty jurisdiction and without regard to the rate at which it is taxed by the foreign country where it is earned.

Following the practice of other nations which exempt foreign source income, such an exemption would apply generally to the branch profits of any U.S. corporation and to dividends received by U.S. corporate taxpayers from foreign corporations. This means that interest income and royalty income, both of which are deductible abroad and therefore not subject to foreign income tax, would be subject to U.S. tax. Under current law, U.S. businesses are often able to shelter interest and royalties earned abroad from U.S. tax through foreign tax credits. Thus, an exemption system would increase the tax on this type of income for many U.S. companies compared to current law.

Definition of Active Business Income

Since active business income but not other types of income earned abroad would generally be exempt, it becomes essential to determine what constitutes eligible active business income. The Internal Revenue Code today does not provide any direct precedent. Nonetheless, the current Code does provide guidance, which probably would be used in defining eligible active business income. Identifying business income eligible for exemption and determining how to treat income not eligible for exemption raise questions parallel to those under current law in determining what income earned through foreign corporations should be taxed currently or eligible for deferral of U.S. tax until repatriated and how the foreign tax credit should apply when that income is subject to U.S. tax. Business income eligible for exemption might be defined first by excluding income that is "passive," drawing on existing Code provisions that identify and tax currently types of passive income earned abroad, particularly Subpart F of the Code. The rationale for excluding passive income from exemption parallels that for taxing such income currently under Subpart F.

Because such income has no nexus to business activity, it is highly mobile and easily shifted abroad to low or no tax jurisdictions. Thus, exempting such income would create an unacceptable incentive to move assets offshore and potentially would lose large amounts of revenue. Consequently, income that constitutes passive income (technically foreign personal holding income) under Subpart F (mostly interest, dividends, rents and royalties) would not be eligible for exemption. Special rules will be necessary when such amounts are earned by entities in which a U.S. corporate taxpayer has a certain minimum ownership interest. (In the latter case, as we discuss below, "look-through" rules would be applied to characterize some types of passive income.) The distinction between income eligible for exemption and nonexempt passive income would raise definitional issues similar to those long debated under Subpart E. For example, banks, securities dealers, insurance companies and other finance-related businesses earn interest and other types of "passive" income that are considered active business income under current law; we believe that such businesses should probably be eligible for exemption as are other active businesses, at least when their financial-service business is located predominately in the country of incorporation.

Once passive income earned abroad by U.S. corporations is excluded from exemption—as we believe it should and will be— the risk occurs that an exemption system might become about as complex as current law. For example, every active foreign business utilizes working capital, and earns passive income from the temporary investment of such capital. Without a de minimis rule which ignores small amounts of passive income, every corporation will have to take into income some amount of passive income and presumably calculate foreign tax credits allowable with respect to such income. A de minimis rule based on a proportion of total gross income or total assets might promote substantial simplification by allowing the income of foreign corporations engaged in an active business to be completely exempt without leading to an unacceptable level of tax planning.

A separate question is whether other "non-passive" types of Subpart F income should be exempt from U.S. taxation. In some cases, for example, Subpart F currently taxes certain sales and services income. In most cases such sales and services income, which is active business income, is taxed currently under Subpart F because of the ability of taxpayers to locate the activities that generate this income in low-tax jurisdictions thereby minimizing both U.S. and foreign source-based income taxes. These Subpart F rules were first adopted in 1962 and some business organizations have recently called for revision, urging, for example, that the transfer pricing rules are adequate to address "abuse" cases. The fundamental policy issue to be faced by an exemption system is whether these (and other) types of "mobile" active foreign business income, which can sometimes be moved to low tax jurisdictions, should be eligible for exemption. Transfer pricing enforcement throughout the OECD has become more vigorous and sophisticated. A simpler system would no doubt result if the transfer pricing rules (which in this case would be enforced by the country from which the sales or services income is deflected to a low or no tax jurisdiction), rather than an exclusion from exemption, could be relied on to constrain tax avoidance.

* * *

TREATMENT OF NON–EXEMPT INCOME EARNED BY U.S. TAXPAYERS

Foreign Tax Credits

The discussion above makes clear that not all foreign source income earned by a U.S. corporation will be eligible for exemption. Non exempt income would surely include foreign source interest, rents and royalties not attributable to an active foreign business, dividends on portfolio stock, income from export sales not attributable to an active foreign business and any other types of active business income (perhaps such as space or shipping income or interest and royalties attributable to an active business) that are specifically determined to be ineligible. However, to the extent that these types of income are potentially subject to foreign tax (including withholding tax) on a basis, the U.S. should make an effort to avoid double taxation. Thus, as under today's rules, such income should probably continue to be allowed a credit for the foreign taxes paid on that income.

If a foreign tax credit is permitted for any income, in principle all the questions that exist today regarding limitations on foreign tax credits would have to be resolved. However, if the nonexempt income were limited to only these classes of income, much simplification would be possible. For example, given this limited application, a single worldwide foreign tax credit limitation could be applied. A worldwide limitation seems reasonable since taxpayers almost always will be subject to tax abroad on these types of income at rates lower than the U.S. corporate tax rate, and therefore they will almost always have foreign tax credit limitations in excess of creditable foreign taxes. A single worldwide limitation would be far simpler than the baskets of current law, and the fact that taxpayers would virtually always have excess foreign tax credit limitations both permits additional simplifying changes and lowers the stakes in applying some rules that would be retained.

If, however, averaging of credits across types of income is of great concern, separate limitations might be applied based on categories of income (similar to today's limitations) or types of taxes (e.g., withholding taxes versus income taxes normally applied to residents). Finally, a separate limitation could be applied to each item of foreign source income not eligible for exemption (much like the so-called "high-tax kickout" limitation on passive income under the current foreign tax credit). However, we see no justification for this level of complexity. In a system that generally exempts active business income, we do not find any policy justification for multiple separate limitations that outweighs the simplification advantages of a single worldwide foreign tax credit limitation.

Treatment of Non–Exempt Foreign Corporation Earnings

If not all income earned by a foreign corporation is eligible for exemption, the question occurs whether non-exempt income should be subject to current inclusion by U.S. corporate shareholders or, alternatively, should not be taxed in the U.S. until distributed as a dividend. Most passive types of income are today subject to current inclusion under Subpart F when earned by controlled foreign corporations. Investors in non-U.S. controlled foreign corporations, which earn mostly passive income, may be subject to current taxation (or roughly equivalent consequences) under the Passive Foreign Investment Company (PFIC) regime or other "anti-deferral" regimes. We see no reason that shifting from a foreign tax credit to an exemption system should delay the imposition of U.S. tax on passive income (which exceeds a de minimis amount) that is taxed currently under present law. Thus, we assume that the U.S. would continue to subject passive types of foreign source income to current inclusion.

If some types of active business income also are not exempt, a decision must be made whether to subject that income to current taxation. Here we believe that avoiding the complexity of having three categories of income for U.S.-controlled foreign corporations—exempt income, currently included income and deferred income—is sufficiently important to argue for current taxation of all non-exempt income. If non-exempt income is taxed currently and dividends are exempt, the timing of dividends becomes of no consequence under U.S. tax law. On the other hand, if a category of deferred income is retained, look-through treatment of dividends might be necessary.

Assuming that all income of U.S. controlled foreign corporations is either exempt or currently included, rules are necessary to measure the income in two categories. For example, rules allocating expenses between the two categories of income would be necessary. Likewise, loss recapture rules (similar to those in Subpart F today) would be necessary to prevent losses from income-producing activities from permanently reducing nonexempt currently includable amounts.

In addition, an "indirect" (or "deemed-paid") foreign tax credit would be appropriate to allow U.S. corporate taxpayers to claim foreign tax credits for foreign taxes paid by foreign corporations on non-exempt income. Such a foreign tax credit would require rules allocating foreign taxes between exempt and currently includable income. The rules would also require integration with the foreign tax credit limitation rules discussed above with respect to foreign source income earned directly by U.S. taxpayers. Thus, many of the foreign tax credit issues that exist today would remain although they would apply to a much smaller category of income earned by foreign corporations and therefore might be substantially simplified.

DISTINGUISHING AMONG U.S. CORPORATE SHARE-HOLDERS

In addition to rules establishing the scope of exemption and the treatment of dividends received from foreign corporations, it becomes necessary to decide whether all U.S. corporate shareholders should be entitled to exemption. In theory, the answer to this question should be yes; otherwise some international double taxation at the corporate level will occur. However, applying an exemption system, as discussed above, requires that U.S. corporate shareholders receive significant amounts of information from those foreign corporations in which they have the requisite level of ownership. The U.S. recipient would, for example, have to know the amount of the foreign corporation's passive earnings and the amount of foreign taxes imposed on those earnings. It thus seems impractical to apply an exemption system on a look-through basis to all U.S. corporate shareholders of foreign corporations.

In determining whether U.S. tax applies currently or is delayed until earnings are repatriated and for foreign tax credit purposes under current law, the U.S. has three different regimes relevant to this issue:

(1) Subpart F limits deferral but allows foreign tax credits to shareholders owning 10 percent or more of the voting

stock in controlled foreign corporations (CFCs). (CFCs are defined as foreign corporations in which U.S. persons each owning 10 percent of the voting stock own a total of more than 50 percent of the stock by vote or value).

(2) To avoid international double taxation, the "indirect" foreign tax credit is allowed to U.S. corporations that own at least 10 percent of voting stock in a foreign corporation which is not a CFC.

(3) No foreign tax credit and no limitation on deferral applies to a U.S. corporation whose ownership in a foreign corporation is less than 10 percent of the voting stock.

In designing an exemption system these categories should be rethought. Today a U.S. corporation, which owns less than 10 percent of the voting stock of a foreign corporation, is treated as a "portfolio" investor. Full double taxation of foreign source income at the corporate level is justified largely on the assumption that such corporate investors cannot get the information necessary to determine their foreign tax credits under U.S. law.

A 10 percent voting stock threshold could also be adopted for distinguishing "portfolio" from "direct" investment for the purpose of applying exemption. The issue remains, however, whether U.S. corporate investors owning less than 10 percent should be fully taxed or fully exempt on dividends (and capital gains). If, as we assume, rules similar to the current Passive Foreign Investment Company regime continue to apply to all investors in foreign corporations that hold predominately passive assets, dividends (and gains) from non-PFIC foreign corporations might be treated as exempt by U.S. corporate shareholders owning less than 10 percent of voting stock in all cases without requiring any significant information and without creating undue potential for tax planning mischief.

* * *

CONCLUSION

We have attempted here to identify the issues that Congress must resolve if it were to replace the existing foreign tax credit system with an exemption for active business income earned abroad. In this discussion we have stuck rather close to present law in addressing how these issues might be resolved under an exemption system. In other words, we have treated a potential change to exemption as an incremental move in U.S. international tax policy rather than viewing such a shift as an occasion to rethink fundamental policy decisions reflected in current law.

Our analysis reveals that virtually all of the questions that must be answered in a foreign tax credit regime must also be addressed in an exemption system. There is little simplification necessarily inherent in moving to an exemption system, but such a move does provide an opportunity to reconsider a variety of issues that might simplify the taxation of international business income. While, in principle, much simplification of current law is possible without abandoning the foreign tax credit, it may be politically unrealistic to think that such simplification will occur absent a substantial revision of the existing regime, such as that entailed in enacting an exemption system.

Our analysis suggests that much of the complexity of an exemption system occurs in the scope and treatment of non-exempt income. If this category generally can be limited to passive non-business income with meaningful de minimis rules applied to the treatment of such income, the impact of these rules can be minimized. Surely the basket system limiting foreign tax credits could be eliminated. Moreover, under an exemption system along the lines we have described here, the timing of the payment of dividends would be of no consequence. Thus, under an exemption regime significant simplification could be achieved for many companies and the costs of complying with U.S. international tax rules might well decrease substantially for U.S. corporations.

A major concern surrounding the adoption of an exemption system, particularly among adherents of capital export neutrality, is the incentive it might create for U.S. companies to invest their resources abroad. However, in the next excerpt economists Roseanne Altshuler and Harry Grubert conclude that no significant locational distortions would occur under an exemption system compared to current law, nor do they find that adopting an exemption system would result in a substantial outflow of capital from the United States.

Rosanne Altshuler & Harry Grubert, *Where Will They Go if We Go Territorial? Dividend Exemption and the Location Decisions of U.S. Multinational Corporations*, 54 NAT'L TAX J. 787 (2001).

We approach the question of how location incentives under the current system are likely to be altered under dividend exemption from three different angles. We start by comparing the U.S. allocation of foreign direct investment (FDI) in manufacturing across low-tax versus high-tax jurisdictions with that of two major dividend exemption countries, Canada and Germany. Both Canada and Germany exempt dividends paid by foreign affiliates from home country tax by treaty. An interesting question is whether, relative to U.S. FDI, the distribution of Canadian and German FDI is more skewed toward low-tax countries.

The second part of the paper uses effective tax rate calculations to quantify the burden of U.S. taxes on the typical investment in a low-tax affiliate under the current system and under dividend exemption. * * * Although the small effective repatriation burden on dividends would be eliminated under dividend exemption, royalties would be fully taxed at the U.S. rate since no excess credits would be available to offset home country taxes on these payments. Whether effective tax rates increase or decrease relative to the current system depends on how firms respond to the dividend exemption system enacted.

The main focus in our effective tax rate analysis is on the role played by expense allocation rules under dividend exemption. These rules govern whether expenses incurred in the U.S. in support of investment abroad, such as headquarter charges and interest payments, are deductible against U.S. or exempt foreign income. In the absence of any expense allocation rules, parents would minimize tax payments by deducting expenses associated with investments in low-tax countries at the higher U.S. tax rate. This behavior could result in negative effective tax rates on investment projects placed in low-tax jurisdictions.

* * *

Our final approach involves using data from the tax returns of multinationals to gauge how location decisions will be affected by a move towards dividend exemption. As explained above, not all parents pay tax at the U.S. rate when they receive active income from operations located in low-tax countries under the current system. The last section of the paper compares the actual behavior of firms that face no residual U.S. taxes on low-tax foreign earnings (those with excess foreign tax credits) with those that are taxed at the U.S. rate (those without excess foreign tax credits). The idea is to use the former group of firms as a control group to predict the extent to which low taxes will attract U.S. affiliate investment under dividend exemption.

We use Treasury tax return data from the 1996 files to estimate the sensitivity of investment location decisions of U.S. MNCs [(multinational corporations)] to host country taxes. Since firms may switch into and out of situations in which they have excess credits (and this may affect economic behavior), we use measures that indicate whether a parent is likely to be exempt from residual U.S. taxes on foreign income in any year. These measures, which include the parent's average tax rate on foreign source income and foreign tax credit carryforwards as a fraction of foreign source income, allow us to test if parents that are "deep in excess credit" are any more sensitive to differences in effective tax rates abroad.

Taken together, our analysis provides no consistent or definitive evidence that location decisions would be significantly changed if dividend remittances were to be exempt from U.S. corporate taxation. However, each of our three approaches suggest that there is some possibility that U.S. MNCs will make adjustments to the allocation of assets held in operations abroad. Although we find that U.S. investment in Asia is more skewed towards the low-tax countries with which Germany and Canada have exemption treaties, the picture that emerges for Europe is mixed. Compared to the U.S. (and Germany), Canadian investment in the European Union is heavily weighted towards Ireland. Whether U.S. firms will shift towards a similar regional distribution in Europe is an open question. However, the evidence from our cost of capital and empirical analysis does not seem to support any large outflow of U.S. investment to low-tax locations.

Our effective tax rate calculations show that expense allocation rules and the full taxation of royalties under dividend exemption play a fundamental role in determining how the relative attractiveness of low-tax countries will change. Under the current system, we estimate that the typical investment in a country with an effective local tax rate of seven percent faces an overall (home plus host country) effective tax rate of only five percent. If the U.S. were to exempt dividends and, at the same time, eliminate required expense allocations (or impose allocations that are easily avoidable), overall effective tax rates on low-tax investments abroad would fall somewhat to three percent. In contrast, if firms were required to allocate overhead expenses to exempt income under the new system, the same investment would face an overall effective tax rate of about nine percent. As a result, investment in low-tax countries would not be encouraged relative to the current system.

The results from our third approach raise the possibility that U.S. MNCs may be somewhat more responsive to differences in effective tax rates under dividend exemption. We find that the sensitivity of location choices to host country effective tax rates does not increase as the parent's average tax rate on foreign source income increases. Other alternative measures of the extent to which a firm is "deep in excess credit" also failed to distinguish an effect on tax sensitivity. However, when we use the size of foreign tax credit carryforwards as an indicator of the likelihood that dividend remittances will face residual U.S. taxation, we do uncover a differential effect. The influence of host country taxes on location choice increases as a parent's foreign tax credit carryforward grows. Although the size of the effect is not quantitatively very significant, the results indicate the possibility that there will be an increase in investment in low-tax countries under dividend exemption.

* * *

Table 3

**Effective Tax Rates of Investment
Abroad in a Low-tax Country**

	Investment comprised of:		
	All tangible assets	All intangible assets	85% tangible and 15% intangibile assets
Dividend exemption	4.8%	35.0%	9.3%
Current system (assuming 25% of firms in excess credit)	1.7	26.3	5.4
Excess limitation firms	0.7	35.0	5.8
Excess credit firms	4.8	0.0	4.1

NOTES

1) *U.S. Multinationals Do Not Favor an Exemption System.* As Table 3 from the Altshuler and Grubert article indicates, the effective tax rate on a typical investment abroad by a U.S. corporation in a low-tax jurisdiction would be higher than current law under an exemption system. One of the main reasons for the low rate under the present system is the ability of companies to defer U.S. taxes on foreign source income and to repatriate dividends selectively in order to cross-credit foreign tax credits from high and low-tax jurisdictions. As the Graetz–Oosterhuis excerpt indicates, royalties and interest paid from foreign subsidiaries to their U.S. parents, which can be sheltered by foreign tax credits under current law, would be subject to tax under an exemption regime. As a result, the NFTC has announced its opposition to shifting to an exemption system. An NFTC report concluded that "on balance, legislative efforts to improve current international tax rules are better spent on reform of our current deferral and foreign tax credit system" than on seeking to adopt an exemption system.[9]

2) *Philosophical Opposition to Exemption.* Shifting from the foreign tax credit to an exemption system is also opposed philosophically by govern-

9. National Foreign Trade Council, Inc., The NFTC's Report on Territorial Taxation, 27 Tax Notes Int'l 687, 689 (2002).

ment officials and academics who remain convinced that U.S. tax policy should use worldwide residence-based taxation to further capital export neutrality. They continue to pursue the illusive goal of eliminating deferral. Ironically, in their opposition to the exemption system their most effective allies are the NFTC and its membership of U.S. multinationals.

Chapter 6

Inbound Transactions: Business Taxation

6.1 INTRODUCTION

Nonresident foreign individuals and corporations who bring their financial and human capital to the United States face two mutually exclusive regimes of taxation, which separate roughly into active business income and nonbusiness income. Chapter 7 covers the taxation of nonbusiness income (often referred to as passive income) associated with inbound transactions. In general, a flat-rate gross-basis withholding tax is imposed on such income, although there are various subtleties.

This chapter focuses on the taxation of business income earned by nonresident individuals or corporations in the United States. The statutory test for the treatment of income from nonresident persons as business income is whether the income is "effectively connected" with a "trade or business within the United States." See §§ 871(b), 882, 884, 864(c) & 864(b). If the United States has a bilateral treaty with the home country of the foreign individual or corporation, as is true for the OECD countries and many others, taxation turns on whether the foreigner has a "permanent establishment" in the United States. These tests are considerably more complicated than they appear at first glance, and substantial stakes rest on their interpretation for foreign persons doing business in the United States. For example, the challenge that e-commerce poses to traditional understandings of the permanent establishment requirement highlights how international tax policymakers must constantly adapt tax principles to a changing business environment.

6.2 THE CONCEPT OF "ENGAGED IN A TRADE OR BUSINESS"

Unless a tax treaty provides otherwise, the Internal Revenue Code taxes income that is effectively connected with a trade or business within the United States at regular U.S. corporate rates. The first question is whether a nonresident alien individual or corporation is "engaged in a trade or business within the United States." This determination is sometimes difficult, because of the uncertainty that surrounds what constitutes a trade or business. In the following excerpt, Ernest Larkins

266

explores this ambiguity and lays out the basic contours of judicial and administrative rulings interpreting the phrase "trade or business within the United States."

Ernest R. Larkins, *U.S. Income Taxation of Foreign Parties: A Primer*, 26 SYRACUSE J. INT'L L. & COM. 1, 5–7 (1998).

Though the Internal Revenue Code and Treasury Regulations use the phrase "trade or business" ubiquitously, neither defines it. Moreover, Rev. Proc. 98–7, 1998–1 I.R.B. 222, 4.01(3), indicates that the IRS ordinarily will not rule on whether a party is engaged in a U.S. trade or business nor whether income is effectively connected with a U.S. trade or business. Prior judicial and administrative rulings provide the most relevant guidance on trade-or-business-type questions.

Generally, a trade or business is any considerable, continuous, and regular activity engaged in for profit. Rev. Rul. 73–522, 1973–2 C.B. 226, normally characterizes minimal, sporadic, or irregular transactions as investment, rather than business, activities. I.R.C. 875 treats a foreign party as engaged in a U.S. trade or business if the partnership of which the foreign party is a member is so engaged. *United States v. Balanovski*, treats partnerships as carrying on business when one or more of their partners are conducting business on the partnership's behalf. For example, the ABC partnership is organized in Brazil, and each of its three partners are Brazilian citizens and residents. Partner A conducts business in the United States on behalf of the partnership. As a result, the partnership is considered to be engaged in a U.S. trade or business, as are partners B and C. A similar rule applies to the beneficiaries of estates and trusts.

Beyond this general definition, certain specific activities have been held to constitute trades or businesses. For example, a foreign party that regularly sells goods into the United States through a dependent or exclusive, independent agent is conducting a U.S. trade or business. Similarly, an agent that regularly exercises broad powers to manage a foreign party's U.S. real estate investments (beyond mere ownership or collection of rent) causes the principal to be engaged in a U.S. trade or business.

Rev. Rul. 56–165, 1956–1 C.B. 849 treats a foreign enterprise as engaged in a U.S. trade or business when it sends an employee or other dependent agent to the United States to sell goods and conclude contracts. Employees that do not have the power to conclude contracts but who must send solicited orders to the home office for approval is one arrangement that can avoid trade or business status. However, if marketing representatives or employees are technically precluded from concluding contracts but the home office approves virtually all orders through no more than a "rubber stamp" procedure, the IRS will likely view the activity as a trade or business; the fact that the representative cannot conclude contracts must be more than a formality.

In contrast to the situations above, direct sales into (or purchases from) the United States are not considered a trade or business if the foreign seller (or purchaser) has no office, employee, or agent in the United States or if sales are made through a nonexclusive, independent agent with multiple principals. Also, technical services performed in the United States incident to the sale of goods are not, by themselves, a trade or business. Absent other activities, the mere creation of a corporation, collection of passive income (e.g., in relation to a net lease), ownership of realty or corporate stock, investigation of business opportunities, or distribution of earnings do not constitute a trade or business.

Higgins v. Commissioner confirms that mere investment activities on one's own account, even if actively and continuously engaged in, are not considered a trade or business. Thus, a foreign investor that trades commodities (of the type normally listed on organized exchanges), stocks, and securities in the United States on its own behalf or through an independent agent is generally not carrying on a U.S. trade or business. However, I.R.C. 864(b)(2) indicates that a trade or business does exist if the investor is a dealer in such stocks and securities or, in the case of trading through an independent agent, the investor has a U.S. office or other fixed place of business at any time during the taxable year through which trading is directed.

Occasional or single, isolated transactions generally do not lead to a finding of trade or business activities. However, the IRS and the courts have held that a single event (often involving substantial personal service income) can be a trade or business. For example, a prize fighter's engagement in one or more boxing matches has been held to be the conduct of trade or business activities. Rev. Rul. 67–321, 1967–2 C.B. 470 held that a French company that contracts to perform a floor show or night club revue in a U.S. hotel over a ten-week period is engaged in a U.S. trade or business. Similarly, the purse winnings of a horse entered in only one race within the United States may be taxable since the IRS has ruled that a single race is a U.S. business activity. On the other hand, *Continental Trading, Inc. v. Commissioner* held that numerous but "isolated and non-continuous" sales transactions do not constitute a trade or business when motivated for tax avoidance, rather than profit-making, reasons.

The rendition of personal services is generally considered carrying on a trade or business. However, a nonresident alien performing de minimis services in the United States, whether as an employee or independent contractor, is not engaged in a U.S. trade or business when the three conditions of I.R.C. 864(b)(1) are met. First, the compensation cannot be more than $3,000 for the U.S. services. Second, the U.S. presence during the taxable year cannot exceed 90 days. Third, the services must be rendered for either a foreign party not engaged in a U.S. trade or business or a foreign office or place of business of a U.S. party.

NOTE

No Comprehensive Definition. As this excerpt indicates, Congress has generally left the determination whether an activity constitutes a trade or business to the IRS and the courts. But the Supreme Court has not defined conclusively what constitutes a trade or business. This point is best illustrated by *Commissioner v. Groetzinger*, 480 U.S. 23 (1987), a case concerning the deductibility of a professional gambler's gambling losses as business losses. In *Groetzinger* the Court held that the sale of goods or services is not essential to find a trade or business and found the gambler to be engaged in a trade or business. The Court added: "the difficulty rests in the Code's wide utilization in various contexts of the term 'trade or business,' in the absence of an all-purpose definition by statute or regulation, and in our concern that an attempt judicially to formulate and impose a test for all situations would be counterproductive, unhelpful, and even somewhat precarious for the overall integrity of the Code," Id. at 38.

The absence of any comprehensive definition of "trade or business" may create the potential for unpredictable results. In some circumstances, this may prevent foreigners from being able to determine in advance the extent to which their U.S. activities will expose them to U.S. tax liability. The next excerpt, however, suggests that these difficulties are not great.

The following excerpt from an article by Nancy Kaufman indicates that judicial decisions determining whether a foreign person is engaged in trade or business tend to involve the distinction between active commercial activities and passive investment, a dichotomy that occurs in other areas of the Code.

Nancy H. Kaufman, *Common Misconceptions: The Functions and Framework of "Trade or Business Within the United States,"* 25 VAND. J. TRANSNAT'L L. 729, 776–782 (1993).

The question of whether a foreign person is engaged in trade or business has been litigated almost exclusively with respect to noncorporate taxpayers, probably because the Code tends to presume that corporations are engaged in trade or business. The "trade or business" issue arises most commonly with respect to activities in securities and commodities markets, investments in real estate, and, more recently, working interests in oil and gas. Judicial opinions in these cases draw heavily upon cases decided under other areas of the Code that utilize the term "trade or business." The upshot of these opinions is a distinction between activities that are actively conducted and those that are more in the nature of passive investment.

The real estate cases provide a good illustration. Few, if any, of these cases arise under current law. Since 1960 foreign persons have been able to elect net-basis taxation for income from real property. Moreover, since 1980 the Code has treated gains from the disposition of United States real property interests as effectively connected with the conduct of a trade or business within the United States. The real estate cases remain relevant, however, for other types of investment. An early real estate case illustrating the active/passive dichotomy is *Neill v. Commissioner*. Neill was a nonresident alien whose United States source income consisted of rent paid to her under a long-term ground lease of a single parcel of Philadelphia real property. Neill employed a Philadelphia law firm to receive the rents due from the tenant and pay the interest due on the mortgage and incidental expenses. The tenant had full responsibility for the upkeep of the property. The Board concluded, after very little discussion, that "the rule is settled that the mere ownership of property from which income is drawn does not constitute the carrying on of business within the purview of the cited section." In reaching its conclusion, the Board relied upon *Higgins v. Commissioner,* a well-known Supreme Court decision in the domestic tax context holding that expenses incurred by an individual in managing investments held for capital appreciation and current income could not be deducted as expenses incurred in a trade or business.

In contrast to Neill's "mere ownership of property," the courts have had very little difficulty finding that a trade or business exists when a foreign person owns several pieces of real estate managed by an agent who signs leases, collects rents, and supervises maintenance and other activities necessary to operate the properties, even though the degree of discretion actually exercised by the agent is quite limited. For example, in *Lewenhaupt v. Commissioner,* a nonresident alien owned several pieces of United States real estate that were managed by his agent in California. Under the power of attorney establishing the agency, the agent had broad discretionary authority to act for Lewenhaupt, including the authority to negotiate leases and purchase and sell properties. Nonetheless, the parties understood that the agent would not, and did not, take any important action, such as consummating a sale, without first consulting with the taxpayer or the taxpayer's nonresident alien father. The Tax Court held that the taxpayer was engaged in a trade or business within the United States. In reaching this conclusion, the court stated that the activities carried on by the agent were beyond the scope of mere ownership of real property or the receipt of income from real property. The court found that the activities constituted engaging in a trade or business within the United States because the activities were "considerable, continuous, and regular."

The application of the active/passive dichotomy to real estate leads to curious results. A foreign person who owns real property in the United States subject to a long-term net lease is not engaged in trade or business within the United States. A long-term net lease, which shifts to the lessee the day-to-day activities and expenses necessary for the upkeep of the property, leaves the foreign person with the "mere ownership of property." The I.R.S. apparently agrees with this position, even where the foreign person engages in significant oversight activities. The sale of the foreign person's holdings does not appear to be relevant. * * *

The distinction between active and passive activity may be extended to other endeavors as well. A foreign person's receipt of royalties for the use of intangible property, taken alone, should not rise to the level of a trade or business within the United States. A foreign person's receipt of interest on a loan negotiated outside the United States, particularly a loan arising in a noncommercial context, should not result in a trade or business within the United States.

The results in the cases applying the active/passive dichotomy make a sharp contrast to the Code provisions relating to foreign persons' interests in partnerships, trusts, and estates. The Code imputes the trade or business within the United States of a partnership, trust, or estate to the entity's partners or beneficiaries. For example, a foreign person who is a limited partner in a limited partnership conducting a real estate business in the United States is engaged in trade or business within the United States. Likewise, a foreign person who is the beneficiary of a trust is engaged in trade or business within the United States if the trust is engaged in trade or business within the United States. Under the analysis employed in the cases utilizing the active/passive dichotomy, it is doubtful whether limited partners or the beneficiaries of trusts or estates would be found to be engaged in trade or business within the United States solely on account of the activities of the partnership, trust, or estate. The entity would shield them from the activity necessary to support such a finding.

The passive characterization cannot readily apply to many activities other than those producing interest, dividends, rents, and royalties. For example, sales of goods are inherently active. Where the nature of the foreign person's endeavors is active, the existence of a trade or business depends upon whether the foreign person's activities are considerable, continuous, and regular. On the one hand, a single isolated sale of goods generally does not rise to the level of a trade or business. There are scenarios, however, when an isolated sale might involve a magnitude of activity as to constitute a trade or business.

NOTE

Agents. As this excerpt highlights, activities conducted by U.S. agents of foreign persons pose some of the most difficult questions regarding what constitutes a U.S. trade or business. For example, as Nancy Kaufman notes, in *Lewenhaupt v. Commissioner*, Lewenhaupt himself was involved in a purely passive way, but his agent's activity was attributed to him. Similarly, a partner may be entirely passive—indeed a limited partner—yet the partnership's activities are attributed to her. The distinction between "active vs. passive" activity can be tricky, because if *anyone is active*, then even passive participants may find themselves deemed to be engaged in an active trade or business depending on their relationship to the actor.

Meaning of "Within the United States"

The second element of the term "trade or business within the United States" concerns whether the business is located within the United States. No Code provision offers a comprehensive definition of whether an activity takes place within the United States. The parameters can be gleaned, however, from examples. At one extreme are foreign corporations that have major offices in the United States and conduct business through their U.S. offices; these activities clearly take place within the United States. At the other extreme is a foreign producer, whose business activities do not occur within the United States, who ships directly to customers from abroad. Between these two extremes is a spectrum of commercial activities that the IRS and the courts assess on a case-by-case basis considering the relevant facts and circumstances.

The seminal case for whether an activity occurs "within the United States" is *United States v. Balanovski*, 236 F.2d 298 (2d. Cir. 1956). In *Balanovksi* a foreign taxpayer came to the United States to buy trucks and other equipment that he then sold to the Argentine government. Upon receiving bids from American suppliers, the foreign taxpayer would mark-up the bids and send them to the Argentine government. If the government approved the price, the foreign taxpayer then bought the equipment with funds wired from Argentina. The foreign taxpayer conducted this business out of a hotel room with the help of a secretary, and in this "office" he solicited orders, inspected merchandise, and purchased and sold merchandise. The *Balanovski* court assessed all of the facts and circumstances of the foreign taxpayer's activities and concluded that the fact that Balanovski purchased and sold within the United States meant his activities constituted "a trade or business within the United States."

In contrast, a "mere purchasing agent," who takes goods home to his foreign country to sell, would not be engaged in a trade or business within the United States.[1] It is more difficult to determine whether a "mere seller" is engaged in a trade or business within the United States; this determination turns on the level of the seller's activities. For example, a completely foreign catalog business that advertised and had sales in the United States would not be engaged in a trade or business within the United States. However, if the foreign catalog company had a salesman or a store in the United States, its activities would constitute a trade or business within the United States, unless the company had only isolated U.S. transactions.[2]

A Proposal for Reform

In the following excerpt, Nancy Kaufman argues that courts' reliance on two "common misconceptions" of the phrase "trade or business within the United States" makes the term "trade or business" poorly serve its administrative and jurisdictional functions. She urges courts to find the existence of a trade or business within the United States only if the foreign person demonstrates an ongoing commitment to participate in the U.S. economy in a considerable, continuous, and substantial way.

Nancy H. Kaufman, *Common Misconceptions: The Functions and Framework of "Trade or Business Within the United States,"* 25 VAND. J. TRANSNAT'L L. 729, 788–798 (1993).

The term "trade or business within the United States" serves both administrative and jurisdictional functions in the provisions of the Code relating to the taxation of the income of foreign persons. It is the dividing line between net-basis and

---

1. The Balanovski court created a clear negative inference by rejecting the district court's determination that Balanovski was a "mere purchasing agent." In turn, this determination led to the conclusion that Balanovski was purchasing and selling the property in the United States and therefore "engaged in a trade or business within the United States." See 236 F.2d 298, 304 (2d. Cir. 1956).

2. See Ernest R. Larkins, U.S. Income Taxation of Foreign Parties: A Primer, 26 Syracuse J. Int'l L. & Com. 1, 7 (1998).

gross-basis taxation of foreign persons. The term also defines the limits of United States taxation of the sales income of foreign persons. Finally, the term serves as the threshold for the imposition of the branch-level tax provisions on a foreign corporation.[3]

Equity considerations favor the imposition of net-basis tax on foreign persons, the same basis upon which the Code taxes the income of United States persons. However, net-basis taxation is administratively infeasible in the case of a foreign person with relatively few economic contacts with the United States. Net-basis taxation then gives way to a gross-basis tax withheld at source from periodical income and an exemption from tax for sales income, unless the foreign person deriving the income is engaged in a trade or business within the United States. Thus, in its administrative functions, the term should reflect that point at which a foreign person's activities in the United States are such that net-basis taxation is administratively feasible.

As the threshold for the United States taxation of sales income and the imposition of the branch-level tax provisions on a foreign corporation, the term "engaged in trade or business within the United States" also performs a jurisdictional function. However, the primary formulation of United States jurisdiction to impose the income tax is found in the Code's source of income rules. Income rules provide the economic nexus between the United States and the income of foreign persons necessary to support source jurisdiction. With the jurisdictional basis for the taxation of the income of foreign persons already provided for in the source of income rules, the jurisdictional boundaries imposed by the term "trade or business within the United States" do not so much derive from jurisdictional principles as from the administrative considerations inherent in taxing the income of foreign persons.

An examination of the case law applying the term "trade or business within the United States" demonstrates that the framework developed to date does not wholly serve the functions the term must perform in the Code. This mismatch between function and framework is due to two early misconceptions of the term. The first misconception arose out of an attempt to define the term "trade or business" identically in each place it appears in the Code. The second arose out of the discontinuities between the taxation of foreign persons engaged in trade or business within the United States and those not so engaged. These common misconceptions of the term "trade or business within the United States" have distracted the courts

---

3.   Chapter 7 discusses the branch profits taxes.

from the task of developing a cogent framework for the consistent application of the term.

Once the misconceptions of the term "engaged in trade or business within the United States" are stripped away, a framework for the application of the term that comports with its functions begins to emerge. The existing case law provides a foundation for finding a trade or business within the United States only if the foreign person has an ongoing commitment to participate in the United States economy. This standard requires the foreign person to engage in activities that involve the exercise of entrepreneurial judgment within the United States and are considerable, continuous, and substantial.

The adoption of this standard for being engaged in trade or business within the United States would serve equity by treating similarly situated foreign persons similarly and by ensuring that foreign persons whose activities bring them into the mainstream of the United States economy compete on equal footing with United States citizens and residents and domestic corporations. The clearer set of criteria involved in the standard would assist the I.R.S. in the efficient administration of the income tax without imposing unreasonable compliance burdens on foreign persons. The adoption of this standard would serve economic considerations by enabling foreign persons to determine in advance the United States income tax consequence of their activities and ensuring that foreign persons compete in the United States on equal footing with their United States counterparts. Although the standard proposed herein is higher than the activity currently thought to give rise to a trade or business within the United States, it would exclude from net-basis taxation largely marginal cases in which administrative and compliance considerations outweigh equity and economic concerns and in which compliance under current law is questionable.

The meaning of "trade or business within the United States" is not self-evident. Nancy Kaufman's approach offers the prospect of making this critical concept a bit more coherent. This issue is tightly linked to the idea of "effectively connected" with a trade or business, discussed in the following section.

6.3 INCOME EFFECTIVELY CONNECTED WITH A U.S. TRADE OR BUSINESS

Once it is established that a foreign person is "engaged in a trade or business within the United States," the Internal Revenue Code taxes any income that is "effectively connected" to that trade or business at the rates applicable to U.S. residents. § 864(c). However, if the United States has a treaty with the foreign taxpayer's home country, taxation turns on whether the foreign taxpayer has a "permanent establishment" in the United States, a topic considered in Section 6.5. For now, the important question is what "effectively connected" with a trade or business within the United States entails.

U.S. and Foreign Source Income

In some instances income can easily be identified as effectively connected to a U.S. trade or business. However, it is often not readily apparent when income is treated as effectively connected income without a close reading of the Internal Revenue Code and the pertinent regulations. The rules in section 864 for effectively connected income require two steps for determining whether income is effectively connected to a U.S. trade or business. First, taxpayers must identify income as U.S. or foreign source. Second, different categories of income have separate tests for determining when income should be treated as effectively connected to a U.S. trade or business. In the following excerpt, Ernest Larkins lays out the tests for determining what constitutes "effectively connected" U.S. and foreign source income.

Ernest R. Larkins, *U.S. Income Taxation of Foreign Parties: A Primer*, 26 Syracuse J. Int'l L. & Com. 1, 9–11 (1998).

Once the existence of a U.S. trade or business is established, whether a given income item is taxable as ECI [Effectively Connected Income] is often clear. For example, the net profit from sales a foreign corporation earns from a sales branch or retail outlet in the United States is ECI. However, types of income that traditionally have been classified as investment or passive in nature are ECI in some cases; it depends on the income's source.

The manner in which ECI is determined differs for U.S. and foreign source income. U.S. source income that satisfies either the asset use test or business activities test of I.R.C. 864(c)(2) is ECI. Under both tests, one must give due regard to how the U.S. trade or business accounts for the item in question.

The asset use test treats U.S. source income as ECI if the income is derived from assets currently used or held for current use in the U.S. trade or business. This test applies primarily to passive income such as interest and dividends. Treas. Reg. 1.864–4(c)(2)(i) indicates that interest from a temporary investment of idle working capital in U.S. Treasury bills is ECI since it is held to meet the present needs of the business. In contrast, the income from a long-term investment of excess funds in U.S. Treasury bills with the expectation of using the accumulations for the future expansion of product lines or to meet future business contingencies is not ECI.

The business activities test concludes that income from U.S. sources is ECI whenever the activities of a U.S. trade or business are a material factor in realizing the income. This test applies to income that, though generally passive, arises directly from business activities. Treas. Reg. 1.864–4(c)(3)(i) indicates that interest income of a financing business, premiums of an insurance company, royalties of a business that primarily licenses intangibles, dividends and interest of a dealer in stocks and securities, and fees of a service business are ECI under the business activities test. * * *

Prior to 1966, foreign parties often used the United States as a tax haven for sales activities. The United States, at that time, did not tax foreign source income. Thus, a foreign party might establish a U.S. sales office through which it could sell to third countries. The home country did not tax the profit on such sales because, for example, it was derived from foreign sources. The United States did not tax the profit as long as title passed abroad. The third country did not tax the profit because the seller had no permanent establishment there. Thus, the profit on these sales often escaped income tax altogether.

Under current U.S. law, foreign parties are not taxed on most foreign source income. However, to prevent abuses such as those described above, foreign source income is considered ECI when the three conditions in I.R.C. 864(c)(4) and (5) are met. First, the foreign party (or the party's dependent agent) must have a U.S. office or fixed place of business. Second, the office must be a material factor in the production of the foreign source income and must be regularly used in business activities that produce the type of income in question. Third, the foreign source income must be one of the following: (1) royalties from the use of intangible property abroad or (2) dividends or interest derived in the active conduct of either a U.S. banking or finance business or a corporation whose principal business is trading stocks and securities for its own account.

I.R.C. 864(c)(4)(B)(iii) indicates that foreign source income a foreign party earns through the material effort of a U.S. office is ECI. However, the interaction of this provision with the source of income rules assures that foreign source ECI will never result. In particular, sales of personalty (including inventory) through a U.S. office generally result in U.S. source income, which is ECI through the business activities test. On the other hand, if a foreign office materially participates in the sale and the property is sold for consumption abroad, the income is from foreign sources and is not ECI. In effect, when a foreign party sells inventory through a U.S. office, the profit must be either U.S. source ECI or foreign source income that is not ECI; it cannot be foreign source ECI.

NOTE

The "Asset Use" Test. The most difficult of these tests to apply may be the "asset use" test for U.S. source income, because of the potential ambiguity concerning what assets are "held for use" by a trade or business. The Treasury regulations provide additional guidance and define three categories of assets that fall under the "asset use" test: assets (a) whose "principal purpose" is "promoting the present conduct of the a trade or business," (b) that are "[a]cquired and held in the ordinary course of business," or (c) that are "[o]therwise held in a direct relationship to the trade or business conducted in the United States." Treas. Reg. § 1.864–4(c)(2)(ii). As the foregoing excerpt indicates, the third category of assets includes working capital held to meet the operating expenses of a U.S. trade or business. However, investment capital does not count as assets for ECI purposes; for example, ECI does not include income from assets used for future diversification into a new trade or business, for the expansion of a trade or business conducted outside of the United States, or for future plant replacement. See Treas. Reg. § 1.864–4(c)(2)(iv).

ECI in the Absence of a Trade or Business or Linkage with a Trade or Business

Limited circumstances exist under which a foreign person can opt into ECI or the IRS can find that income effectively connected with a trade or business exists, even if there is no trade or business or no linkage between the trade or business and the targeted income. In the following excerpt, Harvey Dale sets forth the provisions that expand or limit the reach of the effectively connected income principle.

Harvey P. Dale, *Effectively Connected Income*, 42 TAX L. REV. 689, 711–713 (1987).

Having once defined the effectively connected concept, Congress has used it in dozens of sections. * * * Most of them are designed to conform various parts of our taxing pattern to the ECI rules. * * *

Several provisions make ECI status mandatory without regard to the tests of section 864(c)(2). Some of these are designed to be helpful, that is, to reduce the U.S. income tax on particular transactions. Others look in the opposite direction— they are intended to increase U.S. tax revenues. One example of the helpful variety is section 882(e). It affects banks organized and doing business in U.S. possessions. Interest on obligations of the United States derived by such banks is automatically ECI, thus eliminating withholding at the source and allowing offsetting deductions for interest paid, and other relevant deductions. A second example applies to make ECI the income of participants in certain exchange or training programs. The 1986 legislation added an election, also intended to be helpful, to treat as ECI some types of income of certain foreign corporations insuring U.S. risks.

The best example of a revenue-raising ECI rule is section 897, * * * making ECI most gains from disposition of U.S. real estate. Several other Code provisions, however, are also designed to protect the revenue by making ECI status mandatory. For example, certain distributions from corporations electing the possessions tax credit of section 936 are automatically ECI. * * * There is at least one (now anachronistic) instance of the attempted use of this sort of mandatory ECI status not by Code provision but by regulation: for a foreign corporation to make a consent, under section 341(f) (dealing with collapsible corporations), obsolete regulations provide that the corporation had to agree that any subsequent gain on disposition of the assets would be treated as ECI.

Deferred Gains from U.S. Source or Foreign Source Income

Foreign individuals and corporations cannot avoid taxation merely by deferring income to a later period. In the following excerpt, the Joint Committee on Taxation explains the conditions under which deferred profits are treated as effectively connected with a trade or business.

STAFF OF THE JOINT COMMITTEE ON TAXATION, EXPLANATION OF PROPOSED INCOME TREATY BETWEEN THE UNITED STATES AND THE UNITED KINGDOM, March 5, 2003.

Any income or gain of a foreign person for any taxable year that is attributable to a transaction in another year is treated as effectively connected with the conduct of a U.S. trade or business if it would have been so treated had it been taken into account in that other year (I.R.C. § 864(c)(6)). In addition, if any property ceases to be used or held for use in connection with the conduct of a trade or business within the United States, the determination of whether any income or gain attributable to a sale or exchange of that property occurring within ten years after the cessation of business is effectively connected with the conduct of a trade or business within the United States is made as if the sale or exchange occurred immediately before the cessation of business (I.R.C. § 864(c)(7)).

NOTE

It May be Income But Can We Collect the Tax? The shortcoming of efforts to tax deferred gains from U.S. or foreign source income is that individuals and corporations may take all of their property out of the United States, thereby placing their assets beyond the reach of the IRS. So long as individuals and corporations are repeat players economically within the United States, IRS officials can collect tax on deferred gains. However, even the mere transfer of funds from one corporate entity to another may make it practically difficult, if not impossible, for the IRS to collect taxes on deferred gains.

6.4   THE SIGNIFICANCE OF TAX TREATIES

In cases in which the United States does not have a tax treaty with the foreign taxpayer's nation, the fact that the individual or corporation has income effectively connected with a trade or business is sufficient to trigger U.S. income tax exposure. However, when a tax treaty exists with the home nation of the foreign individual or corporation, the treaty generally requires that a foreign individual or corporation must have a "permanent establishment" in the United States to be subject to U.S. taxation on its net business income.

The Internal Revenue Code is only one piece of the framework for determining what tax rules apply to international income. Sometimes treaties play a more significant role in determining what tax rules apply to the investments or businesses of foreign parties in the United States or of U.S. residents outside of the United States. For example, treaties have introduced the concept of a "permanent establishment" to supplant the application of the ECI rules in many cases.

Income tax treaties generally cover only federal income tax issues. State and local tax issues are generally not addressed in treaties, yet they may be affected by treaty provisions. Most tax treaties are bilateral treaties with individual countries based on one or more model treaties provided by the United States, the OECD, or the United Nations. In the following excerpt, Joseph Henderson and Michael Pfeifer lay out the basic purposes of tax treaties and the process for their creation and ratification.

Joseph H. Henderson & Michael G. Pfeifer, *Effect of Tax Treaties on U.S. Activities of Nonresidents*, International Trust and Estate Planning: American Law Institute–American Bar Association Course of Study Materials 555, 557–558 (October 4–5, 2001).

> Accompanying the exponential growth of international commerce of the past century has been the exposure of multinational investors and business operations to taxation in more than

one country. In 1939, the United States signed its first income tax treaty ever, with France. Thus began a process to resolve conflicts between the United States and other countries in the area of taxation. This has resulted in the United States entering into some 63 income tax treaties currently in force.

A tax treaty is a bilateral agreement between two countries in which each country agrees to modify its internal tax laws, thereby resulting in a reciprocal benefit. As a result, a tax treaty is an independent source of tax law that must be consulted in advising the multinational investor (in addition to the internal tax rules of the investor's country of residence as well as those of the country in which the investment is located). The most prevalent U.S. tax treaties are those addressing taxes applicable to income and capital gains. In addition, the United States has entered into treaties with 16 countries focusing on estate, gift and generation skipping taxes.

The basic purpose of an income tax treaty is to facilitate international trade and investment by removing—or preventing the erection of—tax barriers to the free international exchange of goods and services, and the free international movement of capital and persons. This goal is achieved, as the IRS has stated, by means of the three functions that tax treaties serve: (i) preventing double taxation; (ii) preventing discriminatory tax treatment of a resident of a country; and (iii) permitting recip-rocal administration to prevent tax avoidance and evasion.
* * *

The U.S. Treasury Department negotiates U.S. tax treaties; however, as with all U.S. treaties, every tax treaty must be ratified by the U.S. Senate before that treaty will enter into force. As part of this process, the Treasury Department will issue a Technical Explanation for a treaty. In addition, the Senate Foreign Relations Committee will hold public hearings to discuss whether a particular treaty should be ratified by the Senate and will issue a companion Committee report. In many cases, Letters of Understanding will be issued by the United States and the treaty partner clarifying certain points regarding the treaty. All of these sources must be reviewed to determine the scope and impact of a particular treaty provision when advising a client. Finally, a treaty may be modified by a Proto-col, which generally will have its own separate Treasury Techni-cal Explanation, Senate Foreign Relations Committee Report and possible Letters of Understanding that must also be re-viewed in determining the applicability of a tax treaty.

Each U.S. tax treaty is unique. However, the starting point for U.S. tax treaty negotiations is the appropriate U.S. model tax treaty. Income tax treaty negotiations are based upon the model income tax treaty published by Treasury in 1996. Estate tax treaty negotiations are based on Treasury's 1980 model estate tax treaty. Each model treaty is accompanied by Treasury's technical explanation of the treaty's provisions. In interpreting treaties, it is helpful to refer to the current model treaty and its technical explanation.

NOTE

Other Models. The OECD, an international organization whose members include the world's major industrialized countries, has published model income and estate tax treaties that have influenced tax treaty policies of the United States as well as its other member countries. The United Nations also publishes a model income tax treaty, which is often the basis for negotiations between industrial and developing countries.

One of the most-cited advantages of tax treaties is the reduction of barriers to foreign direct investment. In the following excerpt, Bruce Blonigen and Ronald Davies highlight the arguments for how tax treaties may reduce barriers to foreign direct investment, but they suggest that tax treaties may not live up to these expectations and may actually decrease levels of foreign direct investment across countries.

BRUCE A. BLONIGEN & RONALD B. DAVIES, DO BILATERAL TREATIES PROMOTE FOREIGN DIRECT INVESTMENT?, Working Paper 8834, National Bureau of Economic Research, at 4–8 (March 2002).

Although individual treaties include a wide range of specific investment incentives, overall treaties reduce the barriers to FDI [Foreign Direct Investment] in two ways. First, by harmonizing the tax definitions and the tax jurisdictions of treaty partners, a treaty can reduce the double taxation of investment. For example, income is typically taxed in a host country when it is generated through a permanent establishment. However, without a treaty each country can form its own definition of a permanent establishment. If this definition differs between countries, it can lead to double taxation of overseas profits. * * * Since treaties standardize tax definitions and jurisdictions (often by matching them to those provided by the OECD's model tax treaty), they have a similar potential to increase FDI.

Second, tax treaties affect the actual statutory taxation of multinationals. They do so through the rules affecting double taxation relief and the withholding taxes levied on repatriations by FDI. Following the OECD model treaty guidelines, most tax treaties specify that both countries must either exempt foreign-earned profits from domestic taxation or offer foreign tax credits when calculating the domestic tax bill. Although most countries already offer their investors credits or exemptions, certain treaties do alter the relief method applied by one or more treaty partners. In addition to the provisions for double taxation relief, treaties usually reduce maximum allowable withholding taxes on three types of remitted income: dividend payments, interest payments, and royalty payments. Some treaties lower these withholding rates to as low as zero. Most treaties specify that the same maximum rates apply to both treaty partners. If these reductions in the withholding tax reduce the tax burden on overseas investment * * * this should increase FDI. Note that even though withholding tax rates fall under a treaty, this does not imply that tax receipts from inbound investment must decline. Since withholding taxes can be tailored to the specific investment from a treaty partner, it may be possible to set tax rates which encourage tax-sensitive inbound investment and actually raise total tax receipts. In addition, treaties are accompanied by improved information exchange between partner governments. Because of this, tax evasion may fall under a treaty, leading to increased tax revenue.

Combining these arguments, it is easy to understand the common expectation that tax treaties serve to increase the amount of FDI activity between tax partners. Nonetheless, there exist several economic and legal arguments which suggest treaties may have no effect on FDI. [Tsilly] Dagan asserts that the use of treaties to promote foreign direct investment is "a myth." He claims that since a parent country could unilaterally adjust its tax policy to eliminate distortions caused by differing parent and host country tax policies, promotion of efficiency plays little role in treaty formation. Instead Dagan suggests that treaties are intended to reduce administrative costs, reduce tax evasion, and to extract tax concessions from treaty partners. * * * Furthermore, there is the concern that tax treaties arise due to lobbying efforts by profit-seeking investors. If this is the case, then treaties may be geared towards maximizing investor profits rather than promoting efficient incentives. In addition to uncertainties about government objectives in treaty formation, it is by no means clear that firms' investment activities will necessarily respond to reductions in withholding tax rates. * * *

Finally, it is even possible that tax treaties may actually increase the tax barriers for certain types of investment. * * * [I]nformation exchange treaties can reduce the firm's ability to engage in transfer pricing. This is the practice by which, through manipulation of the price of goods trade between their various subsidiaries, firms can shift profits to low tax locations and minimize their global tax revenues. * * * Since treaties streamline and promote the exchange of tax information by governments, this reduces firms' ability to avoid taxes through misrepresentation of costs. As a result, treaties may reduce the incentive to engage in investment for tax minimization reasons, leading to decreased FDI activity. In addition, recent tax treaties have sought to eliminate treaty shopping. Treaty shopping is a practice in which investments are funneled through a treaty country by a third nation for the purpose of avoiding or reducing taxes. * * * [C]oncerns over treaty shopping have been a primary focus of many new treaties and have prompted the U.S. to renegotiate many of its older treaties. In addition, certain so-called "tax haven" countries (particularly Aruba, Malta, and the Netherlands–Antilles) have seen several of their treaties cancelled due to perceived insufficient efforts to prevent treaty shopping. If a treaty is revised to close this possibility, then this could easily reduce the investment activity between treaty partners as third nation investors choose to simply send their capital directly to the ultimate host. * * *

With these conflicting arguments in mind, it is by no means certain that bilateral treaties will increase the amount of FDI between partner countries. * * *

NOTE

Greater Uniformity and More Disclosure. Whether tax treaties increase the level of foreign direct investment or not, they do promote greater uniformity of tax policies and enhance information disclosure across countries. Tax treaties may bring benefits to ratifying states, but they also create additional issues, for example, how treaty obligations interact with national laws and regulations.

The Relationship Between Tax Treaties and the Code

Article VI of the United States Constitution declares that federal statutes, including the Internal Revenue Code, and treaties, such as tax treaties, are the supreme law of the land.[6] When conflicts arise between a Treasury regulation, IRS ruling, or other administrative pronouncement and a tax treaty, the tax treaty provision prevails. However, the United States Congress can unilaterally override treaty obligations with statutes, as the statute or treaty provision that is later in time prevails. This fact is a cause for dismay among many of our treaty partners, such as France, where a treaty overrides statutory provisions regardless of when a statute is enacted. In the following excerpt, Meenakshi Ambardar shows how federal courts strive to interpret U.S. statutes to honor the intent of both U.S. treaty obligations and statutes. When conflicts

---

6. "Laws of the United States which shall be made in Pursuance thereof; and all Treaties made, or which shall be made, under the Authority of the United States, shall be the supreme Law of the Land." U.S. Const. art. VI, cl. 2.

occur, however, U.S. federal statutes trump treaty obligations whenever a conflicting statute is later in time and the statute evidences an intent to override a treaty obligation.

Meenakshi Ambardar, Comment, *The Taxation of Deferred Compensation under I.R.C. 864(c)(6) and Income Tax Treaties: A Rose Is Not Always a Rose*, 19 FORDHAM INT'L L.J. 736, 771–774 (1995).

Tax treaties affect taxation under the Code by reducing or eliminating tax liability. In cases of conflict between the Code and tax treaties, courts give both equal authority under the U.S. Constitution ("Constitution"). Courts construe the language of the tax treaty so as to make it harmonious with the Code. The possibility of a treaty override, however, occurs when subsequent amendments to the Code cannot be reconciled with existing provisions of a tax treaty.

In determining the force of treaties in the United States, the Supremacy Clause of the Constitution subjects all treaties and laws to constitutional scrutiny. The U.S. Supreme Court ("Supreme Court") has interpreted the Supremacy Clause as putting statutes and treaties on equal footing because both are part of the domestic law. Accordingly, in trying to interpret the relationship between an earlier treaty provision and a statute enacted after the treaty has been adopted, courts must decide whether the two provisions, both of equal authority, can both be given effect.

As in the case of statutes, courts construe tax treaties by first considering the text of the treaty. Courts begin with a general presumption of harmony between treaties and statutes, regardless of which was first enacted. In resolving conflicts, courts may also rely upon the legislative history of a tax treaty when interpreting its provisions. Historically, absent specific legislative history or explicit statutory override, courts have upheld existing treaties that conflict with subsequent revenue laws.

Treaty overrides occur when subsequent domestic legislation by the source country conflicts with earlier obligations assumed under a binding tax treaty with another country. Treaty overrides are thus linked to the incorporation of tax treaty provisions into domestic law. Tax treaty overrides can be classified into two groups: intentional and unintentional. Intentional tax treaty overrides occur when one country enacts legislation knowing and intending that it will conflict with a tax treaty obligation. An unintentional tax treaty override occurs when the country does not express such intent. In the latter situation, U.S. courts may reconcile the existing tax treaty and the new law. In cases of intentional override, however, the new domestic law prevails over the treaty.

NOTE

The Later-in-Time Principle. I.R.C. § 7852(d)(1) codifies that the later-in-time principle reconciles code and treaty conflicts by having the most recently enacted provision prevail. The Supreme Court has held that courts should not easily infer a legislative override and has stated that a "treaty will not be deemed to have been abrogated or modified by a later statute, unless such purpose on the part of Congress has been clearly expressed."[7] The Court has also held, however, that "tax provisions should generally be read to incorporate domestic tax concepts absent a clear congressional expression that foreign concepts control."[8]

6.5 THE TREATY CONCEPT OF A "PERMANENT ESTABLISHMENT"

If an alien individual or foreign corporation is a resident of a country with an income tax treaty with the United States, the treaty will alter the applicability of certain Internal Revenue Code rules. For example, as Chapter 3 discusses, most U.S. income tax treaties signed since 1967 contain treaty articles defining "residents," with tie-breaker rules for dual resident individuals. The treaty concept of a "permanent establishment" for corporations is an analogue to the "engaged in a trade and business concept" in the Code. Similarly, the statutory concept of "effectively connected income" is often replaced by treaty with the concept of income "attributable to" a permanent establishment. Income "effectively connected with a trade or business" is a much broader concept than income "attributable to a permanent establishment." While finding that a foreign individual or corporation maintains a permanent establishment in the United States typically means that a U.S. trade or business exists, a foreign entity may be engaged in a trade or business within the United States but not maintain a permanent establishment in this country.

One of the salutary effects of the permanent establishment concept is to relieve pressure on the sometimes indeterminate rules concerning when an individual is "engaged in a trade or business in the United States." Ordinary "engaged in a trade or business" concepts do not

---

7. Cook v. United States, 288 U.S. 102, 120 (1933); see also Estate of Burghardt v. Commissioner, 80 T.C. 705, 717 (1983) (stating that "the intention to abrogate or modify a treaty is not to be lightly imputed to the Congress"); Reid v. Covert, 354 U.S. 1, 18 (1957) (holding that courts will always try to reconcile treaty obligations with statutes when the two relate to the same subject, but that the later in time rule applies when the treaty and statute are inconsistent with each other).

8. See United States v. Goodyear Tire & Rubber, 493 U.S. 132, 145 (1989) (holding that accumulated profits for indirect tax credits under the I.R.C. should be calculated in accordance with domestic tax principles).

provide good answers for questions such as whether mail-order or sporadic businesses should be taxed in the United States. The permanent establishment requirement sweeps many of these difficulties away by allowing foreign persons to engage in quite a lot of business activity before they become subject to U.S. taxation. The permanent establishment concept has historically served the basic function of defining which business activities are subject to U.S. taxation quite well. The permanent establishment clause is far from a panacea, however, as this framework does not provide easy answers to complications posed by new challenges, such as e-commerce. In the following excerpt, Randolph Buchanan highlights some of the basic differences between the statutory "effectively connected" standard and the treaty-based "permanent establishment" test.

Randolph J. Buchanan, Comment, *The New-Millennium Dilemma: Does the Reliance on the Use of Computer Servers and Websites in a Global Electronic Commerce Environment Necessitate a Revision to the Current Definition of a Permanent Establishment?*, 54 S.M.U. L. Rev. 2109, 2113–2116 (2001).

[T]he "effectively connected" test has a lower threshold than the [permanent establishment (PE)] test because there is no requirement that the U.S. trade or business has a fixed place of business. Consequently, if at the end of the analysis it is determined that a foreign company is engaged in a U.S. trade or business and has income that is "effectively connected" with that business, it is only necessary to determine whether the foreign company also has a PE in the United States if a tax treaty exists between the country of residence of the foreign company and the United States. * * *

[A] low level of activity is all that is required for the courts to conclude that the activities of a foreign corporation located outside of the United States is engaged in a U.S. trade or business. Consequently, all activities that are considerable, continuous, and regular will be treated as "effectively connected" with a U.S. trade or business. Continuous is defined as a day-to-day activity, rather than a sporadic activity. Moreover, to pass this test, an activity must occur regularly rather than irregularly, and it must be considerable as opposed to minimal. * * *

If a tax treaty exists between the country of residence of the foreign enterprise and the United States, the tax authorities will apply the PE test in an attempt to impose a tax on the foreign enterprise. This involves answering two questions. First, does the foreign enterprise have a PE in the United States or elsewhere that would subject them to the imposition of an income tax? Second, assuming that it does have a PE, what amount of its business profits are taxable and at what rate under the applicable tax treaty with that particular contracting state? Since having a PE necessitates the existence of a tax treaty, once the elements of a PE have been met under Article V of the tax treaty, the calculation of business profits under Article VII becomes crucial.

The purpose of the PE requirement was to determine a particular point in time when a foreign entity providing goods or services had established a sufficient taxable presence or connection with a jurisdiction to entitle that jurisdiction to tax the transaction, including the business profits generated from it. Thus, it was essential to determine whether the enterprise had a PE in a particular contracting state since the business profits of the enterprise, operating in a contracting state that was different from the source state, could not be taxed by the source state unless their business activities were attributable to a PE. * * *

The U.S. Model Treaty

One significant goal of tax treaties is to make more predictable the tax exposure of U.S. companies operating abroad and foreign companies operating in the United States. The U.S. Model Treaty establishes the framework for U.S. efforts to create a uniform understanding of a permanent establishment for which attributable profits are taxable in both the United States and other ratifying countries. In the following excerpt, Ernest Larkins describes the standard permanent establishment provisions that exist in the U.S. Model Treaty and most U.S. tax treaties.

Ernest R. Larkins, *U.S. Income Tax Treaties in Research and Planning: A Primer*, 18 VA. TAX REV. 133, 148–155 (1998).

U.S. income tax treaties generally preclude the United States from taxing residents of foreign treaty countries on business profits unless the income is attributable to permanent establishments in the United States. Similarly, treaties do not permit foreign treaty countries to tax U.S. residents on business profits unless those profits are attributable to permanent establishments in the foreign treaty countries. Thus, the existence or absence of a permanent establishment is the pivotal element when determining the taxation of most categories of business profits under a U.S. tax treaty. Nonetheless, the I.R.S. indicates that it will ordinarily not rule on the existence of a permanent establishment or whether income is attributable to a permanent establishment.

Business profits of a permanent establishment are determined on a net basis, i.e., after allowable deductions. Generally, the same methods of accounting are used from one year to the next. All business profits attributable to a permanent establishment are generally subject to taxation in the host country, even if received in a later year when the permanent establishment no longer exists. Assume a treaty country enterprise sells goods on an installment basis in 1991 through a U.S. permanent establishment. At the end of 1991, the permanent establishment and all business activities in the United States are terminated. During 1992, the installment obligations are collected. Though no permanent establishment exists in the United States at any time during 1992 when the installment profits are realized, the income is nonetheless attributable to the permanent establishment. Thus, the United States is entitled to tax the business profits during 1992 from the installment sale in 1991.

The concept of a permanent establishment is not found in the Code except as it relates to U.S. treaties. A permanent establishment can assume one of three forms: a fixed place of business, a specified duration of business activity, or a dependent agent. All fixed places of business in a host country are not permanent establishments since treaties often carve out several exceptions. Similarly, all agents operating within a host country are not permanent establishments. * * *

Generally, a fixed place of business through which a resident of one treaty country wholly or partially conducts business activities in the other treaty country is a permanent establishment. Thus, a person can carry on a trade or business in a treaty country and be exempt from that country's income tax if the profits of the activity are not attributable to a permanent establishment in that country. A permanent establishment typically includes any place of management, branch, office, factory, store, or workshop. It also includes any place from which natural resources are extracted such as a mine, oil or gas well, or quarry.

Nonetheless, certain activities are not considered carrying on business through permanent establishments, even though they satisfy the general meaning of the term as given above. An enterprise generally does not have a permanent establishment if it is merely maintaining the following:

● Facilities for storage, delivery, or display of goods or merchandise (e.g., a warehouse);

● Inventory for storage, delivery, or display;

● Inventory that another enterprise will process;

- Facilities for the purchase of goods or merchandise or for collecting information (e.g., an office from which marketing studies are done);

- Facilities for preparatory or auxiliary activities of the enterprise (i.e., advertising, promotion, supplying information, basic scientific research, and similar supportive services); and

- Facilities for some combination of the activities above (e.g., for displaying merchandise and collecting information). * * *

- Advertising, supplying information, or scientific research; and

- Concluding or signing loan contracts, contracts for the delivery of goods or merchandise, or contracts for the performance of technical services.

The use of an office for reasons other than those exceptions listed in the treaty generally results in permanent establishment status. * * *

An enterprise's temporary use of a fixed location is generally not considered to be a permanent establishment. * * *

The fact that a resident of one treaty country controls a company that resides or conducts business in the other treaty country does not, absent other factors, cause the first resident to have a permanent establishment in the latter country. For example, a U.S. corporation is not considered to have a permanent establishment in France merely because it owns all the stock in a French subsidiary that does business in France. Similarly, a company that resides or conducts business in France and controls a U.S. subsidiary does not, by itself, cause the subsidiary to have a permanent establishment in France. * * *

The location of some activities constitutes a permanent establishment only if the activities continue beyond a certain time period, which is generally 12 months but which can range from three to 24 months depending on the underlying treaty. Usually these activities are conducted at building or construction sites or involve installation or assembly projects. * * *

Under U.S. income tax treaties, some agency relationships cause the principal to have a permanent establishment in the host country, even when a fixed place of business is lacking. Whether an agent creates a permanent establishment for the principal depends on whether the agency relationship is classified as independent or dependent, which depends on the authority and activities of the agent.

An independent agent must be legally and economically autonomous of its principal. Independent agents are those that act in the ordinary course of their own business and generally have nonexclusive relationships with more than one principal. Independent agents are not considered permanent establishments and, absent other factors, do not subject their principal's business profits to taxation in the host country. Thus, brokers, general commission agents, local sales representatives, and other agents of independent status are not permanent establishments. A subsidiary corporation in one country that sells goods on behalf of its parent generally is considered to be an independent agent and, thus, does not cause the parent company to have a permanent establishment in the subsidiary's country.

When a dependent agent has the authority to conclude contracts in an enterprise's name and regularly exercises that authority to bind the enterprise, the agent is considered a permanent establishment and, thus, subjects the enterprise to taxation in the host country. Three conditions must exist before an enterprise is considered to have a permanent establishment because of the activities of a second party. First, the relationship between the parties must be that of an agent and principal, where the agent party represents and acts on behalf of the other party, known as the principal. Second, the agent must be dependent on the principal. A dependent agent generally is one subject to the principal's detailed instruction and comprehensive control (e.g., an employee of the principal). In many cases, the dependent agent bears little or no business risk (i.e., risk of loss) from its own activities. Third, the dependent agent must possess and regularly exercise authority to conclude contracts that legally bind the principal.

Nonetheless, if the dependent agent's activities are restricted to the non-permanent establishment activities listed earlier, the dependent agent is not considered a permanent establishment. For example, an employee who has the authority to conclude contracts for advertising his or her principal's merchandise and regularly concludes such contracts, absent other activities, is not treated as a permanent establishment since facilities used for advertising generally are not permanent establishments. Similarly, a news reporter engaged in collecting information is generally not considered a permanent establishment since a facility used for this purpose likewise avoids permanent establishment status.

In most cases, a subsidiary that operates through a permanent establishment in a treaty country does not cause its parent company to have a permanent establishment. However, a subsidiary that regularly exercises its authority to negotiate and conclude contracts on behalf of its parent can be treated as the parent's dependent agent. Likewise, a partnership that conducts business in a treaty country through a permanent establishment results in similar permanent establishment treatment for each of its partners (whether general or limited). * * *

NOTE

Related Provisions. The U.S. Model Treaty also has specific provisions for the taxation of transportation, real property, and personal services income, as well as provisions governing particular professions such as entertainers, athletes, teachers and students. An important treaty provision distinguishes between independent and dependent agents, a distinction that may not always be as easy to make as this excerpt suggests. The difficulties are well illustrated by the challenge that e-commerce poses for permanent establishment determinations, an issue explored later in this section.

Permanent Establishment Under the OECD and U.N. Model Income Tax Conventions

The OECD Model Income Tax Convention and U.N. Model Income Tax Convention offer alternative frameworks for determining what constitutes a permanent establishment. In the following excerpt, Brian Arnold shows that the OECD and UN approaches are very similar to each other (and implicitly to the U.S. Model Treaty described in the Ernest Larkins excerpt). He also notes some differences between these frameworks for determining the existence of a permanent establishment.

BRIAN J. ARNOLD, *Threshold Requirements for Taxing Business Profits Under Tax Treaties*, forthcoming, Canadian Tax Foundation,[9] 14–20, 25–27 (2003).

* * * Under Article 7(1) of the OECD Model Convention a resident of one contracting state is not taxable on business profits derived in the other contracting state unless the business is carried on through a PE in that state. Even if a PE exists, only the profits attributable to the PE are taxable. The existence of a PE is clearly a minimum threshold that must be satisfied in order for a country to tax a nonresident on business profits derived from sources in the country.

The PE concept also plays an important role in allocating tax revenues from cross-border business transactions between the country in which the income is derived and the country in

---

9. A summary of the proceedings of the conference where this paper was presented is provided in Brian J. Arnold, Jacques Sasseville and Eric M. Zolt, Summary of the Proceedings of an Invitational Seminar on the Taxation of Business Profits under Tax Treaties, 57 Bull. Int. Fiscal Dec. 187 (2003).

which the owners of the business are residents. In the absence of a PE, the business profits derived in the source country by a nonresident are exempt from tax there and taxable only in the country of residence. Once a PE is established in the source country, the source country not only acquires the right to tax the business profits attributable to the PE, but also its right to tax takes precedence over the residence country's right to tax those profits. The residence country becomes obligated either to exempt the business profits attributable to the PE in the source country or to provide a credit for the source country tax.

The PE concept is obviously the most important threshold for source country taxation of business profits. This importance is illustrated by the fact that the term "Permanent Establishment" is the only term, other than "resident," the definition of which takes up an entire article in the Model Treaty. Although there are other threshold requirements for special types of business profits in the OECD Model Convention, as discussed below, the PE threshold is the one that is generally applicable.

A PE is defined in Article 5(1) to be "a fixed place of business through which the business of an enterprise is wholly or partly carried on." The term and the definition both suggest something that is fixed in a geographical sense and permanent in a temporal sense.

Most of the examples provided in Article 5(2)—office, factory, workshop, mine, oil or gas well—serve to reinforce the idea that only physical facilities can constitute a PE. This aspect of the definition of PE has the virtue of certainty. In most cases, the existence of a fixed place of business will be obvious. Moreover, the OECD Commentary has attempted to eliminate any issues related to the taxpayer's use of the fixed place. It is not necessary for the taxpayer to rent or own the premises or to have some legal right to use them. It is sufficient if the taxpayer uses the premises. The only uncertainty comes from the time period that the fixed place must continue to be used by a taxpayer. The other obvious advantage of the existence of physical facilities used by the taxpayer is that, usually, the tax authorities will be able to enforce any tax liability effectively.
* * *

From the outset, the drafters of the predecessors to the OECD Model Convention recognized that a fixed place of business threshold was too limited. They recognized that source countries should be entitled to tax some types of business that could be carried on in a country by nonresidents without the necessity of establishing a fixed place of business in the country. Therefore, * * * a taxpayer is deemed to have a PE in a country if the taxpayer has a dependent agent in the country who has and habitually exercises an authority to conclude contracts on behalf of the taxpayer. Under the dependent agent rule, it is unnecessary for either the taxpayer or the agent to have a fixed place of business in the country. Thus, the OECD Model Convention has recognized from its beginning that the fixed place of business part of the PE definition was not appropriate for all types of business, and that a different threshold was necessary and appropriate for certain businesses. The dependent agent rule is noticeably different from the fixed place of business threshold. Whereas the latter focuses on a fixed place, the former focuses on the activities carried on by dependent agents for the taxpayer. The activities must be central to the income-earning process: the concluding of contracts. They may be carried out at different locations in a country, but they must be carried out habitually.

* * * [T]he advantages of a fixed place of business threshold—namely, certainty for taxpayers and tax authorities and the practical ability to enforce any tax obligations against a nonresident—do not apply to the dependent agent threshold. The application of the dependent agent rule requires several difficult determinations based on the facts of each situation. If a nonresident is considered to have a PE by reason of the activities of a dependent agent, in most countries, the nonresident's tax liability can be enforced against the agent. However, the ability to take enforcement action against someone who is not the taxpayer and is only physically present, perhaps only temporarily present and not necessarily in one place, is unlikely to be as effective as taking action against a nonresident with a fixed place of business in the country.

The fixed place of business and dependent agent aspects of the definition of a PE are both modified by the exceptions in Article 7(4) for preparatory and auxiliary activities. If a fixed place of business is used solely for such activities, or a dependent agent's activities are limited to concluding contracts regarding such matters, the fixed place of business or the activities of the dependent agent are deemed not to constitute a PE. The rationale for the exclusion of preparatory and auxiliary activities is that such services "are so remote from the actual realization of profits that it is difficult to allocate any profit to the fixed place of business in question." This statement confuses the existence of a PE and the amount of profit attributable to a PE. As discussed earlier, these are two separate and distinct issues. A PE may exist even though little or no profit is attributable to the PE. Moreover, in terms of accepted transfer-pricing practices, even preparatory and auxiliary activities * * * are functions that should be compensated on an arm's length basis.

* * *

In summary, the PE concept, viewed from the perspective of a threshold requirement for source country taxation of business profits, is much more complicated than the fixed place of business aspect of the definition would suggest. The fixed place of business requirement reflects the nature of the presence that a nonresident must have in a country. It is not enough that the nonresident is physically present in the country. The nonresident must have the use of some type of fixed location, such as an office at a particular place in the country, for a significant period. This aspect of the definition is modified by a requirement related to the nature of the activities carried on at the fixed place of business. The activities carried on must go beyond preparatory and auxiliary activities. Further, the fixed place of business requirement is augmented by the dependent agent rule. This rule can be seen as the converse of the preparatory and auxiliary activities rule. Concluding contracts on a regular basis is so central to any business that if such activities take place in a country the taxpayer is deemed to have a PE, even though activities do not take place at a fixed place of business of the taxpayer. In contrast, preparatory and auxiliary activities are considered to be so remote that even if the activities are carried on at a fixed place of business, no PE is considered to exist. Finally, a specific time requirement is provided for construction sites and installation projects. * * *

The UN Model Convention is broadly similar to the OECD Model Convention. In general, the UN Model Convention provides greater opportunities for taxation by source counties compared to the OECD Model Convention. Not surprisingly, the threshold requirements in the UN Model are somewhat different from those in the OECD Model. The following discussion is intended to highlight the significant differences.

Perhaps most significantly, the UN Model Convention provides that a nonresident is considered to have a PE in a country if the nonresident renders services in the country through employees or other personnel for more than 6 months in any 12–month period. This aspect of the PE definition is accompanied by a parallel rule in Article 14, which, unlike the OECD Model Convention, was not repealed in the 2001 revision of the UN Model Convention. Under Article 14(1)(b), a nonresident who stays in a country for more than 183 days in any 12–month period is taxable in that country on income from professional services and other activities of an independent character. In this regard, the UN Model Convention reflects the judgment that a fixed place of business threshold for service businesses is inappropriate. Instead, the minimum threshold for source country taxation of profits from service businesses is based on the service activities taking place in the country and the physical presence of the nonresident in the country for a significant time (more than 6 months).

The UN Model Convention also considers a construction site or an assembly or installation project, including supervisory activities, to be a PE if the site, project, or activities last more than 6 months, rather than the 12–month period used by the OECD. This 6–month rule for construction sites and installation projects is consistent with the 6–month rule for other service businesses. The UN Model Convention deems a PE to exist if a nonresident insurance company collects premiums in the country or insures risks in the country through employees or agents other than independent agents. No fixed place of business is required and, unlike the OECD Model Convention, it is not necessary for the employees or agents to have and habitually exercise the authority to conclude contracts. The threshold for insurance is simply that the relevant activities (collecting premiums or insuring risks in the country) take place in the country. In this regard the threshold and the source rule for insurance profits are the same.

The Potential Shortcomings of Permanent Establishment in an Electronic Age

The permanent establishment concept was initially a compromise to resolve competitive efforts by nations to maximize their tax revenues from international business transactions in the wake of World War I. In the following excerpt, Walter Hellerstein describes how the physical presence standard for permanent jurisdiction may have fit the world of the 1920s quite well, but may be ill-suited for the distinctively different challenges facing tax policymaking in today's economy.

WALTER HELLERSTEIN, JURISDICTION TO TAX INCOME AND CONSUMPTION IN THE NEW ECONOMY: A THEORETICAL AND COMPARATIVE PERSPECTIVE (Working Paper, April 1, 2003) 29–31.

* * * The permanent establishment concept originated in the work of the Committee of Technical Experts who drafted the League of Nations model income tax treaty in the 1920s. At that time, the American business community was becoming increasingly concerned over what it viewed as the aggressive assertion of source-based taxing claims by foreign governments, which were under great pressure to raise revenues after World

War I. According to one contemporary observer, foreign governments:

> began to try to tax the earnings of the visiting businessman
> and the profits of the foreign company on the goods sold
> through him. Canada even tried to tax a United States firm
> on profits from advertising its wares and receiving mail
> orders from customers in its territory. * * * In the early
> 1920s, the British Board of Inland Revenue sought to
> impose liability * * * [on] sales through a local commission
> agent * * * [e]ven if the nonresident and his British inter-
> mediary took pains to conclude the contract abroad.

"In the face of this concern with expanding jurisdiction
over business income, the Committee of Technical Experts
adopted the 'permanent establishment' safeguard: only the nation in which the permanent establishment of a business enterprise was located could legitimately levy source-based taxes on
the enterprise's income." * * *

But times have changed over the three-quarters of a century since the permanent establishment concept first became a
fixture of international income tax jurisdiction. Indeed, if there
is one proposition upon which virtually all observers agree, it is
that the way in which income is generated in the "new economy" is materially different from the way it was generated
during the formative era of international income tax rules."
* * * Suffice it to say that services and intangibles have become
increasingly important (relative to goods) in today's economy
and electronic commerce pervades (when it does not dominate)
many forms of income-producing activity. Consequently, today's
economy bears a fading resemblance to the economy of the
1920s in ways that bear directly on both the theoretical and
practical underpinnings of income tax jurisdiction. Specifically,
the significance of the relationship that traditionally existed
between the physical location of activities and the income they
produce has diminished. The implications for jurisdictional analysis are apparent. The concept of a permanent establishment,
rooted as it is in indicia of physical presence, has become a less
accurate gauge of the source of income than it was when the
concept was first adopted. * * *

Electronic-commerce transactions made through computer servers
or websites that may be located anywhere in the world pose one of the
greatest challenges to traditional understandings of permanent establishment. In the following excerpt, Richard Doernberg considers whether

the principles underlying the OECD Model Income Tax Convention are sufficiently adaptable to address this new challenge.

Richard L. Doernberg, *Electronic Commerce: Changing Income Tax Treaty Principles a Bit?*, 21 TAX NOTES INT'L. 2417, 2417–2422 (Nov. 20, 2000).

In the world of international taxation, perhaps the most significant change brought about by the electronic commerce (sometimes referred to as e-commerce) revolution is the ability to produce income with little or no physical presence. Consider a typical traditional transaction where R Corp., a resident of state R manufactures thermostats in state R for sale to state S customers. After production, the thermostats are transferred to a facility (e.g., a retail establishment) in state S where a state S sales force markets and distributes the thermostats to state S customers. By international consensus, the income that is produced by the sale of the thermostats is allocated between states S and R so that state S has primary taxing authority with respect to the income attributable to the marketing and distribution in state S while state R has taxing authority with respect to the income attributable to the manufacturing.

Now consider the same transaction in the world of electronic commerce. The thermostats are still manufactured in state R but now can be marketed and sold to state S customers through an Internet web site, designed and maintained by programmers in state R, that might be located on a server in state R. Credit could be checked and payment made online, and then the goods would be shipped to state S customers. If, instead of thermostats, R Corp. produced a digital output (e.g., investment advice, a video), delivery could be made digitally through the Internet. Of course, it has always been possible for R Corp. to sell to customers in state S without having a physical presence there. Mail order or telephone order sales may permit R Corp. to penetrate markets in state S. However, the rise of electronic commerce through the Internet makes it possible for out-of-state vendors such as R Corp. to reach customers in state S with greater ease and in far greater numbers than was previously possible. Accordingly, what may have been a de minimis trading pattern historically has become and will continue to evolve into a substantial trading pattern. Electronic commerce also, in some cases, allows for the delivery of goods and services digitally, which may result in a de-emphasis on physical presence and which also poses enforcement problems for tax administrators because of the lack of an audit trail. * * *

The digital transaction poses a variation of the old philosophical conundrum: if a tree falls in the forest and no one hears it, does it make a sound? In the electronic commerce context, the issue might be posed. if all the value of the thermostat is created in state R but the customers that determine value are in state S, where is the income generated? From an economic standpoint, one might suggest that only state R should have income taxing authority because all of the wealth was created in state R. Certainly, under traditional international income tax principles, state S, which boasts only of a customer base, would have no income taxing authority over R Corp. All profit would be taxable in state R. Arguably, however, R Corp. is conducting business in state S, even if it is not physically present there. * * *

But regardless of the economic arguments championing how e-commerce will benefit all states, there are some political realities that cannot be ignored. The perception, whether right or wrong, that the current tax system, built on the concepts of physical presence, will benefit e-commerce-exporting states (i.e., state R) may portend that the current multilateral consensus on basic international tax principles will not endure. Conversely, notwithstanding arguments by some that origin-based (source) taxation is the answer to ever-mobile residence by companies, countries where entrepreneurs reside will not surrender their right to tax. The current international consensus, reflected in the OECD Model Income Tax Convention, balances residence and source state taxation, but that balance may now be called into question. * * *

What are the major problems under existing treaties that are exacerbated by the growth of electronic commerce? To the extent that treaties divide taxing authority between residence and source states, there will be treaty problems where the contracting states differ on the meaning of the source and residence concepts. With respect to source state taxation, double taxation may result in a situation where state S thinks there is a permanent establishment in state S, but state R does not. For example, suppose that R Corp., a state R resident, has a server in state S that hosts a Web site that transacts all aspects of a business transaction. If state S concludes that R Corp. has a state S permanent establishment, it will have the authority to tax all profits attributable to the permanent establishment. However, if state R does not agree with the permanent establishment characterization, then double taxation might result if state R does not provide taxation relief, by exempting the income or giving a credit for the state S taxes paid. Currently, the OECD is attempting to clarify when a server (or more accurately the geographical location where the server is situated) can constitute a permanent establishment and how profits are to be attributed to any permanent establishment that is found to exist. * * *

Aside from differences in determining what constitutes a permanent establishment, state R and state S may also disagree about allocation of the tax base resulting from other definitional differences. For example, suppose that R Corp. makes available to state S customers the benefit of accounting software the output of which can be downloaded for a fee from R Corp.'s Web page on its server in state R. State R might view the transaction as a sale that is only taxable in state R in the absence of a state S permanent establishment. Or state R might view the transaction as a performance of services taxable only in state R in the absence of a state S permanent establishment. In either case, article 7 of the OECD model grants exclusive taxing authority to state R, in the absence of a state S permanent establishment to which the income is attributable. However, state S may view the payment by a state S customer as a royalty that may be subject to a state S withholding tax. If state R does not recognize the taxing authority of state S, state R may be unwilling to relieve double taxation by granting a tax credit for any withholding tax imposed.

Currently, under income tax treaties and the domestic international tax provisions of most countries, income is categorized, and different treatment may apply to different categories of income. For example, under the OECD model treaty, sales proceeds, income from the performance of services, royalties, dividends and interest may all be treated differently. Categorization of income from an economic standpoint is inherently artificial. In the marketplace, a seller does not care (aside from tax considerations) how a payment received is categorized, as long as the payment is fair value for what was transferred. The artificiality of categorization has manifested itself in the growth of derivative financial instruments, which can turn one category of income into a category that is more tax-favored (e.g., dividends into interest). Similarly, determining the difference between a royalty for licensing an intangible, and sales proceeds (or rental income) for the sale (or lease) of an article that embodies the intangible, may be untenable. Problems of categorization are likely to intensify as electronic commerce becomes more widespread.

Under OECD model principles, state S cannot tax business profits of R Corp. not attributable to a state S permanent establishment. Even if those business profits are royalties, under article 12 of the OECD model there is no source-state taxation. However, many treaties do permit source-state taxation of royalties. Where permitted, that taxation is on a gross basis. Those treaties that do permit source-state taxation of royalties set up the possibility of inconsistent characterization, where the source state considers a payment to be a royalty while the residence state considers the payment to be business profits, taxable exclusively in the residence state in the absence of a permanent establishment in the source state. * * *

While the challenges that e-commerce poses for the permanent establishment concept may appear daunting, the OECD has tried to adapt the OECD Model Treaty to the world of e-commerce. In the following excerpt, Sandra McGill and Lowell Yoder lay out the OECD's proposed revisions to the permanent establishment concept. They also suggest some of the difficulties that the OECD faces in building an international consensus behind this proposal and some potential shortcomings of the OECD's approach.

Sandra P. McGill & Lowell D. Yoder, *From Storefronts to Servers to Service Providers: Stretching the Permanent Establishment Definition to Accommodate New Models*, TAXES, March 2003, at 141, 156–157.

On December 22, 2000, the OECD issued a proposed final draft of amendments to the OECD Commentary on Article 5 (PE) of the OECD Model Treaty to address the application of the PE definition currently contained in Article 5 to e-commerce business activities. The draft provides guidance as to when the activities of a server and/or a Web site may constitute a PE under the current PE definition contained in the OECD Model Treaty. A separate committee has been charged with the task of analyzing whether any changes should be made to the PE definition to address e-commerce business activities.

The proposed OECD Commentary draws a fundamental distinction between the software and data that comprise a Web site, which, according to the Commentary, can never constitute a PE, and the computer equipment (server) on which the software and data is used or stored, which can constitute a PE under certain circumstances. A Web site by itself cannot constitute a PE because it is only "a combination of software and electronic data that does not, in itself, involve any tangible property," and therefore, cannot create a fixed place of business than could constitute a PE.

A server, however, on which the Web site is stored and through which it is accessible is a piece of equipment having a physical location and may thus constitute a fixed place of business of the enterprise that operates (i.e. owns or leases) the server, if the other requirements of a PE are satisfied. In order for a server to constitute a PE, it must first be located at a certain place for a sufficient period of time, so as to become "fixed." In addition, if an enterprise operates a server at a particular location (i.e., it is "fixed"), a PE may exist "even though no personnel is required at that location for the operation of the equipment." A server will not constitute a PE, however, "where the electronic commerce operations carried on through computer equipment at a given location in a country are restricted to the preparatory or auxiliary activities."

Therefore, in the example set forth above, under the proposed OECD commentary the foreign corporation would not have a PE in the United States if its Web site was hosted by an ISP or if the foreign corporation owned or leased its own server located outside the United States. However, if the foreign corporation owned or leased a server located in the United States, it would be considered to have a PE in the United States.

Several countries have already indicated that they will apply the PE provision to e-commerce activities in their country differently from the proposed OECD Commentary. The United Kingdom, for example, has indicated that a server (as well as a Web site) located in the United Kingdom will not be considered to create a U.K. PE for the foreign enterprise that owns the server. This is presumably driven by the United Kingdom's desire to attract e-commerce businesses to the United Kingdom.

Spain and Portugal, by contrast, have dissented from the OECD consensus and have indicated that a Web site alone may give rise to a PE, depending on the nature of the Web site. Both countries have indicated that they are looking forward to subsequent OECD guidance as to the need to change the PE definition to deal with e-commerce activities.

As a result of the amendments to the Commentary on Article 5, enterprises that operate in countries that follow the OECD Model Treaty (and follow the OECD's Commentary regarding the application of the PE provision to e-commerce) have relatively clear guidelines as to how to structure their e-commerce operations in order to avoid creating a PE in a high-tax jurisdiction. The new guidance also offers opportunities for shifting income from e-commerce operations to a low-tax (or no-tax) jurisdiction. For example, a foreign sales company that wants to expand its market to the United States may lease a server in a low- or no-tax jurisdiction (e.g., Bermuda) that has the software to advertise the products to U.S. customers through a Web site, take an order and process payment and shipping. The foreign sales company will not be considered to have a PE in the United States under the proposed OECD Commentary as a result of its e-commerce sales and will, therefore, not be subject to U.S. tax on any of its sales income.

NOTE

A Computer Server as a Permanent Establishment. The excerpt from Nancy Kaufman's article describing what constitutes being engaged in a trade or business, in Section 6.2 supra, suggests the potential futility of the OECD's new standards for treating computer servers as permanent establishments. The use of a computer server in a given state would not alone necessarily demonstrate an ongoing commitment to participate in the economy of the state in which the server is located. For example, a server in the United States may facilitate business activities directed exclusively toward other countries and therefore would fail the test for being engaged in a trade or business within the United States. Under the proposed OECD standard, this same server would constitute a permanent establishment in the United States. This seems contrary to common sense and may merely succeed in providing incentives to relocate servers to offshore havens.

Richard Doernberg has offered his own innovative solution to some of the potential shortcomings of the current approach to permanent establishment. He calls this a "base erosion" approach. Like the OECD's efforts to amend its Model Treaty's conception of permanent establishment, Doernberg seeks to mend rather than end the use of the concept of permanent establishment to address the challenges posed by e-commerce.

Richard L. Doernberg, *Electronic Commerce: Changing Income Tax Treaty Principles a Bit?*, 21 TAX NOTES INT'L. 2417, 2424–2427, 2430 (Nov. 20, 2000).

The approach set forth below (hereinafter sometimes referred to as the "base erosion" approach) is offered as one possible avenue to explore, should current OECD treaty concepts prove ineffective in generating a worldwide consensus on the allocation of tax revenue. * * *

The base erosion approach is premised on the maintenance of the permanent establishment principle which has the advantage of longevity and familiarity. Under the current permanent establishment principle, R Corp., which has no presence in state S other than a customer base, would not be subject to income tax in state S merely because R Corp. reaches customers in state

S through a Web site or through some other means of electronic commerce. This conclusion holds even if R Corp. has extensive business dealings in state S in this manner. Even if a server were located in state S, in many cases a server alone is not likely to constitute a permanent establishment. Nor would the use of a telecommunications network, or the shipping of goods from state R to state S, constitute a permanent establishment. In some cases the geographical location where a server is located may constitute a permanent establishment, but only if the server conducts the core functions of the taxpayer's business, and the taxpayer has the premises where the server is located "at its disposal." Accordingly, if a taxpayer's server software is hosted by a third party in state S, it is unlikely that the taxpayer will have a state S permanent establishment.

Keeping the permanent establishment principle intact may be widely viewed by electronic commerce importing states as unacceptable, because they will not be able to share in the tax base generated by electronic commerce income. Yet, expanding the permanent establishment concept may not be a practical solution to the tax problems caused by the growth of electronic commerce. Forcing taxpayers to file net basis tax returns all over the world may impose administrative burdens that are unrealistic.

Indeed, the concern that administrative burdens be realistic explains, in part, the current use of gross base withholding taxes in international tax law. Gross base taxes are easy to administer, but the trade-off is that a gross base tax may be imposed when there is no net income. That trade-off has been accepted in tax treaties for dividends, interest, and royalties. The base erosion approach maintains the use of gross basis withholding taxes and, in some situations, may expand their use. However, in order to minimize the likelihood of imposing a gross base withholding tax when there is no net income, the suggested withholding tax rate would be set very low. * * *

To illustrate how the base erosion approach might work, consider the following hypothetical. Suppose that R Corp. maintains servers in state R that contain a database. R Corp. has no presence in state S, except that unrelated customers in state S use the R Corp. database for a fee. For example, assume that S Corp., a state S corporation, earns 1,000 in state S. In order to earn that income, it incurs a 300 expense for accessing the R Corp. database. Assume also that a state S individual resident, S, earns 1,000 in wage income. S accesses the R Corp. database for personal purposes (e.g., to download personal reading material), paying 300.

From the perspective of state S, the 1,000 of income earned by S Corp. is taxable, but that 1,000 of gross income is reduced by the 300 paid to R Corp., resulting in 700 of net income. If the 300 paid to R Corp. constitutes business profits, then state S will not have taxing authority over the 300, as R Corp. has no permanent establishment in state S. On the other hand, if the 300 payment is deemed to be a royalty, and if the R–S treaty permits source state taxation of royalties, then state S can withhold on the payment to R Corp.

Because countries in the position of state S fear an erosion of their tax base, it is likely that ever-expansive views of what constitutes a royalty may result. * * *

Rather than focus on whether a particular payment is a royalty or constitutes business profits, the base erosion approach renders labeling unimportant. Rather, the focus should be on whether the payment erodes the tax base of state S. The tax base of state S is eroded if the payment is deductible. If it does erode the tax base, then state S would be entitled to withhold; if the tax base is not eroded (i.e., nondeductible payment), no withholding would be permitted. So, in the example above, state S could withhold on the payment by S Corp. to R Corp., but would not withhold on the payment from individual S to R Corp., which is a consumer transaction. Whether a payment is labeled a royalty makes no difference under this approach; the issue is base erosion. Note that this approach would permit state S to tax R Corp.'s business profits, even if they are not attributable to a state S permanent establishment, so long as the payor could deduct the payment. * * *

The key to this base erosion approach, if it were ever able to generate a consensus, would be the tax rate to apply to base eroding payments. The higher the tax rate on gross income, the more likely that the tax may be imposed even in the absence of income (or that will result in a very high effective rate of tax on net income). For example, a 20 percent withholding tax on 300 of gross income is a 100 percent tax if the expenses of earning the 300 of income are 240. If the expenses exceed 240, then the source state collects a tax in excess of 100 percent of the net income, and, if expenses equal or exceed 300, state S collects a tax even though no net income has been generated.

What tax rate is the "appropriate" rate? In large part, this is a political question. From an economic perspective, any gross base tax is problematic because it may produce a tax that exceeds net income. Obviously, the lower the tax the more likely that the tax will not exceed net income. The political issue focuses on how the residence and source states will divide tax revenue. As long as any change in that division does not increase the tax burden on a taxpayer, and does not result in additional inefficient tax planning or behavior, then which government ends up with the tax revenue is an uninteresting question from a global economic perspective, albeit a very interesting question from the economic perspective of each country involved.

Because a gross base tax, by nature, is inefficient, and because the base erosion approach is going to permit source state taxation of many payments that are not currently subject to source state taxation, it is reasonable to set the rate very low. This is particularly important because the proposed reallocation of tax revenue between residence and source countries is not intended to increase taxation—merely to reallocate tax proceeds. If residence countries are fully to relieve any new source country taxation, the withholding rate should be set very low. A low tax rate applied to many base eroding payments can work a reasonable reallocation of tax proceeds. But ultimately, what the rate should be would, in part, be an empirical decision based on how different rates would divide tax revenues. The OECD is well equipped to undertake such an empirical study. Armed with that information, countries could then try to reach a consensus on what would be an appropriate rate. * * *

One of the basic principles * * * to which any change to existing principles should adhere is that the overall level of taxation should not be increased. Accordingly, if the source state is to gain taxing authority over transactions not currently taxable under existing international tax principles, and if there is to be no overall increase in the level of taxation, then the residence state must decrease its tax collection to the extent of the source state's increase. * * *

State R might find this result as unacceptable as state S finds the tax result under existing tax principles. * * *

There is no doubt that this presents a problem with no perfect solution. * * * Unless state S is willing to permit net basis elections, state R is willing to waive domestic tax credit limitation rules, and R Corp. is willing in some cases to make a net basis election, the base erosion approach is not likely to generate much enthusiasm. But in the interest of certainty, simplicity, and a more realistic allocation of tax revenue, these concessions could prove to be reasonable. * * *

The base erosion approach, while somewhat of a leap from current tax treaty concepts, is not nearly as radical as some other approaches to international taxation that have been discussed in light of the rise of electronic commerce. For example, even before the growth of electronic commerce, some have advocated abandoning the general arm's-length approach under current tax principles in favor of some type of formulary approach that allocates a taxpayer's overall income based on an agreed weighting of factors, such as property, payroll, and sales. Some have advocated abandoning residence-based taxation in favor of taxation based on source or destination. At the very fringe of radical approaches lurk proponents of a "bit tax," suggesting a totally new approach for taxing income generated from electronic commerce where users of electronic commerce would be taxed based on the number of bits generated. These approaches deviate more from the status quo than the base erosion approach, and each has its own set of problems that may not represent much improvement from the current approach.

The advent of e-commerce has not only challenged traditional understandings of what constitutes a permanent establishment, but also may have wider implications for the development of international income tax rules. In the following excerpt, David Noren discusses the relationship between developments in the taxation of e-commerce transactions and a trend towards source-based taxation over residence-based taxation.

David G. Noren, *The U.S. National Interest in International Tax Policy*, 54 TAX L. REV. 337, 343–344 (2001).

Isn't the United States a net technology exporter? Shouldn't its revenue interest favor residence-based e-commerce tax rules? This was the position taken by the Treasury Department in its 1996 White Paper on e-commerce, arguably with these revenue considerations in mind. But if corporate residence is practically meaningless, and if these e-commerce activities are highly mobile, a residence-based approach will not work in the long run; such rules would favor the fisc only until they drive all of this e-commerce activity out of the country. Basically, we are all "source countries" now—even a net technology exporter like the United States must behave as though it is importing the fruits of these activities from nationless MNCs and from the highly mobile factors of production that generate value in this environment. In this regard, Graetz's proposal to move further in the direction of source-based taxation and away from residence-based concepts makes good sense and seems likely to be implemented in one form or another at some point in the future.[10] * * *

10. See Michael J. Graetz, Taxing International Income: Inadequate Principles, Outdated Concepts, and Unsatisfactory Policies, 54 Tax L. Rev. 261, 320–23 (2001).

One recent development suggests that U.S. tax policy in the e-commerce area already may be starting to shift in this direction. The United States recently signed on to an OECD pronouncement that determined that computer servers alone, under some circumstances, may constitute a permanent establishment (and thus a basis for source-country taxation of e-commerce business income). Some may view the U.S. agreement to this position simply as a concession by the United States to the rest of the world, but it arguably reflects the beginning of a more fundamental evolution in the way in which some U.S. policymakers conceive the national interest in this area—a realization that we have more in common with e-commerce importers than we might think, and that a drift in the direction of source-country-protecting rules might not be such a bad thing for the United States in the long run, contrary to the views initially expressed in the White Paper. (On the other hand, perhaps the server issue just doesn't matter all that much in the long run, since the location of servers is itself so easily manipulable.)

NOTE

No Silver Bullet. The concept of a permanent establishment standard agreed to by nations on a reciprocal basis has considerable appeal in enhancing uniformity and predictability. In spite of this fact, the increasing ability of businesses to function through computer servers and the Internet may be eroding the relevance of traditional understandings of permanent establishment. This problem defies an easy solution as the mobility and potential financial gains from e-business may make it difficult to avoid a race to the bottom in the tax treatment of electronic business. Unfortunately for tax policymakers, thorny tax problems abound concerning both tax policy design and enforcement in this area.

6.6 EARNINGS STRIPPING

The permanent establishment concept is a useful tool for identifying what income the United States or foreign countries should tax, but corporations possess various means to disguise income from taxation. Earnings stripping and transfer pricing are two tools that United States branches or subsidiaries of foreign companies use to sidestep U.S. income taxes while shifting income from the United States to the foreign parent company. Chapter 9 addresses the challenges Congress and the Treasury Department face in overseeing transfer pricing. This section highlights the equally difficult challenge posed by earnings stripping and Congress's and Treasury's attempts to address this problem.

At its core, the cross-border problem of earnings stripping stems from a problem encountered in many purely domestic transactions: the potential for abuse that attends the different tax consequences of debt and equity and the difficult task of drawing a line between the two. Because interest payments are tax-deductible to the payor corporation, while dividend payments are not, corporations have an incentive to obtain capital in the form of debt rather than equity. Usually a corporation's choice to use debt financing is uncontroversial. However, in certain cases a taxpayer might try to characterize capital as debt when the Internal Revenue Service believes it should more properly be characterized as equity. To police the debt-equity line, the IRS and the courts use a facts-and-circumstances case-by-case approach, considering such factors as the company's debt-to-equity ratio and the source of the capital. As Julie Roin has noted, this generally applicable "thin capitalization" law is applied relatively infrequently, often when a related party, especially a shareholder, "loans funds to a company that is already in severe financial difficulties."[11] Often there is a question about "whether an independent party would have loaned money to the debtor at such a time, or whether the loan should be characterized as simply an attempt to salvage past capital investments by injecting more equity."[12]

In the purely domestic context, however, unless the lender is tax-exempt, one party's interest deduction will usually result in another party reporting interest income, so at least one level of tax will generally be collected. In contrast, a foreign lender will typically not be taxed on the interest income by the United States. The United States does not tax portfolio interest, and many tax treaties lower or eliminate withholding taxes on interest payments between related parties. Thus, interest payments by U.S. subsidiaries to foreign parents not only result in tax deductions but also may escape any U.S. tax on the interest income. Concerned about foreign companies financing their U.S. subsidiaries or branches with a disproportionate amount of debt in order to use deductible interest payments to "strip" the U.S. corporation of its earnings, Congress enacted Code section 163(j). This so-called "earnings stripping" rule denies interest deductions to corporations for interest payments to related, "tax-exempt" parties under specific circumstances. Robert Culbertson and Jaime King review the history and some details of 163(j) in the following excerpt.

Robert E. Culbertson & Jaime E. King, *U.S. Rules on Earnings Stripping: Background, Structure, and Treaty Interaction*, 29 TAX NOTES INT'L 1161, 1161–62, 1166–68 (Mar. 24, 2003).

[T]ax administrations may take the view that the stakes [of a proper characterization as debt or equity] are often higher in the cross-border context. This concern relates generally to the

---

11. Julie A. Roin, Adding Insult to Injury: The "Enhancement" of § 163(j) and the Tax Treatment of Foreign Investors in the United States, 49 Tax L. Rev. 269, 273 (1994).

12. Id.

fact that while in a purely domestic setting one taxpayer's deduction is another's income item, that symmetry often breaks down in the cross-border context. For example, while a payment of interest between the residents of a single country would ordinarily be deductible by the payor and includible by the recipient, a cross-border payment of interest may be deductible by the payor but includible by no one, particularly if treaty benefits are available with respect to the payment. It is possible that the foreign recipient of the payment may bear full home country tax on that receipt, but in many circumstances such a tax may be deferred indefinitely or excused altogether. Accordingly, tax administrations have increasingly taken the view that a cross-border investor may have a particularly compelling incentive to structure its investment in a corporation as debt rather than equity. * * *

[In the 1980s] * * * the U.S. Congress made an initial attempt to address its own concerns about the use of debt capitalization by foreign investors and others who bore little or no tax on the receipt of interest payments. In particular, the U.S. Senate passed an earnings stripping rule as part of its version of the legislation that was ultimately enacted as the Tax Reform Act of 1986. The provision was vigorously opposed by Treasury, in part based on its stated inconsistency with U.S. treaty obligations, and it was not included in the final version of the bill that emerged from conference.

Three years later, however, a substantially identical provision was adopted by the House, and although (in a reversal of roles from 1986) the provision was not adopted by the Senate, a slightly modified version of the provision emerged from conference and was enacted as part of the 1989 tax bill. The House report noted the absence of debt/equity regulations under section 385, and expressed the committee's belief that "the uncertainty of present law (particularly the debt/equity distinction) may allow taxpayers to take aggressive positions that inappropriately erode the U.S. tax base." The committee more generally expressed its belief that—

> it is appropriate to limit the deduction for interest that a taxable person pays or accrues to a tax-exempt entity whose economic interests coincide with those of the payor. To allow an unlimited deduction for such interest permits significant erosion of the tax base. Allowance of unlimited deductions permits an economic unit that consists of more than one legal entity to contract with itself at the expense of the government.

Accordingly, Congress enacted the provisions of section 163(j), described in the next section.

B. Mechanical Operation of the U.S. Rules Under Section 163(j)

Section 163(j) establishes as an initial threshold that its rules only apply to a company that has a debt/equity ratio that exceeds 1.5 to 1.[13] For purposes of this threshold test, a corporation's debt/equity ratio is the ratio that total indebtedness bears to total assets minus total indebtedness.[14] * * * Assuming that a company is not excused from further testing by the debt/equity test (i.e., that the company's debt/equity ratio exceeds 1.5 to 1), the following calculation would be required. First, the amount of the company's "excess interest" must be determined.[15] This is essentially an interest coverage test, in which the company's interest expense is compared with its cash flow. Specifically, net interest expense that exceeds 50 percent of "adjusted taxable income" constitutes "excess interest."[16] In other words, if a company is paying out more than half of its cash flow as interest expense, then the excess will be treated as excess interest.[17] * * *

Second, the amount of the company's "disqualified interest" must be determined. This is simply the amount of interest paid to related tax-exempt recipients.[18] For this purpose, tax-exempt recipients would include both domestic tax-exempt entities and foreign recipients not subject to U.S. tax on receipt of the interest.[19] In the case of a treaty resident that benefits from a reduced rate of withholding tax under the treaty, a pro rata amount of the interest is treated as paid to an exempt recipient, based on the extent of the reduction from the otherwise applicable 30 percent withholding rate.[20] Thus, for example, if the applicable treaty withholding rate on the interest paid to a foreign recipient was 10 percent, then one-third of the interest paid would be treated as paid to an exempt recipient (and thus as disqualified interest). In addition, pursuant to an amendment

---

13. I.R.C. § 163(j)(2)(A); Treas. Reg. § 1.163(j)–1(b).

14. I.R.C. § 163(j)(2)(C); Treas. Reg. § 1.163(j)–3.

15. I.R.C. § 163(j)(2)(B); Treas. Reg. § 1.163(j)–2(b).

16. I.R.C. § 163(j)(2)(B); Treas. Reg. § 1.163(j)–2(b).

17. These are the NOL deduction under IRC § 172 and deductions for depreciation, amortization, or depletion. Because these deductions do not affect the company's cash flow, they would not affect the company's ability to service its debt, and thus are excluded from the rules' calculation of the amount of debt that the company can incur without being treated as thinly capitalized.

18. I.R.C. § 163(j)(3); Treas. Reg. § 1.163(j)–4.

19. I.R.C. § 163(j)(5)(B); Treas. Reg. § 1.163(j)–4(b).

20. I.R.C. § 163(j)(3)(B)(i).

to the statute enacted in 1993, interest paid to an unrelated recipient may nevertheless be treated as disqualified interest if it is subject to a guarantee by a related tax-exempt or foreign person.[21]

Finally, the lesser of excess interest or disqualified interest is not deductible in the current year.[22] However, rather than treating this as a permanent denial of deductibility (as would occur if the instrument were recharacterized as equity), the rules permit the nondeductible amount to be carried forward indefinitely.[23] Thus, if the company's interest coverage ratio improves in future years, it may be able to take that deferred deduction into account in the later year.

In addition, in a similar effort to smooth out annual variability in a company's interest coverage ratio, the statute interestingly provides for an excess limitation carryover.[24] Although functionally similar to a carryback of nondeductible interest, the limitation carryover approach avoids the need to modify previously filed returns. Instead, in any year in which additional interest would have been deductible if paid (and thus a year which could have absorbed a carryback), the amount of additional interest that could have been deducted is carried forward as an excess limitation carryforward, and increases the amount of interest that may be deducted in the following three years.

Finally, related party status for purposes of section 163(j) is generally determined under sections 267(b) and 707(b)(1).[25] Section 267(b) provides that two corporations are related if they are members of the same "controlled group" within the meaning of section 1563(a)[26] * * * Under section 1563(a) as modified by section 267(f)(1), two corporations are members of the same parent-subsidiary controlled group if, with the exception of the common parent corporation, more than 50 percent of the total voting power or more than 50 percent of the total value of shares of each corporation in the group is owned by another corporation in the group, and the common parent corporation owns more than 50 percent of the total voting power or value of shares of all classes of stock of at least one of the corporations.[27] Under section 1563(a) as modified by section 267(f)(1), two corporations are members of the same brother-sister controlled

---

21. I.R.C. § 163(j)(3)(B)(i).

22. I.R.C. § 163(j)(1)(A); Treas. Reg. § 1.163(j)–1(a)(2).

23. I.R.C. § 163(j)(1)(B); Treas. Reg. § 1.163(j)–1(c).

24. I.R.C. § 163(j)(2)(B)(ii); Treas. Reg. § 1.163(j)–1(d).

25. I.R.C. § 163(j)(4)(A); Treas. Reg. § 1.163(j)–2(g).

26. I.R.C. §§ 267(b)(3), 267(f)(1).

27. I.R.C. § 1563(a)(1), as modified by IRC § 267(f)(1).

group if five or fewer persons who are individuals, estates, or trusts own more than 50 percent of the total voting power or value of all classes of stock of each corporation in the group, taking into account the stock ownership of each such person only to the extent such stock ownership is identical with respect to each such corporation.[28]

The principle embodied in the earnings stripping rule—that a taxpayer should not be able to take a deduction for interest payments if the party receiving those payments is exempt from tax on the interest income and has economic interests that coincide with the taxpayer—seems fair enough. But as Julie Roin argues in the next excerpt, interest payments on which the normal 30% withholding tax has been eliminated or lowered under a tax treaty are not necessarily exempt from all tax. Rather, the foreign creditor is still potentially subject to tax in its home country. Treasury theoretically agreed to exempt this interest income from U.S. tax in a tax treaty in order to receive "enhanced residence tax opportunities, created by the treaty partner's reciprocal limitation of its source tax on interest income earned within its borders by U.S. residents."[29] For Roin, then, I.R.C. § 163(j) results in the United States's "attempting to claim the benefits of the treaty * * * without paying the agreed upon price in terms of its own lost source tax revenues."[30]

Julie A. Roin, *Adding Insult to Injury: The "Enhancement" of § 163(j) and the Tax Treatment of Foreign Investors in the United States*, 49 Tax L. Rev. 269, 277, 279–285, 288–289 (1994).

Interest payments made by a foreign-owned U.S. business constitute U.S. source income,[31] and thus, fall within the scope of the U.S.'s primary taxing jurisdiction. If the United States chose to tax such interest payments at full rates, it would have little reason to worry about excessive leveraging of foreign-owned corporations—at least, no more to worry about than with domestic corporations.

The United States, however, does not tax all such income. Following a period in which tax was withheld from both interest and dividend payments to foreigners, Congress, in 1984, decided not to tax foreign corporations and nonresident aliens on "portfolio" interest paid by unrelated U.S. debtors. Thus, a French individual holding a bond issued by General Motors may receive interest payments made with respect to the bond free of U.S. income tax. * * *

28. I.R.C. § 1563(a)(2), as modified by IRC § 267(f)(1).
29. Roin, supra note 11, at 284.
30. Id. at 289.
31. See I.R.C. §§ 861(a)(1), 884(f)(1).

Congress restricted the repeal of the portfolio withholding tax to interest paid to unrelated foreign creditors. Interest paid to foreigners by related U.S. debtors continued (and continues) to be taxable in the United States. Of each interest payment, 30% is required to be withheld and paid to the United States by the related debtor unless (1) such interest is attributable to a U.S. trade or business of the related creditor or (2) the creditor is a resident of a country which has a tax treaty with the United States. In the former case, the foreigner pays tax at normal rates on all business income, including the interest income. In the latter case, tax at the rate specified in the treaty is withheld and paid to the United States. Virtually all income tax treaties provide for interest income to be taxed at less than the statutory 30% [withholding] rate; some exempt it from tax entirely. For example, if Toyota–Japan lends money to its subsidiary corporation, Toyota–U.S.A., only 10% of each interest payment made on that debt by Toyota–U.S.A. must be withheld and paid to the United States. In contrast, if a Kenyan company lends money to its U.S. subsidiary, 30% of each interest payment must be withheld and paid to the United States because the United States has no tax treaty with Kenya. * * *

This synopsis of the rules for taxing foreigners' interest income demonstrates the possibilities for seemingly advantageous leveraged combinations involving a foreign creditor. Combinations are advantaged under U.S. tax law whenever the creditor is unrelated to (that is, not a major shareholder of) the debtor. For example, Toyota could lend money to Ford; Ford's interest payments (and Toyota's interest receipts) would be free of U.S. tax. Alternatively, prior to § 163(j)'s enactment, combinations involving related corporations diminished or eliminated the U.S. tax burden whenever the creditor was in a position to claim the protection of a favorable tax treaty (as in the Toyota–Japan/Toyota–U.S.A. example above). In both situations, the debtor's interest payments reduced its income tax liability without triggering a corresponding U.S. tax liability for the creditor. Thus, no (or limited) U.S. income taxes could be paid on the bulk of the operating profits of the debtor's U.S. business; the earnings could be successfully "stripped" from the corporate earner. The first of these options is as open to domestic businesses as foreign-owned ones, as the Toyota–Ford example illustrates. The latter, by definition, was only available to foreign-owned businesses; it is the only one affected (potentially) by the operation of § 163(j). But does taking advantage of such opportunities, particularly the second, constitute abusive tax avoidance * * * ? The answer to this question is far more equivocal and perhaps a definitive no, thus undercutting the justification for the enactment of § 163(j).

In the first place, the avoidance of U.S. income tax (in the Toyota–Japan/Toyota–U.S.A. case) may not confer a tax advantage on the affected taxpayers. The apparent advantage of reducing U.S. income tax evaporates whenever U.S. forbearance triggers a correspondingly higher tax by the creditor's home country. If the withholding tax on Toyota–Japan's $100 interest income is reduced by treaty from $30 to $10 (or by statute from $30 to zero), Japan may itself increase its income tax on that interest income from $20 to $40, in which case neither the treaty nor U.S. tax law helps Toyota. Rather, the Toyota combination would pay a combined tax of $40 on its interest income of $100, which is more than Toyota would pay in U.S. tax if both Toyota companies were U.S. corporations and the intercorporate contribution were in the form of equity rather than debt. When residence taxation substitutes for source taxation, the creditor corporation (and, hence, the leveraged combination as a whole) is no better off than it would have been had it paid U.S. income tax. It therefore has little incentive to substitute debt for equity in the financing of its U.S. business. All that changes is the identity of its tax collector. Foreign creditors simply are not tax-exempt in the same way as are domestic tax-exempt entities.

In jurisdictions, like the United States, which utilize a credit mechanism to avoid double taxation in international transactions, no treaty is necessary for the substitute tax to appear; a resident's tax automatically increases as the source tax decreases. Even jurisdictions which ordinarily do not tax their residents on foreign source income generally do so when the source tax has been waived by treaty. Indeed, the United States often refuses to enter into treaties with foreign countries unless they ensure that their residents pay a reasonable residence tax on income on which the United States waives its source tax pursuant to the treaty. Moreover, the United States generally refuses to enter into such treaties with known "tax haven" countries, that is, countries whose income tax levies are far lower than its own. Thus, foreign creditor corporations that avoid U.S. income tax on their U.S. source interest income under a tax treaty usually pay at least as much as the forgone tax to their home country, at least if the home country finds out about the interest receipts. Given that most tax treaties also provide for at least a limited exchange of tax information between the signatory countries, residence countries may well be able to identify and tax interest recipients claiming relief under a treaty.

Of course, the identity of the collecting government has revenue implications for the affected governments; they may not be indifferent as to the taxpayers' mix of financing sources even if the taxpayers themselves are unconcerned. When, however, the exemption from U.S. tax stems from a treaty obligation, the revenue loss to the United States is less than appears from consideration of the foreign taxpayer's tax situation. The elimination of the U.S. source tax is supposed to be coupled with enhanced residence tax opportunities, created by the treaty partner's reciprocal limitation of its source tax on interest income earned within its borders by U.S. residents. Consider the Toyota–Japan/Toyota–U.S.A. example once again, and the impact of the treaty on an interest payment of $100. The treaty appears to deprive the United States of $20 of revenue to which it is otherwise (that is, by statute) entitled by reducing the tax imposed on Toyota–U.S.A.'s $100 interest payment to Toyota–Japan to $10. One must look at both sides of Japan's treatment of interest payments made by a Japanese subsidiary to its U.S. corporate parent before concluding that a tax avoidance problem exists. If IBM–Japan pays $100 in interest to IBM–U.S.A., then under the treaty, Japan may levy only $10 of tax on that interest payment. If Japan would have levied additional tax on that interest payment absent the treaty, the treaty costs Japan money, the difference between its statutory withholding rate on such payments and $10, shifting that difference to the United States, since under our U.S. tax rules, each additional dollar of tax paid to Japan reduces the U.S. tax burden on IBM–U.S.A.'s interest income. If, for example, Japan (like the United States) would have imposed a $30 tax on the interest payment in the absence of the treaty, then in a world with no treaty, the United States would have collected only another $5 of tax from IBM–U.S.A. on its interest income. The treaty increases the U.S. tax to $25, thus recouping the loss the United States suffered from Toyota–U.S.A.'s interest payment. In short, with the right set of investment flows, the extra tax collected on the foreign source interest payments of U.S. entities offsets the source tax forgone on interest payments made to foreign entities, leaving the United States in about the same position that it would have been in absent the treaty. Once again, substitute taxation occurs, although this time it is the payors, rather than the payees, that change places.

* * * Further, it is also clear that when revenue is lost due to the operation of a treaty, this nontaxation (or undertaxation) cannot be compared to the nontaxation of domestic tax-exempt entities. The contrast is not only in the uncertainty as to whether any revenue is in fact lost, but also the justification for

any loss that actually exists. Tax exemption for domestic entities stems from a legislative act; what Congress grants unilaterally it may freely rescind. Treaties, however, are bilateral agreements with foreign nations—nations which have given up rights
to enter into the treaty. Both parties pay a price for the
existence of the treaty; the willingness of each to pay that price
depends on the assurance of reciprocity. If Congress unilaterally
revokes the benefits flowing from a treaty, as § 163(j) indisput-
ably would do whenever it applies, it essentially is reneging on
that bargain. In other words, it is attempting to claim the
benefits of the treaty (for example, reduced source tax on U.S.
taxpayers investing in the foreign country, among other benefits) without paying the agreed upon price in terms of its own
lost source tax revenues—and is doing so across the board,
without investigating whether the particular government or
taxpayer affected is, in fact, a party to an (unintended) unequal
trade of tax revenues.

NOTES

1) *Section 163(j) and U.S. Treaty Obligations: Nondiscrimination.* Roin
argues that the application of § 163(j) essentially involves the U.S.
"reneging" on its tax treaty obligations. Further, in their article above,
Culbertson and King noted that Treasury "vigorously opposed" the
initial earnings stripping rule passed by the U.S. Senate in 1986 in part
because of its "stated inconsistency with U.S. treaty obligations." Specifically, Treasury was concerned then—and numerous commentators
continue to be concerned today—that § 163(j) violates the nondiscrimination provisions of the OECD and U.S. Model Treaties. The nondiscrimination issue is discussed in Chapter 11.

2) *Earnings Stripping and Corporate Inversions.* Chapter 3 explores the
trend of corporate inversions, in which U.S. corporations reincorporate
in a tax haven country to become a subsidiary of a foreign holding
company. One major advantage of such inversions is that they may
facilitate earnings stripping, particularly when the foreign parent is in a
no-tax country and a comprehensive income tax treaty with the United
States is applicable.[32] The flood of corporate reorganizations in tax
havens prompted congressional proposals in 2002 and 2003 on reorganizations, earnings stripping and corporate inversions.[33] The Treasury
Department's position had been that directly blocking inversion transactions would simply redirect companies toward start-up incorporations in
tax havens or encourage foreign acquisitions of U.S. companies that
would have the same effect.[34] Instead, Treasury Department officials

---

32. See Treasury Department Office of Tax Policy, Corporate Inversion Transactions:
Tax Policy Implications 12–13, 21–22 (May 2002).

33. See the discussion of these proposals in Chapter 3.

34. See Senate Appropriations Committee, Treasury and General Government Sub-
committee, U.S. Senator Byron Dorgan (D ND) Holds Hearing on Corporate Moves to Tax

focused on limiting the ability of foreign corporations to engage in earnings stripping in an effort to remove the major incentive for inversion transactions and reincorporations.[35]

A new section 7874 of the Code, passed by the Senate in 2003, but not included in the final legislation, would have incorporated Treasury's recommended approach.[36] Specifically, this provision would strengthen the "earnings stripping" rules for inverted corporations, by eliminating the debt-equity threshold generally applicable under section 163(j) and reducing the 50–percent thresholds for "excess interest expense" and "excess limitation" to 25 percent. Only corporations having engaged in inversions would be subjected to these more stringent rules (generally for ten years following the inversion). The Senate bill would define an inversion as a "transaction in which, pursuant to a plan or a series of related transactions: (1) a U.S. corporation becomes a subsidiary of a foreign-incorporated entity or otherwise transfers substantially all of its properties to such an entity; (2) the former shareholders of the U.S. corporation hold (by reason of holding stock in the U.S. corporation) 50 percent or more (by vote or value) of the stock of the foreign-incorporated entity after the transaction; and (3) the foreign-incorporated entity, considered together with all companies connected to it by a chain of greater than 50 percent ownership (i.e., the 'expanded affiliated group'), does not have substantial business activities in the entity's country of incorporation, compared to the total worldwide business activities of the expanded affiliated group."

Havens, Oct. 16, 2002, FDCH Political Transcripts (testimony of Pamela Olson, Assistant Secretary of the Treasury for Tax Policy).

35. See generally Treasury Department Office of Tax Policy, Corporate Inversion Transactions: Tax Policy Implications (May 2002).

36. The bill was sponsored by Senator Charles Grassley and adopted by the Senate.

Chapter 7

Non-Business Income—Inbound and Outbound Transactions

7.1 Introduction

Chapter 6 addressed the taxation of income earned by nonresidents "effectively connected" to a U.S. trade or business. As explained in Chapter 6, such income is taxed by the U.S. on a net income basis. The first part of this chapter addresses inbound income that is not effectively connected with a U.S. trade or business, but which is U.S. source income and, in the words of sections 871 and 881 of the Internal Revenue Code, is "fixed, determinable, annual or periodical" (also known to tax aficionados as "FDAP"). The subsequent part deals with the taxation of "non-business income" earned by U.S. resident corporations and taxpayers investing abroad.

This chapter considers many different types of income, grouped here under the term "non-business income." Given the heterogeneous nature of the various types of income discussed here, this is a somewhat difficult category to label. The term "non-business" is a considered compromise, which does not perfectly capture the nature of the various kinds of income that are addressed. We considered the more commonly used term "passive," but rejected it because not all forms of income considered here are passive. FDAP includes many items of income that are not truly passive in nature. We also discarded the term "portfolio" as a general label because, for example, not all dividends are from portfolio investment; some result from the repatriation of income realized through direct investments.

In the United States, investment is classified as direct whenever a U.S. individual or company owns, directly or indirectly, at least ten percent of the voting rights of a foreign corporation or, contrariwise, when a foreign individual or company owns, directly or indirectly, at least ten percent of the voting rights of a U.S. corporation. Investment is classified as portfolio whenever the individual or corporation owns less than ten percent of the foreign entity. Obviously, one can quarrel with whether the ten–percent ownership threshold is the right place to draw the line between direct and portfolio investment. The ten–percent ownership threshold is, however, commonly used throughout the OECD, although some countries use a lower threshold—five or even one percent. The precise dividing line between direct and portfolio investment may be controversial, but that is not important to us here. What is important is that some dividing line exists, however arbitrary.

Both direct and portfolio investors may receive "non-business income" from foreign corporations. Equity investors, for example, receive dividends periodically and experience capital gains or losses when they sell their shares. In a "classical" corporate income tax system, the income distributed through dividends is taxed twice. Dividends are not deductible by the corporation in computing its net income, and they are typically taxed again when received by the shareholder. To avoid multiplying the levels of taxation, most countries grant some relief from dividend taxation when one corporation pays dividends to another. Section 243 of the Code, for example, allows corporations, in effect, to exclude 70 percent of dividends they receive. In so-called integrated tax systems, countries also give full or partial relief from this double taxation to individual shareholders, either by giving them a credit for all or a portion of the corporate taxes that have been paid or by excluding all or part of the dividend from shareholders' income.

In contrast to dividends, interest is deductible and therefore not taxed at the corporate level. Thus a tax on net business income does not tax income attributable to those who have supplied capital to a corporation in the form of debt. Likewise, rents and royalties are deductible in measuring net business income. Thus, if source countries taxed only net business income, they would collect no tax revenues from debt capital used by businesses in their countries, nor any tax from intangible capital supplied in exchange for a royalty. In addition, they would collect only one level of tax on income produced by equity investments. As a result, source countries have often exercised their power not only to tax net business income, but also to tax dividends, interest, rents and royalties paid to foreigners.

There is a crucial difference, however, between the taxation of business income generated by a nonresident and the taxation of nonresidents's non-business income. The difference is that active business income is generally taxed on a "net basis." The expenses incurred in producing business income are deductible in determining the nonresident's tax liability. Therefore, taxes on active business income are levied only to the extent that revenues exceed expenses; they are levied on what is colloquially understood as "profit." This contrasts sharply with the "gross-basis" withholding tax imposed on non-business income. Gross-basis taxation ignores any expenses that may have been incurred in generating the income. Instead, a flat rate of tax—called a "withholding" tax—is applied to gross non-business income. Gross-basis withholding is a final one-shot method of taxing income at source. The level of the source country's withholding tax on non-business income often depends on whether the source country has an income tax treaty with the country of the foreigner's residence. Indeed, the taxation of non-business income is one of the most treaty-dependent areas in international taxation.

A simple example of the tax treatment of an outbound portfolio investment makes the distinction between gross-basis and net-basis taxation clear. Assume a U.S. investor invests $1,000 in the common stock of a nonresident corporation. Suppose further that the foreign corporation is resident in a country with a classical tax system that imposes an income tax both at the corporate level and on the individual taxpayer. The investor receives $50 in dividends annually for five years. On January 1 of year six, the U.S. investor sells her shares in the foreign corporation. Assume that at all times during the five-year period, the $1,000 investment represents less than ten–percent ownership of the corporation. In each of the five years the investor receives $50 in dividends and will pay a withholding tax to the host country on the receipt of that dividend income of $50. Suppose the applicable rate of withholding is 30 percent. Thus, in each year, the U.S. resident will receive only $35 of her $50; the remaining $15 will be remitted by the payor directly to the foreign tax authorities on behalf of the U.S. resident. The withholding tax the U.S. investor pays the host country each year is creditable against the taxpayer's U.S. income tax liability.[1] For portfolio income, there is no indirect tax credit for taxes paid by the foreign corporation as exists for foreign direct investments under § 902 (see Chapter 3). Thus, the withholding tax generally will be the only source-country tax for which a U.S. investor will receive a foreign tax credit. Therefore, the U.S. investor will report the dividends as $50 of taxable U.S. ordinary income, and apply the $15 credit from paying withholding tax in the host country against her U.S. tax liability on the foreign portfolio income.[2]

Gaining credit for the full amount of foreign tax paid is, however, subject to both major and minor caveats. The major caveat is that, ordinarily, the foreign tax credit is limited by the amount of U.S. tax payable on the income. Thus, if a country imposes a 40% tax on a U.S. investor in the 15% bracket, the foreign tax would be creditable only at a 15% rate. The minor point is that with the enactment of the Taxpayer Relief Act of 1997, Congress simplified the foreign tax credit for individuals with only foreign portfolio income by eliminating this limitation on the foreign credit for an individual claiming less than $300 in foreign taxes or a married couple filing jointly and claiming credit for less than $600 in foreign taxes.[3]

1. See I.R.C. § 901 (granting a credit for foreign income taxes up to a maximum of the United States taxes on equivalent U.S. source income).

2. See I.R.C. § 904 (d)(2)(a). Alternately, a shareholder may elect to deduct the foreign taxes paid; see I.R.C. § 164.

3. See I.R.C. § 904(j)(2)(b).

Gross-basis taxation of non-business income was adopted largely for administrative reasons, not out of concern for economic efficiency or equity. Taxing the net income of nonresident investors has long been regarded as impractical because (1) tax authorities in source countries usually cannot obtain accurate information about nonresidents' expenses of earning portfolio income, and (2) nonresidents often do not have significant assets in the source country, making enforcement other than through a gross-basis withholding tax difficult. For example, one result of the information problem is that owners of intangible property are unable to offset royalty income by either deducting or amortizing the costs of developing the intangible asset that produced the income. But, in the absence of a withholding tax, if the nonresident did not remit taxes to the source country, it would be difficult, if not impossible, for the foreign tax authority to seize the nonresident's intangible asset to satisfy its tax claim.

One alternative would be for source countries to forgo taxation of non-business income and leave income taxation of such income to the country of the recipient's residence. However, residence-based taxation raises two problems. First, source countries—including developing countries—would lose a significant amount of tax revenue if they decided to tax on the basis of residence only. Second, the administrative difficulty for residence countries attempting to tax portfolio income is the potential unavailability of information concerning the income-producing activities of its residents abroad. Indeed, the existence of tax havens often makes it relatively easy for taxpayers to keep portfolio income from coming to the attention of domestic tax authorities.

The thorny enforcement and informational problems associated with the taxation of non-business income by both source and residence countries have made the admittedly crude gross-basis withholding tax a fixture of international tax law since the first League of Nations model treaty of 1928. Despite the crude nature of these rules, their importance has grown dramatically in recent years in step with the increasing globalization of investment and business activities. At the end of 1976, nonresident ownership of U.S. debt and equity securities (including Treasury securities) totaled $62 billion. By the end of 2001, this figure had increased to $3.02 *trillion*. This is nearly a fifty-fold increase in twenty-five years. Likewise, U.S. ownership of foreign securities also grew nearly fifty-fold over the 1976–2001 period from $44.2 billion at the end of 1976 to over $2.11 trillion at the end of 2001.[4] The tremendous growth of international portfolio investment suggests that the tax treatment of income associated with such investment is increasingly important to the welfare and efficiency of the global economy. However, as will be demonstrated in this chapter, the taxation of international non-business income is at best problematic.

---

4. See Elena L. Nguyen, International Investment Position of the United States at Year-End 2001, 82 Survey of Current Business 10 (2002).

7.2   FIXED, DETERMINABLE, ANNUAL, OR PERIODICAL (FDAP) INCOME: INBOUND TRANSACTIONS

As indicated above, the Internal Revenue Code distinguishes between income from non-business investments by foreigners in the U.S. and income of foreigners associated with a U.S. trade or business. More technically, sections 871 and 881 of the Code impose withholding tax on income from a U.S. source which is "fixed, determinable, annual, or periodical" ("FDAP"), but is not "income effectively connected with the conduct of a U.S. trade or business."[5] Section 894 allows the reduction of these taxes by tax treaties. The following table identifies the various types of FDAP income and sets out the rules determining the source of such income:

Summary of Source Rules for FDAP Income

Type of Income:	Source Determined by:
Pay for personal services § 861(a)(3) and § 862(a)(3)	Where services are performed
Dividends § 861(a)(2) and § 862(a)(2)	Residence of payor corporation (U.S. or foreign)
Interest § 861(a)(1) and § 862(a)(1)	Residence of payor
Rents § 861(a)(4) and § 862(a)(4)	Where property is located
Royalties, patents and copyrights, etc. § 861(a)(4) and § 862(a)(4)	Where property is used
Royalties and natural resources § 861(a)(4) and § 862(a)(4)	Where property is located
Pensions due to personal services performed § 864(c)(6)	Where services were performed while a nonresident alien
Scholarships and fellowship grants § 117 and § 1441(b)	Generally, residence of payor

Source: IRS, Publication 515: Withholding of Tax on Nonresident Aliens and Foreign Entities For Withholding in 2003, (November 2002) at 12.

The Internal Revenue Code imposes a 30–percent withholding tax rate on income fitting the FDAP definition. This rate, however, is commonly reduced by bilateral tax treaties. Tax treaty withholding rates can vary substantially. For example, the treaty rate on "direct dividends" (certain qualifying parent-subsidiary dividends) in the U.S.–Greece Tax Treaty is the same as the statutory withholding rate—30 percent. However, in the U.S.–U.K. tax treaty, signed in 2001, the withholding tax on certain direct dividends has been eliminated entire-

---

5.   See IRC § 871(a).

ly.[6] Under U.S. tax treaties, most portfolio income is taxed between the extremes of "not at all" and the statutory withholding rate of 30 percent. The following chart lists the withholding rates applying in 2003 to various types of income in many U.S. bilateral tax treaties:[7]

	General Interest	General Dividends	Direct Dividends [8]	Industrial Royalties
Statutory Withholding Rate	30	30	30	30
Australia	10	15	15	10
Austria	0	15	5	0
Barbados	5	15	5	5
Belgium	15	15	5	0
Canada	10	15	5	0
China	10	10	10	10
CIS	0	30	30	0
Cyprus	10	15	5	0
Czech Republic	0	15	5	10
Denmark	0	15	5	0
Egypt	15	15	5	0
Estonia	10	15	5	5
Finland	0	15	5	5
France	0	15	5	5
Germany	0	15	5	0
Greece	0	30	30	0
Hungary	0	15	5	0
Iceland	0	15	5	0
India	15	25	15	10
Indonesia	10	15	10	10
Ireland	0	15	5	0
Israel	17.5	25	12.5	15
Italy	15	15	5	10
Jamaica	12.5	15	10	10
Japan	10	15	10	10
Kazakhstan	10	15	5	10
Korea	12	15	10	15
Latvia	10	15	5	5
Lithuania	10	15	5	5
Luxembourg	0	15	5	0
Mexico	15	10	5	10

6. "The proposed treaty was signed on July 24, 2001. The United States and the United Kingdom exchanged notes on the same day to provide clarification with respect to the application of the proposed treaty. The proposed protocol was signed on July 19, 2002." See Congressional Committee Reports: Senate Foreign Relations Committee Report on Tax Convention with United Kingdom (Treaty Doc. 107–19), Exec. Rept. No. 108–2 (March 13, 2003). Article X of the treaty provides for no withholding on "direct" dividends.

7. See IRS, Publication 515: Withholding of Tax on Nonresident Aliens and Foreign Entities For Withholding in 2003, (November 2002) at 33–34. There are many caveats and details not reflected in the chart as it is reproduced here that are described in the notes to the original table. Reference to the treaties for detailed guidance is essential.

8. Direct dividends are dividends paid from a foreign subsidiary to a parent corporation that holds more than 80 percent of voting control of the foreign subsidiary.

	General Interest	General Dividends	Direct Dividends [8]	Industrial Royalties
Morocco	15	15	10	10
Netherlands	0	15	5	0
New Zealand	10	15	15	10
Norway	0	15	15	0
Pakistan	30	30	15	0
Philippines	15	25	20	15
Poland	0	15	5	10
Portugal	10	15	5	10
Romania	10	10	10	15
Russia	0	10	5	0
Slovak Republic	0	15	5	10
Slovenia	5	15	5	5
South Africa	0	15	5	0
Spain	10	15	10	8
Sweden	0	15	5	0
Switzerland	0	15	5	0
Thailand	15	15	10	8
Trinidad & Tobago	30	30	30	15
Tunisia	15	20	14	10
Turkey	15	20	15	5
Ukraine	0	15	5	10
United Kingdom	0	15	5	0
Venezuela	10	15	5	5

In the following excerpt, Max Holmes describes the fundamental statutory provisions imposing United States withholding taxes on domestic payors of FDAP to nonresidents.

Max Holmes, *The Scope of the Withholding Tax on Payments to Aliens: A Survey*, 22 COLUM. J. TRANSNT'L L. 359, 359–364 (1984).

The United States taxes the income of foreign nationals (both individuals and corporations) in two ways. If the foreign national is actually conducting business operations in the United States, the foreign national will be taxed at the standard rates applicable to domestic businesses or individuals. However, if the foreign national's income is derived from passive investment activities, or if the contacts with the United States are fleeting, direct taxation becomes difficult. The United States, therefore, taxes such passive income, without deductions, at a flat rate of 30%. In order to facilitate collection of the flat 30% tax, the United States requires that the full tax be withheld at the source of the payments involved. Finally, in order to encourage the flow of capital into the United States, some forms of income, notably [portfolio interest] and certain capital gains, are entirely exempt from tax.

The foreign national who pursues investment opportunities in the United States must plan carefully in order to maximize his after-tax return. Ideally, the investment will fall into a category where no United States tax is due. If that is impossible, the foreign national must decide whether to structure his activities to incur the flat 30% tax or the standard graduated rates. In most cases the standard rates will be preferable, either because the standard rate in the foreign national's tax bracket is below 30%, or, through deductions, tax credits, and tax treaties, the foreign national's effective tax rate is below 30%. Since the 30% flat tax is a withholding tax, it is the domestic American payor's responsibility to collect the tax. Americans dealing with foreign investors must therefore be aware of the relevant tax laws: if an American payor fails to collect and pay over the tax, he may be liable for the full amount himself.

* * *

CONDITIONS FOR WITHHOLDING

For the withholding tax to be imposed, six different conditions must be fulfilled:

(1) The amount being paid must go to some foreign entity, either a nonresident alien individual, a foreign corporation, a foreign partnership, a foreign trust, or a foreign estate. The most difficult problem here is the distinction between resident and nonresident aliens. Resident aliens are taxed at standard progressive rates, while nonresident aliens are subject to the 30% withholding tax. The taxpayer must determine which status would be more favorable, and then take steps to achieve or maintain the desired status. The United States payor has the responsibility to determine the residency status of the alien payee for purposes of withholding. Distinguishing between resident and nonresident alien status can be complicated.

* * *

(2) The amount being paid must be income from sources within the United States.

* * *

(3) The amount being paid must be income of a type enumerated by Congress, or of a type generally described as 'fixed or determinable annual or periodical.'

* * *

(4) The amount being paid must not be effectively connected with the conduct of a trade or business in the United States.

* * *

(5) The payor must be considered a withholding agent under the terms of the Internal Revenue Code.

* * *

(6) The amount being paid must not fall into one of several categories of income which are exempt from withholding.

* * *

The six different conditions for withholding are complex and contain issues which cut across taxation and immigration law. Nevertheless, in the great majority of cases, application of the tax will not be problematic.

* * *

THE STRUCTURE OF THE WITHHOLDING TAX

Because the operative provisions of the withholding tax on nonresident aliens are scattered throughout the Code, a brief glance at how these provisions fit together is necessary before the substantive aspects of the tax are examined.

Only income from sources within the United States is subject to the withholding tax. "Sources within the United States" is defined in Section 861 of the Code. "Sources without the United States" is defined in the Code at Section 862, much of which simply refers to exceptions carved out in Section 861.

The income involved cannot be effectively connected with the operation of a trade or business within the United States. "Effectively connected" is defined in Section 864(c). "Trade or business" is defined in Section 864(b). Taxes on income that is effectively connected with the operation of a trade or business are dealt with in Section 871(b).

The withholding tax is imposed on individuals by Section 871(a) and on foreign corporations by Section 881(a). These Sections define the income that is covered by the tax. Capital gains earned by individuals receive separate treatment in Section 871(a)(2). The calculation of the tax is a complicated procedure, dealt with in Sections 863, 872, 873 and 874 for individuals, and in Sections 882 and 883 for corporations. Under Section 894, the withholding tax may be reduced or eliminated pursuant to tax treaties.

Collection of the tax (as distinct from imposition of the tax) is accomplished through the withholding mechanism. Section 1441 provides for the withholding on payments to individuals, and Section 1442 provides for the withholding on payments to foreign corporations. Pursuant to Section 1461, the American payor is held liable for failure to withhold.

———————

As Holmes suggests, the existing statutory framework providing for and implementing the withholding tax is complex. Nonetheless, its application to the most common elements of FDAP income is relatively straightforward. The following sections build and extend upon Holmes's description of the basic framework by (1) explaining the withholding tax treatment accorded to dividends, (2) discussing the details of the branch profits tax, (3) describing the tax treatment of portfolio interest, and (4) providing an account of how capital gains realized by nonresidents in the U.S.—on both personal and real property—are taxed.

Treatment of Dividends

A 30–percent withholding tax is imposed on U.S. source dividend payments to nonresidents unless certain specific statutory or treaty exemptions apply either to reduce or eliminate this rate of withholding. Section 861(a)(2) of the Code provides that—with some exceptions—dividends paid by U.S. resident corporations constitute income from a source "within the U.S." Section 871(a)(1)(A) provides that any U.S.–source dividends paid to a nonresident individual are subject to 30–percent gross withholding. Section 881(a)(1) provides that any U.S.–source dividends paid to a nonresident corporation are also subject to a 30–percent withholding rate.

The gross-basis withholding tax on dividends is troubling for several reasons. The most significant is the "double taxation" issue. Corporations are taxed at an entity level on a net basis on their income. Thus, since the gross basis withholding tax is imposed indiscriminately on dividends paid by U.S. corporations to nonresidents (depending, of course, on the provisions of any applicable tax treaty) it often results in an inefficient and unfair total level of taxation.

A closely related "double taxation" problem arises in any domestic "classical system" of taxation, which imposes income tax at both the corporate and individual level. However, as indicated previously, many countries have devised means of "integration" whereby, with varying degrees of efficacy and accuracy, the sum of the taxes imposed at the corporate level and taxes imposed at the individual taxpayer level equals or is close to what the total tax burden would be if the income had been earned directly by the individual taxpayer. The most common means of achieving integration is by providing tax credits to individual taxpayers for the corporate taxes paid on the income they receive as dividends, but many countries instead opt to exempt all or a substantial part of dividend income received from the recipients' income.

As described briefly above, the U.S.–U.K. tax treaty imposes no withholding tax on dividends paid directly from a controlled subsidiary to its nonresident parent corporation, so long as the parent controls at least 80 percent of the voting stock of the subsidiary. This development demonstrates increased awareness of the problems associated with double, or even triple, taxation—at least within international corporate groups. In the following excerpt, the Senate Foreign Relations Committee provides the details of the zero withholding tax rate arrangement with the United Kingdom and analyzes this innovation in U.S. treaty policy.

Senate Foreign Relations Committee Report on Tax Convention with United Kingdom (Treaty Doc. 107–19), Exec. Rep. No. 108–2 (March 13, 2003).

Zero Rate Of Withholding Tax On Dividends From 80–Percent–Owned Subsidiaries

* * *

The proposed treaty would eliminate withholding tax on dividends paid by one corporation to another corporation that owns at least 80 percent of the stock of the dividend-paying corporation (often referred to as "direct dividends"), provided that certain conditions are met (subparagraph 3(a) of Article 10 (Dividends)). The elimination of withholding tax under these circumstances is intended to reduce further the tax barriers to direct investment between the two countries.

Unlike the United States, the United Kingdom currently does not impose withholding tax on dividends paid to foreign shareholders as a matter of domestic law. Thus, the principal immediate effect of this provision would be to exempt dividends that U.S. subsidiaries pay to U.K. parent companies from U.S. withholding tax. With respect to dividends paid by U.K. subsidiaries to U.S. parent companies, the effect of this provision would be to lock in the currently applicable zero rate of U.K. withholding tax, regardless of how U.K. domestic law might change in this regard.

Currently, no U.S. treaty provides for a complete exemption from withholding tax under these circumstances, nor do the U.S. or OECD models. However, many bilateral tax treaties to which the United States is not a party eliminate withholding taxes under similar circumstances, and the same result has been achieved within the European Union under its "Parent–Subsidiary Directive." In addition, subsequent to the signing of the proposed treaty, the United States signed proposed protocols with Australia and Mexico that include zero-rate provisions similar to the one in the proposed treaty.

Description of provision

Under the proposed treaty, the withholding tax rate is reduced to zero on dividends beneficially owned by a company that has owned at least 80 percent of the voting power of the company paying the dividend for the 12–month period ending on the date the dividend is declared (subparagraph 3(a) of Article 10 (Dividends)). Under the current U.S.–U.K. treaty, these dividends may be taxed at a 5–percent rate (although, as noted above, the United Kingdom currently does not exercise this right as a matter of domestic law, whereas the United States does).

In certain circumstances, eligibility for the zero rate under the proposed treaty is subject to an additional restriction designed to prevent companies from reorganizing for the purpose of obtaining the benefits of the provision. * * *

Benefits and costs of adopting a zero rate with the United Kingdom

Tax treaties mitigate double taxation by resolving the potentially conflicting claims of a residence country and a source country to tax the same item of income. In the case of dividends, standard international practice is for the source country to yield mostly or entirely to the residence country. Thus, the residence country preserves its right to tax the dividend income of its residents, and the source country agrees either to limit its withholding tax to a relatively low rate (e.g., 5 percent) or to forgo it entirely.

Treaties that permit a positive rate of dividend withholding tax allow some degree of double taxation to persist. To the extent that the residence country allows a foreign tax credit for the withholding tax, this remaining double taxation may be mitigated or eliminated, but then the priority of the residence country's claim to tax the dividend income of its residents is not fully respected. Moreover, if a residence country imposes limitations on its foreign tax credit, withholding taxes may not be fully creditable as a practical matter, thus leaving some double taxation in place. For these reasons, dividend withholding taxes are commonly viewed as barriers to cross-border investment. The principal argument in favor of eliminating withholding taxes on certain direct dividends in the proposed treaty is that it would remove one such barrier.

Direct dividends arguably present a particularly appropriate case in which to remove the barrier of a withholding tax, in view of the close economic relationship between the payor and the payee. Whether in the United States or in the United Kingdom, the dividend-paying corporation generally faces full net-basis income taxation in the source country, and the dividend-receiving corporation generally is taxed in the residence country on the receipt of the dividend (subject to allowable foreign tax credits). If the dividend-paying corporation is at least 80–percent owned by the dividend-receiving corporation, it is arguably appropriate to regard the dividend-receiving corporation as a direct investor (and taxpayer) in the source country in this respect, rather than regarding the dividend-receiving corporation as having a more remote investor-type interest warranting the imposition of a second-level source-country tax.

Since the United Kingdom does not impose a withholding tax on these dividends under its internal law, the zero-rate provision would principally benefit direct investment in the United States by U.K. companies, as opposed to direct investment in the United Kingdom by U.S. companies. In other words, the potential benefits of the provision would accrue mainly in situations in which the United States is importing capital, as opposed to exporting it.

Adopting a zero-rate provision in the U.S.–U.K. treaty would have uncertain revenue effects for the United States. The United States would forgo the 5–percent tax that it currently collects on qualifying dividends paid by U.S. subsidiaries to U.K. parent companies, but since the United Kingdom currently does not impose any tax on comparable dividends paid by U.K. subsidiaries to U.S. parent companies, there would be no offsetting revenue gain to the United States in the form of decreased foreign tax credit claims with respect to withholding taxes. However, in order to account for the recent repeal of the U.K. advance corporation tax and related developments, the proposed treaty also eliminates a provision of the present treaty requiring the United States to provide a foreign tax credit with respect to certain dividends received from U.K. companies. On balance, these two effects are likely to increase revenues for the U.S. fisc. Over the longer term, if capital investment in the United States by U.K. persons is made more attractive, total investment in the United States may increase, ultimately creating a larger domestic tax base. However, if increased investment in the United States by U.K. persons displaced other foreign or U.S. investments in the United States, there would be no increase in the domestic tax base.

Revenue considerations aside, the removal of an impediment to the import of capital from the United Kingdom into the United States is a not-inconsiderable economic benefit. Further, it should be noted that, although U.K. internal law currently does not impose a withholding tax on dividends paid to foreign persons, there is no guarantee that this will always be the case. Thus, the inclusion of a zero-rate provision in the treaty would give U.S.-based enterprises somewhat greater certainty as to the applicability of a zero rate in the United Kingdom, which arguably would facilitate long-range business planning for U.S. companies in their capacities as capital exporters. Along the same lines, the provision would protect the U.S. fisc against increased foreign tax credit claims in the event that the U.K. were to change its internal law in this regard.

Although the United States has never agreed bilaterally to a zero rate of withholding tax on direct dividends, many other countries have done so in one or more of their bilateral tax treaties. These countries include OECD members Austria, Denmark, France, Finland, Germany, Iceland, Ireland, Japan, Luxembourg, Mexico, the Netherlands, Norway, Sweden, Switzerland, and the United Kingdom, as well as non-OECD-members Belarus, Brazil, Cyprus, Egypt, Estonia, Israel, Latvia, Lithuania, Mauritius, Namibia, Pakistan, Singapore, South Africa, Ukraine, and the United Arab Emirates. In addition, a zero rate on direct dividends has been achieved within the European Union under its "Parent–Subsidiary Directive." Finally, many countries have eliminated withholding taxes on dividends as a matter of internal law (e.g., the United Kingdom and Mexico). Thus, although the zero-rate provision in the proposed treaty is unprecedented in U.S. treaty history, there is substantial precedent for it in the experience of other countries. It may be argued that this experience constitutes an international trend toward eliminating withholding taxes on direct dividends, and that the United States would benefit by joining many of its treaty partners in this trend and further reducing the tax barriers to cross-border direct investment.

* * *

The Committee believes that every tax treaty must strike the appropriate balance of benefits in the allocation of taxing rights. The agreed level of dividend withholding for intercompany dividends is one of the elements that make up that balance, when considered in light of the benefits inuring to the United States from other concessions the treaty partner may make, the benefits of facilitating stable cross-border investment between the treaty partners, and each partner's domestic law with respect to dividend withholding tax.

In the case of this treaty, considered as a whole, the Committee believes that the elimination of withholding tax on intercompany dividends appropriately addresses a barrier to cross-border investment. The Committee believes, however, that the Treasury Department should only incorporate similar provisions into future treaty or protocol negotiations on a case-by-case basis, and it notes with approval Treasury's statement that "[i]n light of the range of facts that should be considered, the Treasury Department does not view [elimination of withholding tax on intercompany dividends] as a blanket change in the United States' tax treaty practice."

The Committee encourages the Treasury Department to develop criteria for determining the circumstances under which the elimination of withholding tax on intercompany dividends would be appropriate in future negotiations with other countries. The Committee expects the Treasury Department to consult with the Committee with regard to these criteria and to the consideration of elimination of the withholding tax on intercompany dividends in future treaties.

NOTE

Harbinger of the Future? The U.S.–U.K. Treaty may augur a fundamental change in U.S. international tax policy. This suspicion is fed by the fact that recent protocols with Mexico and Australia have also provided for the elimination of withholding taxes on certain qualifying dividends. According to BNA Daily Tax Reports:

> Treasury International Tax Counsel Barbara Angus said at the March 5 Foreign Relations Committee hearing on the treaties that, while the United States is interested in pursuing treaties that reduce withholding taxes and eliminate double taxation wherever possible, the zero dividend rate has to be assessed on a case-by-case basis and cannot be made an automatic feature of U.S. treaty policy. In order for the United States to include that withholding rate on dividends, Angus said, the agreement would have to include "effective anti-treaty shopping provisions of the highest standard."[9]

Unsurprisingly, such anti-treaty shopping provisions play a key role in eliminating double taxation while protecting the U.S. tax base. Anti-treaty shopping provisions prevent abuse of the advantageous treaty provisions by denying parties only weakly associated with treaty partner countries access to the lower withholding rates provided for in treaties (see Chapter 3).

As we have discussed, the Code nominally imposes a full two-tier tax on corporate dividends originating in the United States. Tax treaties routinely reduce the rate of withholding tax, and there may be a trend to

---

9. See Senate Ratifies Tax Accords with U.K., Mexico, and Australia, BNA Daily Tax Report (March 17, 2003).

lower withholding rates even further. In the meantime, the IRS and Congress have attempted to defend the U.S. classical system with a regime called the "Branch Profits Tax," the aim of which is to ensure that the United States collects two levels of corporate tax on U.S. source earnings, regardless of whether a foreigner invests in branch or subsidiary form.

The Branch Profits Tax

Congress enacted the Branch Profits Tax (the "BPT") in an attempt to mitigate the differences in the tax treatment between foreign corporations with U.S. subsidiaries and foreign corporations with U.S. branches. Before enactment of the BPT, earnings repatriated by a U.S. branch to its nonresident corporate owner were not subject to U.S. tax if the gross income effectively connected to U.S. operations accounted for less than 50 percent of the parent company's worldwide income over the previous three-year period (changed in 1986 to 25 percent).[10] Foreign corporations with U.S. subsidiaries complained of a competitive disadvantage as a result since dividends paid by U.S.-based subsidiaries were subject to U.S. taxation in a way that U.S. branches were not. In the following excerpt, Richard Doernberg describes the motivation for the BPT and outlines its basic features.

Richard L. Doernberg, *Overriding Tax Treaties: The U.S. Perspective*, 9 EMORY INT'L L. REV. 71, 84–87 (1995).

The branch profits tax became a part of the tax landscape in the Tax Reform Act of 1986. Prior to 1987, a foreign corporation owned by foreign investors and doing business in the United States was taxed at the corporate level under the regular graduated corporate rates on income effectively connected with a U.S. trade or business. If the foreign investors operated in the United States through a domestic corporation, the outcome was the same. Differences in treatment arose when the corporation distributed its corporate earnings to foreign investor-owners.

For a domestic corporation, the dividend is subject to the 30% ([or] reduced treaty) tax rate under Code section 871(a) (or section 881), collected under the withholding rules of Code sections 1441 and 1442. For a foreign corporation, prior to the Tax Reform Act of 1986, a dividend paid to foreign investors by a foreign corporation was much less likely to be subject to any U.S. tax. In the first place, if less than 50% of the gross income of a foreign corporation for the three preceding taxable years was derived from income effectively connected with a U.S. trade or business, dividends were free from U.S. taxation anyway. Moreover, if the corporation had income 50% or more of which

---

10. See I.R.C. § 861(a)(2).

was effectively connected with the conduct of a U.S. trade or business, only the portion of the dividend paid by the foreign corporation proportional to the percentage of its connected income was subject to the U.S. tax. Most importantly, many treaties exempted those dividends paid by certain foreign corporations to non-U.S. residents or citizens.

Congress's stated intention in legislating the branch profits tax is to subject the income earned by foreign corporations operating in the United States to two levels of taxation just like income earned and distributed by U.S. corporations operating here. In the latter case, the income is taxed at a maximum marginal rate of 35% when earned, and it is subject to a maximum 30% tax when the corporation makes a dividend payment. In the case of a foreign corporation, under the branch profits regime, income is taxable at a maximum marginal rate of 35% when it is earned and an additional 30% branch profits tax when the income is repatriated by the foreign corporation (or deemed repatriated because it is not reinvested in "U.S. assets"). In effect, the branch profits tax treats the branch as if it were a U.S. corporation.

The 30% tax is levied on the "dividend equivalent amount" in lieu of a secondary withholding tax on dividends paid by the foreign corporation. The dividend equivalent amount equals the foreign corporation's earnings and profits that are effectively connected with the conduct of a trade or business in the United States subject to certain specified adjustments. To the extent that the effectively connected earnings and profits are invested in "U.S. net equity," the dividend equivalent amount is decreased. Thus, the branch profits tax decreases because the branch is deemed not to have repatriated the earnings. Conversely, to the extent that a foreign corporation's U.S. net equity decreases because of an actual repatriation of assets or because U.S. property of the branch previously invested in "U.S. net equity" is converted into other nonqualifying domestic assets, the dividend equivalent amount will be increased. The increase in the dividend equivalent amount reflects the fact that earnings of a previous year are being repatriated or are treated as having been repatriated.

The term "U.S. net equity" is defined as U.S. assets reduced by U.S. liabilities. The term "U.S. assets" is defined as money plus the aggregate adjusted basis of property used by the foreign corporation that is treated as effectively connected with the conduct of a trade or business in the United States. The term "U.S. liabilities" means the liabilities of a foreign corporation treated by the Secretary as effectively connected with a U.S. trade or business. * * *

As part of the branch profits tax legislation, Congress imposed a 30% tax on interest paid (or deemed paid) by a branch of a foreign corporation engaged in a U.S. trade or business. Absent Code section 884(f), which imposes this branch level tax on interest, it would be possible for a foreign corporation to decrease or even avoid the branch profits tax by making interest payments to its foreign shareholders. The interest payments would decrease taxable income effectively connected to earnings and profits and, ultimately, the dividend equivalent amount on which the branch profits tax is based.

Code section 884(f) contains two rules for taxing interest paid by the U.S. branch of a foreign corporation. Section 884(f)(1)(A) provides that, for a foreign corporation engaged in a U.S. trade or business, interest paid by the U.S. trade or business is treated as if it were paid by a domestic corporation. Consequently, under section 861(a)(1) the interest is U.S. source income, so it generally is subject to a flat 30% tax under Code sections 871(a) or 881. Section 884(f)(1)(B) provides that, to the extent that the amount of interest allowable as a deduction under Code section 882 in computing taxable income exceeds the interest actually paid, it shall be treated as interest paid by a fictional U.S. subsidiary (the branch) to its parent, thereby subjecting the interest payment to a 30% tax under Code section 881.

Again, a foreign corporation with a U.S. branch is subject both to the regular U.S. corporate income tax on income effectively connected with a U.S. trade or business and to the branch profits tax to the extent that the income is not reinvested in "U.S. assets," as defined in Code section 884(c)(2). Normally, there is no further tax when the foreign corporation makes an actual dividend distribution to its foreign investors. The branch profits tax on the U.S. earnings and profits of foreign corporations is intended to serve the same function as the 30% tax on dividend distributions from domestic corporations to foreign investors.

Congress has preserved, however, a 30% tax on dividend distributions from foreign corporations when a treaty prohibits the application of the branch profits tax, but allows imposition of the 30% tax on dividends. Essentially, the withholding tax on dividends serves as a back-up for the branch profits tax.

NOTE

Treaty Overrides. One significant challenge for implementation of the BPT has been how to harmonize this tax with existing U.S. obligations under international tax treaties. International tax treaties contain nondiscrimination articles that provide that residents of the treaty partner will not be discriminated against as compared with domestic taxpayers (see Chapter 10). The BPT arguably discriminates against nonresidents by imposing a tax that U.S. residents do not have to pay. In enacting the BPT, Congress effectively overrode existing treaty commitments by its interpretation of U.S. nondiscrimination obligations, which raises troubling concerns about how seriously Congress regards U.S. income tax treaty obligations. In spite of these concerns, the BPT appears to have served its purposes of increasing federal revenues and placing foreign branches in the United States on approximately the same tax footing as domestic corporations and foreign subsidiaries in the United States.

Treatment of Portfolio Interest

In deciding how and to whom to lend money, investors anticipate the withholding taxes they will have to pay on the interest that their investments will yield. As a consequence, firms that are located in countries that impose gross-basis withholding taxes on interest payments to nonresidents will have to pay more to borrow than firms located in countries that do not impose gross-basis withholding taxes on interest payments. In 1984, the U.S. eliminated all withholding taxes on "portfolio" interest payments both to make debt financing more affordable for U.S. firms and to place U.S. borrowers on a competitive footing with firms in countries not imposing withholding taxes on portfolio interest.

In the following excerpt, Reuven Avi–Yonah examines the 1984 changes in the taxation of portfolio interest and discusses their desirability from both the U.S. perspective and a multilateral international standpoint.

Reuven Avi–Yonah, *Globalization, Tax Competition, and the Fiscal Crisis of the Welfare State*, 113 HARV. L. REV. 1573, 1579–82 (2000).

In 1984, the United States unilaterally abolished its withholding tax of 30% on foreign residents who earned portfolio interest income from sources within the United States. "Portfolio interest" was defined to include interest on U.S. government bonds, on bonds issued by U.S. corporations (unless the bond holder held ten percent or more of the shares of the corporation), and on U.S. bank accounts and certificates of deposit. This "portfolio interest exemption" is available to any nonresident alien (that is, any person who is not a U.S. resident for tax purposes) and does not require any certification of identity or proof that the interest income was subject to tax in the investor's country of residence.

The portfolio interest exemption resulted from a fortuitous combination of three factors. First, the Reagan tax cuts of 1981, which dramatically lowered the U.S. effective tax rate, and the accompanying defense buildup created a significant budgetary deficit that the U.S. government could finance only by borrowing abroad. Second, unlike other U.S. tax treaties with developed countries, which provide for zero withholding rates on interest paid from one treaty partner to the other, the Japan–U.S. tax treaty imposed a 10% withholding tax. Third, in 1987, the United States decided to terminate its tax treaty with the Netherlands Antilles, which had a zero withholding rate on interest and no limitation on benefits to Antilles residents. By channeling the loans through a Netherlands Antilles finance subsidiary, U.S. corporations had been able to borrow abroad without having a withholding tax imposed on the interest. Thus, the portfolio interest exemption was motivated by the desire of both the U.S. government and U.S. multinationals to borrow abroad without having to bear the cost of any withholding tax, which, under the circumstances of 1987, was likely to be shifted to the borrower.

Arguably, none of these reasons for the portfolio interest exemption is valid today. The U.S. government is in budgetary surplus, and Japan is an unlikely source of funds. Moreover, given the size of the U.S. bond market and the widely held perception of U.S. bonds as relatively safe investments in turbulent economic times, both the U.S. government and U.S. corporations can probably afford to borrow abroad despite any withholding costs. However, the portfolio interest exemption remains with us.

* * *

[M]ost developed countries levy no withholding tax on interest paid to nonresidents on bank deposits and on government and corporate bonds. These nations do levy taxes on dividends, but dividends (unlike interest) are not deductible, and the underlying income has therefore already been taxed once. In reality, the discrepancy between interest and dividends may be [small], for two reasons. First, a significant portion of the return on equity comes in the form of capital gains, which are not subject to source-based taxation in any of the countries included in the table. [The table referred to is omitted.–ed.] Second, the withholding tax on dividends is generally easy to avoid for sophisticated investors. For example, a foreign investor can construct a "total return equity swap" in which she receives payments equivalent to dividends from an investment banker in the source country, who in turn hedges by holding the underlying stock and receiving the actual dividends. Most countries do not subject the dividend-equivalent payments to withholding, and the underlying dividends are free from withholding because they are paid to a domestic recipient. This situation has led to calls for a "portfolio dividends exemption."

Treatment of Capital Gains

Section 871 of the Internal Revenue Code provides that, as a general rule, nonresidents are not taxable in the U.S. on transactions that give rise to capital gains. However, there are three important exceptions to this general rule.

First, as described in detail below, capital gains generated by the sale of U.S. *real property* or the stock of certain U.S. *real property* holding corporations are subject to withholding tax. Second, transactions yielding capital gains that are *effectively connected* with the conduct of a trade or business will be taxable as ordinary income under IRC § 871(b). Third, an exception to the general rule of nontaxability of capital gains, contained in § 871(a)(2), concerns nonresident aliens who are present in the U.S. 183 days or more during the taxable year. Ordinarily, persons who are resident in the U.S. for 183 days or more in a year are deemed to be residents by the substantial presence test of § 7701(b) of the Code. However, those staying temporarily in the U.S. on certain visas (such as students) are considered to be "exempt persons" and do not have to count days spent in the U.S. toward establishing residency under § 7701(b). However, § 871(a)(2) is an entirely separate provision of the Code, and the "exempt persons" exclusion for not counting days in the U.S. does not apply. The general rule is that any nonresident individual present in the U.S. for 183 days or more during the taxable year is subject to withholding tax on her U.S.-source capital gains.[11] Thus, under this third exception, nonresidents may be subject to gross-basis taxation on capital gains even if they are ordinarily considered to be "exempt persons" and, thus, nonresidents under the "substantial presence" test of § 7701(b) of the Code.

In the following excerpt, Stephen Shay, Clifton Fleming, and Robert Peroni examine the efficacy of the withholding tax regime in protecting the tax base. They also briefly discuss the theoretical consistency of the rationales for imposing mandatory withholding taxes on some types of passive income, such as some interest, dividends, rent, and royalties, but not on others, such as capital gains on personal and intangible property.

---

11. Section 871(a)(2) provides (in part) that: "In the case of a nonresident alien individual present in the United States for a period or periods aggregating 183 days or more during the taxable year, there is hereby imposed for such year a tax of 30 percent of the amount by which his gains, derived from sources within the United States, from the sale or exchange at any time during such year of capital assets exceed his losses, allocable to sources within the United States, from the sale or exchange at any time during such year of capital assets."

Stephen E. Shay, Clifton Fleming, Jr. & Robert J. Peroni, *"What's Source Got to Do With It?" Source Rules and U.S. International Taxation*, 56 TAX L. REV. 81, 121–22 (2002).

Withholding tax at source has the appearance of being a secure and reliable mechanism to assure payment of source tax on fixed and determinable income. In practice, however, the withholding tax regime has proven to be a blunt instrument. A withholding tax regime is easiest to administer and enforce if tax is withheld from the gross amount of every payment at the same rate. Yet, this has never been the case.

It is particularly difficult to administer exceptions to withholding and at the same time protect against the risks of both tax evasion by U.S. persons and granting treaty relief to foreign persons not eligible for treaty benefits. Because the U.S. withholding agent often is remote from the beneficial owner of the income, it cannot obtain information to evaluate self-certified claims of eligibility for relief from the tax.

The withholding rules exclude several important items realized by nonresidents from U.S. investments. The most significant statutory exclusion from gross taxation at source is for gains from the sale of personal property, other than U.S. real property interests, that are not effectively connected with a U.S. business. This exclusion includes most gain from the sale of stocks and securities in a U.S. corporation (unless the corporation is a U.S. real property holding corporation) and intangible property (unless the consideration is contingent on use).

The exception for gains is justified on the grounds that (1) the source country does not have a strong claim to tax the income, and (2) absent information regarding the taxpayer's basis, it is not feasible for the source country to determine the correct amount of net gain. (A tax on the gross amount realized could result in a very high effective tax rate on the net gain.) If the market access rationale, however, is sufficient to support a source tax on dividend income derived from U.S. economic activity, as a matter of logic it should equally support a source tax on capital gains from the same instruments since the capital gain is essentially a market capitalization of future earnings.

Moreover, the failure to tax a nonresident's stock gains offers her an opportunity to completely avoid the shareholder tax on U.S. corporate income to the extent that the nonresident's capital gains are exempt in her residence country or she may successfully avoid residence country tax through use of a tax haven. U.S. residents are comparatively disadvantaged because they do not lawfully have this opportunity. Accordingly, the decision not to tax capital gains at source would seem to rest largely on administrative and enforcement considerations and not on principles of substantive tax policy.

Capital Gains Taxes on Foreign–Owned Real Property: "FIRPTA"

Before 1980, nonresident individuals and foreign corporations were exempt from withholding tax on capital gains from the sale of real property not effectively connected with the conduct of a trade or business within the U.S. In 1980 Congress enacted the Foreign Investment in Real Property Tax Act of 1980 (FIRPTA)—resulting in § 897 of the Code—to close this gap. Section 897 provides that gains on the disposition of U.S. real property interests by nonresidents are taxed as if the gains were effectively connected income of a U.S. trade or business under § 871(b)(1) of the Code.

The IRS relies on section 6039C(a) of the Code to learn about the U.S. real estate holdings of nonresidents through information returns. These information returns must include the name and address of the nonresident and a description of all U.S. real property interests held by the nonresident during the year. A nonresident is treated as holding a U.S. real property interest if the nonresident did not engage in a trade or business in the United States during the year and the fair market value of the U.S. real property interests exceeds $50,000. Separate look-through provisions address U.S. real property interests held indirectly by nonresidents through holding companies. As an aid to the enforcement of FIRPTA, purchasers are required to deduct and withhold a tax equal to 10% of the amount realized on the disposition of a U.S. real property interest by a nonresident. See § 1445(a).

In the excerpt below, Richard Kaplan argues that the loophole ostensibly addressed by FIRPTA was minor and was created because of the difficulty of collecting taxes on the capital gains of non-business nonresident investors. According to Kaplan, FIRPTA complicates the tax code, overrides bilateral tax treaty provisions, and creates an intrusive and administratively difficult collection scheme. Professor Kaplan asserts that FIRPTA can only be understood as an attempt to discourage foreign investment in U.S. real estate. He recommends that FIRPTA be repealed.

Richard L. Kaplan, *Creeping Xenophobia and the Taxation of Foreign–Owned Real Estate*, 71 Geo. L.J. 1091, 1092–1128 (1983).

For many years the subject of foreign ownership of United States property was the concern primarily of international investment advisors and economic theorists. In the decade of the

1970's, however, this arcane topic became the focus of widespread concern and intense debate. The popular television news program, "60 Minutes," devoted an entire segment to foreign purchases of United States farmland, and the American Bar Association began sponsoring annual courses on foreign investment planning geared toward general practitioners, not just international law specialists. * * * The increased attention given to foreign holdings of United States real estate is directly related to the perceived phenomenal expansion of such holdings in recent years. International investors had long been attracted to United States investments because of the relative stability of this country's economic and political systems, as well as the sheer enormousness of the investment market itself. But this attraction became even stronger in the 1970's because of favorable foreign currency fluctuations, the rise of local communist movements overseas, and other destabilizing events. At the same time, skyrocketing petroleum prices concentrated more investable funds in the hands of some foreign investors than had ever been the case before. By the end of 1980, in fact, the Arab oil exporting nations had invested $340 billion worldwide, a tripling of their cumulative investment since 1975, and fully 80% of this total came from just four countries: Iraq, Kuwait, Saudi Arabia, and the United Arab Emirates.

In 1974 * * * Congress asked the Department of Commerce to prepare a "benchmark" study of foreign investment in the United States, and two years later, a nine-volume tome was completed. Congress then responded with the International Investment Survey Act of 1976, which requires the President to obtain information concerning foreign acquisitions of 10% ownership interests, whether direct or "indirect," in American businesses. * * * Thus, Congress created a mechanism to monitor foreign investment on an annual basis.

* * *

Congress then enacted a new statute, the Agricultural Foreign Investment Disclosure Act of 1978. This Act requires reports of foreign ownership of "agricultural land," including land used in timber production, and once again, substantial fines are provided to deter nonreporting. As is the case with the International Investment Survey Act, however, the objective is simply more information about foreign investments. No attempt is made to limit or otherwise dissuade foreign investors from coming to this country.

* * *

So it was in 1978 that opponents of such investments came to see the root of their dilemma in, of all places, the federal tax code. Senator Wallop of Wyoming introduced legislation to close what came to be described as a "loophole"—namely, the long-standing exemption of certain foreign investors from tax upon the disposition of their capital assets, including land. Although this amendment was withdrawn to give the Treasury Department time to study the problem, it eventually culminated in the Foreign Investment in Real Property Tax Act of 1980, commonly known as FIRPTA. The highly complex provisions of this statute were then amended by the Economic Recovery Tax Act of 1981 to "plug" further holes, and implementing regulations were first promulgated on September 21, 1982. These enactments are the focus of this article, although many of the policy considerations discussed apply with equal force to the federal disclosure statutes and to the state prohibitions mentioned previously. Unlike those earlier manifestations of creeping xenophobia, however, these tax amendments are not essentially harmless. For reasons of tax complexity, international relations, and economic policy, this article argues, FIRPTA should be repealed in its entirety posthaste.

* * *

[T]he ability of some foreign investors to avoid tax on their United States real estate gains results primarily from the statutory requirement that such gains be derived from a "trade or business" in order to be subject to United States tax. This, then, is the rule that FIRPTA and its subsequent amendments had to address. Doing so, however, was not as straightforward as it might seem.

* * *

When Congress enacted FIRPTA, it chose not to disturb the basic rule that capital gains are taxable only when "effectively connected" with a United States "trade or business." Instead, FIRPTA supplies the rule's condition precedent by statutory fiat. Thus, the gain of a nonresident alien individual or a foreign corporation from the disposition of a United States real property interest shall be taken into account * * * as if the taxpayer were engaged in a trade or business within the United States during the taxable year and as if such gain were effectively connected with such trade or business.

In other words, there no longer is any need to consider the extent of an investor's involvement in his property's operation, or the scope of that troublesome phrase, "trade or business." If the gain results from a "United States real property interest," it is treated as if it were "effectively connected" income and is taxed at the rates applicable to domestic taxpayers.

The pivotal element in this regime, obviously, is the newly created term of art, "United States real property interest." This phrase is defined as any "interest in real property (including an interest in a mine, well, or other natural deposit) located in the United States or the Virgin Islands." Moreover, FIRPTA recognizes that an investor can profit from real estate without actually owing it and accordingly includes as a "real property interest" all "leaseholds of land or improvements thereon, options to acquire land or improvements thereon, and options to acquire leaseholds of land or improvements thereon." Clearly, the new statute reaches far beyond fee simple ownership of undeveloped land, encompassing even a humble option to lease an apartment or a small storefront. Such comprehensiveness is not unusual in legislation that responds to perceived "abuses," but the inevitable result is that FIRPTA affects transactions that are not typically thought of as real estate deals.

FIRPTA also addresses the common situation in which real estate is held by a corporation with the foreign investor owing stock in that corporation but not the real estate itself. To counter the circumvention possibility created by such an arrangement, FIRPTA defines "real property interest" to include "any interest (other than an interest solely as a creditor) in any domestic corporation."

* * *

[T]he broad inclusion of corporate stock as "real property interests" is subject to two important exceptions. The first exception covers stock that is "regularly traded on an established securities market," unless the investor holds more than five percent of that company's stock. * * * In any case, this exception means that most investors in Exxon Corporation, for example, are not affected by FIRPTA, even though Exxon has vast holdings of United States real estate.

The second exception applies to stock of a corporation that was not a "United States real property holding corporation" during the period in which the foreign investor held its stock. A "United States real property holding corporation" is defined as any corporation whose "United States real property interests" comprise at least fifty percent of its real property interests, including foreign holdings, plus any other assets that are used or held for use in a "trade or business." Thus, the exception would not apply to a company whose principal function is to own or develop United States real estate. Moreover, the statute requires that market values, not actual costs, be used in making this calculation.

* * *

Such piercing of the corporate veil, though a bit convoluted, is certainly sound conceptually. If real estate is the object of FIRPTA's concern, real estate held in corporate form must be attributed to the corporation's foreign investors or else the statute would be virtually meaningless. The statute's use of fair market values, however, imposes an unavoidably speculative character on this rather central definition.

* * *

In any case, investors cannot avoid that status by concocting intricate holding structures because FIRPTA contains an impressive battery of "look-through" provisions in its arsenal. * * * The statute's point seems clear: formalities of title holding are irrelevant, whether they involve foreign or domestic corporations, partnerships, or other conduits. A company's status as a "United States real property holding corporation" is a function of its substantive asset ownership and nothing else.

* * *

Before 1980 a foreign investor often realized his gain in a company's real estate holdings by selling the stock of that company rather than having the company sell its assets. The company, in many cases, was engaged in a "trade or business" (of managing the property), while the investor was not so engaged, stock ownership itself not constituting a trade or business. The investor's gain, therefore, was usually tax-free. Now, however, that gain is taxable, because FIRPTA treats the stock of companies that own real estate as "real property interests."

* * *

Inherent in any tax statute is the problem of its enforceability. Can the government really collect the levy it purports to impose? This problem is particularly acute in the case of FIRPTA because the class of persons affected by this statute is effectively exempt from customary enforcement sanctions. For example, an individual who does not reside in the United States is less susceptible to being arrested and, accordingly, is less concerned about the Code's imprisonment provisions than a resident would be. Similarly, someone who does not engage in a trade or business in this country is likely to have fewer assets subject to the Code's property seizure provisions than a person who is so engaged. Hence, the enforceability of FIRPTA is fraught with serious problems because the taxpayers affected are neither residents nor persons engaged in United States trades or businesses.

In point of fact, these very problems are the raison d'etre of the "loophole" that FIRPTA now closes.

* * *

The exemption of United States source capital gains from tax was not some legislative oversight. Rather, it represented a deliberate recognition of the limitations of enforceability, coupled with a hope that the revenue forgone by its creation would be offset by taxes on the increased earnings of stockbrokers and other middlemen. * * * Among the responses available to Congress are information reporting requirements and withholding of sales proceeds. * * * [T]here are significant chinks in FIRPTA's armor with respect to enforceability, raising the question whether this new statute ought to exist at all.

* * *

As analyzed thus far, FIRPTA seems to be an almost perverse enactment. To repeal a relatively limited exemption of some forty-four years standing, Congress expended inordinate legislative effort in five separate sessions. The resulting statute is complex, difficult to enforce, and disrespectful of existing tax treaty obligations.

* * *

If an American citizen, or an alien who resides in the United States, or a nonresident alien who engages in a United States trade or business, invests in United States land, his gain upon disposition of that land is usually taxable. Oftentimes, this gain will qualify for favorable treatment as a capital gain, but it is taxable nevertheless. In contrast, certain foreign investors who do not engage in a United States "trade or business" are exempt from tax on their United States source capital gains, including gains derived from sales of United States real estate. That, in a nutshell, is the dichotomy FIRPTA abolishes. Under FIRPTA, real estate profits are now taxable, no matter how limited a foreign investor's United States contacts may be.

But it is not so clear that this principle really applies to domestic and foreign taxpayers. Domestic taxpayers, after all, enjoy all of the protections and benefits of United States law and participate fully in the commercial life of this country. Foreign investors who do not engage in a United States "trade or business," on the other hand, are prototypically passive. Their involvement in United States commercial activity is not ongoing and extensive, or else they would probably be taxable even under pre-FIRPTA law. These investors, quite simply, are not similarly situated to domestic taxpayers, and disparate tax treatment for these two groups, therefore, is not necessarily inappropriate.

But the whole notion that the purpose of FIRPTA was to correct a breach of "horizontal equity" is itself rather spurious. In point of fact, the breach persists, even after FIRPTA, whenever an investor's gains derive from listed securities, commodities, bonds, or any capital asset other than real estate. If preferential treatment of foreign investors is such a pernicious affront to horizontal equity, why was its eradication limited to real estate gains? It is this limitation that shows unmistakably that FIRPTA was intended to do far more than simply correct a disparity between foreign and domestic investors. Notwithstanding the statement quoted previously from the Committee Report, FIRPTA was intended to discourage foreign investment in United States real estate. The question then becomes whether this statute will indeed have that effect.

* * *

Foreign investors are attracted to United States real estate for many different reasons. * * * The absence of a tax upon disposition, however, does not seem to be a major consideration; in comparison with the other factors at play, it is downright trivial. After all, a tax upon disposition has absolutely no impact on a foreign investor unless he disposes of the property. Until then, any tax advantage, or "inducement" as the Committee Report called it, is irrelevant.

That being the case, how can FIRPTA hope to affect foreign investment in United States land? It might deter foreign speculators perhaps, but most foreign investors come to the United States for long term, even permanent, investments. To them, the panoply of relevant investment incentives—stable economy, "safe haven," and so forth—remains unchanged. Hence, FIRPTA is unlikely to affect the level of aggregate foreign investment in United States real estate to any discernible degree.

Yet, proponents of the new statute apparently believed that the capital gains exemption had not only increased aggregate foreign investment in United States real estate, but had also, by itself, precipitated higher land prices. In the words of Senator Church, one of FIRPTA's cosponsors:

> This tax loophole gives foreign investors a special advantage in the purchase of U.S. land by enabling them to pay higher prices than can any U.S. investor or farmer, who must take

into consideration that he will have to pay the full capital gains tax in the event he should sell or transfer the land.

The validity of this proposition is open to serious question. A detailed study prepared by the General Accounting Office before FIRPTA was enacted found that "foreign purchasers did not consistently pay more than U.S. buyers for similar land." In other words, foreign investors typically bought at market prices and did not exploit their pre-FIRPTA tax advantage by making higher bids. Even if this had not been the case, those higher prices would presumably have gone to the landowners who sold their properties to the foreign investors—usually, American citizens. But the fact remains that the tax advantage eliminated by FIRPTA was not a significant factor affecting United States real estate prices.

* * *

The Foreign Investment in Real Property Tax Act (FIRPTA) of 1980, as amended in 1981, is an unmitigated disaster. The "loophole" it closes was consciously created as a practical necessity and was restricted to a relatively limited class of foreign investors. To abolish this loophole, FIRPTA imposes a complex statutory regime that, despite an intrusive system of reporting requirements, is of questionable enforceability. Furthermore, for the new statute to have even facial effectiveness, it was necessary for Congress to override conflicting tax treaty provisions, a move that is without modern precedent or foreseeable long-term consequences.

Even more problematic are FIRPTA's confused policy objectives. The supposedly horrific inequity of foreign versus domestic taxation actually remains unchanged, except for the special case of real estate dispositions. The clear intention of this statute, therefore, is not to eradicate inequities, but rather to discourage foreign investment in United States real estate, a goal for which FIRPTA is singularly unsuited. In any case, the goal itself manifests a disturbing xenophobia that lacks any economic rationale or common sense foundation. The new statute, quite clearly, is flawed beyond amendatory repair and should be repealed in its entirety at the earliest opportunity.

NOTES

1) *Here to Stay and Tough to Gainsay.* Despite the many problems with FIRPTA and notwithstanding Richard Kaplan's call for its demise, it perseveres and remains an established fixture of U.S. tax law two decades after its enactment. The legitimacy of U.S. taxation of capital gains realized on U.S. real estate is difficult to question apart from the unfavorable comparison of FIRPTA with the general exclusion of capital gains realized in the U.S. on personal property owned by nonresidents.

The U.S. has a strong case for asserting its source country tax jurisdiction over U.S. real estate gains; the property is indubitably part of the U.S. Thus, the nexus of such income with the U.S. is clear.

2) *Administrative Nightmare?* Despite Kaplan's strong contrary opinion, it is not entirely clear that FIRPTA constitutes an egregious affront to U.S. tax policy, to principles of equity more generally, or even to administrative convenience. By the dictates of § 1445, purchasers of real estate from nonresidents are expected to withhold and pay to the IRS 10% of the purchase price. The IRS then credits this 10% to the nonresident who can then file for net basis treatment of the capital gains earned on the transaction, if any. This system appears to work quite well, with those nonresidents most adversely affected by the withholding tax—for example, those who have realized losses on their U.S. real estate holdings—filing tax returns, opting for net basis taxation, and receiving a refund of the withholding tax.

3) *Read the Treaty.* Inbound non-business income is taxed through a curious mixture of statutory gross-basis withholding taxes, lower treaty-based withholding rates, and provisions that deem non-business income (in the case of FIRPTA) to be income effectively connected with a U.S. trade or business. In addition, with some narrow exceptions, certain categories of inbound non-business income are not taxed at all by statute, such as portfolio interest and personal property capital gains (including stocks and bonds), whereas others, such as direct dividends in the case of the U.K., escape U.S. taxation through treaties. In sum, the U.S. taxation of nonresident non-business income presents no united front and few generally applicable guidelines can be discerned. The withholding tax system established through the international networks of bilateral tax treaties admits of few consistencies and few, if any, overarching principles. The gross-basis withholding tax on non-business income payments to nonresidents ignoring, as it does, the costs of producing the payments, is a blunt instrument motivated more by administrative ease and certainty than by principles of equity or efficiency. Needless to say, resort to the treaties themselves is indispensable whenever one is dealing with inbound transactions.

7.3 NON-BUSINESS INCOME: OUTBOUND TRANSACTIONS

The taxation of inbound non-business income presents only part of the picture of the taxation of non-business taxation—i.e., how nonresidents are treated by the United States tax system and its treaties. More salient for many U.S. residents is the tax treatment that Americans earning non-business income abroad may expect from foreign jurisdictions.

The Important Differences Between Portfolio Income and FDI Income

Unlike the discussion of portfolio income in the context of inbound transactions where U.S. law and treaties are paramount, a discussion of portfolio income arising from outbound transactions involves the tax laws of nearly every nation in the world. This is because the foreign investment activities of Americans are broad, complex, extensive and growing. However, not all investments of Americans abroad have the same character; far from it. In the context of inbound transactions in the U.S., the main distinction is between income associated with or effectively connected to a U.S. trade or business and FDAP income. In the context of outbound transactions, there exists an equally important distinction, in this case between direct and portfolio investments.

The key differences between portfolio income and foreign direct investment income have largely been neglected for a long time. In the following excerpt, Michael Graetz and Itai Grinberg highlight the various ways in which portfolio income and income from foreign direct investments differ.

Michael J. Graetz and Itai Grinberg, *Taxing International Portfolio Income*, (forthcoming, Tax Law Review).

When the U.S. regime for taxing international income first came into place, policymakers were focused on direct investment abroad by U.S. corporations: "[T]he United States says, in effect, to its citizens—go abroad and trade." U.S. international tax policy was essentially mercantilist, driven largely by concerns that double taxation of international income by both the United States and the country where the income was earned would inhibit U.S. direct investments abroad and also would be unfair. The U.S. decision unilaterally to grant a tax credit for foreign income taxes was also grounded in the policymakers' convictions that the source country—the country where the income was earned—had a right to tax such income and inevitably would exercise that right.

Soon after the U.S. enacted its foreign tax credit, the League of Nations, spurred in part by the United States, examined the problem of international taxation, and in 1928 The League produced a model bilateral income tax treaty. The decades since have seen some changes, to be sure, but the basic structure of the League's 1928 model undergirds today's model treaties of the United States, the OECD, and the United Nations, which, in turn, form the basis for the more than 2000 bilateral income tax treaties now in effect throughout the world. Like the instigators of the U.S. foreign tax credit, the drafters of the League's 1928 model treaty were overwhelmingly concerned with international business income. A few moguls may have owned widespread international portfolio investments, but portfolio investments simply were not of much importance to the world economy at that time.

The tax literature frequently labels the League of Nations' basic allocation of income taxes in its model treaty between countries of source and countries of residence as the "International Tax Compromise." That compromise typically is described as allocating active business income to the jurisdiction where it is earned (the source jurisdiction) and passive or portfolio income to the jurisdiction from which the capital is supplied (the residence jurisdiction). But this description buries the fact that source countries frequently impose income taxes on income from passive portfolio investments in the form of so-called withholding taxes: final taxes imposed at a flat rate on gross dividend or interest income paid to foreigners.

In 1984—both to encourage foreigners to purchase U.S. debt to help finance federal deficits and to help U.S. companies borrow in world markets—Congress repealed the U.S. withholding tax on portfolio interest income. Since then zero taxation by source countries of portfolio interest income has become commonplace. But source countries typically continue to impose withholding taxes on dividend income earned by foreigners. The U.S. tax code imposes such a tax at a 30% rate, but the U.S. commonly reduces that rate to 15% by treaty. * * *

Analysis and reassessment of U.S. tax policy regarding international portfolio income is long overdue. With the exception of routine bows to the "International Tax Compromise" and sporadic discussions of the practical difficulties of residence countries in collecting taxes on international portfolio income, the taxation of international portfolio income has generally been ignored in the tax literature. But the amount of international portfolio investment and its role in the world economy has grown exponentially in recent years. Since 1990, the value of U.S. persons' foreign portfolio investments has exceeded the total market value of U.S. corporations' foreign direct investments, and the total amount of U.S. taxpayers' foreign portfolio income has exceeded their income from foreign direct investments. Cross-border portfolio investments are no longer a tiny tail on a large direct-investment dog. International portfolio investments now play a major role in the world economy, a role quite different from that played by foreign direct investments. We can no longer afford simply to assume, as we have in the past, that the way the U.S. taxes the latter obviously is appropriate to the former.

* * *

As we have indicated, U.S. policy for taxing income from foreign portfolio investments followed—without any serious independent analysis—the policies developed for U.S. foreign direct investments. But there are important economic differences between direct and portfolio investments, which may imply quite different tax treatment of their income. Indeed, these economic differences suggest that the principal normative concepts used to evaluate international tax policy generally—capital export neutrality and capital import neutrality—have far less relevance to the taxation of international portfolio income than for evaluating the taxation of income from direct investments. This section describes how these two types of investments diverge economically and outlines the key distinctions in the current taxation of income from direct and portfolio investments.

The Key Tax Distinction Between FDI and FPI

Foreign portfolio income is often earned today by both individuals and corporations, while foreign direct investments are virtually always made by corporations. As we have indicated, whether an investment in a foreign entity by a U.S. corporation is classified as direct or portfolio technically turns on the degree of ownership of the foreign company; to qualify as a direct investment, some minimum threshold of ownership—generally 10 percent of voting stock—must be crossed. It may be simpler analytically however, to regard income from foreign direct investments (FDI) as representing the profits from conducting business activities abroad—the profits of the firm—and income from foreign portfolio investments (FPI) as representing passive investment income—the profits realized by investors in the firm. Although we follow the technical definitions here, it may be helpful to think of investment as a direct investment when a U.S. taxpayer has sufficient control over the business decisions of the foreign entity; when the U.S. taxpayer has little or no control over the foreign entity's business decisions, the investments are typically FPI.

Although a number of U.S. tax consequences turn on the distinction between FDI and FPI, which generally corresponds to the tax law's distinction between active and passive income, here we emphasize one: Whenever a U.S. company has sufficient control over a foreign corporation, it is permitted to credit against its U.S. tax liability corporate income taxes imposed by the foreign country on the foreign corporation's earnings, either when those earnings occur or when dividends paid out of those earnings are received by the U.S. corporation. In other words, a direct investor is entitled to the "indirect foreign tax credit." In contrast, portfolio investors generally are not allowed any U.S. tax credit for corporate income taxes imposed abroad but instead are allowed to credit only foreign withholding taxes paid on dividend or interest income. * * *

In the OECD countries where U.S. corporations have substantial FDI, corporate income taxes range from a low of 12.5 percent (in Ireland) to a high of 40 percent (in Belgium). Most corporate tax rates in OECD countries today are in the range from 25 to 35 percent. By imposing these corporate income taxes, source countries exercise their rights to tax international business income. On the other hand, source countries today rarely exercise any right to tax interest income earned by foreign portfolio lenders and, where bilateral treaties are in force, tend to tax portfolio dividend income at a 0 to 15% withholding rate. This is why commentators frequently describe the "International Tax Compromise" as generally allocating the taxation of portfolio income to the country where the investor resides, although that is a bit of oversimplification.

The Key Economic Distinctions Between FDI and FPI

Foreign direct investment is undertaken by corporations that often expect to earn economic rents. Foreign direct investment decisions therefore are frequently driven by opportunities to exploit economies of scale, economies of scope, or proprietary business advantages. Furthermore, considerable evidence suggests that foreign direct investments by U.S. multinationals are complementary to domestic investments, rather than a substitute for them. Empirical economic evidence, however, also suggests that foreign direct investment decisions are sensitive to differences in tax burdens.

In contrast, portfolio investment is highly volatile and seeks the highest return possible for a given level of risk. In portfolios managed by investment professionals, investments in one foreign country are frequently interchangeable with investments in countries with similar risk/return profiles. Indeed, portfolio investment dollars move rapidly throughout the world in an effort to find the best return for a given level of risk. One consequence is that portfolio investment dollars abroad may substitute for investments at home.

Surprisingly, economic analysis to date offers no clear consensus about the extent to which U.S. portfolio investors are tax-sensitive. While economic theory suggests that portfolio investors should be tax sensitive, seeking the greatest after-tax returns, the empirical data is mixed. For example, empirical research by Joel Dickson and John Shoven suggests that as recently as 1993 investors did not pay much attention to the effect of income taxes on the rates of return of their portfolio investments. Shoven and Dickson examined 147 of the 150 largest U.S. mutual funds in existence on October 31, 1992. They convincingly showed that for these funds the relative ranking based on rates of return was substantially different pre-tax and post-tax. However, in 1993 only one analyst, among the very large number of information sources dedicated to providing investors with mutual fund information, published after-tax returns. Nor had prior academic papers evaluating mutual fund performance adjusted mutual fund returns for shareholder level taxation. The lack of easily available data regarding after-tax performance, combined with the disparity between pre-tax and post-tax rankings for mutual funds, suggests that—as recently as 1993 at least—most mutual fund investors did not make their mutual fund portfolio investment decisions on a post-tax basis. And most mutual funds apparently were little concerned with the tax consequences of their investments for their fund's shareholders. Since 1993, however, after-tax information and after-tax results have become increasingly available and possibly important to mutual fund investors.

In January 2001, the SEC approved a rule requiring mutual funds to disclose after-tax returns. New mutual funds have emerged in the decade subsequent to the Shoven–Dickson study advertising themselves as "tax-efficient" or "tax-sensitive." Furthermore, major non-proprietary sources of information about mutual funds, such as Morningstar, now rank mutual funds based on after-tax performance. These changes suggest that both mutual fund investment managers and individual mutual fund shareholders are becoming more sensitive to tax effects on portfolio investment returns. Nevertheless, tax-efficient funds accounted for only 12 percent of all inflows into equity funds in the first 10 months of 2001. This figure represents significant growth compared to the 2 percent of tax-efficient equity fund inflows in 2000, but still represents only a relatively small portion of mutual fund investments. And the decline in stock market values since 2001 has decreased the attractiveness of tax-efficient funds. It therefore remains unclear the extent to which U.S. portfolio investors' investment decisions are now tax-sensitive.

Portfolio Investors Favor Their Home Country

Economic theory, which emphasizes the role of risk diversification, in investment choices of portfolio investors, predicts a full worldwide diversification of portfolio investments. The problem for the theory, however, is that portfolio investment exhibits a substantial "home bias"; a very large percentage of the debt and equity issued in any country is in the hands of the country's residents.

Economists, have, to date, been unable to explain the home-bias phenomenon. Indeed, given the difficulties of enforcing residence-country income taxes on foreign portfolio investments, * * * we might expect to see a bias in favor of foreign rather than domestic investments.

In many countries, corporate-shareholder tax integration regimes favor domestic over foreign investment. But these tax effects are far too small to explain the home-country bias seen in the data.

A large economic literature is devoted to efforts to explain the home bias, but no explanation is yet regarded as convincing. Hedging explanations are to little avail, and neither transactions costs nor tax differentials have much explanatory power. Intuitively, the most convincing explanation is grounded in information asymmetries, that investors have better information about domestic than foreign securities. But, whatever the reason, "the aggregate demand for domestic equity is much less elastic than would be implied by standard models of portfolio choice." This means that the economic impact of taxes on domestic portfolio investment income is less than might be expected.

Portfolio Capital Flees When the Milk Goes Sour.

Unlike direct investments, portfolio investments are highly volatile. Portfolio investments move through the international capital markets quickly in response to changes in economic circumstances. In the 1990's, for example, the decision by the United Kingdom not to participate in the European Union's currency rate mechanism, the Mexican Peso crisis, the Asian financial crisis, and the financial fallout associated with the demise of the Long Term Capital Management hedge funds all demonstrated the volatility of portfolio investments. The most dramatic instances of the volatility of portfolio capital during the past decade involved the flight of capital from developing countries. The serious political and economic consequences that resulted often were not caused by specific policy decisions within the country, but rather resulted from flows of portfolio capital triggered by changes in market expectations and herd behavior.

Institutional investors, especially from the United States, dominated the flow of portfolio equity to the developing world in the 1990's. Modern risk management techniques used by portfolio managers, including such techniques as computerized portfolio program trading strategies, value-at-risk and mark-to-market models, exacerbate the effects of changes in asset prices and increase the risks of portfolio contagion. The five developing economies that received the largest flows of portfolio capital from the United States in the 1990's were Mexico, Brazil, Chile, Hungary, and Malaysia. Each experienced serious economic shocks due to the flight of portfolio investor capital during the 1990's. In a study of twenty emerging markets in the aftermath of the 1996 Mexican Peso crisis, Jeffrey Sachs found that the degree of a country's financial and currency vulnerability is systematically correlated with the composition of its capital inflows. In particular, he found that the larger the short-term foreign portfolio flows, the greater the disarray in the local financial markets.

The pain of these shocks, however, was not limited to developing countries. Particularly in response to the Asian financial crisis and the demise of Long Term Capital Management, financial turmoil reached markets in Europe and the United States when portfolio equity churned as investments turned sour. In response, debates emerged over the appropriate international economic policies in light of the dangers posed by foreign portfolio flows. Nobel prize-winning economists, world-renowned financiers, and central bankers have all debated whether and how global portfolio capital flows should be constrained. Numerous popular books as well as major works of economic scholarship have addressed the subject. * * * The debate over policies appropriate to deal with global capital flows in international economic policymaking circles has, however, had no impact on the international income tax literature, which, as we have indicated, generally has ignored the question whether FPI should be taxed differently from FDI.

The Taxation of Portfolio Investment Does Not Affect the Location of Plant and Equipment

The empirical economic evidence demonstrates that corporate decisions about where to locate plant and equipment and headquarters activities, such as research and development, are quite sensitive to differences in the corporate-level taxes applicable to the income generated by these investments. But taxes on portfolio investment income generally will not affect the location of corporate investments in plant and equipment.

Economic theory holds that effective marginal tax rates on FPI might influence the locational decisions of companies if a change in tax policy changes world interest rates. However, if, as most policy-makers believe, capital markets are sufficiently integrated that the world interest rate is unaffected by the domestic amount of saving in any one country, personal taxes generally will not affect the investment behavior of companies. Along these lines, the staff of the European Commission recently examined a set of simulated tax reforms in which either the domestic elements of various European corporation tax regimes, the international elements of those regimes, or the relationship between the corporation tax regime and the personal tax regime were harmonized across EC countries. The Commission Staff concluded that "personal taxes have little effect on the economic impact of various policy scenarios."

Changes in the marginal income tax rates for portfolio investors might, to some extent, affect the allocation of portfolio investments throughout the world. But in a classical corporate income tax system, taxes on portfolio investors generally will not influence the decisions of companies about where to locate their plant or equipment. Decisions about where to locate productive plant and equipment are made at the corporate level. So long as business decision-makers cannot know the identity and tax position of their marginal shareholders, they will take only corporate-level taxes into account in making their business decisions. As a practical matter, this seems accurately to describe corporate behavior, at least for publicly traded companies. In a classical corporate income tax system, while corporate level taxes may vary depending on where investments are made, the residence country's taxation of dividends and capital gains of portfolio investors typically does not vary based on the location of the corporation's investments.

Our conclusion that taxes on the income from FPI do not influence the locational decisions of companies is true only if internationally mobile portfolio capital is available to a company. This holds generally for large publicly traded multinational companies, which account for the bulk of FDI, but internationally mobile portfolio capital may not be available for small and medium-sized companies. As a result, tax policy changes for FPI might affect these companies in a way such changes would not affect larger multinationals. However, small and medium sized companies are also less likely to base their foreign locational decisions on tax rates, and, in any event, are relatively unimportant in terms of the international allocation of productive plant and equipment.

Thus, the taxation of FPI—in sharp contrast to the taxation of FDI—has, at most, a small impact on where productive plant and equipment will be located. It might affect the national origin of the owners of the company which owns the plant and equipment, the nations from which the capital to finance the plant and equipment has been raised, but not the location of the plant and equipment itself.

NOTE

A Deduction Rather than a Credit? Based on their analysis of the differences between foreign direct investment and foreign portfolio investment, Graetz and Grinberg contend that both capital export neutrality and capital import neutrality are inapt as a basis for U.S. tax policy toward outbound portfolio investments. They urge that source-country taxation of portfolio income be eliminated and that such income be taxed only by residence countries. Toward this end and to increase the welfare of U.S. citizens and residents, they suggest that the U.S. might replace its foreign tax credit for withholding taxes on foreign portfolio income with a deduction for foreign taxes paid. This proposal, however, does not seem likely to be embraced by U.S. policymakers anytime soon.

Issues of enforcing residence-based income taxes on foreign portfolio income are also discussed by Graetz and Grinberg. These issues are taken up in Chapter 8.

Outbound FPI Invested Through Mutual Funds and the PFIC Regime

Another important variation in the taxation of portfolio income occurs because portfolio income can be earned either directly or through pass-through entities such as partnerships or mutual funds. In the Code, mutual funds are known as "Registered Investment Companies" or "RICs." If a pass-through entity is used, that entity may be either a U.S. or a foreign entity. U.S. investors held over $700 billion in foreign portfolio investments in U.S. (domestic) mutual funds at the end of 1999.[12] Foreign portfolio income (FPI) earned through U.S. funds represented almost 30 percent of total U.S. FPI.[13]

Under Code sections 851 through 855, mutual funds are taxed as corporations but reduce their taxable income by their distributions to their shareholders if they distribute at least 90% of their earnings to shareholders each year.[14] For the most part, funds elect to distribute their earnings, effectively making them pass-through entities for federal income tax purposes.[15] Under section 853 of the I.R.C., mutual funds are also allowed to pass through to their shareholders foreign taxes paid.[16] Individual mutual fund shareholders may elect to take the foreign tax

12. Lipper Analytical Services, World Equity Database (2000). Data specially assembled by Derek Lewis at author's request.

13. Id.

14. To do so a fund must meet the requirements of § 852(a). Under this subsection, the mutual fund must distribute 90% of its investment income and 90% of its tax-exempt interest.

15. Virtually all funds choose to comply with the various statutory requirements and distribute their earnings annually. Tim Krumwiede, Ron Worsham & Mary Sue Gately, Tax Planning Can Maximize Mutual Fund Returns for Multinationals, 7 J. Int'l Tax'n 157 (1996).

16. See I.R.C. § 853.

credit (FTC)[17] or deduct foreign taxes; typically the credit is more valuable.[18] Earnings distributions and the foreign tax credit pass through combine to make the taxation of FPI earned through U.S. mutual funds functionally equivalent to that earned through the direct purchase of foreign securities.

A limited quantity of U.S. taxpayers' outbound FPI also takes place through investments in foreign mutual funds. The Passive Foreign Investment Company (PFIC) rules were created principally to govern the taxation of these foreign mutual funds. The following two excerpts describe the structure, purposes and pitfalls of the PFIC regime.

Kevin M. Cunningham, *The PFIC Rules: The Case of Throwing the Baby Out with the Bathwater*, 21 Va. Tax Rev. 387, 389–91 (2002).

In the mid–1980s, U.S. investors established foreign investment corporations in tax havens in order to defer taxation on their investment income and to convert the income into capital gain. A foreign investment corporation, unlike a RIC [Registered Investment Company] organized in the United States, could earn dividends, interest, capital gains, and other income without its U.S. investors having to report these amounts annually. The U.S. investor would recognize the income only when it sold its interest in the foreign investment corporation, and the income would be treated as capital gain.

Although U.S. withholding tax could be imposed on dividends and interest that the foreign investment company earned from U.S. sources, the portfolio interest rule would prevent withholding on interest on obligations issued after July 18, 1984. Moreover, some tax havens in which the foreign investment corporation could be organized, such as the Netherlands Antilles, offered a treaty with the United States that reduced dividend withholding to only 15%.

Investment corporations that are organized in the United States, many of which are commonly referred to as mutual funds, generally elect RIC status. Congress created RICs to allow small investors to diversify their investments and obtain supervision over their investment choices in a tax efficient manner. However, the RIC rules do not exempt a RIC from an entity level tax, but instead permit a RIC to deduct the income that it distributes to its shareholders each year. As a result, a foreign investment corporation organized in a tax haven achieved a tax result a RIC could not: it incurred no entity level

---

17. See I.R.C. § 901 (granting a credit for foreign income taxes up to a maximum of the United States taxes on equivalent U.S. source income).

18. See I.R.C. 164.

tax and its shareholders did not report their share of its earnings annually.

The foreign investment corporation could avoid most of the existing U.S. anti-deferral tax rules by not allowing U.S. investors to acquire 50% of the company. The Subpart F rules require U.S. ownership of more than 50%, and the foreign personal holding company rules require that five U.S. citizens or residents own more than 50% of the corporation. The foreign investment company rules require that a foreign corporation either be registered under the Investment Company Act of 1940 as a management company or as a unit investment trust, or be primarily engaged in the business of investing or trading in securities or commodities at a time when 50% or more of the stock is held by U.S. investors.

Foreign investment corporations could prevent U.S. investors from owning 50% of the company by issuing two classes of shares, one of which was designated for U.S. investors. Depending upon local law, the foreign investment corporation had the right to redeem and approve the transfer of a U.S. investor's shares. As long as U.S. investors did not acquire 50% of the company, the foreign investment corporation would not become subject to these anti-deferral rules.

Another anti-deferral rule, the accumulated earnings tax, imposes the highest rate of tax on a foreign corporation's income from U.S. sources that accumulates beyond the reasonable needs of the business. Any amount accumulated by an investment corporation is usually considered to be beyond the reasonable needs of an investment company. Unlike the other anti-deferral rules, the accumulated earnings tax is imposed without regard to the level of U.S. ownership. The accumulated earnings tax, like the RIC rules, would require the foreign investment corporation to distribute its U.S. source income annually in order to avoid an entity level tax on the company.

To avoid the accumulated earnings tax, foreign investment corporations did not distribute their U.S. source income to their investors, but instead organized a holding company in the tax haven, which held all the shares of the foreign investment corporation. The foreign investment corporation could reduce its U.S. source income subject to the accumulated earnings tax under the accumulated earnings tax rules by distributing its income to the holding company. The amount that the holding company receives would be foreign source income to the holding company because the foreign investment corporation is not engaged in a U.S. trade or business and its indirect U.S. ownership is less than 50%. The holding company would then have no U.S. source income, and neither the holding company nor the foreign investment corporation would be subject to the accumulated earnings tax.

In light of the transfer restrictions, the different classes of shares, and the U.S. tax planning already discussed, creating a foreign investment corporation required significant administrative costs. Therefore, ownership of foreign investment corporations was generally limited to investors that could make an investment large enough to justify these costs. In fact, many foreign investment corporations were offered only to senior employees of the companies that created them. In addition, because most of these corporations were not registered with the Securities and Exchange Commission (SEC) in order to avoid the foreign investment company rules, they could not solicit customers or deliver shares in the United States. Lack of SEC involvement and general nervousness about transferring funds to a Netherlands Antilles company limited U.S. investor interest further. Therefore, the extent to which these corporations were offered in the U.S. was narrower than one might expect given the U.S. tax benefits that they offered.

Robert J. Peroni, J. Clifton Fleming, Jr. & Stephen E. Shay, *Getting Serious About Curtailing Deferral of U.S. Tax on Foreign Source Income*, 52 SMU L. Rev. 455, 486–88 (1999).

The enactment of the PFIC rules in the 1986 Act represented a sea change in the scope of the U.S. anti-deferral rules. The definition of a PFIC was intended to identify companies that were engaged in passive or portfolio investments, so there was little rationale to permit deferral. Targeted at investors in offshore investment funds structured to avoid existing anti-deferral rules, the PFIC regime implicitly recognized the substantially greater role of portfolio capital in U.S. international investment. * * * Although ostensibly targeted at offshore investment funds, the PFIC rules have a far broader reach. The principal reason for the broad reach of the PFIC rules is the use of an asset test. The passive asset test proved extremely powerful as an indirect measure of the accumulated earnings deferred from even an active business.

* * *

Once a foreign corporation is determined to be a PFIC, the U.S. shareholder's entire share of income of the PFIC is subject to the rough economic equivalent of current taxation. * * * All U.S. persons owning stock in a PFIC, regardless of how small their shareholding, are subject to the PFIC taxing rules. * * * The PFIC rules' taxing mechanism is to apply an interest charge in respect of all of the deferred income of the PFIC unless the shareholder elects to include its share of the PFIC's earnings currently in income. Although defective in specific design, the interest charge represented a break-through approach to economically recapturing the deferral benefit. As an alternative, shareholders could elect to report income currently (subject to obtaining information from the PFIC). The interest charge taxing mechanism effectively permitted the PFIC rules to be applied to an extremely small U.S. shareholder interest because it does not require the shareholder to obtain information from the corporation.

The PFIC rules are widely viewed as a possible model for ending deferral altogether simply by changing the definition of a PFIC to include any foreign corporation in which a U.S. shareholder holds a material interest.

* * *

A foreign corporation is a PFIC with respect to a U.S. shareholder if, for any tax year in which the U.S. shareholder holds shares, either (i) 75% or more of the gross income of the foreign corporation for the tax year is passive income; or (ii) the average fair market value of its assets during the tax year that produce passive income or that are held for the production of passive income is at least 50% of the average fair market value of all of the foreign corporation's assets for such year. For this purpose, passive income means, in general, dividends, interest, royalties, rents (other than rents and royalties derived in the active conduct of a trade or business and from unrelated persons), annuities, and gains from the sale of assets that would produce such income, other than sale of inventory. A foreign corporation could elect to apply the asset test using the average adjusted tax bases of assets (as determined for purposes of computing earnings and profits) during the tax year. [In the Taxpayer Relief Act of 1997, Congress provided that a United States shareholder in a CFC would not be subject to the PFIC rules in respect of that investment.][19]

PFIC look-through rules. For purposes of the PFIC tests, if a foreign corporation owned directly or indirectly at least 25% by value of the stock of another corporation, the foreign corporation would be treated as owning its proportionate share of the assets of the other corporation, and as if it had received directly its proportionate share of the income of such other corporation.

19. Pub. L. No. 105–24, 1121, 111 Stat. 788, 971 (1997).

* * * Income of the foreign corporation's subsidiaries that does not constitute "passive income" will be treated as non-passive income of the foreign corporation for purposes of the PFIC tests. Significantly, if a foreign holding company is not a PFIC, after application of the look-through rules, a less than 50% U.S. shareholder would not be attributed ownership of stock in a lower-tier PFIC.

NOTE

Deferral and Subpart F. The deferral problems combated by the PFIC rules are only one aspect of the more general deferral issues faced in international tax. The CFC rules in Subpart F of the Code are discussed in Chapter 5.

7.4 PROPOSALS FOR INTEGRATING TAXES INTERNATIONALLY

The traditional apportionment of the international taxation of income is that the residence country has primary jurisdiction over investor income (although the source country will often impose withholding taxes) while the source country has primary jurisdiction over corporate taxation (although the residence country may impose a residual tax). Therefore, dividends and interest received from foreign corporations are typically taxed by the recipient's country of residence, usually subject to a foreign tax credit for any taxes imposed by the source country. The source country often collects withholding taxes. There are many potential ways of dealing with the problems associated with the crudeness—both in terms of equity and efficiency—of gross-basis withholding taxes on dividends. The overriding goal of such alternatives is to devise a sensible and administratively feasible method of allocating corporate income between corporations and shareholders in both the source and the residence jurisdictions of the relevant corporate and individual taxpayers.

In the following excerpt, Alvin Warren describes some of the issues associated with the international division of corporate and investor income for tax purposes and suggests some alternatives for reform aimed at minimizing the adverse effects of the system in terms of double taxation and the impairment of horizontal equity and economic efficiency.

Alvin C. Warren, *Alternatives for International Corporate Tax Reform*, 49 TAX L. REV. 599, 603–614 (1994).

The most fundamental problem with the conventional approach [to the taxation of dividends paid to nonresidents] is that it is based on a premise, separate taxation of corporate and shareholder income, that is no longer the premise of the domestic income tax systems of most industrialized countries. When the consensus for dual and separate taxation of corporate and investor income was developed originally under the auspices of the League of Nations, separate taxation of corporations and their shareholders was the norm for major countries engaged in international commerce. * * * Over the last 30 years, however, most developed countries, other than the United States, have fully or partially integrated their corporate and shareholder income taxes as a matter of domestic law. [In 2003 legislation, the United States lowered its maximum tax rate on dividends received by individuals to 15 percent.–ed].

Separate taxation of corporate and shareholder income produces several undesirable economic distortions, including a disincentive for investment in new corporate capital, an incentive for corporate financing by debt or retained earnings, and incentives to distribute or retain corporate earnings. Integration reduces or eliminates these distortions by a shareholder credit for previously paid corporate taxes, an exemption for dividends received by shareholders, or a corporate deduction (or equivalent rate reduction) for income distributed as a dividend.

The premise of these domestic methods of integration is that corporate and shareholder income should be considered together when designing a national income tax system. The premise of the international consensus remains the opposite, because the conventional division of the tax base between source and residence countries depends on separate taxation of corporations and shareholders.

* * *

The discontinuity between the conceptual bases of national tax systems and their international relationships might not be troubling if it did not involve its own distortions. The interaction of domestic integration and classical international separate taxation, however, creates two significant tax differentials: (1) In a source country, foreign investment can be subject to higher taxation than domestic investment, because shareholder integration credits are not generally available to foreign investors. (2) In a residence country, income from investment abroad can be taxed more heavily than income from investment at home, because the foreign tax credit or exemption for corporate income earned abroad is not generally available to shareholders when that income is distributed as dividends. In short, international income can be taxed more heavily than domestic income from both a source country and a residence country perspective, when corporate and shareholder taxes are integrated.

There has been some attenuation of these differentials in recent years. In some tax treaties, source countries have extended shareholder credits to foreign portfolio investors, subject to the applicable withholding tax, an approach that has been endorsed by the American Law Institute. As a residence country, the United Kingdom recently has taken steps to mitigate the effects of failing to pass through foreign tax credits to shareholders. None of these developments, however, has produced a general response to the tax differentials inherent in the current system. As a result, the consensus on how income should be divided between source and residence countries, which originated more than 60 years ago as a way of reducing the double taxation of international income, today can result in higher taxation of international income than of domestic income.

The longstanding conceptual foundation of the international division of the income tax base, which assumes separate corporate and investor income taxes, is no longer consistent with the domestic tax systems of many developed countries, which have integrated those taxes. As a result, transnational income flows can be taxed more heavily than purely domestic income in both source and residence countries. Even on it own terms, the traditional system of dual and separate taxation of corporate and investor income suffers from operational problems. Finally, some analysts argue that particular implementations of the traditional system have resulted in a competitive disadvantage for particular countries.

* * *

Summary and Conclusions. The longstanding international system of dual and separate taxation of corporate and investor income is no longer adequate. Not only does that system suffer from a number of well-known operational problems, it can result in heavier taxation of incoming and outgoing international income than of domestic income. Most fundamentally, the current international system no longer reflects the premises of the domestic tax systems of most developed countries, which have fully or partially integrated their corporate and investor income taxes.

There are a number of possible approaches to reform, but each has disadvantages. The structural features of the current system certainly could be improved, but such improvement is unlikely to remove the fundamental tension between domestic and international taxation. Harmonization of national systems also might improve the current situation, but even member states in free trade areas have been unwilling to surrender significant control over their income tax policies.

Accordingly, more fundamental reform should be considered beyond the limitations of dual and separate taxation of corporate and investor income. One possibility would be to substitute cash flow taxation for income taxation as the international norm, but that would require a dramatic change in domestic, as well as international, tax policy in most major countries. A second possibility would be to ask either source or residence countries to surrender jurisdiction, but such a surrender appears unlikely in the foreseeable future.

A more modest approach would be to relax the assumption of classical corporate income taxation that is embedded in the current international consensus. One way to accomplish that result would be to reformulate the idea of nondiscrimination for source countries and neutrality for residence countries on an integrated basis, eliminating the constraint of withholding tax reciprocity. This approach, however, would require residence countries to take more seriously the idea that income earned abroad should not be taxed more heavily than income earned at home. Whatever one thinks of this particular approach, it suggests that there are likely to be new ways of thinking about the division of the international tax base, once the assumption of separate corporate and investor taxation is relaxed.

In the following excerpt, Robert A. Green offers a detailed discussion of a taxation regime in which corporate income would be passed through to shareholders who would then be taxed on the corporation's income as if it were their own. In 1992, the United States Treasury Department published a detailed report entitled *Integration of the Individual and Corporate Tax System: Taxing Business Income Once*, which regarded the idea of passing income through shareholders as infeasible for a whole host of administrative and technical reasons. In light of this determination, Professor Green's proposal constitutes a substantial departure from conventional opinion.

Robert A. Green, *The Future of Source–Based Taxation of the Income of Multinational Enterprises,* 79 CORNELL L. REV. 18, 60, 70–74 (Nov. 1993).

[I]f national governments were to forgo attempts to impose source-based corporate income taxes and instead taxed corporate income exclusively on the basis of residence, national corporate income taxes would be largely insulated from the pressures of tax competition. This is because in all but exceptional cases, individuals are unlikely to change their national residence in response to tax differentials. Thus, moving to an international system of residence-based corporate income taxation would not ensure governmental efficiency or responsiveness to citizens' preferences any more than a system of source-based corporate income taxation. Residence-based taxation would, however, enable governments to continue to rely on income taxation as a cornerstone of a redistributive fiscal policy.

Moving to an international system of residence-based corporate income taxation may not be feasible, however, because of implementation and enforcement problems and the difficulty of obtaining international agreement.

* * *

A pure residence-based system of income taxation would require that corporate income be allocated to individual shareholders on a passthrough basis. The shareholders would include their allocable share of corporate income on their personal income tax returns and pay tax on their total income to their country of residence. To avoid double taxation by the residence country, the shareholders would increase their stock basis by the amount of corporate income allocated to them. Shareholders would then treat actual corporate distributions as a return of capital to the extent of their stock basis, and would treat any excess as capital gain. Withholding taxes on dividends, interest, royalties, and other transnational financial flows would be eliminated.

The approach described above would replace the classical corporate income tax system with a pure passthrough integration system, similar to the current U.S. system for taxing shareholders of subchapter S corporations. However, any country that wished to retain a system under which corporate income was taxed twice could do so by imposing a separate "corporate income" tax on its resident individual shareholders with respect to the corporate income allocated to them. Individual countries would be free to set individual income tax rates (and, if applicable, residence-based corporate income tax rates) at any level they desired.

This system could be implemented by having each corporation calculate its taxable income based on its separate accounts, as is done under current law. The corporation would then allocate this income among its shareholders, both individual and corporate. This process would continue through any chains of corporate ownership until all corporate income was allocated to individual shareholders.

Under this approach, the taxable income of each separate corporate affiliate of a multinational enterprise would still depend on transfer prices and on the multinational's global financial structure. However, as long as all of the corporate affiliates of the multinational were under the same ultimate individual ownership, the total amount of corporate taxable income passed through to each individual shareholder would not be affected by income shifting within the multinational. Because all taxes would be paid by individuals exclusively to their country of residence, income shifting under these circumstances would have no effect on the tax liability of any taxpayer or on the tax revenues of any country. If the corporate affiliates of the multinational were not under identical ownership, however, transfer pricing and financial manipulation could affect tax liabilities and revenues. In that case, the existence of adverse interests among the individual shareholders would likely be sufficient to deter income shifting.

Under a residence-based system of corporate income taxation, corporate income would be taxed identically by the individual shareholders' countries of residence, regardless of where the corporation invested its capital and earned its taxable income. International tax competition would be eliminated, except in the form of competition among countries to be the place of residence of individual shareholders. Because individuals do not readily move between countries in response to tax differentials, it is not likely that this form of tax competition would be very significant.

Residence-based taxation does present several potential problems. First, if each country continued to maintain its own definition of the corporate income tax base, corporations would have to calculate their taxable income under the rules of each country in which any of their ultimate individual shareholders resided. Second, enforcement would be difficult, because each country would have to monitor the worldwide operations of every multinational enterprise in which any of its residents were shareholders. Third, shareholders might have cash-flow problems, because they would have to pay tax on the corporate income allocated to them regardless of whether the corporations actually distributed the income.

Thus, as a practical matter, the approach outlined above would probably be feasible only if governments were to agree on a uniform definition of the corporate income tax base. Corporations would then be required to make only a single calculation of their taxable income. Governments, however, would have to give up sovereignty to define their own corporate income tax bases. As a consequence, they would have to forgo using national tax policy as a means of controlling corporate behavior.

The shareholder cash-flow problem and the enforcement problem could be alleviated by imposing a corporate-level income tax purely as a withholding mechanism. Because this corporate-level tax would not affect ultimate tax liabilities, it might be relatively easy to obtain international agreement on the assignment of jurisdiction to impose the tax. It would be logical to assign corporate-level tax jurisdiction on the basis of ability to enforce the tax. This would likely mean assigning such jurisdiction exclusively on the basis of the source of income.

Under this system, each corporation would allocate to shareholders not only its corporate income, but also tax credits for the amounts of corporate-level tax that it paid to each country in which it earned income. The tax credits would be refundable by the countries whose tax gave rise to the credits. This use of a corporate-level tax as a withholding mechanism would directly ameliorate the shareholder cash-flow problem. It would also alleviate the enforcement problem, at least insofar as the source countries conscientiously enforced the corporate-level tax.

Such a system would entail, however, all of the administrative difficulties inherent in a system of passthrough integration. To be successful, the system would have to address the problems of how to allocate corporate income among shareholders, how to treat corporate losses, how to deal with changes in stock ownership during the reporting period, and how to solve various reporting and auditing issues.

This type of residence-based system would require a high degree of international agreement and coordination. The system would provide some benefit, however, even if it were not universally adopted. Multinationals based in non-participating countries would continue to be taxed under the current international tax system. With respect to multinationals based in participating countries, intercompany transactions and financial flows involving subsidiaries located in non-participating countries would also continue to be taxed under the current international tax system.

A substantial obstacle to moving to a residence-based system would be that it would alter the international division of the tax base in favor of countries that are net exporters of capital ("residence" countries) and to the detriment of countries that are net importers of capital ("source" countries). However, many countries that are net importers nevertheless export large amounts of capital; they merely import even more than they export. Such countries would have sufficiently strong residence-country interests that they might support an effective and efficient residence-based tax system. By contrast, countries that are not significant exporters of capital, particularly developing countries, would likely lose tax revenue under an international system of residence-based corporate income taxation. Note, however, that participation in the system of residence-based corporate income taxation would not preclude source countries, including developing countries, from imposing benefits taxes or taxes on location-specific rents, such as those based on the extraction of natural resources. These source-based taxes would not, however, be creditable in the residence country.

NOTES

1) *Pure Pass–Through is Passé.* The 1992 United States Department of Treasury report, *Integration of the Individual and Corporate Tax Systems: Taxing Business Income Once*, did not even consider "pure pass-through integration," but rather discussed a modified version. Even so, this modified version was deemed undesirable because of the administrative and policy issues:

[If a pass-through system of integration] is to retain parity between retained and distributed earnings, the shareholder allocation prototype must extend tax preferences to shareholders and exempt from U.S. tax foreign source income that has borne no U.S. tax. While the shareholder allocation prototype reduces (but does not eliminate) current law's bias in favor of debt financing, the same is true of the dividend exclusion prototype, which is a simpler regime. Administratively, shareholder allocation integration would require corporations and shareholders to amend governing instruments for outstanding corporate stock to provide for income allocations, would require corporations to maintain capital accounts similar to those used under the partnership rules, and could create significant reporting difficulties for shareholders who sell stock during a year and for corporations that own stock.

2) *President Bush's More Modest Proposal.* In January 2003, President Bush proposed elimination of shareholder income taxes on dividends paid out of corporate earnings. The President's proposal provided that only dividends paid out of fully taxed corporate income would be eligible for exclusion by individual shareholders. In determining whether dividends are eligible to be excluded from the recipients' income, the proposal would treat foreign income taxes paid by the corporation—up to the foreign tax credit limit—as equivalent to U.S. income taxes. Thus, assuming that the corporation cares whether it pays excludable or

taxable dividends to its shareholders, the proposal would prevent dividend exclusion integration from changing the impact of current corporate level taxes on companies' decisions about where to locate their productive investments. However, the Bush dividend exclusion proposal is unconcerned with achieving neutrality in the investment choices of portfolio investors. It provided an exclusion for dividends paid directly to U.S. portfolio shareholders by foreign companies only to the extent that U.S. income taxes have been paid; dividends paid to U.S. investors out of foreign earnings subject to tax abroad would not be exempt. In this regard, the Bush plan would introduce into U.S. tax law a new preference for U.S. portfolio investors in favor of investments in domestic rather than foreign corporations.

In 2003, Congress watered down the President's proposals and delinked the exclusion of dividends from the taxes paid at the corporate level. Ultimately, Congress simply reduced the maximum tax rate on dividends received by individuals to 15 percent (and reduced the maximum rate on capital gains to the same level). The law makes no distinction between dividends paid by foreign and domestic corporations.

Chapter 8

Portfolio Income—Enforcement and Administration

8.1 CHALLENGES CONFRONTING THE TAXATION OF FOREIGN PORTFOLIO INCOME

Few areas of tax enforcement policy offer more of a study in contrast than IRS efforts to enforce taxation of domestic and foreign portfolio income. The IRS has the power to impose and enforce virtually comprehensive information-reporting requirements on financial institutions concerning domestic portfolio income.[1] Widespread compliance by financial institutions means that American investors and the Internal Revenue Service receive annual reports of dividend and interest income on Form 1099. Thus, investors have little ability to evade taxes on their domestic portfolio income; they know the IRS is receiving information on their investment income and likely matching that information with their tax returns.

In contrast, the Service confronts stark limits to its enforcement powers when attempting to monitor and tax foreign portfolio income.[2] Historically, recipients of foreign portfolio income have been able to use anonymity to sidestep IRS scrutiny and to engage in tax evasion. Individuals' ready access to the world financial system limits the efficacy of each nation's ability to enforce income taxation of foreign portfolio income, making unilateralism largely a futile endeavor. The pursuit of U.S. policy objectives in taxing foreign portfolio income necessitates cooperation both with foreign financial intermediaries and with other nations. The increasing flows of foreign portfolio income make the practical difficulties of taxing this income an important matter of concern for U.S. policymakers and their foreign counterparts.

---

1. See Stephen Shay, J. Clifton Fleming, Jr. & Robert Peroni, "What's Source Got to Do With It?" Source Rules and U.S. International Taxation, 56 Tax L. Rev. 301, 354 (2002). See also §§ 6042 (mandating disclosure of dividend payments) and 6049 (mandating disclosure of interest payments) and the associated regulations.

2. In theory no limits exist on U.S. tax policy jurisdiction, save those imposed by national policy and attitudes towards popular obligations to the government. See Stanley S. Surrey, Current Issues in the Taxation of Corporate Foreign Investment, 56 Colum. L. Rev. 815, 817 (1956). In practice, however, the U.S. faces significant constraints on exercising its jurisdiction over foreign portfolio income, which this chapter highlights.

The material that follows describes the evolution of the U.S. approach toward enforcing income taxation of foreign portfolio income. It explores the potential and pitfalls of a strategy of withholding tax at source and suggests how bilateral and multilateral attempts to heighten reporting requirements across nations may redress some of the shortcomings of the current system. Recent efforts by both the European Union and OECD to develop bilateral and multilateral reporting requirements and the U.S.'s innovative efforts to enhance information reporting by foreign financial intermediaries offer the promise of real progress in collecting tax on this income. Efforts to address the obstacles to taxation of foreign portfolio income are a work in progress, but both developed and developing countries are now beginning to confront these challenges.

Defining the Enforcement Problem

Effective tax policy depends on the credibility of its enforcement mechanisms. The IRS enjoys great success in collecting taxes on domestic portfolio income, because widespread compliance with reporting requirements by financial institutions essentially compels individual compliance. In contrast, as Stephen Shay and his co-authors highlight in the following excerpt, a striking gap exists between the almost unlimited theoretical jurisdiction of the United States and the real practical limits on the reach of the IRS in the international context.

Stephen Shay, J. Clifton Fleming, Jr. & Robert Peroni, *"What's Source Got to Do With It?" Source Rules and U.S. International Taxation*, 56 Tax L. Rev. 301, 336–339 (2002).

A conventional statement of the U.S. view is that there is no limit on the jurisdiction of the United States to prescribe tax rules. The ALI position is that a country may tax: (1) worldwide income of a national or a resident natural or juridical person.
* * *

This statement of generally accepted bases to tax (jurisdiction to prescribe), however, is incomplete without also taking into account the limits on jurisdiction to adjudicate and enforce. A country cannot enforce an income tax in the absence of information and the ability to compel compliance. The United States taxes the worldwide income of its residents and taxes certain income of foreign persons at source. In order to enforce an income tax imposed on nonresidents and on income earned outside the United States, it is necessary to have sufficient information to determine whether the correct amount of income is subject to tax and to collect a tax judgment. The scope of jurisdiction to enforce delineates a country's ability to compel production of information by imposing civil and criminal sanctions and to compel collection of tax obligations. * * *

U.S. courts have exercised their jurisdiction to compel production of information of a U.S. resident held abroad, including information held by a subsidiary of a U.S. parent corporation and information held by a foreign parent corporation and information held by a foreign parent corporation of a domestic subsidiary (where the foreign parent corporation exposed itself to U.S. jurisdiction). Section 6038A also provides a powerful inducement for foreign affiliates of a foreign-controlled domestic corporation to consent to U.S. jurisdiction for the limited purpose of the enforcement of an administrative summons. Absent an income tax convention or the application of § 6038A, however, it is difficult to obtain information located abroad where a U.S. court does not have jurisdiction over the person controlling the information. * * *

In addition to jurisdictional limitations on the ability to obtain information to make an assessment, the so-called "revenue rule" holds that one country will not provide assistance to another country in collection of the other country's final revenue claim. This hoary and archaic common law doctrine dates back to 1775. In 2001, the Second Circuit affirmed that this revenue rule is alive and well in the United States. [See Attorney Gen. of Canada v. R.J. Reynolds Tobacco Holdings, Inc., 268 F.3d 103 (2d. Cir.2001).] * * *

————

The problems posed by the limits to effective U.S. jurisdiction contribute to a significant gap in tax revenues. As Michael Graetz notes in the excerpt below, the largest problem the U.S. faces today with respect to outbound foreign portfolio income is often outright evasion. Taxpayers have recognized the difficulties of IRS enforcement and frequently take advantage of them by not reporting foreign portfolio income earned abroad.

Michael J. Graetz, *Taxing International Income: Inadequate Principles, Outdated Concepts, and Unsatisfactory Policies*, 26 Brook. J. Int'l L., 1357, 1414 (2001).

Collectability is an essential attribute of any tax. Enacting rules that cannot be enforced is pointless. In the international tax arena, considerations of enforceability have always shaped the law and always will. Source-based taxation of income, for example, has long been justified, at least in part, on the ground that the country of source is in the best position to collect income tax. * * *

Underreporting of transnational portfolio income is apparently quite substantial. For example, in March, 1994, the U.S. Treasury, for the first time in 50 years, conducted a comprehensive survey of outbound portfolio investments from the United States. As a result of this survey, the Department of Commerce revised its 1993 estimates of portfolio interest upward by $6.1 billion, from $17.2 billion to $23.3 billion, and its estimate of portfolio dividends upward by $4.1 billion, from $6.8 to $10.9 billion. A similar 1997 Treasury survey reduced the reported U.S. balance of payments deficit by more than $10 billion due to increased interest and dividends received by U.S. residents from foreign securities. The 1993 estimate of U.S. holdings of portfolio stock was increased from $302.8 billion to $543.9 billion. The magnitude of these adjustments suggests massive gaps in tax reporting of interest, dividends, and capital gains.

The problem of increasing foreign portfolio income flows coupled with easy tax evasion is not limited to the United States. In the following excerpt Reuven Avi–Yonah suggests that Graetz's observations apply with equal force to other developed and developing nations. This excerpt highlights the interdependence of national tax policies for collecting tax on foreign portfolio income.

Reuven S. Avi–Yonah, *Globalization, Tax Competition, and the Fiscal Crisis of the Welfare State*, 113 HARV. L. REV. 1573, 1584–1585 (2000).

Even in the case of sophisticated tax administrations like the IRS, tax compliance substantially depends upon either withholding at the source or information reporting. When neither is available, as in the case of foreign source income, compliance rates drop dramatically.

The result is that much of the income from overseas portfolio investments escapes income taxation by either source or residence countries. Latin American countries provide a prime example: after the enactment of the portfolio interest exemption, about $300 billion fled from Latin American countries to bank accounts and other forms of portfolio investment in the United States. Most of these funds were channeled though tax-haven corporations and therefore escaped taxation in the country of residence. Estimates of the capital flight from all developing countries to the United States in the 1980s range as high as $148 billion in a single year.

Nor is the problem limited to developing countries. Much of the German portfolio interest exemption benefits German residents who maintain bank accounts in Luxembourg, and much of the U.S. portfolio interest exemption benefits Japanese residents who hold U.S. Treasuries and do not report the income in Japan. It is questionable how much tax even the United States actually collects on portfolio income that its residents earn abroad other than through mutual funds. One estimate puts capital flight from the United States between 1980 and 1982 as high as $250 billion.

Thus, in the absence of withholding taxes or effective information exchange, income from foreign portfolio investments frequently escapes being taxed by any jurisdiction. This immunity from taxation is particularly significant because the flows of portfolio capital across international borders have been growing much faster than either world gross domestic product or foreign direct investment (FDI). Current estimates indicate that international capital flows amount to $1 trillion per day. Although this figure is much larger than income from capital, it gives a sense of the magnitudes at stake.

NOTE

No Vaccination Against Evasion. The problem of overseeing foreign portfolio income flows is growing, and no nation appears immune to its effects. The United States, the European Union, and the OECD have all made some progress in recent years in strengthening information reporting requirements. However, reciprocal information exchange remains limited across nations, and nations resist implementing withholding taxes for fear of driving capital elsewhere. This creates obvious opportunities for taxpayers to engage in tax evasion or underreporting without being detected. Ironically, past U.S. responses to competitive pressures from Europe helped to produce this situation at the very time when foreign portfolio flows began to increase dramatically.

8.2 EVOLUTION OF THE UNITED STATES'S APPROACH TO TAXING FOREIGN PORTFOLIO INCOME

The evolution of the United States's approach to foreign portfolio income reflects the interdependence of world financial markets and the difficulties of sustaining a unilateral tax policy on foreign portfolio income. The shift in the U.S. approach in 1984, when it eliminated the withholding tax on portfolio interest, had reverberations for tax policies for foreign portfolio income in many countries. Ultimately, these changes helped pave the way both for the dramatic expansion in foreign portfolio income and the companion problem of pervasive tax evasion.

Most source countries, including the United States, currently forgo imposing any withholding tax on the portfolio interest income of foreign investors. As Chapter 7 relates, until 1984 the Internal Revenue Code maintained a 30% withholding tax on interest income paid to foreign persons or corporations when that income was not effectively connected with the conduct of a U.S. trade or business. Various bilateral treaties had provided exemptions from this withholding tax, but the treaties always forced detailed income reporting by the foreign investor. The U.S. withholding tax and reporting requirements were far more stringent than the practices in other developed nations, but the American ability to sustain this policy collapsed in 1984.

Competition from the Eurobond market, the largest bond market outside the United States, which was created in the immediate aftermath of World War II, helped drive changes in the U.S. tax treatment of foreign portfolio income.[3] The competitive advantages of the Eurobond market prior to 1984 were that it allowed international investors to provide capital without paying withholding taxes or being forced to reveal their identity or other financial details. Interest on Eurobonds is free from withholding, and the borrower bears the risk of tax at the source by agreeing to indemnify the lender for any such tax imposed.[4] Eurobonds are issued in bearer form; thus, these debt obligations do not indicate the identity of their beneficial owners.[5] Eurobond issuers therefore know only how much interest they are paying, but not to whom. As a result, they cannot assist governments seeking to impose taxes on the interest income earned by their residents.

International investors through the early 1980s demanded higher interest rates for U.S. source borrowing than for borrowing in the Eurobond market in order to offset the U.S. portfolio interest withholding tax and the lack of anonymity associated with U.S. source borrowing.[6] This regime placed U.S. companies at a competitive disadvantage in acquiring capital. American companies responded by using offshore financial centers to access the withholding-free interest and anonymity of the Eurobond market.

The Treasury Department had paved the way for this subversion of our tax policy toward portfolio income by entering into tax treaties with offshore financial centers. The extension of the U.S. tax treaty with the

3. See Richard Benzie, The Development of the International Bond Market 7–15 (1992) (detailing the development of the Eurobond market).

4. See James P. Holden, Repeal of the Withholding Tax on Portfolio Debt Interest Paid to Foreigners: Tax and Fiscal Policies in the Context of Eurobond Financing, 5 Va. Tax Rev. 375 (1987).

5. Bearer bonds stand in contrast to registered form bonds. The transfer of a registered form bond can only be effected by 1) surrender of the old instrument to the issuer followed by either a new issuance or a reissuance to the new creditor or 2) rights to principal and interest that are transferred through a book-entry system that records ownership. § 163(f). In the United States, any obligation offered to the public with a maturity of over one year must be registered unless it is sold to a non-U.S. person, yields interest payable only outside the United States, and bears a statement saying that any U.S. person who holds it will be subject to U.S. income tax law.

6. See Leslie E. Papkie, One–Way Treaty with the World: The U.S. Withholding Tax and the Netherlands Antilles, 7 Int'l Tax & Pub. Fin. 295, 298 (2000).

Netherlands to the Netherlands Antilles in 1955 opened the floodgates to U.S. companies' sidestepping of U.S. bond restrictions. A host of island nations, such as Aruba, Bermuda, the Cayman Islands, and the Isle of Man, followed the Netherlands Antilles and became offshore financial centers. These islands combined tax treaties with the U.S., the development of sophisticated financial infrastructures, and bank secrecy laws to become intermediaries for American firms for access to the Eurobond market.

Financial subsidiaries of offshore banks would float bond issues in London and pass the borrowed funds through the offshore financial center to a U.S. parent corporation. In turn, interest payments on the bonds made by the parent corporation flowed back through the offshore financial conduits to foreign investors. U.S. corporations received loans at below U.S. rates, offshore financial institutions received a spread for their role as intermediaries, and the islands taxed a percentage of the financial institutions' spread. In the early 1980s, U.S. corporations' bond issues in the Eurobond market averaged $2.4 billion annually from the Netherlands Antilles alone, a figure which represented eleven percent of the total dollar denominated bonds issued by U.S. corporations at that time.[7]

Everyone seemed to benefit from this system; that is, everyone but the U.S. treasury. By 1984 an increasing federal budget deficit, tight domestic credit, and complaints from the U.S. corporate community and securities industry about their competitive disadvantages coalesced in the Deficit Reduction Act of 1984. This Act unilaterally eliminated the U.S. withholding tax on portfolio interest earned by foreign individuals and corporations. Equally significantly, this legislation allowed U.S. corporations and the U.S. Treasury to tap into foreign capital markets by issuing bearer bonds in the Eurobond market.

Congressional fears that the issuance of bearer bonds abroad by the U.S. Treasury would foster tax evasion by U.S. citizens and residents led then Secretary of the Treasury Donald Regan to assure Congress that no U.S. agency would issue bearer bonds.[8] Instead, the Treasury issued a limited quantity of "foreign-targeted registered obligations." These bonds represented a hybrid between bearer and U.S. registered bonds and offered partial anonymity. Treasury did not receive the names and addresses of purchasers, but required banks to certify that all beneficial owners were not citizens or residents of the United States.

---

7. The material in this discussion draws from id. at 299–300.

8. Congress recognized that U.S. investors might buy obligations abroad in bearer bond form, claim to be foreigners, and thereby avoid taxation on their interest income, despite their status as U.S. investors and the fact that they were receiving income from a U.S. corporation or even the U.S. Treasury. See Marilyn Doskey Franson, The Repeal of the Thirty Percent Withholding Tax on Portfolio Interest Paid to Foreign Investors, 6 J. Intl. L. Bus. 930, 953–55 (1984); Corporations May Issue Bearer Bonds to Foreigners, but Treasury and Fannie Mae Will Not, 24 Tax Notes 734, 734 (1984) (quoting Secretary of the Treasury Donald T. Regan).

The 1984 legislation, however, unambiguously allowed U.S. companies to issue bearer bonds. Thus, although the Treasury's hands might be clean (or only a little dirty) in providing outlets for tax evasion through U.S. Treasury offerings, U.S. corporations could issue bearer bonds abroad in the Eurobond markets, even to U.S. citizens and residents. This provided an outlet for U.S. persons to evade domestic reporting requirements for interest income and to engage in tax evasion.

The following excerpt by James Holden relates Congress's contradictory goals. Congress simultaneously sought to help American multinational corporations remain competitive internationally in raising funds, while preventing new opportunities for U.S. investors to evade U.S. taxes on U.S. source income. In the end, Congress appeared to be content to satisfy only the former goal of creating a level playing field in debt financing for multinational corporations. This ultimately has created a substantial problem for the enforcement of U.S. tax law.

James P. Holden, *Repeal of the Withholding Tax on Portfolio Debt Interest Paid to Foreigners: Tax and Fiscal Policies in the Context of Eurobond Financing*, 5 VA. TAX REV. 375 (1987).

Congress believed that it was important for U.S. business to have access to the Eurobond market as a source of capital. Congress recognized, moreover, that the withholding tax might impair such access by placing U.S. corporations at a competitive disadvantage in their efforts to raise capital offshore, since foreign governments do not usually subject international bond issues to either withholding or estate taxes. * * *

The second major congressional concern that shaped [the 1984 legislation] was * * * that the repeal could lead to both "legitimate" and "illegitimate" increases in the volume of bearer debt issues. In addition to an increase because of lowered costs to borrowers, an increase might result from U.S. investors buying obligations overseas in bearer form, claiming to be foreigners, "without concern * * * that their ownership of the obligations [would] come to the attention of the IRS." The increase in the number of U.S. bearer obligations would, Congress feared, "exacerbate existing compliance difficulties associated with bearer obligations." In response to these concerns, Congress concluded that the Secretary should have "full discretion" to disqualify obligations [from the provisions of the exemption]. * * *

It is uncertain how Congress intended the purpose of combating tax avoidance to mesh with the purpose of providing access to the Euromarket. If Congress expected to extract from the Treasury ironclad assurances that regulations implementing [the portfolio interest repeal] would preclude all avoidance, then Congress was wasting its time in ostensibly permitting issues in bearer form: some increase in avoidance was inevitable.

If Congress instead recognized that the achievement of broad access to the Eurobond market would necessarily entail a certain amount of avoidance by determinedly dishonest taxpayers, then Congress must have faced the question of whether the benefit to the economy of access to cheap foreign capital outweighed the cost to the Treasury of some lost tax dollars. Because Congress anticipated that the portfolio interest exemption would eliminate the usefulness of the [International Finance Subsidiary] by providing a lower-cost alternative, Congress must have intended a broad exemption. [The 1984 Act] is, after all, described as a "repeal." If broad access to foreign capital was intended, Congress must have intended that the goal of compliance, while important, should be pursued only insofar as broad access to the Eurobond market would not be threatened.

Congressional resistance to the Treasury's eagerness to issue bearer debt *may* have simply reflected a change of heart on the part of some congressmen. It is far more probable, however, that Congress initially did not perceive the inherent contradictions in its goals, or that some congressmen understood the contradictions but simply did not care to become mired down in resolving them. These two characterizations tend to explain why the plain language of [the 1984 Act] is so broad and yet why the Secretary is given such discretion to narrow it. Congress may have foisted upon the Treasury the responsibility for attaining two irreconcilable goals.

This result suggests an approach on the part of Congress that was more wishful than rational. * * * In determining what action to take [in the future], * * * Congress' response should not be an automatic attempt to achieve near-absolute compliance through measures that might detect those few U.S. tax avoiders who will not be deterred by an extreme penalty tax, where to do so is to undermine access to a valuable source of cheap capital. By providing efficient, largely unrestricted, tax-free access to the Eurobond market, Congress can (1) help U.S. industry remain competitive by keeping its financing costs down, and (2) substantially lower the borrowing costs that the Treasury—and ultimately the U.S. taxpayer—bears. Congress should not let its justified aversion to tax avoidance interfere with a careful attempt to identify the financing alternative that will ultimately prove least costly to the U.S. economy as a whole.

NOTES

1) *An Example.* A simple example highlights the dilemma that, due to this contradictory approach, the U.S. Treasury now confronts. Suppose that residents of country A invest in bearer bonds issued by corporations of country B and receive interest income on these bonds. Even if countries A and B have tax information exchange agreements, country B will not be able to assist country A in taxing this particular category of income, because it has no information about to whom the interest is paid. The private issuers of the bearer bonds do not possess this information either.

Both the tax base of country A and the tax base of country B are threatened by such arrangements. Country A can ask only for assistance collecting information regarding the investments made by its residents. Since country B does not know to whom the interest originating in its own jurisdiction is paid, it cannot be sure that the interest has not been paid to its own residents. If country B imposes a lower tax (in the form of a withholding tax) on outbound interest income than the tax country B imposes on its domestic interest income, country B residents can engage in virtually undetectable fraud by shifting funds to accounts abroad and investing in country B debt obligations through their foreign accounts.

Even if the U.S. could create a mechanism to prevent U.S. companies from selling bearer bonds to U.S. residents in the Euromarkets, U.S. residents may still anonymously purchase bearer bonds issued by foreign corporations in the Euromarkets. A U.S. resident may find a bearer bond in that market that pays the same rate of return and has the same risk as a comparable investment in a bearer bond issued by a U.S. corporation. This leaves U.S. tax policymakers in a bind. The U.S. cannot unilaterally rectify this situation, and both the U.S. and foreign governments suffer from tax evasion on interest income by their residents.

2) *The IRS Pursues John Doe.* The IRS has taken several steps to stem offshore tax-avoidance schemes. Among the most promising of these actions are the John Doe summonses, which do not identify those whose liability is at issue, requesting from VISA, MasterCard, and American Express information about U.S. citizens and residents with offshore credit and debit cards. The IRS has received information on offshore credit and debit card accounts from 77 countries—many of them tax havens—all around the world as a result of these John Doe summonses. It is not illegal to have offshore credit cards, but prior to these summonses, taxpayer self-disclosures on Form 1040 had revealed to the IRS fewer than 170,000 accounts of U.S. citizens offshore. The results of the summonses suggest that there are at least one million (and perhaps up to two million or more) of these suspicious accounts. According to Tax Division U.S. Assistant Attorney General Eileen O'Connor, "The information that is coming in from these summonses has been astounding,

absolutely amazing." She continued, "The IRS knew that this would be huge, but I think it's even huger than they had imagined." At the end of the 2002 fiscal year, the IRS had 600 agents working on approximately 1000 cases arising out of the John Doe summonses. By the end of the 2003 fiscal year, they expect to have as many as 1400.[9]

In the wake of this mountain of information, the IRS launched its "Offshore Voluntary Compliance Initiative" (OVCI), which provided that taxpayers with offshore accounts could "come clean" by disclosing previously undisclosed offshore tax avoidance arrangements by April 15, 2003. To make use of the program, taxpayers were required to disclose who promoted the scheme to them, how it operated, and the extent of their involvement. Those who did so were guaranteed that they would avoid civil and criminal fraud proceedings, though they would still have to pay their back taxes, certain accuracy and delinquency penalties, and interest on back taxes.[10] The OCVI was aimed at bringing ordinary taxpayers who engaged in these avoidance techniques back into compliance with the law, while gathering information about those who promoted the schemes in the hopes of stemming the promotion and use of such tax avoidance schemes in the future. Its overall efficacy remains to be seen, although the early indications have been promising.

8.3 STRATEGIES FOR MONITORING INTERNATIONAL PORTFOLIO INCOME

The underreporting challenge stems from the fact that nations tax portfolio income principally on a residence basis and active business income principally on a source basis. The paradox is that it is difficult to trace highly mobile passive income on a residence basis; portfolio income can be more effectively monitored on a source basis. At the same time, efforts to tax on a source basis may be stymied by the existence of tax havens, fears of capital flight, and negative redistributive consequences. For this reason, residence-based taxation of portfolio income is preferable on the grounds of equity, efficiency, and political accountability.[11] In the following excerpt, Reuven Avi–Yonah lays out two complementary strategies to overcome the difficulties of monitoring portfolio income.

Reuven S. Avi–Yonah, *The Structure of International Taxation: A Proposal for Simplification*, 74 TEX. L. REV. 1301, 1336–1338 (1996).

There are two complementary ways to develop a solution to this dilemma. The first is to enhance the information exchange

9. See Alison Bennett, Offshore Credit Card Summonses Generating Huge Amount of Information, O'Connor Says, BNA Daily Tax Report (October 25, 2002).

10. See Dale Hart, IRS Small Business Testimony at Finance Committee Hearing on Tax Scams 2003 Tax Notes Today 63–64 (April 1, 2003).

11. See Reuven S. Avi–Yonah, The Structure of International Taxation: A Proposal for Simplification, 74 Tex. L. Rev. 1301, 1336 (1996); Michael J. Graetz & Itai Grinberg, Taxing International Portfolio Income, (forthcoming, Tax L. Rev., 2003).

programs under tax treaties, so that developed countries can share with developing countries the data necessary for effective enforcement of residence-based taxation, especially data on tax haven investments. The development of information technology and its spread throughout the world promise significant progress in this direction in the next century. Another promising development is the increasing number of treaties, with their attendant information exchange benefits, between developed and developing countries. The combination of these two developments may mean that in the twenty-first century, even the least advanced tax administration in a developing country will be able to benefit from the computerized databases of the most advanced administration, currently the IRS, in a developed country.

The second way is for developed countries to establish a concerted program of withholding taxes at the source of income for the benefit of the residence country. All developed countries lose from the competitive abolition of withholding taxes, which impedes their efforts to collect taxes from their residents on investments in other developed countries. Instead, developed countries could agree to levy a uniform backup withholding tax on all portfolio investments that would be retained by the country imposing the tax unless the investor furnishes documentation showing that the income has been declared in his or her residence country; in that case, the source country would transmit the withholding tax to the residence country through a clearinghouse mechanism similar to the one used by some European Community countries for [other income tax] purposes.

The efficacy of withholding taxation or information exchange strategies depends on bilateral or multilateral cooperation. The following section explores possibilities for bilateral or multilateral solutions and their potential to address the challenges for monitoring and taxing foreign portfolio income.

8.4 THE POTENTIAL AND LIMITS OF MULTILATERAL SOLUTIONS

Many countries face problems similar to the United States's with respect to tax evasion on portfolio interest income earned by their nationals in the Euromarkets.[12] The following excerpts from Michael Graetz and Vito Tanzi explore the theoretical potential and shortcom-

---

12. Though many OECD countries have territorial tax systems, they generally create exceptions to territoriality for the purpose of taxing the passive investment income of their residents.

ings of multilateral solutions for heightened information reporting requirements. Following these excerpts, we describe the multilateral solutions for withholding tax and information reporting requirements proposed by the European Union and the OECD. Michael Graetz argues that a stronger multilateral information reporting regime is needed to collect tax on international portfolio income.

Michael J. Graetz, *Taxing International Income: Inadequate Principles, Outdated Concepts, and Unsatisfactory Policies*, 26 BROOK. J. INT'L L. 1357, 1415–16 (2001).

When source-based countries forgo imposing income tax, as so many now do, for example, with portfolio interest, other enforcement mechanisms become essential. Over the past three decades, the United States has demonstrated the power of information reporting in lieu of withholding in improving the collection of income taxes on domestic interest, dividends, and capital gains. A cooperative multilateral information-reporting effort might prove quite fruitful in improving enforcement of residence-country taxes on portfolio income.

The agreement by the countries of the European Union to expand information reporting of cross-border income flows is an encouraging development. It demonstrates the willingness of countries to collaborate to limit tax evasion, even when they are unwilling to impose low-rate withholding taxes, as had been long urged by E.U. officials. And, despite the gaps in coverage, it shows both the potential benefits and necessity of international cooperation in improving tax enforcement. Although U.S. portfolio investments are widespread throughout the world, two-thirds of such investment is in 10 countries, with five countries (the United Kingdom, Canada, Japan, the Netherlands, and Germany) attracting more than $100 billion each of such investments.

The European move toward more information reporting, especially in the face of the bank secrecy laws of certain member countries, offers an important policy opportunity for the United States. In the 1980's, when this nation was anxious for foreign purchases of U.S. debt in order to help finance federal deficits, Congress repealed our withholding tax on portfolio interest and allowed bearer bonds to be issued to foreigners. As a result, the U.S. government is currently unable to provide other countries with any information about the owners of these bonds. To protect against tax evasion by U.S. residents, however, these bonds contain a stamp indicating that they may not be sold to U.S. persons. Of course, the Eurobond market also provides bearer bonds, so that U.S. persons who want bearer bonds (without paying withholding taxes) may purchase bonds abroad. Today, fiscal surpluses are permitting the federal government to reduce the national debt held by the public, and national economic policy seems likely to produce an ongoing reduction of such debt in the years ahead. Since combating tax evasion on portfolio investment is clearly in our national interest (and in the interest of the European nations), the time seems ripe to seek a multilateral agreement eliminating bearer bonds and simultaneously otherwise improving mechanisms for information exchange on portfolio investments (especially when no substantial withholding tax is collected at source).

This excerpt paints a hopeful picture in which multilateral coordination might solve the enforcement problems tax administrators face with respect to portfolio interest. Not all commentators are similarly optimistic about the potential for a multilateral solution. In the excerpt below, Vito Tanzi identifies three "fiscal termites" that he regards as undermining the collectibility of income tax on portfolio investments. These "fiscal termites" are (1) the pressures arising from the growth of off-shore financial centers and tax havens and the falling transaction costs connected with using their services, (2) the increasing availability of derivatives and hedge funds as vehicles for portfolio investment, and (3) the general difficulty of taxing financial capital as the international capital market becomes more integrated and efficient. Tanzi believes that these difficulties, combined with other difficulties he identifies in connection with taxing mobile capital and labor, will force the developed economies to become more reliant as time passes on taxes on immobile factors.[13] He argues that it would be prudent for developed countries with high tax levels to prepare themselves for significant downward pressures in future years.

Vito Tanzi, *Globalization, Technological Developments, and the Work of Fiscal Termites*, 26 BROOKLYN J. INT'L L. 1261, 1271 (2001).

Many hedge funds operate from off-shore centers and are not, or are weakly, regulated. Even those operating from industrial countries are relatively unregulated. The funds use new and exotic instruments that raise new challenges for tax author-

---

13. For more details regarding the types of transactions Vito Tanzi is concerned about, see Jeffrey Colon, Financial Products and Source Basis Taxation: U.S. International Tax Policy at the Crossroads, 1999 U. Ill. L. Rev. 775, excerpted in Chapter 2, discussing source of income. While Colon focuses on transactions by foreign investors into the United States, similar strategies can be employed by U.S. investors investing abroad.

ities, which often do not have the skills necessary to deal with them. * * * In relation to the earnings from derivative instruments, there are huge problems identifying individual beneficiaries, transactions, incomes, and jurisdictions where the individuals live or where the incomes are generated. The reporting requirements to the tax authorities on the part of the hedge funds that operate from tax havens are very limited or nonexistent. In many cases, unless or until these incomes are repatriated and are declared as incomes by those who receive them, their taxation will remain problematic. The amount of funds channeled through them is now estimated at around one trillion dollars. Hedge funds are likely to continue growing as channels for the investments of wealthy peoples.

One of the challenges from the growing use of complex financial instruments, such as derivatives and similar instruments, is that these can be used in tax avoidance schemes by exploiting uncertainties and inconsistencies in their tax treatment. Most tax systems do not capture, sufficiently well, the special nature of financial derivatives even when the funds that use them are domestic ones. As an example, the distinction between capital income and capital gains or losses becomes fluid when a contingent claim (gain or loss) can be created on a structure of certain cash flows (income). Likewise, the separation in tax legislation between dividends and interest becomes arbitrary since derivatives allow for easy modification between the external attributes of various financial arrangements. Furthermore, any kinks in tax schedules will lead to incentives for tax smoothing and the trading of tax positions around which financial instruments can be designed.

Income from cross-border portfolio investments could be taxed at the source by withholding taxes. However, with the widespread use of derivatives, this approach becomes less appropriate. First, for a derivative that consists of several contracts, for tax purposes each contract is treated as if standing on its own, leading to incentives to use the most tax efficient combinations of contract components. Second, withholding taxes only apply to positive cash flow, whereas an increasing number of derivatives envisage both positive and negative cash flows. Furthermore, for tax purposes, in most instances, cash flows from derivatives are not considered income from capital in the same sense as dividends and interest. New financial instruments are being created all the time. These new instruments will challenge the ingenuity of the tax administrators to deal with them. This trend will set the best paid and best trained minds in the financial markets against the modestly paid employees of the tax administrations.

NOTE

Tanzi's Pessimism. Vito Tanzi focuses on the difficulties derivatives, swaps, and other novel financial instruments pose for administration of the international tax system. It is unclear whether multilateral coordination of the type suggested by Michael Graetz could address these administrative problems. Heightened information reporting may offer the beginning of a solution. However, the efficacy of heightened information exchange depends on the ability of legislators and regulators to respond quickly to novel financial transactions and to apply information effectively in enforcement actions.

Vito Tanzi's excerpt highlights the fact that bearer bonds are only one type of financial transaction that makes the identities of the recipients of investment income opaque and creates opportunities for evading residence taxation. A wide (and ever increasing) range of vehicles for international portfolio investment will make it difficult for the IRS to ensure that U.S. persons are not benefiting from treaty and statutory exemptions from taxation intended for nonresidents. Despite Tanzi's pessimism about the efficacy and relevance of multilateral solutions, the European Union and OECD are pioneering multilateral information reporting requirements.

The European Union's Approach to International Enforcement

The European Union is leading the way in trying to strengthen information reporting requirements and withholding tax requirements through multilateral agreements. Historically, Europeans have enjoyed even simpler channels for tax evasion on portfolio investment income than bearer bonds. Investors commonly moved savings into countries with no withholding taxes and simply failed to report the resulting investment income. For over thirty years, members of the European Union debated a Union-wide withholding tax on interest income, but the EU's requirement of unanimity has blocked this goal.[14] Little was done to address the pervasive tax evasion until the European Union began to create a common framework for addressing portfolio income in 1997.[15]

In 1997 the European Union considered a proposal to tackle harmful tax competition that included a draft directive on the taxation of savings.[16] The draft directive lays out a "coexistence" model that gives EU member states two options: to cooperate in an exchange-of-information program or to levy a withholding tax on interest payments made to

14. See H. Onno Ruding, Tax Harmonization in Europe: The Pros and Cons, 54 Tax L. Rev. 101 (2000); see also Commission of European Communities, "Proposal for a Council Directive on a common system of withholding tax on interest income", COM (89) 60 final.

15. See Tom Buerkle, EU Resolves Dispute Over Tax Evasion, Int. Herald Tribune, Nov. 28, 2000; EU Plan to Fight Tax Evasion Leaves Bankers Calm, Int. Herald Tribune, Nov. 29, 2000.

16. See Conclusions of the ECOFIN Council Meeting on 1 December 1997 Concerning Taxation Policy, 1998 O.J. (C 2) 1.

residents of other member states.[17] The information reporting require-ments would require disclosure of the identities of beneficial owners of income and of amounts paid to them. The original proposal for a withholding option was a requirement for member states to levy a twenty percent withholding tax, unless the beneficial owner could pro-vide certification from her resident country's tax authority that it was aware of the amounts received. The withholding tax would have to be credited against the tax liability in the beneficial owner's resident country.

For more than five years, Luxembourg and Austria, whose bank secrecy laws have made them tax havens, fiercely resisted the draft savings tax directive, because it would disadvantage them vis-à-vis other tax shelter states outside the European Union, particularly Switzerland. However, in January, 2003 the finance ministers of the European Union reached a multilateral agreement. This settlement called for a gradual phase-in of withholding tax on member states with bank secrecy laws and the right of these states to maintain their bank secrecy so long as (non-EU member) Switzerland does. Developments in March 2003, how-ever, seem to have at least temporarily derailed the savings tax scheme. To take effect, all EU tax agreements must be ratified by all 15 member countries. Italy refused to ratify the savings tax agreement without an agreement by the other EU nations on certain unrelated demands regarding tax breaks for diesel fuel.

If the agreement is ultimately passed as agreed in January 2003, Belgium, Luxembourg, and Austria will have the choice of phasing out their bank secrecy laws, beginning in 2004, or implementing a fifteen percent withholding tax, which will increase to twenty percent in 2007 and to thirty-five percent in 2010. Much of the revenue from these withholding taxes on funds of anonymous owners—if any is collected—will be shared with other EU member nations to replace funds that they otherwise would be earning if their nationals' income were properly reported.

While this proposal may address some tax evasion in Europe, funds can easily flow outside of the European Union. European Union officials hope that the settlement with non-EU member Switzerland will stick, since that country accounts for an estimated one-third of the world's private savings.[18] However, the settlement with Switzerland also suffers from the limited coverage of the withholding requirement and the mobility of funds. Even if the coverage of this plan were more compre-hensive, at least one commentator remains concerned that even the

---

17. See Resolution of the Council and the Representatives of the Governments of the Member States, Meeting within the Council, of 1 December 1997 on a Code of Conduct for Business Taxation, 1998 O.J. (C 2) 2.

18. See Alison Langley, Europeans Want Swiss to Tell All, N.Y. Times, Oct. 9, 2002.

highest tax rate of thirty-five percent may only partly offset nontaxation in the host country and, in some cases, may be too low.[19]

The OECD's Model Agreement for Bilateral Treaties

The European Union's attempt at a multilateral solution is a step forward, albeit not a complete solution. The OECD has also offered proposals to promote a broader consensus on uniform information reporting requirements. In April 2002, the OECD issued a Model Agreement on Exchange of Information on Tax Matters.[20] This agreement grew out of ongoing efforts to enhance tax information exchange that began with the 1998 OECD Report *Harmful Tax Competition: An Emerging Global Issue*, which identified "the lack of effective exchange of information" as the core obstacle to reducing harmful tax competition.[21] (For further discussion of the OECD Report, see Chapter 11.)

The 1998 Report had recommended that countries unilaterally adopt "foreign investment fund" rules modeled on controlled foreign corporation rules to force individuals to disclose foreign portfolio income.[22] It recommended that countries pass laws to produce a transparent tax regime and allow for the effective exchange of information.[23] The 1998 Report also recommended that countries renegotiate tax treaties to heighten information sharing, terminate tax treaties with tax havens, exclude entities and income benefiting from preferential tax regimes from the benefits of treaties, and incorporate more provisions promoting coordinated enforcement efforts across countries.[24]

The 1998 Report led to the creation of the OECD's Forum on Harmful Tax Practices.[25] By 2000 this group had identified a list of potentially harmful preferential regimes in OECD member countries based on the factors laid out in the 1998 Report.[26] The Forum also put pressure on forty-seven other jurisdictions that were identified as tax havens based on the 1998 Report.[27] The Forum's 2000 Progress Report suggested that OECD members should subject uncooperative tax havens to coordinated defensive measures unless these tax havens make a public

---

19. See Reuven S. Avi–Yonah, Globalization, Tax Competition, and the Fiscal Crisis of the Welfare State, 113 Harv. L. Rev. 1573, 1657 (2000) (arguing that a forty percent withholding tax may be necessary to offset the advantage of non-taxation in the resident country in the European Union).

20. See OECD, Model Agreement on Exchange of Information on Tax Matters (available at http://www.oecd.org/pdf/M00028000/M00028528.pdf).

21. See Organization for Economic Co-operation & Development, Harmful Tax Competition: An Emerging Global Issue 21–25 (1998).

22. Id. at 40–43, para. 97–103.

23. Id. at 43–45, para. 106–112.

24. Id. at 46–51, para. 114–120, 125–132. 136–137.

25. Id. at 53, para. 140.

26. See Organization for Economic Co-operation & Development, Report on Progress in Identifying and Eliminating Harmful Tax Practices 6 (2000).

27. Id. at 6, 10.

commitment to "adopt a schedule of progressive changes to eliminate harmful tax practices by 31 December 2005."[28]

A year later in the Forum's 2001 Progress Report, the OECD retreated somewhat from its aggressive posture, although in a manner that on its surface is expansive. The 2001 Report indicated that the coordinated defensive measures against tax havens will apply to tax havens only when they also apply to OECD members that fail to remove harmful preferential regimes by December 31, 2005.[29] The coupling of defensive measures against OECD members and tax havens alike will tend to make it more difficult for members to agree on which defensive measures to adopt.

The Forum's 2001 Progress Report expressed more clearly than the 1998 Report what the Forum believes a commitment to transparency and exchange of information entails.[30] The Forum stated that transparency requires the elimination of secret tax rulings and the ability of persons to negotiate the rate of tax to be applied to them. The Forum also indicated that transparency requires that states mandate that financial accounts are produced in accordance with generally accepted accounting standards and that accounts be either audited or filed. The Forum suggested that governments should have access to beneficial ownership information regarding the ownership of all types of entities and to bank information that is relevant to tax matters. The 2001 Forum Report also suggested that governments make this information available to other national authorities upon request, provided that the information is used only for the purpose for which it is sought. [31]

The 2002 Model Agreement moved toward the creation of a framework that countries may use to adopt new bilateral and multilateral treaties to enhance portfolio income disclosures. This OECD initiative effectively builds on the European Union's work. The Forum panel that produced this agreement included representatives from many OECD countries and from most of the significant tax shelter "islands" in the world, including Aruba, Bermuda, Bahrain, Cayman Islands, Cyprus, the Isle of Man, Malta, Mauritius, the Netherlands Antilles, the Seychelles and San Marino.[32] Including offshore financial centers in developing a

28. Id. at 7, 18–19, para. 20–21.

29. See Organization for Economic Co-operation & Development, Report on Progress in Identifying and Eliminating Harmful Tax Practices 10, 12, para. 33, 39 (2001).

30. Id. at 11, para. 37; see also Organization for Economic Co-operation & Development, Improving Access to Bank Information for Tax Purposes (2000) (supporting the Forum's 2001 Progress Report's recommendation for greater information exchange and transparency by calling for OECD members to take steps to prevent bank secrecy from facilitating illegal behavior).

31. Organization for Economic Co-operation & Development, supra note 29, at 11, para. 37–38 (2001).

32. See OECD Press Release, OECD Releases Model Agreement on Exchange of Information in Tax Matters, Apr. 18, 2002 (available at http://www.oecd.org/EN/document/0,,EN-document–590–17–no–12–28532–590,00.html).

common framework with developed nations was aimed at producing an agreement with the potential for gaining widespread acceptance and compliance.

The Model Agreement consists of both multilateral and bilateral model agreements for information reporting requirements. Nations can choose to ratify the model agreements either with a single other nation or groups of nations and not others. This allows progress to be made without universal agreement. The Agreement commits nations to providing assistance through the "exchange of information that is foreseeably relevant to the administration and enforcement of the domestic laws of the Contracting Parties concerning taxes covered by the Agreement."[33]

The shortcoming of the OECD model is that it is more an aspiration for information sharing than a description of reality. The Agreement itself states that "[t]he OECD members and committed jurisdictions have to engage in an ongoing dialogue to work towards implementation of this standard."[34] But nations have complete discretion to tailor the scope of taxes that are covered under any given agreement and to enter into an agreement with any party to whatever extent they agree. Thus, the Agreement is essentially a first step. It is an open blueprint for encouraging bilateral and multilateral agreements. But it is only a modest step forward. While the Model Agreement may help to promote greater dialogue about information sharing and may serve as an impetus towards the creation of additional bilateral and multilateral agreements, it is too early to tell how much it will heighten information sharing.

The Case for a Multilateral Agreement for Uniform Withholding Taxes

In the excerpt below, Reuven Avi–Yonah expresses doubt about the efficacy of multilateral reporting regimes, such as those proposed by the European Union and the OECD. Avi–Yonah argues that nations have raced toward the bottom in their failure to tax foreign portfolio income. He argues for the multilateral implementation of a uniform withholding tax as the best solution.

Reuven S. Avi–Yonah, *Globalization, Tax Competition, and the Fiscal Crisis of the Welfare State*, 113 HARV. L. REV. 1573, 1583–1585 (2000).

The current situation resembles a multiple-player assurance ("stag hunt") game: all developed countries would benefit if all re-introduced the withholding tax on interest because they would gain revenue without the risk that the capital would be shifted to another developed country. However, no country is willing to attempt to spark cooperation by imposing a withhold-

33. See OECD, supra note 20, at 4.
34. *Id.* at 2.

ing tax unilaterally; thus, they all "defect" (that is, refrain from imposing the tax) to the detriment of all.

In global terms, this outcome would make no difference if countries were able to tax their residents on foreign source interest and dividend income as a portion of all income "from whatever source derived." However, as Joel Slemrod writes, "although it is not desirable to tax capital on a source basis, it is not administratively feasible to tax capital on a residence basis," because residence-country fiscal authorities generally have no means of learning about the income that their residents earn abroad. Even though tax treaties contain an exchange-of-information procedure, it is fundamentally flawed in two respects. First, the lack of any uniform, worldwide system of tax identification numbers means that most tax administrations are unable to match the information they receive from their treaty partners with particular domestic taxpayers. Second, there are no tax treaties with traditional tax havens, and routing the income through a tax haven suffices to block the exchange of information. For example, if a Mexican national invests in a U.S. bank through a Cayman Islands corporation, the Mexican authorities would gain nothing from the exchange-of-information article in the U.S.-Mexico tax treaty; given the Caymans' bank secrecy, the American IRS would have no way of knowing that the portfolio interest paid to the Caymans was beneficially owned by a Mexican resident covered by the treaty. * * *

Avi–Yonah contends that the time is ripe for the U.S. to lead in reintroducing a withholding tax on interest income as efforts by the EU and the OECD suggest that support for multilateral action is building. In the following selection, he suggests that a default forty percent withholding tax on portfolio income might remedy many of the problems of the existing system, even if tax haven nations do not participate.

Reuven S. Avi–Yonah, *Globalization, Tax Competition, and the Fiscal Crisis of the Welfare State*, 113 HARV. L. REV. 1573, 1667–1670 (2000).

[T]he problem of nontaxation of cross-border interest flows stems largely from the unilateral enactment of the portfolio interest exemption by the United States in 1984. That enactment was driven by the need to finance a growing budget deficit and by the fear that any tax withheld on portfolio interest flows from the United States would simply be shifted forward to the U.S. borrowers, including the U.S. Treasury.

Whatever merit these contentions had in 1984, they have none now. The United States is enjoying a budgetary surplus, and because it is perceived as a safe haven in financially troubled times, its borrowers are unlikely to bear the cost of any withholding tax on interest. Thus, the United States could probably repeal the portfolio interest exemption immediately without suffering adverse consequences. Further work in this area by economists is clearly desirable.

Even if the repeal of the portfolio interest exemption on a unilateral basis were to lead to adverse consequences for the United States, the prospective OECD report and the EU position render multilateral action much more likely. As observed [earlier], the nontaxation of cross-border interest flows is an assurance game: each player (the EU, the United States, and Japan) refrains from taxing for fear of driving investment to the others, even though they would all benefit from imposing the tax. Nevertheless, such assurance games can be resolved if parties can credibly signal to each other their willingness to cooperate.

The EU draft Directive represents just such a signal. The EU is telling the United States that it is willing to go forward with taxing cross-border interest flows, and even Luxembourg and the United Kingdom are indicating willingness to cooperate if the United States and Japan agree to follow the EU's lead. Thus, if in the context of the OECD Report on taxation of interest the United States and Japan were to commit themselves to taxing cross-border interest flows, the assurance game could be resolved and a new, stable equilibrium of taxing, rather than forgoing taxation, be established.

The prospects for agreement in this area are particularly good because only a limited number of players need be involved. The world's savings may be parked in traditional tax havens, but the tax havens' cooperation is not needed. To earn decent returns without incurring excessive risk, investors must use the markets in the EU, the United States, Japan, and Switzerland. Thus, if the OECD member countries could agree to the principles adopted by the EU in its draft Directive, they could effectively tax cross-border portfolio interest flows.

This Article therefore proposes that the OECD implement, on a coordinated basis, the principles contained in the EU draft Directive on taxation of savings. However, although in the EU context exchange of information plays a large role in ensuring taxation because there are few traditional tax havens there, in a global context withholding taxes must be the primary means of enforcement. As noted above, traditional tax havens with strong bank secrecy laws render it very difficult to exchange information effectively among OECD member countries. If the investment is made through a tax-haven intermediary, exchange of information is likely to be useless because tax authorities will not know the identity of the funds' owner.

Therefore, instead of the "co-existence" model of the EU, the OECD should adopt a uniform withholding tax on cross-border interest flows, which should also be extended to royalties and other deductible payments on portfolio investments. To approximate the tax rate that would be levied if the payments were taxed on a residence basis, the uniform withholding tax rate should be at least 40%. However, unlike the withholding taxes that were imposed before the current race to the bottom began in 1984, the uniform withholding tax should be completely refundable. To obtain the refund, as suggested by the EU draft Directive, a beneficial owner need only show the tax authorities in the host countries a certificate attesting that the interest payment was reported to the tax authorities in the home country. No actual proof that tax was paid on the interest income is required; from efficiency, equity, and revenue perspectives, the country of residence needs only the opportunity to tax foreign investment income just as it taxes domestic. Thus, * * * even if the home country imposes a low generally applicable tax rate on its residents (or even a zero tax rate, as long as it applies to all bona fide residents), the resident could obtain a refund by reporting the income to the tax authorities in his home country.

Neither the proposed withholding tax nor the refund mechanism would require a tax treaty. Nevertheless, countries could reduce or eliminate the withholding tax in the treaty context when payments are made to bona fide residents of the treaty partner. In those cases, the exchange of information among treaty countries should suffice to ensure residence-based taxation. Because most OECD members already have tax treaties with most other members, the proposed uniform withholding tax would generally apply only to payments made to non-OECD member countries, including traditional tax havens.

Were OECD members to enact such a uniform withholding tax, it would go a very long way toward solving the problem of under-taxation of cross-border portfolio investments by individuals. Such under-taxation is unacceptable from either an efficiency or an equity perspective. Moreover, unlike the under-taxation of direct investment, this type of under-taxation is illegal (which is assessing its magnitude is so difficult). By adopting a uniform withholding tax, the OECD could thus strike a major blow at tax evasion, which is a major problem for most developing countries and some developed countries (including OECD members) as well. * * *

NOTE

Political Never-land. The European Union has long failed in its efforts to impose a uniform withholding tax, even at a rate much lower than Reuven Avi–Yonah proposes. In the unlikely event that such a withholding tax could be adopted within the European Union or even the OECD, it seems unrealistic to expect non-OECD nations to go along. In the absence of a worldwide tax, individual tax evaders will still be able to sidestep this system. As Julie Roin has emphasized, even if Avi–Yonah's system were somehow adopted, individuals will still be able to go residence shopping to minimize their tax exposure.[35] Prospective tax evaders would then report their income to low-tax countries of "residence" or countries that maintain territorial systems of taxation and request the refund of withheld taxes. Like information reporting, Avi–Yonah's plan would only reduce rather than eliminate the ability to evade tax on foreign portfolio income.

Multilateral proposals for both heightened information reporting and uniform withholding taxes face significant challenges. The following section considers an alternative of co-option of the financial intermediaries themselves, a path the United States is currently pursuing vigorously.

Cooperating with Foreign Financial Institutions: The Qualified Intermediary Regime

The foregoing excerpts highlight both the potential and limits of multilateral solutions to taxing foreign portfolio income. But the IRS has not stood idly by, waiting for a multilateral solution to bear fruit. Since 1997 the IRS has tried to induce foreign financial intermediaries into cooperating with U.S. reporting requirements. The basic quid pro quo offered is that the U.S. will grant anonymity to foreign investors of foreign financial intermediaries in exchange for intermediaries' cooperation with the IRS in prohibiting tax evasion by U.S. investors and confirming treaty eligibility for non-U.S. investors.

This "Qualified Intermediary" regime shifts the focus of the IRS's strategy away from a multilateral effort to identify individual earners of income toward unilateral cooperation with foreign financial intermediaries in reporting and collecting tax owed by U.S. citizens. Participating financial intermediaries will now shoulder some of the compliance costs of the U.S. income tax.

The IRS's objectives in promoting the Qualified Intermediary regime are two-fold: (1) to identify all U.S. persons investing in the United States through non-U.S. financial intermediaries, and (2) to eliminate

---

35. See Julie Roin, Competition and Evasion: Another Perspective on International Tax Competition, 89 Geo. L.J. 543, 596–597 (2001).

"treaty shopping" abuses, so that only actual residents of treaty countries will obtain lower treaty withholding rates. The Qualified Intermediary regime is targeted at almost every form of foreign portfolio investment except bearer bonds. Bearer bonds are excluded because the reporting requirements created by the Qualified Intermediary regime would end the anonymity of the bearer bond market. The following excerpt discusses how this regime attempts to trade off higher compliance by U.S. residents with concessions to foreign taxpayers.

Stephen Shay, J. Clifton Fleming, Jr. & Robert Peroni, *"What's Source Got to Do With It?" Source Rules and U.S. International Taxation*, 56 TAX L. REV. 301, 344–347 (2002).

The [Qualified Intermediary] regime is an innovative development in the international withholding system. It essentially attempts to "privatize" assistance in enforcement of reductions in source taxation. The fundamental exchange is that the foreign financial institution's customer is granted anonymity in relation to the U.S. tax authorities provided that the foreign financial institution cooperates with the [IRS] in prohibiting tax reduction benefits to U.S. investors and confirming treaty eligibility for non-U.S. investors. Under the withholding rules of the final regulations, the United States seeks to surmount the practical limitations on its enforcement jurisdiction without having to request foreign tax authorities to obtain or certify residence information from investors,[36] or implement a refund system as the mechanism to obtain the information.[37]

Before adoption of the [QI regime], there was no practical regime for a U.S. withholding agent to collect documentation from a foreign beneficial owner of income holding a security through a foreign financial institution. The final withholding regulations address this problem by (1) placing the burden of investigating beneficial ownership on foreign financial institutions rather than on U.S. custodians, and (2) providing clear rules requiring withholding in the absence of documentation (whether or not through the qualified intermediary structure).[38]

* * *

36. In contrast, withholding regulations proposed in 1984 would have required Certificates of Residence from treaty partners.

37. After the repeal of the withholding tax on portfolio interest, the Treasury and IRS determined that a refund system would not be feasible because there would be insufficient "float" to finance the costs of a refund system. It was believed that a refund system would require a new and separate processing center and there would not be sufficient interest income from the amounts withheld until repaid to foreign investors to pay for the costs of such an operation.

38. The final regulations also eventually provided rules for nonqualified intermediaries to be able to supply the required documentation in a manner that did not expose foreign customers to back-up withholding if they did not disclose their identities.

Generally, a QI is a non-U.S. financial institution that is subject to know-your-customer rules that have been approved by the Internal Revenue Service (IRS) and has entered into a contractual agreement with the IRS to report annually certain aggregate information concerning the beneficial owners of U.S. source payments and to make any necessary tax payments. The QI must agree to engage an external auditor to verify that it is in compliance with the QI agreement. In return, the QI avoids the burden and competitive drawback of forwarding documentation with respect to each customer that is a beneficial owner of U.S. income subject to withholding to a U.S. withholding agent in order to claim reductions in the U.S. withholding tax. The QI, however, must identify U.S. customers that hold accounts covered by the QI agreement. A foreign financial institution that executes a QI agreement does not have to identify U.S. customers that hold accounts not covered by the QI agreement. There are special rules permitting a QI that discovers a U.S. person in such an account to avoid disclosure of the person to the Service if back-up withholding is imposed with respect to the assets in the account (including on gross proceeds). * * *

To avoid administrative burdens and excess withholding (and the consequent need for the foreign investor to file a U.S. tax return and claim a refund), the final withholding regulations contain at least three important concessions that limit the identification of beneficial owners and the reach of disclosure. These concessions reflect the strength of the tension between the need to ensure eligibility for relief from the tax while not interfering with efficient operation of the capital markets.

First, the regulations treat a foreign corporation as the beneficial owner of its income, irrespective of whether it is located in a tax haven, and its owner(s) need not be identified. * * * This was a significant decision by the Service to limit the extent to which the withholding tax rules would be used as a means to catch U.S. tax evaders (or to obtain information that could be exchanged with treaty partners regarding their residents' investments in U.S. securities through offshore entities).

Second, the regulations employ so-called presumption rules to permit a withholding agent to presume that an investor is a foreign person and thereby avoid imposition of back-up withholding in the absence of documentation of foreign status. This permits a presumptively foreign payee to accept a 30% withholding tax on income (instead of 30% withholding on gross proceeds) as the sole price for not providing withholding documentation. * * *

Third, as discussed above, the final withholding tax regulations provide that a foreign beneficial owner customer of a QI may claim exemption from withholding on interest without disclosing her identity to the Service (or the U.S. withholding agent).

Notwithstanding these concessions, the new withholding regime for the first time holds at least a modest promise of defending against U.S. taxpayers taking advantage of source tax exemption—with a major exception for foreign-targeted bearer bonds. In due course, if the QI system proves workable and even is adopted by other countries, these concessions should be re-examined. * * *

NOTE

More on QIs. The Qualified Intermediaries scheme is, by design, a partial solution. Given the difficulties of monitoring foreign portfolio income and the absence of a multilateral agreement, this shortcoming is understandable.

The federal government has stiffened requirements for qualified intermediaries to make the regime more effective. For example, the Treasury has required qualified intermediaries to report payments if they know a withholding agent has not reported it, even if the agent withheld the correct amount. Treasury has also required qualified financial intermediaries "to disinvest a U.S. non-exempt recipient who does not waive its local law non-disclosure privileges" and allow its portfolio income information to be reported to the U.S. At the same time, Treasury has increased the reach of the qualified intermediary regime by expanding eligibility for the program beyond foreign branches of U.S. persons or of foreign persons with U.S. branches to include foreign persons with no U.S. ties. [39]

Despite these measures, one can imagine that some U.S. investors will migrate from foreign financial intermediaries that assume the role of qualified intermediaries to foreign financial intermediaries that preserve the anonymity of U.S. investors. The qualified intermediaries approach does expand the reach of the IRS and may allow the IRS to cast an even wider net in the future. At the same time, it merely patches some of the holes in the current system, and it is not likely to be an adequate substitute for an OECD-wide multilateral approach.

Nonetheless, the Qualified Intermediary approach represents an innovative way for the U.S. to expand effective tax administration over U.S. citizens and residents. Multilateral solutions to heighten information exchange or to secure uniform withholding levels may be more ideal,

---

39. See Treasury Department, Revisions to Regulations Relating to Withholding of Tax on Certain U.S. Source Income Paid to Foreign Persons and Revisions of Information Reporting Regulations, 65 Fed. Reg. 32152–32159 (May 22, 2000).

but the Qualified Intermediary regime may serve as an opening wedge for the United States to obtain information from foreign financial intermediaries. The United States and other developed nations face daunting challenges in collecting tax on foreign portfolio income. This area of enforcement challenges is likely to see significant new developments in the years ahead.

Chapter 9

Transfer Pricing and the Allocation of Income Among Related Parties

9.1 INTRODUCTION

The transfer pricing problem is one that reappears in many different guises throughout tax law. The general tax avoidance strategy involved in transfer pricing involves income that is earned by a high tax rate entity being somehow realized instead by a closely related entity that pays tax at a lower tax rate. In this way, the total tax burden faced by a group with common interests can be reduced, sometimes dramatically. The transfer pricing rules under § 482 of the Code are an attempt to prevent earnings shifting schemes from significantly reducing the total tax obligations faced by corporate groups operating internationally.

Suppose that Company A, a U.S. corporation, manufactures contact lenses. Most of Company A's product is sold abroad through a wholly owned subsidiary, Company B. Each lens costs $5 to manufacture and is sold to the public abroad for $9 by Company B. Suppose that Company B is situated in a low-tax foreign jurisdiction. If Company B is a wholly-owned subsidiary of Company A, then Company A may, by controlling the sales price of the lenses, be able to choose in which jurisdiction its taxable income is realized. Company A may attempt to realize the bulk of its income in the foreign jurisdiction by selling contact lenses to Company B for say, $5.25, resulting in a token profit of $0.25 per lens in the U.S. Company B will realize profit of $3.75 per lens ($9.00 minus the $5.25 it paid for each lens from Company A). Absent a challenge by the IRS, for the purpose of allocating income from the sales of each lens for determining income tax owed, the profit will be split between Companies A and B, with only 25 cents of profit realized in the U.S. and $3.75 in Company B's low-tax jurisdiction for each lens produced and sold.

Transfer pricing—setting prices in transactions between related entities—is a problem for tax administrators because different countries have different income tax rates. In the example above, Company A has an incentive to realize as much of its income as possible in the lower tax jurisdiction. Company A may not escape tax liability on that income indefinitely, however. For example, if Company A repatriates income earned through Company B into the U.S. by dividends paid, then the

U.S. will tax the payment as dividend income, allowing a foreign tax credit for only the low-rate taxes imposed by the foreign jurisdiction (unless Company A can find a way to average that tax rate with higher taxes in another jurisdiction). But the opportunity for Company A to defer tax on this income is valuable because it will allow the company to compound its income at a higher effective after-tax rate of return.

Transfer pricing is a problem because of the existence and tax treatment of different corporate entities that are related through ownership. In the example above, U.S. tax law does not consolidate the accounts of Companies A and B. That is, the IRS treats these companies as two different entities for tax purposes, and the total profits accruing to the corporate family (i.e. $4 per transaction) are not considered relevant for U.S. tax purposes. But if the same people own the two companies, the owners will care only about the total return after taxes from the sale of the contact lenses. The economic reality is that Company A, whose profits include the profits of all the entities it owns, evaluates its operations based on its worldwide income; in this example the corporate family makes a total profit of $4 per transaction, regardless of how this income is formally allocated.

Wherever there are different rates of taxation in different jurisdictions, multinational companies will have an incentive to engage in strategic transfer pricing by shifting profits among multiple entities to the lower tax jurisdiction *without lowering the overall economic profit per transaction*. Reasoning from first principles, one might speculate that tax authorities would ignore the fact that Company A and Company B are separate *legal* entities and would mandate the consolidation of the accounts of related corporate parties for the purpose of determining taxable income. But for a variety of reasons, including lower compliance costs for many taxpayers and the arguably increased ease of administration, tax authorities generally accept the separate legal identities of the parent corporation and its subsidiaries. It is important, therefore, that the Treasury Department and the Commissioner of Internal Revenue (and tax authorities in other nations) promulgate rules that require related parties to allocate the income they realize from transfer pricing transactions to each jurisdiction in a way that is fair and appropriate.

9.2 THE QUESTIONABLE PREMISE OF AN ARM'S LENGTH STANDARD

Notwithstanding the difficulties posed in determining fair and appropriate transfer prices, there are often compelling business reasons motivating the form of the transactions underlying the transfer pricing problem. It is common for multinational enterprises (MNEs) to engage in transactions that implicate transfer pricing issues in order to take advantage of the economies of scale and the reduced transaction costs that dealing with related corporate entities affords. Dealing with related entities also allows companies to keep trade secrets and other corporate knowledge within the corporate family. MNEs may legitimately want to limit the number of people who have access to the fruits of their research and development by keeping their intellectual property from the open market. As Charles McLure writes, "An influential body of literature emphasizes that modern corporations exist precisely because of the difficulties of relying on market transactions under certain circumstances. When know-how or other intangible assets are important inputs, there are 'transactions difficulties.' "[1]

Intangible assets present a particularly difficult problem for tax administrators. Since the early 1960s, the IRS has adopted the practice of using prices from similar transactions between unrelated parties to allocate income from transactions among related entities wherever possible. But intangible property is often unique, and there are often not any comparable transactions among unrelated entities for the IRS to use as a basis for establishing the prices (and thereby determining the appropriate income allocations) from the contested related-party transaction.

As Professor Richard Caves emphasizes:

The transactional model of the MNE holds that international firms arise in order to evade the failure of certain arm's length markets, especially those for intangible assets. Premier among those assets is the knowledge that represents new products, processes, proprietary technology, and the like. Thus, theory implies and empirical evidence confirms that MNEs appear prominently in industries marked by high expenditures on R & D and rapid rates of new product introduction and productivity advance. * * * MNEs arise because of shortcomings in arm's length markets for intangible assets, and the statistical evidence establishes the prominence of MNEs in high R & D industries.[2]

The irony and the essential difficulty is that MNEs may exist because of the absence or imperfections of an arm's length market, yet an arm's length standard is the standard that the U.S. Treasury Department and other OECD nations (at least putatively) employ to ascertain appropriate transfer prices for tax purposes. A brief review of the history of transfer pricing legislation in the United States reveals how Congress and the IRS have attempted to resolve this fundamental tension between the needs of efficient and fair tax administration and the realities of the organization of international businesses.

1. Charles E. McLure, Jr., U.S. Federal Use of Formula Apportionment to Tax Income from Intangibles, 14 Tax Notes International 859 (1997), at 861.

2. Richard E. Caves, Multinational Enterprises and Technology Transfer, in Alan M. Rugman, ed., New Theories of the Multinational Enterprise (New York: St. Martin's Press, 1982), 254, 254.

9.3 HISTORY OF TRANSFER PRICING LEGISLATION IN THE UNITED STATES[3]

Section 482 of the Internal Revenue Code governs transfer pricing transactions. The Commissioner was first authorized to allocate income and deductions among affiliated corporations in the War Revenue Act of 1917: "Whenever necessary to more equitably determine the invested capital or taxable income."[4] The Revenue Act of 1921 went even further by authorizing the Commissioner to prepare consolidated accounts to correct income received from commonly controlled trades or businesses. Specifically, the 1921 Act provided:

> in any case of two or more related trades or businesses (whether unincorporated or incorporated and whether organized in the United States or not) owned or controlled directly or indirectly by the same interests, the Commissioner may *consolidate the accounts* of such related trades and businesses, in any proper case, for the purpose of making an accurate distribution or apportionment of gains profits, income, deductions, or capital between or among such related trades or business.[5]

The legislative history suggests that this provision was enacted to arm the Commissioner with an effective tool to combat tax avoidance and prevent companies from shifting income to tax-favored foreign subsidiaries through manipulative transfer pricing practices. For example, the House Ways and Means Committee's Report states "subsidiary corporations, particularly foreign subsidiaries, are sometimes employed to 'milk' the parent corporation, or otherwise improperly manipulate the financial accounts of the parent company."[6] The Senate Finance Committee described this provision as "necessary to prevent the arbitrary shifting of profits among related businesses, particularly in the case of subsidiary corporations organized as foreign trade corporations."[7]

The Revenue Act of 1928, in contrast, eschewed the authorization of the consolidation method of the 1921 Act, substituting for the phrase "consolidate the accounts" a rule authorizing the Commissioner "to distribute, apportion or allocate gross income or deductions between or among such trades or businesses, [as] necessary in order to prevent evasion of taxes or clearly to reflect the income of any such trades or businesses."[8] This change was intended to "broaden [the Act] considerably in order to afford adequate protection to the Government made

---

3. Much of what follows is taken from Section 482 Historical Compilation, by Ryan Walker (unpublished manuscript on file with the editor).

4. T.D. 2694, 20 Treas. Dec. Int. Rev. 294, 321 (1918). See also War Revenue Act of 1917, ch. 63, 40 Stat. 300 (1917).

5. Ch. 136, § 240(d), 42 Stat. 260 (1921) (emphasis added).

6. H.R. 350, 67th Congress, 1st Sess. (1921)

7. S., 67th Cong., 1st Sess. (1921)

8. Revenue Act of 1928, ch. 852, § 45, 45 Stat. 791.

necessary by the elimination of the consolidated return provisions."[9] Congress also reiterated its goal "to prevent evasion by the shifting of profits, the making of fictitious sales, and other methods frequently adopted for the purpose of 'milking.' "[10]

The IRS issued the first transfer pricing regulations under the predecessor to § 482 in 1935. These regulations explicitly created the arm's length standard, the norm used to this day by the Commissioner to analyze and allocate the income from transfer pricing transactions. The provision established the Commissioner's authority to make adjustments "expressly predicated upon his duty to prevent tax avoidance and to ensure the clear reflection of the income of the related parties."

By the 1960s, Congress had recognized that both the predecessor to § 482 and its associated regulations were not working properly. Many U.S. companies were succeeding in shifting U.S. taxable income to their foreign subsidiaries, fueled in their efforts by court decisions favoring MNEs in the intervening decades. For example, in *Seminole Flavor Co. v. Commissioner*, 4 T.C. 1215 (1945), the court focused on whether payments made under a distribution agreement were "fair or reasonable," not on whether the distribution agreement would have been concluded at the same price had it been negotiated at arm's length. In other cases around this time the courts adopted a range of similarly worded fairness tests, most concerned mainly with whether certain payments between related parties were "fair" and/or "reasonable" in determining whether a given transaction was conducted at an appropriate price.[11] In most (if not all) of these cases, courts did not try to find comparable transactions in order to arrive at an arm's length standard price for the contested transactions.

As a result of these cases and the intractability of the transfer pricing issue more generally, the Treasury complained in 1961 that "transactions between related domestic and foreign entities cause extreme administrative difficulties."[12] Congress responded by directing the Treasury Department to issue new regulations under the broad authority granted to it under § 482.[13] According to Reuven Avi–Yonah, these

9. H.R. Rep. 2, 70th Cong., 1st Sess. 16–17 (1927).

10. Id.

11. See, e.g., Grenada Industries, Inc. v. Commissioner, 17 T.C. 231 (1951), aff'd, 202 F.2d 873 (5th Cir. 1953) (holding that the Commissioner's judgments may be reversed if they are proved to be "unreasonable, arbitrary, or capricious" by the taxpayer); The Friedlander Corp. v. Commissioner, 25 T.C. 70 (1955) (holding that the sale of goods inventory between a related corporation and partnership at cost constituted "fair full value"); and Polak's Frutal Works, Inc. v. Commissioner, 21 T.C. 953 (1954) (holding that payments for services rendered between related parties were "fair and reasonable" and therefore not reallocable).

12. Hearings on the President's 1961 Tax Recommendations Before the Committee on Ways and Means, 87th Cong., 1st Sess., vol. 4 at 3549 (1961).

13. In conference concerning the Revenue Act of 1962, the House gave authority to the Treasury to promulgate new regulations that would clarify section 482: "Section 482

regulations, which remained in effect until 1993, attempted to clarify the application of the arm's length standard (ALS):

> [T]he regulations attempted to establish rules for applying the ALS to specific types of transactions, but with different degrees of specificity. For services, the regulations merely recited the ALS without any guidance as to its application in the absence of comparables. For intangibles, the regulations contemplated a failure to find comparables. They list twelve factors to be taken into account, but without establishing any priority or relative weight among them.[14]

For tangible property, the regulations set out three methods for analyzing transactions: the comparable uncontrolled price (CUP)[15] method (i.e. the price at which unrelated parties have conducted similar transactions), the resale price method (i.e., the price at which goods are distributed less an appropriate mark-up), and the cost-plus method (i.e., the cost of producing the goods plus an appropriate mark-up), in that order of priority.[16] All three methods rely on finding an appropriate way to allocate profits accruing from cross-border related party transactions, either through direct comparison with similar transactions or by reference to "appropriate" markups.

The comparable uncontrolled price method is described by the Treasury Department as "likely to achieve the highest degree of comparability of any method potentially applicable to a transfer of tangible property." Since the regulations emphasized comparability, the Commissioner attempted to find comparable unrelated party transactions to evaluate related-party transactions. But comparable transactions were often "either absent or misused when transfers of intangible property are at issue."[17] Intangible property, such as a license for a patent or some other sort of intellectual property, is often unique and indeed may derive a substantial part of its value from its uniqueness. When such intangibles are involved, there will likely not be transactions involving comparable properties for the Commissioner to use to analyze transfer pricing transactions. Thus analyzing transfer-pricing transactions involv-

---

already contains broad authority to the Secretary of the Treasury or his delegate to allocate income and deductions. It is believed that the Treasury should explore the possibility of developing and promulgating regulations under his authority which would provide additional guidelines and formulas for the allocation of income and deductions in cases involving foreign income." H.R. Rep. No. 2508, 87th Cong, 2d Sess. 18–19, reprinted in 1962 U.S.C.C.A.N. 3732, 3739.

14. Reuven Avi–Yonah, "The Rise and Fall of Arm's Length," 15 Va. Tax Rev. 89, 107 (1995).

15. "The comparable uncontrolled price method evaluates whether the amount charged in a controlled transaction is arm's length by reference to the amount charge in a comparable uncontrolled transaction." 1994 Treasury Regulations, § 1.482(3)(b).

16. Id., § 1.482(2)(e).

17. A Study of Intercompany Pricing under Section 482 of the Code, 1988–2 C.B. 458, at 5 (hereinafter the White Paper).

ing intangible property has been and continues to be difficult and controversial.

In 1986 Congress amended § 482 in an effort to remedy transfer pricing problems associated with licenses of intangibles.[18] The Conference Committee Report on the 1986 amendment to § 482 also invited the Treasury Department to create new transfer pricing regulations.[19] In response, the Treasury Department issued a white paper in 1988, "A Study of Intercompany Pricing under Section 482 of the Code,"[20] to solicit comments for the proposed regulations. The Treasury Department issued "Proposed Regulations under Section 482[21] in January 1992," "Temporary and Proposed Regulations"[22] in January 1993, and "Intercompany Transfer Pricing Regulations under Section 482"[23] in July 1994. There are substantial differences between the 1992, 1993, and 1994 regulations: "The most noteworthy feature of the 1993 regulations in comparison to earlier versions of the regulations under § 482 was the emphasis on comparability, and the resulting flexibility. * * * The final regulations adhere to this emphasis, and in some cases increase it."[24] One of the sources of this increased flexibility is the best-method rule, which gives the Commissioner discretion in determining which method to use: "The arm's length result of a controlled transaction must be determined under the method that, under the facts and circumstances, provides the most reliable measure of an arm's length result. Thus, there is no strict priority of methods, and no method will invariably be considered to be more reliable than others."[25]

It is clear "that the changes made might have been directly influenced by, among others, U.S. trading partners, in particular the members of the Organization for Economic Cooperation and Development (OECD)."[26] Indeed, the OECD's reaffirmation of the arm's length standard in 1995 signaled an ongoing international endorsement of that

18. Section 482 was amended to read, "In the case of any transfer (or license) of intangible property (within the meaning of section 936(h)(3)(B)), the income with respect to such transfer or license shall be commensurate with the income attributable to the intangible."

19. "The conferees are also aware that many important and difficult issues under section 482 are left unresolved by this legislation. The conferees believe that a comprehensive study of intercompany pricing rules by the Internal Revenue Service should be conducted and that careful consideration should be given to whether the existing regulations could be modified in any respect." H.R. Cong. Rep. No. 841 at II–638, reprinted in U.S.C.C.A.N. at 4726.

20. The White Paper, supra note 17.

21. 57 Fed. Reg. 3571 (hereinafter the 1992 regulations).

22. 58 Fed. Reg. 5263 (hereinafter the 1993 regulations).

23. Regs § 1.482 (1994).

24. 1994 Regulations, preamble, 59 Fed. Reg. 34971.

25. Id., 1.482(c)(1).

26. Dora Cheng, General Comments and Comparison Chart on the 1994 Final Section 482 Regulations and the 1995 OECD Guidelines, 11 Tax Notes Int'l 1184 (1995) at 1184.

standard and is often cited as evidence of an international consensus in its favor. Critics of proposals to substitute some other transfer pricing methodology for inquiries about comparable arm's length prices insist that the OECD's endorsement makes clear that the current international consensus requires the U.S. to use as its standard the arm's length approach. Deviating from the arm's length standard in the face of this international consensus might burden MNEs with different inquiries from the tax authorities in the U.S. and elsewhere. They would then have to keep at least two sets of books: one following the accounting requirements of the arm's length standard and another following the accounting requirements of an alternative standard. The Treasury's endorsement of the arm's length standard conforms to the current OECD policy preference.

9.4 THE ARM'S LENGTH STANDARD

Today the regulations under § 482 state that, "In determining the true taxable income of a controlled taxpayer, the standard to be applied in every case is that of a taxpayer dealing at arm's length with an uncontrolled taxpayer."[27] Furthermore, "A controlled transaction meets the arm's length standard if the results of the transaction are consistent with the results that would have been realized if uncontrolled taxpayers had engaged in the same transactions under the same circumstances (arm's length result)."[28] The arm's length standard requires that each party calculate its profits separately; that is, without consolidating its accounts with related taxpayers and demands that related party transactions be priced as if unrelated parties had entered into them. The arm's length standard is supposed to reflect the pricing and allocation of profits of a transaction that would have occurred had the transaction occurred between unrelated parties: "The current regulations adopt a market-based approach, distributing income among related parties the way a free market would distribute it among unrelated parties."[29]

Should the Treasury Department continue to use the arm's length standard, or are there better approaches to the transfer pricing problem? In the excerpt below, Reuven Avi–Yonah criticizes the current methods of regulating transfer pricing, which he believes have failed to tax the income of MNEs accurately. Avi–Yonah argues that the arm's length standard ignores the reasons that MNEs are organized as they are, and he is concerned about the lengthy fact-based litigation, involving expensive and contradictory expert testimony, required by prevailing transfer pricing methods. Avi–Yonah's fundamental question is: Does the arm's length standard uncover any underlying economic reality?

27. 1994 Final Regulations 1.482(b)(1), 59 FR 34971 (hereinafter1994 regulations).

28. Id.

29. The White Paper, supra note 17, at 6.

Reuven S. Avi–Yonah, *The Rise and Fall of Arm's Length: A Study in the Evolution of U.S. International Taxation,* 15 Virginia Tax Review 89–159 (1995).

The question is now whether the new, expanded definition of arm's length can be used to replace the current approach with a more simple and practical solution to the transfer pricing problem and whether such a solution may gain world-wide acceptance.

To answer this question, it is first necessary to understand why the traditional ALS [arm's length standard] has failed. To do so, let us reexamine the theoretical criticism of the ALS, as developed by a succession of critics from 1976 onward. On the most fundamental level, the basic criticism of the ALS is that it does not reflect economic reality. As the courts and Congress have stated, multinational corporations do not regard each subsidiary as a separate entity which bargains with other sub-sidiaries at arm's length. Multinationals are usually integrated entities to which each subsidiary contributes, and the transfer prices among the constituent subsidiaries are fully under the control of the multinational which naturally considers the tax implications in setting such prices. This fact has been recog-nized by the Treasury since the promulgation of the first set of transfer pricing regulations in 1935, which stated "the interests controlling a group of controlled taxpayers are assumed to have complete power to cause each controlled taxpayer so to conduct its affairs that its transactions and accounting records truly reflect the net income from the property and business of each of the controlled taxpayers."

Moreover, the very existence of integrated multinationals is evidence that the ALS does not reflect economic reality. The predominant explanation for the existence of multinationals is the internalization theory which posits that, like any organiza-tion, multinationals exist because of market and non-market advantages that are derived from their structure. The multina-tional's structure allows it to avoid (internalize) transaction costs, which increases efficiency in raising capital, advertising products, achieving economies of scale, and protecting valuable intangibles. Thus, if one applies a market rate of return sepa-rately to each of the components of the multinational, the result is less than the actual return of the organization as a whole. This residual, the result of the interaction among the constitu-ent parts of the organization, cannot be assigned to any compo-nent. Any transfer pricing rule which arbitrarily assigns the residual to one part of the organization distorts economic reali-ty.

* * *

Beyond the theoretical critique of the ALS, which may explain some of its practical problems, one is left with the fact that the experience of the last twenty-five years indicates that the ALS creates a climate of uncertainty and an immense administrative burden for the taxpayers, the IRS and the courts and provides ample opportunity for abuse. The burden imposed by the ALS has been documented and commented upon extensively. This burden results from the need to apply the ALS on a factual, case-by-case basis, without any general rules in the majority of cases in which there are no comparables. The GAO, after an extensive survey of the practical problems involved in administering the ALS on a case-by-case basis, recently concluded "transfer pricing cases in general can be very burdensome, time-consuming, and expensive for the courts, IRS, and the companies involved." Former Chief Judge Nims of the Tax Court has stated that transfer pricing cases have absorbed a substantial part of the Tax Court's pretrial, trial, and post-trial resources. The dollar amount of tax in controversy in section 482 cases docketed in Tax Court in 1992 was * * * twice the amount it was in 1989. The figures in the appeals process are even more substantial. The costs for the government in such cases are very high and are likely to be even higher if the IRS is allowed to hire outside counsel to aid it in litigation, as has been proposed. The IRS spent about $15 million on expert witnesses in section 482 cases in 1992, and a recent Treasury report recommends increased use of such experts. The Treasury report concludes that "the IRS has not been widely successful in developing and litigating section 482 cases" and "for the foreseeable future, transfer pricing litigation will place a heavy burden on the Service and the Tax Court."

Moreover, the traditional ALS leads to a pervasive uncertainty. In the absence of clear rules, neither the taxpayer nor the IRS can know in advance the likely revenue outcome in a transfer pricing case. For the vast majority of taxpayers, the result is years of uncertainty before a case can be settled or litigated. The inability to forecast the taxes on international ventures with reasonable certainty may discourage taxpayers from undertaking such ventures despite higher potential returns. Such an inability also has multibillion dollar implications on the government's ability to plan its revenues in advance.

The traditional ALS also leads to the widespread possibility of abuse. While it is impossible to prove that transfer pricing underlies the widely documented and substantial disparities between the profitability of foreign controlled corporations [CFCs] and domestic corporations, there is a distinct likelihood, as recognized by the Treasury and the GAO, that multinationals are underpaying taxes in the billions as a result of the "fiscal no-man's land" created by the continuum price problem. Moreover, the perception of lack of competitive fairness resulting from such disparities in profitability may be almost as bad as an actual underpayment of taxes by [CFCs]. This is because it can lead to hasty and discriminatory reactions such as the recent proposals to apply minimum profit standards only to [CFCs] but not to domestically controlled U.S. corporations.

It is likely these problems will get worse in the future despite the new final regulations, the increased resources employed by the IRS in transfer pricing cases and the new statutory penalties enacted by Congress to combat transfer price abuses. Several trends are likely to lead to an increased focus on transfer pricing in the twenty-first century. First, as trade becomes more global and multinationals proliferate, a larger proportion of such trade is conducted between affiliated corporations. Such intercompany trade accounted for nearly a third of world manufacturing trade and a quarter of world trade in the 1980's. In 1986, trade among affiliated domestic and foreign corporations accounted for 38% of total U.S. exports and imports. This globalization is likely to continue as corporations shift production of parts to locations where wages are lower. Second, more of this trade consists of high technology goods. * * * High technology goods tend to be manufactured using intangibles unique to the multinational; therefore, comparables are unlikely to be found and the case tends to be litigated.

NOTE

Achilles Heel? No one can doubt that the administrative and compliance issues associated with the arm's length standard are serious. The key question, however, is whether they are severe enough to consider abandoning the arm's length standard in favor of another approach. In responding to that question, we need to know whether the problems associated with other approaches are substantially less severe than those arising with the arm's length standard or whether they are just different. In formulating your thoughts, consider the main alternative to the arm's length standard—the "unitary" or "formulary" standard—described in the next section.

9.5 OTHER ALLOCATION METHODS

The arm's length standard is frequently a fiction imposed upon MNEs by tax rules intended to elicit a fair and appropriate international allocation of profits to various tax jurisdictions. There are often no comparable arm's length transactions precisely because transferring property within commonly controlled entities may be the only economically feasible way to use the property. Because the Commissioner's (and the OECD's) adherence to the arm's length standard in many cases produces an unavoidably arbitrary transfer price and, consequently, allocates income inaccurately, critics of the arm's length standard have devised other approaches to the transfer pricing inquiry.

Among the most popular alternatives is the "unitary" standard, which looks to the total profits earned by firms that are under common control and engaged in similar or related activities.[30] Under this approach, related entities would be treated as two parts of the same company—as composing a "unitary" business. The income that all transactions between these parties generate would be allocated using a predetermined formula to each part of the business. This is sometimes referred to as "formulary apportionment." Under this approach, the income generated by a transaction is typically allocated using a predetermined formula consisting of three elements: sales activity in each jurisdiction, property in each jurisdiction, and payroll in each jurisdiction. For each variable, the ratio of the MNE's income earned in the taxing state to the income earned worldwide is calculated, i.e., sales in state/sales worldwide, property in state/property worldwide, and payroll in state/payroll worldwide.

Developing these terms into a formula, the percentage of income allocated to a particular state is equal to: (sales in state/sales worldwide + property in state/property worldwide + payroll in state/payroll worldwide) divided by three. An MNE's worldwide income is then multiplied by this average, with the product being the amount of taxable income allocable to the MNE's operations in that state. The formula above, which gives equal weight to sales, property and payroll is, of course, only one among many possibilities. Indeed, in the U.S. states where such formulas are generally used, it is common to weight sales more heavily than the other two factors. In Canada, most of the provinces use a formula with only two equally weighted apportionment factors—payroll and sales. In the following excerpt, Daniel Simmons describes the main theoretical underpinnings of the unitary standard and identifies its main shortcomings.

Daniel L. Simmons, *Worldwide Unitary Taxation: Retain and Rationalize, or Block at the Water's Edge?* 21 Stan. J. Int'l L. 157, 162–65 (1985).

> Unitary taxation rests on the theory that activities in each of the states where an enterprise operates contribute to its overall profit. The system apportions that profit to the states [or jurisdictions] based not on the company's own internal—and manipulable—accounting conventions, but on a mathematical

---

30. See, e.g., White Paper, supra note 17, at 136, for a discussion of the theoretical and practical advantages of a unitary system of apportionment.

"rough approximation" of the income "that is reasonably related to the activities conducted within the taxing state." The apportionment is generally based on a three-factor formula that takes into account the proportion of the company's property, payroll and sales attributable to its operations in each of the states [or jurisdictions]. Income may be allocated on this unitary basis even though the company maintains detailed accounts of the separate income earned within a state [or jurisdiction], or where an integrated operation is conducted through related incorporated entities that maintain separate books of account.

Since the theory of unitary taxation involves hidden exchanges of value within an enterprise, it becomes essential to identify which enterprises are sufficiently integrated or "unitary," for such exchanges to occur. In the case of a vertically integrated enterprise, where different stages of the operation add value to the ultimate product, it is easy to see that all of the factors within the enterprise are essential and that each contributes to the realization of profit. The mutual exchange of value within an enterprise is not, however, limited to intra-company purchases and sales of goods and services typical of vertically integrated operations. * * * An enterprise may be integrated on the basis of the unity of use and management of a business scattered throughout several states [or jurisdictions].

* * *

The unitary tax system functions reasonably well with respect to an enterprise located within the United States, where income is computed in a single currency under uniform accounting standards. This would include a domestic multinational required to report its worldwide income to the United States taxing authorities. Nonetheless, lack of uniformity in the appreciation of the unitary tax system can cause substantial problems. A multistate enterprise may face taxation as a unitary business in one state, for example, while another state seeks to tax a local part of the business as a separate operation. The result can be the taxation of the same income by two states. There is also some conflict between a state's taxation of so-called "situs income," income derived from specific activities within the state such as real property rental or extraction of natural resources. The inclusion of such income in the unitary tax base by a non-situs state [or nation] provides another example of the double-taxation of income. Differing interpretations of the factors included in the apportionment formula can also lead to the same value being included in more than one state. These problems are mitigated to some extent by the Multistate Tax Compact and the Uniform Division of Income for

Tax Purposes Act, which provide for uniform definitions and central administration of the unitary tax system. If the unitary tax system were applied uniformly, of course, the sum of the income of a unitary business allocated to each state [or nation] would just equal its total income.

NOTE

Boundary Questions. The "unitary" method offers a sharp contrast with the individual transaction-based analysis that the arm's length standard employs. Like the arm's length standard, however, the unitary method suffers from complications. Among other problems, there are difficulties in defining the boundaries of a "unitary business." The demarcations between various lines of business within many MNEs are apt to be fuzzy and inchoate.[31] Without the clear legal boundaries provided by the incorporation of separate entities and the arm's length standard, it is difficult to determine which operations are sufficiently integrated to constitute a "unitary business," especially within well-diversified MNEs.

Stanley Langbein, a proponent of the unitary method, argues that the arm's length standard is *not* the international norm, despite the apparent reliance upon the arm's length standard embodied in the U.S. regulations and the emphasis placed upon the arm's length standard by the OECD. Instead, Professor Langbein insists that the use of comparable uncontrolled prices, supplemented by resort to various formulary apportionment methods when CUP transactions are unavailable, is more characteristic of international practice. In the following passage, he argues that this "true" norm is close to a unitary standard and, therefore, that contrary to the claims of many adherents of the arm's length system, the explicit and widespread adoption of a true unitary standard would not be overwhelmingly difficult to adopt. His ultimate contention is that adopting a unitary approach would make the tax laws governing transfer pricing clearer and more determinate *ex ante*, qualities that Langbein believes are currently inadequately fulfilled by the arm's length approach to international transfer pricing.

Stanley I. Langbein, *The Unitary Method and the Myth of Arm's Length,* 30 TAX NOTES 625, 625–681 (1986).

I think we can say the method of using comparable prices, when demonstrably available, and fractional methods, otherwise, is the true, descriptive, prescriptive, and theoretically desirable substantive international norm. * * * One can argue

31. See Charles E. McClure, Jr., Operational Independence Is Not the Appropriate "Bright Line Test" of a Unitary Business—At Least Not Now, Tax Notes, Feb. 28, 1983; Jerome Hellerstein, The Basic Operations Interdependence Requirement of a Unitary Business: A Reply to Charles E. McClure, Jr., Tax Notes, Feb. 28, 1983; Charles E. McClure, Jr., The Basic Operational Interdependence Test of a Unitary Business: Rejoinder, Tax Notes, Oct. 10, 1983.

whether this is a 'separate enterprise' or a 'fractional apportionment' international norm: I call it an international norm of formulary apportionment, because of the predominance of formulary features, invariably as expense allocation measures and because, given that comparable prices are ordinarily available in only a trivial range of cases, its status as a backup method does not mean that it is other than the method most frequently used. Others may term it 'arm's length' because of the primacy given the comparable price method when usable. Terminology is not important if we truly understand the 'norm' history, theory, and common sense conjointly coax us to obey. Terminology is only important if it is distorted in an effort to get us to abandon a system close to that norm in favor of one much further away.

[This] brings us to the unitary system. I have suggested the unitary system is very close to the true international norm. In substance it differs only in not starting with comparable uncontrolled prices. But comparable uncontrolled prices exist in only a trivial range of cases anyway—three percent in dollar volume, according to the GAO study. So this deviation should as a practical matter not be of great concern.

The true norm uses fractional methods liberally, but only on an ad hoc basis; only when a controversy arises, i.e., only according to the hit-or-miss proposition whether an agent raises it; and only accordingly to criteria and guidelines which are a priori indeterminate. The unitary method, by contrast, sets forth determinate, universally applicable criteria which leave little for conjecture, or manipulation. And its terms are authored by statute, not by administrative or judicial discretion.

* * *

The problem at the international level is particularly acute. The United States has spent the last 20 years as the apostle of the 'new' arm's length system, which it is not extreme to say the United States has to a substantial extent forced upon the world. We would have a great deal of explaining to do if we shifted support to a mandatory fractional system, particularly after an Administration has endorsed the federal legislation to prohibit the unitary system. But at some point we must be candid with ourselves and the international community about the nature of our experience with the comminution [i.e., recharacterization as a series of transactions] of shared factor relationships, the creation of income, and the single component methods. At a minimum we should address whether the progressive degeneration of procedural principles and method priorities in the cases is evidence that the use of fractional methods in the absence of comparable prices is inevitable regardless whether one calls one's system a 'separate enterprise' approach or not.

NOTES

1) *California's Formulary Approach*. Stanley Langbein wrote this article when California used a unitary method, which "combines the income of related corporations within a multijurisdictional enterprise for tax purposes. * * * To make unity determinations, auditors reviewed a wide range of information on corporate ownership and business operations."[32] MNEs unsuccessfully challenged the constitutionality of California's system in federal court. See *Barclays Bank PLC v. Franchise Tax Board of California*, 512 U.S. 298 (1994). Mostly due to pressure from our allies, especially from the United Kingdom, California abandoned this method.

2) *The Current Regulations and Profit Splitting*. As Langbein notes, the regulations did and still do allow for profit splitting, Reg. § 1.482–6(a). "The profit split method evaluates whether the allocation of the combined operating profit or loss attributable to one or more controlled transactions is arm's length by reference to the relative value of each controlled taxpayer's contribution to that combined operating profit or loss. The combined operating profit or loss must be derived from the most narrowly identifiable business activity of the controlled taxpayers for which data is available that includes the controlled transactions (relevant business activity)." This sounds very much like the apportionment of profits of a unitary business to its constituent parts, but it is nevertheless quite different than the formulary apportionment computations used by state governments in the U.S.

Formulary Apportionment vs. Separate Accounting—a Necessary or False Dichotomy?

Despite the sharp distinctions sometimes drawn in the literature and in discussions among tax authorities from different countries, formulary apportionment and separate accounting may not be irreconcilable alternatives. Tax authorities may be able to develop systems that employ elements from both the arm's length standard and the unitary standard. Valerie Amerkhail, Director of Transfer Pricing with Economic Consulting Services, argues that the Treasury Department should be allowed to use both the traditional ALS transactional method *and* the formulary approach.

Valerie Amerkhail, *Pricing Methodology: Arm's Length or Formulary Apportionment? Sometimes, the Best Choice is Both*, 8 Tax Management Transfer Pricing Report 94 (1999).

Selective use of formula apportionment, such as applying it to the MNE's risk-sharing core, can increase greatly the feasibil-

---

32. Report to the Honorable Byron L. Dorgan, U.S. Senate, Tax Policy and Administration: California Taxes on Multinational Corporations and Related Federal Issues, GAO/GGD 95–171 (1995), at 8–9.

ity of choosing and applying a formula appropriate to the facts and circumstances of a specific MNE.

* * *

Although use of a composite approach to transfer pricing is not recognized explicitly by either the U.S. Section 482 regulations or the Organisation for Economic Co-operation and Development transfer pricing guidelines, this relatively simple solution is consistent with the provisions of both. Further, both the Internal Revenue Service's proposed regulations on global dealing and OECD recommendations on the tax treatment of global trading offer precedents for this combined method approach.

* * *

Under either the U.S. regulations or the OECD guidelines, the provision of a profit split option is an acknowledgment that for some intercompany transactions there are no good uncontrolled comparables. Also, both the U.S. regulations and the OECD guidelines describe ways that may be appropriate for allocating the income attributable to intangibles in particular circumstances, rather than prescribing a particular method that must be used.

The primary concern of the U.S. regulations is to discourage the use of any transfer pricing method that is not based on independent comparables. However, when the circumstances warrant a profit split, the best method rule will provide the authority to select a profit split approach, to choose appropriately between the residual method or a direct, one-step allocation, and to choose the appropriate formula for allocating either the residual or the total profit. The guidelines show less concern for the importance of independent comparables, and more concern that testing only one side of a controlled transaction might impose an inappropriate result on the other side. As a result, the guidelines are relatively flexible regarding the use of profit splits, and very flexible regarding the form of profit split that might be used.

Thus, despite different language and priorities, both provide enough flexibility for the use of profit splits when they are more appropriate than transactional methods, and for the use of the customized profit allocation formula that will be most appropriate for the facts and circumstances of each individual case.

Problems with Following the Lead of the States

Adopting a formulary method would not require the Treasury Department to create a completely new wheel; many states use formulary apportionment already. But there are serious difficulties facing the international adoption of the states' methods. In the following excerpt, Joann Weiner, writing as an international economist with the Treasury Department's Office of Tax Analysis, disagrees with the view that implementing a unitary worldwide system for the taxation of MNEs would be straightforward, arguing instead that it might well be quite difficult for the Treasury Department to replace the arm's length standard.

Joann M. Weiner, *Using the Experience in the U.S. States to Evaluate Issues in Implementing Formula Apportionment at the International Level,* TAX NOTES TODAY 181–76, TREASURY DEPARTMENT WORKING PAPER (1999).

To begin, it is helpful to identify conditions that have enhanced the abilities of the states to use formula apportionment. The states' success with formula apportionment is largely due to factors that are unique to the states, such as the ability to work under the umbrella of the federal tax system, to rely upon federal tax administration through the Internal Revenue Service, and to use common accounting and tax conventions. Because U.S. companies already compute their total income for federal tax purposes, it is a simple matter for the states to use that amount as the base for total income. [I]t would have been impracticable for the states to adopt the corporate income tax in the absence of the federal corporate income tax.

Another factor that enhances use of formula apportionment in the states is the similar tax environment at the state level relative to the international level. For example, there are no tax barriers to cross-state expansions or mergers. No state imposes a withholding tax on payments from a taxpayer in one state to an affiliate located in another state. These common elements, combined with the lack of barriers to cross-state business and income flows, create the conditions that encourage companies to become functionally integrated, to have centralized managements, and to pursue economies of scale. When a company integrates its separate elements into a unitary business, then the formula apportionment method is often viewed as more practical than the separate accounting method.

The above conditions do not exist in the international economy, where tax barriers can impede enterprises from expanding across national borders. For example, most countries levy a withholding tax on cross-border payments to parties. Many countries tax cross-border mergers more harshly than mergers taking place within a single country. Economic conditions also vary considerably more among nations than among the states.

State tax practices are also remarkably similar when compared with cross-country differences in tax systems, tax rates, and tax bases. For example, some countries have a classical corporate income tax system, others integrate the corporate and individual income taxes, and others operate a split-rate system. Among the OECD countries, corporate income tax rates range from 10 percent to above 50 percent. In contrast, state corporate income taxes range from zero to 12 percent. The corporate income tax is a more important revenue source to countries than to the states. Compared with the roughly six percent of revenue in the states, the corporate income tax accounts for nearly 20 percent of federal revenue in Japan, above 13 percent in Luxembourg and the United Kingdom, and greater than 10 percent within the OECD as a whole. Since the corporate income tax looms so large in the revenue base, countries may not be willing to make compromises that jeopardize their revenue stream.

A.   Unilateral or multilateral implementation?

Based on the inability of the states to reach agreement on all elements of the formula apportionment system, it might be impossible to gain sufficient agreement at the international level, where the underlying conditions are already so disparate. Since reaching agreement seems so difficult, some have argued that the only way to implement global formula apportionment is for one or more countries to take the lead and adopt the approach as a way to encourage other countries to follow.

As desirable as this suggestion may sound to its advocates, pursuing a multilateral approach is essential for several reasons. First, a relatively harmonious tax system helps commerce run smoothly by reducing the tax barriers to doing business in several countries. Each country must work with its trading partners to reach a consensus on the key elements of the system. Without cooperation in establishing the starting position, countries may be unable to agree on ways to resolve the double taxation problems that would inevitably arise if countries adopted separate approaches. The United States and other nations recognized this principle more than half a century ago when they set out to adopt a common method to divide multinational income. Through continued cooperation, the nations have been able to enforce that common system, while allowing individual countries to pursue their own independent tax policies.

Second, no country can unilaterally enforce its chosen standard for dividing income among nations. Every country requires the cooperation of other nations to gather information regarding a multinational company's global income and factors. Without agreement on such definitions, it would be impossible to enforce the system. Unlike the U.S. states, which generally use federal income as their tax base, countries have no common tax base for measuring a multinational enterprise's global income. Given the much greater amount of international investment today than when countries first set out to adopt a common system, such international agreement on a common standard would be even more important today.

* * *

Third, countries may have to renegotiate or reinterpret their network of bilateral income tax treaties to incorporate the apportionment method. The treaties presently in place allow formulary methods in certain cases, but they do not allow use of a predetermined formula. If countries agreed to adopt another treaty standard, they would work together to develop guidelines for uniform application of that standard.

Finally, a multilateral approach helps prevent countries from retaliating against foreign companies doing business within their borders. If one country unilaterally adopted a measure that appeared to violate international practices, other countries might impose punitive measures against companies from that country that would harm the first country as a whole. Cooperation is more effective than confrontation and would better ensure a continued smooth economic environment for multinational enterprises. Without international agreement on the basic tax rules, the resulting conflicts could severely disrupt world trade and investment.

NOTE

Down Under. As of July 1, 2002, Australia introduced full scale consolidation of accounts for tax purposes for controlled groups of corporations operating within the country. In commenting on the relative merits of the competing arm's length and unitary approaches to dealing with transfer pricing domestically and internationally, Australian Professor Richard Vann remarked that "the group approach contradicts the separate entity approach that underlies tax treaties and countries wish to avoid clashes between the two ways of dealing with companies in tax law." Vann continues: "one way of mounting the argument in favour of formulary apportionment is that the consolidation concept is increasingly being adopted into tax laws which leaves the separate enterprise principle of tax treaties the odd one out."[33]

33. See Richard J. Vann, Taxation of Business Profits and the Arm's Length Principle: Thoughts in Progress, unpublished manuscript on file with the editor, at 2–3.

A *Federal Formula To Tackle Intangibles*

As discussed above, intangible property presents particularly diffi-cult problems for the Treasury Department in applying arm's length methods and generally has been left out of account altogether in the standard apportionment formulas of the states. In the following article, Charles McLure discusses the possibility of manipulating the standard formula used by the states to include another variable to measure more accurately income from intangible property.

Charles E. McLure, Jr., *U.S. Federal Use of Formula Apportionment to Tax Income from Intangibles,* 14 TAX NOTES INTERNATIONAL 859 (1997).

[Professor Paul] McDaniel suggests that 'a more refined approach would be required to capture the 'knowledge' factor in income from intangibles' [in a formula] and that 'sophisticated factors can be developed that both reflect and capture the complexities of the multinational corporations of the 1990s.' I am not so sure. One cannot generalize from either the develop-ment of formula-based taxation of global trading companies or the development of special formulas for such industries as transportation, communication, financial intermediaries, pipe-lines, and professional sports. After all, those are industries that are reasonably easy to identify. By comparison, income from intangibles cuts across industries and is not easy to identify. Perhaps one could hive off a few industries (such as pharmaceu-ticals) that are known for their dependence on intangibles based on R & D. But how far can one go? While some of the electronics industry would clearly fall in this category, much probably would not. Would some of the income of an MNE in this industry be apportioned using one formula and some using another, even though the firm arguably is involved only in a single unitary business? Beyond that, intangible assets are of some value in all industries. How would we draw the line between 'intangible-intensive' industries and others? Finally, what would go into the formula for the former?

Having recorded my reluctance to speculate on the contours of a formula that would be appropriate for intangible-intensive industries, I offer the following thoughts for consideration, but without much conviction or inclination to defend them. Suppose that, as in state formulas, the apportionment factors in the federal formula are payroll, property, and sales, weighted in some manner; the formula would be applied to the combined activities of a group of related corporations deemed to be engaged in a unitary business. One alternative would be to include the cost of creating intangibles in the property factor.

To be commensurate with other property values, this would be a cumulative value, not current expenditure.

NOTE

Another Factor. A second alternative would be to create a fourth factor, consisting of a measure, for example, the cost of activities that give rise to intangibles. While this might represent cumulative value (like the property factor) or current expenditure (like the payroll factor), the former seems more appropriate from an economic point of view and would be less subject to manipulation. Determining which costs should count will, however, inevitably be controversial. To prevent this factor from assuming undue importance in industries in which intangibles are not especially important, there should probably be a threshold (perhaps defined in terms of the costs of creating intangibles, or research and development costs over time, as a fraction of total expenses) below which this factor is eliminated. (The mathematically inclined can play endless variations on this theme. For example, the weight accorded this factor might depend on the ratio of costs of creating intangibles to total expenses.) Of course, the flexibility of measuring such a factor may well simply prove an invitation to mischief by both taxpayers and states.

9.6 ENFORCEMENT

As discussed above, the enforcement of transfer pricing rules has long been a problem for the IRS, since taxpayers have so much to gain from manipulating transfer prices in their favor and do not have so much to lose upon reassessment as to make this manipulation unattractive. One of the responses to the enforcement problem has been the enactment of penalties. These penalties provide for amounts in addition to tax to be paid, under certain conditions, by taxpayers who are deemed by the IRS to have misstated transfer prices, where the transfer pricing misstatements lead to an underpayment of tax.

In 1990, Congress adopted new transfer pricing penalties—known collectively as the "Substantial and Gross Valuation Misstatement" penalties—in § 6662(e) of the Code. There are two main categories of transfer pricing penalties. The first is the "Transactional Penalty" of § 6662(e)(1)(B)(i) and Treas. Reg. § 1.6662–6(b). In general, a 20 percent penalty is imposed when, under the auspices of § 482, the IRS determines that the price asserted for any good or service is less than 50 percent or more than 200 percent of the "correct" transfer price. This penalty is increased to 40 percent if the price asserted by the taxpayer for any good or service is less than 25 percent or more than 400 percent of the "correct" transfer price.

The second penalty is the "Net-adjustment Penalty" of § 6662(e)(1)(B)(ii) and Treas. Reg. § 1.6662–6(c). A 20 percent penalty is imposed when the IRS concludes that the net transfer pricing adjustments exceed the lesser of $5 million or 10 percent of a taxpayer's annual gross receipts. This penalty increases to 40 percent if the adjustments exceed the lesser of $20 million or 20 percent of a taxpayer's annual gross receipts.

These penalties are not automatically applied; there are threshold and good faith exceptions. For example, under § 6662(e)(2), no penalty will be exacted from a corporation unless the misstatement for the year results in an underpayment of tax of at least $10,000. There is a "reasonable cause" exception in § 6664(c), which provides that if the taxpayer had reasonable cause and acted in good faith with respect to an underpayment, there will be no penalties imposed under § 6662.

One way to meet the "reasonable cause" exception requirement is for a taxpayer to meet the "contemporaneous transfer pricing documentation" requirements of Treas. Reg. § 1.6662–6(d)(2)(iii). These regulations require the taxpayer to make extensive disclosure of the background surrounding related intercompany transactions and also the method by which the appropriate transfer price was determined by the company. According to the IRS, acceptable documentation "should tell the Service the Who, What, When, Where, Why and How of the intercompany transactions" and demonstrate that the transfer price used reflects "a reasonable method reasonably applied."[34]

Litigation under Section 482

A brief perusal of the case reports and periodicals with the words "transfer pricing" in their titles demonstrates that transfer pricing is a big business. Consultants, lawyers, and experts are in demand because in many cases involving large MNEs the threatened reassessments are very costly. The nature of transfer pricing disputes—setting the most appropriate arm's length transfer price coupled with the large stakes—means that they are especially amenable to legal squabbles, with respected experts on each side insisting that a higher or lower transfer price is more or less appropriate.

Taxpayers and the IRS both often have adopted hardball litigation tactics involving "scorched earth" policies. In *DHL Corp. v. Commissioner*, T.C. Memo 1998–461, in which DHL challenged the Commissioner's determination of deficiencies and additions to tax arising from trademark sale adjustments, royalty deficiencies and the transactions between DHL and a related foreign company, the court placed the burden of explaining why a transfer pricing system is appropriate on the taxpayer. Dolores Wright has described the litigation as follows:

> Before the transfer pricing penalty legislation, a "scorched earth" approach to audits was fairly common. Briefly, this

---

34. IRS, The Section 6662(e) Substantial and Gross Valuation Misstatement Penalty, available at http://www.irs.gov/pub/irs-apa/penalties6662_e.pdf (last visited March 10, 2003) at 14.

approach tended to be non-cooperative, refusing to provide the information needed to properly evaluate the transfer pricing issue in the case. Now, the burden of explaining why a transfer pricing system is appropriate is the responsibility of the taxpayer if the taxpayer wants to avoid transfer pricing penalties. Today, the "scorched earth" policy is less effective than it was before the penalty legislation, and *DHL* clearly indicates that the Tax Court is willing to impose penalties when it deems them appropriate.[35]

The Tax Court has clamped down on taxpayers in transfer pricing litigation. It has required clear and thorough documentation of transfer pricing transactions and has legislative backing for this enforcement. But, remembering the tension inherent in transfer pricing, the question remains whether resolving these issues through litigation is consistent with business or administrative needs.

Alternatives to Litigation

Historically, the IRS often took a very aggressive stance whenever a U.S. subsidiary owned an intangible asset. However, this approach has backfired several times for the IRS in litigation. See, for example, *Bausch & Lomb Inc. v. Commissioner,* 933 F.2d 1084 (1991) and *Exxon Corp. v. Commissioner,* T.C. Memo 1993–616 (1993). In order to avoid losing additional cases, the Commissioner offered to begin to arbitrate difficult transfer pricing cases involving intangible assets owned by U.S. subsidiaries. The Apple Computer case, Apple Computer, Inc. v. Commissioner, (U.S. Tax Court, 1993, No. 21781–90), was the first to settle in arbitration; David Korteling describes it in the following excerpt.

David P. Korteling, *Let Me Tell You How It Will Be; Here's One For You, Nineteen For Me: Modifying the Internal Revenue Service's Approach to Resolving Tax Disputes,* 7 AMERICAN UNIVERSITY ADMINISTRATIVE LAW JOURNAL 659 (1993).

The *Apple* arbitration concerns the transfer pricing agreements between Apple and its Singaporean subsidiary ("Apple Singapore"), and involves a determination of the total income earned by Apple Singapore in 1984, 1985, and 1986. The arbitration agreement provides for a "baseball" type format. In this format, each party submits to the arbitrators its view of the correct income figure for the three years in dispute. The arbitrators must decide on one of the figures, but cannot make adjustments.

35. See Deloris R. Wright, "Transfer Pricing in the United States: Recent Events and Expectations for the Future," Bulletin International Bureau of Fiscal Documentation (Sept/Oct 2001), 417, 420.

The presentation of evidence is governed by principals [sic] set forth in the arbitration agreement and essentially follows the Federal Rules of Evidence. After the arbitration panel reaches a decision, the parties present the decision to the Tax Court. The judge assigned to the case reviews the decision of the arbitrators, and the decision is enforced by the Tax Court as if it were a decision of a Tax Court judge.

This format encourages each party to submit a reasonable estimate of Apple's total income for each of the years in dispute. Because the arbitration proceedings will require each side to justify its figure, rather than attack the other figure as unreasonable, neither side is encouraged to assume an extreme position for bargaining room. If either side submits an unreasonable figure, it is likely that the arbitrators will accept the other position.

Additionally, the taxpayer has a lower burden of proof than the normally required showing of arbitrary, capricious, and unreasonable action by the IRS. Under arbitration, taxpayers must show only that their position is more reasonable than the Commissioner's. Even if the taxpayer does not meet the burden of proof, the IRS is likely to assert a lower deficiency, because both parties are encouraged to submit a more "reasonable" estimate.

NOTES

1) *All's Well That Ends.* Both parties claimed to be satisfied by the arbitration. Eric D. Ryan, Tax Director for Apple Computer, stated that Apple was pleased with the results it obtained. Apple submitted only three binders of information to support its transfer prices. IRS Deputy Associate Chief Counsel stated that had the issue gone to litigation, "Apple would probably have had to generate three boxcars of information."[36] But despite Apple's apparent satisfaction with the arbitration outcome, as Jay Soled states below, there were problems with the process:[37]

Because the use of FOA [final offer arbitration] was an uncharted path, however, both parties struggled to design mutually acceptable ground rules that would produce accuracy in results.[38] When the matter was finally resolved before the arbitration panel, both parties proclaimed the virtues of FOA for the following reasons: (i) the parties narrowed their differences

36. David P. Korteling, at n. 116.

37. The following is excerpted from Jay A. Soled, Esq., Transfer Tax Valuation Issues, the Game Theory, and Final Offer Arbitration: A Modest Proposal for Reform, 39 Ariz. L. Rev. 283 (1997).

38. "It was reported that Apple and the IRS spent nine months negotiating a stipulation and developing a procedure to meet their mutual needs." Id.

prior to their submissions to the arbitrators; (ii) the interval between the arbitration proceedings and the decision was shortened; and (iii) the process was much less expensive than it otherwise would have been if the case had gone to trial.[39]

2) *The End of Arbitration?* In 1998, the Internal Revenue Code was amended to include § 7123, which provides, in part, "The Secretary shall prescribe procedures by which any taxpayer may request early referral of 1 or more unresolved issues from the examination or collection division to the Internal Revenue Service Office of Appeals." This move constituted the adoption into the Code of procedural developments that had occurred much earlier in the Tax Court. Tax Court Rule 124 provides as follows:

Rule 124. Voluntary Binding Arbitration

(a) Availability: The parties may move that any factual issue in controversy be resolved through voluntary binding arbitration. Such a motion may be made at any time after a case is at issue and before trial. Upon the filing of such a motion, the Chief Judge will assign the case to a Judge or Special Trial Judge for disposition of the motion and supervision of any subsequent arbitration.

Despite the existence of these procedural rules and the promise that they hold for reducing the costs of litigating expensive factual questions, such as those arising in transfer pricing disputes, it appears that apart from the *Apple* arbitration no other significant transfer pricing case has been resolved using voluntary binding arbitration. According to the IRS, "The new ADR procedures have not had significant application in section 482 cases, because these cases frequently require competent authority assistance and thus are appropriately handled under the simultaneous appeals/competent authority provisions."[40] Unlike arbitration in Tax Court, the competent authority process involves tax authorities from both countries which have a stake in the transfer price between related entities. The failure of arbitration to resolve transfer pricing disputes *ex post* perhaps contributed to the innovative development of advanced pricing agreements (APAs), discussed in the next section.

9.7 ADVANCED PRICING AGREEMENTS

By the early 1990s, it was becoming clear that the process by which the IRS then reviewed and adjusted transfer prices not only imposed high costs on taxpayers but has also created serious difficulties for the

39. "After Successful Use of Baseball Arbitration, Apple, IRS Both Declare Themselves Winners," 11 Alt. High Cost Litig. 163 (December 1993). "The parties did acknowledge, however, a number of flaws in the process: (i) the selection of arbitrators took too long and was too costly and (ii) the method of discovery and document production needed improvement." Id.

40. Department of the Treasury & Internal Revenue Service, Report on the Application and Administration of Section 482 at 52 (April 21, 1999).

IRS. Unlike the arbitration procedures, APAs have been gaining in popularity and are an important way in which the Service and taxpayers have been able *ex ante* to avoid expensive and time-consuming litigation. APAs typically involve the tax authorities from both countries in a procedure designed to reach agreement about the methods applicable to determining the price at which property will be transferred between the jurisdictions *before* the actual transactions occur. An APA gives the corporate group a significant degree of confidence that transfer prices based upon the agreed methodology will be accepted by the tax authority in each jurisdiction.

The General Accounting Office reported in 1995 that, of all tax cases on appeal and litigated that were closed in fiscal year 1993 or the first half of fiscal year 1994, "IRS spent about a third of its total international examiner time, and a much higher percentage of its economist time, on those cases that had a section 482 issue." The results from litigating transfer pricing cases were especially discouraging:

> [Among] four major section 482 cases that had been decided in court between January 1, 1993, and May 20, 1994, [all] took an average of 15 years from the earliest tax year audited until resolution in the courts. * * * [Cases] like these illustrate how disputes over section 482 issues can become extremely expensive for taxpayers and the government by requiring the employment of outside experts, resulting in long, drawn out litigation and keeping corporate tax liabilities in an uncertain status for years.
>
> In three of the cases, the Tax Court expressed its displeasure with IRS and found its reallocation of income to be arbitrary, capricious, or unreasonable.[41]

Moreover, the GAO found that "the most prevalent reason why the IRS reached a settlement of transfer pricing issues in cases closed during fiscal year 1993 was concern about whether a court would apply the same judgment to the evidence as the IRS had."

The IRS's response to these difficulties was remarkable: the IRS revised its procedures in a number of ways that conveyed a surprisingly flexible conception of tax administration. The most important of these procedural innovations was the APA regime. First introduced in 1991,[42] the APA scheme combines diverse elements from a number of traditional IRS mechanisms; yet the resulting arrangement seems to deviate from all past models of tax administration, stimulating subtle conceptual debate for scholars and practitioners alike. The following analysis of the APA process is taken from one extended scholarly inquiry.

---

41. GAO Report: Transfer Pricing and Information on Nonpayment of Tax, April 25 (95 TNI 93–16, GAO/GGD–95–101).

42. See Rev. Proc 91–22, 1991–1 C.B. 526 (first introducing the APA process); Rev. Proc. 96–53, 1996–2 C.B. 375 (revising and superseding Rev. Proc. 91–22).

Diane M. Ring, *On the Frontier of Procedural Innovation: Advance Pricing Agreements and the Struggle to Allocate Income from Cross Border Taxation*, 21 MICH. J. INT'L L. 143 (2000).

Under the APA program introduced by *Rev. Proc. 91–22*, taxpayers initiate the U.S. APA process by requesting an APA from the Office of the Associate Chief Counsel International. The request must identify the taxpayer and all parties to the transactions; describe the business operations and history, the ownership structure, capitalization, financial arrangements, and principal business; provide relevant tax and financial data for the past three years, descriptions of financial accounting methods used as well as differences between tax and financial accounting; and explain the taxpayer's and the government's positions on previous and current audit, appeal, or litigation issues. The request also must include a detailed description of the transfer pricing method being proposed by the taxpayer and demonstrate this method by applying it to the taxpayer's three prior years' data. To establish and evaluate the proposed transfer pricing methodology, the taxpayer may need to provide party profitability data, functional analyses, economic analyses of the general industry, a list of competitors, and a detailed discussion of comparable transactions. Regardless of whether an APA is signed or not, factual oral and written representations or submissions made during the APA process may be introduced by either the Service or the taxpayer in any administrative or judicial proceeding.

Finally, the APA request must outline the proposed set of critical assumptions. These are the objective business and economic criteria that are fundamental to the operation of the proposed transfer pricing methodology—any facts about the taxpayer, industry, or tax regime that would significantly affect the substantive terms of an APA, if such facts changed. As part of the APA process, the Service may require that the taxpayer provide, at its own expense, an independent expert acceptable to both the Service and the taxpayer (and if necessary the foreign government) to review and opine on the proposed method.

After the request is completed, it is sent to the Chief Counsel (National Office) who coordinates with the district office. These interactions form an interesting facet of the APA process. Normally, taxpayers deal with the local district or regional offices for most of the audit, appeal and litigation of a tax matter. The APA process, however, is handled by the National Office. Thus, the APA process brings new people into the dynamic without removing the district office from the negotiations. * * * [T]he change in personnel focus from the district to the National Office plays a key role in drawing taxpayers into the APA process.

The Service representatives then meet with the taxpayer, often on a number of occasions, to discuss facts and economic analysis, and to negotiate. If the parties reach agreement and the Service grants the request, an APA can be signed. If the taxpayer seeks to involve a foreign government in the negotiations then [the procedure under Rev. Proc. 96–53 requires that] the foreign country [be brought] into the process prior to an established understanding between the taxpayer and the Service. Then the U.S. competent authority negotiates the issue with the foreign country. Because such "bilateral" APAs involve competent authorities, generally they are available only when the other country is a treaty party.

* * *

[A]voidance of double taxation is a primary attraction of the APA program. [For instance,] some taxpayers are drawn to the process because of current audit difficulties. The APA process, with its possibility for rollback application, can be an attractive alternative for dealing with existing and future problems, saving interest, penalties and current dispute costs. [Moreover,] taxpayers in a particular industry may consider the APA program, with its ability to rely on treaty authority, as a useful way to combat serious gaps or irrationalities of current rules. For example, taxpayers engaged in global trading sought "recognition" of interbranch transactions (to achieve more economic taxation), an outcome not directly possible under the Service's interpretation of the Code but achievable through the APA program. Also a foreign manufacturer could be [assured] that its U.S. subsidiary would not be considered its permanent establishment (and thereby subject to more extensive U.S. income taxation) by building that assumption into the terms of the APA. Such strategic participation in the APA program is the logical outcome of any system that offers participants choice.

Assuming agreement is reached (either with United States alone, or with a foreign country as well), the APA is binding between the Service and the taxpayer and typically effective for about three years. If the taxpayer complies with the APA terms, then the Service will regard the results obtained from applying the transfer pricing methodology specified in the APA as satisfying the arm's length standard and generally will not contest the application of the methodology to the transactions outlined in the APA. As part of the APA, the taxpayer is required to file an annual report describing the actual operations of the business for the year and demonstrating compliance with the terms of the agreement. In certain cases, compensating adjustments to the calculations for that year might have to be made. In the event of fraud or malfeasance by the taxpayer with respect to material facts provided or good faith compliance with the terms of the APA, the Service can revoke the APA.

* * *

[Why] would taxpayers participate [in the APA, since] it requires disclosure to the government of significant information, some of which might otherwise be withheld? Ideally participating taxpayers obtain tax certainty before actually engaging in their transactions. In addition they obtain a tax treatment that is uniformly accepted by all of the taxing authorities, thereby eliminating conflict. There is also an expectation that this alternative mechanism for dispute resolution might reduce overall costs of addressing transfer pricing problems.

[Why] should governments be willing to engage in this one-on-one process with taxpayers? Governments may hope to gain information about pricing practices and transaction specific issues, to utilize a different forum, and to interact with other countries in a setting conducive to more comprehensive resolutions of transfer pricing "problems." Additionally, governments have historically borne a significant burden for transfer pricing, both in terms of time and money. They now look to the APA program to provide less costly dispute resolution and to enhance their information base for future improvements to the taxation of related party transactions.

The participating taxpayers and governments represent the central but not exclusive parties significant to the APA program. Nonparticipating taxpayers (those with and without transfer pricing issues) are impacted by both the tax system's problem with transfer pricing and by the addition of APAs to the mix of procedural options. On the positive side, a successful APA program might reduce government administration and enforcement costs, providing a generalized benefit. Also, to the extent the Service gains more detailed knowledge about transfer pricing practice and can translate that learning into improved rules, then all taxpayers with transfer pricing questions may benefit. On the negative side, the program's use of private individualized agreements raises a number of risks that might not be acceptable in an administrative regime, including the specter of uneven application of substantive law.

* * *

The APA involves the National Office in the discussion at the outset. This new participant not only acts on its own views and authority, but it can also help mediate the views of the taxpayer and district. In part, the National Office is able to do this because of the absence of an intense one-on-one history with the taxpayer. Plus, its role in the process begins before positions have become entrenched (a problem experienced by appeals). In fact, where the focus is future transactions, not only are positions not yet fixed, the actual subject matter has yet to occur. As a result, the APA process attracts taxpayers by granting the opportunity to sidestep or modify an unproductive relationship at the district level and obtain a bit of a "fresh start."

* * *

A common district reaction, at least at the outset, was that APA participants were "deceiving" the National Office, which has much less familiarity than the district with the taxpayer's detailed history and operations. This concern (as well as an appreciation of the learning curve savings in time and resources that the district can bring to the process) may have prompted the Service to make the district a more formal and active part of the National Office APA process in the 1996 updated procedure [Rev. Proc. 96–53].

Another source of concern regarding the participant changes is the potential for manipulation of the process. Given that the district-taxpayer relationship may be mutually strained, but that the APA process can be initiated only by the taxpayer, strategic uses of the program may be possible, leaving the district averse to the APA program. Again, the 1996 changes to the program may reflect sensitivity to this concern and to the importance of having the districts as partners in a process in which they are both up-front and tail-end (in the audit of the APA years) participants. Furthermore, the introduction in late 1997 of a "program" that encourages field examiners to recommend appropriate taxpayers for the APA process could have a balancing effect.

What marks APAs as an unusual procedural device in the tax system is the fact that they permit the taxpayer and the government to discuss and resolve substantive tax issues voluntarily, prior to the transactions occurring, and to reach agreement on their tax treatment. At first blush this may not seem unusual; a student of the tax system could identify other existing mechanisms that allow this kind of interaction. The APA differs because of the precise nature and context of the interaction. Unlike an audit or settlement agreement, the primary function of the APA is to cover future transactions. Although advance tax rulings exist in the United States (for example letter rulings), APAs are different for several reasons: the agreements involve foreign countries; the issues are intensely factual (and the facts very complex) and require significant negotiation between the government and taxpayer, the agreements can cover a number of years; and the terms of the agreements are confidential with no redacted versions released to the public. These APA characteristics stand in contrast to the operation of the most common advance ruling, the letter ruling. Such rulings, which are primarily legal determinations applied to relatively generic facts, involve only the Service and are published in redacted form.

NOTES

1) *Two Sources of Discomfort.* In the more theoretical parts of her article, Diane Ring explores whether the APA process belongs to which, if either, side of the rulemaking versus adjudication dichotomy, which has been central in American administrative law. Ring also asks whether the process is excessively non-transparent, leaving IRS officials sufficiently unaccountable to the public, to justify alarms that a new form of "private justice" is being created. Among practitioners, it is the impression of private justice, not deviation from traditional legal paradigms, which is the more urgent source of concern about the operation of the APA process.

2) *Other Innovations.* The APA was the dominant administrative innovation in the field of transfer pricing in the 1990s, but not the only one. A flexible conception of tax administration also undergirded the changing role of the competent authority process in resolving transfer pricing disputes. Each of two treaty partners typically designates its own "competent authority" who can negotiate with its counterpart in the other country to resolve disputes, for example, in transfer pricing cases. The two competent authorities reach agreement in specific cases according to what is called the Mutual Agreement Procedure. As the following excerpt from an article co-authored by an IRS insider shows, some IRS officials and practitioners recognized early on that the competent authority process had greater potential for resolving transfer pricing disputes than was commonly known. After the IRS began to promote the APA procedure, it also took steps to integrate the competent authority process with the appeals process.

Christine Halphen & Ronald Bordeaux, *International Issue Resolution Through the Competent Authority Process*, 64 TAX NOTES 657 (1994).

By its very nature, the competent authority procedure is intended, and does work, as a dispute resolution mechanism under tax treaties. The competent authority procedure plays a major role in resolving disputes involving re-allocation of income or deductions under *section 482*, particularly for taxpayers who determine that correlative relief[43] will provide adequate relief in their case. These taxpayers tend to have less of an incentive to pursue their domestic remedies to protest an unagreed adjustment before proceeding to competent authority. Despite encouragements in *Rev. Proc. 91–23* that taxpayers pursue their administrative Appeals remedies before requesting competent authority assistance, many taxpayers choose to by-pass Appeals with respect to their unagreed issues. These taxpayers are, as a general rule, accepted in the competent authority process. It is then up to the competent authorities to evaluate the merits of the proposed adjustment and, through a negotiated process, to reach a mutual agreement with the foreign competent authority on what the amount of the adjustment should be. The purpose of the mutual agreement is to grant full relief, i.e., correlative relief is granted for the full amount of the agreed-on adjustment. This means that, if the competent authorities agree on an amount less than the adjustment originally proposed, the U.S. competent authority will generally withdraw any amount of the proposed adjustment in excess of the negotiated settlement. Thus, where the process is successful, it allows the resolution of a domestic dispute without prior recourse to traditional channels.

* * *

Traditionally, the IRS has encouraged taxpayers that disagree with a proposed IRS adjustment to pursue their rights to administrative appeals before seeking competent authority assistance. This reflects the long-standing belief that the competent authority process is at its best when limited to the resolution of disputes between treaty partners, and is not the appropriate vehicle for resolving disputes with taxpayers.

Traditionally, each IRS function has a strictly defined role: the Examination function is responsible for identifying an audit issue and developing supporting facts and methods; Appeals is responsible for exploring the range of a reasonable settlement given the strengths and weaknesses of the case and hazards of litigation; and, if the adjustment entitles the taxpayer to assistance under a treaty, the competent authority is responsible for obtaining correlative relief for the amount that the taxpayer

---

43. If taxpayer T has operations in countries A and B and is subject to tax under both, then, after country A reallocates T's income or deductions in connection with transactions between related parties, T is entitled to request country A's competent authority to negotiate "correlative relief" from country B so that T is not subject to double taxation in country B.

and the IRS agree is a justified, or at least reasonable, adjustment.

Also, it is true that appeals and competent authority are each guided by a different philosophy and use a different approach. In the case of a U.S-initiated adjustment, the goal of the U.S. competent authority is to present the adjustment so as to best defend it to the foreign competent authority. In that process, a taxpayer's agreement or disagreement with the adjustment has little relevance. What is important is that the taxpayer support the process (particularly if it does not support the adjustment). This entails that the taxpayer participate in the process by responding to requests for information and analysis it may receive from either side in a manner that is consistent with helping the two parties reach a fair agreement. While there is nothing wrong with the taxpayer pointing to weaknesses in the case, it is important to understand that the process is not adversarial and should not be used for the primary purpose of reducing or reversing the adjustment (even though, as part of the process, such a result may occur). Use by the taxpayer of the competent authority process in an adversarial manner may diminish the chances of a successful outcome between competent authorities and, therefore, increase the risks that the taxpayer will suffer double taxation.

On the other hand, the Appeals process is specifically designed for taxpayers who feel that the proposed adjustment should be reduced or withdrawn. As such, it is expected that the taxpayer will treat the process as an adversarial procedure, in which it will vigorously advocate its position.

Yet, the theory that the competent authority process should be limited to the negotiation of correlative relief does not always hold true in practice. Experience shows that the U.S. competent authority can effectively handle disagreements with taxpayers while conducting an effective and successful mutual agreement procedure. * * * Where the taxpayer cooperates in that process, it appears that a prior Appeals procedure would add little to the successful outcome of the competent authority process. * * *

[IRS's Announcement 93–144] on the coordination of the administrative appeals process with competent authority evidences a significant change of policy. * * * Announcement 93–144 describes procedures by which taxpayers that disagree with a proposed adjustment may seek competent authority assistance and request simultaneous Appeals consideration of the issue in competent authority.

* * *

[APAs and Competent Authority]

In situations where an APA may affect the tax liability of a related company in one or more foreign countries with which the United States has an income tax treaty, *Rev. Proc. 91–22* contemplates involving the competent authorities in the APA process. The purpose of a competent authority agreement within the APA process is to avoid double taxation between the taxpayer and its related foreign entities that otherwise may arise if the taxpayer is subsequently audited in the foreign country. As of March 1994, the IRS had completed 19 APAs, 16 of which involved an affiliate in a treaty country. Of these 16 APAs, 9 include a bilateral agreement with the treaty partner. Therefore, the IRS has been generally successful in its policy to encourage taxpayers to seek bilateral agreements whenever possible. The main reason for this success is the fact that most treaty partners have been receptive to these advance determinations, particularly with respect to situations involving complex derivative financial product transactions.

* * *

Once the U.S. competent authority accepts a case for consideration, the U.S. competent authority will contact the treaty country to negotiate an acceptable transfer pricing methodology (TPM). The treaty country can present its views through written communications and/or face-to-face negotiations. Competent authority APA negotiations are largely similar to negotiating a double tax case. Each side presents its views on the TPM, and terms and conditions are negotiated to provide a basis for an APA.

The APA process is flexible as to when the foreign competent authority gets involved. Some treaty partners have expressed a specific preference for being involved at the very beginning of the APA process. Others prefer to review and comment on the agreement reached by the IRS and the taxpayer.

NOTE

APA Use Increasing. Since this article was authored, there have been several developments in the IRS experience with the APA process. Foremost among these has been the increasing use of the APA mechanism. In 1992, 21 applications for APAs were filed with the IRS, with only nine agreements completed (three unilateral and six bilateral). In contrast, in 2001 the IRS entertained 77 applications for APAs and negotiated 55 agreements. Of these, 34 were entered into with foreign-owned U.S. corporations, reflecting the IRS's auditing focus on these firms. In addition, approximately one-third of the APAs were bilateral (i.e., entered into with the taxpayer with the knowledge and agreement of a foreign competent authority) and approximately two-thirds were unilateral (i.e. entered into by the IRS with the taxpayer alone). At the end of 2001, 166 requests for new APAs were outstanding.[44]

The debate surrounding the best approach to allocating income among related companies internationally is one that continues to vex commentators, legislatures, and the international community. The arm's length standard is intuitive and easy to understand (at least from a theoretical perspective), but suffers from administrative complexity and uncertainty. It also frequently imposes the fiction of comparable arm's length transactions in a context where arm's length transactions may not even be feasible. The unitary or formulary apportionment may trade lowered administrative complexity (though to what extent is debatable) for somewhat more arbitrary and ad hoc allocations of income than the arm's length standard (although this too is debatable).

The choice—if indeed one must be made—between these two standards is apt to continue to be an uneasy one. Procedural developments such as APAs have somewhat decreased the costs associated with coping with the factual burden associated with the arm's length standard, thereby making it somewhat more efficient and less burdensome for MNEs to comply with. At the same time, however, international business continues to grow at a rampant pace. Whether the administrative burdens associated with the application of the arm's length standard can continue to be met in the future remains to be seen. Further procedural innovations in the application of § 482 and its regulations and the streamlining of transfer pricing rules, perhaps including the greater incorporation of elements of unitary taxation and formulary apportionment, may ultimately become the most attractive outcome. But the future of the transfer pricing debate and administrative practice is extremely difficult to predict.

44. See IRS, Announcement 2002-40: Announcement and Report Concerning Advance Pricing Agreements (March 29, 2002) at 8, 12.

Chapter 10

The Nondiscrimination Principle

10.1 INTRODUCTION

Nondiscrimination is one of those motherhood and apple pie issues. Everyone applauds it; no one attacks it. How, after all, can one voice support for discrimination? Certainly the embrace of nondiscrimination in taxation is sweeping. The U.S. Supreme Court has long regarded nondiscrimination in interstate commerce as a linchpin of our federalist constitutional order. The European Court of Justice has recently used nondiscrimination as a basis for striking down national tax laws of member nations. Students should, however, be aware that the tax concept is quite different from the civil rights principle which comes to mind when the term "nondiscrimination" is used.

The nondiscrimination norm in international taxation deals with *source country taxation*. Nondiscrimination clauses, which bar source countries from discriminating against foreign investors, are standard features in bilateral and multilateral tax treaties. Their goal is not necessarily allocative efficiency, but rather similar tax treatment for similarly situated persons and businesses, regardless of residence. As we shall see, there is a contested relationship between the nondiscrimination norm and both capital import neutrality (CIN) and capital export neutrality (CEN). When we delve into the treaty requirements of nondiscrimination—as we do in this Chapter—both nondiscrimination's meaning and its purpose become unclear.

Nondiscrimination requirements do *not* preclude all distinctions in the taxation of foreign and domestic taxpayers. Foreign and domestic taxpayers are not "similarly situated," an implied requirement of a nondiscrimination principle; thus they can be taxed differently. In the United States, for example, as we have seen, U.S. residents are taxed on worldwide income, while nonresidents are ordinarily taxed only on income generated in the United States. As the following excerpt suggests, policymakers continue to struggle to achieve clarity and rationality in expressing any standard separating permissible from impermissible discrimination.

Sanford H. Goldberg & Peter A. Glicklich, *Treaty–Based Nondiscrimination: Now You See It Now You Don't*, 1 Fla. Tax. Rev. 51, 51–53 (1992).

Although treating similarly situated taxpayers the same is a laudable goal, there appears to be a great distance between acceptability of the nondiscrimination concept in general and the ease or exactness of its application. * * * The nondiscrimination principle was often incorporated in consular or establishment conventions and in treaties of friendship, commerce, and navigation; the parties to those agreements often attempted to obtain "most favored nation" status for the businesses conducted abroad by their nationals.

The existence of nondiscrimination provisions in treaties has been justified as being consistent with the concept that taxes should not be an impediment to the free-flow of international trade, investment, or the movement of individuals. * * * Rather than leveling the playing field by extending domestic investment incentives to foreign investments made by their own nationals, the level playing field concept has been implemented by having source countries agree to *avoid placing extra burdens upon foreign persons and their businesses conducted in the source countries*. Thus, in practice, a nondiscrimination provision represents a commitment that a source country will not tax the nationals or residents of its treaty partner more heavily than it taxes its own nationals or residents.

In addition to committing to tax foreign nationals no more heavily than source-country nationals, some source countries, including the United States, implement the "level-playing-field" concept by retaliating against foreign nationals of a country that imposes discriminatory taxes against source-country nationals. For example, sections 1091 and 1096 of the Internal Revenue Code [the I.R.C. provisions based on the OECD model treaty provisions] allow the United States to increase taxes applicable to nationals, residents and corporations of another nation that subjects U.S. citizens or domestic corporations to discriminatory or extra-territorial taxes. [These provisions, however, have never been invoked.][1]

NOTE

Definitional and Conceptual Difficulties. Neither sections 1091 or 1096 of the Internal Revenue Code define discrimination, but as the following selections show, the absence of a functional definition presents only half

---

1. See § 1091. (Doubling of rates of tax on citizens and corporations of certain foreign countries); § 1096 (Adjustment of tax on nationals, residents, and corporations of certain foreign countries).

of the challenge. The conceptual rationale for the nondiscrimination principle is also unclear. While justifications for nondiscrimination have most often cited equity and efficiency concerns, neither the intuitive fairness of the nondiscrimination rule nor the economic logic which supposedly undergirds the principle are self-evident. Certainly the classic economic argument for free trade is important:

> Taxes that discriminate against importers * * * distort the optimum geographical distribution of enterprise. Production that could be carried on more efficiently in State A will be carried on in B instead if B's tax on imports from A exceeds the cost advantage of producers in A.[2]

Yet disparate income tax structures are often not equivalent to tariffs or subsidies. Residence countries may vary deductions and credits based upon how a source country describes and applies a particular tax. Moreover, if, as in the United States, a residence country taxes income earned from foreign sources, giving a credit for foreign taxes paid by its nationals, the taxpayer may be indifferent to the actual rate of taxation in the source country so long as the foreign taxes are less than those imposed by the country of residence. As such, the rate of taxation in the residence country may affect the profitability of an investment even if the source country declines to tax its income.

While a functional definition of nondiscrimination and a clear conceptual basis for the principle remain elusive, drafters of bilateral and multilateral tax treaties have consistently included nondiscrimination clauses alongside provisions providing for relief from double taxation. Despite the widespread use and acceptance of the OECD's nondiscrimination clause in bilateral tax treaties, commentators continue to be critical of the clause's inclusion and are struck by its ambiguous and potentially limitless meaning. A skeptical Peggy Musgrave offers one reason a nation might wish to discriminate.

Peggy B. Musgrave, *The OECD Model Tax Treaty: Problems and Prospects*, 10 Colum. J. World Bus. 29, 36 (1975).

> [T]he rule of non-discrimination is not a compelling one. * * * The rates of tax chosen by a country for its internal domestic reasons need not necessarily be those appropriate to its tax share of foreign investment income. A country might choose, for instance, a low or zero rate of profits tax for reasons of domestic growth or equity. Under the non-discrimination rule it thereby foregoes its tax share of foreign investment profits. * * * While the source country should be obliged in its tax treaties to guarantee a non-arbitrary, even-handed and predictable tax

---

2.   Richard A. Posner, Economic Analysis of Law 631 (4th ed. 1992).

regime to investors from abroad, its tax rates as applied thereto should not be bound by the non-discrimination rule.

10.2 THE SCOPE OF NONDISCRIMINATION

The current OECD and U.S. Model Tax Conventions contain blanket, if rather indeterminate, nondiscrimination provisions:

United States Model Income Tax Convention of September 20, 1996

Article 24: Non-Discrimination

1. Nationals of a Contracting State shall not be subjected in the other Contracting State to any taxation or any requirement connected therewith that is more burdensome than the taxation and connected requirements to which nationals of that other State in the same circumstances, particularly with respect to taxation on worldwide income, are or may be subjected. This provision shall also apply to persons who are not residents of one or both of the Contracting States.

2. The taxation on a permanent establishment or fixed base that a resident or enterprise of a Contracting State has in the other Contracting State shall not be less favorably levied in that other State than the taxation levied on enterprises or residents of that other State carrying on the same activities. The provisions of this paragraph shall not be construed as obliging a Contracting State to grant to residents of the other Contracting State any personal allowances, reliefs, and reductions for taxation purposes on account of civil status or family responsibilities that it grants to its own residents.

3. Except where the provisions of paragraph 1 of Article 9 (Associated Enterprises), paragraph 4 of Article 11 (Interest), or paragraph 4 of Article 12 (Royalties) apply, interest, royalties, and other disbursements paid by a resident of a Contracting State to a resident of the other Contracting State shall, for the purpose of determining the taxable profits of the first-mentioned resident, be deductible under the same conditions as if they had been paid to a resident of the first-mentioned State. Similarly, any debts of a resident of a Contracting State to a resident of the other Contracting State shall, for the purpose of determining the taxable capital of the first-mentioned resident, be deductible under the same conditions as if they had been contracted to a resident of the first-mentioned State.

4. Enterprises of a Contracting State, the capital of which is wholly or partly owned or controlled, directly or indirectly, by one or more residents of the other Contracting State, shall not be subjected in the first-mentioned State to any taxation or any requirement connected therewith that is more burdensome than the taxation and connected requirements to which other similar enterprises of the first-mentioned State are or may be subjected.

5. Nothing in this Article shall be construed as preventing either Contracting State from imposing a tax as described in paragraph 10 of Article 10 (Dividends).

6. The provisions of this Article shall, notwithstanding the provisions of Article 2 (Taxes Covered), apply to taxes of every kind and description imposed by a Contracting State or a political subdivision or local authority thereof.

OCED Model Income Tax Convention of April 29, 2000

Article 24: Non-Discrimination

1. Nationals of a Contracting State shall not be subjected in the other Contracting State to any taxation or any requirement connected therewith, which is other or more burdensome than the taxation and connected requirements to which nationals of that other State in the same circumstances are or may be subjected. This provision shall, notwithstanding the provisions of Article 1, also apply to persons who are not residents of one or both of the Contracting States.

2. The term 'nationals' means:
    a. all individuals possessing the nationality of a Contracting State;
    b. all legal persons, partnerships and associations deriving their status as such from the laws in force in a Contracting State.

3. Stateless persons who are residents of a Contracting State shall not be subjected in either Contracting State to any taxation or any requirement connected therewith, which is other or more burdensome than the taxation and connected requirements to which nationals of the State concerned in the same circumstances are or may be subjected.

4. The taxation on a permanent establishment which an enterprise of a Contracting State has in the other Contracting State shall not be less favorably levied in that other State than the taxation levied on enterprises of that other State carrying on the same activities. This provision shall not be construed as obliging a Contracting State to grant to residents of the other Contracting State any personal allowances, reliefs and reductions for taxation purposes on account of civil status or family responsibilities which it grants to its own residents.

5. Except where the provisions of paragraph 1 of Article 9, paragraph 6 of Article 11, or paragraph 4 of Article 12, apply, interest, royalties and other disbursements paid by an enterprise of a Contracting State to a resident of the other Contracting State shall, for the purpose of determining the taxable profits of such enterprise, be deductible under the same conditions as if they had been paid to a resident of the first-mentioned State. Similarly, any debts of an enterprise of a Contracting State to a resident of the other Contracting State shall, for the purpose of determining the taxable capital of such enterprise, be deductible under the same conditions as if they had been contracted to a resident of the first-mentioned State.

6. Enterprises of a Contracting State, the capital of which is wholly or partly owned or controlled, directly or indirectly, by one or more residents of the other Contracting State, shall not be subjected in the first-mentioned State to any taxation or any requirement connected therewith which is other or more burdensome than the taxation and connected requirements to which other similar enterprises of the first-mentioned State are or may be subjected.

7. The provisions of this Article shall, notwithstanding the provisions of Article 2, apply to taxes of every kind and description.

Article 24 (under both the OECD and the U.S. Model) explicitly bars a host country from imposing discriminatory taxes on a business enterprise operating within its territory that is carried on, owned, or controlled by residents of the other treaty country. In the following selection, Robert Green supplies a paradigmatic example of the operative significance of the nondiscrimination principle.

Robert A. Green, *The Troubled Rule of Nondiscrimination in Taxing Foreign Direct Investment*, 26 LAW & POL'Y INT'L BUS. 113, 122–23 (1994).

[S]uppose that the two treaty countries are Home and Foreign. [For the sake of comprehension, the reader may wish to mentally substitute, for example, the United States for "Home," and Spain for "Foreign."] Then if a foreign firm has a branch or other permanent establishment in Home, the treaty nondiscrimination rule prohibits Home from taxing the foreign firm on the income attributable to the permanent establishment less favorably than it would tax a domestic firm carrying on the same activities. Similarly, if a foreign resident wholly or partly owns or controls a domestic firm, the treaty nondiscrimination rule prohibits Home from taxing the domestic firm less favorably than it would tax a similar domestic firm that was owned and controlled by domestic residents. In particular, if a foreign corporation has a domestic subsidiary, Home may not tax the subsidiary less favorably than it would tax a similar domestically owned corporation.

The treaty nondiscrimination rule does not, however, prevent Home from taxing nonresident investors who receive dividends, interest, royalties, or similar payments from an enterprise carried on in Home less favorably than it would tax resident investors receiving similar payments. Indeed * * * host countries generally do tax nonresident investors differently from resident investors. The nonresident investor will be subject to gross-basis withholding taxes, while the resident investor will be subject to a net-basis tax. The nondiscrimination rule, being inapplicable, requires neither that the nonresident be taxed on a net basis nor that the gross-basis withholding taxes be comparable to the net-basis tax.

NOTES

1) *Permissible Discrimination.* As Robert Green's excerpt demonstrates, under the nondiscrimination principle, not all forms of discrimination are precluded. A residence country may impose different rates of taxation on particular categories of nonresidents' income (e.g., dividends, interest, and royalties) but not on others (namely, effectively connected active business income). There are other circumstances in which Article 24 does not oblige a host country that accords special taxing privileges to

its own bodies or institutions to extend those same privileges to the other treaty country. For example, a host country permitting special tax benefits applicable only to public benefit nonprofit institutions (in the U.S. for example, look to tax exempt § 501(c)(3) organizations) is not obliged to grant a treaty partner similar privileges. Likewise, special taxation privileges accorded a host state's own public bodies are not required to be extended to public bodies of another state since the circumstances of the treaty country's public bodies are never comparable to those of the host state.[3]

Yet even where discriminatory treatment is prohibited, it remains unclear what nondiscrimination requires. When is the taxation of a domestic branch or subsidiary of a foreign firm "less favorably levied" or "other or more burdensome" than the taxation of wholly domestic firms? Do these phrases permit any differences at all in taxation? Also, when should two taxpayers be considered to be "in the same circumstances" or "carrying on the same activities?" Neither the language of nondiscrimination clauses nor the OECD commentary provides satisfactory insight into these questions.

2) *Earnings Stripping*. In the United States, the application of the nondiscrimination principle has been enforced somewhat erratically, with Congress sometimes overriding nondiscrimination provisions by statute. By virtue of the U.S. Constitution's Supremacy Clause, a treaty may override a previously enacted statute and a statute passed subsequent to Senate approval of a treaty may supersede that treaty. For example, the 1989 enactment of the "earnings stripping" provision of Code section 163(j) will, in some circumstances, deny interest deductions to corporations for interest payments to related tax-exempt parties. This provision was enacted out of concern that taxable U.S. corporations were improperly reducing their tax liability by taking interest deductions for payments to tax exempt lenders, especially to foreign lenders. Foreign parent companies are not subject to U.S. taxation on interest payments from U.S. subsidiaries whenever there is a lack of an effective connection between the interest income and the U.S. trade or business. Additionally, the 30% withholding tax on interest payments has been eliminated for portfolio interest and in other cases reduced by tax treaty provisions. The earnings stripping provision of § 163(j) has been controversial. Some commentators and foreign governments have contended that the section conflicts with treaty nondiscrimination clauses similar to Article 24(4) of the U.S. Model Income Tax Treaty. And the legality of the code section is questionable under international law.

Disallowing deductions for certain interest payments made to foreign lenders while allowing deductions for the same payments made to related U.S. lenders appears to violate the nondiscrimination principle.

---

3. OECD, Commentary on the Articles of the 1977 OECD Model Double Taxation Convention on Income and Capital art. 24, para. 1–2 (1977).

In its defense, Congress claimed that, in addition to foreign companies, § 163(j) also applies to U.S. tax-exempt lenders. The treaties' explicit permission for deductions to be "disallowed for interest paid other than at arm's length" was also used to buttress the claim that § 163(j) was an appropriate mechanism used to disallow such deductions.[4]

But some analysts regard these claims as a thin veneer for discrimination. Emphasizing that it is limited to interest exempt from taxation, Julie Roin points out that § 163(j) does not exempt interest income from tax in the lender's country.[5] Robert E. Culbertson and Jamie E. King question

> why a treaty resident fully taxable in the treaty jurisdiction should not be properly compared to a U.S. resident fully taxable in the United States, for purposes of determining that the payment to the treaty resident is being made "under the same conditions" that would support equal deductibility in both circumstances.[6]

The issue of earnings stripping is also considered in Chapter 6.

Another specific instance when treaty obligations of nondiscrimination have been advanced to challenge U.S. tax law is the enactment of the Branch Profits Tax, discussed in Chapter 7. In the following excerpt Richard Doerenberg suggests that Congress effectively overrode existing treaty commitments in its interpretation of U.S. nondiscrimination obligations.

Richard L. Doernberg, *Overriding Tax Treaties: The U.S. Perspective*, 9 EMORY INT'L L. REV. 71, 88–91 (1995).

> In enacting the branch profits tax, Congress recognized that many income tax treaties to which the United States is a party contain nondiscrimination clauses that bar its enforceability. Since U.S. corporations are not subject to a branch profits tax on their earnings, it would be discriminatory to subject foreign corporations to such a tax. Congress, however, clearly prefers to take a broader view of treaty nondiscrimination clauses. The General Explanation of the Tax Reform Act of 1986 states that:
>
> > Congress generally believed that a branch profits tax does not unfairly discriminate against foreign corporations because it treats foreign corporations and their shareholders

4. See H. Rep. No. 1010–247, at 1249 (1989); H.R. Conf. Rep. No. 101–386, at 568–69 (1989).

5. Julie A. Roin, Adding Insult To Injury: The "Enhancement" of § 163(j) and the Tax Treatment of Foreign Investors in the United States, 49 TAX L. REV. 269 (1994).

6. Robert E. Culbertson & Jaime E. King, U.S. Rules on Earnings Stripping: Background, Structure, and Treaty Interaction, 29 TAX NOTES INT'L 1161, 1176 (Mar. 24, 2003).

together no worse than U.S. corporations and their shareholders. * * *

In other words, since U.S. corporations are taxed on their
earnings, and U.S. shareholders of such corporations are taxed
on dividend distributions, it is not discriminatory to subject
foreign corporations and their shareholders to two taxes—one
on a corporation's earnings and the other on the repatriation of
those earnings.

The equation of a double tax at the corporate level for
foreign corporations with a single tax at the corporate level and
a second tax at the shareholder level for domestic ones carries a
significant and unproven assumption, however, about the incidence of corporate-level taxes. Unless the incidence of the
branch profits tax falls 100% on the shareholders, the branch
profits tax and the secondary tax on dividend distributions are
not equivalent.

Those who have studied the incidence of the corporate tax
have reached inconclusive results. [C]orporations do not pay
taxes—people do. It may be that the shareholders bear the
burden of a corporate tax increase. On the other hand, customers of the corporation may bear higher corporate taxes in the
form of higher prices, suppliers of the corporation through lower
prices paid for supplies, workers through lower wages, or lenders through lower interest payments.

Although Congress argued that the corporate level branch
profits tax is equivalent to the withholding tax imposed on
individuals, it is a basic tenet of the U.S. tax system that
corporations and individuals are treated as separate taxpayers.
A corporate-level tax is not a tax on individuals. That fiction
enabled the Joint Committee on Taxation to state, with respect
to the Tax Reform Act of 1986, that "the Act produces substantial reductions in individual income tax liabilities." On one
level, the statement is true since Congress shifted $120 billion
of the tax burden from 1981 to 1987 to the corporate sector. If
individual tax liabilities are reduced substantially by a shift to
the corporate sector, however, why in the context of the branch
profits tax would a corporate-level tax be equivalent to a withholding tax on income received by individuals?

In Notice 87–56, the Treasury did recognize that treaty
nondiscrimination provisions could preclude the operation of the
branch profits tax. A foreign corporation, however, can claim
the benefits of a tax treaty only if the corporation is a "qualified
resident" of the treaty country in question. The term "qualified
resident" is determined under U.S. domestic law. A publicly
traded foreign corporation is a qualified resident if its stock is

"primarily and regularly traded on an established securities market" in its country of residence. A non-publicly traded corporation residing in a treaty country is a "qualified resident" if it meets shareholder and base erosion tests. A corporation is not a qualified resident if individuals who do not reside in the treaty country or are not U.S. persons beneficially own more than 50% (by value) of the corporation's stock. Code section 884(e)(4)(A)(ii) prevents non-treaty country foreign investors from treaty shopping by capitalizing a treaty corporation with a large amount of debt while residents of the treaty country hold shares of the corporation having little or no value. That section provides that a foreign treaty corporation is not a qualified resident if 50% or more of its income is used to meet liabilities to persons who are not residents of the treaty country or the United States.

NOTE

Little Practical Effect. Richard Doerenberg's nondiscrimination objection to the Branch Profits Tax and the objections of foreign governments have had relatively little practical impact. Section 884 denies rate reductions for dividends and exemption from the branch profits tax to foreign companies that are not publicly traded or owned by residents of a treaty country. In post–1986 treaties, the U.S. has dealt explicitly with the imposition of the branch profits tax, generally imposing it at the same rate as is applicable to dividends.

10.3 PROFFERED POLICY RATIONALES

Is Nondiscrimination an Incoherent Norm?

While the treaties' nondiscrimination clause is potentially broad in scope—for example, the U.S. decision to tax citizens and residents on worldwide income while taxing non-residents only on U.S.-source income is not, strictly speaking, equal treatment—it is typically thought to bar only certain kinds of taxing practices. In the following selection, Alvin Warren describes permissible and impermissible forms of discrimination in both international tax and international trade law. He is, however, ultimately unable to find a controlling principle, and concludes, "the current distinction between permissible and impermissible discrimination is incoherent."[7]

Alvin C. Warren, Jr., *Income Tax Discrimination Against International Commerce*, 54 TAX L. REV. 131, 149–165 (2001)

Prohibited and Permitted Income Tax Discrimination Against International Commerce

7. Alvin C. Warren, Jr., Income Tax Discrimination Against International Commerce, 54 TAX L. REV. 131, 131 (2001).

There are three principal ways in which a country might discriminate against international commerce. It could favor (1) domestic producers over foreign producers, (2) domestic production over foreign production, or (3) domestic products over imported foreign products (which, for simplicity, here include services). The first two possibilities can be illustrated by considering two countries (domestic and foreign), in each of which there are producers from both countries. The matrix below displays the four possible combinations of production and producers, which I will consider from the perspective of the domestic country.

Table 1

	Domestic production	Foreign production
Domestic producer	1	2
Foreign Producer	3	4

The first form of discrimination, which is based on the nationality of the producer, is shown on the vertical axis. The second form, which is based on the location of the production, is shown on the horizontal axis. To isolate these two forms of discrimination, I initially assume that all products are sold in the country of production, an assumption that is relaxed later.

* * *

1.   Direct Investment

Under [OECD Article 24] provisions, a source country could not apply a tax rate to domestic business income earned by a foreign company that was higher than the tax rate applied to the domestic income of a domestic company. Nor presumably could a country limit accelerated depreciation or an investment tax credit to machinery and equipment owned by domestic companies.

There are, on the other hand, many tax provisions that differentially tax foreign producers, but these provisions usually are justified on the ground that foreign and domestic producers are in different circumstances. * * * The protection against discrimination afforded by the bilateral tax treaties * * * can be more limited in practice than might be suggested by the treaty language.

Discrimination on the vertical axis also could be implemented using policy instruments outside the tax law, which would be tested against the applicable trade provisions. For example, the domestic country might limit licenses to operate retail businesses on its territory to its own nationals. Whether such discrimination would be prohibited would depend on the national treatment clauses of an applicable [bilateral income tax treaty] or, if implemented, the MAI.[8] * * *

2. Portfolio Investment

The nondiscrimination provisions of the tax treaties generally have been interpreted to permit differences in taxation of resident and nonresident portfolio investors, on the ground that they are not in similar circumstances. Many countries that have integrated corporate and shareholder income taxation rely on this reasoning to deny shareholder credits to foreign shareholders.

More generally, the gross-basis withholding tax levied on dividends paid to foreign shareholders could be higher than the net-basis tax levied on domestic shareholders. Although the American Law Institute [ALI] has indicated that in principle withholding taxes should not be used to impede international commerce, the Institute recommended against extending the nondiscrimination article to such taxes, presumably because of the different situations of residents and nonresidents. Rather, the ALI suggested that these considerations be taken into account when the rates are negotiated. This suggestion is curious, given the practice of reciprocal withholding rates, which requires comparison of the tax rates for foreign investors from two different residence countries, whereas nondiscrimination requires comparison of the tax rates for foreign and domestic investors in a single source country. Accordingly, the recommendation will be germane only when the two countries have the same domestic rate structure.

3. Favoring Foreign Producers

Although the principal subject [examined here] is constraints on income tax discrimination against international commerce, it should be noted that there are now some constraints on favoring international commerce. Traditionally, international tax law has not prohibited tax holidays granted to new domestic production, which would favor Cases 1 and 3 over Cases 2 and 4

---

8. The Multinational Agreement on Investment (MAI) has been under negotiation at the OECD since 1995. Under the proposed agreement, the basic nondiscrimination concepts of national and most-favored-nation treatment would apply to foreign investment, along with a commitment to the free flow of funds in and out of member countries. Certain requirements imposed on investors, such as a minimum export target for goods and services, would be prohibited. Expropriation would be limited to public purposes and require prompt compensation. Dispute resolution would include binding arbitration between countries and investors. With the exception of the provisions applying to expropriation, the MAI generally would exclude direct taxation from its application. The official commentary states that the parties recognize the importance of nondiscrimination in the taxation of foreign investors and investments, but that nondiscrimination is to be implemented under the double taxation treaties. [Information in footnote from the original, citation omitted see Warren at 145—ed.]

in the matrix in Table 1. What about a tax holiday for domestic production that was available only to foreign producers, which would favor Case 3 over all the others? The European Union recently has adopted a "code of conduct" that restricts the use of such incentives by member countries. The OECD also recently decided to limit such activity in the financial sector, which it considers "harmful tax competition."

What is the rationale for constraining countries from favoring international commerce with tax incentives limited to foreign producers? According to the OECD, such incentives distort locational decisions, but so do incentives also available to domestic companies. Another way of looking at the prohibited practices is that they discourage source countries from using low rates to attract too much of the international income tax base by requiring that those low rates be extended to domestic taxpayers. From this perspective, the European Union and OECD prohibitions protect the tax revenues of competing source countries. Finally, the current debate in the international tax community about the appropriate limitations on tax incentives is reminiscent of the longstanding trade debate about the appropriate limitations on production subsidies.

4. Recapitulation

Tax and trade law have developed separately with respect to discrimination against international commerce on the vertical axis, but have reached similar results in the generally accepted norm of national treatment for foreign producers, whether that discrimination is accomplished by placing a burden on foreign producers or granting a benefit to domestic producers. On the other hand, given the narrow scope of the tax treaty concept of discrimination, there remains some potential for income tax discrimination against foreign producers. Finally, absence of most-favored-nation treatment means that tax law can be used to discriminate among foreign producers.

A. Discrimination Against Foreign Production

1. In General

International tax law conceptualizes the horizontal axis as a matter of double taxation, rather than discrimination. Framing this issue this way obscures the analysis of whether foreign production is being treated better or worse than domestic production, because the baseline of equivalent treatment is not explicitly articulated. The different methods of reducing double taxation (and the underlying concepts of economic neutrality) permit different results for the comparative treatment of Cases 1 and 2 in the matrix in Table 1. Under the foreign tax credit (and capital export neutrality), the basic idea is that the domestic country should not treat Case 2 any worse than Case 1, given the baseline of equal after-tax returns. Under an exemption for foreign income (and capital import neutrality), on the other hand, a country can treat Case 2 better than Case 1 to achieve equal treatment between Cases 2 and 4, given the same baseline. If equal treatment after deduction for foreign taxes (and national neutrality) were considered the appropriate baseline, both methods of alleviating double taxation would favor foreign over domestic production. From the perspective of those two methods, however, eliminating double taxation by a deduction for foreign taxes, which is not acceptable under the typical tax treaty, would discriminate against foreign production. Although not explicitly framed as a nondiscrimination requirement, the treaty requirement of either a credit or exemption could thus be considered such a requirement.

There is no other provision in either the tax or trade treaties that explicitly precludes a residence country from discriminating against foreign production, whatever the appropriate baseline. To be sure, the method chosen to reduce double taxation will have an effect on a country's ability to discriminate against foreign production. An exemption for foreign business income certainly reduces the possibility of taxing such income more heavily than domestic income. Even under an exemption system, however, it would be possible to discriminate against foreign production by over-allocating (and disallowing) deductions to such income, effectively raising the tax rate on domestic income for taxpayers with foreign income.

Now suppose that a residence country, which used a foreign tax credit to eliminate double taxation, also applied higher rates to foreign income than to domestic income. Although this result would not be consistent with the economic rationale usually thought to underlie the credit (capital export neutrality), such a provision would not seem to violate any treaty obligation, unless the higher rate effectively eliminated the benefit of the credit. [An] * * * example of this * * * is the limitation of accelerated depreciation or investment tax credits to machinery and equipment used domestically.

Turning now to investor-level taxation, a common example of residence-country discrimination against foreign production is the denial under integration systems of shareholder tax credits for dividends paid from foreign corporate income. Income produced in international commerce is accordingly subject to potentially heavier taxation than is domestic income in an integration country exporting capital (due to the denial of shareholder credits for foreign taxes), as well as in an integration country importing capital (due to the denial of credits to foreign shareholders).

Discrimination on this horizontal axis also could be implemented using policy instruments outside the tax law, which would be subject to the constraints of trade law. The domestic country, for example, might grant a subsidy for domestic production, which would be tested under the WTO Subsidies Code. Alternatively, a country could forbid domestic companies from transferring capital to the foreign country to build plants there, which might run afoul of the proposed changes in the IMF Articles.

2. Favoring Foreign Production

Neither the tax nor the trade treaties constrain a residence country's freedom to favor foreign production by its companies. If the source-country tax rate is lower than that applicable in the residence country, either an exemption for foreign income or a credit for foreign taxes coupled with deferral can have this effect.

3. Recapitulation

Tax and trade law, as in the case of discrimination on the vertical axis, have developed separately along the horizontal axis, but here the results seem weaker and less uniform within tax and trade law and across the two domains. Although higher (and lower) taxation of foreign producers is subject to explicit prohibitions, higher (or lower) taxation of foreign production is not.

B. Discrimination Against Foreign Products

So far, the assumption has been that products were sold in the country of production in order to isolate discrimination based on the identity of the producer or the location of the production. Countries, however, may also attempt to discriminate on the basis of whether the products are produced at home or imported from abroad. A third, diagonal, dimension accordingly can be added to the two-dimensional matrix above to reflect the possibility that products could be exported to the other country. The possible outcomes in the two-country example would increase from four to eight, and can be represented in two-dimensional space by expanding the matrix to include the additional outcomes, which are in boldface and can be visualized as lying behind the nonexport results.

Table 2				
	Domestic production		*Foreign production*	
	Local Sales	**Export Sales**	Local Sales	**Export Sales**
Domestic producer	1	**5**	2	**6**
Foreign Producer	3	**7**	4	**8**

Although there is nothing in international tax law that would limit this third form of discrimination, GATT and its successors have been aimed precisely at burdens imposed only on foreign products. The most obvious application is diagonal even in the expanded two-dimensional matrix: Case 10 cannot be too disfavored relative to Case 1 by the importing country.

International trade law constrains not only tariffs on imports, but also subsidies for exports, which are sometimes thought to favor domestic products over foreign products in the foreign market. An example of an export subsidy constrained by international trade law would be an attempt by the exporting country to give an advantage to Case 5 over Case 4 by granting a subsidy to Case 5, but not to Case 1. Like tax holidays limited to domestic production by foreign producers, these prohibited practices discriminate in favor of international commerce over domestic commerce.

Although tax and trade law generally have developed independently on the horizontal and vertical dimensions, tax law has been subordinated to trade law on this third, diagonal dimension. For example, nothing in the tax treaties would prevent a country from exempting from taxation income from domestic production of exported products. Such a tax provision, however, would run afoul of the GATT and it successors, as did the U.S. DISC legislation, which deferred some export income. The European Union subsequently filed a WTO complaint alleging that the partial exemption for income from exports for Foreign Sales Corporations (FSCs) enacted by the United States after DISC repeal violates the new Subsidies Code. A WTO panel recently agreed that partial exemption of export income under these provisions violated the trade treaties.[9]

Similarly, limiting accelerated depreciation or investment tax credits to machinery and equipment produced domestically presumably would be prohibited under the trade treaties, al-

9. In response to the WTO panel's findings, Congress in November 2000 enacted the FSC Repeal and Extraterritorial Income Exclusion Act of 2000 (ETI Act). The EU promptly challenged the ETI Act as inadequate, and in August 2001, the WTO panel issued its report, finding against the ETI Act. The U.S. appeal of the panel's decision is still pending. See U.S. Trade Representative Testimony on WTO Ruling in FSC Case of February 27, 2002, available at http://usinfo.state.gov/topical/econ/wto/020227yy.htm. [Footnote in the original. The U.S. appeal was rejected by the WTO subsequent to the publication of this article.—ed]

though the U.S. investment tax credit was limited to machinery and equipment produced in the United States for a brief period in 1971. Yet another provision that might have run afoul of GATT and its successors was the congressional proposal a few years ago that preferential tax treatment be extended to withdrawals from pension plans used to purchase U.S.-made cars.

C.   Summary

* * * International tax and trade law in principle prohibit (vertical) discrimination by source countries on the basis of taxpayer identity by requiring national treatment of foreign producers. International trade, but not tax, law also prohibits such nontax discrimination among treaty partners through most-favored-nation treatment. * * * International tax and trade law in principle permit (horizontal) discrimination by residence countries on the basis of production location, but there is less consistency within and across the two legal domains than with respect to discrimination on the basis of producer identity. * * * International trade, but not tax, law limits (diagonal) discrimination by importing countries on the basis of whether the product is domestic or foreign.

The consequences of these differences for income taxation can be captured by recalling three hypothesized limitations on accelerated depreciation, with each limitation discriminating against international commerce on one of the three axes. A limitation to machinery and equipment owned domestically would violate the tax treaties, a limitation to machinery and equipment produced domestically would violate the trade treaties, and a limitation to machinery and equipment used domestically would violate neither.

As for the possibility of favoring international commerce, the recent E.U. and OECD actions against "harmful tax competition" constrain (vertical) discrimination in favor of foreign producers, but not (horizontal) discrimination in favor of foreign production.

Potential Norms

It is * * * worth inquiring whether the current distinction between permissible and impermissible discrimination can be justified as implementing some principle or norm applicable to both trade and taxation. Three familiar possibilities * * * are considered here: efficiency, competitiveness, and equality.

A.   Efficiency

The basic idea [behind the efficiency norm is] that taxation should interfere as little as possible with production and consumption decisions in order to maximize global economic welfare. In its strongest form, this norm implies elimination of source taxation in favor of exclusive reliance on residence taxation. The assumption here is that owners of capital bear the burden of the tax and are less mobile than the location of production. Accordingly, taxation on the basis of residence would provoke less tax-motivated reaction than would taxation on the basis of source, which would affect decisions about where to locate production. Taxes tend to be borne by factors that cannot escape, so this view would be particularly apt if the supply of capital in residence and source countries were fixed. More generally, this view is consistent with the standard, though not unanimous, conclusion of economists that the corporate income tax is borne by shareholders or capitalists generally, rather than passed forward in product prices.

[T]he worldwide efficiency norm usually is used to justify the tax credit method of reducing international double taxation by * * * neutralizing tax differentials * * * for investment, thereby promoting capital export neutrality. The overall tax burden for a company in international commerce would be the same, no matter how the revenue was divided among different countries, as long as the tax rate in the source country did not exceed that in the residence country. The worldwide efficiency norm is inconsistent with deferral to the extent that policy affects locational decisions, and capital export neutrality generally is invoked in proposals to repeal or reduce deferral. * * *

[T]ax treaties only prevent (vertical) discrimination against foreign producers. Somewhat surprisingly, the worldwide efficiency norm provides little direct support for prohibiting such discrimination, given the usual assumptions about the incidence of corporate taxes in competitive markets. If such taxes are borne by a company's shareholders or capitalists generally, the company's investment and production decisions in competitive markets will not be affected by the fact that some of its competitors are subject to a different rate of tax. Indeed, if the source-country taxes were fully creditable in the residence country, a foreign producer would not suffer at all from a discriminatory tax.

The tax treaty nondiscrimination requirement, however, might be considered a practical prerequisite of the credit, which is based on the efficiency norm. Otherwise, a low-rate source country could raise taxes on foreign producers up to the creditable amount, effectively taking revenue away from the residence country, without disadvantaging either foreign or domestic producers. From this perspective, the tax treaty provisions can be thought of as protecting foreign governments, as well as foreign producers.

In a world in which all residence countries had exemption systems, a discriminatory source-country tax might cause capital to leave that country, leading to a loss of welfare for source-country workers who would suffer from a less-than-optimal amount of capital, results that are analogous to those produced by a source-country tariff. In such a world, the tax treaty nondiscrimination requirement would advance the efficiency norm if it precluded discriminatory taxes that reduced economic welfare.

Turning now to the second axis, the efficiency criterion is directly contrary to discrimination against foreign production, which is prohibited by neither the tax nor the trade treaties. Worldwide efficiency and capital export neutrality directly imply the elimination of locational distortions, suggesting, for example, that integration residence countries should pass through foreign tax credits to domestic shareholders.

Regarding the third axis, discrimination against foreign products, the efficiency norm suggests that consumption decisions should not be affected by taxation, thereby supporting the reduction of taxes that apply to imported, but not domestic, goods. The principle of comparative advantage further suggests that discrimination against foreign products is undesirable even for producers, because it precludes gains from specialization.

The current distinction between permissible and impermissible discrimination is not consistent with capital-export neutrality, which is the norm traditionally embraced as the cornerstone of international income tax design in the United States. Indeed, the only form of discrimination (against foreign producers) prohibited in the tax treaties is not directly implicated by this norm, whereas the form of discrimination (against foreign production) most inconsistent with the norm is permitted by both tax and trade treaties.

B.   Competitiveness

   1.   The Norm

[Competitiveness] is the norm usually favored by business representatives in discussions of international income taxation. The basic idea * * * that U.S. companies should be treated no worse than their foreign competitors when doing business abroad * * * strongly implies exclusive source jurisdiction and the exemption method of reducing international double taxation. I will consider four possible versions of the case for the competitiveness norm.

[T]he corporate tax is borne by consumers (through higher prices) in the source country. From that perspective, a policy of capital import neutrality makes sense, because the income tax has the same effect as a tax on sales in the source country. The argument for the competitiveness norm on this assumption is similar to traditional arguments for an unrelated business income tax. * * * This argument is not only inconsistent with standard assumptions regarding the incidence of corporate taxes, but also with the longstanding, albeit arguably questionable, GATT distinction between indirect and direct taxes. Border adjustments are permitted for value-added, but not income, taxes, precisely because the former, but not the latter, are thought to increase product prices or decrease wages.

A second argument for the competitiveness norm is that locational distortions reduce economic welfare less than do the distortionary effects of taxing capital income generally, assuming now that the latter is borne by capitalists. The conditions for this view would seem to be most fully satisfied when the demand for capital in both source and residence countries is fixed, and its supply elastic. Even under these conditions, however, economic welfare would be improved by exempting income earned abroad only on the assumption that domestic tax rates could not also be reduced. Accordingly, economists generally consider this argument for capital import neutrality to be weaker than that for capital export neutrality.

Third, [there is scant evidence for the proposition] that lower taxation of foreign competitors will encourage multinationals based in tax-credit countries, such as the United States, to move their tax residences abroad. A fourth and final argument for the competitiveness norm is that U.S. companies, for example, are disadvantaged by a higher cost of capital, because their foreign competitors benefit from residence-country exemptions of foreign income. * * * [T]he idea here seems to be that potential suppliers of capital to U.S. multinationals will prefer to invest in foreign multinationals in order to benefit from the latter's exemption for foreign income, leading to a reduction in the size of U.S. companies producing abroad. [The assumption makes] the link between the hypothesized effect on companies and a negative effect on the tax-credit country often simply a general claim about the spillover effects of headquarter companies or the claim that "what is good for our companies is good for our country."

A clear implication of the competitiveness norm is that foreign producers should be treated no worse than their domestic counterparts, directly supporting the tax treaties' prohibition of discrimination on the first axis. Similarly, this norm would support the prohibition of discrimination against foreign products under the trade treaties, our third axis. The issue of whether a residence country should be able to tax companies more or less heavily on foreign production than on domestic production (the second axis) does not generally arise on this view, because foreign production should be exempt in the residence country, and subject to taxation only in the source country. A fortiori, discrimination against foreign production would be prohibited.

3. Evaluation

The competitiveness norm would seem more consistent with the current scope of prohibited discrimination than is the efficiency norm. On the other hand, the economic assumptions of arguments based on the competitiveness norm often are unstated or dubious. Without further clarification of those assumptions, it is difficult to identify many of the implications of the competitiveness norm, such as the appropriate treatment of international commerce by integration countries.

C. Equality

1. The Norm

A general prohibition of tax discrimination against international commerce is the logical concomitant of a requirement of equality of treatment for domestic and international commerce. There are substantial legal precedents for such a requirement in the United States and the European Union. * * * [But alone] such precedents do not constitute a rationale for extending into the international arena a strong requirement of equal treatment, which is simply another way of expressing a broad prohibition against nondiscrimination.

2. Implications for Discrimination

The strongest version of nondiscrimination based on a norm of equality for domestic and international commerce would go further than the current treaties on all three of the axes. Integration source countries, for example, could not collect a greater total tax on income produced by incoming investment than on income produced by domestic investment. Nor could integration residence countries collect a greater tax on income produced by outgoing investment than on income produced by domestic investment. Taking nondiscrimination more seriously in international taxation would also call into question the long-standing practice of reciprocal withholding rates, which do not achieve equal treatment of domestic and foreign investors in any particular source country. Similarly, a general requirement of nondiscrimination could prohibit a residence country from favoring domestic over foreign production by its own nationals.

The equality norm thus has both important precedents and strong implications for a prohibition of tax discrimination against international commerce. The idea of equality does not, however, provide an independent rationale for a requirement of nondiscrimination, because the latter is just another way of expressing the former. Moreover, the concept of equality, by itself, cannot be a guide to international policy, because the very idea of sovereign nations implies some differences in the treatment of domestic and foreign interests. What is needed is a set of principles on which to base limitations on that sovereignty.
* * *

NOTES

1) *A Principle in Search of a Policy.* Alvin Warren argues that efficiency does not explain the current constraints on income tax discrimination against international commerce. Indeed, he claims that efficiency—by which he means capital export neutrality—suggests that constraints should be the strongest where they have been the weakest. For Warren, competitiveness—which is often equated with capital import neutrality— offers a better rationale for the current situation, but he views the assumptions of this norm as inconsistent with the standard views of corporate tax incidence and the distortionary effects of taxation. Warren also concludes that equality neither explains the current situation nor provides an independent rationale for extension of the considerable U.S. and E.U. constraints on tax discrimination to international commerce.

2) *A Fairness Rationale.* Michael Graetz regards the idea of nondiscrimination as a fairness-based norm, grounding the idea of nondiscrimination in fairness and reciprocity:

Taking the demands of fairness seriously in the formation and implementation of tax policy is always a daunting challenge. * * * [T]he foreign tax credit was a response to concerns about unfair "double taxation" or unfairly burdensome taxation of income earned internationally. The income tax treaty requirement of nondiscrimination against foreigners was developed virtually simultaneously to guarantee fair treatment by the source country for foreigners and foreign businesses. The fundamental idea that everyone, including foreigners (once they are in the country legally), is entitled to equal treatment before the law (including the income tax law and tax treaties) is grounded in concern for fairness and mutual respect. Whether the nondiscrimination requirement of existing tax treaties also furthers worldwide economic efficiency is, at most, a secondary consideration.[10]

10. Michael J. Graetz, Taxing International Income: Inadequate Principles, Outdated Concepts, and Unsatisfactory Policies, 26 BROOKLYN J. INT'L L. 1357, 1391 (2001).

No one has yet examined in detail the relationship of fairness norms to the treaties' requirement of nondiscrimination.

3) *CEN or CIN?* The classic argument for free trade rests on the assumption that the reduction of tariffs eliminates locational distortions and thereby enhances efficiency, but tax treaties do not attempt to eradicate taxation. Rather, they seek to alleviate the burden of double taxation by assigning primary taxing authority to either the country of source or the country of residence. In this connection, policymakers and commentators have predominantly focused on two types of neutrality: capital export neutrality (CEN) and capital import neutrality (CIN). CEN advocates would allocate primary taxing power to the residence country, thereby "leveling the playing field" among investors within the same country; CIN advocates would allocate primary taxing power to the source country, thereby "leveling the playing field" among those who invest within the same country. Because nondiscrimination seeks to alleviate disparate tax burdens within a country, promoting what Peggy Musgrave has called intra-nation equity, nondiscrimination is typically understood as a CIN principle.

Robert Green, based on simplified assumptions about international capital flows, agrees that the nondiscrimination principle generally promotes CIN. Green also claims that nondiscrimination, in some situations, promotes CEN. Specifically, he argues that the "standard model" used by Warren does not explain the existence of an international nondiscrimination rule because it assumes that there are only one-way flows of investment between countries. In the article excerpted below, Green claims that if one examines cross-flows of foreign direct investment between countries, the tax treaty nondiscrimination rule "facilitates international trade in goods, services, and knowledge, and therefore magnifies the gains from trade competition." Warren notes two assumptions, which he questions, inform Green's analysis.[11] First, that the current practice of combining deferral and cross-crediting is close enough to an exemption system that the implications of the foreign tax credit can be entirely ignored; and second, that under the current regime, international investment is currently taxed more heavily than domestic investment. The latter assumption is empirical; there is some evidence that sophisticated multinationals face lower rates of taxation on international income than they do on domestic income. Emphasizing evidence to the contrary, Green contends that nondiscrimination promotes CEN because it precludes source countries from shifting a greater tax burden to foreign investments and thereby further reducing worldwide efficiency. Green also argues that by promoting "competitiveness," the nondiscrimination norm also promotes economic efficiency. The jury is still out.

11. Email from Alvin C. Warren, Harvard Law School, to Michael J. Graetz, Yale Law School (April 13, 2000) (on file with author).

Does Nondiscrimination Promote Efficiency?

Green's excerpt follows in part, as a response to Warren's arguments as well as an argument that nondiscrimination is an efficiency promoting norm.

Robert A. Green, *The Roles of the Nondiscrimination Principle in International Taxation*, NYU Colloquium on Tax Policy and Public Finance, 1, 10–45, Spring 2003.

II. Non–Discrimination, Capital Import Neutrality, and Capital Export Neutrality

This Part of the article analyzes the effects of discriminatory taxation using a very basic model of international capital flows. * * * In the model there are only two countries, R and S.

The model assumes that markets are perfectly competitive, so that all capital earns a rate of return equal to the marginal product of capital. It also assumes that the actors who make decisions about the allocation of capital have fixed amounts of capital to invest. These actors can most naturally be viewed as individuals who invest their savings, but also could be viewed as firms with fixed supplies of capital. * * *

A. *Baseline Case 1: No Taxation of Capital Income*

It is useful first to consider the baseline case in which there is no taxation of capital income. For generality, this Section makes no assumptions about the size of R and S.

In the absence of international capital mobility, residents of R would invest only in R, residents of S would invest only in S, and the marginal product of capital generally would be different in the two countries. Assume for specificity that, in this initial state, the marginal product of capital is higher in S than in R. Under competitive conditions the rate of return on capital would reflect the marginal product of capital, so capital invested in S initially would earn a higher rate of return than capital invested in R.

Now suppose that capital becomes internationally mobile. Residents of R would then move some of their capital from R to S, where it would earn a higher rate of return. This movement of capital to S would cause the marginal product of capital in S to fall—as the amount of capital invested in S increases, the marginal investment in S becomes less and less productive. Similarly, the movement of capital from R would cause the marginal product of capital in R to rise. This movement of capital would continue until the marginal product of capital was equalized in R and S at some level intermediate between the initial levels in R and S. At that point, capital would earn the same rate of return in the two countries, and so investors would no longer have any incentive to move capital from one country to the other. In this process, capital is reallocated from a country where it had a lower marginal product to a country where it has a higher marginal product, thus increasing global production. In equilibrium, there would no longer be any way to reallocate capital between the two countries in order to increase global production further. Thus, in the absence of taxation, international capital mobility leads to global production efficiency. In addition, in equilibrium, residents of R and S earn the same rate of return on investment.

The equilibrium in the no-tax case is optimal from a national perspective as well as from a global perspective. The flow of capital increases national economic welfare in R, because the residents of R who own the capital that is exported from R to S will earn foreign investment income on this capital in an amount greater than the amount of output the capital would have produced had it remained in R. * * *

Note that, in equilibrium, residents of S, as well as residents of R, would be indifferent between investing in R or in S. * * *

B. *Baseline Case II: Non–Discriminatory Source–Based Taxation*

* * * [A]ssume now that R is a "large" country and S is a "small" country, in the sense that capital flows between R and S will affect the marginal product of capital in S but not in R. Denote the marginal product of capital in R by r. Assume again, for specificity, that in the absence of international capital mobility the marginal product of capital in S would be higher than the marginal product of capital in R. * * * [W]ith international capital mobility and in the absence of taxation, capital would flow from R to S until the marginal product of capital in S was also r.

Now suppose that S imposes a tax at the effective marginal rate t on the income from all capital invested in S. This tax is non-discriminatory; that is, it applies equally to residents of R and to residents of S. For the time being, assume that R continues not to impose any taxes, either residence-based or source-based. Before any adjustment takes place, capital in S that initially earned a pre-tax rate of return r will now earn an after-tax rate of return $(1 - t)r$. Since this after-tax rate of return is less than the after-tax rate of return r that capital can still earn in R, investors will move some of their capital from S

to R. This disinvestment from S will continue until the pre-tax rate of return to capital in S rises to $r/(1-t)$. At that point, equilibrium will be restored, since investors will earn the same after-tax rate of return—r—on their capital regardless of whether it is invested in S or in R.

This source-based tax results in a violation of capital export neutrality. * * *

Capital export neutrality is violated in this case because investors face a higher effective marginal tax rate on investment in S than on investment in R. Capital export neutrality is directly related to the general goal of production efficiency. As discussed in Section A, in the absence of taxes, capital mobility will result in an international allocation of capital that maximizes global production. Thus, any tax system that violates capital export neutrality, and therefore distorts the pre-tax allocation of capital, necessarily must reduce global production. * * *

When S is a small country, the source-based tax imposed by S also reduces aggregate national welfare in S. The burden of the source-based tax imposed by S falls entirely on residents of S. Investors who are residents of R do not bear any of the burden of the tax, because they continue to earn, after taxes, the rate of return r on all of their investments. The same is true of investors who are residents of S. Instead, the burden of the tax is borne by residents of S. * * *

Given that the source-based tax imposed by S reduces aggregate economic welfare in S and is borne entirely by residents of S, one might wonder why politicians in S would enact such a tax. One reason might be fiscal illusion. Although the burden of the tax is borne by domestic labor and landowners, the tax is legally imposed on and paid by owners of capital, including foreign owners. Therefore, the tax might *appear* to be borne by owners of capital and to be exported, at least in part, to *foreign* owners of capital. * * *

C. *Discriminatory Source–Based Taxation*

Suppose now that S imposes a discriminatory tax on the income from capital invested in S. * * * [The] tax [is] at the effective marginal rate t on the income that foreign residents earn from capital invested in S, but not on the income that domestic residents earn from capital invested in S. In that case, before any adjustment takes place, residents of R will earn an after-tax rate of return $(1-t)r$ on capital invested in S. Since this is less than the after-tax rate of return r that they can earn from capital invested in R, they will start to move some of their capital from S to R. As this happens, the marginal product of capital in S will start to rise above r. But this means that residents in S, who are not subject to any tax, will earn a higher rate of return on investment in S than on investment in R. Therefore, they will start to move some of their capital from R to S, causing the marginal product of capital in S to move back down toward r. These cross-flows of capital will continue until residents of S have moved all of their capital from R back to S, and residents of R have moved an equal amount of capital from S back to R. At this point, the amount of capital in S will not have changed; only the ownership of the capital has been affected. Thus, the pre-tax rate of return to capital in S will still be r. Residents of R will then continue to move capital from S back to R, with no offsetting movement of capital in the other direction.

Depending on the initial state, one of two possible equilibria will be reached. In one, residents of R will have moved capital from S back to R until the marginal product of capital in S has risen to $r/(1 - t)$. At this point, residents of R will be indifferent between investing in R and in S. Residents of S will prefer to invest in S rather than in R, but will no longer have any capital to move back to S. In the other equilibrium, residents of R will have moved all of their capital in S back to R, but the marginal product of capital in S will remain below $r/(1 - t)$. At this point, residents of R will prefer to invest in R rather than in S, and residents of S will prefer to invest in S rather than in R, but neither will have any capital to move in the preferred direction.

This analysis is based on the assumption that S was initially a net importer of capital from R. A different equilibrium is possible if S was initially a net exporter of capital to R. In that case, cross-flows of capital would occur until residents of R had moved all of their capital from S back to R, and residents of S had moved an equal amount of capital from R back to S. * * *

D. *Implications for Traditional International Tax Policy Goals*

1. *Capital Import Neutrality*

The international tax system is said to satisfy capital import neutrality if foreign owners of capital obtain the same after-tax rate of return as domestic owners of capital on similar investments in the domestic economy. In the case analyzed in Section B, where S imposes a non-discriminatory source-based tax, foreign owners of capital (*i.e.*, residents of R investing in S or residents of S investing in R) and domestic owners of capital both earn, in equilibrium, an after-tax rate of return of r on all investments. Thus, capital import neutrality is satisfied. In contrast, in the case analyzed in Section C, where S imposes a discriminatory source-based tax, capital import neutrality can be violated. In the first equilibrium, residents of R earn an after-tax rate of return of r on investments in S, while residents of S earn the higher after-tax rate of return of $r/(1-t)$ on investments in S. The second equilibrium does not technically involve a violation of capital import neutrality as the term was defined above, because there is no cross-border investment in this equilibrium. Nevertheless, the principle underlying capital import neutrality is violated: residents of R earn an after-tax rate of return of r on investment, while residents of S earn a higher after-tax rate of return on investment (between r and $r/(1-t)$), so that the international allocation of savings is inefficient. The third equilibrium, which occurs when the source country is a net capital exporter, is the only case in which capital import neutrality is not violated. In conclusion, the discriminatory tax will often produce a violation of capital import neutrality, but the non-discriminatory tax will not.

If the international tax system achieves capital import neutrality and if capital is internationally mobile, then in equilibrium owners of capital in all countries will earn the same after-tax rate of return on investment and consequently they will face the same marginal rate of substitution between present and future consumption. As a result, there will be an efficient allocation of *savings* among countries. * * * [T]he international tax system will achieve capital import neutrality if it is based exclusively on source-based taxation, and if source countries do not discriminate between foreign and domestic investors investing in the source country. Thus, the tax treaty non-discrimination rule is a necessary element of the prescription for capital import neutrality. * * *

2. *Capital Export Neutrality*

The basic model used above assumes that there are no residence-based taxes. [T]he initial state satisfies capital export neutrality because countries impose no source-based taxes or, equivalently, impose source-based taxes at identical effective marginal rates. * * * The standard prescription for achieving capital export neutrality * * * calls for residence countries to maintain tax systems that neutralize the locational distortions caused by the differing source-country tax rates. Specifically, this prescription calls for residence countries to maintain pure foreign tax credit systems; that is, to tax residents on accrued worldwide income, and to grant residents a full credit against their domestic tax liability for any taxes paid to foreign countries on foreign source income. The requirement that residence countries tax *accrued worldwide* income means, in particular, that there must be no deferral of residence-based taxes on profits earned and retained in foreign subsidiaries. The requirement of a *full* foreign tax credit means that the residence country must not limit the foreign tax credit; indeed, if the amount of foreign tax credits exceeds the precredit residence-country tax, the residence country must refund the difference, resulting in a negative residence-country tax.

If a residence country adopts such a system, its tax system will neutralize any taxes imposed by source countries, so these taxes will have no effect on the location of investments. Thus, *any* restriction on source-country taxation would be irrelevant from the standpoint of capital export neutrality. In particular, the tax treaty non-discrimination requirement * * * would be irrelevant. * * * The appropriate rule from the standpoint of capital export neutrality would prohibit *residence* countries from discriminating on the basis of the *location* of their residents' investments. Tax treaties do not contain such a residence-based, locational non-discrimination rule. * * * [T]here appears to be complete disjunction between the form of non-discrimination rule found in tax treaties and the goal of capital export neutrality. * * *

[If] in the initial state all countries impose source-based taxes at the same rate, and if one country is considering raising its tax rate, then in some circumstances it will make no difference from the standpoint of capital export neutrality whether the increase is discriminatory, while in other circumstances the discriminatory increase will be *less* distortionary than the non-discriminatory increase. This suggests that, from the standpoint of capital export neutrality, a discriminatory tax should be *preferred* to a non-discriminatory tax at the same rate.

In practice, however, the choice will seldom be between discriminatory taxation and non-discriminatory taxation at the same rate. The relevant choice is more likely to be between a high discriminatory tax and lower non-discriminatory tax. * * * [P]oliticians are likely to find it much more attractive to impose a high tax that applies only to foreigners. * * * [T]he burden of a source-based tax imposed by a small country is borne entirely by domestic residents. With either a non-discriminatory tax or a discriminatory tax, foreign residents continue to earn the after-tax rate of return r in all equilibria, and therefore bear none of the burden of the tax. Nevertheless, * * * the government of S might find the source-based tax attractive because * * * (the tax *appears* to be borne at least in part by foreigners) or because of interest group politics. * * * [T]he discriminatory tax, which appears to be borne *exclusively* by foreigners, would be more attractive [and] * * * the discriminatory tax benefits domestic owners of capital more than the non-discriminatory tax—the non-discriminatory tax does not change the after-tax rate of return to domestically owned capital, while the discriminatory tax can raise it from r to $r/(1-t)$ when S is a net capital importer. This suggests that the * * * non-discrimination rule can play a role in promoting capital export neutrality by restraining politicians from enacting abnormally high source-based taxes applicable to foreign direct investment.

* * * [W]e must consider an initial state in which countries impose source-based taxes at heterogeneous rates. * * * [A] change in tax rates could actually reduce distortions. * * * [S]uppose that initially R imposes a source-based tax at the effective marginal rate of 40% and S imposes a source-based tax at the effective marginal rate of 20%. In the case where R is a large country, S is a small country, and capital in R earns a pre-tax rate of return of r, equilibrium will occur when the pre-tax rate of return on capital in S is $0.75r$. Given the assumption of competitive markets, in equilibrium capital in R will have a marginal product of r, and capital in S will have a marginal product of $0.75r$. Because the marginal product of capital is different in the two countries, world production is not maximized.

S would bring about an optimal allocation of capital if it were to raise its tax rate to 40%—this is the prescription of harmonizing source-based taxes. * * * But suppose that, for domestic political reasons, politicians in S are unwilling to increase the rate of taxation of domestically owned capital. An alternative would be to leave the rate applicable to domestically owned investment at 20%, but to impose a discriminatory tax of 40% on foreign-owned capital. If S was a net importer of capital, this would cause a net flow of capital from S to R, until in the new equilibrium the marginal product of capital was r in both countries. Thus, the discriminatory tax would result in an efficient allocation of capital, consistent with capital export neutrality. Th[e] question [whether discriminatory taxation will make the international allocation of capital more or less efficient, under the realistic assumption that countries initially impose source-based taxes at different effective marginal rates] can be studied systematically by comparing the pre-tax rates of return on the marginal investment (*i.e.*, the required pre-tax rates of return described in Part I) for cross-border investment with those for domestic investment. Suppose that, for a given residence country and a given source country, the required pre-tax rate of return for investment in the source country was greater than the required pre-tax rate of return for investment in the residence country. In that case, there would be a violation of capital export neutrality, and the violation would be exacerbated if the source country were to raise its effective marginal tax rate applicable to investors from the residence country. A treaty rule that restrained source countries from doing so would therefore be beneficial from the standpoint of capital export neutrality. The tax treaty non-discrimination rule provides such a restraint.

The empirical evidence indicates that, at least among OECD countries, for any residence country the required pre-tax rates of return for cross-border investment generally *are* higher than the required pre-tax rate of return for domestic investment. * * * The higher pre-tax rate of return required on foreign as compared to domestic investment is a measure of the tax system's deviation from capital export neutrality with respect to outbound investments by U.S. companies. [An] OECD report * * * shows that the international system of taxation discourages foreign companies resident in each of the other OECD countries from investing in the United States relative to investing at home. * * * To a significant extent, this bias against cross-border investment is due to discriminatory aspects of source-country tax systems that are permitted by tax treaties. For example, source countries are free to impose high withholding taxes on dividends that local subsidiaries of foreign corporations pay to the parent corporations, or to refuse to extend the benefits of integrated tax systems to foreign shareholders. The tax treaty non-discrimination rule prevents source countries from increasing this bias against cross-border investment, and therefore contributes to capital export neutrality.

In conclusion, the international tax system results in deviations from capital export neutrality in every OECD country, and the direction of the deviations is usually in favor of domestic investment over foreign investment. This means that if an OECD country were to increase its rate of taxation of foreign-owned firms, the increase generally would exacerbate the deviations from capital export neutrality. The tax treaty non-discrimination rule tends to constrain countries from doing so. This empirical survey, therefore, suggests that, at least among the OECD countries, the tax treaty non-discrimination rule generally advances the goal of capital export neutrality by constraining countries from raising taxes on foreign-owned firms.

This analysis is subject to two qualifications, however. First [is] * * * the possibility of non-compliance. If there is significantly greater tax avoidance and evasion associated with cross-border investment than with domestic investment, the international tax system in reality might be biased in favor of cross-border investment over domestic investment. * * * In this case, discriminatory taxation could actually reduce the deviations from capital export neutrality. This suggests in particular that violations of the non-discrimination rule might sometimes be justified on the ground that they are needed because of the difficulties of enforcing a tax on foreign investors.

Second, the results of the studies show substantial variation from country to country in required pre-tax rates of return. Multinationals often have flexibility to take advantage of this variation by choosing the most tax-favored locations for their investment. Moreover, even where the *general* tax systems of countries tend to favor domestic investment over cross-border investment, countries sometimes offer preferential tax regimes * * * *in favor* of foreign investors. [T]hey result in a deviation from capital export neutrality that is in the opposite direction from the usual deviation. In this case, the appropriate non-discrimination rule for promoting capital export neutrality would be one prohibiting discrimination *in favor* of foreign firms. This would involve an extension of the tax treaty non-discrimination rule, which prohibits only discrimination *against* foreign firms.

3. *Summary*

* * * [T]he tax treaty non-discrimination rule is necessary to achieving capital import neutrality [and] * * * under reasonable assumptions, * * * leads to the conclusion that the tax treaty non-discrimination rule often tends to promote capital export neutrality as well.

III. Competitiveness, Multinational Firms, and Non–Discrimination

* * * If one accepts th[e] argument that discriminatory or differential taxation will tend to cause low-taxed firms to drive high-taxed firms from the market, one might still go on to ask why this outcome should be a matter of national concern. Warren [has asked this question]. * * *

This question could be given a * * * satisfactory answer if the "competitiveness" argument could be recharacterized as an efficiency argument. * * *

[F]oreign firms often will be able to realize the benefits of their firm-specific advantages only if they can extend their control through foreign direct investment. This means that discriminatory taxation will not merely shift control of investments from one firm to another that differs only in residence or nationality. Instead, it can shift control over investments from a firm that would operate the investments more productively to one that will operate them less productively.

This will happen as long as the discriminatory tax raises the more productive firm's required pre-tax rate of return by an

amount that more than offsets the advantage that the firm had
because of its greater productivity (which would be reflected, if
all else were equal, in a lower required pre-tax rate of return).
* * *

* * * [E]xcluding otherwise competitive foreign firms from
the domestic market, discriminatory taxation can cause further
inefficiencies as well. It can reduce opportunities for the excluded firms to achieve economies of scale and scope. In addition, it
can make the market in the source country less efficient by
reducing competition.

Another way to see the efficiency costs of discriminatory
taxation is to conceptualize foreign direct investment as a
device for facilitating international trade. When arm's length
transactions among unrelated parties are replaced by transactions among affiliates of a multinational enterprise, transaction
costs can often be reduced; this is part of the reason that
multinationals exist in the first place. In some cases, transactions that would not occur at all in arm's length transactions
might be feasible if carried out between affiliates of a multinational enterprise. In particular, it is often difficult or impossible to trade knowledge or goods that embody intellectual capital in arm's length transactions, due to problems of markets in
information. Therefore, the well known benefits of free trade,
resulting from comparative advantage, economies of scale, and
increased competition, will be enhanced if multinational enterprises are permitted to invest in all markets on an equal
footing with domestic firms. In particular, this requires a commitment to non-discrimination in international taxation.

It is difficult to quantify the extent to which these industri-
al-organization related benefits are enhanced by a non-discrimination rule. Ultimately, however, these enhanced benefits might
be the most persuasive rationale for the tax treaty non-discrimination rule, rather than the benefits that the rule produces by
promoting the more traditional international tax policy goals of
capital export neutrality or capital import neutrality. * * *

Conclusion

* * * [The] non-discrimination rule tends to promote efficiency * * * [by] promot[ing] capital import neutrality. * * *
[T]hough capital import neutrality and capital export neutrality
are often perceived to be incompatible goals, the tax treaty nondiscrimination rule also tends to promote capital export neutrality in many situations. In addition, the "competitiveness"
argument leads to an efficiency argument: by prohibiting discrimination against foreign multinational enterprises, the nondiscrimination rule facilitates international trade in goods, ser-

vices, and knowledge, and therefore magnifies the gains from trade that result from comparative advantage, economies of scale, and enhanced competition.

10.4 LOCATIONAL NEUTRALITY

Because state and local governments exercise taxing power alongside the federal government, the threat of discriminatory taxation exists in the domestic as well as the international sphere. The CEN norm also emerges in the domestic context, albeit under the label of locational neutrality. Within the federalist paradigm, in the following excerpt Daniel Shaviro considers what he regards as the primary theoretical goal underlying the nondiscrimination principle: locational neutrality.

Daniel Shaviro, *An Economic and Political Look at Federalism in Taxation*, 90 MICH. L. REV. 895, 898–929 (1992)

Tariffs, Taxes, and Locational Neutrality

* * * [T]he principal argument for attaching such great importance to locational neutrality is one of efficiency. As an economic matter, all else being equal * * * it is optimal that the tax levied on a given amount of profit or a given taxpayer be invariant with regard to where property or persons are located. * * * [U]nder standard economic assumptions, locational neutrality minimizes the real social costs of production and ensures that low-cost producers will out-compete high-cost but otherwise equivalent producers. * * *

B. *The Definition of a Tax and Its Significance for Locational Neutrality*

* * * Conceptually, a locationally efficient tax is one that does not affect people's decisions about where to live, travel, invest, and so forth. * * * [A] locationally equitable tax is one in which real tax burdens do not vary with location, and therefore are the same as under a uniform national taxing scheme. * * *

C. *The Comparative Value of Locational Neutrality*

Even if one accepts the view that taxes should usually be neutral, locational neutrality presents special complexities and difficulties. The key difference between it and, say, neutral treatment of different types of investment income under an income tax is that the cost and value of the services people receive in different geographical areas from the operation of their state and local governments are likely to differ, whereas there may be no reason to expect differences in the government services that holders of different types of investments receive.

* * * Governments that charge more taxes often may provide more value in the form of services, and may be able to direct most of this value to resident taxpayers. These residents, in their capacity as voters, rationally may take a different view of taxes than in their capacity as taxpayers. A voter is helping to determine everyone's tax burden, not just her own, and therefore has less reason to be tax-averse. Voting for higher taxes does not automatically create an externality problem: one may receive significantly more services if everyone pays more. * * * If a government provides insufficient value in exchange for the taxes it extracts, residents may be able to "vote with their feet" by leaving. If exit costs are sufficiently low, state and local taxes *are* user fees, voluntarily exchanged for the state or local government's service package.

Thus, higher taxes in one jurisdiction are not locationally inequitable to the extent that those paying the higher taxes also receive greater value from government services, and are not locationally inefficient to the extent that this value is effectively linked to the payment of tax. * * *

* * * [O]ne particular form of locational disparity merits special attention: the problem of tax exportation, which occurs when governments succeed in placing tax burdens on outsiders. * * * [T]ax exportation may pose unusually serious equity and efficiency problems by placing tax burdens on what may often be non-consenting non-beneficiaries.

* * * Differences in tax level may arise, however, even if people in all jurisdictions have identical preferences. The social costs of what all deem to be essential services may vary, * * * [and m]any of these differences would efficiently be reflected in user fees varying with location if it were feasible to finance all government operations through user fees rather than taxes. How, then, can it be argued that locational neutrality, rather than a system of highly nuanced variation in local tax levels, is optimally efficient?

The answer to this challenge, in part, is that locationally neutral taxation concededly is not optimally efficient. No taxation can be, given that it is an imperfect substitute for user fees, made necessary by the public goods problem. The argument for locationally neutral taxation * * * is * * * that absent differences on the service side taxes should be neutral and minimize behavioral responses. * * *

D.   *Broader Ramifications of Locational Neutrality*

1.   *Differences Between Tax Systems as Inherently Distortive*

* * * In a locationally neutral system, the level, kinds, and geographical distribution of all activity would be the same as if the country had a uniform national taxing system, disregarding any effects that such a reallocation of taxing authority would have on the types of taxes levied or tax rates. Unfortunately, this notional touchstone for measuring locational neutrality is not only abstract and counterfactual, but utterly unattainable other than by actually establishing a uniform national taxing system. Consider the administrative and compliance effects of having federal rather than national taxation. The existence of multiple taxing authorities * * * inevitably creates burden, unevenly distributed among taxpayers, that changes outcomes.

* * * As soon as there are any differences in the taxes levied by such jurisdictions, locational neutrality disappears. * * * Tax base disparities present obvious planning opportunities for both taxpayers and governments. The taxpayer side of maximizing after-tax returns by minimizing tax liability is obvious. The government side is significant as well, however. [For example,] states can choose tax bases that seem likely to draw tax revenues from outsiders. * * *

* * * [D]isparities in state and local taxation would defeat locational neutrality even if no person was present in more than one jurisdiction. When taxpayers straddle jurisdictions and thus become directly subject to more than one tax system, the disparities grow worse. * * * For each of the major taxes widely employed at the state and local level, a set of coordination problems between jurisdictions, commonly lacking easy solution, has emerged over the years. These problems involve determining which states have taxing authority, and to what degree, over a particular taxpayer or transaction, as well as how one state's exercise of authority should affect another's. Imperfect coordination, which often is unavoidable, tends to distort taxpayers' choices regarding entry into multiple jurisdictions. * * *

2. *Multi-jurisdictional Coordination Problems*

a. *Personal income taxes*

If income could be taxed only in the state where it was earned and the identity of that state were always clear, the personal income tax might present no coordination problems. At the other extreme, if all states could and did tax all income, regardless of whether the earner or earning activity had any connection with the taxing state, coordination problems would not arise. In that instance, multiple taxation would be a fact of life to which all persons were subject without regard to their locational decisions.

[However,] [s]tates can and do tax their residents on all income, and nonresidents on income earned within the state. The resulting threat of double taxation when a taxpayer resides in one state and earns income in other states is widely addressed by tax credits for liability incurred elsewhere, or by states' declining to exercise their full taxing powers. However, these countermeasures are not constitutionally required, are not universally employed, and provide incomplete protection due to built-in limitations and disparities in their application. * * *

B. *Business taxes*

Stat[e] * * * taxes on * * * business entities * * * commonly resemble general income, property, or sales taxes in that they are based on a measure of the taxpayer's profits, value, or gross receipts. Thus, they present many of the same coordination problems as these provisions, but in a particularly significant setting, given that legal entities such as corporations do such a large share of the interstate business in this country.

Taxing companies that are involved in interstate business would present no coordination problems if each company could neatly be divided, such that each piece belonged for tax purposes to one state. Where the proper lines of division are unclear, however, some pieces may be taxed more than once or not at all, leading to over-or under-taxation of interstate business relative to other business. * * * [The Supreme Court] now holds that interstate business may be taxed, whether directly or indirectly, but that the Commerce Clause bars undue relative burdens on such commerce, such as duplicative "multiple" taxation.

The differences between the tax bases of profits, value, and gross receipts, along with the difficulty of defining each, guarantee that states will not achieve the outcome of taxing everything exactly once. States can opportunistically choose whatever base, within the permissible range, appears most favorable to themselves, and thereby collectively engage in effective multiple taxation. Businesses can opportunistically exploit disparities in state tax bases in the effort to avoid even single taxation. * * *

Coordination problems would remain even under a uniform tax base, however, because for large interstate businesses there often is no definite place where gross receipts or income are earned or value exists. The problems go to substance, not just administration or record keeping. For example, consider a merger between two previously separate businesses in different states, creating synergies, * * * the increased value and income resulting from the synergy * * * not inherently belong[ing] to either state. * * * [F]actors of production in more than one state are deployed cooperatively [and] that which is being taxed may have no "real" location. * * *

The difficulty of determining where income, value, or gross receipts are located need not prevent the development of a set of consistent and plausible allocation rules. Such a set of rules may impose social costs * * * but at least the rules might solve the basic coordination problem of multiple or nontaxation of a portion of the tax base.

* * * [A]t least in principle, extraterritorial value cannot be taxed. Where in-state and out-of-state operations, even if conducted by separate corporations that belong to the same control group, constitute a "unitary business," however—another not very demanding standard that affects incentives at the margin—the state can use any number of apportionment methods in identifying the in-state component that is subject to tax.

* * * [S]tates can choose their apportionment standards opportunistically and make overlapping or inconsistent claims, although this will not necessarily lead collectively to over-taxation of interstate business relative to intrastate business. Businesses also can respond opportunistically * * *—for example, by tax planning to minimize liability, deploying superior resources to win contested factual issues at audit, and applying in-state political pressure, backed by the threat of leaving, to obtain favorable rules. * * *

E. *Responding to the Problems Caused by Locational Disparity*

* * * Differences between state and local tax systems also give rise to serious coordination problems, potentially inducing taxpayers to seek or avoid a multi-jurisdictional presence purely for tax reasons, and presenting strategic opportunities, as for tax exportation or protectionism, to state and local governments. Such differences also impose massive costs of compliance, administration, tax planning, politicking, and litigation.

* * * [E]ven if the tax burdens on intrastate and interstate activity are roughly equivalent overall, the result may still be allocatively inefficient. Opposing inefficiencies of over-and un-der-taxation of interstate commerce in different sectors of the economy may compound each other as distortions, rather than cancel each other out. Moreover, shifts between interstate and intrastate commerce are only one category of allocative ineffici-ency resulting from federalism in taxation. Other examples include the shifting of investment to low-tax jurisdictions, to activities whose proper apportionment between jurisdictions is unclear and manipulable, and to more mobile forms of capital, which can flee when jurisdictions raise their taxes.

Costly departures from locational neutrality are inevitable under a federal system. * * * How are we to define and identify impermissible departures from locational neutrality, given that many departures will be permitted? Particularly if courts are in charge of applying the anti-tariff principle, some sort of general legal standard is needed. * * *

The legal standard most widely accepted in this area is one barring discrimination against outsiders or interstate commerce. The leading * * * [case], *Complete Auto Transit, Inc. v. Brady,* lists four requirements for upholding such taxes, the most stringent and important of which is the absence of discrimination against interstate commerce. [However, w]hat constitutes discrimination against outsiders or interstate commerce is far from clear.

NOTES

1) *Locational Neutrality.* Whatever its theoretical appeal, locational neutrality is unattainable in the United States other than by actually establishing a uniform national taxing system applicable to all of the states and unattainable among nations in the absence of uniform world income taxes. Indeed the hurdles are compounded in the international context where taxing regimes are often drastically different, markets are not readily integrated, and the value of currencies and interest rates are subject to considerable fluctuation. Treaties may seek to harmonize incongruencies; yet worldwide locational neutrality is not a realizable goal. Moreover, harmonization of taxes may seriously conflict with the principle of sovereignty, as Chapter 11 illustrates.

2) *Does Nondiscrimination Provide an Answer?* While the nondiscrimination principle has been adopted as the controlling legal norm in the federalist context, its content and purpose has proven almost as illusory there as in the international context. After reviewing the cases and the relevant academic literature, and noting that the Supreme Court has itself described its Commerce Clause jurisprudence as a "quagmire," Edward Zelinsky recommends abandoning the nondiscrimination principle in U.S. taxation.

Edward A. Zelinsky, *Restoring Politics to the Commerce Clause: The Case for Abandoning the Dormant Commerce Clause Prohibition on Discriminatory Taxation*, 4 TAX L. & POL'Y 1, 2 (2003).

The doctrinal problems of the dormant Commerce Clause nondiscrimination principle are insurmountable. Despite the extensive efforts of judges and scholars, we cannot, for these purposes distinguish convincingly between taxes and equivalent direct subsidies nor have we found workable standards with which to differentiate between those state taxes which are discriminatory and those which are not. [A]t the core of the Commerce Clause nondiscrimination principle, that principle is indeterminate.

In light of this logistical indeterminacy, the only plausible courses before the Court today are the abandonment of the nondiscrimination principle in the context of state taxes or the unprecedented expansion of the dormant Commerce Clause to cover states' and localities' direct expenditure programs.

* * * [R]ather than enlarging the scope of the nondiscrimination principle to an unprecedented scope, the Court should abandon that principle as to taxation.

As in the international context, the nondiscrimination rule is enforced highly selectively: Outsiders are compared to insiders as they stand, and outsiders are considered victims of discrimination if, in cases where members of the two groups are alike in some relevant sense, the tax system treats the outsiders worse, either by directly taxing them more or otherwise by imposing a burden that places them at a competitive disadvantage.

10.5 NONDISCRIMINATION IN THE EUROPEAN COMMUNITY

Nowhere in international tax law has the principle of nondiscrimination had a more important role in recent years than in the European Union. The European Court of Justice has been quite active in overturning member states' taxing measures as violating the Treaty of Rome. There is a rapidly growing body of case law by the European Court of Justice that applies nondiscrimination principles to national tax laws in interpreting the European Union's treaties.

Specifically, the EU Treaty prohibits discrimination on the ground of nationality and further guarantees the "four freedoms": the freedom of movement of people, the freedom of establishment, the freedom to provide goods and services, and the freedom of movement of capital. International income tax systems are at risk of violating these provisions since they often treat nonresidents differently from residents. In the following selection, Kees van Raad reviews some of the ECJ decisions and proposes a method to overcome differential treatment of nonresident taxpayers where significant disparities among tax systems exist.

Kees van Raad, *Non-Discriminatory Income Taxation of Non–Resident Taxpayers By Member States of the European Union: A Proposal*, 26 BROOKLYN J. INT'L LAW 1481, 1482–1492 (2001).

In its 1995 decision in *Wielockx*, the Court of Justice * * * observed that * * * while the income tax law among the EU

Member States hardly has been harmonized, it must meet the requirements regarding non-discrimination laid down in the EC Treaty rules on the fundamental freedom of movement. These rules went largely unnoticed by the Member States' legislators and executives until * * * the EC Court issued its first decision on the compatibility of a domestic income tax rule of a EU Member State with the fundamental freedom of movement provisions of the EC Treaty. * * * About half of [twenty subsequent decisions on the issue] * * * deal with the question of whether the tax treatment of non-resident taxpayers, as compared to resident taxpayers, meets the non-discrimination standards of the freedom of movement provisions of the EC Treaty.

* * * It should be noted that, while "nationality" generally is not used by EU Member States as a relevant criterion in the taxation of individuals, the EC Court has interpreted the Treaty's prohibition on discrimination on the basis of nationality as forbidding not only overt discrimination on the basis of nationality, but also covert forms of such discrimination. * * *

The pattern that arises from the various decisions by the EC Court on the tax treatment by source states of non-resident taxpayers is not entirely coherent. * * *

Gross Income Items and Deductible (Business) Expenses

The EC Court has not yet decided any case that directly deals with the issues: (1) whether a source country may tax a nonresident taxpayer on items of income in respect of which residents of that country are not taxed (e.g., non-business capital gains, in respect of which in a given country resident individuals are not subject to tax, are taxed to non-resident individuals that derive such a gain); and, (2) whether a source country may deny to a nonresident taxpayer a (business) deduction in respect of a given item of income to which a resident taxpayer is entitled (e.g., while resident employees are entitled to a deduction for commuting expenses, frontier workers who are resident of the other country are denied such a deduction).

While there is indeed no precise case on point, from the Court's decision in *Avoir Fiscal*, it may be derived that the Court interprets the EC Treaty's freedom rules as indeed requiring equal treatment of non-resident and resident taxpayers with regard to both the taxable items of income and the deductibility of expenses.[12] The Court ruled that:

12. The *Avoir Fiscal* decision dealt with the denial by France of the imputation credit that it grants to its resident (corporate and individual) shareholders, to a company that was a resident of Italy and that operated in France through a permanent establishment whose business capital included the French shares concerned.

Since the rules at issue place resident companies and [non-resident] companies on the same footing for the purposes of taxing their profits, those rules cannot, without giving rise to discrimination, treat them differently in regard to the grant of an advantage related to taxation such as shareholders' tax credits.

* * * France, unlike most countries, does not subject resident companies to tax in respect of foreign source income. Strictly speaking, there is, therefore, no difference between the income in respect of which resident companies and non-resident companies are liable to tax. In effect * * * the denial of the imputation credit to non-resident shareholders results in a taxation of non-resident taxpayers * * * less favorabl[y] than the taxation of resident taxpayers on the same type of income. * * * The *Avoir Fiscal* decision provides a strong indication of the Court's feeling vis-à-vis cases in which items of income of gain of non-resident taxpayers are subjected to less favorable taxation than such income and gains that are in the hands of residents.

Where dividends, interest, and royalties are concerned (and in some states also other items of income) that typically are taxed to non-residents on a gross basis (and at a flat rate), the Court may take a different approach. By not taxing such items on a net basis as is done where resident taxpayers are concerned, discrimination arises in cases where the amount of tax that would be due under a net basis is lower than the gross-basis tax.

Personal Deductions

In its *Schumacker* and *Wielockx* decisions, the EC Court ruled that a source state must grant personal deductions to non-resident taxpayers if they derive their worldwide income "entirely or almost exclusively" from sources in that country. The Court based its decision on the reasoning that such taxpayers cannot effectuate their personal deductions in their residence state in the absence of (adequate) income from that country. These decisions are in line with the 1993 Recommendation of the EC Commission that non-resident taxpayers, who derive at least 75 percent of their worldwide income from the source country, are entitled to taxation by that country on equal footing with resident taxpayers.

By restricting its ruling to taxpayers who derive all, or virtually all, their income from a country other than their country of residence, it left unrelieved all cases where a taxpayer derives all, or virtually all, of his worldwide income from more than one non-residence state, as well as cases where the fraction of a taxpayer's foreign income is lower, but still too high to be able to obtain full relief in his residence country. Unlike the Court's (probable) treatment of items of gross income and related expenses, the Court's rulings on personal deductions fall short of providing adequate relief.

Tax Rate

The first case decided by the EC Court of Justice, on possible discriminatory application of tax rates, was *Biehl.* * * * Biehl was a resident of Luxembourg for only a part of the taxable year concerned. The issue was whether * * * Luxembourg was allowed to refer to the income that the taxpayer would have earned in the entire taxable year (12 months), while the given individual earned his monthly salary only during a period of 10 months. This issue has some similarity to the question whether, with regard to the taxation of non-resident individuals, a source country may determine the applicable individual income tax rate on the basis of the worldwide income of the non-resident taxpayer rather than on the income this person derives from the source country only.

In its *Biehl* decision, the Court ruled that to determine the appropriate tax rate, Luxembourg only might take into account the income the taxpayer earned during the part of the year that he lived and worked in Luxembourg. On the basis of this ruling it may be concluded that also the country to which the taxpayer moved from Luxembourg (i.e., Germany) would be allowed, in determining the applicable tax rate, to take into account only the income earned in that country. As a result, Mr. Biehl would not only pay a lower effective tax on the income earned in his first residence country (Luxembourg)—in comparison to a taxpayer that earns during the entire taxable year the same amount of income as Mr. Biehl earns in the first and second country combined—but Mr. Biehl also pays less tax in his new residence country (i.e., Germany) than a full year resident of that country would pay on the same monthly income earned during the months that Mr. Biehl resides and works in Germany. As a result of the Court's ruling, Mr. Biehl is treated by each of the two countries more favorably than either a Luxembourg or a German resident taxpayer who earns exactly the same monthly salary in the given year as Mr. Biehl does.

A few years later the Court took the same approach in the *Asscher* case. This case * * * concern[ed] a person * * * who received a part of his income from sources in one EU Member State (the Netherlands) [but was] a resident of another EU Member State (Belgium) where he also derived income. * * * One of the arguments forwarded by the Netherlands was that non-resident and resident taxpayers are, with regard to rate application, not in the same position because the tax rate to which resident taxpayers are subject in respect of their Netherlands-source income is upwardly adjusted by the amount of their foreign income with respect to which they are entitled to an exemption from Dutch taxation. It, therefore, should be considered non-discriminatory if, in determining the tax rate at which non-resident taxpayers are subject to Dutch taxation, non-Dutch income is taken into account. (It should be noted, however, that rather than effectively requiring non-residents to report their foreign source income for purposes of establishing the applicable tax rate, the Netherlands simply applied a somewhat higher first bracket rate than it applied to resident taxpayers.)

The EC Court ruled that the Netherlands might not apply to nonresident taxpayers a higher tax rate than it applies to resident taxpayers in order to take into account that the nonresident may have received items of income from other countries. It is not known, of course, whether the Court would have decided differently if the source state (the Netherlands) would have applied to nonresident taxpayers not a generally applicable approximating rate but, on a case-by-case basis, a rate based on the worldwide income of the nonresident taxpayers (as, for example, Switzerland does). From the Court's approach in the *Biehl* case, however, it does not seem likely that the judgment would have been different. The *Asscher* ruling itself provides an indication for such a conclusion. The ground for the Court's decision appears not to be the general applicability of a higher rate (instead of an application on a case-by-case basis), but the (incorrect) belief of the Court that, since Belgium as a residence country provides an exemption with progression, there is no need for the Netherlands to take into account in determining the applicable tax rate the income derived by the taxpayer from sources in Belgium or third countries.

According to the Netherlands Government, the higher rate of tax is intended to offset the fact that certain non-residents escape the progressive nature of the tax because their tax obligations are confined to income received in the Netherlands.

It must be noted that, under Article 24(2)(1) of the [tax treaty between the Netherlands and Belgium], modeled on Article 23A(1) and (3) of the OECD Model Convention (exemption with maintenance of progressivity), income received in a State in which the taxpayer pursues an economic activity but does not reside is taxable exclusively in that State and exempt in the State of residence. The State in which the taxpayer resides may nevertheless take that income into account in calculating the amount of tax on the remaining income in order, inter alia, to apply the rule of progressivity.

The fact that a taxpayer is a non-resident thus does not enable him, in the circumstances under consideration, to escape the application of the rule of progressivity. In other words, the Court believes (again, incorrectly) that since Belgium as the residence country takes into account the Netherlands source income in determining the appropriate tax rate on the Belgian part of the income, there is no need for the Netherlands to do the same in respect of the Netherlands part of the income. The Court thus demonstrates a complete lack of understanding of the operation of "exemption with progression" as applied by many exemption countries in determining the amount of double taxation relief.

A simple example may illustrate the foregoing. Let us assume that both EU Member States R(esidence) and S(ource) apply in their individual income taxes the following rate structure: On the first income slice of 10 the tax rate is 0% (tax on this slice amounts to 0). On the second income slice of 10 the tax rate is 10% (tax on this slice amounts to 1). On the third income slice of 10 the tax rate is 20% (tax on this slice amounts to 2). On the fourth income slice of 10 the tax rate is 30% (tax on this slice amounts to 3). On the fifth income slice of 10 the tax rate is 40% (tax on this slice amounts to 4).

The tax due by a State R resident, who has income of 50 that is entirely derived from sources in State R, therefore amounts to $0 + 1 + 2 + 3 + 4 = 10$. (The same is true for a resident of State S who receives income amounting to 50 from sources in State S). If the State R resident derives of his worldwide income of 50, an amount of 20 from sources in State S, and State R relieves double taxation through "proportional tax exemption" (often, imprecisely referred to as "exemption with progression") State R will compute the amount of the tax reduction as follows: $20/50 \times 10 = 4$, indeed resulting in tax to be paid of $10 - 4 = 6$.

It will be clear that if State S, which is assumed to apply exactly the same tax rates as State R, will subject the income that is sourced in State S (20) to a tax of 4 only if it would take into account in determining the applicable tax rate not only the 20 of income derived from sources within its territory, but also—as Switzerland does—the 30 income from State R, and computes the amount of tax by deducting from the tax computed in respect of the worldwide income of 50 (10), that part of the tax of 10 that refers to the income derived from sources in State

W (30/50 × 10 = 6), resulting in a tax to be paid to State S of 10 − 4 = 6.

Instead of having State S apply such an "exemption with progression," an equitable result also would be obtained if State R would apply an "exemption at the bottom," i.e., reducing its tax computed on the basis of the worldwide income by that part of such tax that would have been imposed on income that the taxpayer derives from the source country (i.e., 1). In this approach State R would compute the tax to be paid as follows: 10 − 1 = 9.

The problem, illustrated in the preceding paragraph, with the divergence between the taxation by the source state and the relief granted by the residence state, is not so much the difference in the tax amounts as such (such difference will always arise where states apply different tax rates and compute taxable income differently), but the difference in the computation of these amounts: The source state computes the tax at the bottom of the progressive rate scale whereas the residence state provides an exemption at a (higher) average rate reflecting the worldwide income. The same phenomenon may occur when the residence state applies the foreign tax credit, namely when the limit on the credit ("ordinary credit") is computed through a proportional allocation of the domestic tax to the foreign income and this limit applies in the given case, while the source country applies its tax rate without taking into account any income the taxpayer receives from sources elsewhere.

Proposal

The various issues that have been highlighted in the preceding paragraphs can be solved if each of the EU Member States, from which a non-resident individual derives income, treats this individual pro rata parte with regard to the taxable items of income and related deductible expenses, the personal deductions, and the tax rate on the same footing with a resident taxpayer. At the same time, the residence state of this individual should restrict his right to personal deductions to that fraction thereof that is equal to the fraction: aggregate amount of income items derived from sources in his residence State divided by worldwide income.

Source states can effect such a pro rata parte approach only if they have at their disposal the necessary information with regard to the amount of income the non-resident taxpayer derives from sources abroad, along with the data required for computing his personal deductions. Because both types of information are not available in the source country, and need to be provided by the taxpayer, the source state may want to be able

to verify such data. The EC 1977 Directive on Mutual Administrative Assistance provides the means to verify the information
produced by the taxpayer. It is clear, however, that the administrative burden for the source state in making such verification
is relatively great. It, therefore, seems preferable to restrict the
application of the pro rata parte approach to instances where
the taxpayer so requests (i.e., makes such a request to all
(source) states from which he derives income) and, in the
absence of such a request, to permit the source states: (a) to tax
capital income (and perhaps employment income as well) on a
gross basis; (b) not to permit personal deductions; and, (c) to
apply tax rates, the lowest of which is higher (e.g., 30%) than
the lowest rate applicable to resident taxpayers.

The pro rata parte approach by the source State implies
that this State first determines the taxable income of the
pertinent non-resident taxpayer fully in accordance with the
rules that apply to residents of that State. The tax computed on
the basis of that income subsequently will be restricted to that
part thereof that is determined by the fraction: Net income from
sources in the source state divided by net worldwide income.
Both the numerator and the denominator of this fraction are
determined on the basis of the tax law of the source state.
Consequently, a taxpayer who is a resident of one EU Member
State and who receives, in addition to income from sources in
the residence state, income from two other EU Member States,
and who opts for taxation by the source states on a pro rata
parte basis, needs to compute his worldwide income under as
many tax systems as there are EU Member states from which
he derives income. The denominator of the fraction (the amount
of the worldwide income), therefore, will differ from country to
country. In this "slice of the pie" approach, the various slices
will not, as a result of the existing differences among the tax
systems of the individual states, jointly form a nice round pie.
Given the differences among the tax systems, however, this
approach represents the highest possible degree of equal treatment of a nonresident taxpayer with resident taxpayers of each
of the countries concerned, because in each source state the
non-resident is treated pro rata parte on equal footing with
resident taxpayers.

An important issue is presented by how much the tax rate
that source states may impose on non-resident taxpayers, that
do not opt for taxation at a pro rata parte basis, may exceed the
tax rate applicable to resident taxpayers of that state. Apart
from the extra effort that the exercise by the taxpayer of the
option to be taxed proportionally as a resident taxpayer means
for him, his choice whether or not to exercise this option will be

guided by any resulting tax savings that the option produces over gross basis taxation by the source state. Such saving may occur on the one hand as a result of the difference between the gross and the net amount of the income, and on the other hand because of the difference between the regular tax rate and the flat rate that is applied to non-opting non-residents.

NOTES

1) *Freedom of Movement of Capital*. The ECJ's June 6, 2000 *Staatssecretaris van Financiň v. B.G.M. Verkooijen* decision further elaborated the EU's principle of nondiscrimination. This case held the Dutch government in breach of the freedom of movement of capital guarantee due to an income tax provision exempting part or all of Dutch dividends distributed to Dutch residents from Dutch companies, while failing to provide a similar exemption for dividends received by Dutch residents from companies resident in other EU countries. The ECJ made clear that nondiscrimination provisions in bilateral income tax treaties (within the EU) applied to the disparate taxation of corporate dividends. The ECJ rejected the Dutch argument that the exemption was to avoid double taxation in the Netherlands of the same profits, and that its extension to dividends out of profits not taxed in the Netherlands would interfere with the cohesion of the Dutch tax system. Instead, the ECJ regarded the corporate and shareholder taxes as two different taxes involving two different taxpayers. The ECJ regarded as irrelevant the fact—and the fiscal import—that the Netherlands collected corporate income taxes only from companies resident in the Netherlands. The Netherlands, joined by the United Kingdom, also argued that the EC Treaty permitted distinctions between resident and nonresident taxpayers with regard to the location of invested capital. The Court, however, ruled that this principle could not be used as a means of "arbitrary" discrimination or restriction on the free movement of capital. The ECJ concluded that the Dutch government's economic goal did not constitute an overriding reason justifying a measure contrary to the principle of free movement of capital. In doing so, the ECJ has raised a serious challenge to the continued independence of member states' taxing authority.

2) *A Workable System*. Kees van Raad's proposal suggests that there may be better approaches to equitable treatment of nonresident taxpayers. As he emphasizes in his concluding comments, the increasing mobility of individuals and the rising awareness of the disparate tax practices by states in dealing with cross-border income makes a search for novel approaches in the taxation of such income increasingly worthwhile. The following excerpt, however, demonstrates that achieving nondiscrimination in the context of so-called imputation systems, where shareholders are allowed credits for all or part of corporate-level taxes, is far from straightforward.

Confédération Fiscale Européene, Opinion Statement on the Consequences of the *Verkooijen* Judgement, to the European Commission in 2002.

Since June 2000 when the judgment was handed down, some European countries have amended their laws and have taken the opportunity to end the differences in the treatment of foreign dividends as compared to domestic dividends. * * * [Only Germany and Luxembourg have] extended the same treatment to all foreign dividends, regardless of their source. France has also recently changed some rules in order to take the *Verkooijen* case into account, although with a limited scope, which means that it is still among the countries that do not treat domestic and EU dividends in the same way. It seems that Italy is also considering abolishing the imputation system. * * *

* * * It is obvious that, in the case of imputation countries, the main obstacle to compliance with the judgment—i.e. applying the same treatment to all EU dividends—is how to apply the imputation mechanism to a corporate tax that is not the one for which the imputation mechanism was originally designed. The simplest way would be to treat the foreign dividend in exactly the same way as the domestic dividend, by applying the same mechanism to all dividends.

Of course, this could result in a somewhat inaccurate (or incomplete) prevention of economic double taxation, since in the other 14 Member States; the actual corporate income tax rate is not exactly the tax rate for which the national imputation mechanism was originally designed. In some countries it might be higher and in other countries it might be lower. Thus, a slight distortion in the economic effect could occur. But, with respect to discriminatory treatment, it would certainly be avoided (even if a distortion of capital markets would appear). Moreover, the nominal tax rates in the 15 Member States have become gradually approximated. A more accurate solution could be for every company in a Member State with shareholders resident in other Member States to communicate to its shareholders the rate that has been applied to the profits out of which the relevant dividend is paid. The state of residence of the shareholder then should apply to the dividend the same mechanism it applies to domestic dividends but adjusted to the rate effectively borne by the EU company. The greater accuracy of this method, however, may be outweighed by its lack of practicality.

* * * [However,] nominal rates do not reflect the differences in the effective tax burden that falls on a company in the different Member States, because of the differences in the tax

base. But again, the lack of harmonization in this regard makes it impossible to know the exact tax burden.

* * * A third solution * * * consists in giving non-residents a refund of corporation tax equivalent to the tax credit. * * * [This may result, however,] in a double relief: that is the case where the source country grants the credit to the shareholder and in the country of residence of the shareholder the applicable method is that of exemption.

NOTE

President Bush's Dividend Exclusion Proposal. In response to decisions of the European Court of Justice, some European countries, most notably Germany, have moved away from imputation methods of integrating corporate and shareholder taxes to an exclusion of all or part of dividends from shareholders' income. The German exclusion applies equally to dividends from domestic and foreign companies. In 2003, President Bush proposed a dividend exclusion for the United States, which would treat dividends from foreign companies less favorably than dividends from U.S. companies when received by U.S. residents and citizens. Obviously, the United States need not heed decisions of the ECJ. The question arises, however, whether such a distinction would—or should— violate the nondiscrimination clauses of bilateral U.S. tax treaties. This question was avoided when, instead of exempting dividends, the 2003 legislation adopted a maximum tax rate of 15% applicable to dividends from both domestic and foreign companies.

10.6 RETHINKING THE GOALS OF NONDISCRIMINATION

As David Rosenbloom suggests, countries host to foreign direct investment may want to discriminate (or at least may find that they must discriminate in order to enforce their tax laws dealing with inbound investment). Rosenbloom argues in the final selection of this Chapter that the treaty nondiscrimination rule should be omitted, scaled back, or made a government-to-government commitment with no private rights.

H. David Rosenbloom, *Toward a New Tax Policy Treaty for a New Decade*, 9 AM. J. TAX POL'Y 77, 90–91 (1991).

There is * * * one aspect of U.S. treaty policy toward inbound investment that warrants a separate word. As important as the double tax provisions of the model are for that investment, a provision of the typical tax treaty that has nothing in concept to do with double taxation has come up again and again as the United States has attempted to adjust to the investment inflow that has occurred: I refer to the nondiscrimination article.

Each of the major steps along the road toward greater taxation of foreign investment in the United States has had to come to terms with this provision, and each time a struggle has ensued. FIRPTA [The Foreign Investors and Real Property Tax Act of 1990] gave foreign corporations the option to elect treatment as domestic corporations. The branch profits rules overrode the treaties to the extent of treaty shopping (even though nondiscrimination reflects respect for formal allegiance of the foreign person to the treaty partner, and is arguably a peculiar subject for an anti-treaty shopping provision). The earnings-stripping rules of section 163(j) lean heavily on taxation of non-foreign exempt organizations to defend against the charge of discrimination. Congress may be satisfied with these jerry-rigged and disingenuous solutions, but there is surely a better way—rethink the nondiscrimination clause itself and either omit it, scale it back, or make it a government-to-government agreement, with no private rights, in upcoming treaties.

As one of our treaty partners once patiently explained when I was pressing the U.S. view on the sanctity of nondiscrimination, countries that tax at source usually want to discriminate or, if not, find that they must discriminate to enforce their laws dealing with inbound investment. We have discovered this in recent years, and it has made us uncomfortable. Nevertheless, it would be preferable to face up to the problem, rather than crafting elaborate fictions or, worse, asserting baldly that differential provisions are not discriminatory because there is an economic justification for them or they are needed for some other good purpose. The nondiscrimination article of the U.S. model probably stands in more urgent need of review than [any other] article.

Chapter 11

Tax Competition, Harmonization and National Sovereignty

11.1 APPROACHING "HARMFUL TAX COMPETITION"

It has become trite to observe that the "globalization" of the world economy limits the ability of any nation to act independently, to act without taking into account the reactions and counter-actions of other nations. In the domain of taxation, the international movement of both inputs—capital and labor—and outputs—goods and services—limits national sovereignty, the ability of a nation to adopt whatever policies it chooses, free from external forces. And one nation's sovereignty, its freedom of action, may be impinged upon by the tax policies of another.[1] We have seen that a nation's tax policies may, for example, affect the location of investments in plant and equipment and of financial activities. We have also seen that when countries' tax rates are different, companies have incentives to shift income to the lower-tax jurisdiction and deductions to the jurisdiction with higher rates.

As a result, the question arises whether and how to establish multilateral "rules of the game"—a framework setting parameters to guide national decisions about international taxation. In the area of monetary policies, such a framework was established after World War II in an agreement at Breton Woods and subsequently modernized multilaterally. In international trade, the multilateral General Agreement on Trade and Tariffs (GATT) both sets forth the rules of trade and establishes a decisionmaking body, the World Trade Organization (WTO), to resolve disputes. No such agreement or dispute-resolution mechanism operates in the area of international taxation. Nothing comparable to the thoroughgoing multilateral restructurings of international monetary relationships and rules of trade has affected the system of international income taxation. As the Australian law professor Richard Vann has observed: "The failure to adopt any new approach to international tax after the second World War, compared to trade law and the international monetary system, meant that effectively the solution

---

1. See Charles E. McLure, Jr., Globalization, Tax Rules and National Sovereignty, 55 Bull. Int'l Fiscal Doc. 328, 328–29 (2001).

adopted after the first World War continued by default."[2] The critical question is whether the international tax solutions and processes of the 1920s will serve as well in the 21st century as they did in the 20th.

In recent years, both the OECD and, in a more limited geographical area, the European Union have attempted to fill this vacuum and, in particular, to inhibit what the OECD labels "harmful tax competition." As we shall see, these efforts have had mixed results. The United States has been ambivalent in its participation in this endeavor, supporting the OECD efforts during the Clinton Administration but withdrawing some of this support in 2001 after the election of President Bush.

In international trade, consensus reigns—at least among policymakers—about both the sizable economic benefits from global trade and the large losses to the world economy that would result from an unfettered "race to the bottom." Thus, achieving multilateral trade agreements is relatively easy, despite contentious disputes over its details. In the income tax area, however, the circumstances, if any, which render tax competition "harmful" are hotly contested by theorists and political actors alike. Everyone knows what tax competition is: policies adopted by one nation to attract capital or labor or induce financial activity. The question becomes: When is such competition harmful? In 1998, the OECD Committee on Fiscal Affairs issued a report, *Harmful Tax Competition: An Emerging Global Issue*,[3] which triggered the debate that this chapter reports. The OECD Report was hardly off the press before critics accused it of "repeatedly assert[ing]" that the existence of harmful tax competition is "self-evident," while giving only " 'elephant' tests ('you'll know one when you see it') as the basis for separating beneficial from 'harmful' international tax preferences."[4] Yet that study remains the essential starting point for a discussion of policy about tax competition.

The OECD's Committee on Fiscal Affairs launched its "harmful tax competition project" in 1996 in response to a request from a ministerial meeting of OECD countries. In 1998 it delivered the Report, which included specific recommendations. The well-publicized Report addressed "harmful tax practices in the form of tax havens and preferential regimes in OECD Member countries and non-Member countries and their dependencies."[5] It announced principles and guidelines for combating and preventing the spread of such practices, created a new Forum to oversee the implementation of these principles and guidelines, and prescribed implementation deadlines. The following excerpt from the

---

2. Richard J. Vann, A Model Tax Treaty for the Asian–Pacific Region?, 45 Bull. Int'l Fiscal Doc. 99, 103 (1991).

3. OECD Committee on Fiscal Affairs, Harmful Tax Competition: An Emerging Global Issue (1998) [hereinafter OECD Report].

4. Arthur W. Wright, Review: OECD Harmful Tax Competition Report Falls Short, 17 Tax. Notes Int'l 461, 462 (1998).

5. OECD Report, supra note 3, at 3.

Report is fairly representative of the Report's style of discussion. Buried within it are the Report's most important arguments.

OECD COMMITTEE ON FISCAL AFFAIRS, HARMFUL TAX COMPETITION: AN EMERGING GLOBAL ISSUE 13–14, 15–16, 19–20, 22–29 (1998).

The accelerating process of globalization of trade and investment has fundamentally changed the relationship among domestic tax systems. * * * [The] removal of non-tax barriers to international commerce and investment and the resulting integration of national economies have greatly increased the potential impact that domestic tax policies can have on other economies. Globalization has also been one of the driving forces behind tax reforms, which have focused on base broadening and rate reductions, thereby minimizing tax induced distortions. Globalization has also encouraged countries to assess continually their tax systems and public expenditures with a view to making adjustments where appropriate to improve the "fiscal climate" for investment. Globalization and the increased mobility of capital has also promoted the development of capital and financial markets and has encouraged countries to reduce tax barriers to capital flows and to modernize their tax systems to reflect these developments. Many of these reforms have also addressed the need to adapt tax systems to this new global environment. * * *

* * * Globalization has, however, also had the negative effects of opening up new ways by which companies and individuals can minimize and avoid taxes and in which countries exploit these new opportunities by developing tax policies aimed primarily at diverting financial and other geographically mobile capital. These actions induce potential distortions in the patterns of trade and investment and reduce global welfare. * * * [They] can erode national tax bases of other countries, may alter the structure of taxation (by shifting of the tax burden from mobile to relatively immobile factors and from income to consumption) and may hamper the application of progressive tax rates and the achievement of redistributive goals. Pressure of this sort can result in changes in tax structures in which all countries may be forced by spillover effects to modify their tax bases, even though a more desirable result could have been achieved through intensifying international co-operation. * * *

Tax competition and the interaction of tax systems can have effects that some countries may view as negative or harmful but others may not. For example, one country may view investment incentives as a policy instrument to stimulate new investment, while another may view investment incentives as diverting real investment from one country to another. In the context of this last effect, countries with specific structural disadvantages, such as poor geographical location, lack of natural resources, etc., frequently consider that special tax incentives or tax regimes are necessary to offset non-tax disadvantages, including any additional cost from locating in such areas. Similarly, within countries, peripheral regions often experience difficulties in promoting their development and may, at certain stages in this development, benefit from more attractive tax regimes or tax incentives for certain activities. This outcome, in itself, recognizes that many factors affect the overall competitive position of a country. Although the international community may have concerns about potential spillover effects, these decisions may be justifiable from the point of view of the country in question. * * *

[Sometimes] the spillover effects on the other countries is not a mere side effect, incidental to the implementation of a domestic tax policy. Here the effect is for one country to redirect capital and financial flows and the corresponding revenue from the other jurisdictions by bidding aggressively for the tax base of other countries. Some have described this effect as "poaching" as the tax base "rightly" belongs to the other country. Practices of this sort can appropriately be labeled harmful tax competition as they do not reflect different judgments about the appropriate level of taxes and public outlays or the appropriate mix of taxes in a particular economy, which are aspects of every country's sovereignty in fiscal matters, but are, in effect, tailored to attract investment or savings originating elsewhere or to facilitate the avoidance of other countries' taxes. * * *

At the outset, a distinction must be made between three broad categories of situations in which the tax levied in one country on income from geographically mobile activities, such as financial and other service activities, is lower than the tax that would be levied on the same income in another country:

i) the first country is a tax haven and, as such, generally imposes no or only nominal tax on that income;

ii) the first country collects significant revenues from tax imposed on income at the individual or corporate level but its tax system has preferential features that allow the relevant income to be subject to low or no taxation;

iii) the first country collects significant revenues from tax imposed on income at the individual or corporate level but the effective tax rate that is generally applicable at that level in that country is lower than that levied in the second country.

All three categories of situations may have undesirable effects from the perspective of the other country. However, as already noted * * * globalization has [been a] driving force behind tax reforms which have focused on base broadening and rate reductions, thereby minimizing tax induced distortions. Accordingly, * * * the issues arising in this third category are outside the scope of this Report. * * *

The first two categories, which are the focus of this report, are dealt with differently. While the concept of "tax haven" does not have a precise technical meaning, it is recognized that a useful distinction may be made between, on the one hand, countries that are able to finance their public services with no or nominal income taxes and that offer themselves as places to be used by non-residents to escape tax in their country of residence and, on the other hand, countries which raise significant revenues from their income tax but whose tax system has features constituting harmful tax competition.

In the first case, the country has no interest in trying to curb the "race to the bottom" with respect to income tax and is actively contributing to the erosion of income tax revenues in other countries. For that reason, these countries are unlikely to co-operate in curbing harmful tax competition. By contrast, in the second case, a country may have a significant amount of revenues which are at risk from the spread of harmful tax competition and it is therefore more likely to agree on concerted action.

Because of this difference, this Report distinguishes between jurisdictions in the first category, which are referred to as tax havens, and jurisdictions in the second category, which are considered as countries which have potentially harmful preferential tax regimes. * * *

The necessary starting point to identify a tax haven is to ask (a) whether a jurisdiction imposes no or only nominal taxes (generally or in special circumstances) and offers itself, or is perceived to offer itself, as a place to be used by non-residents to escape tax in their country of residence. Other key factors which can confirm the existence of a tax haven * * * are: (b) laws or administrative practices which prevent the effective exchange of relevant information with other governments on taxpayers benefiting from the low or no tax jurisdiction; (c) lack of transparency and (d) the absence of a requirement that the activity be substantial, since it would suggest that a jurisdiction may be attempting to attract investment or transactions that are purely tax driven (transactions may be booked there without the requirement of adding value so that there is little real activity, *i.e.* these jurisdictions are essentially "booking centers"). * * * In general, the importance of each of the other key factors referred to above very much depends on the particular context. * * *

Four key factors assist in identifying harmful preferential tax regimes: *(a)* the regime imposes a low or zero effective tax rate on the relevant income; *(b)* the regime is "ring-fenced"; *(c)* the operation of the regime is nontransparent; *(d)* the jurisdiction operating the regime does not effectively exchange information with other countries. * * *

There are good reasons for the international community to be concerned where regimes are partially or fully isolated from the domestic economy. Since the regime's "ring fencing" effectively protects the sponsoring country from the harmful effects of its own incentive regime, that regime will have an adverse impact only on foreign tax bases. Thus, the country offering the regime may bear little or none of the financial burden of its own preferential tax legislation. Similarly, taxpayers within the regime may benefit from the infrastructure of the country providing the preferential regime without bearing the cost incurred to provide that infrastructure. Ring fencing may take several forms, including *(a)* Regimes that restrict the benefits to non-residents, * * * [and] *(b)* Investors who benefit from the tax regime are explicitly or implicitly denied access to domestic markets.

NOTES

1) *Focusing on Common Criteria.* While the Report fails to adduce a straightforward definition of harmful tax practices, it does direct attention to the four criteria listed in the penultimate paragraph quoted here: (a) nominal or zero tax rates, (b) practices limiting the exchange of information on taxpayers with other governments, (c) lack of transparency, and (d) a failure to require that economic activity be "substantial" to qualify for preferential tax treatment, including, in the case of preferential regimes, ring-fencing. Criteria (b) and (c) are the most readily defensible and are discussed in Section 11.2. In contrast, the idea that the OECD should have anything at all to say about appropriate tax *rates* (criterion (a)) was regarded by many as an inappropriate impingement on national sovereignty. Criteria (a) and (d) both relate to substantive tax competition and are discussed in Sections 11.3 and 11.4. All four of these criteria have attracted some opposition.[6] For example, Switzerland

---

6. The 1998 OECD Report suggests a list of additional factors that help identify tax havens and harmful preferential regimes. These factors include: (5) An artificial definition

and Luxembourg—nations that insist on bank secrecy—abstained from the 1998 OECD report and the 2000 follow-up document in part because of their objection to the exchange-of-information criterion.[7] Both argued that imposition of withholding taxes is a legitimate alternative to information exchange as deterrence against tax evasion, while the OECD Report identified lack of exchange of information as in itself a harmful tax practice. In contrast, in its 2001 Savings Directive, the European Union endorsed withholding as an alternative to information exchange.[8]

2) *"Tax Havens" vs. "Preferential Tax Regimes."* The Report frequently distinguishes between tax havens and "preferential" tax regimes. For most purposes, harmful preferential regimes are just "part-time" tax havens. However, as the Report points out, a crucial difference between tax haven jurisdictions and jurisdictions with preferential regimes is that the latter can suffer from the harmful tax practices of other countries, whereas "true" tax havens, imposing very low tax and incurring very low public expenditures, have nothing to lose (except for their international reputation), whatever other countries do.

3) *The Limited Scope of the Report.* The OECD Report repeatedly invokes a "race-to-the-bottom" argument, which we revisit in Section 11.3 below. In an open world economy with mobile capital and labor, when "each [country] independently (or 'non-cooperatively') chooses its tax or subsidy policies to maximize the welfare of residents within the [country], its choice affects the size of the tax bases available to other governments."[9] Each country's tax policy may have negative "spill-over" effects, and no single country alone can address these negative effects. One might call this the traditional problem of tax competition. On the other hand, the Report limits its own scope to "geographically mobile activities, such as financial and other service activities, including the provision of intangibles," and excludes from its review "[tax] incentives designed to attract investment in plant, building and equipment."[10]

of the tax base, (6) failure to adhere to international transfer pricing principles, (7) foreign source income exempt from residence country tax, (8) negotiable tax rate or tax base, (9) existence of secrecy provisions, (10) access to a wide network of tax treaties, (11) regimes which are promoted as tax minimization vehicles, and (12) the regime encourages purely tax-driven operations or arrangements. See OECD Report, supra note 3, at 30–34.

    7. Annex II to OECD Report, supra note 3.

    8. See Joann M. Weiner, ECOFIN Makes Significant Progress in Adopting the EU Savings Tax Package, 21 Tax Notes Int'l 2547 (2000).

    9. John Douglas Wilson, Theories of Tax Competition, 52 Nat'l Tax J. 269, 270 (1999).

    10. Although "it is recognized that the distinction between regimes directed at financial and other services on the one hand and at manufacturing and similar activities on the other hand is not always easy to apply." OECD Report, supra note 3, at 8. In fact, the scope of the Report is narrower still, because "the tax treatment of interest on cross-border saving instruments, particularly bank deposits is not considered in this first stage of the project since the Committee is currently examining the feasibility of developing proposals

Furthermore, the Report emphasizes the tendency of tax havens and "preferential tax regimes" to facilitate tax avoidance and evasion. In an unconventional expansion of the term "tax competition," the Report includes these latter phenomena under the rubric of "harmful tax competition." To understand the OECD initiative and the controversies surrounding it, one must separate the various strands of policy considerations that the OECD has unhelpfully lumped together under a single title.

4) *The Range of the Report.* This chapter does not touch on all aspects of the 1998 OECD Report. For example, the Report expresses concern over multinational corporations' exploitation of low-tax jurisdictions for tax avoidance. This issue is distinct from both the traditional problem of tax competition and, to some extent, issues of tax enforcement. The reader is referred to material on corporations' manipulation of residence in Chapter 3, and the discussion of enforcement issues in Chapter 8, as well as to Chapter 9 on transfer pricing, where this technique of tax avoidance by multinationals is extensively discussed. The OECD initiative has evolved through discussions among OECD members and in discussions with non-OECD states which allegedly have harmful regimes. Changes are largely reflected in the OECD's 2000 and 2001 "progress reports" on its harmful tax practices initiative.[11]

11.2 COMBATING EVASION, INCREASING TRANSPARENCY

Of the OECD's four criteria for harmful tax practices, the least controversial and most successful have been those directed at reducing tax evasion and increasing the transparency of tax regimes. As we have mentioned, however, even these proposals did not meet with universal acclaim; the OECD's attack on bank secrecy caused Switzerland and Luxembourg to abstain from approving the Report. Nonetheless, the OECD campaign against tax havens and harmful preferential regimes received positive responses from a large number of countries, especially with regard to regimes that impair enforcement of other countries' tax laws. By April 2002, more than 30 offshore financial centers had pledged to work with OECD countries to counter specific harmful practices. Only seven remaining nations were listed by the OECD as "uncooperative tax havens."[12] As we shall see, this success in enlisting the cooperation of many countries to cease certain practices has been reinforced by other

to deal with cross-border interest flows, including the use of withholding taxes and exchange of information." Id. at 9–10.

   11. See OECD Center for Tax Policy and Administration, The OECD's Project on Harmful Tax Practices: The 2001 Progress Report (2001) [hereinafter 2001 OECD Progress Report]; OECD Committee on Fiscal Affairs, Towards Global Tax Co-operation: Report to the 2000 Ministerial Council Meeting and Recommendations by the Committee on Fiscal Affairs: Progress in Identifying and Eliminating Harmful Tax Practices (2000) [hereinafter 2000 OECD Progress Report].

   12. Seiichi Kondo, OECD Deputy Secretary–General, Ending Tax Haven Abuse, speech (Apr. 18, 2002), available at http://www.oecd.org.

related international agreements. For example, in April 2000, OECD member countries unanimously approved a report on "the desired level of access to bank information" with respect to tax matters.[13] And in November 2000, European Union member states signed an agreement to either participate in information exchange or impose withholding taxes with respect to individual savings income.[14] Chapter 8 contains a discussion of these enforcement mechanisms.

Avoiding Evasion

One way of defining a "tax haven" is as a country that intentionally or foreseeably facilitates evasion of taxes imposed by other countries. If we think that governments generally have legitimate reasons to exercise their taxing power, tax havens so defined are analogous to nations that intentionally facilitate the perpetration of other crimes in their countries. As such, they are clearly objectionable. Under our ordinary understanding of international order, intentionally undermining the legitimate legal systems of other countries is wrong. One does not have to argue whether or not this practice is also "unfairly competitive" or "anti-competitive." When it comes to evasion, competition is not really the issue. If tax havens simply facilitate "tax cheats," the question for the international community would seem to be *how* such wrongs can be corrected, not *whether* a wrong has been perpetrated. Some conservative defenders of tax-haven regimes have attempted to ignore this distinction, insisting a tax haven is merely "a country with tax rates low enough to attract foreign investors," going so far as to claim that the "world's biggest tax haven is the United States," the largest "escape hatch for oppressed taxpayers."[15]

"Harmful tax competition" is too mild a phrase for practices that facilitate tax evasion, and tax havens in that business do more than shelter investors "oppressed" by other jurisdictions. Some countries labeled tax havens are not so much countries that lower their tax rates (and their ability to fund public expenditures) in the hopes of gaining comparative advantage (thereby perhaps sparking a race to the bottom), as they are countries exploiting their situation to abet evasion of residence-based taxes imposed elsewhere. Recent efforts to shore up enforcement mechanisms in offshore financial centers have sometimes also emphasized the potential use of these jurisdictions by international criminal syndicates and terrorists.

13. OECD Committee on Fiscal Affairs, Improving Access to Bank Information for Tax Purposes (declassified March 24, 2000).

14. See Anne–Marie Berthault, A French Perspective on Tax Havens and Bank Secrecy: Is the Future a Transparent One?, 22 Tax Notes Int'l 3171, 3174–75 (2001); Joann M. Weiner, ECOFIN Makes Significant Progress in Adopting the EU Savings Tax Package, 21 Tax Notes Int'l 2547 (2000).

15. Daniel J. Mitchell, Don't Scapegoat Tax Havens (Oct. 5, 2001), available at http://www.heritage.org/Press/Commentary/ed100501.cfm.

It is clear how "lack of effective exchange of information" can frustrate tax enforcement by another country.[16] As the 1998 OECD Report explains:

> Some jurisdictions have enacted laws (*e.g.*, providing anonymous accounts) that prevent financial institutions from providing tax authorities with information about investors. Thus, tax administrators lack the power to compel such information from institutions, and they cannot exchange information under tax treaties or under other types of mutual assistance channels. The most obvious consequence of the failure to provide information is that it facilitates tax evasion and money laundering. Thus, these factors are particularly harmful characteristics of a tax haven and * * * of a harmful preferential tax regime.

> Some progress has been made in the area of access to information, in that certain tax haven jurisdictions have entered into mutual legal assistance treaties in criminal matters with non-tax havens that permit exchange of information on criminal tax matters related to certain other crimes (*e.g.* narcotics trafficking) or to exchange information when criminal tax fraud is at issue. Nevertheless, these tax haven jurisdictions do not allow tax administrations access to bank information for the critical purposes of detecting and preventing tax avoidance which, from the perspectives of raising revenue and controlling base erosion from financial and other service activities, are as important as curbing tax fraud. Thus, the lack of effective exchange of information is one of the key factors in identifying a tax haven since it limits the access by tax authorities to the information required for the correct and timely application of tax laws.[17]

Since its 1998 Report was issued, the OECD has enjoyed substantial success in arranging for better information exchanges. A group of small states sometimes called tax havens—including Aruba, Bermuda, Bahrain, the Cayman Islands, Cyprus, the Isle of Man, Malta, Mauritius, the Netherlands Antilles, the Seychelles, and San Marino—cooperated through the OECD's Global Forum Working Group on Effective Exchange of Information to draft new model exchange-of-information agreements.[18] There appears to be substantial momentum behind adopting the new agreements as a *de facto* international standard.[19] OECD

---

16. For the variety of information exchange mechanisms employed by the U.S. in enforcing its tax laws, see Chapter 8, Sections 8.1 and 8.3.

17. OECD Report, supra note 3, at 24.

18. See OECD, Agreement on Exchange of Information on Tax Matters (2002), available at http://www.oecd.org/pdf/M00028000/M00028528.pdf.

19. See Robert Goulder, OECD Updates Tax Haven Blacklist, Claims Progress in Curbing Harmful Tax Competition, 26 Tax Notes Int'l 375 (2002).

corporate governance initiatives have also focused attention on disclosing corporate ownership, a goal related to the use of corporate entities structured to evade tax.[20]

Clarifying Transparency

By contrast with information exchange, the meaning of the OECD's lack-of-"transparency" criterion may be less clear. One reason is that non-transparency can take a number of forms, including tax bases or rates negotiated with an individual taxpayer, other forms of special treatment, and direct subsidies to offset taxes paid. These features may be a sign of illegitimate competition, but they may not be. As Julie Roin notes, "As a practical matter, one cannot distinguish between expenditures on infrastructure meant to encourage 'economic growth' in general and those meant to benefit the particular investors that end up using the infrastructure so created."[21] Professor Roin illustrates her general point about transparency with the following example of the complications the United States has encountered in attempting to combat one form of non-transparency:

> [The] United States has tried to backstop * * * collusive schemes between foreign governments and U.S. taxpayers to take advantage of the United States' foreign tax credit rules. U.S. taxpayers are supposed to obtain such credits only for taxes actually paid or accrued to foreign governments; such credits are not supposed to be granted for amounts rebated to the taxpayer by the foreign government or paid in return for "specific economic benefits" received from the foreign government. Although the Internal Revenue Service has taken the position that rebates can take the form of subsidies, its regulations target only [the most blatant] schemes—that is, schemes in which the amount of the tax and subsidy are directly linked. Nor is there any evidence that it has attempted to extend the disallowance rules beyond this narrow subset of situations. Enforcement of a related regulation disallowing credits for taxes paid to gain access to a "specific economic benefit" has been similarly limited in scope; the regulation seems to have been enforced only in situations where the taxpayer received access to governmentally owned mineral or petroleum reserves.[22]

The OECD Report describes non-transparency as encompassing a wide range of arrangements:

---

20. See OECD Steering Group on Corporate Governance, Options for Obtaining Beneficial Ownership and Control Information (2002), available at http://www.oecd.org/pdf/M00034000/M00034958.pdf.

21. Julie Roin, Competition and Evasion: Another Perspective on International Tax Competition, 89 Geo. L.J. 543, 571 (2001).

22. Id. at 571–73.

The lack of transparency in the operation of a regime will make it harder for the home country to take defensive measures. To be deemed transparent in terms of administrative practices, a tax regime's administration should normally satisfy both of the following conditions: First, it must set forth clearly the conditions of applicability to taxpayers in such a manner that those conditions may be invoked against the authorities; second, details of the regime, including any applications thereof in the case of a particular taxpayer, must be available to the tax authorities of other countries concerned. Regimes which do not meet these criteria are likely to increase harmful tax competition since non-transparent regimes give their beneficiaries latitude for negotiating with the tax authorities and may result in inequality of treatment of taxpayers in similar circumstances. A lack of transparency may arise because:

— Favorable administrative rulings (*e.g.*, regulatory, substantive, and procedural rulings) are given, allowing a particular sector to operate under a lower effective tax environment than other sectors. As an example of a favorable administrative ruling, tax authorities may enter into agreements with a taxpayer or may agree to issue advance tax rulings in requested cases. However, where these administrative practices are consistent with and do not negate or nullify statutory laws, they can be viewed as a legitimate and necessary exercise of administrative authority. To assure equality in treatment, the ruling criteria should be well-known or publicized by the authority granting the ruling and available on a non-discriminatory basis to all taxpayers.

— Special administrative practices may be contrary to the fundamental procedures underlying statutory laws. This may encourage corruption and discriminatory treatment, especially if the practices are not disclosed. Such practices can also make it more difficult for other countries to enforce their tax laws. Thus, a regime where the tax rate and base are not negotiable, but where administrative practices and enforcement do not conform with the law or do not stipulate the conditions of applicability, may be considered as potentially harmful.

— If the general domestic fiscal environment is such that the laws are not enforced in line with the domestic law, this could make an otherwise legitimate regime harmful. * * * A specific example of this issue is where the tax authorities deliberately adopt a lax audit policy as an implicit incentive to taxpayers not to comply with the tax laws. Such behavior may give these taxpayers a competitive advantage.[23]

Since 1998 the OECD has negotiated with non-OECD countries alleged to be inadequately transparent, but by 2001 only five of thirty-five jurisdictions had agreed to end their non-transparency features. Each of these five countries committed:

that there will be no non-transparent features of its tax system, such as rules that depart from established laws and practices within the jurisdiction, "secret" tax rulings or the ability of persons to "negotiate" the rate of tax to be applied. Transparency also requires financial accounts to be drawn up in accordance with generally accepted accounting standards and that such accounts either be audited or filed. * * * A committing jurisdiction also agrees that its governmental authorities should have access to beneficial ownership information regarding the ownership of all types of entities and to bank information that may be relevant to criminal and civil tax matters. The information to be maintained to meet the transparency criterion should be available for exchange pursuant to legal mechanisms for exchange of information.[24]

Creating a fully transparent tax system, however, may be more difficult than these OECD pronouncements might make it appear. Even where overtly negotiated tax rates are unavailable, other legislative and administrative practices, which give tax authorities broad latitude, may lead to comparable levels of uncertainty. In the following excerpt, former Assistant Treasury Secretary Kenneth Gideon argues that the United States tax system itself is far from fully transparent.

Kenneth W. Gideon, *Tax Law Works Best When the Rules Are Clear*, 81 TAX NOTES 999, 1000–01 (1998).

At its most basic level, "transparency" requires that the rules be written down and uniformly applied. The opposite of transparency can be defined by an annual round of "let's make a deal" with a tax inspector whose priorities, values, and even venality make each year's negotiation idiosyncratic. We Americans have for a long time justly prided ourselves that we did not have a tax system like that: our rules were always written down, sometimes at sleep-inducing length; our revenue agents were honest and conscientious; our senior tax administrators placed a high value on uniformity and predictability.

Without taking issue with the honesty, integrity, and good intentions of those who have formed and administered our income tax system, I suggest that our frequent assertion that

23. OECD Report, supra note 3, at 28–29.
24. 2001 OECD Progress Report, supra note 11, at 11.

we have the best of all possible tax systems is seriously over-stated. * * * One of [our system's] flaws, it is time to admit, is a net loss of transparency in our income tax system over recent years—and, if anything, the trend is accelerating. In terms of issues which regularly arise between taxpayer and the Internal Revenue Service, the "uncertainty" gap is growing and the area open to negotiated outcomes is expanding. * * * Anti-abuse rules, once the regulatory drafter's last ditch "Hail Mary" fling to the end zone against the unexpected, have become a first-line rather than a last-line defense. The current highwater mark of this trend, the partnership anti-abuse rules, contain no substantive rule at all, only an anti-abuse rule. The basic defect of all anti-abuse rules is uncertainty. There is no clear delineation between situations in which the rule applies to deny benefits and those in which it does not.

Ultimately, there still must be a day of decision on whether the benefit sought is available. Anti-abuse rules transfer that decisionmaking process from the open and uniform arena of rulemaking to the uncertainties of the audit process and virtually assure that the results will vary from taxpayer to taxpayer. While it may be harder to craft substantive rules than anti-abuse rules (because you have to decide now what the criteria for allowing or disallowing benefits will be and the risk of failure is higher), the successful substantive rule makes the effort and the risk worth it. The successful rule resolves the issue in a way in which taxpayers and agents can understand and apply.

NOTES

1) *Why Fight Non–Transparency?* The preceding discussion implies at least four ways that non-transparency in a country's tax administration can be bad, though none are fully articulated. First, non-transparency may hamper effective exchange of information with other countries. This, of course, does not make it an independent criterion for identifying tax havens. Second, lack of transparency may simply imply a general laxity in a nation's enforcement of its tax law. This might be taken to be equivalent to a low effective tax rate or other substantive advantage. But again, unless particular taxpayers or categories of taxpayers are favored, it fails to explain why non-transparency is independently a bad thing.

It is only with a third possibility that we begin to see how non-transparency becomes an independent criterion for identifying tax havens or harmful tax competition. The lack of effective information exchange generally prevents non-tax-haven countries from obtaining information about their own citizens or residents, notably those suspected of fraud. When a tax haven maintains a non-transparent regime, by contrast, the information difficult to obtain is about the regime as a whole. When, for example, it is not known whether a country secretly allows subsidies or refunds, other countries may not be able to develop effective defensive measures, such as the disallowance of foreign tax credits.

A final possibility illustrates how non-transparency may result in inequality of treatment of taxpayers in similar circumstances. Suppose that a resident of country A, a non-tax-haven country, creates an investment vehicle in country B, and secretly receives favorable treatment relative to other taxpayers subject to B's laws. One could see how this renders B's legal system unsatisfactory from the perspective of B's own taxpayers. However, the negative impact of this state of affairs on A's tax laws may be less obvious. Suppose that the enforcement of A's laws against its own taxpayer (the first possibility) is not at issue. Suppose moreover that the design of A's tax policy in response to B's general tax law (the third possibility) is not at issue. Why then should A's government care about the lack of rule of law in B? The answer is not clear. The OECD suggests its concern is the following: Simply by allowing residents of country A to benefit from unequal treatment in country B, B's government has undermined "broad social acceptance of tax systems generally."[25] This assertion, however, seems a reach.

2) *Naming and Shaming.* The OECD's approach to both information exchange and greater transparency has combined the carrot of greater OECD cooperation with the stick of an OECD threat to "name and shame" jurisdictions maintaining harmful tax practices. The OECD worked hard to persuade offshore financial centers to commit to information exchange and transparency, extending the deadline for commitment from July 31, 2001 to February 28, 2002. It expressed a strong preference for "dialogue and consensus" over the adversarial deployment of coordinated defensive measures. Yet in 2000, it did envision a framework of such defensive measures, including the following:

- To disallow deductions, exemptions, credits, or other allowances related to transactions with Uncooperative Tax Havens or to transactions taking advantage of their harmful tax practices.

- To require comprehensive information reporting rules for transactions involving Uncooperative Tax Havens or taking advantage of their harmful tax practices, supported by substantial penalties for inaccurate reporting or non-reporting of such transactions.

- For countries that do not have controlled foreign corporation or equivalent (CFC) rules, to consider adopting such rules, and for countries that have such rules, to ensure that they apply in a fashion consistent with the desirability of curbing harmful tax practices. * * *

25. OECD Report, supra note 3, at 8.

• To deny any exceptions (*e.g.* reasonable cause) that may otherwise apply to the application of regular penalties in the case of transactions involving entities organized in Uncooperative Tax Havens or taking advantage of their harmful tax practices.

• To deny the availability of the foreign tax credit or the participation exemption with regard to distributions that are sourced from Uncooperative Tax Havens or to transactions taking advantage of their harmful tax practices.

• To impose withholding taxes on certain payments to residents of Uncooperative Tax Havens.

• To enhance audit and enforcement activities with respect to Uncooperative Tax Havens and transactions taking advantage of their harmful tax practices.

• To ensure that any existing and new domestic defensive measures against harmful tax practices are also applicable to transactions with Uncooperative Tax Havens and to transactions taking advantage of their harmful tax practices.

• Not to enter into any comprehensive income tax conventions with Uncooperative Tax Havens, and to consider terminating any such existing conventions unless certain conditions are met (Recommendation 12 of the 1998 Report).

• To deny deductions and cost recovery, to the extent otherwise allowable, for fees and expenses incurred in establishing or acquiring entities incorporated in Uncooperative Tax Havens.

• To impose "transactional" charges or levies on certain transactions involving Uncooperative Tax Havens.[26]

Whether any of these measures will be used against the seven uncooperative tax havens the OECD identified in April 2002—Andorra, Liechtenstein, Liberia, Monaco, the Marshall Islands, Nauru, and Vanuatu[27]—remains to be seen.

11.3   WHAT IS "HARMFUL" TAX COMPETITION?

Of the four OECD criteria for identifying harmful tax competition, aiding evasion and lack of transparency are by far the easiest to evaluate. The other two criteria—nominal or zero corporate income taxes and a failure of business activities in a jurisdiction to be "substantial"—are harder to appraise, as they relate not to procedures aiding tax avoidance, but rather to substantive competition between tax regimes. Substantive tax competition results whenever different jurisdictions in-

26.   2000 OECD Progress Report, supra note 11, at 25.

27.   Gabriel Makhlouf, Statement, The OECD List of Uncooperative Tax Havens (Apr. 18, 2002), available at http://www.oecd.org.

stitute tax policies in order to attract capital, labor, or other economic goods from outside the jurisdiction.

Substantive competition may threaten the sovereign ability of nations to formulate their own tax rules, for example, by inhibiting a nation's ability to make the tradeoffs between equity and efficiency that the populace and their representatives desire. This echoes widespread concerns about a race to the bottom. Some analysts also think that by threatening the ability of nations to set their own level of taxes, tax competition may also reduce the level of public spending and services that can be provided. Commentators debate whether this is a problem or a benefit. Ironically, multilateral attempts to limit competition, such as by tax law harmonization, may also constrain a nation's sovereignty in setting its own tax policy. The following excerpt describes the many forms tax competition may take.

Thomas F. Field, *Tax Competition in Europe and America*, 29 TAX NOTES INT'L 1235, 1235–37 (2003).

Tax competition occurs when a government alters its tax law in an effort to attract business firms, investment flows, or individuals having needed skills. Typical goals are to create additional jobs, spur investment, and promote or maintain economic growth.

There are hundreds of different ways to engage in tax competition. The commonest include tax holidays, cuts in tax rates in comparison with other taxing jurisdictions (or even abolishing some taxes entirely), providing incentives such as accelerated depreciation deductions or investment credits, and exempting from tax some forms of income, such as interest income.

These competitive techniques can be applied across the board to all individuals or firms that qualify. Or they can be restricted in various ways so as to benefit only nonresidents or new entrants. They can also be targeted narrowly to one or at most a few firms. The first approach involves broadly applicable changes in a state's tax system; the remaining approaches generally leave the basic tax rules unchanged save for a few narrowly crafted exceptions.

Experts have classified the multifarious forms of tax competition into three main groups:

1. Rate Competition. This is competition that involves tax rates (including the zero rate that results when a given activity is not subject to tax).

2. General Incentives. This competition involves tax incentives such as credits or exemptions that are available across

the board to all persons subject to tax within the jurisdiction.

3. Targeted Incentives. This type of competition involves tax incentives which benefit only one firm or individual, or at most a few, or only nonresidents as contrasted with domestic taxpayers.

Rate competition is arguably more acceptable than other forms of tax competition. * * * [C]ompetition-induced cuts in tax rates generally apply across the board to everyone in a rate bracket; for this reason, they are horizontally equitable. Further, they are usually transparent and simple to implement. In contrast, targeted tax competition violates basic principles of tax equity, is difficult to administer, is often needlessly costly in terms of lost revenue, and is frequently nontransparent.

Tax competition is an inevitable result of lowered trade barriers, the elimination of curbs on capital flows, and relaxed employment regulations. These measures have increased the mobility of goods, capital, and labor, which makes it easier to move to low-tax jurisdictions. Another factor facilitating tax competition is the growing importance of services as a percentage of overall economic activity, because the location in which services are performed and taxed is often easy to change, thanks in part to improvements in communications and computer technology.

Political efforts to create broad economic unions are another factor in the growth of tax competition. When sovereign states create a common market, as the United States did in 1789 and Europe has done more recently, it becomes easier for businesses and individuals to migrate to lower-tax jurisdictions within the market. Similarly, the general reductions in worldwide barriers to trade, commerce, and investment have made tax-motivated migration more feasible and attractive. As a result, substantially all nations are now de facto participants in a limited economic union.

The migration of businesses to low-tax jurisdictions within an economic union may be slow or fast, depending on many factors other than taxation, including labor costs, education levels, and transportation and communications infrastructure. But taxes will inevitably be taken into account along with these other factors in the process of deciding where to locate one's business and personal activities. And the migration process will be speeded if professional catalysts, such as investment banking and accounting firms, facilitate the search for tax preferences.

Bank secrecy is another factor in the migration of individuals and business firms to low- or no-tax jurisdictions. In contrast to the economic factors mentioned in the previous paragraph, which are of legitimate concern to law-abiding taxpayers, bank secrecy is especially important to tax evaders. A guarantee of financial secrecy combined with low or no taxation is a sure way to lure tainted money.

Given all these factors, it is natural for states within an economic union to fear tax competition from other members of the union, to react defensively, and to restructure their own tax systems in an effort to remain competitive.

The OECD's Attempt To Develop Substantive Criteria

The most sustained criticism of the OECD's approach to substantive tax competition has concerned its failure to demarcate a clear line between practices that are harmful and those that constitute legitimate competition. The OECD Report generally seeks to identify traits shared by harmful practices, but these traits may or may not indicate that the regime is causing harm from an international perspective, rather than simply from the point of view of a country that stands to lose out in competition against a country with the purportedly offensive trait. The following excerpt tries to explain the OECD's rationale for the line it attempted to draw between acceptable and "harmful" tax competition.

Hugh J. Ault, *Tax Competition: What (If Anything) To Do About It?*, in INTERNATIONAL AND COMPARATIVE TAXATION 1, 2–3, 4 (Kees van Raad ed., 2002).

The OECD Report endorses the international movement in the direction of a broader tax base with fewer preferences and general lower rates which was in part a result of "competitive" reaction to changes in the US and UK systems in the mid–80s. This kind of tax competition has had a positive impact on the development of tax systems. It has forced the elimination of wasteful and inefficient tax preferences and excessively high marginal rates, and in general increased efficiency. This kind of "good" tax competition is consistent with the OECD's general commitment to free market principles.

What then, is "harmful" tax competition? Here the Report focuses on a low or zero effective rate of tax on particular types or classes of income, when that low rate is coupled with other factors which tend to indicate that the particular tax regime was introduced primarily to attract tax base from other jurisdictions. These factors include "ring-fencing", that is, the regime excludes operations in the domestic economy or domestic investors; lack of transparence in the operation of the regime; and lack of effective exchange of information which can prevent other countries from assessing the impact of the regime on their taxpayers.

On the other hand, the issue of what general rate of income tax to have, or whether or not to even have an income tax at all, are basic questions of national policy and sovereignty which every country, at least historically, has been able to decide for itself. In the end, the participating OECD countries accepted the right of each country to establish its own general tax policy. If a country wants to introduce a general low rate of tax, it is free to do so without running afoul of the prescriptions for the Report, even though the effect of the system may indeed be to attract investment from other countries. Thus the countries recognize, on a reciprocal basis, the sovereign right to have whatever tax rate they wish as long as it is applied generally. A country is willing to accept a general low rate of tax in *another* country as a part of preserving its own right to have that rate—or some other rate—a matter of *its* own domestic policy.

Thus what the Report does is to distinguish between an overall low rate which applies to all taxpayers in the jurisdiction and a special regime or practice offering no or low effective taxation and which is combined with other features which make it likely that the effect, and in all probability, the purpose of the regime was simply to attract tax base from elsewhere. The first situation is not covered by the Report and the second may constitute harmful tax competition. So to take two examples, if a country introduces a general non-discriminatory, across the board 20% corporate tax rate, that is not harmful tax competition in terms of the Report. On the other hand, if the country has a special zero tax regime for corporations engaged in off-shore banking where only foreign investors can invest, those corporations are not permitted to do business in the domestic economy, and the country will not exchange information with the other country with regard to the income of such corporations so that country could try to continue to tax its residents on the income arising in the regime, that would constitute harmful tax competition. The Report emphasizes that the decision is to be made on the basis of all the factors taken together in context. * * *

Looking at the definition from a more theoretical point of view, which may not come out so clearly in the Report itself, the Report recognizes that a domestic tax system can in effect create externalities or spillover effects on other countries. That is a necessary aspect of the interaction of tax systems in an open economy. However, if the country is willing to in effect "pay" for the negative effects it causes, by foregoing the revenues from its own domestic taxpayers through a low generally applicable rate, then that is an acceptable tax system. The positive benefit, recognized on a reciprocal basis, of allowing countries to adopt whatever general tax structure or mix they want, outweighs the possible negative spillover effect which might be created. This is not the case however, where the whole purpose of the specially constructed regime is to create externalities for other jurisdictions. There the harmful effects are not offset by the need to effectuate any general domestic tax policies, and harmful tax competition is present.

NOTES

1) *Ring-fencing.* Once the OECD acknowledged that setting tax rates was an attribute of national sovereignty that could not be assailed, even if the tax rates were set with the goal of attracting capital from abroad, it became difficult to reach consensus on what kinds of "harmful tax competition" to attack. "Ring-fencing" became a prime target. The OECD described "ring-fenced" systems as tax regimes "partially or fully isolated from the domestic economy."[28] This became a criterion for determining that a nation constituted a preferential tax regime. The OECD argues:

> Since the regime's "ring fencing" effectively protects the sponsoring country from the harmful effects of its own incentive regime, that regime will have an adverse impact only on foreign tax bases. Thus, the country offering the regime may bear little or none of the financial burden of its own preferential tax legislation. Similarly, taxpayers within the regime may benefit from the infrastructure of the country providing the preferential regime without bearing the cost incurred to provide that infrastructure.[29]

It is not clear, however, why ring-fencing should be regarded as undermining faith in the fair administration of tax systems generally. The key question is why country *A* should care that a taxpayer residing in *A* is subjected to lower tax on her investment in country *B* than is a taxpayer resident in *B*. Country *A*'s concern may be that *B*'s low tax rate on non-residents will attract capital (or possibly labor) from *A*, but that could occur whenever *B*'s tax rates are lower than *A*'s. Ring-fencing might be less efficient than other forms of tax competition, if only because of the transaction costs imposed by administering a system that discriminates among domestic and foreign taxpayers, but surely this is a minor concern.

The Bush Administration has been particularly critical of the OECD's emphasis on ring-fencing. As then-Treasury Secretary Paul O'Neill explained:

28. OECD Report, supra note 3, at 26.
29. Id.

The ring-fencing criterion is problematic because it does not provide an adequate basis to distinguish regimes that facilitate tax evasion from regimes that are designed to encourage foreign investment but that have nothing to do with evasion of any other country's tax law. Countries may have good reason to provide different levels of taxation to income earned by nonresidents or to income earned by residents from foreign activities, such as to provide investment incentives or to improve access to capital markets. If such policies are not coupled with a lack of transparency or a refusal to exchange information and otherwise do not interfere with the enforcement by other countries of their tax laws, they should not be targeted by the OECD initiative.[30]

Partly in response to these arguments, the OECD in subsequent publications abandoned ring-fencing as a hallmark of a preferential regime.[31] However, for preferential regimes within the OECD, ring-fencing appears to remain a concern. Jeffrey Owens, head of the OECD Center for Tax Policy and Administration, told an interviewer in 2002, "Ring fencing is still applicable as a criteria [sic] to identifying harmful preferential regimes in OECD countries. As regards the offshore jurisdictions, the OECD member countries would continue to welcome the removal of practices that are implicated by the no substantial activities criterion, but this is a choice for them to make."[32] The European Union's Code of Conduct on Business Taxation seems to regard ring-fencing as a *per se* harmful practice, and, as a result, EU countries have in the last five years rolled back a number of ring-fencing arrangements.[33]

2) *Is Ireland a Harmful Preferential Regime?* Consider the case of Ireland, over the last decade one of the fastest-growing, and lowest-tax countries in the OECD. Here is how the *Wall Street Journal Europe* described Ireland in 1997:

> In financial circles, when talk turns to trendy island havens, most people think of sunny resorts.
>
> But for some commercial banks developing securitization businesses, the sunniest haven is a dank, misty place in Ireland, where taxes rarely break the 10% mark.

30. OECD Harmful Practices Initiative: Hearing Before the Senate Comm. on Governmental Affairs, Permanent Subcomm. on Investigations (July 18, 2001) (Statement of Paul H. O'Neill, Secretary of the Treasury), available at http://www.treasury.gov.

31. See Cordia Scott, OECD Releases Harmful Tax Competition Report, Extends Deadline for Tax Haven Compliance, 24 Tax Notes Int'l 831, 832 (2001).

32. Robert Goulder, OECD Updates Tax Haven Blacklist, Claims Progress in Curbing Harmful Tax Competition, 26 Tax Notes Int'l 375, 378 (2002).

33. See European Union Code of Conduct Group, Code of Conduct (Business Taxation) (1999), available at http://www.europa.eu.int.

Formerly a derelict seaport, the area known as the Dublin Docks now houses a cluster of gleaming office towers known as the International Financial Services Centre, or IFSC. It is home to 500 offshore funds and 78 non-Irish banks, including 11 U.S. banks and 18 German banks, according to John Curtin, banking specialist at the Industrial Development Authority of Ireland.
* * *

The main attractions of setting up in Ireland are the absence of tax on dividends, interest income and capital gains for investment funds, and the lowest corporate tax rate in Europe: a 10% tax limit on the profits of financial-services companies. The standard tax rate in Ireland is 38%.[34]

Until it caved to European Union pressure to abandon ring-fencing, Ireland imposed a 10% preferential tax rate that favored Irish manufacturing, financial services, software and data processing, film production, and other industries.[35] In recent years, U.S. multinationals have paid a far lower average effective tax rate in Ireland—7.6%—than in Europe as a whole—30%. In response to EU complaints about its ring-fenced tax system, Ireland substituted a low-rate corporate income tax across the board. As of 2003, Ireland imposes a 12.5% corporate income tax. Now that Ireland is in compliance with the EU Code of Conduct, having abandoned ring-fencing, is Ireland's style of tax competition no longer "harmful"?

One lurking question is the extent to which investment in Ireland is genuine capital investment, as opposed to transactions being booked in Ireland but in fact reflecting investments elsewhere. The return on investments booked in Ireland is substantially higher, at least in some industries, than in the rest of Europe. This has led some observers to suspect that transfer pricing among European affiliates is being manipulated to allocate an unwarranted share of multinationals' incomes to Ireland to take advantage of its low rate.[36] On the other hand, Ireland does not have banking secrecy policies that aid tax avoidance. While European policymakers focus on competition from external tax havens, highly competitive regimes like Ireland's within the EU pose many of the same concerns. Developing countries under attack from the OECD's efforts to limit competition may be especially alarmed by the prospect of a dozen formerly Communist countries entering the EU in the coming years, each with a powerful incentive to attract investment through competitive tax rates.

34. Cecile Gutscher, Commercial Banks Flock to Ireland Seeking Tax Breaks, Wall St. J. Eur., Jan. 15, 1997, at 19.

35. See Martin A. Sullivan, Data Show Europe's Tax Havens Soak Up U.S. Capital, 25 Tax Notes Int'l 551, 551 (2002).

36. See id. at 553–54.

Changes in Attitudes, Changes in Latitudes (or Longitudes)

The politics of tax competition are ever evolving, but the general divide appears to be between actors hoping that tax competition will drive down tax rates generally and thereby make governments more efficient, on the one hand, and, on the other, those worrying that tax competition could drive taxes too low, threatening an under-provision of public services and transfers by governments unable to afford necessary expenditures. The following excerpt from Julie Roin sketches the traditional contours of this dispute.

Julie Roin, *Competition and Evasion: Another Perspective on International Tax Competition*, 89 GEO. L.J. 543, 546–48 (2001).

Tax competition occurs when one country seeks to entice investment within its borders (and possibly enhanced tax revenues) through the expedient of reduced business taxation. That is, the competing country tries to make investments within its borders relatively more attractive by reducing its tax claims on any income generated from such investments, thus raising the investors' post-tax returns. This can become an iterative process, in which other countries attempt to forestall potential investment and revenue losses by dropping their own tax rates on businesses and income thought to be at risk. Whereas some view tax competition as leading to beneficial pressure on inefficient governmental extractions and spending, as well as the efficient location of business activities, others believe that the new competitive equilibrium will result in an unduly and unhealthily low level of governmental expenditure or an unhealthily high level of reliance on more distortionary revenue sources.

The United States traditionally has taken a dim view of tax competition. Its tax credit rules prevent U.S. taxpayers from enjoying the benefits of earning low-taxed foreign income; such taxpayers must pay the U.S. Treasury any difference between foreign taxes paid with respect to such income and the tax that would have been paid if the income had been earned in the United States. Nor has the United States been willing to waive its "capital export neutral" rules by treaty with selected countries. The Senate routinely rejects treaties containing "tax-sparing" provisions.

By contrast, most European nations have historically seemed untroubled by the prospect of tax competition. They traditionally have maintained territorial tax systems, taxing only income earned within their national borders. As a result, only the country of source taxed most of the foreign income earned by European residents; those residents reaped the economic benefits of low or absent source taxation. And so, too, did the source countries, in the form of increased investment.

In recent years, European and other developed nations have been moving closer to the United States' attitude toward tax competition. Rather than following the U.S. lead of eliminating the benefits to be gained from low tax rates through increased residence taxation, however, these nations are trying to encourage low-taxing source countries to raise their tax rates. * * *

NOTES

1) *Changing Attitudes.* These differing attitudes give some sense of the range of policy opinions on tax competition, a topic that has proven both intellectually contested and politically fluid. Even the attitudes described by Professor Roin have not been stable. Some claim that tax competition is "efficiency-enhancing," others that it is "wasteful"; both views depend on a myriad of assumptions, which are debated on both empirical and normative grounds. Even the most influential arguments in the literature serve only as starting points for policy analysis. Yet even this incomplete theoretical literature sheds light on the polemical discourse surrounding proposals to confront tax competition and to advance tax harmonization. The critical question is whether competition for capital through differential tax policies leads to a harmful race to the bottom, or whether tax competition—at least in some circumstances—is a beneficial engine for efficient capital allocation.

2) *Europe vs. the United States.* The advent of the George W. Bush Administration seems to have marked a shift in U.S. attitudes toward tax competition, with the U.S. government, beginning in 2001, viewing it as far less troublesome than it had before. Members of Congress, both Republican and Democratic, urged the Bush Administration to withdraw from the OECD initiative.[37] One influential lobby, named the Center for Freedom and Prosperity, had considerable success in convincing key lawmakers that the OECD's hidden agenda was to harmonize rates upward, to European levels, constraining U.S. sovereignty and limiting American economic growth.[38] Treasury Department officials, including then-Secretary Paul H. O'Neill, also made public statements against the initiative:

> Although the OECD has accomplished many great things over the years, I share many of the serious concerns that have been expressed recently about the direction of the OECD initiative. I am troubled by the underlying premise that low tax rates are somehow suspect and by the notion that any country, or group

37. See Lee A. Sheppard, It's the Bank Secrecy, Stupid, 22 Tax Notes Int'l 2018 (April 13 2001). Sheppard also argues against the claim—ironically, made by American opponents of the OECD initiative—that the U.S. is a tax haven.

38. See Thomas F. Field, Tax Competition in Europe and America, 29 Tax Notes Int'l 1235, 1242 (2003).

of countries, should interfere in any other country's decision about how to structure its own tax system. I also am concerned about the potentially unfair treatment of some non-OECD countries. The United States does not support efforts to dictate to any country what its own tax rates or tax system should be, and will not participate in any initiative to harmonize world tax systems. The United States simply has no interest in stifling the competition that forces governments—like businesses—to create efficiencies.[39]

In fact, the phrase "tax harmonization" does not make a single appearance in the OECD's 1998 report on "harmful tax competition."[40] In throwing its support behind unbridled substantive tax competition, the United States has been increasingly at odds with the European Union, which has undertaken its own efforts to reduce some "harmful" forms of competition among its members as a means of promoting greater efficiency in investment allocation by European firms. The EU's Code of Conduct on Business Taxation, though not binding legislation, has led to the repeal of hundreds of tax rules within EU member states that were thought to constitute harmful tax competition within the Union.[41]

3) *The Cato Institute Report.* Ultimately, most public expenditures can be funded only by tax revenue. At some level, lower taxes are not necessarily a good thing, if they imply inadequate funding for needed public spending. A Cato Institute report on "International Tax Competition"[42] ignores this point, asserting that lower tax rates invariably lead to higher economic growth and simply assuming that higher economic growth is the only policy objective that government should pursue. The Cato report ignores entirely the issue of optimal provision of public services and assumes that lower taxes are always and inevitably good for everyone:

> In closed economies, high taxes on capital income and skilled workers stunt economic growth. As economies open up, such bad tax policy causes even larger economic losses due to greater impacts on investment and labor flows. * * *
>
> * * * [Some] economists * * * view tax competition as distortionary. It is thought that if different tax rates cause capital and labor to migrate across borders, those resources may

39. Paul O'Neill, Statement on OECD Tax Havens, May 10, 2001, available at http://www.treasury.gov.

40. Nor does it in the subsequent progress reports of the OECD initiative; see supra note 11.

41. See Code of Conduct Group (Business Taxation) / Primarolo Group, Report to ECOFIN Council (1999).

42. Chris Edwards and Veronique de Rugy, International Tax Competition: A 21st Century Restraint on Government (Cato Institute: Policy Analysis No.431, April 12, 2002), reprinted in 27 Tax Notes Int'l 63 (2002).

not end up in their most productive uses. So Ireland is receiving "too much" investment because of its low tax rates, according to that view. But that loses sight of a larger issue: high tax rates shackle economic growth. Thus, to the extent that tax competition creates pressure to reduce tax rates globally, all countries gain from increased growth and higher incomes.[43]

* * * [Large] economic gains made possible by tax rate cuts mean that tax competition is not a negative-sum game for the United States or the world as a whole. As any one country adopts a more efficient tax system to maximize growth, other countries follow suit, with the result that global investment and output rise. The round of income tax reductions following U.S. tax reforms in 1986 is a good example. All countries end up better off as each country pursues its own interest.[44]

The Cato Institute report dismisses theoretical models of tax competition (which are discussed below).[45] The report seems simply to assume that the more wealth is privately held, always and everywhere, the better. If one really were to embrace this assumption, however, the question becomes why there should be any taxes at all, not whether tax competition should be encouraged. Promoting worldwide economic growth may be a key objective of international tax policy, but it cannot be the only objective.

The Economics Behind the Tax Competition Debate

Economists have given extensive attention to the inefficiencies that tax competition may generate. This picture was originally enunciated by Wallace Oates:

The result of tax competition may well be a tendency toward less than efficient levels of output of local services. In an attempt to keep taxes low to attract business investment, local officials may hold spending below those levels for which marginal benefits equal marginal costs, particularly for those programs that do not offer direct benefits to local business.[46]

In effect, foreign governments may compete for taxpayers the way firms in the market compete for customers. Just as competition drives down prices for consumers, jurisdictional competition for tax revenues may drive taxes lower. And, just as a more efficient competitor might be able to maintain prices at a level where a competing firm can no longer

43. Id. at 3.

44. Id. at 21.

45. "As in other areas of academic economics, these mathematical models rely on underlying assumptions that often end up driving the conclusions. Some theorists have tweaked the assumptions and concluded that tax competition is efficient. Others have tweaked the assumptions and concluded that tax competition is inefficient because it leads to a 'race to the bottom' with tax levels that are too low." Id. at 20.

46. Wallace E. Oates, Fiscal Federalism 143 (1972).

be profitable, so too might one competitive tax jurisdiction be able to survive on tax revenues lower than those in other jurisdictions.[47] To shore up revenues, a jurisdiction is apt to turn to tax bases that cannot, like capital, be easily exported, especially taxes on real property and labor.

Despite these worries about substantive competition, there is, however, also a simple argument that tax competition *enhances* collective welfare. The argument, made most famously by Charles Tiebout, begins with the fact that tax revenue is used to fund public expenditures, including the provision of public goods and services. Of two jurisdictions with the same factor endowments and technologies, the one that imposes a higher tax may well provide more public goods and services. Meanwhile, different people have different preferences about the mix of publicly and privately supplied goods and services. Those who prefer more public goods may be willing to live in the jurisdiction with the higher tax. When residence is mobile, therefore, people can "vote with their feet" and select the jurisdictions where the mix of taxes and spending most closely correspond to their preferences. This in turn encourages different jurisdictions to exploit their comparative advantages in public goods provision, as well as to lower taxes to match the cost of the public goods provided. Mobility of residence therefore may make everyone better off in a market-like fashion.

The above argument originates in Tiebout's highly influential hypothesis that inter-governmental competition for households is welfare enhancing.[48] Tiebout's work dealt originally with local government finance, but others have extended the idea to the international context. John Douglas Wilson summarizes Tiebout's model and its descendents in the following excerpt.

John Douglas Wilson, *Theories of Tax Competition*, 52 NAT'L TAX J. 269, 271–72 (1999).

> Tiebout's theory of local public good provision also provides a theory of efficient tax competition. In modern formulations of the theory, it is often assumed that each region's government is controlled by its landowners, who seek to maximize the after-tax value of the region's land by attracting individuals to reside on this land. To do so, the government offers public goods that are financed by local taxes. * * * [T]he equilibria for such models are found to be efficient under the usual definition of efficiency: a central authority cannot feasibly reallocate goods and resources in a way that makes some individuals better off

---

47. See Julie Roin, Competition and Evasion: Another Perspective on International Tax Competition, 89 Geo. L.J. 543, 552–53 (2001).

48. Charles M. Tiebout, A Pure Theory of Local Expenditures, 64 J. Political Econ. 416 (1956).

without making anyone worse off. There is tax competition here in the sense that a region's taxes must be kept low enough to induce individuals to reside in the region, given the public goods that are being provided. These taxes are collected from residents in the form of efficient "head taxes," and they are chosen so that each resident's tax payment equals the cost of providing him with the chosen levels of public goods and services. This marginal-cost-pricing rule results in efficient migration decisions. * * * There is now a vast literature extending these efficiency results in various directions.

NOTES

1) *The Impossible "Head Tax" and Other Conundrums.* Despite the theoretical attraction of so-called head taxes to fund public services efficiently, they have proven to be politically unpalatable. In 1987, the Conservative government of British Prime Minister Margaret Thatcher introduced a flat-rate head tax called the "poll tax" or "community charge" to replace property taxes. The poll tax, pilloried by the Labour opposition as unfairly regressive, proved so unpopular that it was ultimately credited with forcing Thatcher's resignation a few years later. Since then, no major Western government has dared to tread where Thatcher faltered. Head taxes are unlikely to become a realistic policy option any time soon.

Likewise, the idea of setting tax payments to pay for the government benefits of each resident enjoys great theoretical support in the economics and philosophical literature, but is not practical in the real world. Taxes will never become simply prices for public goods. Tiebout assumes that taxes are imposed on each resident to cover the cost of providing him or her with the chosen levels of public goods and services. If taxes indeed worked this way, then any given region would be indifferent between the marginal inflow and outflow of households (or firms, or labor). Although inflow would mean additional tax revenue, it also would create higher budgetary requirements to provide additional public goods; outflow would result in lower revenue, but at the same time fewer public goods would need to be produced. In the real world, however, taxes rarely can be made into a form of efficient user fee. Because of this, for any given region the outflow of productive factors (for example, capital) tends to be a bad thing and inflow a good thing.[49]

49. The reason why this is the case is explained by Wilson, with reference to mobile capital:

The tax rate t * * * represents the discrepancy between the social value of an additional unit of capital and the social opportunity cost of this unit, measured from the single region's viewpoint. [Where r is the after-tax return on capital, assumed to be determined on the inter-jurisdictional capital market,] [t]his social value is the marginal product of capital, MP_K, which firms equate to $r + t$ when they choose their profit-maximizing investment levels. In contrast, the social opportunity cost is only r, since the tax provides revenue for the government and is therefore not a social cost. Thus, t

2) *Countering Tiebout.* When capital is mobile, a government considering raising its level of public goods by raising the tax rate must make sure that the marginal benefit not only covers the marginal cost of additional public goods, but also compensates for the negative impact of the capital outflow on tax revenue. From a worldwide perspective, the outflow of capital from one region, *A*, into others is not necessarily a bad thing: *A*'s loss of revenue from this outflow of capital results in benefits in other regions where the capital ends up. If the governments in *A* were to take these "positive externalities" into account in deciding their tax policies, they would be justified in raising their level of public goods closer to the point where marginal benefit equals marginal cost. However, governments in region *A* are not likely to consider benefits to other regions as compensating for their own losses. Importantly, every government is in the same situation as those in region *A*.[50]

Like Tiebout's hypothesis, this basic political economy model of tax competition has also been extended to a variety of situations to reveal inefficiencies produced by tax competition.[51] Sometimes the inefficiencies take forms other than the under-provision of public goods. Tax competition, for example, may induce a misallocation of the location of real investments. To eliminate these inefficiencies, corrective policies carried out either by a central authority, or, more appropriately in the international context, through coordination among countries, are often recommended. The adoption of such policies would mean that each government no longer independently (or "non-cooperatively") chooses its tax or subsidy policies; pure tax competition ceases. Harmonization of tax systems or multilateral decisionmaking institutions become necessary. Those responses to tax competition are described in Sections 11.5 and 11.6.

3) *Public Choice Theory Enters the Debate.* Both the Tiebout-inspired (pro-competitive) and the Oates-inspired (race-to-the-bottom) models assume that governments engaged in tax competition attempt to maximize the welfare of their residents. Public choice theory, however, challenges this assumption, arguing that when self-interested bureaucrats in gov-

---

$= MP_K - r$. It is this discrepancy between the value and opportunity cost of capital at the margin that implies that the region benefits from a capital inflow and is harmed by a capital outflow. In a more general model, we would recognize that capital investments impose various burdens on the public sector, such as the increased demands for public infrastructure and various public services. If capital were taxed to cover the marginal costs of these public goods and services, then the region would be indifferent about a marginal inflow or outflow of capital[.] * * * But if capital is not taxed efficiently and we view the term t more generally as the difference between the social value and social opportunity cost of capital at the margin, then [capital outflow must be viewed negatively.]

Wilson, supra note 9, at 274–75.

50. This paragraph is based on Wilson, supra note 9, at 273–75.

51. The model originally derives from George R. Zodrow and Peter Mieszkowski, Pigou, Tiebout, Property Taxation, and the Underprovision of Local Public Goods, 19 J. Urban Econ. 356–70 (1986).

ernment benefit personally from the budget they control, they have incentives to maximize the size of the public sector, whether it enhances the welfare of citizens or not.[52] Tax competition improves welfare precisely because it counters the effect of such bureaucratic incentives: Citizens can constrain officials not only by voting them out of office but also by "voting with their feet" and threatening to reduce the tax base on which the officials rely.[53] Although under Tiebout models governments respond to signals about their residents' desired mix of tax and public spending because they are motivated to maximize public welfare, public choice theory suggests that government officials may do so only (or at least principally) out of self-interest. It does not necessarily follow, however, that tax competition produces the dismantling of inefficient government programs put in place due to public-choice pathologies. Public officials may also raise public expenditures to benefit the capital and labor attracted by tax competition, and thereby enhance their own bureaucratic stature. Economic models exploring these issues have concluded that the total size of government may be greater *or* smaller as a result of tax competition.[54]

4) *Both Sides Now.* There exist strong theoretical considerations that point to both efficiency-enhancing and efficiency-diminishing effects of tax competition. Which prevails depends very much on specific conditions, which is why it is futile to argue, as a general matter, that tax competition is either good or bad. This is why many commentators are dissatisfied with the 1998 OECD Report's failure to adduce specific, meaningful criteria to identify harmful forms of substantive tax competition. Merely identifying a regime as competitive does little to indicate whether it is on the whole beneficial or harmful. And while most theoretical models have considered only the short-term results of competition, some studies suggest that the initial winners and losers under competition may not be the same as the long-term winners or losers.[55] These more complicated models underline the need to examine specific competitive practices. Moreover, to understand the policy debate over tax competition, one must look beyond efficiency arguments to other norma-

52. For representative statements of public choice theory, see Geoffrey Brennan & James Buchanan, The Power to Tax: Analytical Foundations of a Fiscal Constitution (1980); William A. Niskanen, Jr., Bureaucracy and Representative Government (1971). For a thoughtful and sophisticated critique, see Jerry L. Mashaw, Greed, Chaos and Governance (1997).

53. The details of this interaction might prove to be quite subtle. Eckhard Janeba and Guttorm Schjelderup argue, for example, that Westminster (parliamentary) and American (presidential-Congressional) democracies fare somewhat differently under competition, with the latter enjoying more benefit than the former. See Eckhard Janeba & Guttorm Schjelderup, Why Europe Should Love Tax Competition—and the U.S. Even More So, NBER Working Paper 9334 (2002).

54. See Wilson, supra note 9, at 296–98.

55. See, e.g., Richard E. Baldwin & Paul Krugman, Agglomeration, Integration and Tax Harmonization, NBER Working Paper 9290 (2002).

tive disputes, most notably about the nature and size of government and the desirability of wealth redistribution.

5) *The OECD's Retreat from Substantive Tax Competition Criteria.* Under pressure from the Bush Administration, the pro-competition side has, for now at least, triumphed. The OECD harmful tax practices initiative has now essentially given up attempting to reduce or eliminate substantive tax competition by low-tax or zero tax non-OECD countries. Since the 1998 report, the "no or only nominal taxes" and "no substantial activity" criteria effectively have been abandoned. The 2001 OECD progress report indicates that the "no or nominal tax criterion is not sufficient, by itself, to result in characterisation as a tax haven. The OECD recognises that every jurisdiction has a right to determine whether to impose income taxes and, if so, to set the tax rate."[56] Similarly for the substantiality criterion:

> The 1998 Report indicates that the lack of substantial activities is one of the criteria to be applied in identifying a jurisdiction as a tax haven. However, the determination of whether local activities are sufficiently substantial is difficult, as was anticipated in paragraph 55 of the 1998 Report. Consequently, in interpreting the no substantial activities criterion, the Forum sought to determine whether there were factors that discouraged substantial domestic activities. In the light of the discussions with the jurisdictions, the Committee concluded that it should not use this method to determine whether or not a tax haven is uncooperative. * * * Thus, the Committee has decided that commitments will be sought only with respect to the transparency and effective exchange of information criteria to determine which jurisdictions are considered as uncooperative tax havens.[57]

The OECD will continue to look at the substantive criteria, but an "analysis of the other key factors"—those relating to enforcement and transparency—is necessary for a jurisdiction to be deemed a tax haven.[58] This narrowed focus on "special tax regimes that abet the evasion or abusive avoidance of tax in other countries"[59] makes the benefits of the OECD approach much clearer. Combating tax havens, which facilitate tax avoidance and engage in related practices, requires international coordination, for at least two reasons. First, tax haven countries may have little incentive to roll back their objectionable practices if other tax havens do not; the former would merely be losing their business to the latter. Second, if some countries are determined to remain tax havens,

---

56. 2001 OECD Progress Report, supra note 11, at 7.

57. Id. at 9–10.

58. Id. at 7.

59. Letter by OECD Secretary General Donald J. Johnston, quoted in Sheppard, supra note 37, at 2019.

the most effective means to neutralize their impact is by concerted adoption of defensive measures. This is because if non-tax-haven countries fail to adopt defensive or retaliatory measures, they, in effect, help sustain the continued operation of the tax havens' practices. This in turn will translate into added administrative and economic costs for those countries that do adopt defensive or retaliatory measures against tax havens.

Consequences: What To Expect from Tax Competition

Tax competition may force changes in the way tax burdens are allocated within a jurisdiction and the amount and nature of public goods provided there. The two following excerpts describe some potential changes that may be in the offing. First, Reuven Avi–Yonah argues that changes in tax base driven by competition may have the effect of driving countries away from income tax, and toward a consumption tax, and worries about the effect of tax competition on the social safety net. Then, Julie Roin contends that tax competition is not likely to produce changes which are important in either efficiency or distributional dimensions.

Reuven S. Avi–Yonah, *Globalization, Tax Competition, and the Fiscal Crisis of the Welfare State*, 113 HARV. L. REV. 1573, 1576–78 (2000).

Two recent developments have dramatically augmented individuals' and corporations' ability to earn tax-free overseas income: the effective end of withholding taxation by developed countries and the rise of production tax havens in developing countries. Since the United States abolished its withholding tax on interest paid to foreigners in 1984, no major capital-importing country has been able to impose such a tax for fear of driving mobile capital elsewhere (or increasing the cost of capital for domestic borrowers, including the government itself). As a result, individuals can generally earn investment income free of host-country taxation in any of the world's major economies. Second, tax havens with strong bank secrecy laws have made it exceedingly difficult for developed countries—let alone developing countries with their weaker tax administrations—to collect tax on the foreign income of their individual residents in the absence of withholding taxes in the host countries. Thus, cross-border investment income can largely be earned free of either host-or home-country taxation. * * *

If much of both passive and productive income from capital can escape the tax net, the income tax becomes in effect a tax on labor. * * * As a result, countries that formerly relied on income tax revenues now must increase relatively regressive taxes, such as consumption and payroll taxes * * * .

At some point, developed countries find themselves politically unable to raise income taxes on labor, consumption taxes, or payroll taxes any further. High income taxes on labor discourage work, high payroll taxes discourage job creation and contribute to unemployment, and high consumption taxes (for example, on luxury goods) drive consumption overseas. If developed countries are unable to tax income from capital and if alternative taxes are not feasible, their only recourse is to cut the social safety net—a net that is needed more than ever both because of demographic factors and because of the increased income inequality, income volatility, and job insecurity that tend to result from globalization. Thus, globalization leads to a more pressing need for revenues at the same time that it limits governments' ability to collect those revenues. * * *

Julie Roin, *Competition and Evasion: Another Perspective on International Tax Competition*, 89 GEO. L.J. 543, 568–575, 579–580 (2001).

[It is often argued that] tax competition reduces the amount of revenue derived from the corporate income tax that can be directed to redistributive purposes. Affected governments are left with two alternatives: reduce redistributive government expenditures or find another source of revenue to make up the shortfall created by tax competition. Proponents of tax harmonization argue that neither of these alternatives is acceptable. * * *

* * * The harms associated with the "breakdown" in the redistributive process have been exaggerated in several respects. First, opponents have overestimated the amount by which corporate tax revenues' contributions to redistribution will be reduced by tax competition. Second, they have in some respects underestimated the amount of revenue shortfalls that can (will) be recouped without creating additional social burdens. Third, they have ignored the substantial economic literature arguing that the distributional differences between a tax which explicitly taxes only labor income and one which explicitly taxes both labor and capital income is small to nonexistent. * * *

Rules against tax competition do not prevent jurisdictions from trying to attract favorable investments. All they do is push such competition elsewhere. One obvious "elsewhere" is increased governmental expenditure on goods or services that benefit such investors. Government money may be used to create desirable infrastructure (such as water, sewage purification facilities, or roads) which the investors might otherwise have to fund on their own. The more such money is funneled into benefits for investors, the less it is available for redistribution to others. * * *

The experience outside of the United States gives no additional grounds for optimism. GATT has long imposed restrictions on subsidies that operate to increase exports or decrease imports. However, implementation of those restrictions has proved unsatisfactory because "the search for a standard for restraining domestic subsidy policies * * * has proven * * * difficult." Although GATT panels have agreed that certain tax subsidies targeted specifically at imports violate the rule, they have thus far proved largely unwilling to rule against "upstream" subsidies. Moreover, the rules allow recourse only against "specific" subsidies; a considerable amount of litigation has ensued over the meaning of that term without generating any clear answer. The rules have been limited in this fashion precisely because of a general reluctance to interfere with "benefits and services * * * that governments routinely provide to their population at large." Other scholars have expressed skepticism that such distinctions are workable. If they are not, all that harmonization is likely to do is to push competition into spending programs rather than taxing provisions[, producing] few if any [redistributive] consequences.

Opponents of tax competition have expressed the fear that such competition will lead to the elimination of tax on income generated by mobile capital, leading to an unfair and inefficient concentration of the tax burden on labor income. Meanwhile, a number of economists and academicians (and even a few politicians) have been advocating the replacement of the income tax with various forms of a consumption tax. The major difference between an income tax and a consumption tax lies in the latter's explicit and purposive exclusion from the tax base of income generated by capital. One of the lessons to be drawn from the debate over the desirability of consumption taxes is how little is at stake in the choice between an income tax and a tax that exempts returns from capital. * * *

[Many commentators] now agree that consumption taxes treat only two elements of the return on capital—real riskless return and inflation premia—more favorably than does an income tax. Studies of historic rates of return show the "real riskless return" to be almost vanishingly small, while most scholars dispute the desirability of taxing inflation premia to begin with. Indeed, so small are the differences between the consumption tax base and the income tax base that economists now agree that virtually all of the "efficiency gains" claimed by proponents of consumption taxes can be attributed to the one-time tax on accumulated capital created by the transition from an income tax to a consumption tax system. The systems are very similar in effect—whether viewed in terms of economic efficiency or distribution—on an ongoing basis.

This analysis suggests yet another reason to regard the fears of opponents of tax competition as overblown. Exempting capital income from tax appears to be a more significant change than it really is. Even should the "worst case" scenario develop, with countries forced to switch their income tax systems to consumption tax systems, the consequences would be far from devastating. * * *

NOTES

1) *More Debatable Propositions.* Professor Roin treats the proposition that the major difference between a consumption tax and an income tax is that the latter taxes the riskless return on capital while the former does not as though it were uncontroversial. But other commentators view an income tax as taxing returns to capital and consumption taxes as exempting them altogether. Choosing between these views turns on differing empirical assumptions.[60]

2) *Sources of Revenue.* United States taxes as a percentage of GDP are relatively low compared to those in Europe and other OECD countries, as illustrated by Figure 11.1. One important reason is that European

Figure 11.1
Total Tax Revenues as a Percentage of Gross Domestic Product, U.S. and OECD Countries (on Average), 1970 to 2000

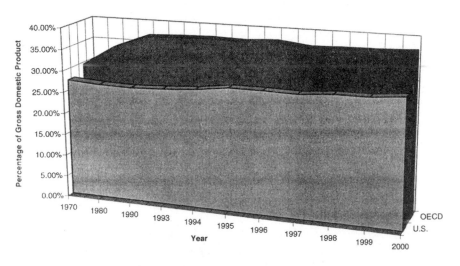

Source: OECD, REVENUE STATISTICS (2002), at 18 tbl.A.

---

60. For a detailed analysis, see Alvin C. Warren, Jr., How Much Capital Income Taxed Under an Income Tax Is Exempt Under a Cash Flow Tax?, 52 Tax L. Rev. 1 (1996).

states publicly fund higher education and health care to a greater extent than the United States does.

The United States also relies substantially less on consumption taxes than do other OECD countries, most of which impose consumption taxes in the form of a value added tax. Figure 11.2 illustrates this disparity.

Figure 11.2.

Consumption taxes (including VAT) as a Percentage of Total Taxation: 1999.

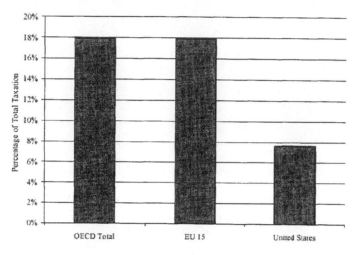

Source: Adapted from OECD, CONSUMPTION TAX TRENDS (2001) at tbl.3.1.

As the OECD notes, "Globalisation has also been one of the driving forces behind tax reforms, which have focused on base broadening and rate reductions, thereby minimising tax induced distortions."[61] Across the developed world, since 1960 corporate income taxes have in general shrunk as a share of GDP and personal income, consumption, and employment taxes have risen. This is why some analysts claim that there is "strong evidence supporting the conclusion that many countries' tax bases are being shifted from capital and business income to labor and consumption."[62]

Hence the threat Reuven Avi–Yonah sees in his excerpted article above may have a different and perhaps more benign effect in the United States than in Europe. While the United States could afford to maintain

61. OECD Report, supra note 3, paragraph 21

62. See William B. Barker, Optimal International Taxation and Tax Competition: Overcoming the Contradictions, 22 Nw. J. Int'l L. & Bus. 161, 166, 169 (2002).

its (relatively lower) level of public expenditures in the face of tax competition by shifting its domestic revenues from income to consumption taxation, Europe has already substantially tapped that source.

3) *The Impact of Tax Competition on Redistributive Goals.* Standard theoretical models of tax competition tend to make the simplifying assumption that the residents of a single region are homogeneous. Thus, they do not consider the distributive consequences of tax competition. Yet some people regard tax competition as harmful precisely because it may undermine the redistributive agenda of modern welfare states. This may happen in two ways: Competition may directly reduce tax revenue and thereby the size of the public fisc that funds redistribution, and/or governments, in order to continue to meet budgetary needs, may use tax instruments aimed at less mobile factors of production (e.g., labor as opposed to capital), which tend to be associated with residents who have lower incomes. Some advocates of tax competition have responded by challenging the desirability of wealth redistribution;[63] others have contested the extent to which tax competition is likely to defeat redistributive goals.

11.4 THE PERSPECTIVE OF DEVELOPING COUNTRIES

Theoretical Dimensions

As discussed in Section 11.2, the OECD's Report on harmful tax practices criticized procedural defects in tax havens that enable or abet tax evasion. In 1998, the OECD also objected to some substantive tax competition engaged in by the small jurisdictions that are usually singled out as tax havens. The problem is that, unlike the secrecy or non-transparency that abet evasion of other nations' taxes, it is often quite defensible economically for small economies to maintain the zero or very low tax rates that OECD countries may view as inappropriate or unfair tax competition. Concerns about substantive tax competition tend to assume the existence of "source-based" capital income taxes—taxes levied on capital income earned within a region's borders. Quite independently of the tax competition literature, economists have shown that for a small economy open to world markets, a source-based capital income tax may be inefficient. The following excerpt explains this conclusion.

---

63. See the Cato Institute report, supra note 42, at 3, 26: "Redistribution involves taxing some people at high rates and others at low rates. The 'free rider' would seems to be the latter group, who pay a less than proportionate share of this income in taxes. * * * [While] international tax competition may indeed hamper income redistribution, that seems to be a positive outcome because redistribution has reached severe proportions."

Roger H. Gordon & James R. Hines Jr., *International Taxation*, NATIONAL BUREAU OF ECONOMIC RESEARCH WORKING PAPER 8854, 4–5 (2002).

The nature of optimal tax policy often depends critically on whether the economy is open or closed. The importance of this distinction is evident immediately from the difference that economic openness makes for tax incidence. In a closed economy, the incidence of a tax on the return to capital depends not only on the elasticity of saving with respect to the interest rate but also on the elasticity of factor demands and the elasticity of consumer substitution between capital-intensive and labor-intensive goods. The presumption has been that, for plausible elasticities, the burden of a corporate income tax falls primarily on capital owners.

In a small open economy, in contrast, a tax on the return to domestic capital has no effect on the rate of return available to domestic savers, since the domestic interest rate is determined by the world capital market. [This follows from the standard assumptions that capital is costlessly mobile internationally and that there is no uncertainty.] Domestic investment falls in response to higher tax rates. For firms to continue to break even, in spite of the added tax, either output prices must rise or other costs must fall by enough to offset the tax. When output prices are fixed by competition with imports, the tax simply causes the market-clearing wage rate to fall. As a result, the burden of the tax is borne entirely by labor or other fixed domestic factors. While a labor income tax would also reduce the net wage rate, it would not in contrast distort the marginal return to capital invested at home vs. abroad. * * * [A] labor income tax dominates a corporate income tax, even from the perspective of labor. As a result, one immediate and strong conclusion about tax policy in an open economy setting is that a "source-based tax" on capital income should not be used since it is dominated by a labor-income tax.

NOTE

Source and Residence Bases. Economists generally agree that a small open economy can improve upon a source-based capital income tax by adopting either a residence-based capital-income tax or a labor-income tax, for reasons that may have little or nothing to do with the collective action problems identified in the tax competition debates. In other words, if a country rejects a source-based capital income tax, it need not be because of its views about tax competition.

The analysis of residence-based capital income taxes can be much more complex. It is true that the availability of a residence-based capital income tax—of which the U.S. international tax rules constitute one example—might change the picture for tax competition.[64] For example, raising the tax rate may cause a lesser capital outflow under residence-based tax than under source-based tax, since only non-residents escape the higher rate. This, in turn, might help mitigate the inefficiencies of tax competition. However, the ability of foreign corporations to defer the resident country's income tax until profits are repatriated and of domestic parent companies to cross-credit taxes from low and high tax countries may provide incentives for investing abroad in low or zero tax countries.

The Rationale for Tax Havens

Some small economies may benefit from exploiting a balance of source-and residence-based rules to attract foreign investment that will not be taxed in the source jurisdiction *or* in the residence jurisdiction. It is these low-tax states that are sometimes known as "tax havens" for substantive reasons, quite apart from issues of secrecy or non-transparency. The following excerpt describes the basic functioning of such systems.

William B. Barker, *Optimal International Taxation and Tax Competition: Overcoming the Contradictions,* 22 Nw. J. Int'l L. & Bus. 161, 176–77 (2002).

Tax havens and similar tax preference regimes largely remove the effect of the economic laws [governing foreign direct investment (FDI)] by insulating themselves from the effect of FDI and non-resident business. This is accomplished principally in two ways: by ring fencing and by maintaining the currency of business enterprise in foreign specie.

First, ring fencing is the process of restricting the benefits of limited taxation to so-called non-resident enterprises that are not permitted to do business in local markets and to compete with local enterprises. Thus, the serious economic consequences of competition are eliminated. Similar economic effects are found in other countries where special enterprise zones are provided.

Second, nations can protect themselves from these economic effects by requiring the business enterprise to conduct its affairs in non-local currency. * * * Thus, these non-resident businesses do not affect the haven's essential economy by increasing imports or increasing currency value. Though transactions are booked in the havens, much of the real economic activity occurs elsewhere.

---

64. See generally Chapters 4 and 5 (concerning outbound transactions).

Overall, low tax rates typically found in small havens, and not in hosts that provide significant markets for goods and services, favor capital intensive over labor intensive activities. The relative mobility of investment permits the separation of this income factor from the market host (or the home) country and its placement in havens. Though financial services are capital intensive, there is a substantial service component. Any service factor requiring large labor costs can be performed outside the offshore financial center. * * * Examples of this are the widespread use of havens for insurance and banking. * * * Few banks or insurance companies have an actual physical presence. There is little true investment by these financial intermediaries in haven countries.

Many tax havens are referred to as offshore financial centers (OFCs), which are principally involved in the financial services sector and in [foreign portfolio investment]. Many OFCs are countries having less than 200,000 inhabitants. For example, the Cayman Islands is reported to be the fifth largest banking center in the world, having approximately 580 banks (with $500 billion in holdings), 2,238 mutual funds, 499 insurance companies and 40,000 off-shore entities in total. The Bahamas is also another major center, with sixty insurance companies, 580 mutual funds, 418 banks and 100,000 off-shore entities in total. The Channel Islands and the Isle of Man have approximately $525 billion in foreign-owned assets. Financial services account for 80% of Isle of Jersey's income, the minimum nonresident account now being $100,000. The list goes on, with the result that the country of Niue, a state with only 2,000 inhabitants, has 3,000 offshore business entities. In all, statisticians estimate that about $8 trillion worldwide is invested in offshore accounts and entities. Thus, considerable amounts of capital are temporarily located in tax havens, and significant financial service sector activity is at least nominally located in these states.

The View from the Developing World

One persistent criticism of the 1998 OECD Report's approach to harmful tax competition has been its emphasis on the concerns of developed countries. Accordingly, the Report has been said not to represent adequately the legitimate interests of developing countries in competing for investments through, *inter alia*, aggressively competitive tax policies. In the following excerpt, Karen Brown argues that the OECD's emphasis on the interests of OECD members blinds the Report to the inconsistent treatment of tax rules when they arise in OECD and developing states.

Karen B. Brown, *Harmful Tax Competition: The OECD View*, 32 Geo. Wash. J. Int'l L. & Econ. 311, 313–14, 316–19 (1999)

[I]t is remarkable that the industrialized nation-members of the Organisation for Economic Cooperation and Development (OECD), including the United States, have issued two recent reports, Tax Sparing: A Reconsideration (Tax Sparing Report) and Harmful Tax Competition: An Emerging Global Issue (Harmful Tax Competition Report), that fail to re-examine the hegemony of the principle of capital export neutrality. The absence of a discussion of the possible merits of a system founded on exemption of foreign source income by the home country of a multinational corporation calls into question the usefulness of the reports. In particular, the recommendations have been made without consideration of the position of developing countries. * * * [T]he Harmful Tax Competition Report does not acknowledge the primacy of the tax regimes of many developed countries, such as the United States, and its influence on the economies of developing countries.

While noting the positive effects of the globalization of trade and investment, the Harmful Tax Competition Report constructs its arguments against "tax havens" and "harmful tax competition" from the isolated perspective of the developed world. This is demonstrated in the definitions of tax haven and harmful tax competition, which exclude some of the practices of developed countries that are OECD members. Excepted from the definition of practices having undesirable effects is the circumstance in which one country collects significant revenues from a tax imposed on individuals or corporations and competes for the tax base of another country by instituting an effective income tax rate generally lower than that existing in the other country.

The exception describes * * * the base-broadening and rate-reducing measures enacted by the 1986 Tax Reform Act in the United States, when the maximum marginal tax rate on corporate income was reduced to thirty-four percent, a low rate when compared to the tax rates of other industrialized nations at that time. * * *

There is no apparent difference between the excepted practice of imposing excessively low income tax rates and a system in which a country collects revenues from a generally imposed income tax but has preferential features for selected types of income. The Harmful Tax Competition Report offers no explanation for the distinction, other than a statement that tax reform based on base-broadening and rate-reducing measures has the effect of minimizing "tax-induced distortions" in the international economy. * * * Without detailed factual information, it is impossible to determine the distortion created by a given tax provision or examine countervailing welfare effects.

The Harmful Tax Competition Report also ignores the tax competitive features of the national tax systems of the leading OECD members, such as the United States. U.S. law provides multinational firms significant opportunities to reduce or eliminate U.S. tax on foreign source income. The primary avenue of tax reduction is through manipulation of the foreign tax credit limitation. * * * Other features of the U.S. tax system reflect preferential treatment for targeted income items. Since 1984, for example, the United States has allowed an exemption from tax for portfolio interest income derived from U.S. firms by foreign investors. This type of exemption is common among industrialized nations. Yet, it appears to escape harmful competition classification because it lacks the factors determined by the Harmful Tax Competition Report to be possessed by tax havens or harmful tax competition jurisdictions.

Further examination, however, suggests the limited perspective of the Harmful Tax Competition Report. Assume, for example, that the law of a developing country does not tax income from sales of inventory within its jurisdiction. It appears that such a regime would be viewed as harmful, especially if accompanied by another factor, such as lack of effective infor mation exchange by the country's tax administration. Further assume that a firm of an industrialized nation takes advantage of the tax exemption for inventory sales income by arranging for passage of title to the goods in the developing country without any physical presence there. This action is taken to maximize the credit available against home country taxes for foreign taxes paid. Since no taxes are paid to the developing country, it is apparent that this action will increase the credit available for taxes paid to other foreign countries, possibly an industrialized country with a tax rate higher than that in the United States.

It seems misguided to treat a tax preference for inventory sales income as indicative of a harmful tax regime. As demonstrated by the example, the developing country's law is used by the industrialized firm as a means to exploit a preferential rule in its home country tax regime. It seems inappropriate to depict the regime as harmful when it is serving a legitimate purpose of the developed nation to allow its own firms to moderate domestic tax rates.

NOTE

The View from Compliant Jurisdictions. Under OECD pressure, a number of small and developing countries have, sometimes reluctantly, agreed to change some tax practices singled out as harmful. In the case of offshore financial service centers, compliance is a two-way street: In return for surrendering some of its comparative advantages vis-à-vis more developed countries by beefing up enforcement and transparency, a developing jurisdiction may reasonably expect that the OECD will demand at least as much from its own members. With a "level playing field" assured, the offshore jurisdictions have in most cases proven willing to sacrifice their allegedly harmful tax regimes in order to maintain a "clean" reputation internationally—i.e., staying off the OECD blacklist. As one Panamanian commentator noted,

> [Panama] cannot pretend to be efficient in the international financial services market if we have an international banking center and a country isolated from other financial centers [while other] countries [are] fighting to minimize the possibilities of their own financial centers * * * being used for illicit activities, without suffering the consequences of such uncooperative behavior.[65]

In order to ensure that the OECD does not advantage its own members once the offshore financial centers' regimes have been dismantled, the agreements between the OECD and non-OECD jurisdictions are made conditional on principles of equity and non-discrimination.[66] These principles attempt to institutionalize a level playing field.

11.5   TAX HARMONIZATION AS A "SOLUTION" TO TAX COMPETITION

In the context of tax competition, "tax harmonization" has a specific connotation: If countries choosing tax policies independently tend to create collective inefficiencies, then it arguably makes sense for them to coordinate—"harmonize"—their tax policies to eliminate these inefficiencies. Even though critics of tax harmonization—and they are many— sometimes portray it as requiring countries to adopt identical or similar tax policies, or even to embrace a supra-national central taxing authority, coordination of tax policy need not involve either. For example, when countries acting independently set their rates of withholding tax on interest or dividend income too high, they can, and do, enter into bilateral tax treaties to reduce the withholding rates.[67] Such forms of cooperation do not require elimination of efficient differences across countries in the packages of tax and public goods levels they offer—

65.   J.S. Acuna, Es necesario un Tratado de Intercambi de Información Tributaria con Estados Unidos?, 7 Revista Legislación y Economia (2002), quoted and translated in Rafael Rivera Castillo, Tax Competition and the Future of Panama's Offshore Center, 29 Tax Notes Int'l 73, 81 (2003).

66.   Castillo, supra note 65, at 81.

67.   See Chapter 7. For further discussion, see Roger H. Gordon and James R. Hines Jr., International Taxation, National Bureau of Economic Research Working Paper 8854, 21, 77 (2003).

efficiencies that Tiebout has emphasized. The most effective international harmonization initiative to date has been the European Union's enactment of a common base—but not a common rate—for value added taxes (VAT). In the following excerpt, Thomas Field describes recent European efforts to extend harmonization from indirect taxes like the VAT to the corporate income tax.

Thomas F. Field, *Tax Competition in Europe and America*, 29 TAX NOTES INT'L 1235, 1237–38 (2002).

To date, the most far-reaching harmonization measure has been the imposition by the EU in 1977 of a 15 percent minimum rate for the value added taxes levied by member states. The justification was that the EU would be partly funded by member-state VAT contributions. In effect, the minimum rate guaranteed the revenues on which the EU depended.

Still under active discussion are 1992 recommendations advanced by the Ruding Committee to impose a minimum tax rate on business income earned within the EU. Similar proposals were made by earlier EU groups in 1962, 1970, and 1975. The basic goal of the Ruding Committee recommendations is to curb member-state business tax competition, which has already resulted in broad reductions in European corporate tax rates. Under one current draft proposal, a mechanism to establish minimum member-state corporate tax rates by a majority vote of EU countries would be written into the future EU constitution.

The EU tax harmonization effort has drawn criticism from observers who think that EU tax rates are too high, and that countries such as Ireland should be allowed to reduce their rates if they wish to do so. In addition, some EU member states such as Great Britain resent the infringement on their tax sovereignty attributable to tax harmonization.

NOTE

Extending the Harmonization Concept. Europe does not seem likely to harmonize its corporate income tax rates anytime soon, despite numerous analyses that demonstrate the distortions in the location of corporate investments that occur with the current disparities. In the context of the increasing difficulty of enforcing residence-based taxation, the meaning of "tax harmonization" is less clear than in the case of European VAT harmonization. For example, if countries agree to impose varying withholding taxes on portfolio investment income—in order to deter individuals from shifting income abroad for evasion purposes—they could be said to be engaged in tax harmonization. Unfortunately, advocates of tax harmonization have not always carefully distinguished between the different kinds of problems that the international mobility of capital and labor can create.

Harmonization, Pro and Con

Corporate income tax rate harmonization is but one form of possible tax harmonization. Other proposals have urged harmonization of a tax base through a unified international definition of income. In the next excerpt, Hans–Werner Sinn advances arguments in favor of tax harmonization by assuming that residence income taxation (along with taxation of cross border consumption according to the destination principle) is unworkable. Moreover, by pointing out that a residence-based income tax will not preclude tax minimization by immigration, he suggests that only radical measures of harmonization will allow countries to retain policies characteristic of the traditional welfare state. In the succeeding excerpt, Julie Roin canvasses the reasons why tax base harmonization remains unappealing to policymakers concerned with national sovereignty and to taxpayers who benefit from arbitrage under the current patchwork system.

Hans-Werner Sinn, *Tax Harmonization and Tax Competition in Europe*, 34 EUR. ECON. REV. 489, 490–91, 499, 500–01 (1990).

In response to the high tax sensitivity, two protective devices have been developed in the past to prevent international commodity and capital flows from being governed by tax considerations. The need for harmonization can only meaningfully be studied when these protective devices are taken into account.

The first device is the destination principle for indirect taxes. According to this principle, commodity exports are exempt from the exporting country's tax and are instead subjected to the tax of the country of import. * * * The destination principle ensures that firms compete on the basis of 'producer' prices; i.e., of prices net of the taxes. * * * Under competitive conditions this implies that the sectoral structures of the national economies satisfy the requirement of an efficient international specialization. * * *

The second protection device is the residence principle for border crossing interest income flows. This principle says that interest income is not taxed in the country where it is earned, but in and by the lender's country of residence. * * * The residence principle makes investors indifferent between domestic and foreign assets when the gross or pre-tax interest rates are the same. Despite international differences in income tax rates, it ensures under ideal conditions that market forces equate gross interest rates and allocate the available stock of capital efficiently to the different countries. * * *

[The] problem with the residence principle is that it does not work well when wealth owners are dishonest and can more easily conceal their foreign than their domestic interest income. * * *

In order to avoid the problem, strict notification would have to be introduced. Banks would have to send statements of their customer's interest income to the revenue offices of the respective countries of residence. A good notification system is not impossible to implement; after all it exists in the United States. However, in the light of the European bank secrecy laws and the tax loopholes offered by Luxembourg and Switzerland, it cannot easily be perfected.

A feasible alternative is a [harmonized] system of source taxation. * * *

The basic lesson from the theory of optimal taxation is that a country cannot, and should not, impose high taxes on activities whose supply and demand are price elastic. Elastic activities can escape taxation and thus imply a high excess burden relative to the tax collected. This is Europe's new problem. The fall of the barriers will increase the possibility of tax avoidance and provide more elasticity to a number of economic activities. Those who perform these activities will in future be handled with kid gloves. They will be the winners in an uncoordinated process of tax harmonization, for they cannot be forced to pay more than simply benefit taxes.

The group of winners will include the mobile part of the labor force and, regardless of whether the source or the residence principle applies, will also include the owners of capital. Source taxes are investment taxes that can be avoided by investing abroad. Residence taxes are savings taxes which can be avoided by emigration. Admittedly, most savers will not consider such a radical solution. However, large savers like corporations and rich individuals, will not find it very difficult to change their country of residence, if only by buying post office boxes in Liechtenstein.

Consumers will also belong to the winners group. As argued above, they can easily escape the domestic VAT by buying foreign products or by simply purchasing domestic products via foreign retailers. The competition of tax systems will exert strong downward pressures on European VAT rates.

The losers of tax competition will be those who cannot escape and those who benefit from a large government sector.

The first group includes immobile workers and landowners. They are the natural victims of the Tiebout equilibrium, since they will serve as the lenders of last resort to Europe's impoverished governments. The second group consists of the poor. The poor will lose because governments will no longer be able to maintain their current scales of redistribution.

On the one hand, for the reasons explained and with the exceptions mentioned, it will be difficult for a single country to extract the required funds from the rich. On the other hand, net benefits being given to the poor in one jurisdiction will attract poor people from everywhere and so make this policy unsustainable. The New York city effect will be the death of Europe's welfare states if the unmitigated competition of tax systems is allowed.

Julie Roin, *Taxation Without Coordination*, 31 J. LEGAL STUD. 61, 78–81, 83–84, 87 (2002).

Though economists have emphasized the need for international tax base harmonization—either in conjunction with or instead of tax rate harmonization—for over 30 years, there has been little discussion, let alone movement, in that direction in the income tax context. Instead, tax rate harmonization has been accorded higher priority, despite widespread knowledge of the toothlessness of such proposals in the absence of tax base harmonization. * * * Any serious tax base harmonization proposal will significantly impinge on preexisting legislative prerogatives. In addition, it is likely to threaten the interests of powerful taxpayers—in many cases, the very taxpayers who would most benefit from the administrative advantages of a harmonized rate base. This inbred resistance to tax harmonization will be hard to overcome by appeals to others, whose interests in the issue will be far more remote. * * *

National legislatures and legislators are the natural enemies of tax base harmonization proposals. Tax base harmonization reduces legislative control over national tax policy without creating a corresponding increase in control over worldwide tax policy. National legislators thus would lose a significant element of political power, power that generates benefits in the form of campaign donations, honoraria, and other in-kind benefits. * * * No national legislature (or group of legislators within such a legislature) could expect to exert as much control over the shape and contents of an internationally harmonized tax base definition as they would over a national definition. Additional interests—some of which may be at odds with domestic political considerations—will have to be taken into account to achieve a multilateral agreement. * * *

* * * [T]he most important impediment to legislative acquiescence in a harmonization scheme comes from the probability that any such scheme would provide for the establishment of a new, international organization for the consideration of tax legislative proposals. * * * It would be hard to overstate the unwieldiness of a decision-making procedure requiring concurrent majorities of the legislatures of all the harmonizing countries, or even a majority of such countries.

* * * Though some additional tax revenues will be raised by foreclosing arbitrage opportunities, the amount that will be gained is uncertain. Most arbitrage transactions, like tax shelter activity in general, are largely hidden from view to prevent attracting the attention of regulators and legislators who might look for ways to foreclose them. It is possible that the amount of revenues at stake would not justify the social costs of harmonization. * * * The biggest beneficiaries of arbitrage are multinational corporations; most of the additional revenues raised by foreclosing arbitrage opportunities would be collected from this relatively small group of taxpayers. These taxpayers, already a potent political force in many national jurisdictions, would undoubtedly fight such attempts to increase their tax burden. And they may well succeed * * * .

[T]ax base uniformity has the potential for conferring both benefits and costs on taxpayers. On the benefit side, taxpayers save administrative costs and avoid the possibility of inadvertent double (or multiple) taxation. On the cost side, taxpayers lose favorable arbitrage opportunities. At first glance, these costs and benefits may appear equivalent, counterbalancing one another sufficiently to make taxpayers relatively indifferent to tax harmonization proposals. However, such indifference is unlikely for two reasons. First, not all taxpayers will reap administrative gains, while all will suffer some transition costs. Second, taxpayers face not only the loss of arbitrage opportunities but also the possibility of losing favorable tax rules inscribed in current statutory law. Together, these factors suggest that base harmonization proposals are more likely to engender substantial taxpayer opposition than support.

NOTES

1) *A Further Criticism.* In another Julie Roin excerpt in Section 11.4 above, she suggests another problem with an argument such as Sinn's.[68] She contends it is a mistake to argue for harmonization on the ground

68. Roin, supra note 21, at 596.

that enforcement of residence taxation of income is infeasible—for example, on account of the fact that information exchange agreements among countries are hard to obtain. The reason is that mutual assistance in enforcement requires less coordination among countries than tax harmonization. If even the lesser form of coordination cannot be secured, surely the stronger forms of coordination—involving coordination in setting tax policies, not just in enforcing them—will not occur.

2) *The European Commission's Approach.* Given substantial opposition from member states, the European Commission (EC, the executive arm of the European Union) has not been optimistic about harmonization of income taxes (as opposed to the value-added tax). The EC now emphasizes the advantages of harmonizing the corporate income tax base, and notes that countries would still control the rates imposed on that common base.[69] The EC initiative expresses concern that because many multinational European firms have come to identify the whole of the EU as their "home market," tax planning with an eye toward allocating income among European subsidiaries will impose an increasing burden on European corporations. A "consolidated corporate tax base for EU-wide activities" would also be intended to reduce tax-related distortions in allocation decisions. The Commission argues that the international competitiveness of EU firms—competitiveness with firms located elsewhere—depends on their allocating investment within the EU efficiently, and that differential tax bases within the EU will likely lead to inefficient allocation of plants and offices for purely tax-driven reasons. Finally, the Commission contends that differentials in tax base among EU states are dwarfed by differentials in effective rates, meaning that base harmonization would not substantially impede the ability of jurisdictions within the EU to engage in healthy tax competition with one another.[70] Of course, tax rate competition also will affect companies' decisions about where to locate business and financial assets. These EC tax base harmonization proposals coexist alongside other EU initiatives such as the EU's proposal for a Europe-wide "code of conduct" to reduce harmful tax practices.[71]

3) *The View from Economics.* Despite significant research in recent years, the likely consequences of tax harmonization—and the prerequisites for successful harmonization—are not well understood, with economists reaching differing conclusions. We have already seen Hans–Werner Sinn's view of the potential gains from harmonization. Assaf Razin and Efraim Sadka investigate a simplified model of competing tax jurisdic-

---

69. See European Commission, Towards an Internal Market Without Tax Obstacles, COM(2001) 582 (2001); European Commission, Commission Staff Working Paper, Company Taxation in the Internal Market, COM(2001) 582 (2001).

70. European Commission, Towards an Internal Market Without Tax Obstacles, COM(2001) 582 (2001), at 8.

71. See, e.g., European Commission, Towards Tax Co–Ordination in the European Union: A Package to Tackle Harmful Tax Competition, COM(97) 495 (1997).

tions and conclude that tax harmonization will not produce a more efficient outcome:

> [I]f the competing countries are sufficiently coordinated with the rest of the world so as to be able to effectively tax their residents on their income from capital in the rest of the world, then tax competition leads each country to apply the residence principle of taxation * * * . Thus, there are no gains from tax harmonization.
>
> If, however, there is not sufficient coordination with the rest of the world to allow each country to tax its residents on their income from capital in the rest of the world, then tax competition leads to no tax whatsoever on capital income. * * * Thus, in this case too there are no gains from tax harmonization.[72]

Enrique Mendoza offers another pessimistic view of harmonization for Europe, with the exception of the United Kingdom. He models the EC proposal to harmonize capital income taxes and predicts that Europe-wide capital tax harmonization would cause substantial capital flows from Continental countries, with higher taxes on labor but lower taxes on capital, toward the United Kingdom and other countries with relatively lower labor taxes. Depending on the rate at which the tax is harmonized, countries may or may not raise labor taxes as a result.[73] No matter what the mechanics, Mendoza concludes, "[h]armonization of the capital income tax always results in the United Kingdom owning a larger share of the world's capital."[74]

With more extreme differences in initial tax structure between harmonizing nations, the results may be somewhat different. In a two-country, multi-stage model considering a developed, high-rate "north" and an undeveloped, low-rate "south," Richard Baldwin and Paul Krugman find that harmonization at some rate intermediate between the pre-harmonization rates of the north and the south might make one or both areas worse off. The reason is straightforward enough: If the north and south had identical rates, firms would prefer to invest in the north, where the advantages of a developed country are available to support the investment. But with the lower, harmonized tax rate, the north would derive lower tax revenues, while the south would receive less investment than under a nonharmonized regime. If instead the harmonized rate were merely a tax floor, the south might maintain its level of welfare while the north might improve. The reason here is more technical, but the basic idea is that, with a tax floor in the south, the north has some

72. Assaf Razin & Efraim Sadka, International Tax Competition and Gains from Tax Harmonization, NBER Working Paper 3152 (1989), at 4.

73. See Enrique G. Mendoza, The International Macroeconomics of Taxation and the Case Against European Tax Harmonization, NBER Working Paper 8217 (2001), at 34.

74. Id. at 36.

assurance of the limits of possible capital flows from north to south and can raise its rates slightly as a result without fear of triggering a catastrophic outflow.[75] In any event, the economics jury is still out, and it may remain out for some time to come.

11.6 MULTILATERAL INSTITUTIONS AS A "SOLUTION" TO TAX COMPETITION

Several commentators have argued that, short of an ambitious harmonization program, some harmful effects of international tax competition might be mitigated by consolidating the current patchwork of mostly bilateral international tax treaties through more robust multilateral institutions. These analysts hope that new institutions would do for tax competition and tax policy coordination what the GATT and WTO have done for trade and trade policy. They often argue that this is the only way to give due weight to nations' sovereignty over tax policy, while still achieving greater uniformity in tax treatment of international activities.

Recognizing that some global tax institution might help, however, scarcely determines the form the institution should take. In the following excerpt, Victor Thuronyi indicates how a multilateral treaty could avoid some of the loopholes in the current bilateral regime. In the next excerpt, Charles McLure describes the idea behind a "GATT for taxes," and the difficulties of achieving it.

Victor Thuronyi, *International Tax Cooperation and a Multilateral Treaty*, 26 BROOK. J. INT'L L. 1641, 1646– 47, 1649–50 (2001).

The international tax system, as currently constituted, is dominated by the principle of national autonomy, with only a limited degree of international coordination. It has become apparent that the existing system favors private actors—both multinational companies and wealthy individuals—who can take advantage of the lack of coordination to minimize the taxes they pay, and that the growing importance of international transactions increases the potential for such tax minimization. Under longstanding principles of public international law, each country possesses an autonomous jurisdiction to tax persons and transactions that have a nexus with that country. When countries exercise that jurisdiction on their own, transactions that have a connection with more than one country may suffer double taxation or, as a result of luck or tax planning, perhaps taking advantage of favorable tax regimes offered by countries engaging in tax competition, may escape the taxing grasp of any

75. See Richard E. Baldwin & Paul Krugman, Agglomeration, Integration and Tax Harmonization, NBER Working Paper 9290 (2002), at 20–21.

country. A network of tax treaties provides some coordination, in most cases eliminating double taxation between treaty countries. Multinational corporations take advantage of the current situation by planning their affairs to exploit inconsistencies in the network of national tax laws and treaties. By dint of such tax planning, they are often able to pay substantially less tax than that paid by taxpayers whose operations are confined to a single country. * * * Many businesses and individuals use a combination of tax treaties and tax havens to avoid or evade tax. National authorities often are helpless against these tactics because they lack the information to find out what taxpayers are doing, because of practical difficulties in auditing taxpayers, or because the tax planning is allowed under current law.

* * * Individual countries often wish to take steps on their own to deal with international tax avoidance. The current treaty network may fail to facilitate, or may even inhibit, such action * * * [E]xisting tax treaties are often inconsistent (or arguably inconsistent) with various anti-abuse measures that countries take or contemplate taking * * * .

A multilateral treaty could facilitate, rather than hinder, reforms which individual countries wish to pursue. To the extent that contemplated reforms are inconsistent with the existing multilateral treaty, countries could discuss and agree on amendments that would permit reform, or even provide for internationally coordinated action. For example, a multilateral arrangement is needed to deal with the taxation of interest income earned by non-resident investors. Whatever arrangement is agreed to—information exchange, a withholding tax, or some combination—all, or nearly all, countries with significant capital markets (end users of capital) must participate, because individual countries cannot go it alone. * * * The multilateral treaty context could institutionalize the process, by providing a forum and procedure for additional agreements, which would be brought from time to time to legislatures for ratification.

Charles E. McLure, Jr., *Globalization, Tax Rules and National Sovereignty*, 55 BULL. INT'L FISCAL DOC. 328, 340–41 (2001).

[Several writers] have raised the possibility of a "GATT for taxes" or General Agreement on Taxes (GATaxes), * * * a "multilateral agreement on the ground rules for the taxation of international flows of income from business and capital." A World Tax Organization (WTaxO), analogous to the World Trade Organization, would perhaps be needed to oversee the implementation of such an agreement. * * * The coverage of a

GATaxes and the mandate of a WTaxO might be either quite broad—involving substantial harmonization of world tax systems—or quite limited—to cover only the international aspects of taxation or only the "tax haven" problem. The implications of these options for national sovereignty are quite different. * * *

Regarding the function of an international tax organization, [Jack] Mintz has suggested that "[t]he purpose of the coordinating body would not be to collect taxes but instead to put a mechanism in place to achieve global co-operation in tax policy", and one of the responsibilities he would assign to the organization is to "develop a code for a 'model' corporation income tax". There are, however, serious conceptual caveats, as well as overwhelming political obstacles, to the creation of a GATaxes and a WTaxO with broad powers. * * * [T]here is little reason to believe that countries will soon engage in the massive surrender of national sovereignty over tax policy implied by this option. * * * Finally, if ever there were international agreement on a particular system, the tyranny of the status quo would take over, and further change would proceed at a glacial pace, if at all. Once made, mistakes would plague us forever. * * *

Even limited narrowly to international flows of income, a GATaxes/WTaxO arrangement would entail substantial surrender of national sovereignty over taxation, as well as vexing conceptual questions. Given the ever-widening network of treaties, however, most of which conform substantially to the OECD Model, multilateral adoption of a system based on that Model might involve less surrender of sovereignty than at first glance, at least for those countries that already participate in the treaty network. But would the rich countries that comprise the OECD want to share power to revise the OECD Model with poor nations? (The UN Model Convention and the OECD Model, while generally similar, are not identical; the former accords more taxing power to source countries.) The many developing countries and countries in transition that do not now have extensive treaty networks might not wish to participate in such an organization if it meant accepting the terms of the OECD Model. In any event, the lack of success in harmonizing direct taxes within the European Union suggests that gaining multilateral agreement even in this limited sphere is not likely to come quickly.

NOTE

Which Respects Sovereignty? Both of the preceding passages note that much of the work of a multilateral tax body is now done through a network of bilateral treaties, mostly based on the OECD or UN models. Despite the off-the-shelf character of these agreements, countries do make individual decisions to adopt the treaties with another country and often modify the models in particular circumstances. The United States's starting point for treaty negotiations is its own model treaty.

While a multilateral agreement—a GATT for taxes—would have to be adopted through the sovereignty-respecting mechanisms nations now use to enter into bilateral treaties, after agreement is achieved, policy-making would be at a remove from national officials, just as trade policy is now done through the WTO. Perhaps more importantly, the success of the WTO has much to do with its dispute-resolution powers. Given the centrality of tax policy to basic questions of sovereignty, however, an international tax court might be especially unpalatable to national governments and might well also be resisted by multinational corporations. The "smart money" would bet on the continuation of the current system, despite its considerable drawbacks.

†